The Illustrated Guide to
HOME NEEDLECRAFTS

Macdonald

A Macdonald Book

© Copyright Macdonald & Co (Publishers) Ltd, 1989
© Copyright Eaglemoss Publications Limited 1983, 1984, 1989

The material in this book previously appeared in *Superstitch*

This edition published in 1989
by Macdonald & Co (Publishers) Ltd.
London & Sydney

a member of Maxwell Pergamon Publishing Corporation plc

ISBN 0 356 17668 1

Printed in Italy

Macdonald & Co (Publishers) Ltd
66–73 Shoe Lane
London EC4P 4AB

Contents

—————————— PART 2 ——————————

KNITTING 159

PART 3

CROCHET 247

PART 4

SOFT FURNISHINGS 289

PART 1
DRESSMAKING

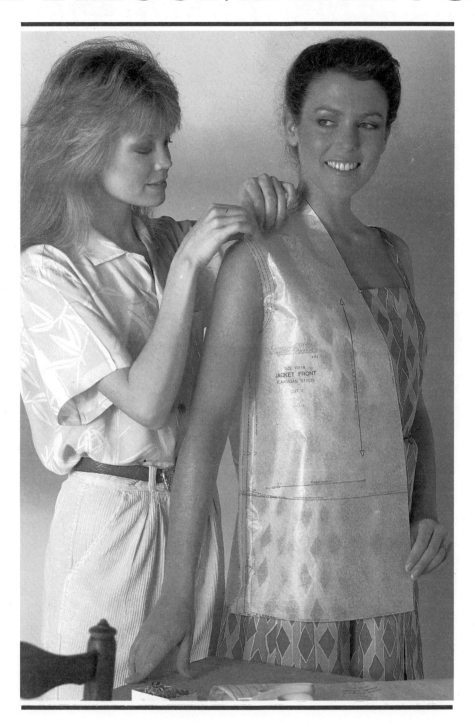

Getting ready to sew

This dressmaking section is designed to teach the home dressmaker all the essential skills necessary for making up a basic classic wardrobe. The introductory chapters in this section contain vital information for the beginner and are also a useful reference for the more experienced home sewer. As well as a glossary of basic stitches and an A-Z of fabrics, there is a checklist of equipment, threads and machine attachments, all of which are invaluable to refer to as a quick reminder.

Graph patterns are given for all the garments described in this book and it is a simple matter to enlarge these multi-size patterns on to dressmaker's graph paper using a flexicurve. Alternatively, the detailed making-up instructions can be applied to any similar commercial patterns – enlarging on their instructions with detailed diagrams explaining the more difficult points and suggesting short cuts or professional touches to use.

As ready-made clothes are designed to fit the average figure, the great advantage of home dressmaking, apart from being able to choose exactly the style you wish to make, is that you can adjust the pattern and make sure it fits perfectly. This section explains how to chart your own measurements for a permanent record.

Finally, why not make up some useful pressing aids and follow the helpful rules on pressing at all stages of making up to achieve a really professional finish to your garments?

Choosing and using fabrics

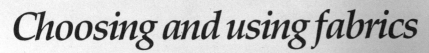

The successful dressmaker develops an eye for colour and pattern and cleverly combines fabrics and styles that complement each other. It's not just a matter of instinct – once you know what a fabric is made of and how to handle it, you'll be able to see the potential it offers.

The best way of envisaging how a fabric will look made up is to see it draped on a model. Then you can appreciate its colour, texture, pattern and weight, just as if it were a completed garment. But this is not always possible, so if a roll of fabric appeals to you, remove it from the rack, stand in front of a full-length mirror and unroll a couple of metres. Hold it up against yourself – will it suit you?

Colour is the first clue. However lovely on the roll some fabrics, when held near the face, seem to drain it of its natural colour. Some fine fabrics may look a suitable colour but lose their density when unrolled. When you find a fabric that flatters your complexion, then you've found one that suits you. Always ask to take the roll to the daylight. If the shop has strip lights, ask to see it under an ordinary tungsten bulb, too.

Feel the texture of the fabric: is it soft, crisp, rough or smooth? Smooth, matt-textured fabrics are more flattering to a larger figure than bulky, loosely woven ones, which are fine for slimmer types. Rough-textured fabrics may need lining, as they can snag lingerie and may irritate the skin. Silky fabrics emphasize curves; matt ones disguise them.

Think about the fabric weight. Will it hang well? Fold the edge under to see how it will hem; try to imagine your finished skirt or dress. Does the fabric have a pronounced pattern? Will it be possible to match it on the seams? Will it mean buying extra fabric? If in doubt, ask the sales staff, who should be able to advise you.

Pattern or fabric first?

Successful dressmaking depends a great deal on how well the fabric works with the style of the garment. There are no rules about buying either the fabric or the paper pattern first, but the advantage of having a pattern first is that it provides valuable guidelines for suitable types of fabric and gives exact quantities for different sizes.

Estimating fabric needs

Beautiful fabrics are the inspiration for lovely clothes. If you choose the fabric first, then search for a suitable style to make it up in, you will need to have some idea of how much to buy. Without a pattern it is impossible to get it exactly right, but there are several ways of making an estimate. The easiest way is to look at a pattern catalogue for the kind of garment you want to make. All fairly straight styles – whether skirts, dresses, trousers, or coats – need roughly the same amount of fabric. Similarly, full-skirted garments take more or

When choosing a fabric, drape it around you and you will get a better idea of what it will look like when made up.

less the same as each other.

If there is no pattern book to hand, hold the fabric against you – from waist to hem for a skirt; from neck to hem for a dress. Add extra for hem and seam allowances. If fabric is narrow (90cm/36in, 115cm/45in) double the measurement (one length for the back and one for the front). If it is wide (140cm/54in, 150cm/60in) only one length is necessary. In either case extra will be needed for sleeves, collars, etc. This is when a paper pattern is invaluable as these extras can take varying amounts of fabric, depending on their shape and pattern layout.

Buying napped fabrics

Some fabrics have a special texture that means they have a right and a wrong way up – this is called the nap. On fabrics with a nap, such as velvet which has a pile that runs in one direction, or mohair, or fake fur, all the pattern pieces must be laid in the same direction.

This will take more fabric – a rough guide is that you will need an extra 20cm/8in per metre/yard. This will also allow you to match pattern repeats if necessary. If you have a commercial pattern, the exact length to buy for a napped fabric should be printed on the envelope. If not, lay the pattern out with all the pieces in the same direction on another length of the same width fabric. This will tell you how much to buy.

Fabrics with one-way designs

If a fabric has a design that must be the right way up, you will also need to lay your pattern pieces in the same direction. To calculate how much extra fabric to buy, measure a complete pattern repeat (from the top of a motif to where the next one starts beneath it) and add this amount to every metre quoted for non-napped fabrics. This will also allow you to match pattern repeats at the seams.

What to look for

Labels The label attached to the fabric roll should state the composition of the fabric and the percentages of the fibres in it. If it does not, ask the assistant to look it up in the order book. For the best results, treat your fabric according to its highest fibre content. For instance, to make a garment in a cotton/polyester blend, treat it as cotton. However, the polyester indicates that a poly/cotton sewing thread should be used. You can expect the garment to handle, wear and wash like cotton, but it will need little ironing.

Colour Check that the fabric has been evenly dyed. Ideally, examine it in daylight.

Check too for colour fastness. Dye should not come off on a dampened finger.

Print Check that the design printed on the fabric meets the selvedges at a right angle. If it does not your garment will look crooked and patterns will not match at the seams.

Weave In all woven fabrics, the weave should be even, and the weft (crosswise) threads should meet the selvedge at right angles. The closer the weave, the stronger the fabric. If you are using a loose weave for a skirt or coat, line it to prevent 'seating'.

A-Z guide to fabrics

Characteristics and uses	Fibre content	Characteristics and uses	Fibre content
ACETATE Silky finish, drapes well. Blended with other fabrics, it adds to their strength and beauty. Makes up into fabrics like taffeta, satin, brocade, jerseys and linings.	Man-made, cellulose based	**BROCADE** All-over raised design with contrasting colours and surfaces, often incorporating metallic threads. Comes in many weights for different garments.	Silk and man-made
ACRILAN Wool-like, bulky and soft. Comfort without weight, good pleat retention, recovers quickly from creasing. Wovens and knitteds. Used for dresses, suits and jumpers.	Acrylic fibre (from oil)	**CALICO** Hard-wearing plain weave, usually printed, in various weights. Shirts and interfacings.	Cotton
BARATHEA Closely woven, pebbly effect. Dresses, suits and coats.	Silk, wool, rayon and blends	**CAMBRIC** Plain weave, medium weight. Summer dresses.	Cotton and linen
BATISTE Plain weave, lightweight, almost sheer. Dresses, lingerie, handkerchiefs.	Cotton, silk, wool, rayon and man-made	**CHALLIS** (ch as in chapter) Soft, lightweight fabric, usually printed in delicate patterns. Dresses and blouses.	Wool, cotton, rayon and blends

wool challis

cambric

brocade

chiffon

cotton

Flaws Check the fabric for flaws. These are often indicated by a tag placed on the selvedge by the manufacturer. If you find a flaw, you may be offered additional fabric to compensate for it, but if you think you may not be able to avoid the flaw when cutting out, you should insist on a fresh length of fabric.

Size Some fabrics are sized – given a finish for extra stiffness. If a powdery dust appears when you rub the fabric lightly between your fingers, too much size has been added. It will wash away, leaving the fabric limp.

Creasing Crumple some of the fabric in one hand. Unless it gradually recovers it will crease constantly in wear.

Price-tag Never buy a fabric just because it is a bargain.

Remnants Chosen with care, a remnant can prove a real bargain. But ask for details if you buy a remnant with no label.

Preparing for cutting out

Press your fabric if it has been folded and creased. Decide on the right side and wrong side of the fabric. The difference is often hardly discernible, but it will show on the garment. Most fabrics are preshrunk during manufacture, but in pure wool and wool blends, up to 2% shrinkage can still take place. This tends to happen when darts and seams are damp pressed, leaving the remaining fabric looking 'baggy' To prevent this, damp press before making up.

To straighten the grain of a woven fabric before pinning on the pattern, pull or mark a thread across the width. Next pin the selvedges together. If the fold does not lie flat, give it a firm tug in the opposite direction to smooth it out.

Ten tips from buyers

Some top fabric buyers were asked to give their ten most helpful hints for choosing fabrics.

1 Is the fabric suitable for the garment you want to make – will it drape or hang correctly?

2 Will the pattern and/or colour suit you. If possible, hold the fabric up against you and look in a full length mirror.

3 Test for creasing. Crumple the fabric in one hand. How quickly does it return to normal?

4 Does the fabric fray? Will you need to spend a lot of time neatening seams?

5 If the fabric is fine, will it need lining?

6 Is it washable, or dry clean only?

7 Check for flaws – not always shown by a marker.

8 Is there a nap or one-way design? Remember to allow extra to compensate.

9 Check fabric width. Some patterns cannot be cut from narrow widths without unsightly joins.

10 Never be rushed into buying. If you can't decide, ask to take away a small snipping and think about it.

Characteristics and uses	Fibre content	Characteristics and uses	Fibre content
CHAMBRAY (ch as in shop) Coloured warp threads and a white filler thread create attractive variations of striped effects in plain cotton fabric. Children's clothes, shirts, pyjamas.	Cotton	**COTTON** Woven and knitted in many weights. (Most cotton fabrics listed under generic names.) All kinds of garments.	100% pure cotton
CHEESECLOTH Loose weave, uneven texture created by twisted yarns. Blouses and fully gathered skirts.	Cotton	**CRÊPE** Woven fabric with crinkled surface; frays easily; various widths. Blouses, dresses, evening wear.	Silk, cotton, wool, man-made
CHIFFON Plain weave sheer fabric with either a soft or a stiff finish. Blouses, scarves, evening dresses.	Silk and man-made	**CRÊPE DE CHINE** Sheer, soft, lustrous, silky fabric. Blouses, lingerie.	Silk and man-made
CORDUROY Ribbed pile fabric, hard-wearing; various weights. Skirts, trousers, jackets.	Cotton and man-made. Stretch cord: cotton/ nylon	**DENIM** Strong, twill-weave fabric; hard-wearing. Various weights and colours. Jeans, skirts and jackets.	Cotton. Stretch denim: cotton/ nylon

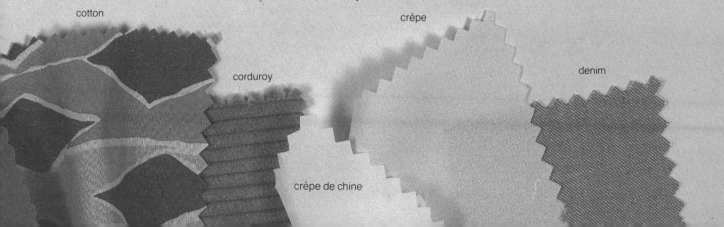

cotton

corduroy

crêpe

denim

crêpe de chine

A-Z guide to fabrics

Characteristics and uses	Fibre content
DIMITY Sheer cotton featuring a fine, corded striped effect (also checks). Blouses, baby dresses.	Cotton
DUETTE Double jersey. Suits, coats, trousers, skirts.	Acrylic and polyester. (Trade names: Courtelle and Lirelle)
FAILLE Fine, horizontally ribbed fabric. Dresses, full skirts, evening wear.	Silk and man-made
FLANNEL Woven fabric, soft surface. Dresses, full skirts, evening wear.	Wool and blends
FLANNELETTE Fine woven cotton fabric with surface brushed to provide warmth. Nightwear, blouses, skirts.	Cotton and man-made
FOULARD Plain or twill weave, soft, lightweight. Scarves, blouses, flowing dresses.	Silk, cotton, rayon
GABERDINE Twill weave, hardwearing fabric which can be shower-proofed. Suits, coats, rainwear.	Wool, cotton, blends. Stretch gaberdines=62% cotton/38% nylon
GEORGETTE Fine, dull textured, chiffon-like (but heavier) with a crêpey finish. Blouses, scarves, evening wear.	Silk, wool and man-made
GINGHAM Firm, washable, hard-wearing, light-weight cotton and cotton-like fabric. Blouses, dresses, overalls.	Cotton and blends
JACQUARD Woven and knitted fabrics of complex structure and colour combinations. Dresses and suits.	Wool and man-made
JERSEY Knitted fabric (single and double knit) in various weights. Soft; good draping qualities; tends to stretch. Dresses, suits. (Double jersey with less stretch is suitable for trousers.)	Wool, cotton, silk and man-made and blends

Characteristics and uses	Fibre content
LACE Delicate, open-structured fabric, woven or knitted. Evening blouses, dresses, trimmings.	Silk, cotton and man-made
LAMÈ (Pronounced larmay.) Woven or knitted base covered with metallic threads, drapes well. Evening and stage wear.	Wool and man-made fabric into which plastic-coated and dyed metallic threads are woven
LAWN Sheer, lightweight, smooth woven fabric. Blouses, handkerchiefs, summer dresses, baby dresses.	Cotton, fine linen, man-made and blends
LEATHER FABRIC Fabrics treated by special finishes to simulate leather. Skirts, jackets, coats, bags.	Cotton, wool with plastic or PVC coating
LINEN Plain weave natural fabric with uneven surface texture. Strong, cool, absorbent. Skirts, trousers, suits.	Linen and blends
MADRAS Fine Indian cotton with interesting stripes and checks in weave. Blouses, skirts, dresses.	Cotton
MOHAIR Knitted and woven fabrics including natural animal hair; soft and warm. Coats, jackets, shawls.	Hair from angora goat plus base of wool
MOIRÉ (Pronounced mwaray.) Watermarked pattern giving a waved effect. Fairly stiff shiny fabric. Evening skirts, dresses and blouses.	Silks, rayons and man-made
NEEDLECORD Finely ribbed plain or printed corduroy. Skirts and dresses.	Cotton and man-made
NET Small, open mesh. Veils, trimmings and dance skirts.	Silk, cotton, rayon and nylon
NYLON Fine woven or knitted fabric. Strong, non-absorbent, best blended with other fibres; useful blended for all garments. Skirts, overalls.	Synthetic: petrochemical fibre

crêpe georgette — net

poplin

organdie

moiré

pongee silk

jacquard

Characteristics and uses	Fibre content
ORGANDIE Sheer, woven fabric; can be very soft or crisp according to finish. Blouses, party dresses, collars and cuffs. The crisp one makes an excellent interfacing.	Cotton and man-made
OTTOMAN Heavy, ribbed fabric, similar in appearance to faille, but with wider, more pronounced ribs.	Wool, silk and man-made
PEAU DE SOIE (Pronounced poderswa.) Soft silk with satin sheen. Dresses and blouses.	Silk, rayon
PIQUÉ (Pronounced peekay.) Firm, medium weight, raised surface. Blouses, dresses and sportswear.	Cotton
POPLIN Smooth, soft-sheened, hardwearing, lightweight woven fabric. Shirts, blouses, summer dresses, children's clothes.	Cotton and blends
P.V.C. Special, non-porous finish applied to woven or knitted base fabric. Aprons, rainwear, coats, capes, jackets, hats and trousers.	Polyvinylchloride
RAYON Fabric made from regenerated cellulose – originally it resembled silk. Now best blended with other fibres.	Regenerated cellulose
SAILCLOTH Strong, plain or basket weave fabric, originally stiff, for sails, now softer. Skirts, jackets, trousers.	Cotton and man-made
SATIN Special weave where threads 'float' over the base threads, giving a sheen. Evening wear, trimmings.	Silk, rayon, man-made
SEERSUCKER Puckered finish on cotton and cotton blends. Summer dresses, beachwear.	Cotton and cotton blends
SHANTUNG Originally wild spun silk with a naturally occurring slub effect (as found in linen). Now a plain weave with an uneven surface from any fibre. Blouses, linings.	Silk and man-made

Characteristics and uses	Fibre content
SILK Many varieties: Pongee (pronounced ponjee): slight slub effect. Surah: twill weave, shiny, often printed, for scarves, blouses, dresses. Thai: takes dyes well in vivid colours. Tussore: wild silk, uneven texture, left in natural colour.	Silk
SUEDE CLOTH Woven or knitted fabric finished to resemble suede. Skirts, jackets, trousers, bags.	Synthetic blends
TAFFETA Interesting crisp fabric, plain or ribbed (faille), moiré (watermarked pattern), paper (lightweight). Evening wear.	Silk, rayon, nylon
TOWELLING Looped fabric for absorbency. Originally pure cotton. Robes and beachwear, stretch baby and children's wear, sports outfits.	Cottons and blends. Stretch towelling=65% cotton/35% nylon
TREVIRA (Trade name) woven or knitted fabric. Skirts, jackets.	Polyester blended with natural fibre
TULLE Very fine net. Evening and party dresses, veils.	Silk and nylon
TWEED Mostly woven but sometimes knitted. Usually checked patterns in particular colours according to place of origin, e.g. Harris tweed. Suits and coats.	Wool and wool blends
VELVET Warp pile fabric, woven. Various types: cut velvet (façonné) panne velvet: (silky pile smoothed one way). Various weights for day and evening wear. Capes, coats, suits, skirts, dresses.	Silk, cotton, man-made and blends
VIYELLA (Trade name) twill weave lightweight fabric. Soft style dresses and blouses. Baby and children's wear.	55% wool, 45% cotton
WOOL Woven and knitted as pure wool and in blends with natural and man-made fibres to form many fabrics. Dresses, coats, suits, skirts.	Pure wool and blends
WORSTED Best quality wool, tightly woven, smooth, strong, wears well. Fine worsteds for winter dresses; suit and coat weights.	Pure wool and pure wool blended with man-made fibres

Note: 100% natural fibres = wool, cotton, linen and silk. 'Man-made' = synthetic fibres produced chemically.

tweed

taffeta

linen look

jersey

gaberdine

suede-look jersey

gingham

Choosing and using commercial paper patterns

Whether you want to make designer outfits or a collection of mix and match wardrobe basics, the paper pattern catalogues offer an abundance of ideas, specially designed to suit the various figure types. Decide which type best applies to you, and you are ready to start.

When you can't find the outfit you are looking for in a shop, don't despair. It is very likely that you will find it in the pages of a pattern book – ready to be made up at a fraction of the shop price.

Though the cost of paper patterns has increased over the years, they still represent good value for money, given the amount of hard work that goes into each design. And if you choose a designer pattern from the wide range that many pattern companies produce – and make it up in a complementary fabric – you will have a designer name outfit you could never otherwise afford. Even making up basic patterns has advantages over shop-bought clothes; you have total control over the fit and the finish, and you can use particularly successful patterns again and again in a variety of fabrics and colourways.

Read on for advice on choosing the patterns that are right for your figure type and will fit without the need for extensive alterations.

Recognising your figure type

Figure types – junior petite, misses, womens etc – are used in pattern books to help you find patterns that are right for you. They are necessary because the female form comes in many shapes and sizes, and one pattern range could not possibly be suitable for them all.

Pattern sizes, however, are based on standard body measurements (see page 20). Ask a friend to help you to take all your measurements over your usual undergarments, with the tape held neither too loose nor too tight. Pay particular attention to your bust measurement and nape of neck to back waist measurement, and check your height, too.

Assess your figure. If you are under 18 years old, you are probably still developing. If not, are you a little short in stature with proportionately small measurements, or well-proportioned and developed, or are you perhaps a little older, becoming fully mature and slightly larger in proportion? All these factors will determine your figure type and the pattern size that is best for you.

The chart on page 17 can be used as a guideline, but do make a final check in the back of a pattern book when buying a pattern. All the sizes are given there in more detailed charts and there are small differences in the way individual pattern companies categorise the figure types.

Do not try to choose a paper pattern size according to the size of garment you usually buy in a shop. Ready-to-wear sizes differ widely – one manufacturer's size 8 can be another's size 10 or even 12 – so be accurate and take your measurements properly.

Pattern books and patterns

The main source of commercial paper patterns is the counter catalogue produced by each pattern company, and displayed in fabric shops and department stores. They contain hundreds of designs, each with several variations, and are updated on a monthly or seasonal basis when some new patterns are introduced, indicating the latest fashion trends.

The key to using a pattern book efficiently is to know your figure type and size. Each catalogue has an information section, usually found at the back. This contains instructions for taking body measurements, explanations and diagrams of figure types, and size charts. The sizes are standard in all catalogues, but some offer a more comprehensive range of figure types to choose from. The best offer a wide range of sizes within each figure type, and cater for the whole family; some produce a separate catalogue for children.

Within the catalogue the designs are grouped together in sections such as Dresses or Sportswear, or in specific figure types, such as Misses or Junior. Between the sections are thick paper dividers, each clearly labelled and visible from the front of the catalogue, to enable you to turn quickly to the section you need.

Right: A selection of outfits from the major pattern companies. Some are special designer outfits – all illustrate how easy it is for today's home dressmaker to make herself a complete range of clothes from commercial paper patterns.

Points to remember when choosing a pattern

Dresses, blouses, coats and jackets Choose a pattern for your figure type in the size corresponding most nearly to your *bust* measurement. If your waist and hip measurements differ from those given, the pattern can be adjusted. Do not choose a size larger for coats and jackets to allow for wearing them over other clothes; this

has already been taken into consideration by the pattern makers.
Skirts and trousers Choose the pattern size by *hip* measurement. If your measurements differ from the pattern, it is easier to make alterations at the waist than at the hip.
When skirts or trousers are part of a multiple choice pattern which

also includes blouses or jackets choose by *bust* size.
Multi-size patterns These patterns eliminate the need for making extensive pattern adjustments if you do not conform to any one size. For example, you can make a jacket in size 10 and a skirt in size 12 from the same pattern.

logue are grouped according to whether the garments are dresses, separates, evening wear and so on, rather than by figure types, check that the chosen style does come in your figure type and is available in your size. Where sizes at either extreme of the size range are not included, or a fabric width is not stated, it means that the style is suitable only for the sizes offered, or that it is impossible or uneconomic to cut from the fabric widths omitted.

Only when you have considered and checked all of these factors is it safe to go ahead and buy, or order the pattern. Large stores usually carry a comprehensive range of patterns in all sizes, but smaller outlets may have to order the pattern for you. If you jot all the details of the pattern down for reference while you are making your choice, you will still be able to go ahead and choose the fabric, threads etc, and put in an order for the pattern – arranging for it to be posted to your home, or to be collected from the store.

The pattern package

The pattern envelope repeats the information given on the catalogue page, with colour sketches or a photograph on the front and all fabric requirements and suggestions, sizes and measurements on the back. The envelope contains the pattern pieces printed on sheets of tissue paper, layouts showing how to position the pieces on different widths of fabric, and step-by-step instructions for making up the styles illustrated.

Pattern pieces for a simple design may be printed on a single sheet of tissue; more complicated designs may cover several sheets. Each pattern piece is numbered for easy reference, and corresponding numbers are used on the layout. Separate the pattern pieces, choose the numbers that are required for the style you are making up and place them on the fabric according to the appropriate layout.

Some pattern companies produce a pattern sheet for beginners with the pattern pieces already in the correct position on the tissue sheet. This is simply pinned directly to the fabric and the pieces cut out.

Look before you buy Patterns are not usually exchangeable, so read the information on the catalogue page with great care before buying, to make sure the pattern is suitable for you. If you are still in doubt, ask the shop assistant for advice; some of the main department stores have staff specially trained to give this guidance.

Each page in the catalogue tells you everything you need to know about the style illustrated, including fabric suggestions and requirements and written descriptions of the style of the garment.

Study the paragraph of detailed description, which tells you what is involved in making up the garment – for example, whether it is lined or cut on the cross. Some pattern companies illustrate all the pattern pieces used as well, which can be a useful guide as to the garment's complexity. Front and back views and any alternative features such as variations of neckline, sleeve or hem length are also shown. A photograph in the catalogue can give you a good idea of the garment, but the artist's impression, combined with the thumbnail sketches of the back views, is most important. It provides style detail such as the position of darts or seams, which do not show up clearly in a photograph. All this information should help you to decide whether you have the dressmaking skills to manage the techniques involved.

Finally, if the patterns in the cata-

Differences to look out for

The cutting line is clearly marked on all patterns so there is never any doubt about which line to follow when cutting out. The seamline is the line along which final stitching takes place, and between these two lines lies the 1.5cm/⅝in seam allowance.

Single size patterns have only one cutting line and a seamline marked 1.5cm/⅝in within it.

Multi-size patterns may have six cutting lines and although the seam allowance is normally included, for the sake of clarity, the actual seamline is not marked.

Continental multi-size patterns may not include the seam allowance at all, in which case first cut out all the pattern pieces following the cutting line for the appropriate size. Then pin them to the fabric and mark the seam allowances all the way round using tailor's chalk or a tracing wheel and dressmaker's carbon paper. The instructions may suggest the amounts to be added on, giving different allowances for different seams.

Study all the information printed on each pattern piece and on the instruction sheet *before* cutting out the fabric. Mark a ring around the fabric layout and view number to be followed. Make all the adjustments necessary to length, sleeves etc before pinning the pattern in place, and make sure you know whether or not seam allowances are included on your pattern. And do make a final check that appropriate pattern pieces are positioned on the fold. Mistakes made when cutting out could prove costly.

Figure types and pattern sizes

Misses

Height (without shoes)	Body description	Nape to waist	Sizes and bust sizes									
			6	8	10	12	14	16	18	20	22	24
1.65–1.68m 5ft 5in–5ft 6in	Well proportioned and developed	Between 39.5–44.5cm 15½–17½in	78 30½	80 31½	83 32½	87 34	92 36	97 38	102 40	107 42	112 44	117cm 46in

Miss Petite (mp)

Height (without shoes)	Body description	Nape to waist						
			6mp	8mp	10mp	12mp	14mp	16mp
1.57–1.63m 5ft 2in–5ft 4in	As above, but shorter overall	Between 37–40cm 14½–15¾in	78 30½	80 31½	83 32½	87 34	92 36	97cm 38in

Junior

Height (without shoes)	Body description	Nape to waist						
			5	7	9	11	13	15
1.63–1.65m 5ft 4in–5ft 5in	Well proportioned, but short-waisted. Taller than Miss Petite	Between 38–41.5cm 15–16¼in	76 30	79 31	81 32	85 33½	89 35	94cm 37in

Junior Petite (jp)

Height (without shoes)	Body description	Nape to waist						
			3jp	5jp	7jp	9jp	11jp	13jp
1.52–1.55m 5ft–5ft 1in	Well proportioned but petite	Between 35.5–39cm 14–15¼in	76 30	79 31	81 32	84 33	87 34	89cm 35in

Women

Height (without shoes)	Body description	Nape to waist						
			38	40	42	44	46	48	50
1.65–1.68m 5ft 5in–5ft 6in	Larger, more mature figure	Between 44–46cm 17¼–18in	107 42	112 44	117 46	122 48	127 50	132 52	137cm 54in

Half-size

Height (without shoes)	Body description	Nape to waist							
			10½	12½	14½	16½	18½	20½	22½	24½
1.57–1.60m 5ft 2in–5ft 3in	Fully developed figure with short back waist length	Between 38–41.5cm 15–16¼in	84 33	89 35	94 37	99 39	104 41	109 43	114 45	119cm 47in

Working with graph and multi-size patterns

These comprehensive instructions on using paper patterns and preparing and cutting out fabric are as valuable to the experienced dressmaker as the beginner. Use them either for the versatile patterns in this book, or for any commercial pattern you choose.

A multi-size pattern is one of the most economical patterns, as it includes several sizes on each pattern piece. Many magazine patterns are prepared this way, and so are a few commercial paper patterns. From the dressmaker's point of view they have an advantage over one-size patterns in that you can make up the same garment in a variety of sizes for family and friends. If the pattern is printed on a graph, find the appropriate cutting line for your size and follow this when drawing up the graph pattern.

Similarly, if the pattern is printed full size, find the appropriate symbol for the cutting line for your size (clearly marked on the pattern) and follow this throughout.

Cutting out multi-size patterns

The full-size pattern pieces are usually printed on sheets of paper (often tissue) and numbered so that you can group together the pieces for each garment. Cut the pieces from the large tissue sheets as they are needed. Alternatively, if you want to make up a garment in more than one size you can trace off the pattern pieces from the original pattern.

If the pieces are creased, run a warm iron over them to smooth them out taking care not to tear them.

This makes it easier to position them on the fabric, and pin them accurately.

Making a pattern from a graph

Enlarging a pattern from a graph is a useful technique which gives you access to graph designs like the ones in this book, rather than always having to buy a pattern. If you use dressmaker's squared paper it is not as time-consuming as you may think or, if you prefer, you can rule up your own squared paper.

Understanding how these miniature patterns work also helps you develop an ability to design and make up your own patterns.

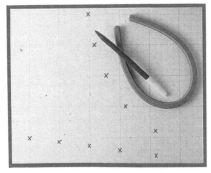
Marking crosses on large-scale paper.

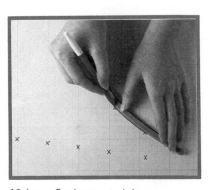
Using a flexicurve to join up crosses.

You will need

Dressmaker's pattern paper marked in centimetres
Pencil, rubber, scissors
Ruler (the longer the better)
A flexicurve or dressmaker's curved ruler for drawing curved areas

The graph is a scaled-down plan of a pattern which has to be enlarged. You can work with plain paper and rule a grid for yourself, but the quickest, easiest and most accurate way is to use pattern paper which is already marked out in 1cm and 5cm squares, and numbered down one side and along the lower edge. Check that the size of the squares on the graph corresponds with your pattern paper. (Some graphs are based on 2cm squares: for these you simply use two squares of 1cm graph pattern paper.)

Work on a firm surface – a piece of hardboard or the kitchen table is suitable. Start by counting the number of squares across and down the graph and mark the same number of squares on the large-scale paper. Draw a rectangle on the paper to correspond with the outer limits of the graph. (This helps you to check later that you have transferred the graph correctly.)

1 Starting with any long straight lines, make a cross on the paper wherever the pattern outline intersects with a gridline on the graph. (Make sure you are transferring the right outline for your size if the graph is multi-sized.)

2 Join up the crosses. You can do this freehand, but a flexicurve, available from good stationers, makes the job very easy. A dressmaker's curved ruler or even a plate are useful alternatives. After completing all the outside lines, indicate other details such as the straight-grain line (use one of the vertical lines on the pattern paper) or the seamlines (usually 1.5cm/⅝in in from the edge). Label each pattern piece and add the size and any other important points such as foldlines and notches. (Notches on patterns are there to help you match two pattern pieces exactly.)

Cut out the pattern pieces with paper-cutting scissors. Where notches are shown on seam edges, cut round them so that they are not forgotten when cutting out the fabric.

Making pattern adjustments

Most commercial patterns and those printed on graphs are designed to fit an average figure. Therefore, to obtain a perfect fit you will probably have to adjust the pattern to make it conform to your figure.

It is worth taking the time and trouble to check the fit of the pattern before cutting out, either by cross-checking your measurements with those of the pattern, or by actually trying on the paper pattern. If the pattern is checked properly at this stage, only minor fitting adjustments should be necessary during making up. If you are still in doubt about the fit of a pattern even after checking, add 1.5cm/⅝in to side and sleeve seams only (*not* the armhole) before cutting out to allow plenty of extra fabric for any alterations.

At whatever stage you make alterations, do remember that the adjustments must be made to all corresponding pattern pieces. For example, if sleeve seams are adjusted, then the side seams must be adjusted in the same way. Always make a record of any alterations carried out on the pattern or at a later fitting stage. This saves time when using the pattern again, or using a similar one.

Finally, to preserve your pattern for future use and to retain an accurate record of the alterations, it helps if you reinforce the pattern with fusible interfacing. See below left for other ideas to preserve your pattern.

Below: Check your measurements against the pattern – trying on the bodice may help. Ask a friend to help you mark any alterations. If they are extensive, make a revised copy pattern (see below left).

Care of paper patterns

Tissue paper tears easily so use these tips to help you preserve your patterns.
● Fold and unfold tissue very carefully, and find the original folds when replacing pieces in the pattern envelope.
● Cut out, mark and remove pattern pieces in one sewing session, as moving the fabric with the pattern still pinned in position will tear the tissue.
● Remove pins carefully, and use the same pinholes when using the pattern again.
● If you have a paper punch use it to perforate the pattern on the appropriate markings and mark fabric with tacks or chalk through the holes to avoid tearing tissue.
● To repair a pattern, iron carefully and mend tears with sticky tape on each side.

Strengthening a new pattern
● Reinforce patterns that are to be used frequently by pressing lightweight, iron-on Vilene on to the printed side of the complete pattern. (On the reverse side it will cling to the fabric.) Perforate pattern to indicate position of markings. Keep pattern rolled, not folded.
● Take copies of your pattern on dressmaker's graph paper, by tracing round the pattern or using a tracing wheel and dressmaker's carbon paper. This is useful if pattern alterations are to be made.

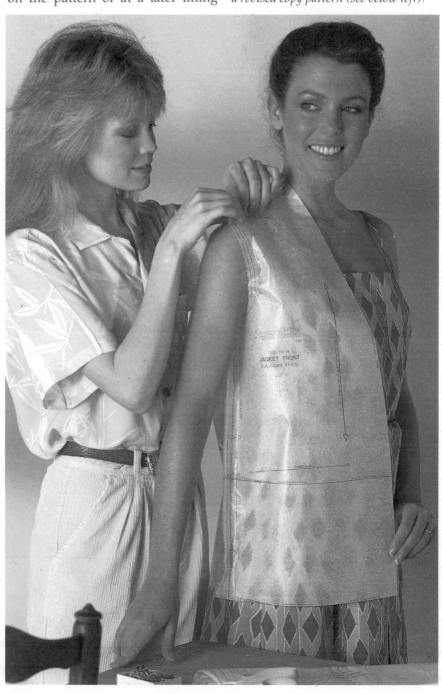

Chart your own measurements

Familiarize yourself with your measurements so that you always know how much you vary from any standard commercial pattern or from the graphs in this book. You can then make accurate adjustments to the pattern before cutting out. In this way you will only need to make minor alterations when you have cut out and tacked the garment.

Measure yourself at the points indicated on the diagram below and keep a note here or in a notebook – and don't forget to recheck your measurements if your weight changes. These measurements are enough for most sewing purposes. Where a style requires other vital statistics – for example the thigh measurement when making trousers – this will be mentioned in the appropriate chapter.

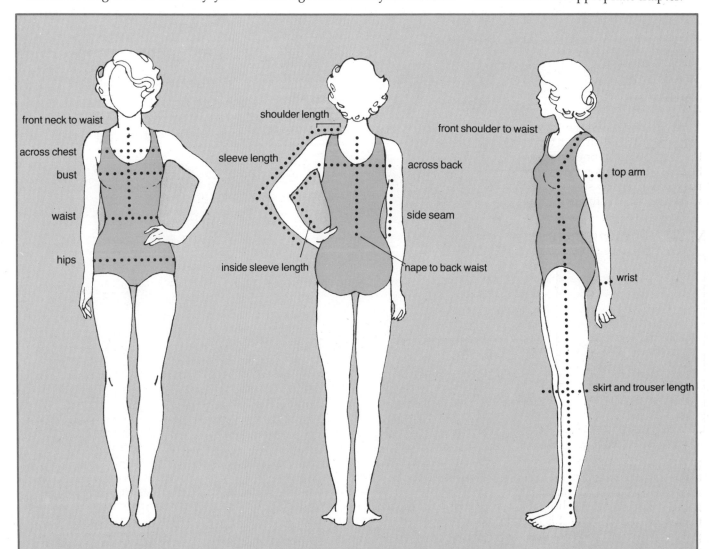

Fifteen vital statistics

Bust Over the fullest part at the front and at the same level straight across the back ....

Waist At your natural waistline, snugly, but not tight.....................

Hips 18cm/7in down from your waist if you are a small size, 24cm/9½in for a large size ....

Across back About 14cm/5½in from nape of neck, over shoulder blades and between armhole seam ....

....

Across chest 7cm/3in from front neck base, straight across between

armhole seams ....

Shoulder length From the side of your neck to the end of your shoulder ....

Nape to back waist From your nape down the spine to your natural waist level ....

Front neck to waist From base of neck to front waist ....

Front shoulder to waist From centre front shoulder, over bust to waist ...

....

Side seam From underarm to side waist ....

Sleeve length With arm bent, from end of shoulder, over elbow, to outside wrist bone ....

Inside sleeve length From under arm out to elbow, and down to inside wrist ....

Top arm Round the fullest part, between the shoulder and the elbow ....

Wrist Over wrist bone ....

Skirt and trouser length From side of waist, over hip to knee, floor, or required lengths in between ....

....

Recognising pattern markings

Each pattern piece contains valuable information to help you make up your garment. These signs and symbols are common to all commercial paper patterns, both multi-size and one-size, so it is worth learning to recognise the important symbols.

────── **Cutting line** Marked by a
─ ─ ─ variety of symbols in multi-size patterns, depending on size. Try to leave it on your pattern by cutting out 1mm/¹⁄₁₆in from the outside edge of the line, to preserve the pattern for future use.

──◇── **Notches** are diamond shapes, found on the cutting line. There may be one or more, numbered to match a notch or pair of notches on a corresponding seam – waist edge to waistband for example.

Cut outwards, not into the seamline.

─ ─ ─ ─ **Seamline** Sometimes shown as a broken line on a pattern. If omitted, the seam allowance is 1.5cm/⅝in from the cutting line, unless otherwise stated.

● ○ **Dots or circles** may be small
● ○ or large and indicate where to start or finish seams or gathers, and the position for pleats, pockets and other features.

◄────► **Grainline** This is shown by a solid straight line with arrows at each end and represents the straight grain (direction of weave) of the fabric. It is important to position the arrow accurately, parallel to the selvedges, because the grain affects the 'hang' of a garment. It is usually placed vertically, running from neck to hem, following the strongest threads of woven fabrics, but there are exceptions. In border-prints the horizontal grain runs down the garment while the border, which is the vertical straight grain, runs horizontally round the garment.

▼───▼ **Fold bracket** This is another grainline marking. The arrows point to the solid outer line which must be placed exactly on the fold of the fabric. It must be left as a fold, so do not cut the fabric when removing the pattern.

════════ **Pattern alteration lines** These are double lines, placed horizontally across a back, front or sleeve indicating the best position for shortening or lengthening the pattern piece without distorting the shape.

Making fitting adjustments

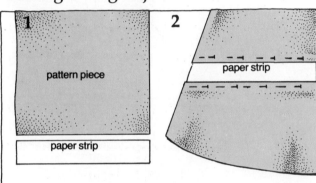
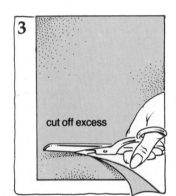
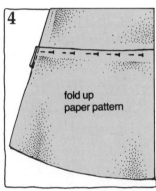

1 pattern piece / paper strip
2 paper strip
3 cut off excess
4 fold up paper pattern

To help you simplify the process of making up, and to see whether any fitting adjustments are necessary, it may help to pin the paper pattern together. If you can see how the pattern works in this way it is easier to put the fabric sections together. Start with any darts, pleats or folds then pin the seams at side and shoulder, handling the tissue very carefully. Hold it up against you in front of a full-length mirror. You can see where it may be necessary to adjust the length, or where to place a pocket, for example.

Multi-size patterns make it possible to use more than one size in a single garment, and so make easy adjustments for your figure. For example, if you are wide hipped you could combine a larger skirt size with a smaller size top in a dress like the camisole dress on page 199. Here are a few general tips on adjusting patterns – subsequent chapters give more detailed fitting instructions.

Lengthening a pattern
1 Garments with absolutely straight lower edges may be lengthened by adding an appropriately sized strip of paper to the pattern at the hem, or drawing a line across with tailor's chalk for the extra amount before cutting out.
2 Garments with shaped lower edges, or where an alteration is to be made in the body of a garment, are lengthened by cutting across the double alteration line. Insert a strip of paper in the gap to extend the piece by the extra amount required, with enough overlap to secure it to either side of the pattern piece.

Shortening a pattern
3 Where there is an absolutely straight lower edge, simply cut off a strip of pattern to shorten it.
4 If there is shaping at the lower edge, or you wish to make an alteration within the body of a garment, measure up from the alteration line the exact amount by which you wish to shorten the pattern. Draw a line across the pattern at this point and fold across the double alteration marking, taking it up to meet the drawn line. Pin to secure and re-draw any shaped seams.

Adjusting pattern width
Commercial patterns are designed to conform to average body measurements, and include an allowance for ease of movement. Fitting problems can be avoided by checking your own measurements against the pattern before cutting. Allow at least 2cm/¾in on top of your measurements across the front and back for ease of movement. If the pattern proves eventually to be a little large, take in more seam allowance at the side seams. If it is too big all over, you should use a smaller size pattern.

Preparing fabric for cutting out

Most fabrics have a right and a wrong side, apart from reversibles which have two right sides. It is easy to tell the difference on printed fabrics, but plain materials can pose a problem. One guideline is to check the way in which the fabric is sold in the shop. If it is rolled around a tube, the right side is inside. Cotton fabrics sold folded have the right side out, while woollens are wrong side out.

It is easier to judge in natural rather than artificial light, and once you have made a decision, mark each pattern piece that you cut on the wrong side of the fabric with tailor's chalk, to avoid confusion later.

Always check your fabric length for flaws before pinning on the pattern. Look carefully for areas of fraying, pulled threads or small holes. Mark them with chalk and avoid them when cutting out.

Cutting layout

A layout gives vital information on how the pattern should be positioned, according to the style and size of your garment, and the width of your fabric. It shows which pieces should be placed to a fold, which ones are to be cut more than once, and indicates when part of the fabric must be opened out for cutting a wide pattern piece, or one from a single thickness.

Pinning pattern to fabric

Fold the fabric right sides together before pinning on the pattern. This means pattern markings can be transferred directly to the wrong side of the material. However, if cutting a napped fabric, or matching the fabric design, fold with wrong sides together.

Pin the pattern to fabric only when you have enough time to cut out the pattern pieces and transfer the markings as well. Never leave pins in fabric for more than a few days – they attract moisture and begin to rust, leaving marks in the fabric when you eventually remove them.

Positioning pins

Never pin into the body of the fabric as even fine, sharp pins can snag. Insert the pins so that the head and point are both within the seam allowance, parallel to the cutting line. This avoids damaging the shears when cutting out, or pulling threads if the garment is folded with the pins in it.

Pin corners first, to secure the pattern. Use one pin every 15cm/6in along straight seams, but more pins are necessary around curved edges – one about every 5cm/2in. Do not pin across folds – it may mark the fabric. Instead, secure the pattern with weights (any small, heavy object will do). Allow enough room between pattern pieces on the fabric to manoeuvre the shears without damaging the pattern.

How to cut out

Use shears with long blades and angled handles. These allow you to cut out without lifting the fabric and the pattern.

Take long, even strokes on straight edges, using the supporting hand to keep the pattern flat, but take shorter strokes around curves. Cut notches outwards into the spare fabric, not into the pattern as this destroys the seam allowances.

Cutting out checklist

Always make a final check of all the points listed below before starting to cut.

1 Are there any flaws in the material? If so, have you positioned your pattern to avoid them?

2 Are all the pattern pieces required for your chosen style pinned on to the fabric? Tick them off on your layout.

3 Are the pattern pieces aligned to grainlines and placed to folds where necessary?

4 If any pieces are labelled 'cut four' (pockets or cuffs for example) have you allowed enough extra fabric to cut the pattern pieces again?

5 Have any alterations to length or width been made on all corresponding pattern pieces?

Pinning on and cutting out

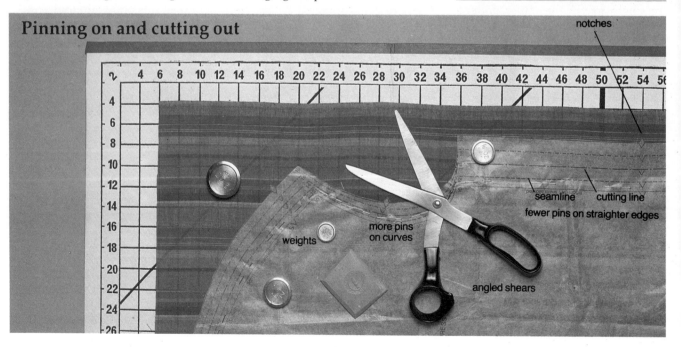

notches

weights

more pins on curves

seamline   cutting line
fewer pins on straighter edges

angled shears

Quick methods of transferring pattern markings

In order to put a garment together accurately, transfer the pattern markings to the garment pieces. This avoids wasting time later in referring back to the pattern.

Markings are usually transferred to the wrong side of the fabric but if you want to interface a piece – a collar for example – mark the interfacing, not the fabric.

When markings are needed on the right side of a garment – buttonholes for example – either choose a marking method that goes through all layers, such as tailor's tacks, or use dressmaker's carbon paper.

If you are using pale-coloured or sheer fabric use only tailor's tacks or pins for marking. Otherwise, you can choose from one of the several methods shown below.

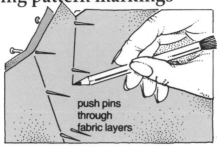

Pins and chalk pencil
Where fabric is folded right sides together, push pins through dots or symbols marking darts, pleats etc, so that they emerge on the other side of fabric. Remove the pattern carefully and make a chalk mark on each wrong side where the pins enter and leave the two layers of fabric.

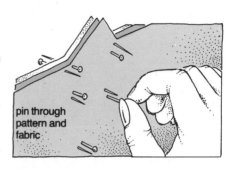

Pins only
This quick method is most suitable for marking darts and pleats. Insert pins as above, but insert a second pin for each mark from opposite side. When the paper pattern is removed a pin will remain at the same point on each garment piece. Deal with the darts or pleats immediately as the pins fall out easily.

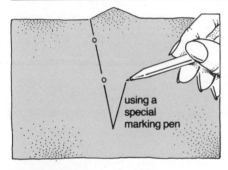

Marking pen
A special marking pen with washable ink can be used on many fabrics. On thin fabrics, the ink shows up on both sides and remains until removed by a drop of water, or by damp pressing.

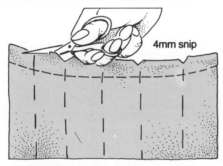

Snipping seam allowances
This is a quick method of indicating pleat and fold positions, gathering points or notches on collar pieces. Use it on seams where the seam allowance will be trimmed down – inside collars for example. Make snips no more than 4mm/⅛in deep.

Carbon paper and wheel
Dressmaker's carbon paper comes in several colours and is used in conjunction with a tracing wheel to transfer whole lines of pattern markings to a garment. Use this method for problem areas – collar edges, for example – where it is difficult to get both sides exactly the same. Choose a colour that is close to your fabric (but still visible). Do not use it on white or sheer fabric where the colour would show through, or on loosely woven fabric, where the marks disappear. Always protect the cutting surface by placing a piece of hardboard or thick cardboard under the work.

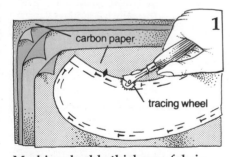

Marking double thickness fabric
1 If fabric is folded right sides together, lay one sheet of carbon paper beneath the double layer and one sheet on top beneath the pattern – coloured side to fabric in both cases. To avoid unpinning the whole pattern, trace off markings required in sections.

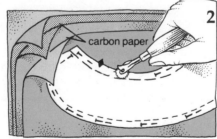

2 If fabric is folded wrong sides together, sandwich two sheets of carbon paper between the two fabric layers, back to back with the colour facing the wrong side of fabric.
Trace as before.

Marking single thickness fabric
When cutting single fabric, pin the pattern to the right side of the fabric and lay the carbon paper under the fabric, coloured side up. Press down firmly on the tracing wheel guiding it along straight edges, using a ruler, and pushing gently round curves.

Basic stitches and seams

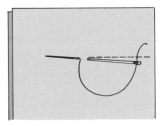

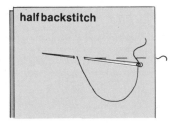

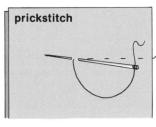

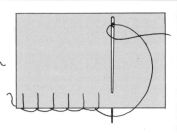

Backstitch
This is a strong hand stitch which has several versions, all useful for different dressmaking purposes. Work from right to left bringing the thread through to the right side. Insert needle to right of first stitch and bring it to right side again, to left of first stitch. Continue in this way, placing stitches in a continuous line.

Half backstitch is not as strong as backstitch. Work in the same way but space stitches one stitch length apart.

Prickstitch gives a strong but almost invisible stitch which is ideal for inserting zips. The stitch taken on the right side is tiny in proportion to that on the wrong side. One backstitch is a very good way of securing thread at the beginning and end of any row of hand stitches.

Blanket stitch
Used as a decorative edging over a turned hem or along a raw edge. Work from left to right with the item away from you and the needle pointing towards you. Insert the needle at A and bring it out at B above the loop of thread from the previous stitch.

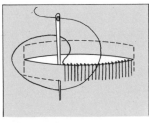

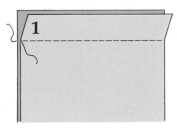

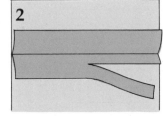

Buttonhole stitch
Work from right to left with the cut edge away from you. Insert the needle into the fabric from the back and, before pulling it through, bring the thread from the needle under the point to form a loop. Draw the needle through the work and pull gently upwards so that a small knot forms on the cut edge. Work the stitches closely together.

Catchstitch
A loosely worked, flexible stitch (see under Blind hem) used for holding two layers of fabric together. Work from right to left between the layers to be joined. Take a few threads only from each fabric and make one stitch at a time. Make stitches no less than 5mm/¼in in length and do not pull sewing thread tightly or stitching line will show on right side.

Flat fell seam
This seam encloses seam allowances of both sides of the fabric and is used on garments needing frequent laundering such as shirts, children's and sportswear. It is also ideal for reversible garments.
1 Place the fabric *wrong* sides together and stitch along the seamline.

2 Trim seam allowance of the back section, or the bodice in the case of a yoke, to 5mm/¼in. Press seam allowance to one side so that the untrimmed edge covers the trimmed edge.
3 Turn under the edge of the upper seam allowance so that it encloses the trimmed edge. Pin, tack and

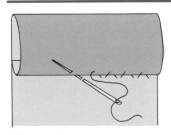

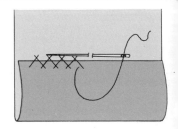

Hemming
This is a closely worked stitch suitable for inner garment areas which need to be strong and durable, but which cannot be machined. Despite its name, hemming is never used around hemlines. Work from right to left inserting needle into main garment taking up one or two threads. Bring needle out diagonally 1–2mm/⅛in along, taking a few threads from the fold to be secured.
Hemming is also used to secure folded edges to a line of machining, such as finishing cuffs and collars, waistbands and pockets.

Herringbone stitch
A strong, flexible stitch used for hems and

All the instructions for hand sewing given in this book are for right-handed dressmakers. Simply reverse the direction of working if you are left-handed.

Blind hem
This type of hem is so called because the stitches holding the hem turning in place should be invisible from both the right and wrong side of the garment. They are concealed between the hem and the main fabric. A blind hem is particularly suitable for medium to heavyweight fabrics. Tack the neatened hem turning to the wrong side of the garment stitching 1cm/½in from the edge. Several types of stitches can be used for the hem.

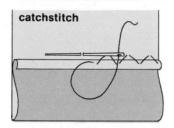
catchstitch

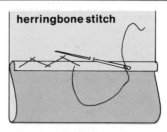
herringbone stitch

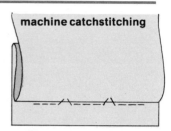
machine catchstitching

Catchstitch (see entry) Fold back ends of hem and, working from right to left, catchstitch hem to garment. Make the stitches between 5mm/¼in and 1cm/½in in length. Do not pull thread tight or an impression of the stitches will show on the right side. Where very heavy fabric is used, two rows

of catchstitches may be needed to support the weight. On a 5cm/2in deep hem, place the first row of stitches 2.5cm/1in from the hem edge and the second row 5mm/¼in to 1cm/½in from the edge.
Herringbone stitch (see entry) An alternative stitch for blind hems, work as for

catchstitching, above.
Machine catchstitching Blind hems may also be stitched on certain zigzag machines and this is particularly helpful where the hem length is considerable, such as on curtains.

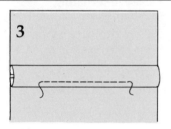

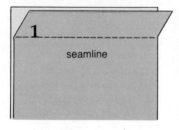

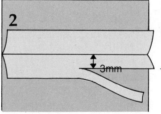

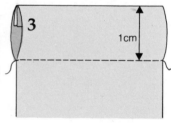

machine stitch, close to the fold.
This seam can also be worked in reverse, placing the *right* sides of fabric together. In this case an additional row of topstitching must be added close to the seamline.

French seam
This is a neat and durable seam which can be made very narrow for comfort on lingerie and nightwear. The finer the fabric, the narrower the finished seam can be made. All raw turnings are enclosed within the seam so there is no chance of fraying.
1 With *wrong* sides

together, machine 5mm/³⁄₁₆in from the seamline, within the seam allowance.
2 Press seam open and trim both raw edges to 3mm/⅛in.

3 Fold along machine line with *right* sides together. Tack and machine on seamline. Press seam to one side.

securing interfacing to wrong side of the fabric. Working from left to right but with the needle pointing to the left, take a few threads of the garment. Bring needle diagonally to the right and take next stitch with needle pointing to the left but in the hem

turning. Continue in this way, alternating between garment and layer to be attached. Do not pull the stitches tightly. This is an ideal stitch for knitted fabrics. For concealed herringbone stitch see Blind hems.

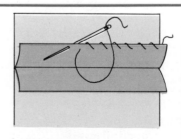

Overcasting
This is used to finish raw edges by hand.

Work from left to right and make evenly-spaced diagonal stitches over the raw edges. Gauge the size and spacing of the stitches to minimize fraying.
Overcasting can also be worked on a zigzag machine using a plain zigzag stitch.

25

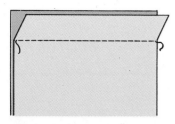

Plain seam

This is the simplest seam which is most often used. Place the fabric right sides together, matching seamlines. Pin and tack along seamline and machine or backstitch by hand. Press

seam open and neaten raw edges if necessary.

Prickstitch

An almost invisible stitch ideal for inserting zips by hand (see Backstitch).

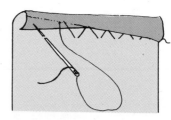

Rolled hem

Used on fine fabrics to give a neat finish when hem is likely to show. Trim hem allowance to 1cm/½in and staystitch 3mm/⅛in from edge with small machine stitches. Trim fabric

away to within a few threads of machining. Turn hem to wrong side along hem foldline, rolling raw edge under so that line of machining just shows. Working from right to left, take small loose stitches through machining and garment. Take several stitches before pulling up thread, causing the hem to roll. When pressing do not iron hem, but leave gently rounded.

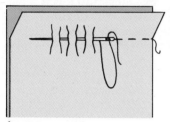

Running stitch

This simple stitch has many dressmaking uses. Work from right to left weaving needle in and out of fabric several times before pulling through.
Gathering Begin with a knot and work small, even stitches.
Tacking Begin with a backstitch and work 1cm/½in stitches 1cm/½in apart.

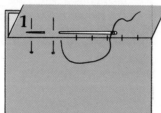 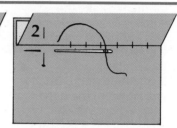

Slip or edge tacking

This is a method of tacking from the right side to ensure accurate matching of designs, checks and stripes at seamlines. It is also used when making fitting adjustments from the right side.
With right sides of garment sections facing upwards, turn under the seam allowance of one

piece along the seamline and lap edge over the adjoining seam allowance, matching both seamlines. Pin at right angles to seam.
1 Begin with a backstitch and work from right to left. Insert needle into fold and take a stitch along for 1cm/½in.
2 Pull thread through and insert needle directly above first stitch but

through the single layer, close to the fold. Bring it out again 1cm/½in along. Pull thread through, drawing the layers together and matching design exactly. Repeat along length to be tacked, alternating between fold and single fabric. When machined on wrong side, the design will be held firmly in place.

Tacking

See under Running stitch. Other tacking stitches follow.

Diagonal tacking

Provides firmer control over an area than ordinary tacking. Work parallel stitches with the needle pointing right to left, so that diagonal stitches form on the right side. For even firmer control, decrease space between parallel stitches.
Tailor's tacks These are used for marking particular points on a garment. Ideally they are used to transfer all

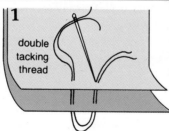 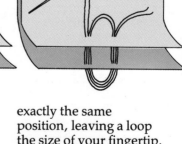 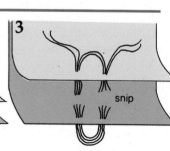

pattern markings to the fabric after cutting out. Use double tacking thread and a fine needle.
1 With paper pattern still in position, take a small stitch where required through all layers, leaving a good tail of thread at the end.
2 Make another stitch at

exactly the same position, leaving a loop the size of your fingertip. Remove pattern.
3 Gently ease the fabric apart and snip the threads between the layers. This leaves tufts of thread as very clear markings which are quickly and completely

removed later.
Thread tacking Used to mark lines on garment prior to making up. Use single tacking thread and alternate long and short stitches working on the right side of the fabric.

Machines and equipment

Having the right equipment to hand and knowing what your sewing machine and its attachments can do will increase your skills and greatly add to the pleasure of your sewing. This guide describes the variations and capabilities of the various machines.

Most homes today possess a sewing machine of one kind or other, yet few machines, whether simple straight-stitchers or sophisticated electronics, are used to their full potential. Modern machines can do so much more than 'running up the seams'.

Choosing a machine

Choosing a machine, new or second-hand, can be a bewildering experience when there is such a wide choice. The most important factors to consider are the processes you want the machine to perform for you. Use this guide to help you work out which sewing machine will best fulfil your sewing needs.

There are three main types: straight-stitch, automatic and electronic. Within one of these areas you should find a machine to suit your needs and price range.

Straight-stitchers

These are available as 'used models' as they are no longer manufactured. They may be hand, treadle or electrically operated and may only stitch forwards. If attachments are used, the machines can perform many extra functions such as buttonholing, hemming, pleating, binding and free embroidery.

Automatic machines

Swing-needle In addition to straight stitching, these stitch from side to side in a zigzag motion, producing a closed or open satin stitch useful for seam neatening and embroidery, but not suitable for stretch fabrics.
Semi-automatic These incorporate several 'embroidery patterns' on cams or discs which have to be inserted by hand.
Automatic The term 'automatic' refers only to buttonholes, which can be made without turning the garment, but these and embroidery patterns are still controlled by hand.

Fully automatic In addition to all previous features, these machines can produce a greater variety of embroidery patterns. Instead of hand-inserted cams for individual patterns, many models in this range have built-in cams controlled by a knob, making them easier to operate than earlier machines.
Super-automatics These machines incorporate a circular motion stitch. The stretch-stitch, flexi-stitch and overlock stitch (simultaneous stitching and overcasting) incorporate side-to-side, forward and reverse, all within the same pattern, for sewing stretch fabrics. They can also seam knitted garments

Microchip machines

Many mechanical parts have been replaced by micro-circuitry, and levers and dials have been replaced by visual control panels. A touch of the finger engages the stitch selected. Fully-electronic machines are controlled by miniature computers which contain silicon chip memories and a micro-processor. Super-electronic machines have eliminated pattern cams completely, storing the patterns in a silicon chip.

Other considerations

Other factors to consider are the size and weight of the machine (these vary considerably from model to model), and whether you require extra convenience features such as a built-in free arm for stitching sleeves. Whatever your choice, ensure there is an 'after-sales' service. A well-cared for machine rarely needs an engineer's attention, but you still need expert advice if something goes wrong.

Make the best of your machine

If you already own a machine that you are happy with, you may be able to make it perform some extra, useful functions by buying the appropriate 'feet' or attachments which are used in place of the normal presser foot. The photographs on page 30 give an idea of the selection available.

Below: A wisely chosen sewing machine will fulfil your sewing needs and give you pleasure for many years to come.

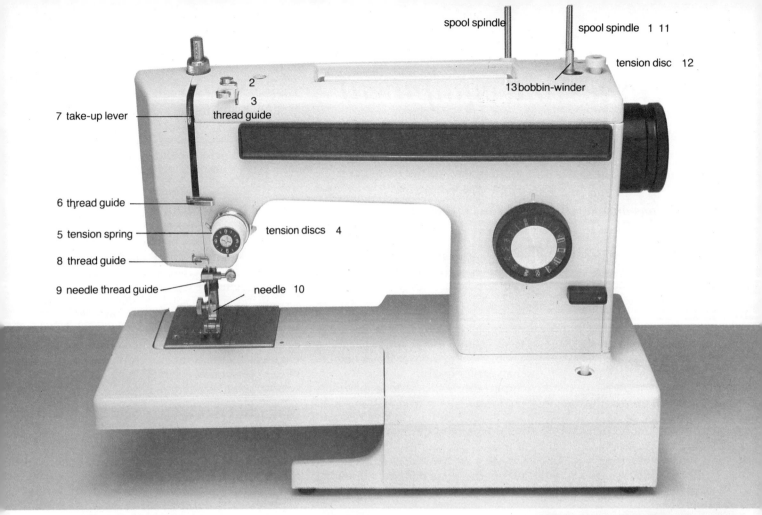

spool spindle

spool spindle 1 11

tension disc 12

13 bobbin-winder

2
3
thread guide

7 take-up lever

6 thread guide

5 tension spring   tension discs 4

8 thread guide

9 needle thread guide   needle 10

Perfect machining

Always check the following areas every time you start to sew: threading, tension, pressures, and correct needle and thread for the fabric. With practice it takes only a few seconds.

Threading

Why is threading so important? Most machines have between eight and ten points through which the thread passes before a stitch can be formed. Some of these points control the thread and stop it tangling. Others are vital to making the stitch. If any are missed the stitch may be affected. Although sewing machines differ in appearance the threading sequences are very similar. Always check with your machine handbook. If you haven't got one, ask the company for a replacement (or photocopy) or advertise for one.

Top threading

Turn the hand (balance) wheel towards you until the thread take-up lever (and therefore the needle) is in its highest position. Place a spool of thread on spindle 1. Lead thread through points shown: thread

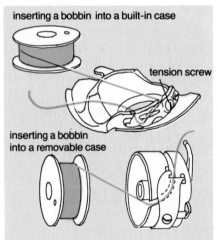

inserting a bobbin into a built-in case

tension screw

inserting a bobbin into a removable case

guides 2, 3, tension discs 4, tension spring 5, thread guides 6, take-up lever 7, thread guide 8, needle thread guide 9 and through needle 10, usually from front to back but on older models from left to right or right to left. Leave about 10cm/4in thread free, ready for sewing.

Lower threading

Always start with an empty bobbin as winding over a different thread will distribute the thread unevenly. The thread should be of the same type and size as the upper thread. Do not overfill the bobbin or the thread will

raising the bobbin thread

be unable to run out freely. Wind the bobbin according to your machine type. Most machines have an external bobbin-winding system. This takes thread from the spool spindle 11 through a tension disc 12 to the bobbin-winder 13. If the tension disc is missed, the winding will be uneven.

Insert the full bobbin into the bobbin-case with the thread running in the same direction as the slit in the side of the case, then pull the thread back under or around the tension spring. Where there is no case it has been built into the machine.

Choose from a wide range of thread types and colours to match your fabric. Some threads, like the bobbin of 'striped' cotton, have novelty finishes, for use in machine embroidery.

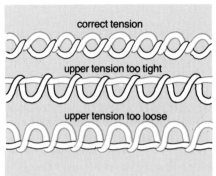

Above: the machine stitches on both sides of your fabric should be identical. If one side is puckered, this may be due to unbalanced tension.

Raising the bobbin thread

The bobbin thread must be drawn up through the hole in the needle plate to meet the upper thread before stitching can take place. Hold the top thread with the left hand, and lower the needle until it draws up the lower thread (by turning the hand wheel). A loop will form. Separate the threads and draw them both to the back of the machine through the slit in the presser foot. You are now ready to sew.

Place the fabric below presser foot. Lower needle into fabric and drop the presser foot. Draw hand wheel towards you before depressing foot control (to avoid going into reverse and snapping thread). This is not necessary on recent machines with variable-speed foot control.

Tension

The tension in the upper and lower threads must be balanced to produce a perfect stitch. Tension discs allow the thread to reach the needle at a controlled rate which ensures an even stitch length. When the presser foot is raised, the discs open and the threads are loose (they can be pulled through the needle by hand). When the foot is lowered, the discs clamp together and stop the thread moving until the machine is started.

It is seldom necessary to adjust the tension from 'normal' for most straight stitching (point 5 on a dial marked 1-10 on most machines) unless different thicknesses of fabric are being sewn or constant changes from straight to zigzag stitching take place. Zigzag stitching needs a lighter tension to prevent the wider stitch drawing up the fabric.

Adjusting the tension

Make a test stitch on a piece of your garment fabric (double thickness). Use the correct size needle and thread for the fabric. (See chart below.) Sew for about 10cm/4in. Remove from machine.

Whenever you stop sewing, make sure the take-up lever and needle are at their highest points, raise the presser foot and draw the threads backwards gently to avoid bending the needle. Cut the threads.

Look at both sides of the stitching. They should be identical. If the top tension is too tight, it will pull the lower stitches up to the surface. Turn the tension control to a lower number (anti-clockwise). If the lower thread is too tight increase the upper tension (by turning the control clockwise). Unlike the tension in the upper thread, the bobbin tension rarely needs changing for normal sewing.

Pressure

The pressure, or force, exerted on a fabric must be heavy enough to keep the fabric layers together while they are machined. Too heavy a pressure affects the stitch length, prevents the fabric moving and spoils the fabric surface. Too light a pressure allows the fabric to slip about and this prevents an even stitch being formed. To adjust the pressure turn the pressure screw or dial clockwise to increase and anti-clockwise to decrease pressure until the presser foot controls the two layers of fabric and a good stitch is obtained.

Needles and thread

Change needles for *each* new garment. Don't throw them away, they can still be used for odd jobs until they lose their sharp point. Never use blunt or bent needles. Always match needle size to thread and fabric.

Choosing needles and threads

Fabric	Needle	Thread	Stitch-length
lightweight chiffon, organza, crêpe de chine, lawn	regular 70–80 (9–11)	fine mercerised cotton, silk, synthetic, poly/cotton	1–1.5mm
medium weight linen, satin, suiting	90–100 (14–16)	mercerised cotton (50), synthetic, silk	1.5–2mm
heavyweight denim, drill, gaberdine, coating	100–110 (16–18)	mercerised cotton (40), synthetic, poly/cotton	2.5–3mm
leather and vinyl	wedgepoint, size according to thickness	mercerised (50)	2.5–3mm

Special feet for special purposes

There is a 'special foot' or attachment for almost every machine sewing process which cannot be managed with the normal presser foot. Some are included when the machine is bought, others are obtainable as extra options and are surprisingly inexpensive. Sewing by machine is quicker, stronger and more accurate than hand-sewing so it is worthwhile finding out which attachments or guides might prove useful for your style of sewing.

Remember that different feet are not interchangeable between models, so consult your machine handbook.

Most of the feet for modern machines are of the 'snap-on' type. Other types may have to be screwed in to the machine.

Experiment with special feet

Most sewers machine seams, neaten raw edges, insert zips and make buttonholes by machine. Then they resort to hand-sewing techniques to finish the hem, catch down the facings, insert elastic and sew on buttons. Hand-sewing is an enjoyable activity but, if you are short of time or would just like to use your machine more fully, think of your next dress-making project as a completely machine-made garment, using the extra feet that came with your machine and perhaps investing in a few time-saving extras.

Other accessories

There are many other attachments and guides for keeping straight lines when sewing or for stitching in circles. One example is a guide-bar for quilting. This protrudes sideways from the presser foot and has a marker which, when kept along the last row of stitching, ensures even rows of quilting.

Zipper foot
This foot stitches close to the zip teeth, covers a cord, pipes a seam and stitches a blind hem. Some machines have a special blind hem attachment.

Narrow hemmer
A useful foot which puts a fine hem on the edge of neck and sleeve ruffles, on frills for skirts and petticoats. It has a slot for attaching lace to an edge at the same time.

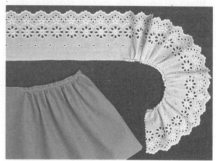

Ruffler
This foot gathers (or pleats), and attaches to a straight edge at the same time. It also has a slot for attaching a trim in the same operation. Use it to gather the frills and ruffles on dresses and skirts.

Even-feed
Also known as a 'walking foot' this seams fabrics which tend to slip or stick. Use it for velvets, silks, quilteds and for matching stripes and checks on two pieces of fabric.

Button foot
Use a button foot for stitching on buttons with surface holes. Put a matchstick between the button and the garment to create a thread shank. Remove the matchstick, draw the top threads through to the inside of the garment and tie off.

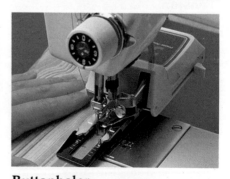

Buttonholer
These attachments vary considerably from one machine to another. Some, like the model shown, make every buttonhole the same size if you put a template in the slot provided (no need to measure). Others need several stages and have to be marked. All make strong buttonholes more quickly than by hand methods.

Useful equipment

Apart from a sewing machine, you need some basic equipment.

Tape measure marked in centimetres and made from glass-fibre or other non-stretch material.

Pins Steel dressmaker's pins, and lace pins for fine work.

Needles for hand-sewing Packets of assorted sizes in two types:

Sharps for general sewing. These are round-eyed, medium-length needles.

Betweens for strong but 'invisible' tailor's stitches. These are short and round eyed.

Machine needles Size 70/9 is best for fine fabrics, size 80/11 for lightweight, size 90-100/14-16 for medium weight and size 100-110/16-18 for heavyweight fabrics. Use ball-point needles for stretch/knitted fabrics.

Thimble Use to protect the middle finger of the hand you sew with. Steel is stronger but plastic is better for white and lingerie fabrics as it will neither mark nor pucker the fabric.

Tailor's chalk or chalk pencil For transferring pattern marks to fabrics.

Tracing wheel and dressmaker's carbon paper For tracing pattern outlines quickly on to fabrics.

Scissors For cutting out fabric, use best quality dressmaker's shears with blades at least 12cm/4¾in long. These are designed so as not to lift fabric as you cut. Use small, sharp scissors for general purposes and keep a separate pair for cutting paper.

Knit and sew gauge A handy gadget for marking regular intervals such as buttonholes and for tracing shapes.

Iron Dry irons have a smooth soleplate and are ideal for smooth-finished fabrics and for pressing small areas with a damp cloth. Steam irons have steam vents in the soleplate; many fabrics develop a shine if touched by the iron so a damp cloth may be necessary, see page 33 and test first.

Ironing board This needs to be firm and designed so that skirts and trousers slip round it easily for pressing. A sleeve board is invaluable for pressing awkward areas as well as sleeves.

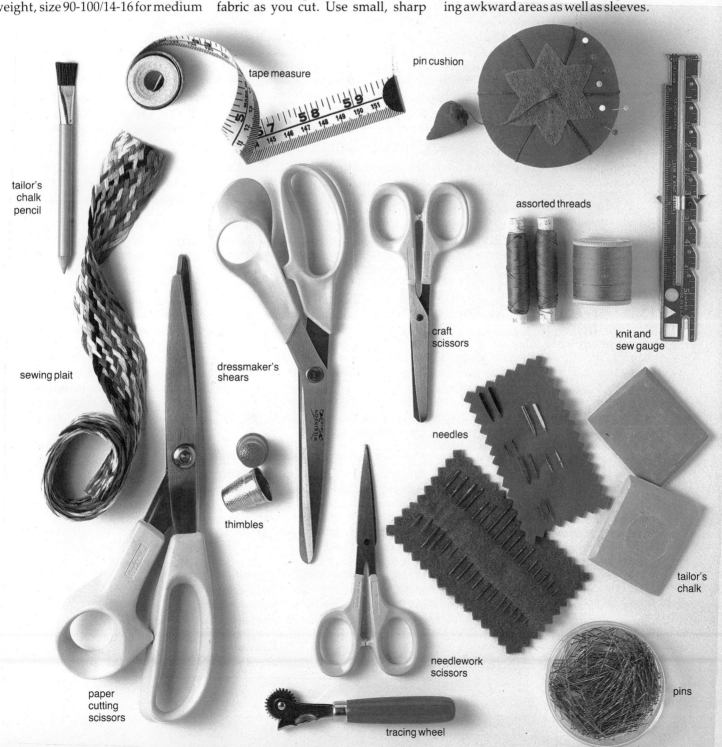

tape measure

pin cushion

tailor's chalk pencil

assorted threads

knit and sew gauge

sewing plait

craft scissors

dressmaker's shears

needles

thimbles

tailor's chalk

needlework scissors

paper cutting scissors

pins

tracing wheel

The art of perfect pressing

Careful pressing at each stage of construction is guaranteed to enhance the appearance of a hand-made garment. Make yourself some basic pressing equipment from the patterns given here, then follow the instructions for a perfect pressed finish.

Pressing and ironing are two different techniques, with different purposes, although some of the same equipment is used. When ironing, you move the iron at random over the fabric to remove creases produced by laundering. When pressing, you concentrate on specific areas, moving the iron by lifting it clear of the fabric and replacing it on the next area, using an up and down movement. You can merely rest the iron on the fabric, holding it so that only the lightest pressure is exerted or you can apply it with pressure.

Pressing equipment

In order to press garments successfully, you need a few basic items of equipment.

The iron A steam iron is the best choice for pressing. The more vents there are in the soleplate the better. Look for an iron with about 20 vents – this ensures good distribution of steam and means that an impression of the vents won't be transferred to the fabric.

When selecting an iron, hold it in your hand and test it for comfort and balance. It should have a toe which is not too pointed and a heel on which it will stand quite steadily. Look for easily accessible control buttons and check if any extra functions are available. A burst of steam is useful when pressing, but irons that spray water are more useful for domestic ironing than pressing. There is a risk of spray leaving a water mark on new fabric so it is safer to use it only for dampening the pressing cloth.

Always use distilled water purchased from a chemist in your steam iron – the sort used for car batteries is not suitable. Do not over-fill – too much water in the iron causes it to bubble and spit, making water marks on the garment.

Serious dressmakers may require a second iron – heavy dry irons are

The three stages of pressing for dressmakers

There are three stages of pressing when dressmaking. First, press the fabric before cutting out so that you can position the pattern pieces accurately. Secondly, press the garment at each stage of construction. Thirdly, give the whole garment a final, careful press.

Before cutting out

Press your fabric before pinning on the pattern pieces.

Woollen fabrics may also need shrinking. Although most are sold pre-shrunk, it is best to damp press a length of wool fabric prior to cutting out. Work on a table protected with blankets and a sheet as previously described. Position one or two chairs, depending on the fabric width, on the far side of the table to support the fabric once it is pressed. Start with the fabric in front of you, folded double and resting in gentle folds on a sheet on the floor so that it does not become dirty.

Lift a length of fabric on to the table, positioning the fold to the left so that you avoid it when pressing, and smoothing the layers together. Spread a damp pressing cloth over the fabric and press, working systematically across from the top left, lifting the iron and replacing it in the next position. Overlap the position of the iron so that every bit of the fabric is covered – the light impression made by the soleplate acts as a guide. Do not move the fabric until the steam has stopped rising and it is cold. Speed up this process in the case of heavy wool fabrics by banging out the steam with a tailor's clapper, the back of a wooden clothes brush or a piece of sanded wood.

As you press each section, fold it lightly on to the supporting chairseats until the entire length is pressed.

If the fabric has an obvious folded edge because it has been rolled on a bale for a long time, open it out to single thickness and press the fold along its entire length.

Pressing during construction

The secret of constructional pressing is never to cross one row of stitching with another until you have pressed the first one. Press on the wrong side wherever possible using a damp cloth and test the iron first on a corner of the fabric.

When in doubt as to the right temperature for pressing your fabric, start on the coolest setting and use a dry cloth. Increase the temperature gradually and introduce moisture until you achieve a satisfactory result. Support as much of the garment as possible when pressing to prevent the fabric weight dragging the warm, damp, newly pressed area out of shape. Do not move the garment until this area is cool and dry again.

Some fabrics take an impression of the seam turnings very easily on the right side, but still require firm pressure, heat and moisture. The answer is to use a pressing roll (see page 34). Lay seam along the top of roll and press from the wrong side. The seam turnings will not create an impression because of the curved roll.

Where it is impossible to use a roll, as on a pleated area, insert a strip of brown wrapping paper under each pleat as it is pressed. Leave the pleat to cool before removing the strip and slipping it under the next pleat.

Wool fabrics are often very resilient and therefore require firm handling when pressing. This means using a lot of steam to penetrate the fabric, but avoiding making it too wet. The moisture must rise out while the fabric is still hot if the garment is to be set in the required way. During pressing, bang the hot, damp area repeatedly using a tailor's clapper, smacking the wood smartly up and down at right angles to the fabric, and working systematically over the area to be pressed until the garment is dry and cool.

useful for pressing heavyweight tweeds, suitings and coats. A solid iron with a mirror-finish chromium-plated soleplate is ideal.

The ironing surface As well as an ironing board, a stable, firmly padded, flat surface is useful for pressing. A table covered with several layers of blankets and then a sheet provides an excellent surface on which to work in conjunction with the pressing aids given overleaf.

If the only suitable tables are too low for comfort, just use an ironing board instead. It is worth investing in a new one if yours is rather old, as much research has gone into the latest designs. Choose a board with an adjustable height so that you can position it at the best level for you, and ensure that the mechanism and catch are

Below: Achieve a professional look on a home-sewn garment by careful pressing at all stages of making up.

easy to operate and well made. Check that the cover is removable for washing or renewing. Ideally you should be able to stand the iron on its heel so that it does not produce steam constantly and waste water. A flex holder is also useful.

The board should curve gently to a point for maximum pressing area and a sleeve board is useful for pressing tricky and otherwise inaccessible areas such as sleeve seams.

Pressing cloths Three cloths of differing fabric weights – calico, poplin and muslin are ideal. Make them large enough so that they can be used for a while without continuous re-dampening – 1m × 50cm/40in × 20in is a good size. Neaten the edges by zigzag stitching or turning a single, narrow hem but avoid this area when pressing so that you do not make an impression on your garment fabric.

A calico cloth holds more moisture than the other cloths and is best for

pressing medium to heavyweight wools. These need firm pressing because the springiness and close construction of the fabric make it difficult for moisture to penetrate.

Use a lightly dampened muslin cloth on fine fabrics. As the muslin is semi-transparent you can see which areas you are pressing and can therefore avoid overpressing delicate fabrics.

The most useful general purpose pressing cloth is one made from fine poplin or lawn, which is suitable for pressing most fabric weights.

The best way to dampen a cloth is to fold it and immerse it in water. Roll it up, still folded, and squeeze out the excess water. Place it on the ironing board, still folded in seven or eight layers, and apply a dry iron to the cloth to disperse the moisture evenly, turning it over several times as you work. The cloth is now ready to use. Do not allow any area to become dry so moisten as necessary.

Final pressing

When the garment is completed a final, all-over press on the wrong side is necessary before it is ready to wear.

Begin by pressing small areas, such as collars, cuffs, frills and bands. Then press the larger areas such as sleeves, back bodice, front bodice, back skirt and then front skirt.

Avoid pressing over the stitching line of a hem, over fastenings or over raised trimmings as these will either leave an impression on the right side of the garment or be flattened. Run the toe of the iron under seam turnings to remove any trace of the impression of the turnings.

Where it is impossible to avoid pressing on the right side, always use a pressing cloth. Complete the pressing of a lined garment *before* anchoring the lining at the hem edge to avoid crushing the lining.

Techniques for pressing difficult fabrics

Fabrics with surface textures such as embossed and flocked cottons, corduroy, velvet and velour, and embroidered voiles, need pressing with great care to avoid flattening or altering the texture irrevocably.

Cushion the right side of the fabric during pressing to prevent this happening, using the method below which is most suitable for your fabric. Whichever method you choose, do not touch or move fabrics with a pile while they are still damp or hot, or you will mark the surface.

Corduroy, embossed/embroidered cotton Lay a soft, folded, Turkish-type towel over the ironing board when pressing firm fabrics with a surface texture like these. If the towel is sufficiently thick you can press hard on the wrong side of the fabric without damaging the pile.

If you are pressing corduroy and do not have a suitable towel, lay an offcut of the same fabric on the ironing board, pile uppermost. Then lay the main fabric down on to it, wrong side uppermost. The piles of both layers will interlock, enabling you to press the wrong side of the fabric without flattening the pile.

Velvet Use a needleboard to press velvet successfully. This is a sheet of small, slightly bent metal pins, just long enough to support the pile of velvet or corduroy. Simply place the fabric face down on the board and press, using a steam iron.

Velour, flocked and shiny fabrics Use a velour sheet, or a large offcut of firm velour fabric as a pressing surface for the best results. Place the fabric face down on it in the usual way and press from the wrong side.

Man-made fabrics – some of the synthetic crêpe-de-chine type fabrics can present pressing problems. If the iron is too hot, it produces shiny areas and permanent impressions of seams and turnings. To avoid this, start with the iron at the coolest setting and test to find the best temperature on an offcut of the fabric. Press only on the wrong side and use brown paper strips or a pressing roll to prevent seam turnings showing through to the right side.

Three pressing aids to make

As you make up a garment its curves and contours start to appear. These too need pressing, but cannot always be dealt with on an ironing board or sleeve board. A pressing roll, a tailor's ham and a pressing mitt should solve all your pressing problems and are indispensable once used.

A pressing roll is a tube of fabric packed hard with sawdust. It is used to prevent impressions of the seam turnings on the main garment when pressing seams.

A tailor's ham is an oval shape with curved sides, also packed hard with sawdust. It is ideal for using when pressing the head of a sleeve, the seat of trousers or princess seams – all areas which need thorough pressing while maintaining a curve.

A pressing mitt is a thickly padded calico mitten which is worn on the hand and pushed inside smaller curves during pressing. The padding protects the hand from heat and steam.

All these items are available from good haberdashery counters, but you can make them yourself using the patterns and instructions below at a fraction of the cost.

You will need
0.50m/⅝yd of smooth wool fabric
0.50m/⅝yd of calico
Matching thread
Bag of sawdust (from pet shops)
Polyester wadding
Blanket fabric

Cutting out
Enlarge the patterns you require on to dressmaker's graph paper. For the pressing roll and tailor's ham, cut one pattern piece in wool and one in calico.

For the pressing mitt, cut two pocket pattern pieces to the fold, and two pad pattern pieces in calico. Cut two single pad pieces in blanketing and two single pocket pieces in wadding.

pressing mitt

pressing roll

tailor's ham

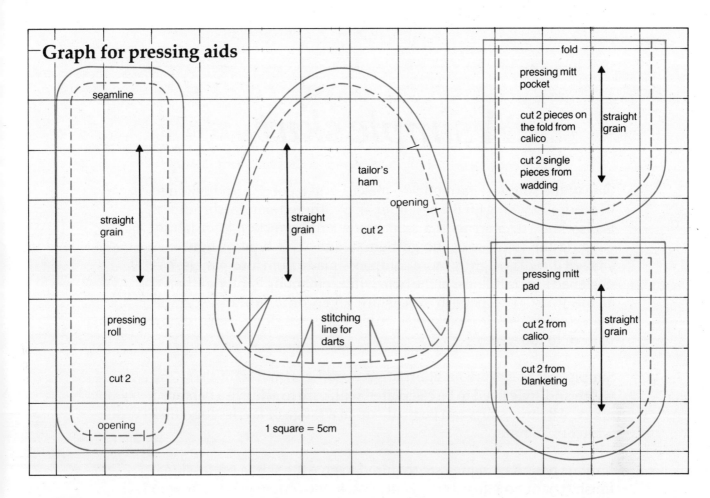

Graph for pressing aids

seamline

straight grain

pressing roll

cut 2

opening

tailor's ham

straight grain

cut 2

opening

stitching line for darts

1 square = 5cm

fold

pressing mitt pocket

cut 2 pieces on the fold from calico

straight grain

cut 2 single pieces from wadding

pressing mitt pad

cut 2 from calico

straight grain

cut 2 from blanketing

Making the tailor's ham

Close the darts on the wrong side of the calico and wool sections with a double row of machining, Begin at the base of the dart, stitch to point, pivot work and stitch back to base. Place the two layers right sides together and stitch starting opposite the marked opening.
Stitch to one marking, pivot the work and stitch all the way round to the other marking. Pivot the work

again and stitch back to beginning of the machining. A double row of stitches is essential for strength. Trim seam to 7.5mm/⅜in and turn to right side.
Fill the ham to capacity with sawdust. A cardboard funnel speeds up the process. Hold the opening closed and bang the ham smartly on to a hard floor or table to pack down the sawdust. Continue to fill in this way until it is

impossible to get in any more sawdust. As a guide, you should use 600–650g/21–23oz of sawdust. Close the opening by backstitching the layers together tightly using four strands of thread in the needle.

Making the pressing roll

Work as for the tailor's ham, omitting the darts. The pressing roll needs about 250–300g/9–10½oz of sawdust to pack it firmly.

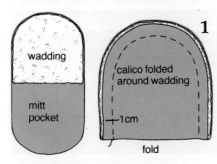

wadding

mitt pocket

calico folded around wadding

1cm

fold

1

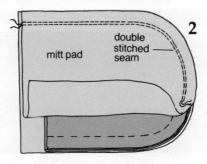

mitt pad

double stitched seam

2

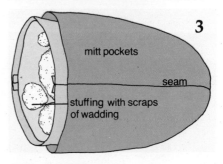

mitt pockets

seam

stuffing with scraps of wadding

3

Making the pressing mitt

1 Lay wadding to the fold on one half of each mitt pocket piece. Fold over the other half and staystitch around outside curve through all three thicknesses, 1cm/½in from cut edge.

2 Place mitt pockets together and add a calico pad section above and below, matching the curve. Machine a double-stitched seam through all layers around the outside curved edge. Trim seam and turn to right side so that wadded pocket pieces

sandwich the pad.
3 Lay a double layer of blanketing inside this centre pad pocket and stuff scraps of polyester wadding inside the blanket layers. Oversew the lower edge of the mitt to close, using double thread.

A simple skirt

One of the simplest garments to make – and a good introduction to home dressmaking for the beginner – is a gathered skirt, or dirndl as it is also known. Start with a skirt made from a rectangle of fabric, gauging the fullness of the gathers to suit your type of figure. A shaped dirndl is slightly more complex – made from four panels, it is designed to give fullness at the hem while remaining lightly-gathered at the waist. The pattern pieces are given on a multi-size graph pattern and this is an ideal project to learn the technique of enlarging a pattern to full size.

Simple soft pleats are an alternative to gathers, and with these the width and style need to be calculated with care to achieve a balanced effect. All three skirts can be made up in a range of fabrics for either winter or summer.

Various basic techniques are required to give the skirt a professional finish. Learn how to insert a centre back or overlapped zip, how to interface and apply the waistband, how to turn up a hem and, to ring the changes, how to apply bold patch pockets.

The dirndl – a basic skirt

A gathered skirt, often known as a dirndl, is one of the easiest skirts to make, needing only a straight length of fabric and a few measurements. You can make a simple pattern from a rectangle of paper or draw the measurements straight on to the fabric.

A gathered skirt may be as narrow or as full as you wish – the wider the hem of the skirt, the more you gather in at the waist. Whether short, mid-calf or full-length, in its fully gathered form it emphasizes a neat waist.

In its narrower version, a gathered skirt lies smoothly over the hips, is only gently gathered at the waist and falls elegantly in a straight line to the hem. Sizes up to about 102cm/ 40in hips can wear the narrower version with confidence.

The art of making a gathered skirt look good lies in the way you position the gathers at the waistline. You can either have fewer gathers over the hips or across the stomach depending on which style flatters your figure most.

Choosing fabrics

The traditional dirndl, designed for Alpine peasant dancing, was made from heavy fabric, fully gathered into a strong waistband and the hem was made to stand out further by bands of embroidery. Today's fabrics make the dirndl a much more versatile skirt, suitable for most occasions and very quick to make because the only fitted area is the waistline. The final effect is determined by the weight and texture of the fabric you choose and the amount of extra fabric added to the hip measurement. No darts are required.

To achieve the most flattering line consider using a lightweight fabric such as silk, lawn, crêpe, crêpe-de-chine, challis (the ch is pronounced as in chapter) or pongee (pronounced ponjee), as these will flow in soft fluid lines. Firmer fabrics such as moiré and paper taffeta, crisp cottons, eyelet embroidered fabrics,

Suitable for a variety of occasions, this dirndl in checked Viyella is simple to sew and needs no commercial pattern.

satins and taffetas usually stand out more from their gathers and create a wider silhouette.

If you choose a patterned fabric, take the trouble to work out how to make the most of the design. Check, for example, to see if it looks best centred at the front of the skirt.

How much fabric?

The following amounts are suitable for all sizes up to 102cm/40in hips.

Lightly gathered skirt If you buy 90cm/36in or 115cm/45in width fabric you need twice the finished skirt length plus 20cm/8in for hem and seam allowances, (eg for a skirt 70cm/27½in long, you need 1.60m/1⅝yd.)

If you buy 150cm/60in width fabric you need the finished skirt length plus 30cm/12in for the pockets, waistband, hem and seam allowances, (eg a skirt 70cm/27½in long would need 1m/1⅛yd of fabric).

Full skirt If you buy 115cm/45in fabric you need twice the finished skirt length plus 40cm/16in for the pockets, waistband, hem and seam allowances, (eg a skirt 70cm/27½in long would need 1.80m/2yd of fabric). 90cm/36in fabric is too narrow to make this skirt with only two seams. If you buy 150cm/60in width fabric you need twice the finished skirt length plus 20cm/8in for hem and seam allowances, (eg

a skirt 70cm/27½in long would need 1.60m/1⅝yd of fabric).

Making a pattern

This chapter shows how to make a pattern for a gathered skirt. When making your own patterns you can decide how much seam allowance you need. Most commercial patterns include a seam allowance of 1.5cm/⅝in, but it is easier to insert a zip into a seam of 2.5cm/1in. (The gathered skirt pattern has no seam allowances, position it on the fabric and then allow for seams and hems before cutting out.) When you make your own patterns it is useful to write all the relevant in-

Patterns for the full and lightly gathered skirts

Use tissue, greaseproof or even a spare roll of wallpaper to make your paper pattern or, if you feel confident, miss out the paper pattern stage altogether and mark the pattern measurements straight on to the fabric with tailor's chalk. If you make this short cut, remember that, having marked the pattern measurements on to the fabric, you must mark the seam and hem allowances before cutting out.

Below: This lightly gathered skirt needs less than two metres of fabric.

Lightly gathered skirt

Cut two rectangles of paper exactly the same size, one for the skirt back and one for the skirt front. When they are placed on folded fabric they give two halves of a skirt which are joined together by a seam at each side. The seam and hem allowances are added at the cutting stage.

The longer side of the paper is the exact finished length you want the skirt to be. The shorter side is one and a quarter times your hip measurement divided by four.

Measure the length of another skirt in your wardrobe which is the right length, from just under the waistband to the hemline. Make a note of this measurement, it is the length of the longer side of the paper pattern.

Measure your hips (see page 20), divide this by four and add this figure to the hip measurement. Now divide the total by four and you get the length of the shorter side of the pattern. For example if your hip measurement is 96cm/38in, divide this by four which equals

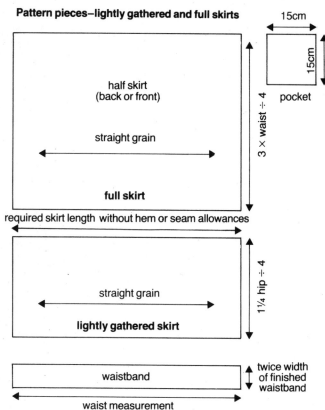

38

formation on the pattern pieces. This way if you want to make the pattern up again you can see all the details at a glance. Mark an edge which has to be placed on a fold, a straight grain line (abbreviated as SG), centre fold (CF), centre back (CB), waist (W), hip (H), length (L), side seam (SS), seam allowance (SA), hem allowance (HA) and name the pattern piece (front, back etc.) if there are more than one.

This chapter shows you how to pin the pattern pieces on to the fabric and how to cut it out. Full instructions for completing a range of gathered skirts, including a shaped dirndl are given in the following pages.

24cm/9½in. Add 24cm/9½in to 96cm/38in which equals 120cm/47½in. Divide by four making 30cm/11⅞in. For the waistband cut a strip of paper exactly to your waist measurement and twice the width you want the finished waistband to be. (Most gathered skirts have waistbands between 3-5cm/1¼-2in wide. Unless you are particularly long waisted a 3cm/1¼in waistband looks best.)

For the pocket cut a piece of paper whatever shape and size you want the pocket to be, provided it will fit on the cutting layout. A good finished size is 15cm/6in square.

Full skirt

Cut out two rectangles of paper exactly the same size, one for the skirt back and one for the skirt front. The longer side of the paper is the required finished length of the skirt. The shorter side is three times your *waist* measurement divided by four, (eg if your waist measures 70cm/27½in, multiply by three to give 210cm/82½in and divide by four to give 52.5cm/20½in). For a less full look, use twice your waist measurement divided by four and for a fuller look use three and a half times your waist measurement divided by four. (Note: for waist measurements above 73cm/29in, the maximum finished width around the lower edge of a skirt cut on 115cm/45in fabric is 219cm/86½in.) Cut out a waistband and pocket pattern piece as described above under the lightly gathered skirt.

Positioning the pattern pieces

Choose the appropriate cutting layout for your fabric and the skirt you are making. Position the skirt pattern pieces as below, leaving room for a 1.5cm/⅝in seam allowance at the waist, a 2.5cm/1in seam allowance at the side and a 6.5cm/2½in hem.

Allow 6.5cm/2½in for the top pocket facing and leave a 1.5cm/⅝in seam allowance round the other three edges, and along the two long edges and one short edge of the waistband. Allow 7cm/2¾in at the other short edge for fastening.

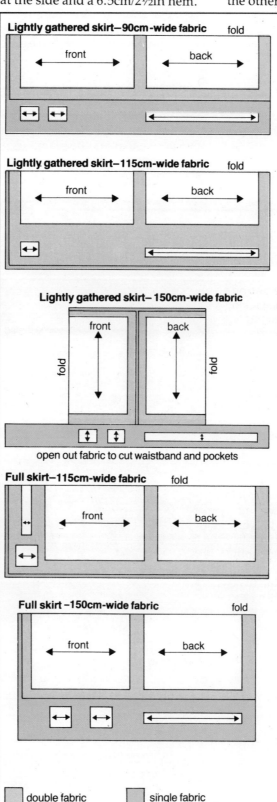

open out fabric to cut waistband and pockets

double fabric   single fabric

Lightly gathered skirt

90cm width Fold the fabric as shown with right sides together and selvedges parallel. Place the two skirt pattern pieces on the folded edge and place the waistband and pocket pattern pieces on the single layer of fabric.
115cm width Fold the fabric in half as shown with right sides together and selvedges level. Place the skirt pattern pieces on the folded edge and place the pocket pattern piece on the doubled fabric as shown. Place the waistband on a single layer of fabric only.
150cm width Fold the fabric as shown with the selvedges meeting exactly in the centre. Place the two skirt pattern pieces on the folded edges giving the centre front and centre back. Open out lower part of the fabric and place pockets and waistband as shown.

Full skirt

115cm fabric Fold the fabric as shown with right sides together and selvedges level. Place the two skirt pattern pieces and the waistband (folded in half) on the folded edge and place the pocket as shown.
150cm fabric Fold the fabric as shown with right sides together and selvedges parallel. Place the skirt pattern pieces on the folded edge and place the pocket pattern pieces and the waistband piece on a single layer of fabric only.

Pinning, cutting out and marking seamlines

Pin skirt pattern pieces to the fabric as close to the pattern edges as possible. Avoid using pins along the folded edges – the centre front and centre back of the skirt – they may leave marks or tiny holes. Before cutting out, mark the cutting lines on to the fabric using tailor's chalk. The cutting line is the paper pattern piece plus the seam allowance so measure out from the edge of the pattern:

  1.5cm/⅝in along waistline edge
  2.5cm/1in along side seam
  6.5cm/2½in along lower edge
  (this represents a 5cm/2in hem
  with a 1.5cm/½in turning)
Cut out the two skirt pieces.
Pin on the waistband pattern piece

as indicated on your chosen cutting layout. Mark a cutting line 1.5cm/⅝in out from the edge of the pattern along long edges and one short edge. Mark a cutting line 7cm/2¾in from edge of pattern at the other short end for the overlap to take a hook or button. Cut out the waistband.
Pin on the pocket pattern piece and mark a cutting line 1.5cm/⅝in from the edge on three sides, and 6.5cm/2½in from the top. Cut out pocket. Because the cutting line is larger than the pattern piece by the exact measurement of the hem and seam allowances, to mark the seamline and hemline simply trace round each pattern piece with tailor's

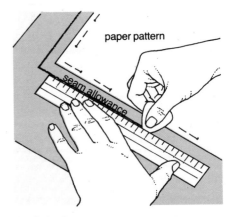

paper pattern

seam allowance

chalk before removing the pattern from the fabric. An alternative method, advisable if using a fine fabric or one with a delicate surface, is to use a row of continuous tailor's tacks.

PROFESSIONAL TOUCH

Tailor's tacks

Single tailor's tack
This is used for marking one particular point such as a button hole or a dart. Use double tacking thread and a fine needle.
1 Make one small stitch.
2 Make another stitch on exactly the same point leaving a loop the size of your fingertip.
3 Gently ease the layers apart.
4 Snip the threads between the layers. This leaves a reference point for making up the garment.

double tacking thread

snip

Continuous tailor's tacks
These are used for marking seamlines to give an accurate line for sewing. Use double tacking thread and a fine needle to work a row of single loops.
1 Make one stitch through both layers of fabric, make the next stitch further along the line to be marked, using the fingertip as a guide for spacing.
2 When the tacking has been completed, gently ease the two layers of fabric apart and snip the threads in between the layers.

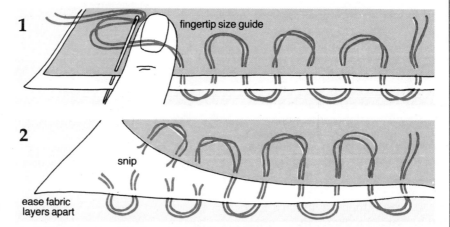

fingertip size guide

snip

ease fabric
layers apart

Marking single layers
For marking a single layer of fabric – for example, the waistband – simply work a row of stitches in single thread around the outside of the pattern.

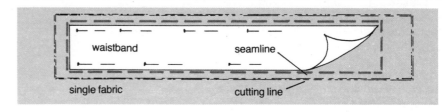

waistband   seamline

single fabric   cutting line

Shaped dirndl skirt

This skirt has four panels (two at the front and two at the back) and four seams – two side seams and a centre seam at front and back. The panels are flared to give fullness at the hem, and it is lightly gathered at the waist. Sizes are as follows:

Size	Waist	Length
10	64cm/24in	70cm/27½in
12	67cm/26in	72cm/28¼in
14	71cm/28in	74cm/29¼in
16	76cm/30in	74cm/29¼in

Making the pattern

From the grid (far right), copy the pattern pieces in the size you require on to dressmaker's 5cm/2in graph paper. Use a ruler to draw the line for the side of the skirt, and follow the lines on the graph paper for the waistband. The curved lines of the waist edge and hem are easy to draw using a flexicurve, as explained in the section on making graph patterns, page 18.

Fabric requirements

For all sizes, on 90cm/36in or 115cm/45in fabric, you need four times the finished skirt length, plus about 50cm/20in for the waistband, hem and seam allowances (eg a skirt 70cm/27½in long would need 3.30m/3½yd of fabric). If you are using 150cm/60in fabric, you need twice the finished skirt length, plus 30cm/12in for the waistband, hem and seam allowances, (eg a skirt 70cm/27½in long would need 1.70m/1¾yd of fabric). If your fabric has an obvious pattern repeat, allow extra fabric to match the pattern across the skirt seams. On 150cm/60in fabric you can easily see how the pattern matches when you lay down the pattern pieces.

Cutting out

Position and pin your pattern pieces as shown on the appropriate layout. Cut out carefully, with the skirt pattern piece positioned on the fold in every case. Remember to add on seam and hem allowances before starting to cut out.

Right: The shaped dirndl is designed to be flattering to all figures. Insert the zip in the left-hand side seam instead of the back as for the simple dirndl.

Copy your pattern pieces from the multi-size grid (right), making four identical pieces for the skirt. This pattern piece represents half your skirt panel, so always place it on the fold, as shown on the layouts below.

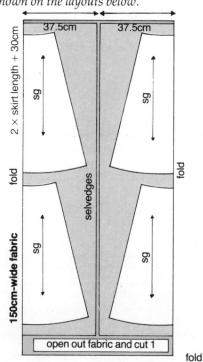

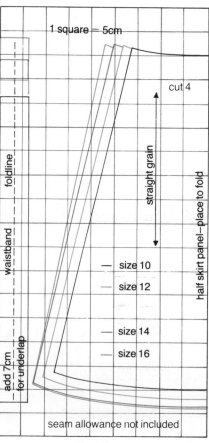

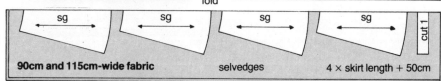

Seams in skirts

The position of the seams in a skirt is most important, for they give a definite 'line' or shape to the garment. A simple skirt has two seams, positioned at the sides. Close-fitting straight skirts hang better with a seam added at the centre back, as this strengthens the 'seat' area and keeps the hem edge firm. When only one seam is preferable, as in a skirt made from a border print, you should position it at the centre back.

A plain open seam is the best type for most skirts. The seam allowance is pressed equally to either side of the seam, giving a flat appearance (see page 26). It is easy to insert a zip into this type of seam.

Most seams are 1.5cm/⅝in wide but allow at least 2.5cm/1in on seams with openings. This not only makes it easier to insert a zip, but also allows you to alter the size at a later date if necessary.

Neatening skirt seams The method used to neaten the raw edges of the seam allowances depends on the thickness of the fabric, and how easily it frays. While all woven fabrics fray and knitted fabrics 'run', only felted fabrics do neither.

When neatening the raw edges, sew the plain seam first. Always sew corresponding seams (the side seams, for example) in the same direction. In a skirt this would be from hem to waistband, unless the fabric has a pile running downwards as in corduroy, in which case stitch from waistband to hem.

On the wrong side, press open the seam allowances, then run the iron lightly over the seam on the right side. If pressed carefully at each stage, no 'final pressing' of the garment is necessary. The raw edges can either be turned under and stitched or finished by either of the methods shown right.

When neatening a seam, try to stitch the edges in the same direction as the seamline was stitched, wherever possible.

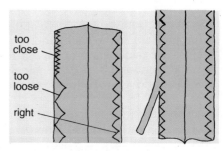

Zigzag overstitching

Before finishing the seam, practise the zigzag stitch on scraps of your garment fabric, experimenting with stitch length and width. The zigzag stitch should be fairly close, so that the fabric does not fray between the stitches, but not as close as satin stitch. If the raw edges curl and form a ridge, try allowing the needle to go just beyond the edge of the fabric on the right-hand stitch. This will keep the edges flat. Alternatively, stitch a line of zigzag just inside the edge of the seam allowance and trim away the excess fabric.

Inserting a skirt zip

Zips come in a bewildering variety of types and forms. Basically, heavyweight metal zips are most suitable for jeans and heavy clothes, and open-ended zips are used in seams that open completely, as in the front of a blouson jacket.

For skirts (and most other garments) use a lightweight metal or synthetic zip, colour matched to your fabric. For fine fabrics, use a nylon zip.

When choosing the size of your zip, remember that the zip opening needs to be long enough for you to get in and out of the garment without putting any strain on the seam or the end of the zip. Generally, an 18cm/7in skirt zip is adequate for small women's sizes, 20cm/8in for medium sizes and 23cm/9in for larger figures. To help you insert the zip into a garment, some zips have a stitching guideline woven into or printed on to the zip tapes. Otherwise, use the weave of the tape fabric as a stitching guide.

There are two main methods of inserting a zip: overlapped insertion and central insertion. The overlapped method is suitable for both side and centre seams, while the central method – used on centre seams only – is shown on page 49.

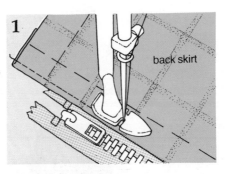

Overlapped zip

1 Prepare and neaten the left-hand side seam, leaving an opening the same length as the zip (measured down from the waist seamline). Press under, or tack, the side seam allowances along seamlines.

Lay back skirt opening edge over front of zip tape, 2mm/⅛in from teeth, with the zip tab 6mm/¼in below waist fitting line. This allows enough space for the zip to open and close when the waistband is attached. Tack, rather than pin, in order to keep flat.

Machine, using zipper foot, from waistline towards lower edge close to fold. The seam should conceal the bottom stop of the zip.

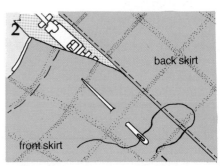

2 Lay front skirt opening edge over entire zip and line up with side seam of back skirt, matching raw edges at waist level.

Tack and machine from waist to zip base. Slide the zip tab down slightly to machine the top of the seam, then slide it back up to the top and machine the rest of the seam with the zip closed. This allows you to stitch the whole seam in a straight line.

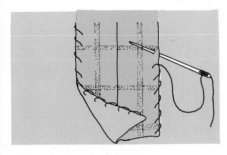

Overcasting by hand

If you do not have a swing-needle device and the fabric is unsuitable for the turned and stitched finish overcast the edges by hand, taking evenly-spaced diagonal stitches over the raw edges. Do not pull the thread too tight or the edge will curl.

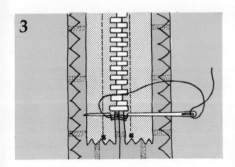

3 At lower end of opening, pull loose ends of machine threads through to wrong side and secure to zip tape with backstitch.
Stitch across lower zip tape through seam allowance by hand. (Machining across bottom of zip on right side can cause a bulge.)
Add a strip of fabric or petersham ribbon behind the zip to protect lingerie and delicate blouses. Sew by hand to one side of opening and across lower end.

Right: Soft pleats are fun to make, and very easy. Checked or striped fabric is particularly suitable for pleating, as the lines help you to match the pleats and make them even. There are many types of pleats to choose from – this variation has side pleats and a central inverted pleat.

Gathers and soft pleats

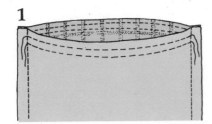

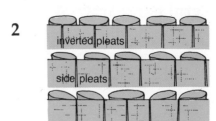

Gathers are small, soft folds formed by drawing the fabric along a row of hand or machine stitches. For small gathers use a small machine stitch (about 8 stitches to 2.5cm/1in) and reduce upper machine tension so that the bobbin thread will pull through easily. Large gathering stitches produce small, flat pleats.
1 Mark the centre front and back of the waist edge of skirt to make it easy to match to the waistband.
Work two parallel rows of machine or handstitching on right side of skirt waist, close to each side of fitting line (about 5mm/¼in apart). Leave loose ends of thread at each end to be pulled up.
Where seams create bulk, work in sections taking the stitches right up to the seams, but avoiding the seam allowances.
Prepare for gathering by pulling up threads a little and securing round a pin inserted on wrong side across seamline at each end of gathering section.

Soft pleats or unstitched pleats, are an alternative to gathering on a full skirt. Here are several possible variations (**2**, above), but you can alter the spacing and size of the pleats for the effect that pleases you, or flatters your figure. Just make sure that the finished pleated skirt top fits your waist, and that the pleats are even in size and evenly spaced.
Soft pleats, and indeed any sort of pleats, work best folded on the straight grain, so the design of the dirndl skirt is ideal for pleating. Make the pleats as shown above, using the pattern of your fabric or the straight grain as a guideline, and check the appearance on the right side.
Pin and tack your pleats in the style you have chosen, tacking a little way down the fold so that the fabric is easier to handle while attaching the waistband. When the skirt is finished, remove the tacking and allow the pleats to fall into soft folds.

Useful hand-sewn stitches

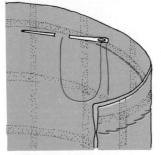 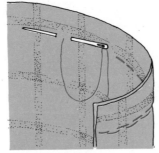 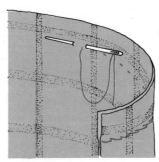 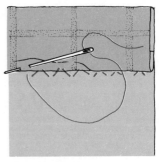

Backstitch
A strong hand stitch, resembling machine stitch on right side.
1 Working from the right side, take a stitch 3mm/⅛in long and bring needle out through fabric 3mm/⅛in ahead on stitching line.
2 Take thread back and insert needle in end of previous stitch, bringing it out one stitch ahead.

Half-backstitch
A neat stitch, evenly spaced on the right side. Work as for backstitch but take needle back only half the length of previous stitch. Continue to bring needle out one stitch length ahead.

Prickstitch
An almost invisible stitch ideal for inserting zips by hand. Work as for backstitch, but take the needle back one or two threads only, so that a tiny stitch forms on the right side.

Catchstitch
A loosely-worked, flexible stitch – not strong, but ideal for hems.
1 Work loosely just inside the hem fold to protect stitches and avoid a ridge on the hem.
2 Catch only a few top threads in the visible part of the garment, but take large stitches in the hem fabric, as shown.

Preparing a straight waistband

The **straight waistband** is the most common method of finishing the waist edge of a skirt. The waistband is backed with interfacing or, for a stiffer finish, petersham ribbon. The most usual (and most comfortable) finished width for the waistband is 3-5cm/1¼-2in.
Attaching the waistband to the skirt is straightforward since the top edge of the skirt is just gathered up until it fits the straight edge of the waistband.
1 Establish the lengthwise centre of waistband by drawing a line on wrong side or pressing a fold.

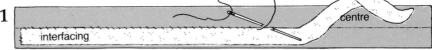

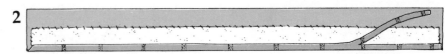

On the wrong side, lay waistband interfacing between one long seam edge and centre. Catch to waistband by hand on all edges, or seal by pressing if interfacing is fusible.
2 Press up seam allowance on non-interfaced long edge. Trim to 6mm/¼in.

3 With right sides together, fold waistband in half along centre line. Machine across ends, trim seams, turn to right side and press.
4 Mark into sections for matching to skirt. With the stiffened side of waistband facing upwards mark off your waist measurement in

Attaching the waistband

1 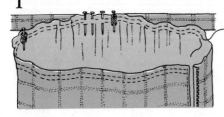 **2** 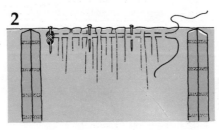 **3**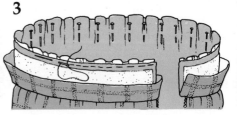

1 With right sides together, lay waistband along waist edge of skirt. Pin across seams at sides and at centres, matching corresponding marks on skirt and waistband. Gently ease the fabric along the gathering thread, holding the loose

ends securely.
2 Gather up each section separately pinning across seams at 2cm/1in intervals, until the skirt is drawn up to fit the waistband. Secure ends of drawn-up thread round a pin, as shown.

3 Tack waistband to skirt along waist fitting line, taking care not to catch in the turned-in free edge of waistband.
Before machining, adjust gathers so that they appear even, taking care that the gathers appear continuous

Instant skirt

You can run up an attractive skirt very quickly from the lengths of ready-shirred fabric that many shops sell. For skirt sizes 10-16 1.5m /1½yd is the recommended amount. Leaving 1.5cm/⅝in seam allowances each side sew fabric in to a tube (from top to bottom to ensure the elastic matches up across the seam). Use a plain seam and neaten the edges by hand or machine overcasting. Fold the bottom selvedge into a narrow hem, fold again to the length required and catchstitch all round on the inside. If you find the shirred section on the waistband too deep, turn half of it to the inside and catchstitch loosely by hand at intervals (to allow 'ease') inside the waistband.

Right: Choose a fabric from the wide range available, complete a seam and a hem and you have an instant skirt.

3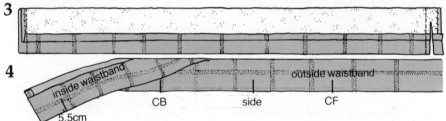

4

inside waistband   CB   side   outside waistband   CF

5.5cm

quarters, working from right to left. Leave the 5.5cm/2in underlap for the fasteners on your left.
5 Before pinning waistband to skirt try it round your waist. Waistbands need about 1cm/½in ease to fit comfortably – more if they are wider than 3cm/1¼in.

Pin the waistband where it fits comfortably, allowing the extra 1cm /½in ease. It will tend to tighten up when it is machined. This fitting is essential – it is very difficult to adjust the waistband after you have machined the gathers.

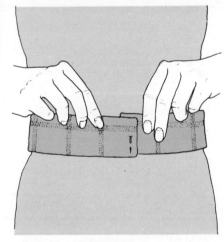

4

across the seams. With practice, you can omit the tacking and machine slowly and carefully over the pins. This allows you to readjust the gathers while sewing.
4 Machine waistband to skirt along fitting line. This is easier if the

5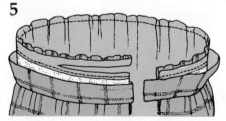

gathers are uppermost, but take care not to catch the free edge of the waistband in the stitching.
5 Remove tackings. Lightly press the seam upwards into the waistband and trim seam allowance to 6mm/¼in.

6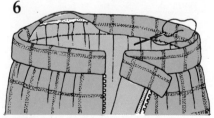

6 Pull free edge of waistband down inside to cover all raw edges and catchstitch to machine stitches of waistline seam. Catchstitch the lower edges of the waistband together, where it extends to form the underlap.

Skirts – the finishing touches

More useful know-how – including simple hemming and how to put in a centre back zip – will help you brush up your dressmaking techniques. Now you have everything you need to know to give a truly professional finish to any type of dirndl skirt that you make.

You can now make a whole wardrobe of skirts – each one completely different – by following these basic instructions. Lightly gathered, fully gathered, softly pleated or gently shaped skirts, made up in winter weight wool or summery cottons – the choice is yours.

When you are completing your skirt, don't neglect the finishing touches – they will help you to achieve a professional finish. Use hooks and eyes, skirt bars, or Velcro to finish the waistband, and always sew in skirt loops so that you can hang up your skirt.

Pockets are an optional extra, but made in contrasting fabric for a plain skirt, cut on the cross for a checked skirt, or trimmed with lace or binding, they can be used to add that special individual touch.

Hemming a dirndl

6.5cm hem.

The easiest type of hem to deal with is one on a straight edge. This is usually finished by just turning up the hem allowance and finishing the raw edge by machine, or with straight seam binding. As the dirndl hem is completely straight, there should be no problems in obtaining an even finish – the side seams should measure the same from waistband to hem, and the centre

Finishing raw edges

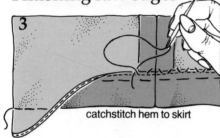

catchstitch hem to skirt

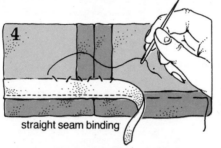

straight seam binding

Two different methods can be used to finish the raw edges of the hem, depending on the fabric's thickness.
3 Light fabrics, for example cottons. Turn 1.5cm/⅝in seam allowance to inside and press. Machine stitch close to this fold if the fabric could fray. Tack hem to skirt, matching seams

on the hem allowance with seams in the body of garment, and catchstitch.
4 Heavier fabrics, for example woollen cloth. Machine straight seam binding to seam allowance, overlapping raw edge of skirt by 1cm/½in. Catchstitch hem to skirt to finish.

Zip protector

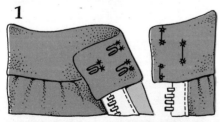

press stud

A protector strip prevents the zip catching your lingerie. Sew the top edge into the waistband when finishing the inside edge. If using petersham ribbon, overcast the top raw edge and press-stud into place.

Skirt fasteners

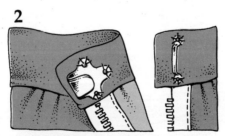

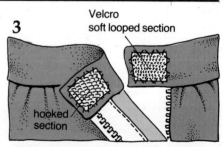

Velcro
soft looped section

hooked section

Skirt waistbands can be finished by a variety of methods. Buttons and buttonholes are dealt with on pages 104, 110 and 114 but other techniques are shown here.
1 Hooks and eyes are, perhaps, the most common finish – use three, positioned as above and sew firmly, securing through interfacing layer.

2 Another alternative is to use a single skirt hook and bar. Sew the base of the hook to inner front edge of overlap, and position the bar above the side seam on the underlap. Sew firmly, making sure the stitches are securely anchored through the layer of stiffening.

3 Velcro can also be used to close the waistband. Cut two pieces the length of the underlap minus 1cm/½in. Trim hooked side by 3mm/⅛in to prevent it catching the skirt. Hem firmly by hand to front inner band. Apply the soft looped section to underlap either by hand or zigzag machine stitching.

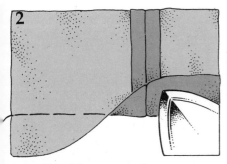

front should measure the same from top to bottom as the centre back.

1 Before marking hem, ensure the bottom edge is even all the way round. With a line of chalk or tacking, mark the finished length required all around the hem, at exactly the same distance from the raw edge.

2 Lightly press to inside along this line.

Useful skirt loops

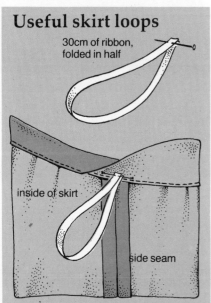

30cm of ribbon, folded in half

inside of skirt

side seam

A shop-bought skirt has loops inside the waistband so that you can hang it in your wardrobe. To make them for your dirndl, cut two pieces of narrow seam binding or ribbon 30cm/12in long. Fold in half and insert at side seams when sewing down free edge of waistband.

Right: A softly pleated skirt made up in fine wool is a versatile addition to your wardrobe. Wear it with a simple, matching jacket and you have a smart but practical outfit that is suitable for any occasion.

Making and attaching patch pockets

Pockets can be many different shapes, with squared or rounded lower edges, made of single fabric or lined. Patch pockets are made up first, then sewn on to the garment like a patch, hence their name. The top edge always needs a facing to prevent it sagging.

It is easier to make up and apply patch pockets in the early stages of the garment, before you have joined the side seams and gathered the top edge. However, you may prefer just to tack them at this stage, adjusting and machining later after you have gathered up the skirt.

1 Cut a rectangle of fabric 18cm× 21.5cm/7in×8½in, or the preferred size for your hand. Cut a piece of lightweight fusible (iron-on) interfacing or ordinary interfacing, measuring 6.5cm×18cm/2½in×7in. Attach this to top of pocket (the facing) by either ironing the fusible interfacing to the wrong side of the fabric, or by catchstitching the ordinary type to the top fold.

2 Neaten edge of facing by hand or machine, trimming seam allowance if necessary.

3 Turn under seam allowances on remaining three sides to wrong side of pocket, folding in bottom seam allowance first. Turn the bottom

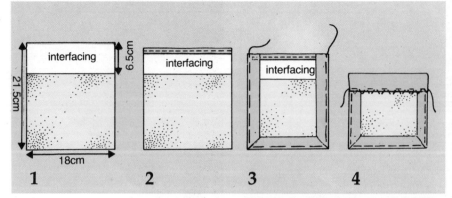

corners of the sides under, to make diagonal folds at the lower corners. Tack and press.

4 Fold top facing over on foldline to inside pocket. Tack, press and catchstitch.

Position pocket on garment with top about 10cm/4in down from waistline and 10cm/4in from centre front. This position will vary, depending on size and fullness of skirt. Tack and machine along sides and lower edges, forming a tiny triangle at the top of each side of the pocket to reinforce the stitching line.

Right: A creative touch for a pocket, making use of the pattern of the fabric to provide a separate, contrasting trim for the pocket top.

Hemming a shaped skirt

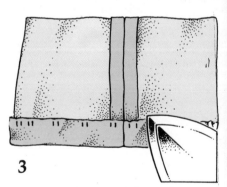

The hem of a skirt that has an A-line design, or is shaped by the flaring of the panels, will have extra fullness round the bottom edge inside the hem. This has to be eased out when completing the hem, to avoid bulkiness.

1 Prepare the hem following instructions for marking a hem on a straight dirndl.
Tack hem to skirt just above the folded bottom edge.

2 Run a line of easing stitches 6mm/¼in from inside raw edge of hem. Distribute fullness evenly along line of easing stitches matching seams on the hem allowance with seams in body of garment.

3 Shrink out excess fullness by pressing hem lightly.
Finish hem by turning raw edge under along line of easing stitches. Tack and catchstitch hem to skirt.

Right: Draw a heart shape on card and use it as a template for cutting a pocket out of fabric or felt. Trim with lace for a soft, feminine finish.

Above: Cut large patch pockets out of plain, toning fabric. Trim with a contrasting piping.

Right: Position your pockets at an angle and flap back to show a contrasting lining. Secure with a button.

Making up instructions

Using the techniques given in this chapter, make up your skirt following these step-by-step instructions.

You will need

Cut out skirt sections with paper pattern pieces removed and seam and hem lines marked
Matching thread
Skirt zip
Your choice of skirt fastener
Waistband stiffening or interfacing

Full and lightly gathered skirts only:

Lightweight interfacing for pocket facings
Straight seam binding for hem (where necessary).

Full and lightly gathered skirts

1 If making pockets, make these first and position on front of skirt, either by tacking, or machining if sure of position.
2 Join left-hand seam, leaving opening for zip. Press seam open and neaten edges. Insert zip by overlapped method.
3 Join right-hand seam, press open and neaten edges.
4 Prepare waistband, skirt loops and protector strip if required.
5 Machine a row of gathering stitches on either side of waist seamline. Join waistband to skirt, following instructions for pulling up gathers given on page 44. Insert skirt loops and protector strip before completing inside by hand. Sew on waistband fasteners.
6 Try skirt on, check length and complete hem.

Shaped skirt

1 Join centre front seam and centre back seam, leaving an opening for zip in centre back seam. Press open and neaten edges.
2 Insert zip by centred method. Join side seams, press and neaten.
3 Follow steps 4–5 above. Remember waistband closes at centre back, not at side, and mark centre front and sides on waistband accordingly.
4 Try skirt on, check length and complete hem, following instructions for a shaped skirt.

Inserting a zip in a centre seam

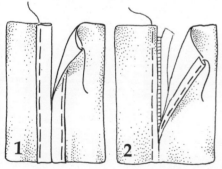 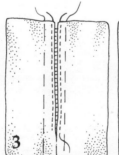 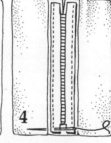

Although a zip can be inserted into a centre seam by the overlapped method, centring it in the opening with an equal allowance on either side gives a neat smooth finish.
1 Stitch the centre back seam, leaving the appropriate opening for the zip. Press under or tack the seam allowances along seamlines.
2 Position seam opening exactly over centre of closed zip, with zip tabs 6mm/¼in below waist seamline.
3 Tack and then machine each side

of the zip separately on the right side, using a zipper foot. Work from the waistline to the bottom of zip. The stitching lines should be equal distances from the centre of the zip on both sides of the opening. Slide the zip tab down while stitching top of seam, then close the zip to stitch the rest of the seam.
4 Finish off loose ends on wrong side, and stitch across bottom of zip through lower zip tape and seam allowances by hand.

A jacket to match

A simple, collarless cardigan jacket with a choice of sleeve lengths is ideal to team with a basic skirt. Start with an unlined version and learn how to set in sleeves and insert shoulder pads using the comprehensive guide to solve any fitting problems.

The basic pattern can be varied in several ways. Design features such as graduated pin tucks at the shoulder or patch pockets will add interest to a plain front. Alternatively, decorative braid and dart shaping will turn it into a Chanel-style jacket.

Interfacing comes in a variety of weights and qualities – learn the facts about interfacing so that you can choose the appropriate type and method of insertion. Full instructions are also given for adding a lining to prolong the jacket's life and give a neat appearance to the inside by concealing all seams and hems.

A wide choice of fabrics can be used for this style which is suitable for both day and evening wear.

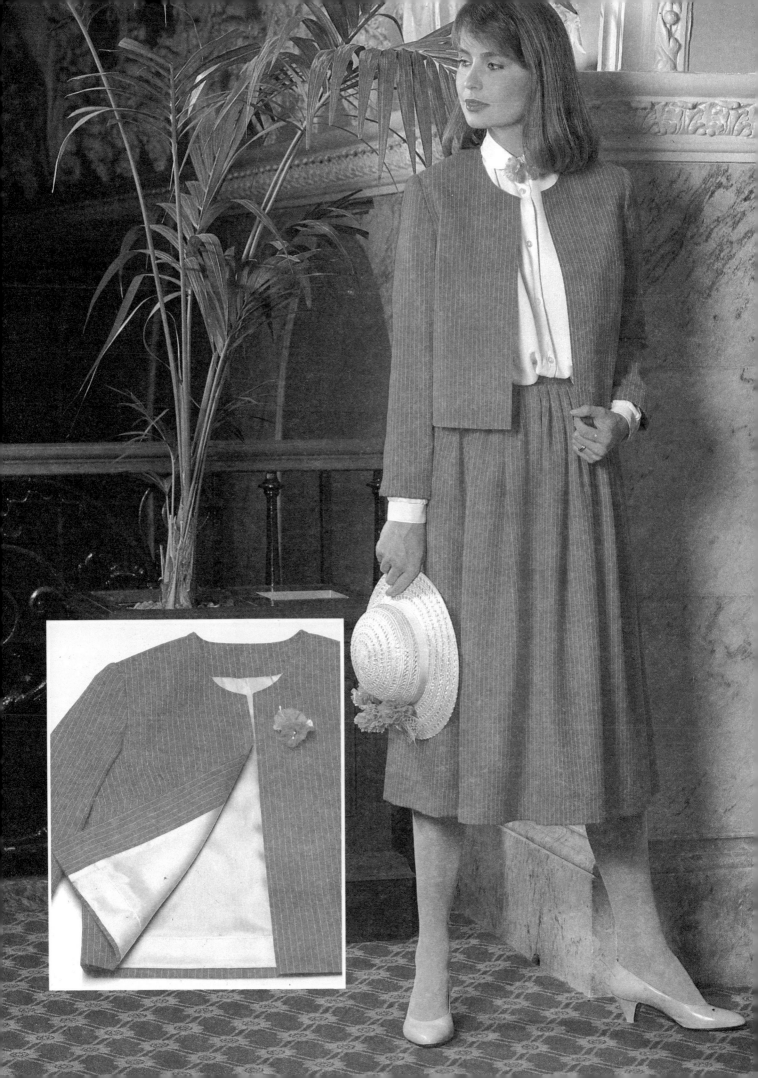

Above: Heavier silk, such as this textured silk shantung, is ideal for an unlined cardigan jacket and makes a smart cover-up for a strappy dress.

Adjusting a jacket pattern

The basic techniques for making a simple jacket are easily mastered, but careful attention to pattern adjustments and fitting are very important. Follow the detailed advice on pattern preparation in this chapter and make yourself a jacket to be proud of.

When you are making a jacket, the most important points to consider are the fit and the finish. A good fabric, crisp front edges, a neat neck-line and professional-looking sleeves provide the finish, but fitting is the key to a perfect garment. It can be the difference between comfort and dis-comfort, as well as influencing the overall appearance.

Making pattern adjustments before cutting out is the first step towards achieving a good fit. Start by pinning the pattern as shown on page 19. Then on the page opposite you can see how to identify the problem areas and make any necessary pattern alterations.

Layouts, fabric suggestions and re-quirements for the cardigan jacket are given on pages 62–63. Compre-hensive fitting instructions are in the next chapter.

Altering the bodice

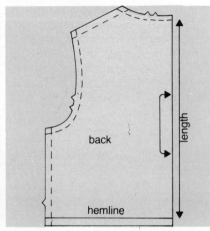

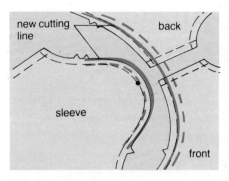

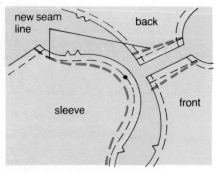

Length

This is usually stated on the envelope of commercial patterns. If not, measure the pattern from centre back neck seamline to the line marked for hem. Compare with your own measurement from nape of neck to proposed length. Shorten or lengthen as necessary (see page 21).

Narrow shoulders

To reduce seam by up to 2cm/¾in, mark the new shoulder point on back and front pattern pieces, measuring from neck point. Re-draw armhole seamline and cutting line on back and front as far as notches. Raise sleeve head if needed to match shoulder position. Do not shorten the shoulder seam too much – instead, slightly extend the shoulder pad into the armhole. If uncertain leave this and following alteration until the fitting stage.

Sloping shoulders

Again, it is better to disguise a pronounced slope with the shoulder pad but if the pattern still requires alteration, re-draw the shoulder seam. Mark a new lower shoulder point on front and back armhole seamlines and connect to neck point.

To remove the surplus from the top of the sleeve, draw a new seamline about 1cm/½in down from centre, curving round top of sleeve to re-join original seamline at notches.

Altering the sleeves

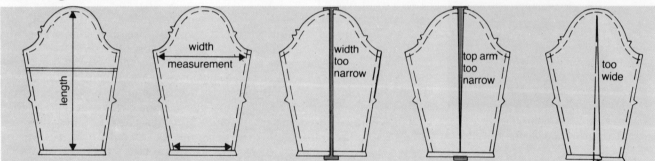

Length

Measure sleeve pattern from top of sleeve to hem fold, excluding top seam allowance. Check your own measurement from shoulder point, over bent elbow to outside wrist, and compare the measurements. Make any adjustments to length on the double alteration line (see page 21), just below the underarm. If alterations are made at the wrist the shape of the sleeve is destroyed.

Width

Jackets are designed to be worn over other garments, so allow plenty of ease. Check your top arm (just below underarm) and wrist measurements and compare with the pattern. Allow enough room to bend your arm comfortably.

Too narrow

If the sleeve is too narrow throughout, draw a line through centre of pattern from top to bottom. Slash open along line and lay the two pieces on to a strip of paper, leaving a gap for the required amount between them. Tape pattern to paper and re-draw seamline.

Trim away excess paper. If the pattern has been enlarged by more than 1.5cm/⅝in let out the bodice shoulder or underarm seams a little to enlarge the armhole for the larger sleeve.

Top arm too narrow

If more room is needed at the top of the sleeve, draw a line through centre of pattern from top to bottom. Slash line from top centre

to within 5mm/¼in of lower edge. Lay pattern piece over paper strip and open pattern at top by required amount. Tape pattern to paper and re-draw seamline. Up to 1.5cm/⅝in extra ease at top of sleeve is acceptable, but let out shoulder or side seams of bodice if necessary.

Too wide

If the sleeve is too wide, draw a line on pattern from centre sleeve at shoulder point to wrist and fold pattern as shown to make a long dart.

If you need to reduce width at under-arm seam of sleeve, make the same reduction on the side seams of the jacket or the sleeve will be too small for the armhole.

Fitting a jacket: the easy way to success

You can give the clothes you make a finish that makes them indistinguishable from expensive shop-bought garments. The secret lies in scrupulous fitting, and the at-a-glance fitting guide given here shows you how to achieve perfect results every time.

Above: Make careful adjustments where necessary during making up, to achieve the good fit characterized by a smooth neckline and shoulderline.

The making up instructions that appear on pages 62–65 should be used in conjunction with the comprehensive fitting chart (below and overleaf). The checklist and diagrams help you to correct any problems that arise during the making up process. Take the time to try on your jacket at the stages indicated and you will be rewarded with a jacket that fits perfectly.

Achieving a perfect fit

Clothes do not necessarily have to fit closely to fit well. They should feel and look good whatever the style, with sufficient ease to allow you to walk, move or sit without straining the seams. When the body is still, they should hang well and keep their shape. Few people would think of buying a garment without first trying it on to see how it looks and fits. The same reasoning should apply to any garment that you make.

For perfect results, try on and adjust at each stage of making up, using the fitting checklist. Do not wait until the end, when alterations might force you to unpick the whole garment. Too many home-made clothes remain unworn because they were not checked for fit during the making up stages, and the prospect of re-making proves too much.

Using a dressmaker's form

Although it is useful to have a dressmaker's form or dummy, the only *true* fitting takes place on the person who is going to wear the garment. Few personal measurements are exactly the same as a dummy – the shoulder slope may be different, for example – and the dummy has to be padded to the correct proportions. However, do use the dummy to work on between personal fittings and to keep the garment in good shape. If you do not have a dummy, keep jackets and coats on padded hangers between sewing sessions, but do not leave heavy fabrics to hang unfinished too long.

When making a personal fitting remember that the garment should always be fitted right side out, the way it will be worn, as the human body is not symmetrical.

Always take into account the clothes you will be wearing under the jacket – a winter version to be worn over jumpers requires more sleeve room than a summer jacket. If possible, ask someone to help you during the fitting process – they will be able to judge the garment's appearance

Jacket fitting problems and how to solve them

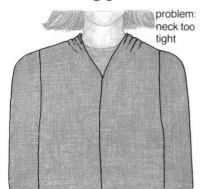

problem: neck too tight

Neck area: too tight
Garment feels too tight and high at neck. Fabric wrinkles at nape of neck, shoulder seams are pulled up and centre front gapes.

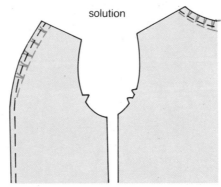

solution

Solution Snip entire neck edge from raw edges to staystitching on seamline. If neckline is still tight and is distorting jacket, mark new seamline on both neck edge and facing.

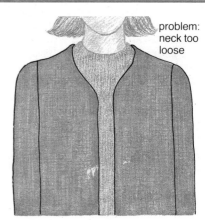

problem: neck too loose

Neck area: too large
Neckline gapes.

Solution Mark a new seamline 5mm/¼in within existing seam allowance to bring it closer to neck,

from every angle more easily than you can, even if you use a second mirror to reflect the back view. The left and right-hand sides should balance and the centre back and front hang vertically.

Fitting checklist

This guide to what makes a 'good fit' applies equally to clothes you have made and shop-bought clothes.

● **Shoulder seam** Straight and slightly sloped, the seam should be towards the back of the shoulder, running from side neck to shoulder point, unless the style dictates otherwise.

● **Neckline** Smooth fit to base of neck with no gaping or pulling across shoulders.

● **Bust** Smooth fit, but enough ease to avoid strained seams, gaping buttonholes or wrinkles at underarm.

● **Back** Enough ease between the shoulder blades for reaching, bending and stretching so that the armhole seam is not strained.

● **Armhole and sleeve** The underarm seam should not be tight in the armpit. Sleeves should be of good appearance both when the arm is straight and when it is bent. Long sleeves should cover the wrist bone when arm is at side.

If problems become apparent in any of these areas during fitting of a garment, use the chart below and overleaf to help you find a solution.

Right: If you have one, work on a dressmaker's form between fittings.

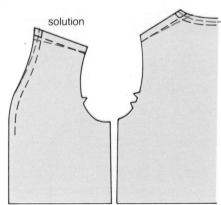

and alter seamline on facing to correspond. If this is insufficient, take a wedge shape out of shoulder seam at neck point, tapering to shoulder point. Alter seamline of facing to correspond.

Jacket fitting problems and how to solve them

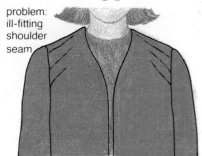

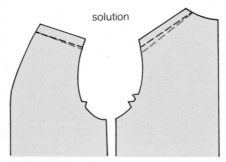

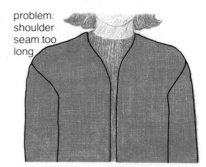

Shoulder area: ill-fitting seam
Folds fall from neck point towards side of armhole, due to sloping shoulders.

Solution Any drastic alteration will simply emphasize the shoulder slope. Instead, use thicker shoulder pad to level off the shoulder or use a normal thickness pad and take out the excess fabric in a wedge shape with the wide end at the shoulder, tapering towards the neck.

Shoulder area: seam too long
More than the 1.5cm/⅝in seam allowance extends beyond the shoulder point.

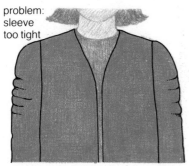

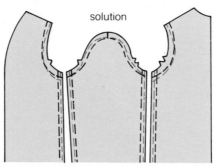

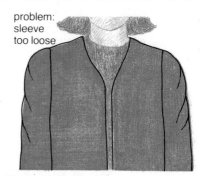

Sleeve: too tight
Upper sleeve too tight, causing fabric to pull into horizontal folds across sleeve head.

Solution Let out top of underarm seam on sleeve, and top of bodice side seams. Take less turning on the sleeve but normal turnings on

bodice between front and back notches of lower armhole. The extra width gained under the arm and from the sleeve seam should be sufficient, but if not, re-draw entire bodice seamline from shoulder point to underarm on each side of jacket. Make corresponding alterations to sleeve.

Sleeve: too loose
Long, vertical folds throughout sleeve due to slender arm in too wide a sleeve.

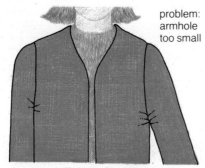

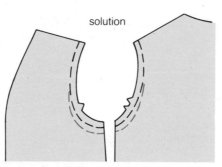

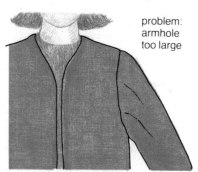

Armhole area: too small
Underarm seam too high and armhole too small. Restricts movement and not enough room allowed for garment underneath.

Solution Clip turnings at underarms to ease curve during fitting. If

necessary lower armhole at bodice side seam by drawing new lower armhole from underarm, tapering upwards to rejoin notches on front and back. Enlarge the sleeve seam by letting out as much seam allowance as possible.

Armhole area: too large
Too much room in armhole.

Solution Take a larger seam allowance at the bodice side seams –in a wedge shape at the armhole, tapering down to join the side seam. If the body of the jacket is the

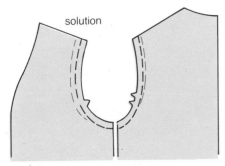

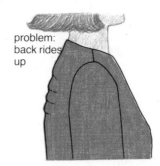

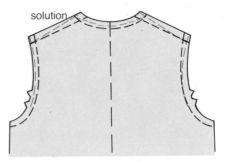

Solution Mark correct shoulder
point, then re-draw the armhole
seamline on back and front armhole
starting from shoulder point and
tapering to notches.
If the sleeve does not now fit
satisfactorily, take only 1cm/½in
turnings at top of the sleeve seam.

Back area: rides up
Garment is stretched across back
between armholes and tends to rise
up at back neck due to a rounded
back. This causes lower hem to stick
out and pulls front open.

Solution Let out shoulder seams of
back pattern piece only, tapering to
the shoulder point. Use a narrower
seam allowance at both back neck
and back armhole. Take smaller
turnings on facings and sleeve to
correspond with alterations.

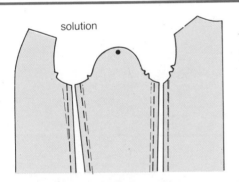

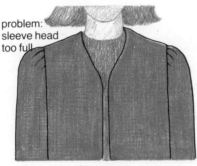

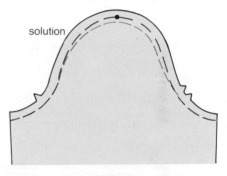

Solution Once the sleeve has been
cut, the only solution is to take in
the seam by the required amount,
either throughout its length, or
tapering from underarm to wrist.
The bodice side seams must be
taken in by the same amount at the
top or sleeve will not fit.

Sleeve: head too full
Too much fullness in sleeve head,
with pleats instead of gathers, due
to too much fabric or incorrect
easing.

Solution Measure both sleeve and
armhole seamline and compare
measurements. The sleeve should

be 2–5cm/¾–2in larger. If it is more,
re-draw the sleeve head, lowering
the centre point (which matches the
shoulder seam of the garment) by
up to 1cm/⅜in. Curve the line
down to meet the notches and
original sleeve seamline. Do not
remove all the ease or sleeve will
not fit the upper arm.

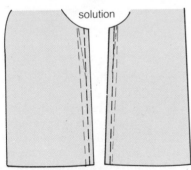

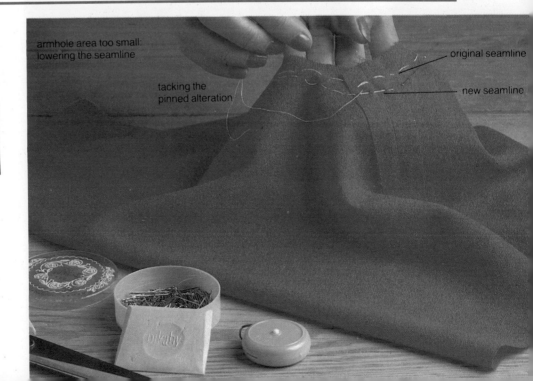

right size make small seam
alterations and raise underarm
seam slightly. If the jacket is too
loose at the hem, take in all down
the side seams.
Take in the sleeve seam at
underarm so that it will fit into the
smaller armhole.

Sleeves and shoulder pads for simple jackets

A cardigan jacket teams with so many other garments that it is well worth making. This chapter introduces the basic techniques you will need for setting in sleeves – useful both for the jacket shown and for any other garment with plain, set-in sleeves.

Unlined, collarless jackets are ideal for day or evening wear and the neat neckline complements frills, ruffles or any collar detail on shirts, dresses or blouses.

The jacket pattern given on page 74 is of this type – a simple, loosely-structured cardigan style. There is a choice of lengths – to just below waist level or to the hip level – and the sleeves can be full length, elbow length or short.

A cardigan jacket is easy to make but,

Plain set-in sleeves

The one piece, set-in sleeve is most frequently used for jackets and coats. When making a jacket, always bear in mind the style of the garment to be worn beneath it and allow sufficient jacket and sleeve width to avoid crushing full gathered sleeves, ruffles or other trims.

Achieving a good fit

The smooth roll at the top of a plain set-in sleeve is achieved by allowing ease (extra fabric) in the sleeve

Setting in a sleeve

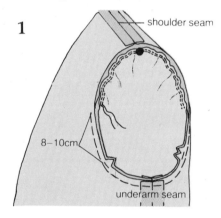

1

— shoulder seam

8–10cm

underarm seam

1 With right sides facing, slip sleeve into armhole. Align underarm seam of garment with sleeve seam, and match front and back notches on armhole and sleeve. Pin and tack underarm section up to notches on each side and run a double row of gathering threads around sleeve top. Working upwards from notches on each side of armhole and matching seamlines, pin, then tack, seam together for a further 8-10cm/ 3¼- 4in towards top of sleeve.

Left: A good shoulderline is achieved by inserting foam or wadding shoulder pads.

as for any jacket – whatever the style – the look of the finished garment very much depends on careful fitting. Having learnt how to make paper pattern adjustments, this chapter is devoted to some of the techniques you need to have at your fingertips when making the jacket. Learn how to set in sleeves perfectly and how to make and fix shoulder pads.
Check the fitting guide on pages 54–57 to achieve a perfect fit at the armhole.

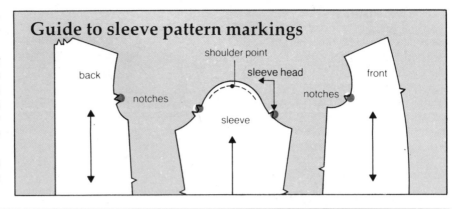

Guide to sleeve pattern markings

head – the top part of the sleeve. The sleeve head is always cut a little larger than the armhole of the jacket so that when the two pieces are joined, the extra fabric allows ease of arm movement where it is most needed – over the top of the sleeve and on the front curve. The back curve of both armhole and sleeve is much less pronounced.
It is important to transfer all armhole and sleeve markings from the pattern to garment sections.

particularly the notches as they are the guides to 'balancing' the sleeve in the armhole so that it hangs perfectly, with the straight grain of the fabric running from shoulder to wrist. The centre top part of the sleeve head (usually marked with a dot or circle on commercial patterns) is a guide to positioning the sleeve correctly at the shoulder. See fitting adjustments on pages 53, 56–57.

Fitting tips

1 Work on both sleeves at the same time, making them up step by step as a pair.
2 Make sure that you cut a left and a right sleeve – it is all too easy to make a mistake and produce two the same.
3 Learn to recognise the shape of sleeves. The front sleeve head has a pronounced curve, whereas the back is fairly straight.
4 Note the difference between front and back notches. The front section of both sleeve and armhole usually has a single notch and the back sections have a double notch.
5 Always join side and shoulder seams and complete all neck and facing details *before* inserting sleeves.
6 Make up sleeves and tack into armhole for an initial fitting. Insert shoulder pads, if used, and check for fit of armhole. Establish sleeve length, allowing an extra few millimetres for tightening up after machining. It is easier to complete sleeve hem before insertion but if you are in doubt about the final length, tack and leave final adjustment until sleeve has been machined in position.
7 If you have never inserted a sleeve before, or are a little unsure about this stage, transfer *all* the markings from the pattern pieces to the garment, including the seamline on both sleeve and jacket, so that you have a very accurate guide to follow.

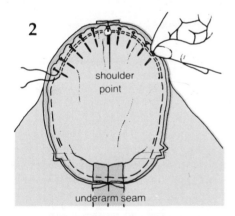

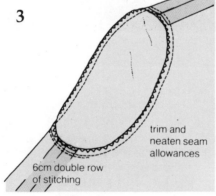

2 Lay the shoulder over one hand and spread the fullness of the sleeve head evenly over it. Pin together the centre shoulder seam and corresponding centre mark on sleeve, then pin round the head of the sleeve at 1cm/½in intervals, inserting the pins at right angles to the raw edges, and matching the seamline exactly. Tack with small stitches, drawing up the gathering to ease sleeve into armhole.

3 Machine sleeve into armhole, with the wrong side of sleeve towards you, starting from the underarm seam. For extra strength, start 3cm/1¼in before the seam and finish 3cm/1¼in after, giving a double row of stitching for 6cm/2½in. Working from the sleeve side makes it easier to avoid creating small pleats in the eased section. Remove tackings and trim seam allowances to 1cm/½in. Neaten both raw edges together, using machine zigzag stitch.

Pressing to finish

The beautifully rounded finish of a sleeve head can be flattened by pressing. If any pressing is necessary, use a tailor's ham, a pad specially designed for the purpose (page 34 shows how to make one), or use a small pad of folded cloth to preserve the roll of the sleeve head. Press only the upper part of the armhole sleeve allowance in towards the sleeve but leave the underarm part upright.

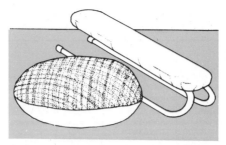

Below: Press the sleeve from the wrong side, using a tailor's ham – its rounded finish maintains the curve of the seam.

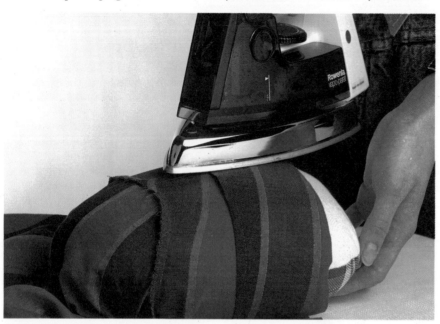

Making shoulder pads

Shoulder pads are not just a fashion gimmick, they are an important detail if you want a really good fit on coat or jacket shoulders. They maintain the shoulder line and the shape of the upper sleeve and give support to the rest of the garment, at the same time disguising any tendency to rounded shoulders or uneven shoulder heights.

Ready-made foam or wadding shoulder pads tend to be expensive so it is worth making your own, especially as they can then be layered to the exact size and thickness you require. Foam pads are suitable for dry-cleaning and washing, but are best covered to avoid irritating the skin, or friction with other garments.

Cutting out the pads

Enlarge the pattern for the shoulder pad (right), following the line for the appropriate size. Use this as your pattern piece.

1 Cut two pieces of wadding to make the outside layers of each pad and as many more pieces as necessary to make up the required thickness.

If using foam sheeting, graduate the two shorter edges of all but the two outer pieces for each pad, slicing them at an angle with a razor blade

Inserting shoulder pads

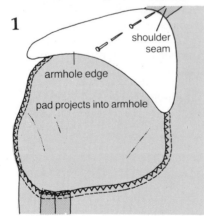

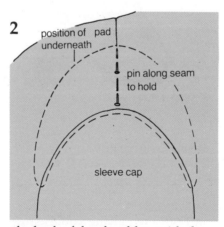

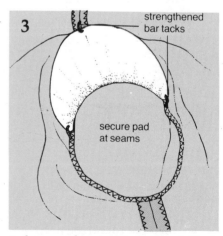

Insert shoulder pads only when the sleeve has been attached to the garment and all raw edges finished at the armhole. (Although they should be inserted temporarily during fitting.)

1 With the wrong side of the garment towards you and the sleeve hanging inside the garment, position the shoulder pad towards the back of the shoulder, with the centre point of the armhole edge of pad just to the back of the shoulder seam. The armhole edge of the pad should align with the armhole seam, but project a few millimetres into the sleeve to maintain the fullness. Pin at seams, to hold.

2 Turn garment to right side and insert pins along the shoulder seam to keep pad in position. Check that it looks smooth.

3 Turn garment back to inside and secure pad to seam allowance on shoulder and armhole seams with 2cm/¾in long bar tacks, strengthened with blanket stitch (see opposite), to allow slight movement, in line with the movement of the body.

or sharp knife. Keep the armhole edge even. Tack diagonally through all layers to secure the pad.

Covering the pads

2 Cut two pieces of lining fabric (such as acetate) for each pad, allowing 2cm/¾in extra fabric all round. Lay pad on wrong side of one lining section, fold the side up over the pad and tack.

3 Position second lining section, wrong side down, on other side of pad. Turn in the edges, taking care not to pull cloth too tight and flatten the pad. Pin and hem to lower section along turned edge with small, neat stitches.

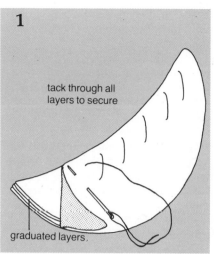

tack through all layers to secure

graduated layers

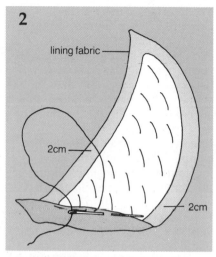

lining fabric

2cm

2cm

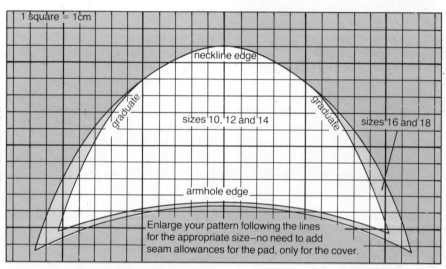

1 square = 1cm

neckline edge

graduate

graduate

sizes 10, 12 and 14

sizes 16 and 18

armhole edge

Enlarge your pattern following the lines for the appropriate size—no need to add seam allowances for the pad, only for the cover.

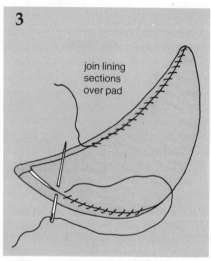

join lining sections over pad

Useful hand stitches

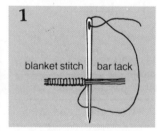

blanket stitch | bar tack

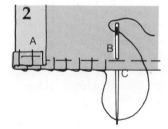

A

B

C

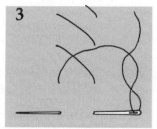

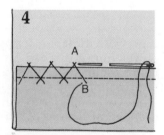

A

B

Bar tack

Used for reinforcement at ends of buttonholes, as thread loop for button or to secure shoulder pads.
Work three or four long stitches closely together to form a loop.
Cover with closely worked blanket stitch (see right).

Blanket stitch

Used as a decorative edging, and in embroidery.
Work from left to right, with fabric edge and needle pointing towards you. Secure thread on wrong side (at **A**) and bring round below edge. Push needle through fabric from right side (at **B**) and bring out (at **C**), within loop of previous stitch.

Diagonal tacking

Provides firmer control over an area than ordinary tacking.
Work parallel stitches with the needle pointing right to left, so that diagonal stitches form on the right side. For even firmer control, decrease space between parallel stitches.

Herringbone stitch

A strong stitch, often used for hems or securing interfacing.
Work from left to right and bring needle through to hem edge.
With needle pointing left, catch a few threads of the garment (at **A**). Take another stitch, with needle pointing left, further along the hem (at **B**). Repeat, alternating from garment to hem.

The facts about interfacing

The interfacing in a finished garment lies between the facing and the wrong side of the garment. This extra layer of a different fabric gives support, strength and body where necessary. It is usually cut to the shape of the facings, whether these are cut in one with the garment, or separately.

Interfacing is never visible on the completed garment – the only indication of its presence should be the general good finish and crisp edges. It is rare to find a garment requiring no interfacing at all – very soft, floaty designs being one of the few exceptions.

Choose interfacing that is slightly lighter in weight than that of the garment, but firmer to handle. It should be lighter in colour than the garment fabric, and have the same washing or dry cleaning properties. There are two main groups of interfacings – woven ones and non-woven ones that form a fabric with the appearance of lightweight felt. Interfacings are further divided into those that are sewn into place, and those that are bonded on to the fabric, using an iron – hence the name fusible interfacing. Both types are available in a wide variety of weights and widths, the heavier, woven interfacings being the narrowest.

Weights of interfacing If you need a heavyweight interfacing, try using a woven type. This is pliable and will move with the fabric. It may be woven from goat's hair, wool, cotton, or linen – all these work well with coatings and suitings.
Non-woven interfacings are more economical in terms of fabric

required. Because there is no grain line, pattern pieces can be closely interlocked.
The choice of woven interfacings for mediumweight fabrics is wide and varied – lawn, organdie, domette, mull, calico and lightweight canvas are all suitable. For a non-woven interfacing, choose Vilene medium sew-in, or Supershape medium – a fusible type with some 'give' on the bias and width.
Choose from organza (silk or man-made), soft cotton lawn, or net for evening wear if you require a woven interfacing in a lightweight fabric. Suitable non-woven interfacings are Vilene Light iron-on, or Supershape light. It may be best to interface some very fine fabrics with the garment fabric instead.

Attaching interfacings Always test fusible interfacings on a scrap of fabric first to make sure they do not alter the character of the fabric. Put a clean cloth over the ironing board to prevent any adhesive sticking to it and press carefully. Do not move the iron to and fro – this will cause air bubbles between fabric and interfacing.
Sew-in interfacings are normally tacked into position during making up and secured in the seam when the garment is stitched. If a free edge remains, it can be held in place with herringbone stitch or catchstitch.
Availability The range of inter-facings on the market is expanding, and many specialist types are now available. Take some of your fabric to the shop and tell the assistant exactly what you require and why. Special interfacings are available for shirts, ties, belts, ball gowns, straps and waistbands.

Cardigan jacket

A jacket is a useful basic garment in any wardrobe – and you can make this one in a variety of fabrics to suit any occasion and to take you right through the seasons. Try a linen-look fabric or raw silk for a smart spring outfit, crisp seersucker for a lovely summery effect and Viyella or light wool for autumn and winter. Later chapters give full instructions for lining the jacket for extra body and warmth.

For an evening look, soft silk is beautiful and luxurious but you could also try velvet, moiré, taffeta or lurex.

You will need
Fabric according to size and style
Matching sewing thread
30cm/12in of 90cm/36in wide interfacing
1 pair shoulder pads
Pattern pieces from pages 74 and 75:
1 Jacket back
2 Jacket front
3 Jacket back facing
4 Jacket front facing
5 Jacket sleeve
7 Pocket (optional – see page 72 for instructions)

Opposite: Waist-length versions of the jacket, showing different sleeve lengths.

Fabric quantity chart
Long cardigan jacket

Size	10	12	14	16	18
Bust (cm)	83	87	92	97	102
90cm	2.25	2.30	2.30	2.35	2.35m
115cm*	1.60	1.60	1.60	1.65	1.75m
140cm	1.45	1.45	1.45	1.45	1.50m
150cm*	1.25	1.30	1.30	1.30	1.35m

Short cardigan jacket

Size	10	12	14	16	18
90cm	1.70	1.70	1.75	1.75	1.75m
115cm*	1.20	1.20	1.25	1.30	1.35m
140cm	1.20	1.20	1.25	1.25	1.25m
150cm*	1.00	1.00	1.05	1.05	1.10m

*without nap. All other fabric widths are with or without nap.
Fabric quantities are given in metres and include amounts for optional patch pockets (see layouts).

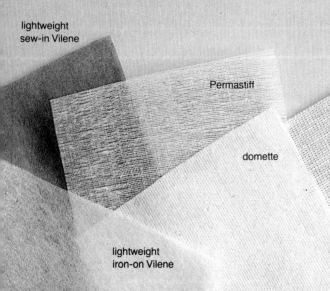

lightweight sew-in Vilene

Permastiff

tie interfacing

domette

lightweight iron-on Vilene

linen duck

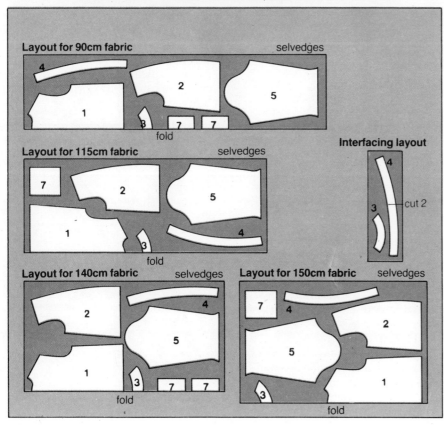

Layout for 90cm fabric

selvedges

4

2

5

1

3

7 7

fold

Layout for 115cm fabric

selvedges

7

2

5

1

3

4

fold

Layout for 140cm fabric

selvedges

2

4

5

1

3

7 7

fold

Layout for 150cm fabric

selvedges

7

4

2

5

1

3

fold

Interfacing layout

4

3

cut 2

long jacket
long sleeves

long jacket
short sleeves

short jacket
short sleeves

short jacket
long sleeves

Preparing to cut out
Make any necessary adjustments to
sleeve width or garment length
remembering that a 4cm/1½in hem
allowance is included.
Fold fabric right sides together, as
shown on fabric layout for your
fabric width. Pin all pattern pieces
to fabric, placing back (1) and back
neck facing (3) to fold. Cut out
carefully. Transfer pattern markings
to fabric and remove pattern pieces.
Using pattern pieces 3 and 4 again,
cut out interfacing for back neck
and front edges. Cut one back neck
interfacing to a fold, and two front
interfacings.

Making up the cardigan jacket

Put the jacket together as follows, paying careful attention to each fitting stage. Before you start fitting, consult the charts on pages 54–57. If possible, ask someone you know to help you make any adjustments that are necessary, as it is difficult to mark accurate alterations with pins or tailor's chalk while you are wearing the garment.

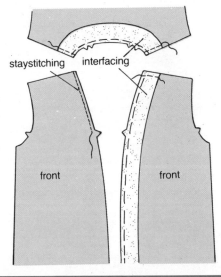

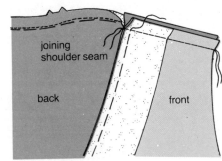

Step 1 Staystitch back and front necklines to prevent fabric stretching. Interface back neck and fronts of jacket, tacking interfacing (or pressing if fusible) to wrong side of fabric.

Step 2 With right sides together, pin and tack side and shoulder seams. Machine shoulder seams only. Remove tacking, press seams open and neaten edges.
Tack one sleeve seam in preparation for first fitting.

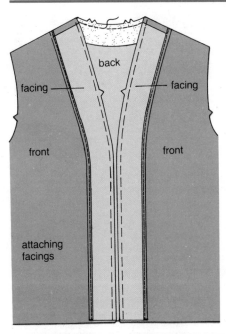

Step 3 Join facings, right sides together, at shoulders. Trim seams to 1cm/⅜in and press open. Neaten outside edge of facing and press. With right sides together, position facings on jacket, matching notches and shoulder seams. Pin, tack and machine all round on seamline. On heavier fabrics reduce seam bulk by layering (see step 4, page 69); for lighter fabrics it is sufficient to snip into neck curve at 1cm/⅜in intervals and trim seam to 5mm/¼in.

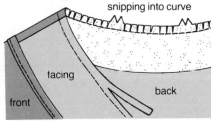

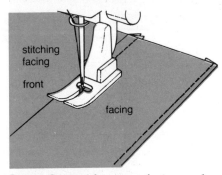

Step 4 On inside, press facing and seam allowances away from bodice. Working on right side, stitch facing to seam allowances as close as possible to seam.
Roll facing back. Tack from wrong side all the way round through facings, catching only a few threads from the front of the garment, 2mm/⅛in in from the edge. Press.

Second fitting

Try on jacket, slipping shoulder pads into position. Check hang of sleeve and width of armhole and mark adjustments if necessary. Remove jacket.

Step 7 Distributing ease evenly, machine sleeves into armholes. Remove tackings and press carefully, using a tailor's ham or roll of cloth (see page 60).
Stitch shoulder pads into jacket as instructed on pages 60–61. Catchstitch facing to garment at shoulder seam.

Third fitting

Try on jacket, align centre fronts and decide final hem length of both jacket and sleeves. Mark with chalk.

Step 8 Unpick about 10cm/4in of tacking from the centre front edges and open out facing. Neaten lower hem edge.
Cut a strip of interfacing 1cm/½in narrower than the width of the hem allowance and the measurement of the hem edge. Tack (or press if fusible) just above foldline of hem on wrong side.

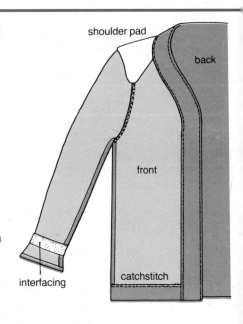

First fitting
Try on jacket bodice and slip shoulder pad inside shoulder area. Mark any necessary alterations at shoulder, remembering that sewing the neckline will draw the shoulder up a little. Check jacket width, and see how it hangs.
Slip the sleeve over your arm and pin to shoulder and underarm of bodice. Check only the sleeve width at this point. Check the width of the back between the shoulders and make sure the centre fronts meet. Remove the jacket and unpin sleeve.

Step 5 With right sides together, matching notches, machine side seams. Remove tacking, press seams open and neaten edges.

Step 6 With right sides together, matching notches, join sleeve seams following the shape of the seam at the wrist. This slopes outwards so it will lie flat at the tapered wrist when the hem is turned up.
Remove tackings, press seams open (using a sleeve arm if you have one), and neaten.
Pin and tack both sleeves into armhole (see pages 58 and 59). Do not try to perfect top ease at this stage – wait until after the second fitting so that you will know exactly how the garment hangs.

Turn up hem over interfacing, tacking and pressing the hem fold edge to give a good finish. Pin, tack and catchstitch neatened hem edge to garment.
Fold front facings back to inside of jacket and catchstitch facings to hem.

Step 9 Finish sleeve hem in the same way as jacket hem, inserting a strip of interfacing at wrist for extra strength.
Remove any tackings left in the garment and gently press out tacking marks.

Making a short jacket . . .
Cut out pattern pieces 1, 2 and 4 along the lines marked for the shorter length. Note that the pattern pieces interlock more closely on the cutting layout. Make up the jacket as above, but to the shorter length.

. . . with short sleeves
The jacket can also be made up with elbow length or short sleeves. Simply measure from shoulder to elbow, or to length required, and

Above: The short jacket, made up with elbow-length sleeves and teamed with a matching softly pleated skirt, from page 43.

transfer this measurement to pattern piece, measuring down from shoulder point. Add 4cm/1½in for hem and re-draw hem shaping. Cut the pattern piece to length required and make up as for long sleeve. (Do not make such a large alteration in size on the double alteration lines – it will distort the shape of the sleeve.)

65

Lining and trimming a Chanel-style jacket

The Chanel-style jacket is another very easy to make and easy to wear variation of the patterns given on page 74.
To make this stylish version, or the short version given on page 51, use the knowhow gained from making the cardigan jacket, adding darts, a braid trim and a simple lining.

The Chanel-style jacket has bust darts, a high, collarless round neck and meets edge to edge at the centre front. It is named after its designer, Gabrielle 'Coco' Chanel (1883-1971), a French fashion designer who played a significant part in the transformation of women's clothing during the twentieth century. Chanel designed casual, yet elegant, easy-to-wear clothes, many of which were inspired originally by men's garments. For example, a polo-necked sweater gave rise to the first jersey dress, and a boy's school blazer was copied and re-cut to make a woman's version. Women appreciated the freedom and comfort afforded by her designs, many of which have proved to have a timeless appeal. The Chanel jacket has re-appeared several times in fashion collections over the years and is as popular now as it ever was. You can turn your jacket into a suit by adding a skirt in a matching or contrasting fabric – an A-line or full dirndl skirt are the most suitable styles to choose. Use a wool mixture for a suit for cooler days, or a slubbed linen for spring or summer. Emphasize the clear cut design lines with parallel rows of braid on the front edges and neckline, and learn how to add a simple lining to make yourself a smart and hard-wearing jacket that will never date.

Adding braid to a jacket

The Chanel jacket is traditionally trimmed with one or two rows of braid, to echo and emphasize the lines of the design and add interest to an otherwise plain finish.

When choosing braid, take a sample of fabric with you and keep the style of the garment in mind. Lay possible trimmings over the fabric and consider points like colour and texture. A heavy braid may be overwhelming, while a dainty trim may be too insignificant.

Scroll braid is most widely associated with the Chanel jacket. It has a textured finish and the best width to choose is 5mm/¼in, particularly if two rows are used. Soutache or Russian braid, ric-rac or any flat, narrow braid are also suitable.

Preparing the braid

If the braid contains a percentage of wool or cotton, it may be subject to shrinkage. It may also have stretched while wound round the card in the shop, so leave it for 24 hours to relax back into shape, then press lightly with a damp cloth. Synthetic trimmings will not require this treatment. The best time to attach the braid is when the hem of the garment is completed. Decide on the best position by laying the braid over the jacket. If you are using a single row of narrow braid, 3cm/1¼in from the front edge looks best. Mark the final position with a line of tailor's chalk or tacking on the right side of the garment. Make sure it is parallel to the front edge, and even around the neckline. If there are two rows of braid, be sure to keep them an equal distance apart.

Applying the braid

Braid can be applied by hand or machine, tacking first. Work from the right side when applying soutache braid, sewing it by machine or by hand using prickstitch. The stitches should be made in the centre groove of the braid, where they will disappear. Thicker, textured braids such as scroll braid are best sewn on by hand, working from the wrong side using fairly loose stitches. If thicker braid is machine-stitched, use a larger stitch with less upper tension than usual, to avoid puckering the garment fabric. Work from the right side, positioning the stitching line where it will be least obvious. Whether stitching by hand or machine, avoid stretching the braid and ease it gently around curves. Take care on sharp, right-angled corners as at the top front neck. Scroll braid and most narrow braids can be bent around right-angled corners and secured with one or two small handstitches. Soutache braid will turn without difficulty.

To prevent fraying or unravelling of ends when cut, bind a piece of sticky tape over the braid, centring it over the point where you wish to cut. Cut through tape and braid – the tape will hold the cut ends in place. Do not remove the tape until you are ready to finish the edges.

Finishing off the braid

If the jacket is to be lined, and the braid is not too thick, the raw edges can be taken round the lower edge and hidden within the hem of the lining. If the jacket is unlined, overcast the raw edges and turn under 5mm/¼in, using tiny slipstitches.

If you are using thick, heavy braid, the raw edges will have to be neatened on the hem fold on the right side. Alternatively, continue the braid round the jacket, parallel to the hem edge.

Right: Flat braid defines the shape of the long version of the Chanel jacket.
Inset: A selection of suitable braids.

Mitring a corner on braid

Flat, woven braid in narrow widths (up to 1.5cm/⅝in) is also suitable for trimming the Chanel-style jacket. It is less flexible than other types of braid and therefore a diagonal fold or mitre has to be made where the braid has to turn a sharp corner.

1 Lay braid on the right side of the garment and pin in position as far as the corner. Turn a right-angled corner by folding braid and stitching diagonally on the wrong side of the braid. Pin across the fold, matching the

pinning across fold

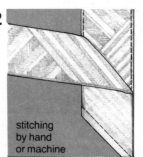

stitching by hand or machine

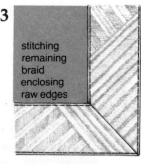

stitching remaining braid enclosing raw edges

pattern where possible.

2 Sew on the braid and when you come to the corner, machine or hand-sew across the diagonal fold on the wrong side and trim the seam, finger pressing it open.

3 Pin the rest of the braid into place along the next straight edge. Continue sewing around the edges of the braid, enclosing the raw edges.

Making a dart

A dart is a method of disposing of unwanted areas of fullness in a garment, shaping it to fit areas like the shoulders, waist and bust. It takes in a triangular area of fabric which is stitched from the wide end to the point.

Darts vary in width, length and shape. Some are short and straight, others curve slightly, according to the effect required and the area being fitted, but all should be unobtrusive. They are shown on paper patterns by small circles, broken or solid lines. On a multi-size pattern several sizes are given so make sure you transfer the correct size dart.

Transfer the dart pattern markings to the fabric using tailor's chalk, tailor's

tacks or a tracing wheel and dressmaker's carbon paper. For complete accuracy, mark the stitching line of the whole dart. The circles should be treated like pattern notches, and placed together accurately.

Pressing finished darts For the best finish, darts should be pressed over a curved surface, such as a tailor's ham or a pad of clean, smooth cloth placed on the ironing board.

Vertical darts, such as those at shoulder and waist, are pressed towards centre front or centre back. Horizontal darts, such as underarm bust darts or elbow darts, are pressed downwards, towards waist or wrist. Darts on bulky fabric are slashed to within 5mm/¼in of the tip, and pressed open.

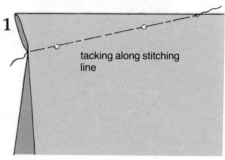

tacking along stitching line

1 Fold dart, right sides together, along centre line matching the pattern markings each side. Pin and tack along stitching line. If you have used tailor's tacks, remove them at this stage.

The Chanel-style jacket

The jacket can be made in two lengths. To make the short version simply cut along the lines indicated on the pattern.

You will need

Fabric according to size and style
Matching sewing thread
0.20m/¼yd of 90cm/36in wide interfacing
2.20m/2⅜yd of 90cm/36in wide lining *or* 1.50m/1⅝yd of 140/54in lining
1 pair of shoulder pads
3.90m/4¼yd of braid (optional)
Pattern pieces, pages 74 and 75:
1 and 3 Jacket back and facing
8 and 9 Jacket front and facing
5 Sleeve

Fabric requirements

Size	10	12	14	16	18
Bust (cm)	83	87	92	97	102cm
(in)	32½	34	36	38	40in

Long version

90cm*	2.20	2.30	2.30	2.35	2.35m
115cm	1.60	1.60	1.60	1.65	1.75m
140cm	1.40	1.40	1.40	1.50	1.50m

Short version

90cm*	1.70	1.70	1.75	1.75	1.75m
115cm	1.20	1.20	1.30	1.30	1.40m
140cm	1.20	1.20	1.20	1.30	1.30m

* without nap

Fabric quantities are given in metres – if your retailer sells fabric in yards, use a conversion chart.

Cutting out

Pin the pattern on the fabric, following the appropriate cutting layout. Cut out carefully and transfer pattern markings using whatever method you prefer. Remove paper pattern pieces and use pieces 9 and 3 to cut out the interfacing for the jacket.

Making up

The jacket is made in the same way as the cardigan jacket (see pages 64 and 65) with the following amendments to the instructions. Complete steps 1, 2 and the first fitting as for the cardigan jacket, stitching the bust darts in the front of the jacket and pressing them down.

Cutting layouts for jacket

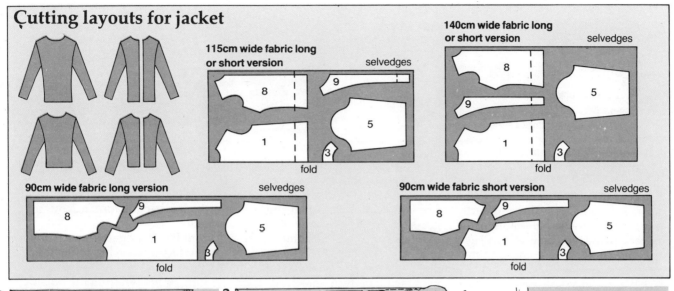

115cm wide fabric long or short version

140cm wide fabric long or short version

90cm wide fabric long version

90cm wide fabric short version

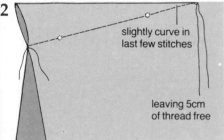

2 slightly curve in last few stitches

leaving 5cm of thread free

2 Stitch, following the tacking line exactly, starting at the wide end and tapering to the point. The last few stitches on the fabric should be curved in slightly towards the tip of the dart to prevent a sharp-angled ending which will make the dart noticeable. Allow the machine to run off the end of the fabric. Leave at least 5cm/2in of thread free.

3 hand sewing loose ends through dart

3 Thread needle and stitch back through the dart to prevent unravelling. Do not tie thread ends in a knot as this will wear a hole in fabrics when pressed. Reverse sewing on the machine is not suitable either – it spoils the fine tapered finish.

4 pressing the dart

4 Press the folded edge and stitching as far as the point, not beyond. Then, opening out the garment, press the fabric either side of the dart before gently pressing it in the appropriate direction. Check the finish on the right side. The stitching line should be flat and the point smooth, with no wrinkles or creases in the fabric.

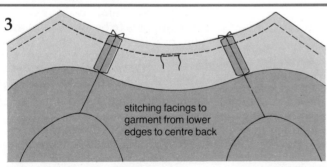

3 stitching facings to garment from lower edges to centre back

Step 3 With right sides together, join facings at shoulder seams. Trim seams to 1cm/½in and press open. If the jacket is to be left unlined, neaten entire outside edge of facing and press or bind all raw edges with seam binding.
With the right sides together, matching notches and shoulder seams, pin and tack facings to jacket.

Starting at the lower edge, machine along seamline up to neck edge. Leave needle in work at corner, take one stitch across corner and continue stitching carefully round neck curve, to centre back. Break stitching, turn work over and stitch the other side working from hem to centre back of neck in the same way, overlapping the stitching at centre back.

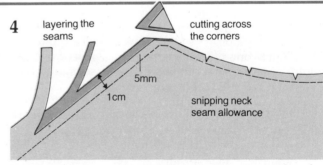

4 layering the seams

cutting across the corners

5mm

1cm

snipping neck seam allowance

Step 4 Reduce the seam bulk by layering the turnings. Trim the jacket front seam allowance closest to the garment surface to just under 1cm/½in, and the facing seam allowance to 5mm/¼in. Trim and snip the neck seam allowances and cut across the corners.
Complete as for the cardigan jacket, pages 64 and 65, from step 4 onwards.

Inserting a simple jacket lining

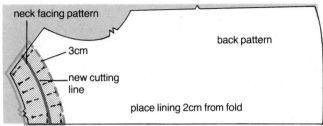

neck facing pattern

3cm

new cutting line

back pattern

place lining 2cm from fold

new cutting line

front pattern

3cm

front facing pattern

A jacket lining is not difficult to make and the finished result amply repays the little extra time it takes. A lining in a jacket adds warmth and body to the garment and hides seams and darts. Buy lining to suit both the fabric of the jacket and the type of wear it will get. A lightweight, silky lining is preferable for an evening jacket, while a jacket for everyday use requires a heavier satin type of lining.

Making the lining pattern
Lining fabric has very little give and therefore it must be cut with extra ease to allow for body movement. If you plan to use the same pattern frequently, it is worthwhile making a separate lining pattern using greaseproof paper or dressmaker's graph paper and incorporating the following adjustments.

Back Pin back pattern over back neck facing pattern, matching notches at neck edge. Draw a new cutting line around neck, 3cm/1¼in up from lower edge of facing, following the curve.

On the centre back seam, mark an instruction to place the pattern 2cm/¾in from the fold. This gives 4cm/1½in extra allowance in the back which is used to form a 2cm/¾in pleat.

Front Pin front pattern piece over front facing, matching notches. Draw a new cutting line for the lining 3cm/1¼in from the outside curved edge of the facing on the front and neck edges.

No alterations to the sleeve pattern are necessary.

Making the lining

Cut out the lining, observing the alterations made to the pattern pieces and remembering to place the back pattern 2cm/¾in from the fold. Join side, shoulder and sleeve seams of the lining as for the jacket. If the lining is attached all the way round the hem, there is no need to neaten any of the raw edges on either lining or the main garment. If the lining is left free at the hem, neaten the side seams of both jacket and lining.

1 Insert the sleeves into the body of the lining as for the main jacket, easing them to fit the armholes. Make the back pleat by folding 2cm/¾in to one side of the centre, press and tack the layers together at the top. Press a 1.5cm/⅝in turning to the wrong side around the front and neck edge of lining, clipping into the curves where necessary. Trim the armhole turnings to 1cm/½in and press them towards sleeve. Turn the completed main garment inside out and the lining right side out. Apply the wrong side of the lining to the wrong side of the garment. Pin in position along side and shoulder seams, smoothing lining over garment to fit.

1

pinning lining to jacket

centre back pleat

1.5cm pressed under

2 Pin lining in position around armholes, inserting pins through all the layers to hold.

Pin pressed edge of lining to jacket all around front and neck edges inserting pins at right angles to seamline. Tack to hold and remove pins. Catchstitch lining to garment, starting 8cm/3¼in above lower hem edge and working up front facing around neck edge and down to 8cm/3¼in above lower edge on the other side.

Trim the lining to 1cm/½in longer than the finished jacket.

If the lining is to be left loose around the hem, press under a turning of 2.5cm/1in and then turn under the raw edge and machine or hand-stitch the hem to finish. The hemmed lining will be 1cm/½in shorter than the jacket. The lining can be secured at the side seams by working a thread chain between the

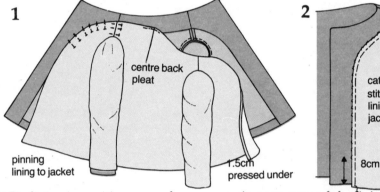

2

catch-stitching lining to jacket

8cm

main garment and the lining. Catchstitch the remaining lower front edges of lining to facings.

If the lining is to be attached at the hem, press under a turning of 2.5cm/1in. Catchstitch the lower, trimmed edge of the lining to the upper edge of the hem turning on the main garment, matching side seams. Take in the excess fabric in a pleat at the lower edge of centre back. When the jacket is worn, the lining will slip down over the stitching, but will not hang below the lower edge. Catchstitch the free lower front edges of the lining to the facings. Remove all pins from side seams. To hem the sleeve, smooth lining towards lower edge and trim to 1cm/½in longer than hemmed sleeve. Catchstitch lower edge of lining to upper edge of hem turning, so that the lining will slip down to hide stitches during wear.

Above: Add graduated pin tucks and patch pockets to the front of a plain jacket.

Pockets and pin-tuck jacket variations

Transform the basic jacket with the addition of pin tucks to the plain front. Learn how to make them, and how to attach patch pockets in a variety of ways, then choose your fabric and make the ideal jacket to complement an evening dress or frilly blouse.

Pockets and pin tucks are both optional features on the cardigan jacket, and this chapter gives you detailed guidance on how to make them. They are valuable and frequently used dressmaking processes – tucks, for example, make an attractive feature on blouses and dresses.

Patch pockets

Patch pockets are just one of a large variety of pocket types. The easiest to make and apply, they are prepared first and then stitched to the outside of the garment, whereas other types of pocket are inserted into seams or cut into the garment.

Making pockets

Where a pair of pockets is required, as on a jacket front, cut, prepare and make them as a pair to ensure that they are exactly the same shape. Use a pattern piece wherever one is supplied, but for full instructions on how to cut out and make simple patch pockets see page 48.

When tacking or sewing pockets by hand, always work on a flat surface. Support the bulk of the garment on the work surface while machining, so that the pocket edges are not pulled out of line.

Apply the pockets as early as possible during the making up of a garment, preferably before joining the side seams. Follow the pocket placement line on the pattern whenever there is one, or else find a comfortable and attractive position, with the top edge parallel to the garment hem and the sides parallel to the centre front of the garment. (As the side seams are often shaped, they are not a good guide.) If there is no pocket placement line, making it difficult to establish the correct position, wait until the garment hem is completed before applying the pockets.

Pin pocket to garment, checking alignment to centre and lower edges and keeping fabric absolutely smooth. Tack diagonally in rows,

Applying patch pockets

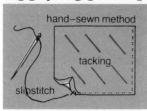
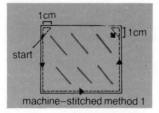
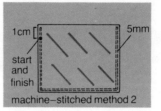
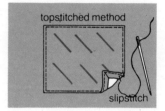

Hand-sewn method Lift pocket edge and slipstitch to garment, keeping stitches very small but not too tight. This method is not suitable for hard wear – to strengthen you can backstitch from inside.

Machine-stitched method (1) A single row of stitches is adequate for most lined pockets. Start about 1cm/½in down from top on side edge. Work diagonally to a point 1cm/½in from top corner, pivot needle, stitch along top edge to top corner, pivot needle and work round outer edges, pivoting needle at each corner until opposite top edge is reached. Complete a triangle to match opposite corner.

Machine-stitched method (2) A double row of stitches is best on unlined pockets to stop seam allowances fraying. Start about 1cm/½in down from top edge and about 5mm/¼in from the side. Work up to top edge, pivot needle and stitch to corner, then pivot needle and work downwards and all around

Tucks – a designer touch

Tucks made on the right side of the fabric add design interest to clothes and may be placed horizontally, across a bodice or yoke for example, or run vertically from neck to waist of a dress or blouse. Some tucks are stitched down their full length, others are only partly stitched and can be used to give shaping to a garment, taking on the function of a dart. These are known as released tucks.

Tucks may be wide or narrow, depending on the fabric and their purpose. Pin tucks are the narrowest, so called because very fine tucks – the width of a pin – were used on the lingerie and fine blouses of the past.

Making released pin tucks

Transfer the pattern markings for pin tucks from the pattern on to the fabric with particular care as they indicate the exact points to join and the stitching lines to follow. Use

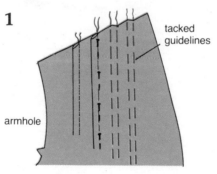
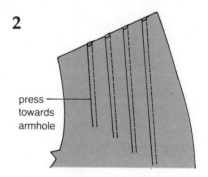

tacking guidelines to avoid marking delicate fabrics.

When sewing, deal with each tuck separately. Do not pin and tack the whole row at once as each perfect stitched tuck is a guide for the next one.

1 With wrong sides together, pin tucks along guidelines, matching marks exactly. Tack, then press before machining to prevent the folded edge from twisting. Machine from shoulder down to end of stitching line as indicated, using an even-feed foot if the fabric is slippery.

Pull loose threads through to inside of garment. Thread each one separately through a needle and run it back through the stitching for 2.5cm/1in, finishing with a back stitch to secure. Never make a knot on fine fabrics – it may press through and make a hole.

2 Press the stitched part of the tuck only towards the armhole. Do not press the area below as this is meant to fall softly in folds.

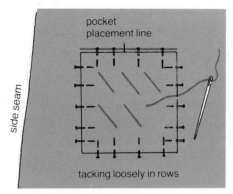

pocket placement line

side seam

tacking loosely in rows

working from top to bottom and keeping stitches loose to avoid drawing up the pocket.

the pocket. Pivot the needle at each corner. When you reach the opposite top edge stitch along about 5mm/¼in, then pivot needle and stitch down and round pocket, parallel to and inside the row of stitching. Finish where you started.
Topstitched method Sewing a thick pocket directly to a garment tends to draw up the fabric. If your design requires a topstitched finish on such a fabric, topstitch the prepared pocket separately, using a fairly large stitch. Then apply the pocket to the garment by hand, using the invisible hand-sewn method.

Pin-tucked jacket

The pin-tucked version of the jacket is ideal for evening and works well made up in soft fabrics. Choose from silks, crêpe or crêpe de chine for evening or soft cottons or Viyella for day wear. Avoid patterned fabric as the effect of the tucks will be lost.

You will need
Fabric, according to size and style
  (see chart)
Matching sewing thread
0.20m/¼yd of 90cm/36in-wide
  interfacing
1 pair of shoulder pads

Making up
Cut out the jacket as instructed on page 63 using the pattern pieces 1, 3, 4, 5, 7 and 6 for the front, instead of piece 2.
Follow the layouts on page 63, noting that the pieces will not

Above: The tucks on this silk evening jacket are all sewn to the same length.

interlock so closely because of the extra fabric required by the pin-tucked front. Follow the instructions, steps 1 to 9 for jacket, on pages 64–65, but pin, tack and machine the tucks on each front during step 1.
Note The pin tucks on the pattern are graduated in length. If you would prefer four tucks the same size, use the shortest tuck as a guide and stitch the others to this length.

Attaching the pockets
Apply the optional patch pockets during step 1, matching the pocket to the jacket front placement line.

Making up a short jacket

To make the short version of the pin-tucked jacket, or a version with short sleeves, follow the making up instuctions on page 65.

Fabric quantity chart

Size	10	12	14	16	18
Bust (cm)	83	87	92	97	102

Long cardigan jacket with pin tucks

90cm	2.25	2.30	2.30	2.35	2.35m
115cm*	1.60	1.60	1.60	1.85	1.85m
140cm	1.45	1.45	1.45	1.45	1.50m
150cm*	1.30	1.30	1.30	1.35	1.50m

Short cardigan jacket with pin tucks

90cm	1.70	1.70	1.75	1.75	1.75m
115cm*	1.20	1.25	1.25	1.45	1.50m
140cm	1.45	1.45	1.45	1.45	1.50m
150cm*	1.30	1.30	1.30	1.35	1.50m

* fabric without nap. All other fabric widths are with or without nap. Fabric quantities are given in metres and include amounts for optional patch pockets.

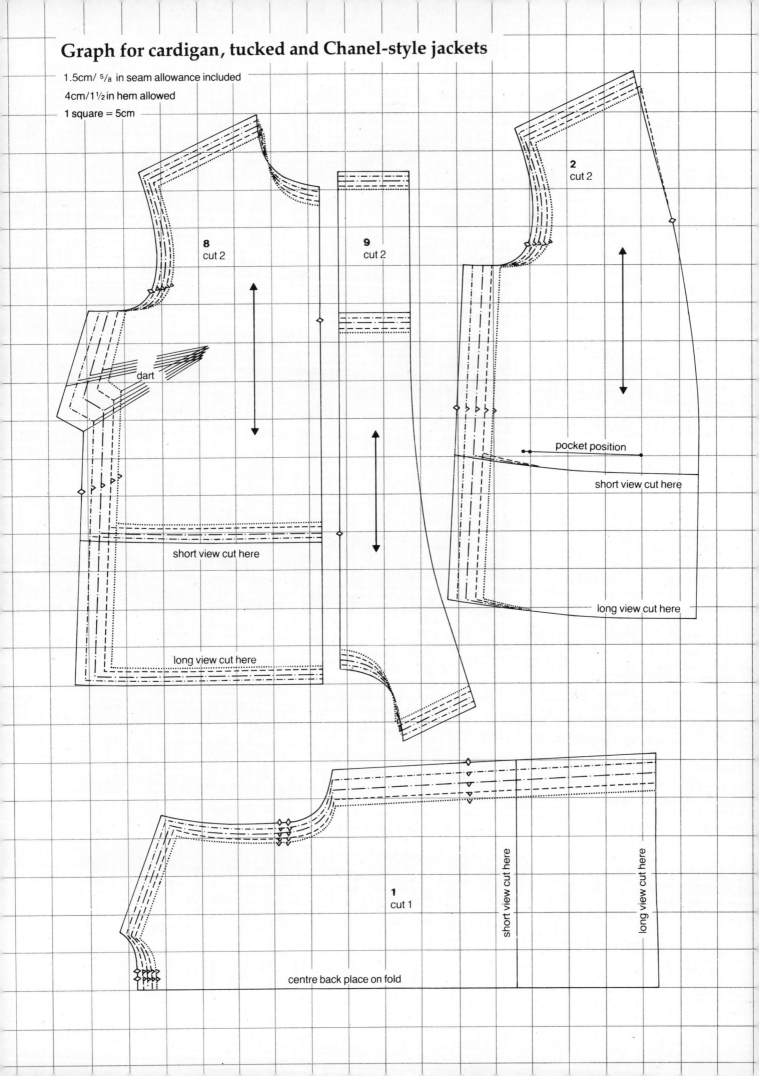

Graph for cardigan, tucked and Chanel-style jackets

1.5cm/ ⅝ in seam allowance included

4cm/1½ in hem allowed

1 square = 5cm

8
cut 2

9
cut 2

2
cut 2

dart

pocket position

short view cut here

short view cut here

long view cut here

long view cut here

long view cut here

1
cut 1

short view cut here

long view cut here

centre back place on fold

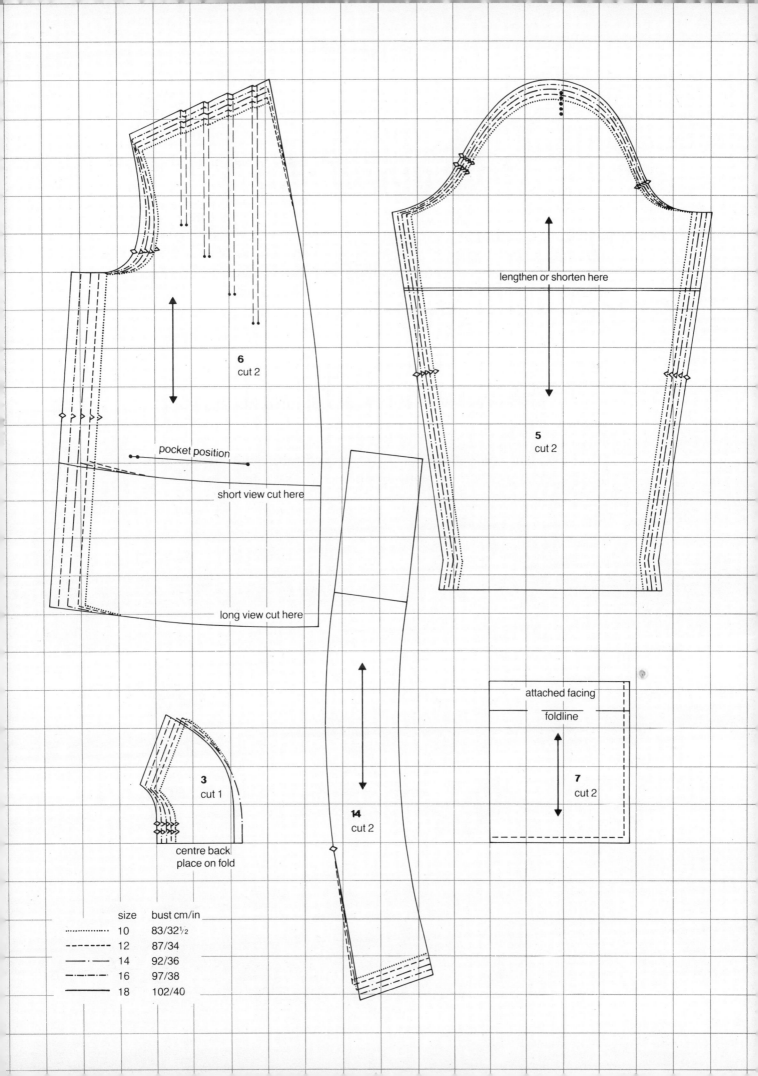

6
cut 2

pocket position

short view cut here

long view cut here

3
cut 1

centre back
place on fold

lengthen or shorten here

5
cut 2

attached facing
foldline

7
cut 2

14
cut 2

size	bust cm/in
10	83/32½
12	87/34
14	92/36
16	97/38
18	102/40

More about skirts

Four-gore and straight skirts are classic styles which may vary slightly but never go out of fashion. Details are given in this section for basic pattern adjustments to cater for all figure types, and careful fitting when making up will achieve a made-to-measure finish. A choice of lining styles can be used to help the skirts keep their shape during wear.

Learn how to add a crisp, inverted front pleat with topstitched variations and handstitched arrowhead detail to the four-gore skirt, and choose between a vent or kick pleat at the centre back of the straight skirt.

Details such as covered hooks and eyes, self-fabric belt carriers and hand sewn zips add the finishing touches to a skirt to be proud of.

Correct fitting for a four-gore skirt

Use the information in this chapter to make a simple but flattering four-gore skirt. Use the fitting guide to learn how to correct some common fitting problems, see how to mark a level hem on your own and discover the secret of keeping checks matched across the seams during machining.

Follow the step-by-step instructions to make this four-gore skirt from the pattern on page 88 or use the sewing and fitting guide for any similar design.

This chapter describes all the common skirt fitting problems and describes how to slip-tack alterations. The same technique is also used to keep checks and stripes aligned at the seams during machining.

Skirt fitting problems

Alterations to size and fit that you are already aware of should be made at

Fitting guide

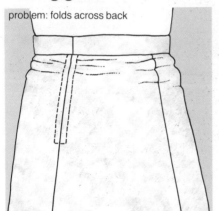

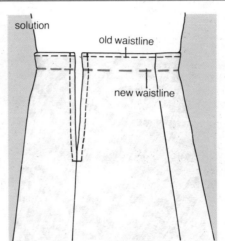

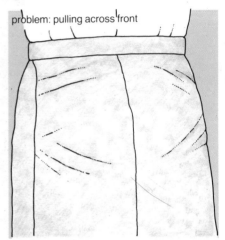

Low waist
Shorter waist to hip measurement than on pattern. Excess fabric forms horizontal folds beneath entire waistline.

Solution Smooth excess fabric upwards above waist. Re-mark waistline at new level. Lower zip. Take out any excess width from side seams at top of skirt and replace waistband at new level, trimming away extra seam allowance.

Round stomach
Skirt pulls across front, forming folds below waistline. The side seams slant towards front and front skirt hem rides up.

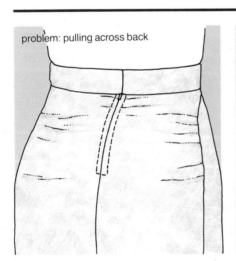

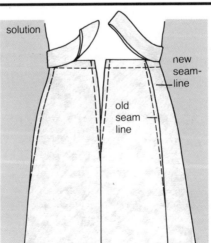

Too tight at rear
Back waistline and hemline ride up, pulling side seams towards back. Pulling also occurs at hip level at back, distorting upper side seams.

Solution Let out seam at centre back and the back part of side seam allowance, tapering up to original waistline. Re-apply waistband.

Too much fullness at rear
Gives baggy appearance in back skirt, especially near seams.

the cutting out stage. Alterations at fitting stages rely on adjustments within the 1.5cm/⅝in seam allowances, so do check all your measurements and compare them with the pattern before cutting out.

Check the waist, hips and hem level to see if they need adjustment. Problems may occur in more than one area – for example, if the waist is too loose, both waistband and side seams will need altering.

Right: Careful fitting is well worth the effort for this four-gore skirt.

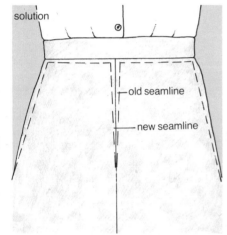

Solution Let out side and centre front seams above hip level, tapering back to original seamline below the hip. Let out some of centre front waistline seam allowance, tapering towards side seams. Re-apply waistband.

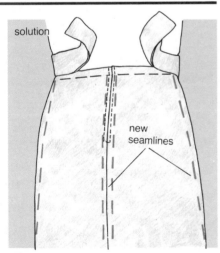

Solution Take in side seams, tapering to original seamline at waist and below the hip. You may need to take in the centre back seam as well, and re-position zip in side seam.

problem: wrinkles at centre back

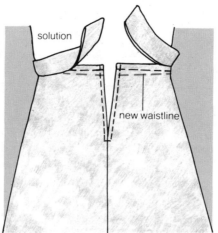

solution

new waistline

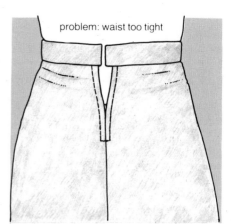

problem: waist too tight

Sway back
A hollow area below back waist causes wrinkles at centre back. Garment fits correctly elsewhere.

Solution Lower waist level at centre back, tapering into original seamline at side waist. Trim away excess seam allowance. If top edge is too wide, take excess fabric out of top side seams on back only. Lower zip. Replace waistband.

Large waist
Zip refuses to close and buttons or hooks strain.

Useful hand stitches

Slip tacking
This stitch, which is also known as edge tacking, ensures accurate matching of checks and stripes at seamlines. It is also used when making fitting adjustments from the right side.
1 Mark seamlines on right side of garment sections. Press one seam allowance to wrong side along its seamline. With right sides of garment sections facing upwards, lap the pressed edge over the

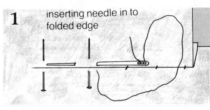

1 inserting needle in to folded edge

adjoining seam allowance, matching both the seamlines and the design on the fabric. Pin at right angles to seam.
To slip tack, secure thread with a double stitch on wrong side. Bring needle to right side of garment

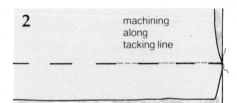

2 machining along tacking line

through folded edge. Insert needle through the single layer close to the fold and bring out again 1cm/⅜in along seam. Pull thread through, matching design carefully. Insert needle into folded edge and bring out 1cm/⅜in further on. Pull thread

The four-gore skirt

You will need
Fabric according to size and style
Matching sewing thread
18cm/7in skirt zip
0.15m/⅛yd of 80cm/32in wide interfacing
Skirt hook and bar
Bias seam binding (if required)

Pattern pieces, page 88:
1 Skirt back
2 Skirt front (four-gore version)
3 Waistband

Cutting out
Pin your pattern pieces to the fabric, choosing the appropriate layout to follow according to the width of the fabric and whether or not it has a nap. Cut out carefully and transfer all pattern markings to fabric before removing the paper pattern.
Use pattern piece 3 to cut the interfacing for the waistband, cutting it to the fold as marked on the pattern.

Stitching curved seams
The side seams of the skirt have a waist to hip curve which requires a little more care when machining to ensure that the fabric is not pulled out of shape. Careful and firm slip tacking is ideal on curved seams. Machine stitch slowly and continuously, working from hem to waist with the weight of the garment supported on a table or working surface. Avoid stitching round the curve in short, sharp bursts as this does not produce a smooth stitching line.

Fabric quantity chart

Size	10	12	14	16	18
Hip (cm)	88	92	97	102	107cm
(in)	34½	36	38	40	42in

Without nap requirements

	10	12	14	16	18
115cm	1.30	1.35	1.45	1.50	1.55m
140cm	0.90	0.95	1.10	1.15	1.25m
150cm	0.90	0.90	0.90	0.90	0.95m

With nap requirements

	10	12	14	16	18
115cm	1.70	1.70	1.70	1.70	1.70m
140cm	1.20	1.25	1.30	1.40	1.50m
150cm	1.00	1.05	1.10	1.15	1.35m

Allow extra fabric for matching checks and stripes at centre seams.

(If your retailer sells fabric in yards use a conversion chart.)

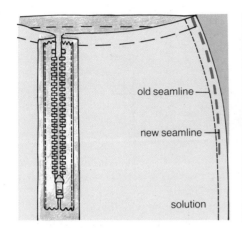

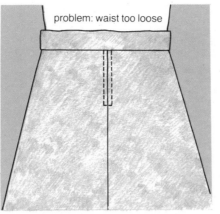

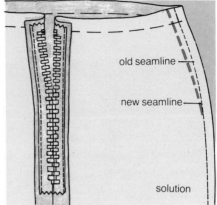

Solution Let out side seam allowance from waist to hip level only. Re-apply waistband.

Small waist
Waistband too loose causing entire skirt to slip down.

Solution Take in side seams, tapering to hip level. Reduce length of waistband and re-apply.

through and continue to end.
2 Remove pins. Turn garment to wrong side and open out fold so that fabric is right sides together. Machine down seam through the centre of straight tacking stitches on wrong side, using an even-feed attachment instead of the normal presser foot. (For an extra firm hold it may be preferable to tack along the centre of the tacking stitches before machining the seam, using an even-feed attachment.) Remove all tacking.

Hemming
A closely-worked stitch which is suitable for inner garment areas which need strong sewing but cannot be machined – inside waistbands, for example. Despite its name, hemming is not suitable for use on garment hems – catchstitch or herringbone stitch is preferable.
Secure thread with a backstitch and, working from right to left, insert needle in main part of garment, catching only a few

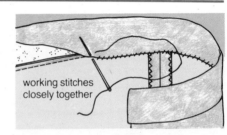

threads of fabric. (On waistbands and binding, work through the line of machine stitching.)
Bring needle out diagonally 1–2mm/ $\frac{1}{16}$in along, picking up a few threads from the fold to be secured.

Cutting layouts for the four-gore skirt

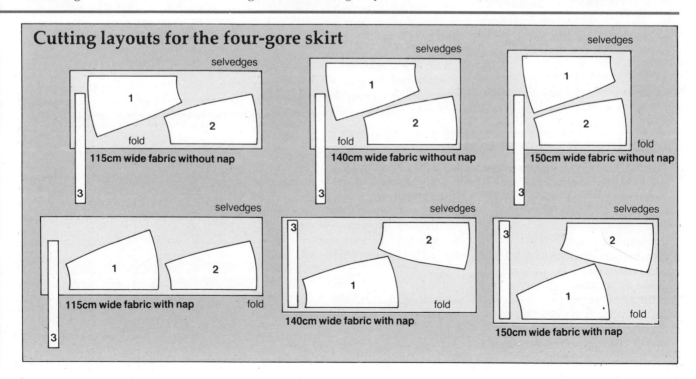

115cm wide fabric without nap

140cm wide fabric without nap

150cm wide fabric without nap

115cm wide fabric with nap

140cm wide fabric with nap

150cm wide fabric with nap

Making up instructions

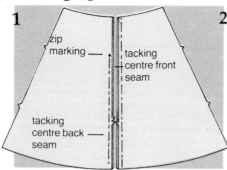

Step 1 With right sides together, matching notches, tack centre back seam from hem up to base of zip marking. Tack centre front and side seams from hem to waist. (Slip tack from right side if using checked or striped fabric. Note that checks will only match at centre seams – not at side seams.)

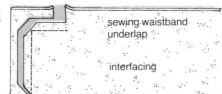

Step 2 Apply interfacing to wrong side of waistband, aligning top edge with fold line of waistband. With right sides together, fold in half lengthwise.
Stitch one short edge and form underlap by stitching other short edge round as far as notch on long edge. Trim end seams and corners and snip to stitching at notch. Turn waistband through and press. Tack waistband to top of skirt.

Step 3 First fitting Try on skirt, checking areas outlined in fitting chart. Mark any alterations.

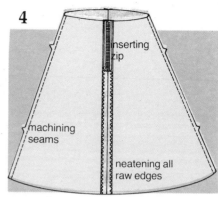

Step 4 Remove waistband and machine centre back seam from lower edge up to circle. Press seam open and neaten edges. Insert zip in top of centre back seam using the central or overlapped method (see pages 42 and 49). Make sure the zip tab is 6mm/¼in below the waist seamline.
Machine the side seams and centre front seam from hem to waist and press open. Neaten raw edges.

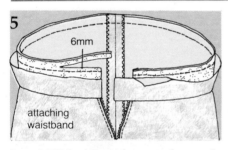

Step 5 With right sides together and underlap to right back, stitch waistband to skirt at interfaced edge. Press the seam upwards into the waistband and trim to 6mm/¼in.

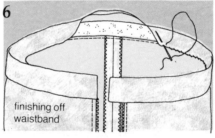

Step 6 Fold free edge of waistband under to cover raw edges and hem to line of machine stitching along waist seamline. Sew on skirt hook and bar.

Step 7 Second fitting. Try on skirt to establish length. Mark the hem level.

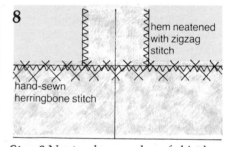

Step 8 Neaten lower edge of skirt by machine zigzag or hand oversewing, or apply bias seam binding to bulky fabric. Complete hem by hand.

PROFESSIONAL TOUCH

Marking a level hem by yourself

The markings and measurements on the pattern are only a guide. Alterations to the length may be necessary after the final fitting. Wear the garment with appropriate shoes and belt if required and measure up from the floor or any level surface. Use a floor-standing hem marker with a bulb of powdered chalk and stand in front of a mirror. Decide on the finished length of the skirt and position the marker accordingly. Stand as still as possible and press the bulb. A line of chalk will mark the hem position. Revolve slowly, leaving the marker stationary, stopping at frequent intervals and allowing the skirt to fall still. Puff a chalk mark each time you stop. After marking, pin up the hem, tack into place and check the length again before completing by hand.

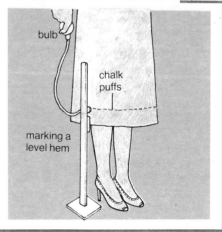

Skirt linings and centre pleats

A crisp front pleat with reinforced topstitching, an arrowhead detail and an integral lining all help to achieve a tailored look. Try out these techniques using the pattern from page 88 to make a skirt which can be both casual and smart.

This skirt is a variation on the four-gore skirt in the previous chapter, with an inverted front pleat. The pleats are constructed by stitching on the wrong side of the garment from waist to about hip level, and then allowing the fabric to fall free. It is usual to reinforce either the whole stitched section or just the base of it in some way.

Topstitching

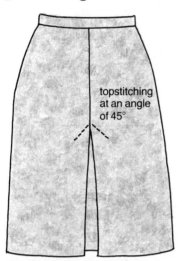

topstitching at an angle of 45°

chevron effect

unobtrusive finish

topstitching close to pleat seam

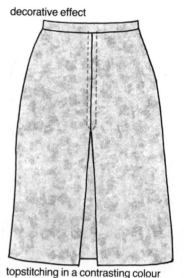

decorative effect

topstitching in a contrasting colour

A simple way of reinforcing the pleat seam is to topstitch it. This anchors the main fabric to the back of the pleat, spreading the strain with a strong, double-stitched seam. Experiment with thread thicknesses and colours and needle size, testing the stitch on three thicknesses of fabric. Use a thicker machine needle – size 100/16 – and adjust the upper tension of your machine if you are using a thicker thread. Always work from the right side of the garment and mark the stitching line with tacking or tailor's chalk.

For a chevron effect stitch down from the end of the pleat seam at an angle of 45° to the fold edge of the back of the pleat on each side.

For an unobtrusive finish edge topstitch just a few millimetres either side of the pleat seam.

For a decorative effect topstitch by hand or machine with a thicker thread, in contrasting or toning colour. Work stitching about 5–10mm/ ¼–³⁄₈in each side of the seam.

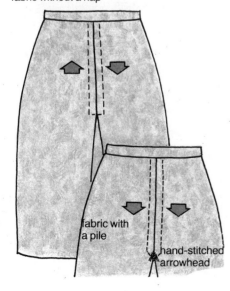

fabric without a nap

fabric with a pile

hand-stitched arrowhead

For fabric without a nap work on the right side and machine a row of stitches parallel to the pleat seam using the presser foot or pattern of the fabric as a guide. Start at the waist edge, one side of the seam and stitch to the lower edge of the pleat. Leave the needle in the fabric and turn the garment, so that you can stitch straight across the seam end at the top of the pleat. Stop the same distance from the pleat seam as the previous row of topstitching, turn the work with the needle in the fabric and machine back up to waist edge. There is no break in the stitching at the point of strain which makes this a particularly strong

method of topstitching. An arrowhead can be added (see overleaf) within the stitching for extra strength and decorative effect.

For fabric with a pile work on the right side, machining both rows of stitching in the same direction, following the nap of the fabric. Slope the stitching at the base to join the pleat seam.

As the stitching line is not continuous, extra strength can be added at the top of a pleat by adding an arrowhead by hand as described overleaf.

Hand-stitched arrowhead

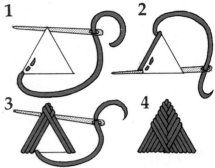

The arrowhead strengthens tops of pleats and sides of pockets, preventing the seam breaking open or the fabric tearing in wear. Work it in buttontwist or thick sewing thread and run the thread through beeswax to prevent tangling during sewing.

Mark a triangle with 1cm/⅜in sides on the right side of the garment, just over the end of the seam for maximum strength, with the point towards the waist edge. Use tailor's chalk or small tacking stitches.

1 Secure thread within triangle on the right side of fabric and bring needle and thread out at lower left-hand corner. At upper point of triangle, take a tiny stitch from right to left and draw needle and thread through.

2 Insert needle at lower right-hand corner and bring out again at lower left-hand side, just to the right of previous stitch.

3 Take a stitch from right to left at the top of the triangle, just below the previous stitch. Repeat step 2, working within previous stitch.

4 Repeat these steps until the triangle is filled. Secure the thread at the back of the work with a backstitch, darning the end in.

Left: Decorative topstitching and an arrowhead add emphasis and strengthen the pleat seam.

How to line a skirt

Most skirts, with the exception of those made for casual, summer wear, benefit from the addition of a lining. It improves the general appearance and hang of the skirt, stops the garment from creasing excessively across the front and helps preserve the shape and minimize 'seating' at the back. A lining also prevents the main fabric from clinging to undergarments, and stops a coarser fabric, such as rough tweed, from irritating the skin.

Lining fabrics

Fabrics suitable for use as lining are grouped together in a fabric department. Man-made linings are the most widely available, but some fabrics may require something a little different. An expensive medium to lightweight wool, for example, is best lined with silk, while cotton and linen garments which may be washed frequently should be lined with cotton lawn or batiste.

When selecting a lining fabric, always take a piece of your main fabric with you for comparison. The lining must be finer and lighter in weight to avoid unnecessary bulk, although it must be strong enough to take the amount of wear it will have.

Rolls of lining are usually marked clearly with fabric content and laundering instructions. These should correspond with your main garment fabric so that both the garment and lining maintain a good appearance during wear.

Cutting out the lining

In most cases, a skirt lining is cut from the main pattern pieces and no special lining pattern is given. If any alterations have been made to the skirt, these must be transferred to the pattern before cutting the lining.

If you are lining a skirt with a pleat the pleat should be omitted from the lining so that the pleat seam continues down to the hem. For ease of movement add vents 20–25cm/8–10in long at the side seams. Apart from this the lining is made in the same way as the skirt. Remember that the raw edges of the lining will face the skirt, away from the body. The lining is usually attached to a skirt before the waistband of the garment is applied.

Lining a skirt with an inverted pleat

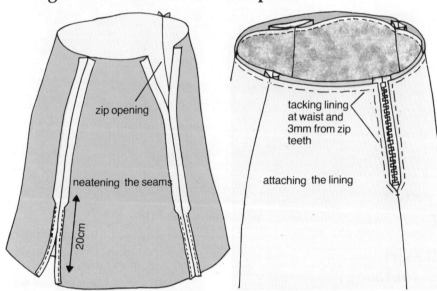

zip opening

neatening the seams

20cm

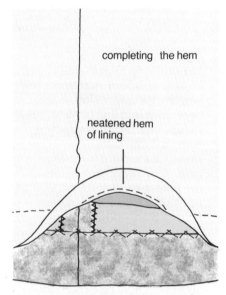

tacking lining at waist and 3mm from zip teeth

attaching the lining

completing the hem

neatened hem of lining

The lining of a skirt with a front inverted pleat should be attached at the waistband and around the zip, but left free at the hem edge.

Cut out and assemble the lining as for the skirt, but omitting the pleat. Either stitch a centre front seam down to the hem or place centre front to fold of fabric. Leave an opening for the zip plus 1cm/½in and at the hem edge leave 20–25cm/8–10in vents in each side seam (see page 96). Do not complete the hem.

Neatening the seams It is best to partially neaten the raw edges of the lining and garment seams. Turn under and machine neaten the lining seam allowances for approximately 20cm/8in from hem edge. Zigzag, bind or oversew the seam allowances of the main garment in the same way. (Neatening the seams all the way to the waist produces unnecessary bulkiness around the hips on a lined skirt.)

Attaching the lining Press the seams open and press under the turnings of the lining around the zip. Place the wrong side of lining to wrong side of skirt, matching seams, and pin raw edges together around waist edge. Tack lining into position around waist and zip, with lining at least 3mm/⅛in from zip teeth. Slipstitch lining to zip tape. (If the garment is to be washed frequently, it is better to leave lining free from zip and machine neaten the edges instead – this will make pressing easier.)

Apply the waistband in the normal way, treating the skirt as if it were made of single fabric and inserting skirt loops at the top of the side seams if required.

Completing the hem During the final fitting, pin the lining up out of the way while finalizing the length of the main garment. Complete the hem, then trim the lining so that it is 5mm/¼in longer than the skirt. Press under a hem allowance of 2.5cm/1in and hem the lining by machine, or machine neaten and finish by hand.

85

Permanent crisp pleats

On heavier fabrics, where it may be difficult to keep a crisp light-weight pleat, Vilene Fold-a-band, which is normally used for waist-bands, can be used. Test it first on a scrap of fabric to make sure it does not produce too stiff a finish. After stitching the pleat seam, measure the length of the pleat from the lower end of the seam to the hem fold. Cut two strips of Vilene Fold-a-band to this length.

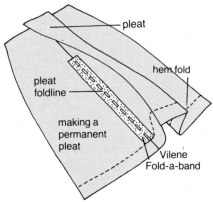

Lay one strip fusible-side-down on wrong side of skirt front, with lengthwise centre slots exactly over front fold line of pleat. Press to fuse interfacing in position, using a damp cloth.
Repeat for second pleat edge. Fold pleat along centre slots of the Fold-a-band and turn skirt to right side. Press edge of pleat using a damp cloth.

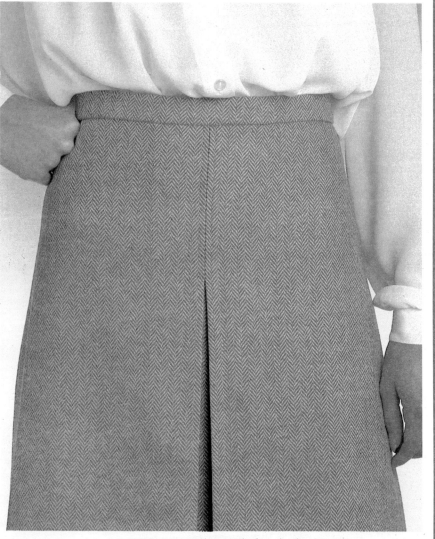

Keep the edges of the pleat tacked together until after the final pressing

Lining a four-gore or straight skirt

The lining of a four-gore skirt and a straight skirt may be either a loose lining, attached at zip and waistband only, or attached at the hem as well.
Make any necessary pattern adjustments before cutting out the lining. If the centre front seam of the skirt is on the straight grain, place to a fold, so omitting seam.
Loose lining Make up the loose lining following the instructions for the four-gore skirt on page 82, steps 1 and 4, remembering that there is no centre front seam. Press the seam allowances under where the lining will be attached around the zip. Neaten the seams, attach the lining at the waist and complete the hem as for the skirt with an inverted pleat.

Attached lining With a lining attached at the hem, there is no need to neaten any of the seams. Attach the lining around waistband and zip tape in the normal way, and establish length of main garment. Complete hem of skirt and trim lining to 5mm/¼in longer than the skirt. Press up 2.5cm/1in hem allowance to the wrong side of lining. Hang garment up inside out and working from the wrong side, pin lining to fabric 15cm/6in from the hem edge. Lay the garment on a flat surface, and push the hem allowance towards the row of pins. Pull back the pressed hem fold and catchstitch lining 1cm/½in from raw edge to garment hem so that all raw edges are enclosed. Remove pins and lining will fall into position.

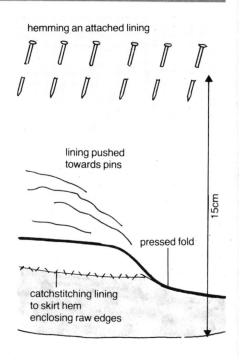

hemming an attached lining

lining pushed towards pins

pressed fold

catchstitching lining to skirt hem enclosing raw edges

15cm

Skirt with inverted front pleat

Follow these simple instructions to make up the skirt with an inverted front pleat (see pattern page 88). The guide on pages 78–81 will help with any fitting problems.

You will need
Fabric according to size and style
Matching sewing thread
18cm/7in skirt zip
0.15m/⅛yd of 80cm/32in wide interfacing
Skirt hook and bar
Pattern pieces, page 88:
1 Skirt back
4 Skirt front
3 Waistband

Cutting out and preparing to sew
Fold fabric length right sides together, following the appropriate layout for your fabric width. Position pattern pieces as shown on the layout with front skirt to fold of fabric. Cut out garment sections carefully, cutting two back sections, one front on double fabric and a single waistband. Transfer the markings from the pattern pieces to the fabric, leaving the front skirt unmarked and with its pattern piece attached.

Making up the skirt

1

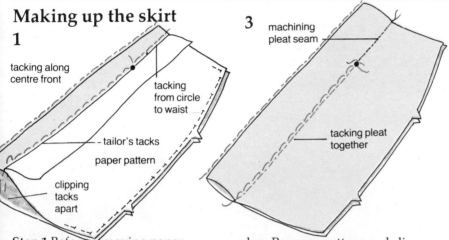

tacking along centre front

tacking from circle to waist

– tailor's tacks

paper pattern

clipping tacks apart

3

machining pleat seam

tacking pleat together

4

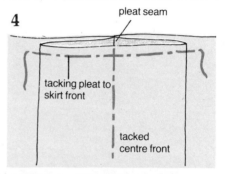

pleat seam

tacking pleat to skirt front

tacked centre front

Step 1 Before removing paper pattern from front skirt, mark centre front line and pleat seam. Remove pins from centre front waist and hem edges and run a line of tacking stitches along the fold of fabric to establish centre front of skirt. Fold pattern back as far as the inner crease line, and tack fabric layers together, from circle up to waist along this line. With tailor's tacks mark pleat fold (creaseline) from circle on pattern to lower edge. Remove pattern and clip tailor's tacks apart.

Step 2 Preliminary fitting
Before machining the pleat, hold the front section against you to determine whether the pleat seam length is too high or too low for you. Mark any alteration required.
Step 3 Having adjusted length of pleat seam if necessary, tack pleat together down to hem. Machine pleat seam, working from circle to waist, and finish off ends securely.

Step 4 Working on wrong side of front skirt, match tacked centre front markings to pleat seam. Fold pleat along outer crease lines and tack to skirt front across waist edge, just within seamline. (The top of the pleat will be secured within the waistband when this is attached.) Topstitch or reinforce pleat seam by whichever method preferred.
Step 5 Tack centre back seam from hem up to circle, and side seams from hem to waist. Complete skirt as for four-gore variation, steps 2 to 8 (see page 82). Check the back of pleat does not hang below front edges. Press well.

Cutting layouts for skirt with inverted front pleat

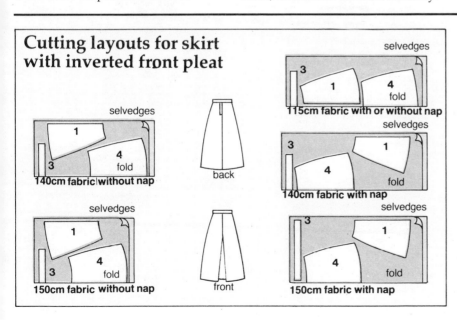

selvedges

1

4
fold

3

140cm fabric without nap

back

selvedges

1

3

4
fold

150cm fabric without nap

front

selvedges

3

1

4
fold

115cm fabric with or without nap

selvedges

3

1

4
fold

140cm fabric with nap

selvedges

3

1

4
fold

150cm fabric with nap

Fabric quantity chart

Size	10	12	14	16	18
Hip (cm)	83	92	97	102	107cm
(in)	34½	36	38	40	42in

Fabric without nap

115cm	1.70	1.70	1.70	1.70	1.70m
140cm	1.15	1.25	1.30	1.40	1.45m
150cm	0.95	1.00	1.05	1.15	1.20m

Fabric with nap

115cm	1.70	1.70	1.70	1.70	1.70m
140cm	1.50	1.50	1.55	1.55	1.65m
150cm	1.30	1.35	1.40	1.45	1.55m

Allow extra fabric for matching checks and stripes.

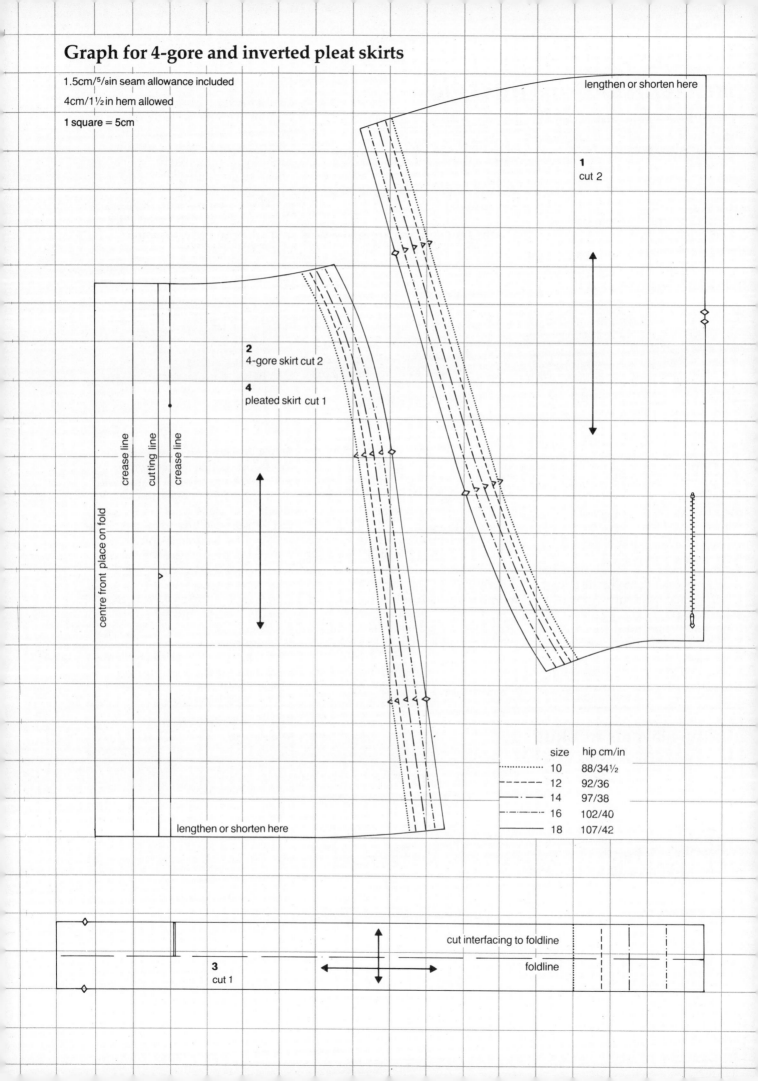

Graph for 4-gore and inverted pleat skirts

1.5cm/⁵⁄₈in seam allowance included

4cm/1½in hem allowed

1 square = 5cm

lengthen or shorten here

1
cut 2

2
4-gore skirt cut 2

4
pleated skirt cut 1

centre front place on fold

crease line

cutting line

crease line

lengthen or shorten here

size	hip cm/in
10	88/34½
12	92/36
14	97/38
16	102/40
18	107/42

cut interfacing to foldline

foldline

3
cut 1

A straight skirt with kick pleat or vent

*This classic but simple skirt can be made in a variety of
fabrics and is suitable for all seasons.
The chapter includes techniques for two new waistband styles
and shows you how to add a professional touch
with belt carriers and covered hooks and eyes.*

Most dressmakers want to make a
classic straight skirt at some time or
other. They have been fashionable
for years and will doubtless endure,
with some minor variations, for years
to come. There are many well-cut
patterns available commercially and,
although this section is geared to the
graph pattern given on page 98, all
the techniques and dressmaking
advice are generally applicable.
Making up instructions for the skirt
are given in the next chapter.

Skirt vents and pleats

Any straight skirt that reaches below
the knee needs some provision for
movement – usually a vent or pleat let
into the centre back seam. This allows
the skirt to open when walking and to
fall back into line when still.

The extension for the vent or pleat is
included in the pattern. The length is
usually about 26cm/10¼in long after
the hem has been turned up. Any
alterations to the length of the skirt
and vent must be made *before cutting
out*. Both the vent and pleat are assembled in the same way, the difference
being the vent is open along its entire
length while the pleat is stitched.

Before machining either version
mark and tack the centre back seam
from the lower end of the zip to the
start of the vent or pleat, continuing
in a straight line to the lower edge.
For a perfect fold edge, leave this
tacking in until you are ready to complete the hem.

*Left: The straight skirt, made up in
lightweight wool. The kick pleat (below)
allows ample walking room.*

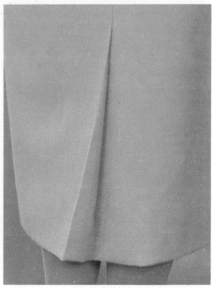

Making a vent

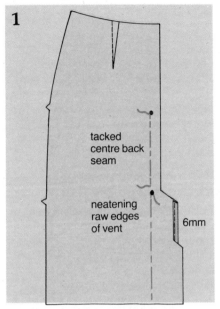

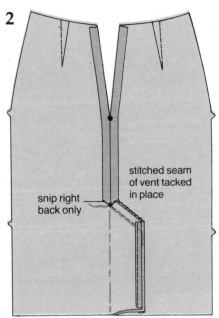

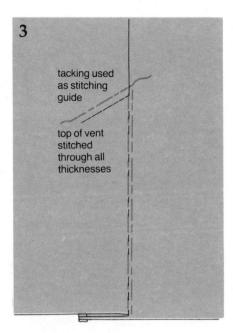

1 If you are using a lightweight fabric, neaten the raw edges of the vent by turning 6mm/¼in to the wrong side and stitch. If you are using a heavyweight fabric, oversew the edge or bind with bias binding to avoid bulkiness.

2 With right sides together and matching circles, join centre back seam from lower zip circle to top of vent, pivot needle at corner and stitch across the top of the vent extension. Snip to seamline at top of vent on *right* back only and neaten the edges. Remove tacking from

centre back seam above vent. Press centre back seam open and press vent towards left back of skirt. Pin and tack into place along seamline across top of vent.
3 On right side of skirt, stitch across top of vent through all thicknesses using tacking as a guide. Take

Making a kick pleat

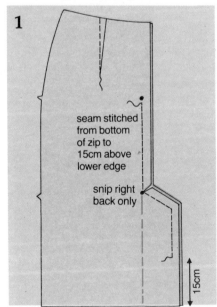

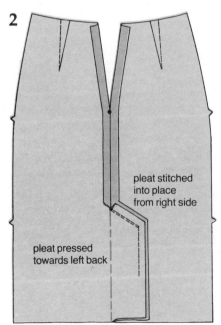

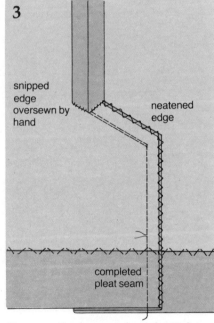

1 With right sides together, matching circles, machine centre back seam from lower zip circle and across top of pleat pivoting the needle at the pleat corners and ending 15cm/6in above lower edge. Snip to seamline at top of pleat on *right* back only and neaten the edges. Remove all tacking above

top of pleat.
2 Press centre back seam open and lightly press pleat towards left back of skirt. Pin and tack across top of pleat and stitch pleat into place from the right side as for the vent (step 3).
3 Remove the tacking in the pleat and open it out at lower skirt edge.

Turn up the hem and catchstitch or blind hem into place, as for the vent (step 4).
Stitch the remainder of the pleat seam together from the break in the stitching to the hem fold. Finish off ends securely, trim seam to 1cm/½in and zigzag or hand oversew seam allowances together to neaten.

4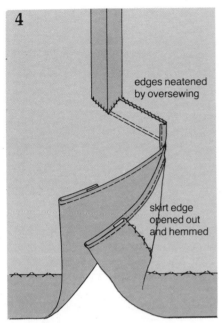

edges neatened
by oversewing

skirt edge
opened out
and hemmed

5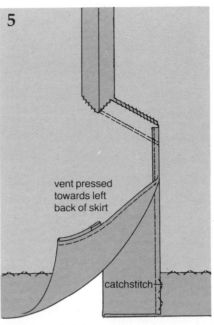

vent pressed
towards left
back of skirt

catchstitch

machine threads through to wrong side and fasten off. Press lightly. Complete rest of skirt and fit before turning up the hem.

4 To hem, undo all tacking in the vent and open it out at lower skirt edge. Turn up hem and catchstitch or blind hem. Neaten top of vent.

5 Fold the left-hand side of the vent extension to the inside along foldline and catchstitch lightly to hem. Press.

Right: The vent is made by neatening the centre-back seam of the pleat extension and leaving it open.

Pattern alterations

Adjusting the length

Shorten or lengthen the pattern on the double alteration lines (see page 21).

If your pattern does not have alteration lines marked, draw a straight line across both back and front pattern pieces, at right angles to centre front and centre back. Draw the line anywhere between hip level and the top of the vent. (The hip level on a pattern is where the side starts to straighten out.)

If you need to shorten a skirt with a vent/pleat by more than 5cm/2in you must alter the length of the vent/pleat to keep it in proportion for a shorter figure and to ensure it does not start too high on the centre back seam.

Draw a second alteration line, parallel to the first, halfway down the vent/pleat on the back skirt pattern. Draw a corresponding line at the same level on the front skirt pattern. Divide the amount by which the skirt is to be shortened equally between the first and second alteration lines on both pattern pieces. Pin tucks of the

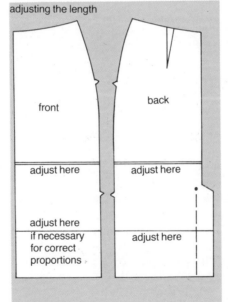

adjusting the length

front

back

adjust here   adjust here

adjust here

adjust here
if necessary
for correct
proportions

adjust here

required size at each of these points and try the pattern against you to check length before cutting out.

Adjusting the waist to hip level

Measure your side waist to hip level and compare it with the paper pattern before cutting out. If the measurement does not correspond to the average hip level of 23cm/9in

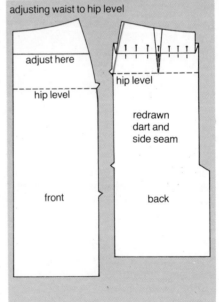

adjusting waist to hip level

adjust here

hip level

hip level

redrawn
dart and
side seam

front   back

below the waist, draw a straight line across the pattern above hip level at the same position on back and front pattern pieces. Lengthen or shorten the pattern pieces as required. Re-draw the side seam to make a smooth curve and re-draw the darts where necessary. Try the pattern against you to check the fit before cutting out.

Ribbon-backed waistband

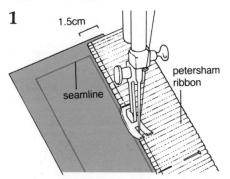

1 1.5cm — seamline — petersham ribbon

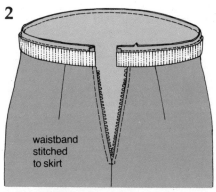

2 waistband stitched to skirt

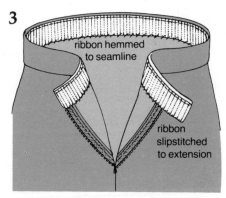

3 ribbon hemmed to seamline — ribbon slipstitched to extension

If you are using thick fabric a double thickness waistband, plus interfacing and seam allowances, can be rather bulky. An alternative is to use the skirt fabric on the outside of the band only, and face it with a firm petersham ribbon. This does away with bulky turnings and means no other interfacing is needed.

Measure the width of the petersham ribbon. Prepare the waistband pattern by folding it lengthwise to the width of the petersham ribbon plus 3cm/1¼in for seam allowances. This will give you a 1.5cm/⅝in seam allowance along each of the long edges.

Position the adjusted pattern on the right side of a single layer of skirt fabric with the grain running lengthwise and cut out. Cut petersham ribbon to the same length as fabric band.

1 With waistband right sides upwards, lay ribbon over upper raw edge, close to the seamline. Machine along ribbon edge, taking a 1.5cm/⅝in seam on the fabric. Fold waistband along this seam with right side of fabric inside and machine across both ends, taking 1.5cm/⅝in turnings. Trim seam

allowances, turn to right side and press waistband.

2 With right sides together, stitch lower edge of waistband fabric to skirt along seamline. Make sure the waistband extension (marked by a notch) is on right back of skirt.

3 Trim turnings, layering the seam allowances if using thick fabric, and press upwards into the band. On the inside of the skirt, hem ribbon edge to waist on seamline and slipstitch ribbon to fabric waistband along the extension.

Sew on hooks and eyes in the normal way.

Ribbon-faced waistline

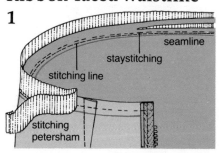

1 seamline — staystitching — stitching line — stitching petersham

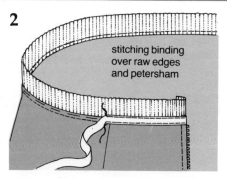

2 stitching binding over raw edges and petersham

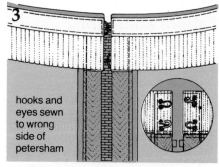

3 hooks and eyes sewn to wrong side of petersham

It is possible to make a skirt without a visible waistband, provided the skirt is straight or fitted, not gathered. Instead of a fabric band, a curved petersham ribbon is stitched to the waistline and tucked inside the skirt top to provide support.

Curved petersham is used because it has one selvedge shorter than the other, giving a curve which moulds round the figure below the waist. The top of the finished skirt then just reaches the waistline without a waistband.

This waistband finish eliminates all bulk at the waistline and is comfortable to wear. It also gives the impression of a longer midriff, which is flattering to short-waisted figures.

After the ribbon has been attached the waist seamline is taped to prevent

the waistline stretching in wear.

1 Measure the required length of curved petersham by laying it around your waist with the inner curve of the ribbon on the waistline and the outer curve below the waist. Mark the required length with chalk, adding 1cm/½in extra at each end for the turnings. A waistband extension is, of course, unnecessary – the ribbon meets exactly at the zip.

Turn under 1cm/½in at each end of length of petersham. Machine across ends to secure.

Staystitch skirt waistline 5mm/¼in from seamline within seam allowance. Working on the wrong side of skirt, lap inner curved edge of petersham over raw edge, close to staystitching, with the 1cm/½in

turnings towards you. Machine close to edge of petersham. Trim skirt turnings to 5mm/¼in.

2 Cut straight seam binding to waist length, plus 2cm/¾in. Lay binding over raw skirt edges and petersham on the right side of skirt, covering the machine stitches. Turn under 1cm/⅜in at each end of the binding. Machine binding into place along both edges and across ends.

3 Sew hooks and eyes to the wrong side of the petersham. Alternate the fastening so that a hook and eye are above an eye and hook to prevent them slipping undone in wear.

Turn the petersham to the inside, concealing the hooks and eyes and press.

Belt carriers

1
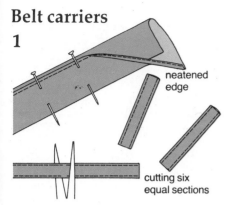
neatened edge

cutting six equal sections

2
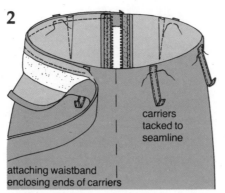
carriers tacked to seamline

attaching waistband enclosing ends of carriers

3
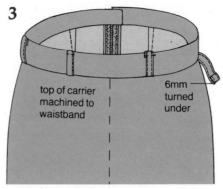
top of carrier machined to waistband

6mm turned under

If you wish to wear a belt with your skirt, you will need belt carriers to keep it in place. Six are best – position one at each side seam and one either side of the centre front and centre back. The carriers should allow the belt to slide through easily – the width of the belt plus 2.5cm/1in to allow for ease and turnings is ideal. The finished width of the carriers is usually just under 1cm/⅜in but varies according to the thickness of the fabric.

Make the carriers from one long strip of fabric and then cut the number required from it, rather than stitching each one individually.

Cut a strip of fabric on the lengthwise straight grain, three times the desired finished width and the total length of all the carriers. Neaten one long raw edge.

1 With right sides outwards, fold the strip in three lengthwise, placing the raw edge inside and the neatened edge on top. Press. With the neatened edge on the underside, machine topstitch 2-3mm/⅛in from the folded edges on both long sides. Mark and cut into six equal sections.

2 With right sides together, taking 6mm/¼in seams on the carriers, tack them into position on the skirt waist seamline. Attach the waistband to the skirt in the normal way, enclosing the lower end of the carrier in the seam.

3 Turn under 6mm/¼in at the top of each carrier and machine it to the front of the waistband close to the foldline. (If the waistband is backed with petersham ribbon, the top end can be enclosed in the upper waistband seam.)

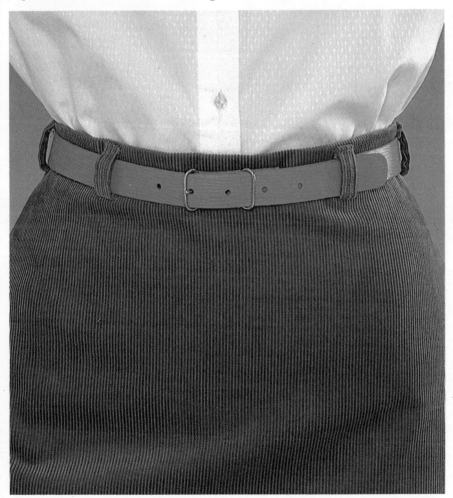

Covered hooks and eyes

blanket stitch

Covering hooks and eyes or hooks and bars with matching thread gives a highly professional finish to skirt waistbands. Use a double strand of thread for small hooks and eyes, choosing a colour to blend with the fabric. The thread hides the metal fasteners while still allowing the hook to fit snugly into the eye.

Secure the hook and eye or bar with overcasting stitches in the normal way. Then continue working in blanket stitch, from right to left, covering the metal as you go. You can use buttonhole stitch instead if you prefer.

Left: Belt carriers prevent a belt slipping round or off the waistband.

Fitting and lining
a straight skirt

Achieve perfect results first time when making a classic straight skirt by fitting frequently and using the professional finishes given here. The fitting checklist and chart will help you know what to look for and how to correct any problems.

This chapter shows you how to cut, fit and complete a straight skirt to perfection. The pattern used comes from the graph pattern on page 98 but the techniques are the same for a commercial straight skirt pattern. Choose either a simple vent or a pleat for ease of movement following the instructions in the previous chapter and making the pattern alterations as described. Alternative waistband styles are given on pages 82 and 92–93 and to give your skirt a really professional finish, insert a lining and a hand-sewn zip.

Follow these techniques and the step-by-step guide to produce a skirt that fits beautifully, wears well and keeps its shape.

Hints for fitting

Make any major alterations to pattern dimensions before cutting out and then fit the skirt frequently between the sewing stages so that you can make minor changes to the shape of your skirt.

General fitting details are given on pages 78–81. The fitting problems which apply specifically to straight

Straight skirt fitting problems and how to solve them

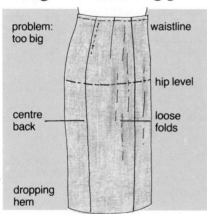

Skirt is too big
Side seam baggy, loose folds and dropping hem.

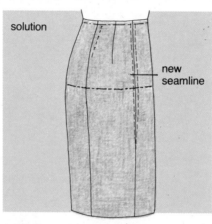

Solution Take in the side seams to fit the curve of the body, following the curve of the original seamline. Reduce the length of the waistband to fit.

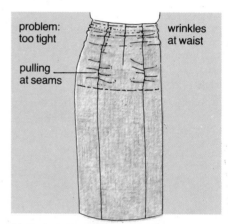

Skirt is too tight
Pulling and wrinkling of fabric across front and at upper side seams.

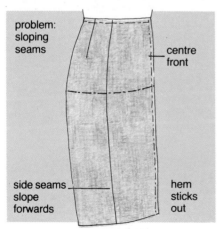

Side seams sloping forward
Hem sticks out, due to high tummy.

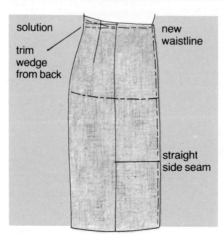

Solution Take a small horizontal wedge from centre back to side seam at waist to lift back skirt and straighten the side seam.

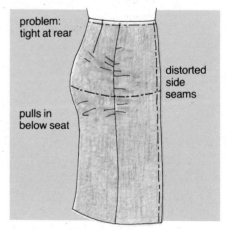

Skirt too tight at rear
Fabric pulls in below seat and side seams distorted.

skirts are dealt with below.

Above all, do not over-fit so that the skirt is skin tight. A reasonably close fit flatters a slimmer figure but a slightly looser fit is kinder to fuller figures.

Special markings for fitting

Fitting is easier if reliable guidelines are established on the skirt as points of reference. They also indicate the grain of the fabric.

After you have cut out the back and front skirt sections and transferred the usual pattern markings, mark the vertical centre front line and the centre back line (if there is no seam) along the fold with a single line of tacking. Run a horizontal line of tacking between the hip notches on front and

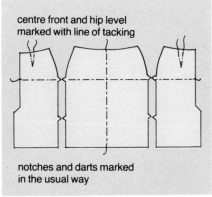

centre front and hip level marked with line of tacking

notches and darts marked in the usual way

back, following the threads of the fabric weave accurately.

Below: The fitting guidelines will help you achieve a smooth fit over the hips – the sign of a well-made skirt.

Fitting checklist

This guide to what makes a good fit applies to any straight skirt pattern and it is also worth bearing in mind when buying ready-to-wear clothes.

General appearance Skirt hangs with centre back and centre front perpendicular to the floor (easy to check using tacked guidelines).

Waistline Close fitting but not tight – there should be 1cm/½in ease.

Hip level Close fit, but with enough ease to sit and walk without straining seams.

Hemline Parallel to the floor.

Darts Tapering to a point, following the curve of the body and stopping 2cm/¾in short of fullest part of hip.

Pleats and vents Firm crisp edges that meet when standing still.

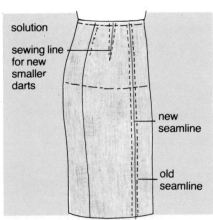

solution

sewing line for new smaller darts

new seamline

old seamline

Solution Let out side seams slightly. This will allow waist to hip area to drop and smooth out. You may also need to make smaller darts. Alter waistband accordingly.

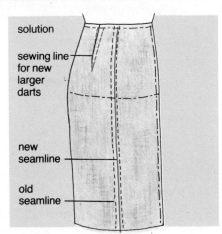

solution

sewing line for new larger darts

new seamline

old seamline

Solution Let out side seams graduating from waist to hem. Any excess fabric can be taken up in back darts. Alter waistband if necessary.

Lining a straight skirt

The straight skirt may be lined in two different ways – with a full lining or with a half lining.

The full lining adds to the comfort of the skirt, preserves its shape, and prevents creasing across the front or back when sitting. It also relieves strain on the vent or pleat and on all the skirt seams. A half lining only covers the back of the skirt and extends down as far as the vent or pleat and helps to prevent seating.

Making a full lining

Cut out lining fabric using back and front skirt pattern pieces. Fold back the vent/pleat extension so that the cutting line extends straight down to the hem. Transfer pattern markings. Close centre back seam from just below marked zip circle to top of vent marking. Press the centre back seam open from waist to hem and neaten. Slipstitch vent turnings back.

Work a bar tack at the top of vent to take the strain, or reinforce with a lining fabric patch. Stitch darts and press away from centre to reduce any

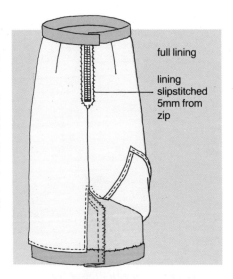

full lining

lining slipstitched 5mm from zip

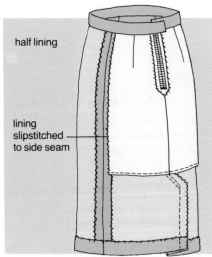

half lining

lining slipstitched to side seam

bulk in waistline. Join side seams and neaten raw edges. With wrong sides together, and making sure side seams and darts match, tack skirt and lining together at waist level (see Making up the skirt, steps 6 and 8 on page opposite). Pin pressed edge of lining around zip tapes, 5mm/¼in from teeth. Slipstitch lining to tapes. Remove pins, complete waistband and skirt hem, then finish hem of lining to 2.5cm/1in above skirt hem.

Making a half lining

Cut the lining from the back skirt pattern, approximately 23cm/9in shorter than skirt. When hemmed this will cover the top of the vent. Complete centre back seam and darts as for full lining. Neaten side seams and hem, then attach to skirt during step 6 tacking along waist seamline to hold in place. Turn under side seam allowances and slipstitch lining to the back seam allowance of each side seam.

Classic skirt

When making a straight skirt, avoid loosely woven fabrics which stretch out of shape easily and tend to seat, or soft fabrics which will cling.

There is a wide variety of suitable fabrics – closely woven wools and worsteds such as flannel, suitings, fine tweeds and barathea, cotton drill, linen and linen/synthetic blends, gaberdine, corduroy and polyester mixtures like Trevira. Straight skirts keep their shape better when lined. The best types of linings to choose are acetate, polyester or viscose twill.

You will need

Fabric according to size
Matching thread
18cm/7in zip
Skirt hook and bar
Hooks and eyes
0.15m/⅛yd of 80cm/32in wide interfacing *or* length of petersham ribbon

Lining requirements

For a full lining, 1.60m/1⅝yd of 90cm/36in wide lining *or* 0.80m/⅞yd of 140cm/54in wide lining

For a half lining, 0.60m/⅝yd of lining, any width
Pattern pieces, page 98:
1 Skirt back, 2 Skirt front
3 Waistband

Fabric quantity chart

Size	10	12	14	16	18
Hip					
(cm)	88	92	97	102	107
(in)	34½	36	38	40	42
Length					
(cm)	70	70	70	70	70
(in)	27½	27½	27½	27½	27½
90cm	1.70	1.70	1.70	1.70	1.70m
115cm*	1.40	1.50	1.60	1.60	1.70m
150cm	0.90	0.90	0.90	0.90	0.90m

*Without nap. All other quantities are with or without nap.

Cutting out the skirt

Make any necessary adjustments to pattern length, then position as shown on the appropriate layout. Cut out and transfer all pattern markings. Mark centre front line and hip levels to help with fitting.

Making up the skirt

Step 1 Machine staystitch waist seamline on back and front

sections, 1.3cm/½in from raw edge.
Step 2 Tack back darts, right sides together. Matching notches and circles, tack back seam between zip circle and vent top, and both side seams.

Step 3 First fitting Place a strip of fabric or petersham ribbon around natural waistline and pin skirt to it for support during fitting. Try on skirt, positioning waist seamline on natural waistline. Pin zip opening edges together. Allow 1cm/½in ease on the waist at this stage. Check that centre front and centre back are hanging correctly. Check that marked hip level is horizontal. Smooth skirt from centre to sides and check that side seams are vertical.

Step 4 Remove side seam tackings. Machine back darts and press towards centre. Pin, tack and machine the vent or kick pleat (see pages 90–91).
Step 5 Insert the zip fastener in the back seam while it can still be spread out flat. Use the central or

Hand-sewn zip

Inserting a zip fastener by hand is the hallmark of a highly professional dressmaker. It is, in fact, very easy to do and the stitching is just as strong as a machine finish if the stitches are worked fairly close together. The prickstitch used (Basic seams and stitches page 26) leaves a row of tiny indentations on the right side of the fabric. In many skirt fabrics, these are hidden within the weave.

For a perfect finish, use a fine, sharp needle and single thread. Tack the zip into place, positioning it according to whether it is to be stitched in by the central or overlapped method (pages 42 and 49).

Overlapped method Follow the instructions for the overlapped zip in step 1, page 42, inserting the zip into the right-hand side of the centre back seam, rather than the side seam as described earlier.

If you prefer, this first row of

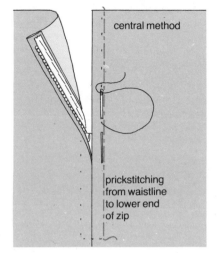

overlapped method
machine or prickstitch concealed stitches
prickstitching left side from waistline to lower end of zip

central method
prickstitching from waistline to lower end of zip

stitches may be machined as the overlap will conceal it. Alternatively, prickstitch the zip into place, working from the waistline to the lower end of zip, with stitches approximately 5mm/¼in apart.

Lay left side of skirt opening over entire zip, just covering the stitching on the right side of the zip. Tack along seamline, then prickstitch from waistline to

lower end of zip.

Work a bar tack across the bottom of the zip on the inside of the skirt.

Central method Work exactly as for a machine stitched central zip (see page 49) but replace all machine stitching with prickstitch worked from waistline to lower end of zip. Work a bar tack across the bottom of the zip on the inside of skirt.

overlapped method.

Step 6 With right sides together, matching notches, join side seams. Make up the lining at this stage and place in position. Make hanging loops from lining fabric (see page 47).

Step 7 Second fitting With lining and skirt together, pin skirt to waistband again. Check the line of the seams, the smooth fit of the darts and the flatness of the zip seam. There should still be some ease in the waistline, but the main body of the skirt should now fit well.

Step 8 With wrong sides together, tack skirt and lining together at waistline. Sew lining around zip tapes, 5mm/¼in from teeth. Attach skirt loops to side seams on waistline.

Step 9 Prepare chosen waistband and attach it to skirt (see pages 82 and 92 for alternative methods).

Step 10 Third fitting Check fit of waistband and position for skirt fastenings.

Step 11 Sew hooks and eyes to end of underlap and add skirt hook and bar.

Step 12 Fourth fitting Pin lining up out of the way and mark hem length on skirt. Tack hem up and check appearance.

Step 13 Complete hem of skirt, then finish lining hem (see page 85).

Cutting layouts for skirt

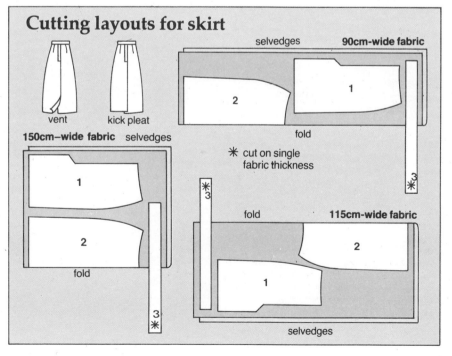

vent   kick pleat

selvedges   **90cm-wide fabric**

150cm–wide fabric selvedges

* cut on single fabric thickness

fold

115cm-wide fabric

selvedges

Graph for straight skirt

1.5cm/⅝ in seam allowance included

4cm/1½ in hem allowed

1 square = 5cm

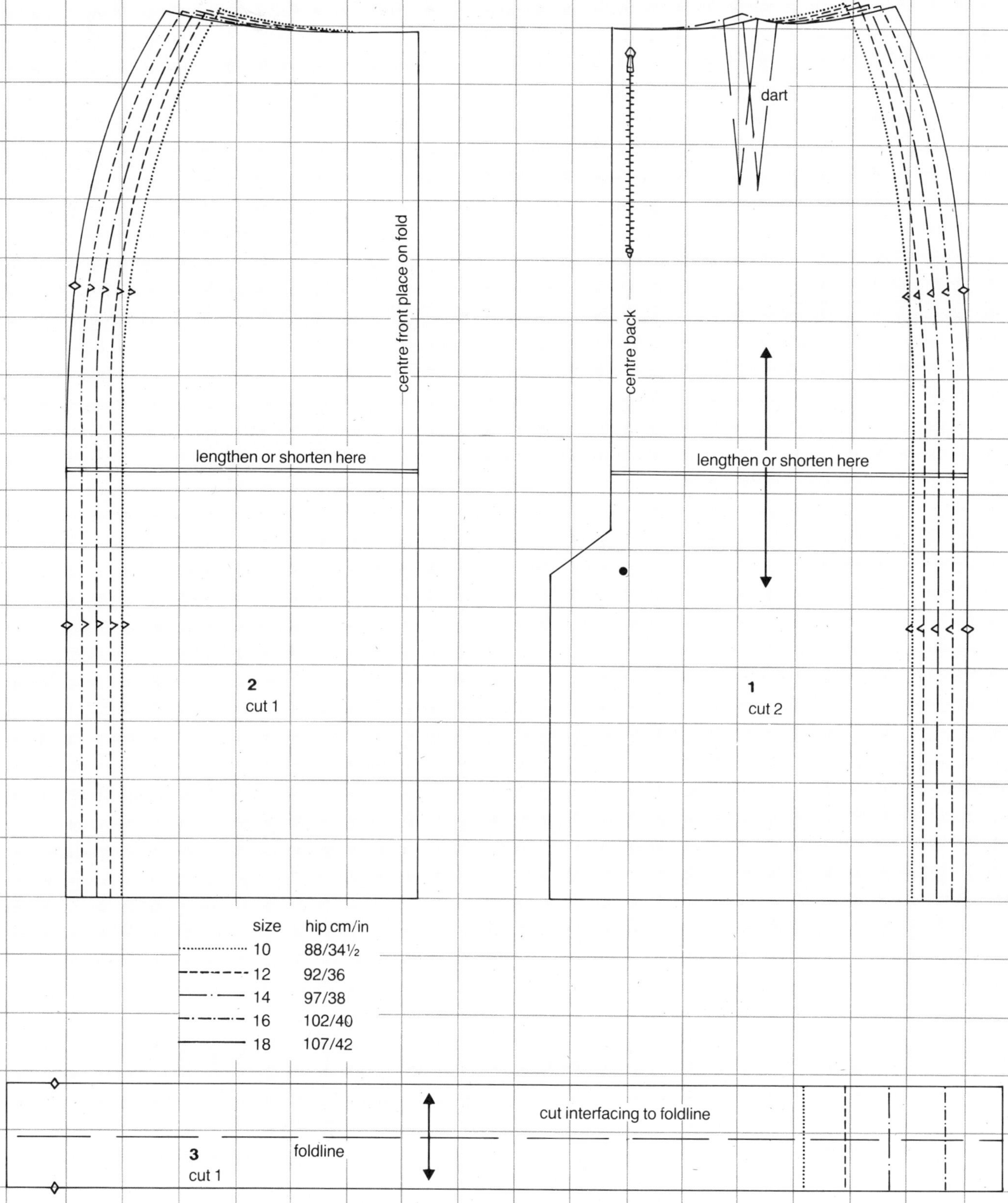

centre front place on fold

lengthen or shorten here

2
cut 1

dart

centre back

lengthen or shorten here

1
cut 2

size	hip cm/in
10	88/34½
12	92/36
14	97/38
16	102/40
18	107/42

cut interfacing to foldline

3
cut 1

foldline

Variations on a theme

The classic high-yoked dress in this section is flattering for most figure types and a clever choice of contrast fabrics for cuffs, collar and yoke can vary the look considerably. The simple collar can be worn open at the neck or tied with a ribbon to form a neat closed neckline. Detailed step-by-step instructions are given for applying the collar and buttoned cuffs for perfect results.

Save money by learning how to adapt a basic pattern to make several garments. A dress, a blouse and a wrapover dressing gown can all be made from this simply styled dress pattern – just extend the facings and length of the pattern pieces to make the dressing gown or cut them to the shorter length for the blouse. Vary the trimmings on the dressing gown by inserting lace round the outside edges of the collar or by adding ribbon to the simple patch pockets.

Cuff details are important and useful tips are given here for making covered buttons and successful hand or machine buttonholes, as well as ideas for dispensing with buttonholes completely.

Cuffs, collars, buttonholes and buttons for a perfect finish

This stylish dress from the pattern on page 120 incorporates some new and useful techniques such as making and attaching simple collars and cuffs. There are also alternative ways of sewing on buttons – useful in many other areas of home dressmaking.

This simply styled dress has several classic features, involving basic dressmaking processes that can be used again and again on other shirts and dresses.

The finish on collars and cuffs, for example, can make or mar a garment – this chapter describes how to fit them to perfection.

Following chapters give you fabric requirements, layouts for the pattern pieces and making up instructions. They also show you how to make a blouse from this versatile pattern.

Coping with collars

Collars are usually made from double fabric, cut as two separate pattern pieces known as the upper and under collar. Interfacing between the two layers preserves the shape. Usually, it is applied to the wrong side of the upper collar so that all bulky seams

are towards the under collar and therefore concealed. However, some iron-on interfacings are better applied to the under collar – follow the advice on your paper pattern instruction sheet.

The shape of the inner or neck edge of the collar determines how it sits on the garment. If the neck edge is straighter than that of the garment, the collar will stand up, then fall away at the neck. If the neck edge is very curved, the collar will lie flat when attached.

Cutting out It is important to transfer pattern markings accurately so that the collar fits perfectly. If any adjustments made to the body of the garment enlarge or reduce the neckline, you may have to adjust the collar slightly.

Careful marking of the garment at the start will save time later. Transfer all

the pattern markings – including seamlines – to the fabric collar, using a tracing wheel and dressmaker's carbon paper.

If the collar is interfaced, transfer the markings to the interfacing instead of the fabric.

Sleeves with cuffs

Long sleeves that are gathered into cuffs usually have a certain amount of fullness to allow ease of movement without constriction at the wrist. The fullness is distributed so that most of it falls to the outside of the arm.

The cuff is made up separately, then attached to the sleeve. To allow the cuff to fit closely at the wrist, but with enough room for the hand to pass through, an opening extends into the sleeve and the cuff fastens with a button.

Techniques for making up a collar

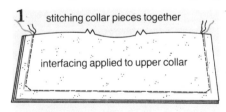

1 stitching collar pieces together
interfacing applied to upper collar

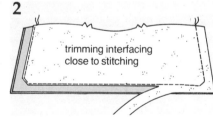

2 trimming interfacing close to stitching

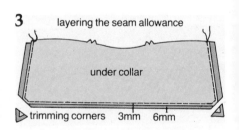

3 layering the seam allowance
under collar
trimming corners   3mm   6mm

Collars are such a noticeable part of a garment, it is essential that they are cut, sewn and turned through precisely. For a perfect finish, you need to know how to layer seams and roll edges.

Layering a seam – which is done before the collar is turned through – helps prevent bulk. This is particularly important on a collar where two seam allowances of fabric plus one of interfacing are sandwiched between the upper and under collar.

Rolling an edge This takes place where an edge consists of a seam – on the edge of a collar or the front edge of a jacket with an attached facing, for example. These have to be finished so that the underside does not roll forwards, exposing the seam.

1 Apply interfacing to wrong side of upper collar. Working with the interfaced side towards you and right sides together, pin under collar to upper collar along the two short edges and long outer edge;

leave the neck edge open. Tack. Machine along seamline on the three tacked edges, using a fairly small stitch. Take one or two stitches diagonally across pointed corners on medium to heavyweight fabric. This produces a better point when the collar is turned through.

2 Layer the seam before turning through the collar by trimming the interfacing on the upper collar close to the stitching.

3 Then trim the under collar seam

100

Right: The short-sleeved version of the dress, gathered into the yoke and belted for a figure-flattering effect.

Above: The dress neckline can be worn in two different ways – here it is left open with the front facing forming revers.

Above: Make a neat, closed neckline by tying a length of ribbon or a fabric rouleau around the collar.

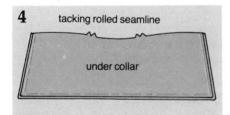

4 tacking rolled seamline

under collar

allowance to 3mm/⅛in and the upper collar seam allowance to 6mm/¼in. Trim corners, clip curves where necessary and turn collar through. Carefully ease out the corners of the collar using a knitting needle or collar-point turner.

4 Roll the outside, seamed edge between the fingers and thumbs until the seam is positioned just to the underside of the collar. Tack close to the outside stitched edges and press on wrong side.

Preparing sleeves for cuffs

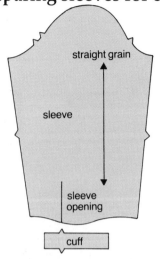

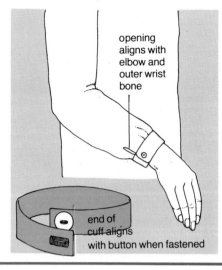

The cuff and the sleeve opening align, and both should be in line with the elbow and outer wrist bones. The opening comes mid-way between the centre sleeve and underarm seam on the sleeve back. The cuff button is stitched to an underlap (an extension of the cuff that laps under the front edge), and the buttonhole is worked so that the end of the cuff lines up with the opening when the button is fastened.

Making the opening

The opening is made before the sleeve seam is joined, as it is easier to manage while the sleeve is flat. The opening is usually marked as a

Binding the sleeve opening

A continuous strip opening – so-called because a single strip of bias fabric is used as a binding – is strong, neat and easy to construct. Use it on fine fabrics, and those that fray easily. From your left over fabric, cut a bias strip 3cm/1¼in wide by twice the length of the opening plus seam allowances. This gives a finished binding width of about 8mm/⅜in.
1 Using a warm iron, crease a seamline 6mm/¼in along one long edge of binding, pressing it towards the wrong side. Repeat on second long side, which will be folded under to form hem.
2 With right sides together, lay sleeve over binding, opening the

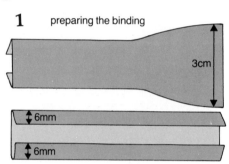

slash out in a straight line. Matching the stitching line on the sleeve opening to the crease line on the bias strip, pin the sleeve opening and strip together along the stitching line, noting that the

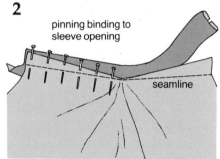

seam allowance on the sleeve opening tapers away to almost nothing in the centre.
3 Working on the sleeve side, machine slowly, keeping just to the left of the original reinforcement

Facing the sleeve opening

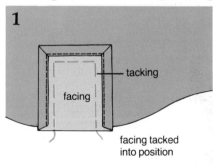

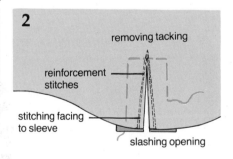

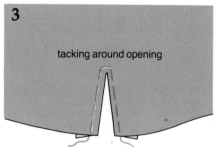

An alternative method of neatening the cut edge of a sleeve opening (best used on medium to heavyweight fabrics), is to use a small facing, instead of a strip of binding. This is applied *before* the opening is slashed through.
1 To make facings, cut two rectangles of fabric 7.5cm×10cm/3in×4in. Press 6mm/¼in to wrong side on two

long sides and one short side and machine stitch to neaten. Reinforce sleeve opening close to stitching line. With right sides together, position facing centrally over cutting line of opening and tack.
2 Working from the sleeve side (where the reinforcement stitches are visible) machine along stitching

line through sleeve and facing, keeping reinforcement stitches within seam allowance. Start at wrist edge, pivot at point, then machine down the second side. Slash through opening along the cutting line as far as point, without cutting the stitches.
3 Turn facing to inside of sleeve, tack around opening and press.

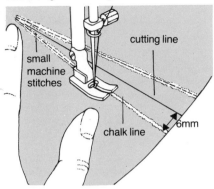

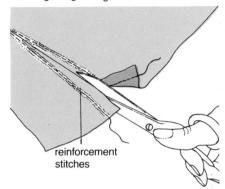

reinforcing the stitching line

slashing along cutting line

straight line on the pattern. Transfer this marking to the wrong side of the fabric with a marking pen, or mark with a tailor's tack at

the top of the opening and a 5mm/¼in snip into the seam allowance at the lower edge.

If only the cutting line is marked on the pattern, mark the stitching line on the wrong side of the fabric with tailor's chalk, starting 6mm/¼in either side of the cutting line on the lower edge and tapering to a point at the top.
Reinforce the stitching line by working small machine stitches exactly on this line. Start at the wrist edge, and work up, keeping fabric taut between finger and thumb so that it doesn't pucker. Pivot needle and machine down the second side.
Slash the opening from lower edge to top along the cutting line, taking care not to cut through the stitches. Do not slash for faced opening.

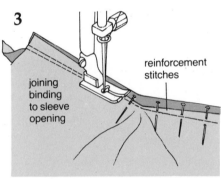

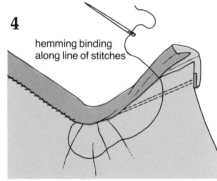

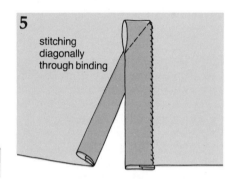

3

4

5

stitches so that they are concealed by the binding.
At the top of the slashed opening, pause with the needle in the work, raise the presser foot and transfer fullness of sleeve above opening to

behind needle. Lower presser foot and continue machining to end of opening.
4 Bring the folded edge of the binding over to the wrong side of sleeve, lining up the fold with the

line of machining. Hem by hand to the machine stitches. Press.
5 On inside of sleeve, machine or backstitch diagonally through binding at top of opening to keep it tucked inside sleeve during wear.

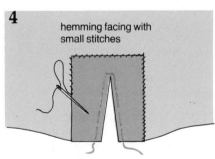

4

hemming facing with small stitches

4 On wrong side, hem facing to garment with small stitches or machine the facing down on to the sleeve. Remove tackings.

Right: The opening of both the cuff and sleeve are aligned. When the arm is bent, the opening lines up with the outer wrist bone and the elbow. The fullness falls to the outer underside of the sleeve.

Making simple cuffs

The simplest type of cuff is made from a single rectangle of fabric, folded lengthwise through the centre. It may be joined to form a circle or, where there is a sleeve opening, cut longer to form an underlap for the button. Like collars, cuffs keep their shape best when interfaced, and some reinforcement is always necessary when buttonholes and buttons are to be added.

The crisp finish of cuffs – again like collars – depends on accurate seamlines and carefully turned through corners. Where seam allowances are to be trimmed use small machine stitches for strength and cut across corners for a well-defined point.

Before stitching the buttonholes make a sample one first on left over fabric. Cut it and check that the button slides through without strain but not too easily.

If you have an automatic or semi-automatic sewing machine, make the buttonholes following the instructions on page 110. Alternatively, make them by hand (page 114).

Cuffs should be made up as a pair so that the underlap for each button is identical and produced in the right place.

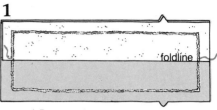

1.5cm seam allowance

Lapped cuff with buttonhole

1 Attach interfacing to cuff, aligning it to foldlines. Transfer all markings from pattern to fabric or interfacing. Where no seam allowances are marked, draw them in 1.5cm/⅝in from raw edges on the wrong side, using a ruler.

Attaching cuffs

Join the sleeve seams before attaching each cuff. If you find it difficult to press an open seam in this area after laundering, use a machine flat fell seam. Alternatively, trim the seam allowance to 3–4mm/⅛–¼in after stitching and machine zigzag or hand overcast together to neaten. Work two parallel rows of large machine or hand gathering stitches on the lower edge of sleeve, placing one row on the seamline and the second row just inside the seam allowance.

1 With right sides together and cuff underlap towards back of sleeve (closest to sleeve seam), pin

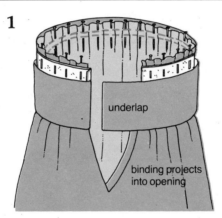

interfaced edge of cuff to sleeve. The binding towards the back of the sleeve (ie below the underlap) projects into the opening, while the

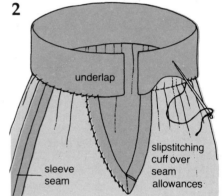

binding towards the front of the sleeve is folded under so it is not visible from the right side.

Pull up gathering threads so that

Sewing on buttons

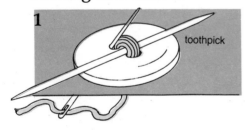

Hand-sewn buttons

Use a double thickness of buttontwist, run through beeswax to prevent the threads parting and tangling. This will also form a firm button shank (the cord of thread that holds the button above the garment and allows room for the buttonhole to slip between button and garment).

1 Start with a backstitch on wrong side of fabric under the button position. Bring needle up through a hole in the button. Centre a

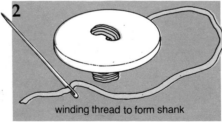

toothpick, matchstick or bodkin over the button, between the holes, to enable you to form the shank. Take several stitches through holes in button, finishing on wrong side of work.

2 Remove toothpick and make sure all extra thread is between garment and button. Take needle through to right side.

Wind thread tightly around strands to form a thread shank. Take thread back to wrong side of work and finish off securely.

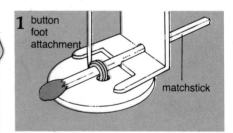

Machine-sewn buttons

You can use your sewing machine to attach buttons – a useful method if you have to sew on several. As long as the ends are finished off properly, the buttons will be secure.

1 Thread machine with ordinary sewing thread to match the garment. Replace presser foot with the button foot which grips button and holds it in place.

Set machine to zigzag stitch and adjust stitch width so that the needle enters the centre of both left

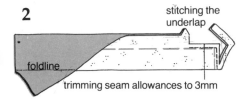

2 stitching the underlap

foldline

trimming seam allowances to 3mm

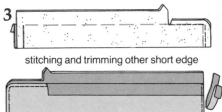

3 stitching and trimming other short edge

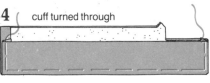

4 cuff turned through

tacking around cuff

2 With right sides together, fold cuff along centre foldline. Starting at marking on long edge, stitch towards short edge, take one stitch diagonally at the corner, and stitch short edge down to fold. This forms the underlap.
Snip into seam allowance from

marking to seam line and trim seam allowances to 3mm/⅛in, cutting across corner.
3 Fold back seam allowance on lower edge or uninterfaced half of cuff and press. Stitch other short end of cuff. Trim seam allowances to 3mm/⅛in.

4 Turn cuff through, using a knitting needle or collar point turner to form neat corners. Tack lightly around the outer edges and press.

Below: Contrasting cuffs for a crisp finish on the long-sleeved dress.

sleeve fits cuff, and distribute the gathers so that there is more fullness near the sleeve opening in line with the little finger. Too much fullness in line with the thumb is unsightly.
Machine gathered sleeve edge from start of underlap to straight cuff edge, being careful not to catch in folded edge of cuff facing. Trim seam allowances to 5mm/¼in.
2 Tuck seam allowances up into cuff and bring free folded edge of cuff over them. Slipstitch folded edge of cuff to line of machine stitching. Make a buttonhole on the flush edge of the cuff and sew a button to the underlap.

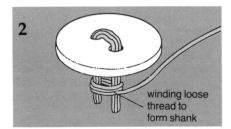

2 winding loose thread to form shank

and right holes in button.
To create a shank, insert a matchstick or thick bodkin over the button between the holes and take about ten zigzag stitches over it. Adjust stitch width to 0 and take several stitches on the spot to secure the threads.
Raise button foot and remove work.
2 Remove the matchstick and push button to end of threads. Wind loose thread around these to form a shank. Finish off loose ends on the wrong side.

An easy-to-wear classic dress

The classic lines of this dress are flattering to most figure types, with gathers falling from a high yoke, comfortable side pockets and a choice of sleeve lengths. The style requires little fitting – shape it at the waist with a sash or elasticated casing.

Using the collar and cuff techniques covered in the previous chapter, you can now make up either the long or short-sleeved version of the dress pattern on page 120. In the next chapter, you can see how to turn this simple, pull-over-the-head style into a blouse, as well as learning how choice and use of fabric can ring the changes in a pattern.

This dress makes up well in a wide variety of lightweight to medium-weight fabrics. The main criteria are that they should not be too stiff or bulky to gather satisfactorily, or too heavy to make the double yoke. Choose polyester/cotton or cool cotton for summer days, silk or polyester crêpe de chine for special occasions. Brushed cotton, pure wool or wool mixtures are ideal for winter.

You will need
Fabric according to size and style
Matching sewing thread
0.25m/2¾yd of 90cm/36in-wide lightweight interfacing
2×13mm/⅝in buttons (long sleeves only)
Pattern pieces, page 120:
  1 Back (dress)
  2 Front (dress)
  3 Yoke
  4 Collar
  5 Front neck facing
  6 Pocket
  7 Long sleeve *or* 9 Short sleeve
  8 Cuff
10 Belt
11 and 12 Waist casing (optional)

Fabric quantity chart

Size	10	12	14	16	18
Bust (cm)	83	87	92	97	102
(in)	32	34	36	38	40
Waist (cm)	64	67	71	76	81
(in)	24	26	28	30	32
Hips (cm)	88	92	97	102	107
(in)	34	36	38	40	42
Length* (cm)	114	115	115	118	119
(in)	44¾	45¼	45¼	46½	46¾
Long-sleeved dress					
90cm	4.00	4.05	4.05	4.15	4.20m
115cm	3.40	3.45	3.45	3.55	3.55m
140cm	2.65	2.65	2.70	2.90	2.95m
Short-sleeved dress					
90cm	3.50	3.55	3.55	3.70	3.75m
115cm	3.05	3.10	3.10	3.20	3.20m
140cm	2.50	2.50	2.55	2.55	2.60m

Allow extra fabric for one-way designs and matching plaids or stripes.
*Length is finished length without belt.

Left: The optional elasticated casing holds the dress waistline in position.

Paper pattern alterations

- **Dress length** Carefully check the finished back length of the dress against your own back length. Remember that the dress is to be belted, or have a waist casing, and allow at least 10cm/4in extra length to take this into account, depending on how much you want the dress to 'blouse' at the waist. If necessary, lengthen or shorten the dress on the double alteration lines and re-position the pockets accordingly.
- **Sleeve length** Alterations to length on a cuffed sleeve must be made on the double alteration lines between the underarm and wrist, not at the shaped lower edge. Remember that the sleeve is full and allow a little extra length so that it is not too short when gathered in to the cuff.
- **Sleeve width** Any extra width in the long sleeve can be gathered in to the cuff. If the short sleeve is too wide, make a vertical dart from the lower edge up to the shoulder point to take it in without altering the size of the armhole seam.
- **Pockets** If you prefer to make the dress without pockets, simply fold back the pocket extensions so that the side seams are even all the way down the dress pattern piece. You will not require pattern piece 6 when cutting out the dress.

Preparing to cut out

Position pattern pieces as shown on the layout for your chosen fabric width. When cutting pieces from double fabric, fold fabric with right sides together. When pattern pieces are shown extending beyond the fold of double fabric, first cut all the double pieces, then open out the remaining fabric and cut all the single pieces, placing pattern to right side of fabric.

Transfer all pattern markings to the fabric, then carefully remove paper. Cut a single piece of interfacing for the collar, using pattern piece 4. Fold pattern piece 8 in half lengthwise and use it to cut two pieces of interfacing for the cuffs.

Cutting layouts for dress

Note: Where pattern pieces are shown white, place paper pattern printed side down to fabric

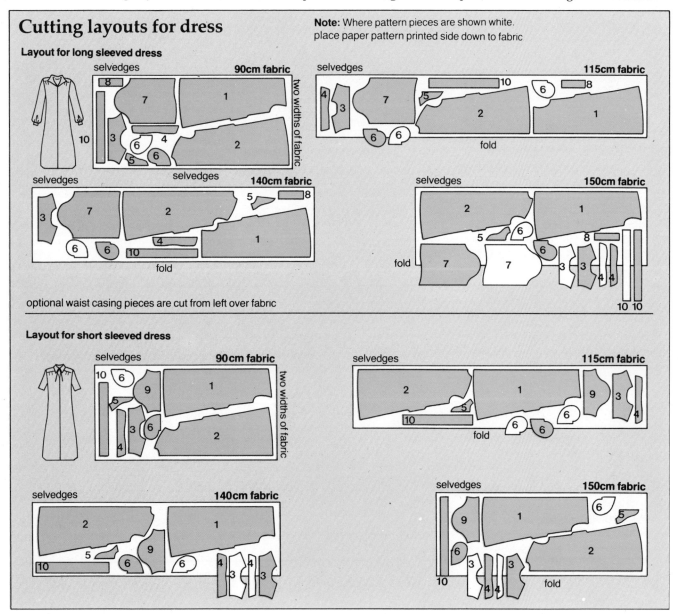

Making the long-sleeved dress

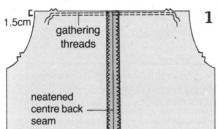

Step 1 With right sides together and matching notches, pin, tack and then machine centre back seam. Press seam open and neaten raw edges.

Staystitch neck curves on both yoke sections and on front facings. Fold yoke sections in half marking centre back on neck edge and lower edge.

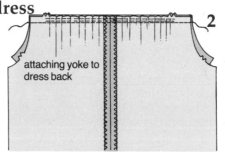

Run a double row of hand or machine gathering threads 4mm/³⁄₁₆in apart within seam allowance across upper edge of back dress between notches.

Step 2 Draw the gathers up to fit the lower edge of upper yoke and with right sides together, matching notches and centre back markings,

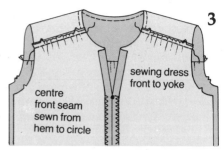

apply back dress to yoke. Spread the gathers evenly between the notches and pin, tack and machine along the seamline.
Make sure that you do not displace the gathers.

Step 3 With right sides together, join centre front seam from lower hem edge to lower circle. Press

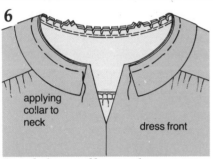

Applying collar to dress

Step 6 Snip seam allowance of dress neckline to staystitching.
Make up collar (see page 100).
Pin and tack collar into position at neckline with upper collar uppermost and under collar next to garment, matching centres and notches.

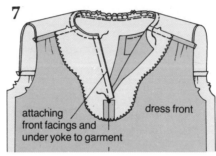

Step 7 Place right side of the under yoke and front facings to the right side of the garment, matching notches and circles. Pin and then tack into position on the seamline around neck.
Work down the centre front from small circles at neckline to base of opening, pinning and tacking

facing to garment. Take care not to catch collar in to this seam.
Before machining, check that the two sides of the collar are identical in length and position, and that no little pleats have formed in the seam around neckline. Snipping into the neckline seam allowance of the garment means the curved seamline can be spread so that the machining is easier.
Machine the seam in two halves, working from base of front opening up to centre back. Pivot the needle exactly on the circle at centre front where the collar joins the neck.
Trim seam allowance to 5mm/¼in, cut across corners and snip turnings if necessary.

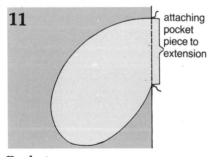

Pockets

Step 11 With right sides together, matching notches, stitch one pocket section to each front and back side seam extension, along seamline as marked. Press turnings towards the pocket and neaten the raw edges separately by machine zigzag or hand overcasting.

Step 12 Join side seams of dress from armhole edge, down to top of

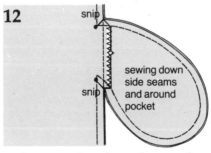

pocket, round pocket to lower edge of sections, then down to hem. Snip to stitching line above and below pocket on back only, press main parts of side seams open and neaten edges. Trim the raw edges of the pocket bag to 6mm/¼in and neaten. Press pocket bags towards front of dress. If you do not require pockets, simply stitch the side seams from armhole edge to hem.

Sleeves

Step 13 Finish the sleeve opening with a facing or strip of binding, join the sleeve seam and make up and attach cuff (see pages 102–105). Insert the sleeve following the method used for the jacket sleeve (pages 58–59).

Step 14: Second fitting
Try on the dress when all neck and sleeve details are complete. Wear the shoes you intend to wear with the dress (heel height makes a difference) and a belt. Arrange the fabric in a bloused effect over the belt and mark the hem length required, getting a friend to help you if possible.

seam open and neaten raw edges from hem to circle.

Run a double row of machine or hand gathering stitches 4mm/³⁄₁₆in apart within seam allowance across two upper front edges of dress between notches.

Draw up gathers on both these edges and with right sides together, matching notches, apply front dress to front edges of yoke. Distribute gathers evenly between notches and pin, tack and machine along seamline. Remove gathering threads and tackings and press all seam allowances on back and front on to yoke, taking care not to flatten gathers.

Trim seams to 6mm/¼in.

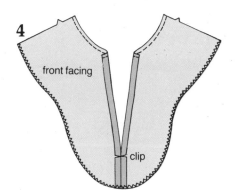

Front facing and under yoke

Step 4 Place front facings right sides together and stitch seam below lower circle. Clip into seam allowance at circle and press seam open. Neaten outer edge of facing.

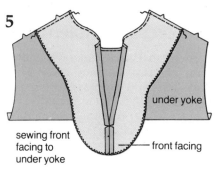

Step 5 With right sides together, pin, tack, and machine under yoke to front facings. Press seam turnings towards under yoke. Press up 1.5cm/⅝in seam allowance to wrong side along back lower edge of under yoke.

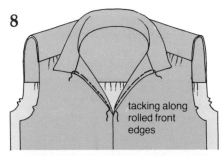

Step 8 Turn under yoke and facings through to wrong side of garment. Tack along centre front edges close to seamline, rolling the facing slightly to the inside of garment. Working on the wrong side with the collar standing upright, smooth the under yoke down to the lower back edge and pin the turned under

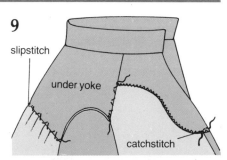

seam allowance to the seamline of dress and upper yoke. Use a dressmaker's dummy if you have one, or slide the dress over the ironing board.

Step 9 Slipstitch pressed edges of under yoke to machine stitching of seamlines. Catchstitch front facing to centre front seam.

Step 10: First fitting

Tack side seams together, leaving pocket opening if pockets are required. Tack underarm seams of sleeves, and tack sleeves into position. Try on dress with a sash or belt and arrange the blouson effect above the waistline.

Check that the centre front and centre back hang vertically, that the shoulder seams are not too long and that the pocket opening is at the right height when the dress is belted. Mark any adjustments with pins and transfer the markings to corresponding sections as soon as the dress is removed.

Hem

Step 15 Neaten lower raw edge and turn hem up, following method used for shaped hem (see page 48), tacking into position.

Try dress on again to check length before finally catchstitching hem into place.

Belt

Step 16 With right sides together, seam two belt pieces together along one narrow end. Press seam open. Fold belt in half lengthwise, right sides together. Seam two short edges and the open long edge, leaving a 10cm/4in opening in the centre of the long edge. Trim seams, clip corners and turn belt through. Stitch up opening by hand, taking small stitches, and press.

Optional waist casing

Join the seams on the waist casing, right sides together, to form one long shaped strip. Press under the seam allowances on both long edges and attach casing to dress.

Making the short-sleeved dress

Make up as for long-sleeved dress as far as step 13. Join sleeve seams, press open and neaten edge. Insert sleeves following the method used for the jacket sleeve (pages 58–59) for a smooth sleeve head.

Press under 5mm/¼in at lower edge of each sleeve and machine stitch to neaten. Try on dress and mark required finished sleeve length. Remove dress and tack up sleeve hems. Try on dress and check that

sleeve lengths are equal. Catchstitch hems in position. Complete as for long-sleeved dress, from second fitting to end. If you are making waist casing you can wear the belt on top for a neat finish.

Successful machine-made buttonholes

Successful buttonholes depend on correct positioning, correct marking and correct selection of stitch width and tension. Always make a test buttonhole using the same materials as in the garment.

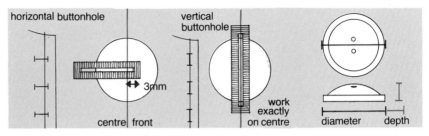

Positioning the buttonhole

In women's and girl's clothes place the buttonholes on the right-hand side, the buttons on the left. Reverse the procedure for men and boys.

The button is always stitched exactly on the centre of a front or back closing. A vertical buttonhole is positioned centrally, but a horizontal one extends 3mm/⅛in beyond the centre to accommodate the button shank and still allow the button to rest exactly on the centre.

Measuring and preparation

Measure the diameter and thickness of the button and add together to work out the length of the cutting line. The finished buttonhole will also have a bar tack worked at each end for additional strength.

Mark a test buttonhole on spare fabric on the same grain as garment, using sharp tailor's chalk or a fabric marking pen, to exact length required. Indicate ends with a short line across top and bottom.

Test zigzag stitch (use slightly less upper tension than for straight stitching). Machines vary, so follow the instructions for your particular model. In general, for the buttonhole sides use a zigzag stitch width *just under* half that of the stitch which forms the bar tack at either end. This ensures a cutting space is left between the two rows.

Machining the buttonhole

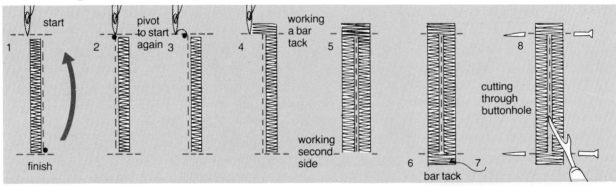

1 Starting at the top left-hand side, work a row of zigzag stitches down the whole length of the marked line, stopping with the needle down in the centre. Raise the presser foot.
2 Carefully pivot the work until the worked row is now on the right-hand side. Lower the presser foot.
3 Using the hand-wheel, take one stitch only to the left, bringing you to a corner.
4 Now change the stitch width to the full width and work four stitches across the entire width of the buttonhole (a bar tack).
5 Return the stitch width to just under half, exactly as for the first row, and work the second row of stitches parallel to it. There should

be only one or two threads of fabric between the rows.
6 Leave the needle down in the lower left-hand corner, change the stitch width to full width and work four stitches to make the second 'bar'.
7 Change the stitch width to zero and work three or four stitches 'on the spot' to prevent stitches coming undone. Raise presser foot. Draw work gently away towards the back of the machine. Cut threads close to buttonhole.
8 Cut through the cutting line, using small sharp scissors or a seam ripper, protecting the 'bar' first by placing pins across each end. Push button through to test for size and adjust length if necessary.

Achieve a professional finish for a shirt with machine-made buttonholes.

Short or long sleeves — a blouse for all seasons

A blouse that can be worn with anything is invaluable, and the simple lines of this one allow you to use fabric as creatively as you please. Useful techniques included in this chapter are hand-sewn buttonholes, covered buttons and quick ideas for cuff fastenings.

The long or short-sleeved blouses from the patterns on page 120 are made up in exactly the same way as the dress on pages 100–109, but you can add some more techniques to your repertoire as you sew.

There are quick ideas for instant cuff fasteners or, for those who prefer the more traditional method, a step-by-step guide to hand-sewn buttonholes.

As the pattern is so simple, why not experiment with colour and pattern to highlight the design features of both garments? For dramatic contrast, you could make up the dress or blouse in dark red, navy or black and add a crisp white collar, front facing and cuffs. For a more subtle effect, cut the main body of the garment in one colour, and the yoke and cuffs in a toning colour as shown below.

Whatever you decide to do, check which pattern pieces are affected, and calculate any extra fabric required accordingly. If you want to cut the yoke or collar on the crosswise grain, for example, you will need to add about half a metre (half a yard) to the fabric requirements – more if you are using stripes that require a one-way layout.

Pattern pieces cut in a different fabric make little difference to the amount of fabric required for most fabric widths. Make a rough layout of the pieces to be cut from the different fabric to help you calculate how much extra fabric to buy.

Below: Back and front views of the blouse, showing different uses of toning fabric.

Fabric ideas for the blouse

The blouse, like the dress, makes up well in a wide range of fabrics, from lightweight cottons to wool mixtures. Try bright seersucker for a casual effect, or use plain white or coloured cotton poplin to make yourself a wardrobe basic. Make a useful long-sleeved shirt in brushed cotton, or a wool mixture, with small checks or a floral design, to be worn belted over trousers.

You will need

Fabric according to size and style
Matching sewing thread
0.30m/⅓yd of 90cm/36in wide lightweight interfacing
2×13mm/½in buttons (long sleeves only)
Pattern pieces, page 120:
1 Back (blouse)

2 Front (blouse)
3 Yoke
4 Collar
5 Front neck facing
7 Long sleeve *or* 9 Short sleeve
8 Cuff (long sleeves only)

Cutting out and making up

Make any necessary pattern alterations and cut out the blouse following the instructions for the dress, cutting the front and back to the shorter length as indicated on the pattern. Omit the waist casing lines and fold away the pocket extensions.

Make up the blouse following the instructions for the long or short-sleeved dress, steps 1 to 9 and steps 12 to 15, referring to the instructions for a dress without pockets during step 12.

Fabric requirements

Size	10	12	14	16	18
Bust (cm)	83	87	92	97	102
(in)	32	34	36	38	40

Long-sleeved blouse

	10	12	14	16	18
90cm*	2.95	3.00	3.00	3.05	3.05m
115cm	2.20	2.25	2.25	2.30	2.30m
140cm*	1.50	1.50	1.50	1.55	1.55m

Short-sleeved blouse

	10	12	14	16	18
90cm*	2.70	2.75	2.75	2.80	2.80m
115cm	1.85	1.90	1.90	1.95	1.95m
140cm*	1.15	1.15	1.15	1.20	1.20m

*without nap. All other quantities are with or without nap.
Allow extra fabric for one way designs and matching plaids or stripes.

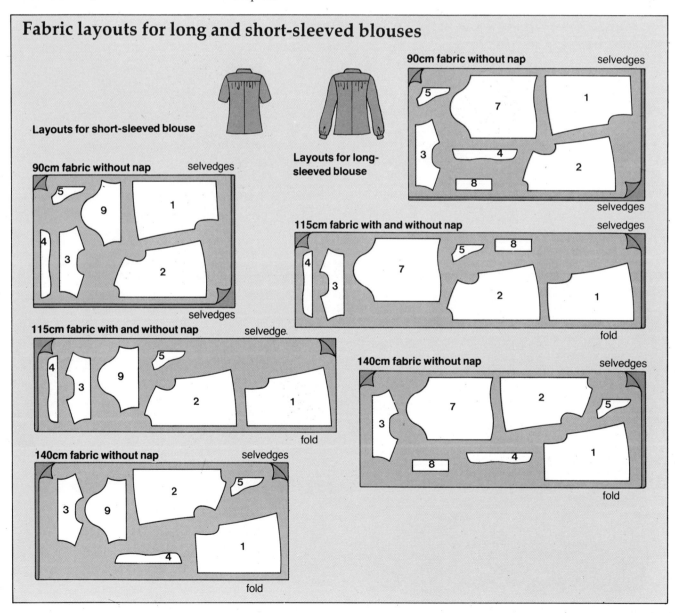

Fabric layouts for long and short-sleeved blouses

Layouts for short-sleeved blouse

90cm fabric without nap — selvedges — selvedges

115cm fabric with and without nap — selvedge

140cm fabric without nap — selvedges — fold

Layouts for long-sleeved blouse

90cm fabric without nap — selvedges — selvedges

115cm fabric with and without nap — selvedges — fold

140cm fabric without nap — selvedges — fold

Clever ways with stripes

This pattern lends itself well to striped fabrics. As the back and front of this dress or blouse are gathered on to the yoke, only the centre front and centre back seams need the pattern to be matched.

In fact stripes can be used as a design feature in themselves. Cut the yoke and collar (and cuffs, if required) so that the stripes run horizontally (that is, on the cross-wise grain), while the stripes on the main body of the dress run vertically.

Learn to recognise the nature of stripes. They may form an even repeat or a one-way design across the fabric. For example, if a striped pattern consists of a red and white stripe, alternating across the fabric from selvedge to selvedge, and ending with a red stripe, then the pattern is even. This is because the sequence of stripes is the same, viewed from either selvedge of the fabric. An even sequence of stripes is easy to match on straight central seams.

If the pattern is made up of a sequence of say, green, blue, pink and white stripes, interspersed with red, it is a one-way design. This is because the pattern is not the same, viewed from either selvedge of the fabric.

The most important thing to ensure with this dress is that the stripes are well-positioned on the pattern pieces. Before cutting, ensure that the stripes match at centre front and centre back seams. Position the pattern pieces so that when they are joined, the stripes balance across the front and back (they will not match at the side seams, which are shaped).

Follow a one-way layout for fabric with a nap, and be sure to follow the straight grain markings, whether cutting on the straight or crosswise grain.

uneven stripes

stripes to highlight yoke

stripes to highlight pocket

even stripes

113

Making hand-sewn buttonholes

Buttonholes worked by hand are especially suitable for fine and delicate fabrics. They are cut first, then stitched. To prevent fraying of the raw edges while stitching, you can insert a scrap of fusible interfacing between the fabric layers at the buttonhole position (unless interfacing is already present). Tack into position, press and then cut through the interfacing to match the cutting line of the buttonhole.

Use buttonhole twist if extra strength is required. Run the thread through a piece of beeswax for firmness and to prevent twisting.

Buttonhole stitch, which can be confused with blanket stitch as they look similar, is used for hand-sewn buttonholes. Both stitches are used to protect and decorate edges, but buttonhole stitch is worked with the raw edge of the fabric away from you, and the thread is twisted round the needle to form a 'purl' stitch. The rounded end of the buttonhole is made towards the edge of the fabric.

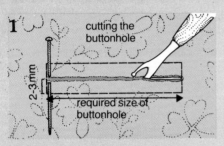

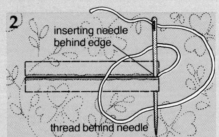

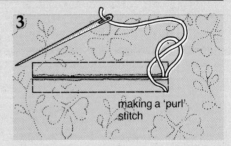

1 Mark centre line of buttonhole on right side of fabric. Machine a rectangle around the marking (or stitch by hand, using small stitches). Begin in the centre of one long side, 2-3mm/⅛in away from marking, and count stitches to ensure opposite sides are the same. Cut buttonhole along marked centre line.

2 Starting at the inner, square edge of the buttonhole, with the fabric edge away from you, secure the thread at the back of the work with a backstitch.

Working from right to left, insert needle behind edge, bringing point out 2-3mm/⅛in down from edge on right side.

With needle in this position take thread behind needle and under needle point from right to left.

Making covered buttons

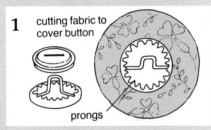

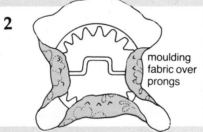

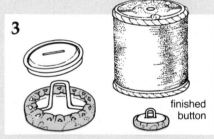

Kits for making covered buttons can be bought from most haberdashery counters. The button is hollow and usually made of metal or plastic, with prongs on the underside to secure the fabric cover. The button back snaps on to the button, hiding the raw edges of fabric. The shank is made of metal, plastic or strong fabric.

Full instructions are usually given with the kits but, in general, buttons are covered as follows:
1 Cut a circle of fabric slightly less than twice the diameter of the button, or use a pattern if supplied. Position any fabric design centrally within the circle.
2 Centre button over wrong side of fabric circle and bring fabric up around button, moulding it over the prongs so that it is held firmly.

3 Ease excess fabric into the hollow of the button and make sure it has a smooth appearance from the front. Place the button back in position and apply pressure until it snaps into place. If this proves difficult, place a cotton reel upright over the shank and rap it firmly with a hammer to force the back into position.

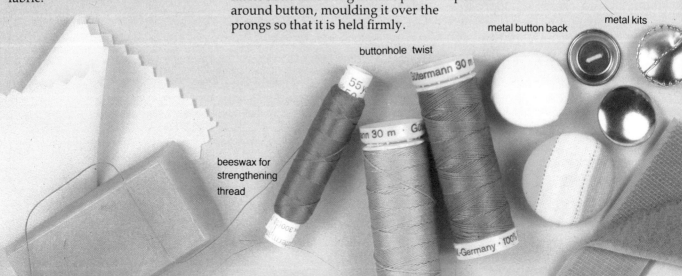

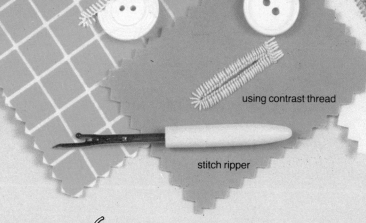

using contrast thread

stitch ripper

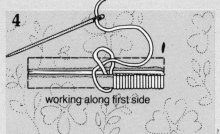

4 working along first side

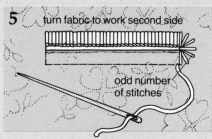

5 turn fabric to work second side

odd number
of stitches

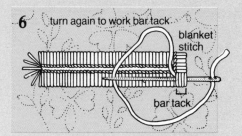

6 turn again to work bar tack

blanket
stitch

bar tack

3 Draw needle through work and pull gently upwards so that a 'purl' stitch forms on the raw edge.
4 Repeat along first side of buttonhole, working stitches close together and of the same length.

5 To stitch round the end nearest the open edge, work an odd number of overcasting or buttonhole stitches, fanning out round the end of the buttonhole. The centre stitch should be in line with the opening for the button.

6 Continue with buttonhole stitch along second side and make a bar tack across the end, the full width of the buttonhole. Blanket or buttonhole stitch over bar tack. Take thread through to wrong side and secure with a backstitch.

SHORT CUT

Doing without buttonholes

If you don't want to make buttonholes on cuffed sleeves, here are two quick alternatives to try. They are ideal on children's wear, for small fingers often can't manage buttons, but they should not be used in areas that take a lot of strain.

Press-stud method Sew the socket of the press-stud to the cuff underlap, and the ball part (which locks into the socket) to the wrong side of the overlap. Attach a button to the right side of the cuff, directly above the press-stud, so that the cuff has the appearance of a traditional

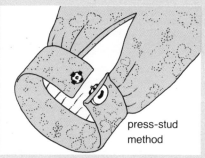

press-stud
method

Velcro method

buttoned cuff when fastened. Sew the button flat to the fabric, without making a shank.
Velcro method Apply a small piece of Velcro – about 1.5cm/⅝in long – to the cuff underlap,

with a hooked piece on the wrong side of the corresponding overlap. Sew a button flat to the fabric on the right side of the cuff directly above the Velcro, for effect.

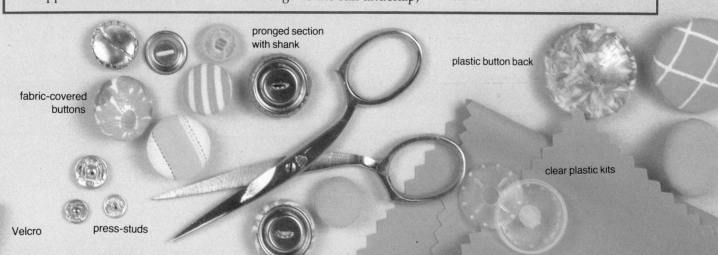

fabric-covered
buttons

pronged section
with shank

plastic button back

clear plastic kits

Velcro   press-studs

Choose a pretty flower-sprigged cotton for this lightweight wrapover dressing gown, then trim the pockets, belt and front edge with toning ribbon.

A lightweight wrapover dressing gown

Adapt the classic dress pattern from the beginning of this section to make a simple housecoat. The sewing techniques are almost the same, just add facings and lengthen to suit your needs. Patch pockets with ribbon trims and a lacy collar frill add a personal touch.

An existing dress pattern with a front seam, like the classic dress on page 101, can be adapted to turn it into a comfortable, full-length wrapover dressing gown.

Simply lengthen the dress and extend the front facings to full length on each side. The dressing gown makes up well in lightweight cotton or cotton blends. Add a lightweight interfacing to the front edges for a crisper look which will hang better and stay in place when wrapped over.

You can adapt the style by adding patch pockets, with a ribbon trim on pockets, sleeves and hem, or insert a broderie anglaise frill around the collar.

Altering the pattern

The dressing gown is made by simply lengthening dress pattern pieces 1 and 2 and front facing piece 5 to ankle length. You can, of course, make it any length you prefer, mid-calf for example; the method used to extend the pattern is the same.

The amount to be added to the pattern depends on your height, but will probably be between 20–30cm/ 8–12in. Finished lengths for the dressing gown, based on average heights, are given in the fabric chart. If you are taller or shorter than the average of 5ft 6in, work out the amount to be added to the dress pattern by comparing your back neck to ankle measurement (or length preferred), with the finished back length for the dress given on page 106. The difference between the two is the amount to be added. A 4cm/1½in hem allowance is already included in the pattern so do not add any extra.

Fabric suggestions

Choose cotton blends such as polyester cotton and terylene and cotton, which are easy to wash and care for. Poplin, piqué, seersucker, brushed cottons or broderie anglaise are also suitable.

Fabric quantity chart

Size	10	12	14	16	18
Bust (cm)	83	87	92	97	102
(in)	32½	34	36	38	40
Length* (cm)	140	142	145	147	150
(in)	55	56	57	58	59
90cm	5.90	5.90	5.95	5.95	6.00m
115cm	4.30	4.35	4.35	4.40	4.40m
140cm	3.10	3.10	3.10	3.15	3.15m

*length is finished back length from nape to ankle without sash.

Allow extra fabric for one-way designs and matching checks and stripes.

Extending the pattern pieces

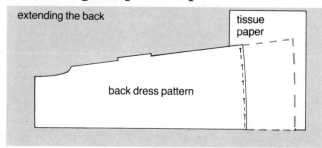

If you are a reasonably experienced dressmaker you can extend the pattern pieces when cutting out. Simply add on the appropriate amount where indicated and mark the new cutting line on the fabric with a ruler and tailor's chalk. If you are less experienced, or wish to make a permanent addition to your pattern, add tissue paper as follows:
Back pattern Pin a sheet of tissue paper to lower edge of pattern, aligning the centre back with the straight edge of the paper. Measure down the amount to be added from the lower edge of pattern at centre back, making marks parallel to the lower edge at 5cm/2in intervals across the width of the pattern. Join the marks, drawing a curve parallel to the lower edge of the pattern. Using a ruler, extend the side seam to the new lower edge, following the cutting line for your size.
Front pattern Lengthen in the same way. The excess tissue is cut away as you cut out.
Front facing pattern Take a strip of tissue paper 20cm × 150cm/ 8in ×60in, joining several small pieces together if necessary. Draw a parallel line 10cm/4in from the straight edge along the full length of the paper. Pin the front facing to the top of the paper, with the centre front to the edge of the paper strip.
Extend the shoulder seam by 2.5cm/ 1in and join this new shoulder point to the line drawn 10cm/4in from the edge of the paper, parallel to the curve of the dress facing.
Trace round the neck curve and shoulder slope of the facing and mark off the length to correspond with centre front edge of extended front pattern. Remove facing pattern from the tissue and cut out the new extended front facing.
Mark a straight grain line parallel to the front edge.

Cutting out and making up the dressing gown

You will need
Lightweight fabric – see fabric
  quantity chart on previous page
Matching thread
1.50m/1⅝yd of 90cm/36in-wide
  lightweight iron-on interfacing
Two buttons for cuffs
Pattern pieces, page 120:
1 Back (dress)
2 Front (dress)
3 Yoke

4 Collar
5 Front neck facing
6 Side seam pocket (or Patch pocket
  pattern piece 7, page 74)
7 Long sleeve
8 Cuff
10 Belt

Cutting out
Position pieces as shown on cutting
layouts for your fabric width. For

economic cutting, 90cm/36in and
115cm/45in fabric is folded across
the width; 140cm/54in fabric is
folded lengthwise. Cut out pattern
pieces carefully and transfer pattern
markings to fabric.
Fold interfacing in half to cut two
pieces for the new long front facing
and two pieces for the cuffs, using
pattern piece 8 folded in half
lengthwise. Cut a single layer of
interfacing for the collar.

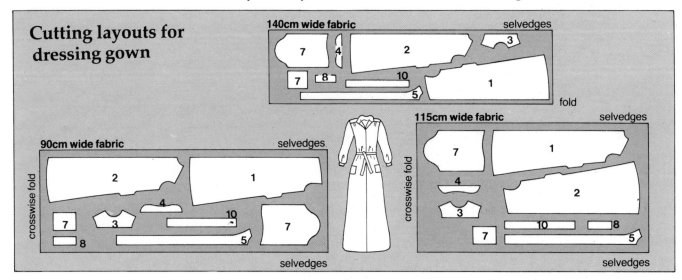

Cutting layouts for dressing gown

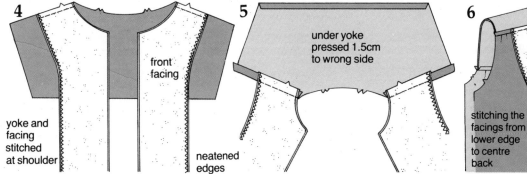

4 yoke and facing stitched at shoulder — front facing — neatened edges

5 under yoke pressed 1.5cm to wrong side

6 stitching the facings from lower edge to centre back

Making up
The dressing gown is made up
following the instructions for the
dress on pages 108–109 with the
following variations:
Steps 1–3 Work as for the dress, but
leave the centre front seam open.
Step 4 Iron fusible interfacing on to
wrong side of extended front
facings and neaten the long curved
edge of the facings. With right sides
together, pin front facings to under
yoke at shoulders. Machine and
press turnings towards under yoke.
Step 5 Press up 1.5cm/⅝in seam
allowance to wrong side on lower
edge of under yoke.
Steps 6–7 Apply collar and facings
as for dress, stitching the facings

from the new lower edge to the
centre back of neck on each side.
Steps 8–14 Complete under yoke,
side seam pockets if required, and
sleeves as for the dress.
Step 15 A narrow machine-stitched
hem (about 1cm/½in) is preferable
for the dressing gown, as there is a
danger of catching heels in a hand-
sewn hem on a full-length garment.
Trim away excess length and press
up hem allowance, easing the fabric
around the hemline curve. Turn
under 5mm/¼in at raw edge and
press, tack and machine hem in
place, keeping line of stitches
parallel to pressed hem fold.
Catchstitch facings into position
over hem.

Step 16 Make the belt as for the
dress.

Adding patch pockets
You may prefer to attach patch
pockets to the dressing gown, using
pattern piece 7 from page 74. Fold
the pocket extensions of pieces 1
and 2 away along the appropriate
seamline when cutting out, and
attach the pockets as instructed on
page 72.
As the dressing gown wraps over at
the centre front, the pockets need to
be nearer the side seams. The exact
position is determined after the
hem has been turned up, and
should be in the most comfortable
position for the hands.

Trimming with ribbon

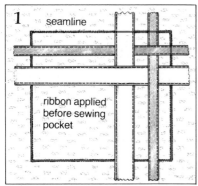

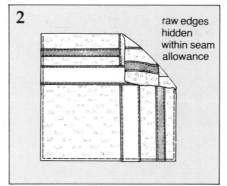

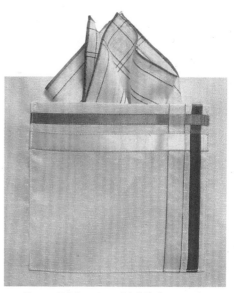

Above: Ribbons can highlight a pocket.

Ribbon is an ideal choice for trimming the dressing gown. You can choose from a wide range of colours and finishes, including satin and velvet. If your dressing gown is to be washed frequently, a polyester ribbon, which will not crease, may be a better choice than nylon, which will have to be ironed.

Ribbons should be attached as invisibly as possible. When machining, try to merge the stitches with the woven edge of the ribbon. Sew each edge in the same direction to avoid diagonal pulling.

1 Ribbon trims look particularly effective on pockets. Apply ribbon to the pocket *before* it is made up.
2 When it is stitched to the garment, the raw edges are hidden within the seamline.
Try combining different widths and colours of ribbon at right angles to one another, overlapping and interweaving the rows where they meet at the top front corner of the pocket. Or, for a simple finish, stitch two parallel rows of 5mm/¼in ribbon across the top of the pocket. Trimmings need not be confined to

the pockets. Add a ribbon band at the edge of the cuff and, instead of using shop-bought buttons, cover your own in a wider, matching ribbon. A hem also benefits from a ribbon trim which can be used to hide the machine stitching and to add weight to a lightweight fabric, so that it hangs well. Small ribbon bows can be tied or sometimes purchased ready-made – use these to add interest at the neckline and on the cuffs.

Trimming with lace

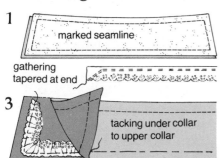

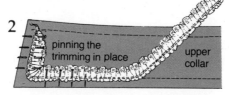

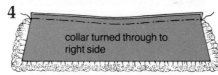

Above: Narrow lace, gathered to make an attractive edging for the collar.

Broderie anglaise and other lacy trimmings can be used very effectively as a dainty, decorative edging for collars. If you buy them ready gathered, you will need about 70cm/¾yd for the collar. Alternatively, you can gather your own using a straight piece of trimming, two to three times the finished length required.

How to apply the trimming
1 Cut out two fabric collar pieces and one piece of interfacing. Mark the seamlines 1.5cm/⅝in from the raw edges all around the collar pieces on the wrong side.
Run two rows of hand or machine gathering stitches 7mm/¼in from the raw edge, along the trimming,

tapering across to the decorative outer edge at each end. Pull up the threads to the required length, distributing the gathers evenly.
2 With right sides and raw edges together, pin the trimming to the interfaced upper collar, matching the gathering line on the trimming to the collar seamline. Start at the front edge of the collar, positioning the tapered end of the trim exactly on the point where the seamlines cross. Pin along one short edge, across the outer edge of collar and back up second short edge to centre front. More gathers are needed at the corners to allow the trimming to spread out evenly when the collar is turned through.

3 Tack the trimming along the seamline, using small stitches. With right sides together, pin and tack upper collar to under collar along seamline, keeping trim well tucked in at corners.
Machine carefully along seamline through all layers. Trim seam allowances to 6mm/¼in and cut across corners.
4 Turn collar through to right side. Tack around outer edges and press. Tack neck edge together, ready to join to garment, and remove all the visible tackings and gathering threads.

119

Graph for pull-over-the-head dress and blouse

1.5cm/⅝in seam allowance included (except where shown)

4cm/1½in hem allowed   1 square = 5cm

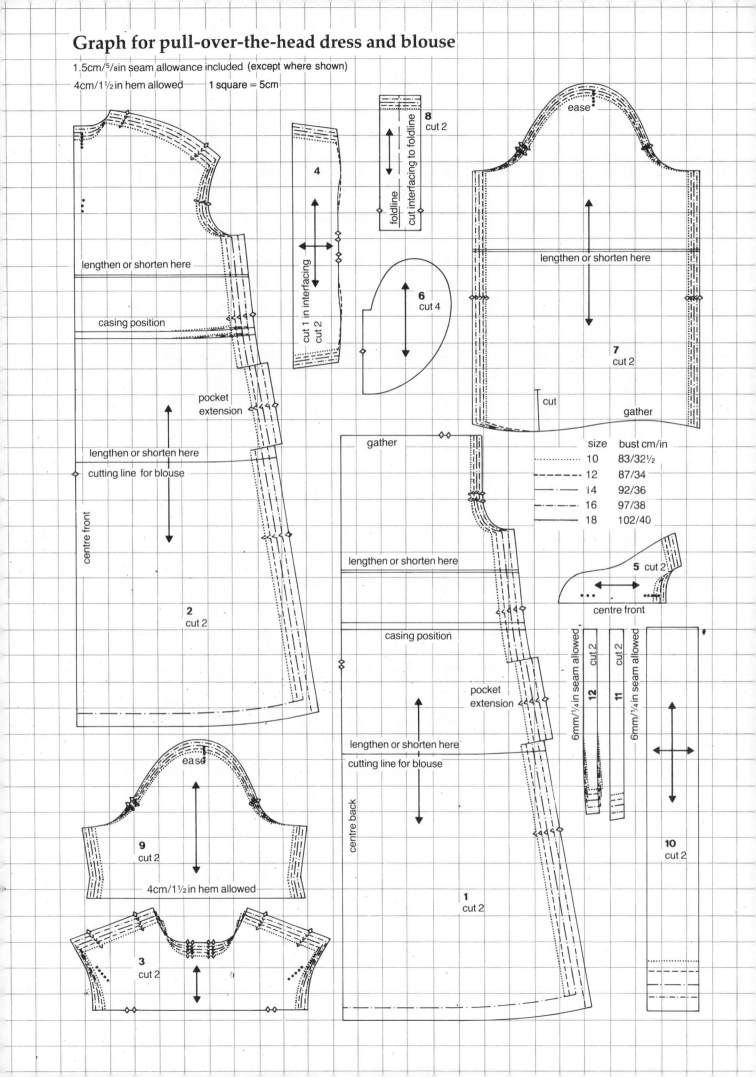

lengthen or shorten here

casing position

pocket extension

lengthen or shorten here

cutting line for blouse

centre front

2 cut 2

4

cut 1 in interfacing cut 2

8 cut 2

foldline

cut interfacing to foldline

6 cut 4

ease

lengthen or shorten here

7 cut 2

cut

gather

size	bust cm/in
10	83/32½
12	87/34
14	92/36
16	97/38
18	102/40

5 cut 2

centre front

gather

lengthen or shorten here

casing position

pocket extension

lengthen or shorten here

cutting line for blouse

centre back

1 cut 2

6mm/¼in seam allowed

12 cut 2

11 cut 2

6mm/¼in seam allowed

10 cut 2

ease

9 cut 2

4cm/1½in hem allowed

3 cut 2

Shirts and shirtwaisters

A classic shirt pattern can form the basis for innumerable variations of style, creating a whole wardrobe of blouses and shirts for day and evening wear for both winter and summer.

The basic pattern has a button band attached to each front and a collar stand with collar. To change the look, replace the pointed collar with a round version or simply use a stand collar on its own. Alternatively, substitute a bias-cut tie for the collar and stand. For a pretty feminine version learn how to make single or double frills to insert into the button band, collar stand or cuffs.

These collar and sleeve variations can also be used on a basic button-through shirt dress. This style, with its fitted bodice and partly-gathered skirt, requires careful cutting out when using patterned fabrics. Learn how to balance the pattern across the front and back, and how to match the design horizontally at the armhole seams and vertically through the bodice and skirt.

Button bands and collar stands for a basic blouse

Add some new techniques to your sewing skills and some attractive blouses to your wardrobe by making up this ideal basic blouse in a range of fabric weights. It has a simple shirt-style neck, button-through front and long, full cuffed sleeves.

This chapter introduces you to the shirt style blouse with button band and collar stand. All the blouses which follow are made from the same main pattern pieces on pages 149–150, with variations of neckline and long and short versions of the full, gathered sleeves. The bodice of the blouse is softly gathered into a yoke at front and back, and all the blouses have a strip button band with vertical buttonholes.

The basic collar stand can be attached

Making a button band

A button band is a vertical band or strip of fabric which is interfaced and attached to each side of the centre front of a shirt, adding a firm, crisp finish. One button band has buttonholes and laps over the other which carries the buttons. If you have altered the length of the blouse, remember to adjust the band. Hem the lower edge of the blouse before applying the button band.
1 Interface the wrong side of each button band (on thicker fabrics cut interfacing to half the width of the button band only, that is up to the fold). Fold band in half lengthwise, right sides together, and stitch across the lower edge. Start 1.5cm/⅝in from long edge and take a 1.5cm/⅝in turning. Clip corner, trim seam and press.
Press 1.5cm/⅝in seam allowance to

Positioning buttonholes

Use horizontal buttonholes where there is some strain, for example at the neckline, cuff or across the chest. Use vertical buttonholes where extra ease has been allowed in the pattern so that the buttons are not pulled undone by undue strain.
A fitted shirt or dress bodice should have horizontal buttonholes down the centre front.
The blouse shown left has extra body fullness gathered into a yoke, allowing enough ease for centre-front buttonholes to be positioned vertically. On both styles the horizontal rule still applies to cuffs and collar stands.

Left: Cut the collar, button band and cuffs in crisp, contrasting white and highlight the buttons by covering them in the main fabric. Wear the shirt-style collar open or closed.

on its own for a simple stand collar, or you can add a shirt-style collar or a round collar. For a sophisticated look you can make a tie-necked version. The instructions are presented in such a way that the sewing techniques involved in a particular style can be used for any similar pattern. Add frills to the button band, cuffs and collar stand instead of a collar. Dress up a plain fabric by topstitching the button band, collar stand, yoke and cuffs in contrasting thread.

This chapter concentrates on the classic shirt-style neck line with a pointed collar joined to the collar stand. It may be worn buttoned to the neck, or with the top buttons left open for a casual effect. The sleeves are long and buttoned at the cuff.
The only new techniques to learn are how to make a button band and how to construct and attach a collar stand and collar to a blouse neckline.
A classic shirt collar has two parts made up separately – the stand or

neckband which fits closely to the neck and fastens with a button, and the fall or visible collar which is joined to the top edge of the stand. This method of construction raises the collar above the level of the garment neckline unlike one-piece collars which fall from the neckline without a stand. The finish of the collar and stand is always very noticeable, so mark the seamlines on all pattern pieces, and particularly on the interfacing, for accuracy.

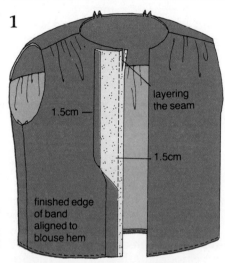

1

1.5cm

layering the seam

1.5cm

finished edge of band aligned to blouse hem

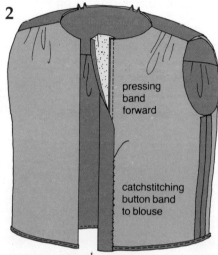

2

pressing band forward

catchstitching button band to blouse

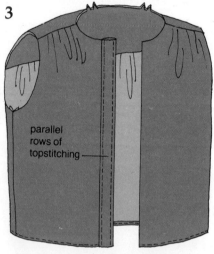

3

parallel rows of topstitching

wrong side along one long edge. Turn band through to right side. Lay button band over blouse front edge, aligning seamed lower edge with blouse hem. Tack and machine the long front seam. Layer turnings.

2 Press band forward so that pressed fold of seam allowance just covers line of machine stitching on wrong side. Catchstitch button band in place to line of machine stitching. Press.

3 Topstitch (see page 209) both long edges from right side if required and repeat all steps to attach button band to other front edge.

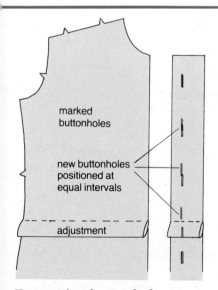

marked buttonholes

new buttonholes positioned at equal intervals

adjustment

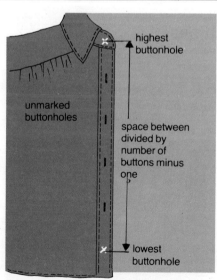

unmarked buttonholes

highest buttonhole

space between divided by number of buttons minus one

lowest buttonhole

Re-spacing buttonholes
Most commercial paper patterns include markings for the position of both buttons and buttonholes. If you have to adjust the pattern length

these must be re-positioned so that they remain an equal distance apart.
Marked buttonholes Measure the distance between the top and bottom buttonhole and space the

rest of the buttonholes evenly between them. Re-space the button markings to correspond.
Unmarked buttonholes Where buttonholes are not marked on the pattern, as in the graph patterns on page 137, make any adjustment to the length as necessary and make up the blouse.
Mark the position of the highest buttonhole – in the collar stand if there is one – and the lowest, making allowances for the hem. Divide the space in between by the number of buttons to be used, minus one. For example, if there are to be six buttons, divide by five as there will be five spaces between them. This amount gives the distance between the buttons. To mark the position of vertical buttonholes, measure from the top of one to the top of the next.

Making a shirt collar with stand

1 applying interfacing to stand

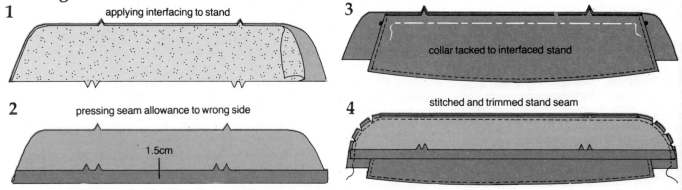

3 collar tacked to interfaced stand

2 pressing seam allowance to wrong side

1.5cm

4 stitched and trimmed stand seam

Make up the collar in exactly the same way as the dress collar on page 100. Tack the layers together along the free edge and topstitch the outer edges if required.

1 Tack the interfacing (or press if fusible) to the wrong side of one of the stand pieces.
2 Press the seam allowance to the wrong side on the long edge of the other stand piece.

3 With right sides together, pin the under collar to the interfaced stand between circles, matching notches. The stand extends beyond the collar ends. Tack along seamline.
4 With right sides together,

8 slipstitching folded edge to blouse

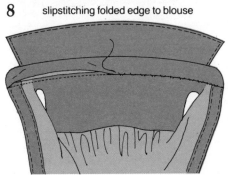

9 topstitching in two sections

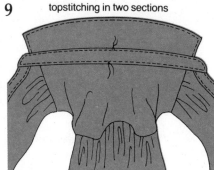

8 On wrong side, bring folded edge of stand down to neck seamline and slipstitch to secure.
9 If you want to topstitch the stand, work from the right side and,

starting at the upper centre back, work across and down to the centre back of the neck seamline on both sides of the stand.

Classic blouse

This style of blouse is ideal for everyday wear so choose a fabric which launders well and is easy to care for. Cotton and polyester blends are ideal for frequent washing, and a high proportion of polyester means that the blouse will drip dry and require little ironing. A higher proportion of cotton or an all-cotton fabric is cooler and more comfortable to wear in warm weather, but requires more ironing. Seersucker and crêpe are also suitable for the blouse, but they must be pressed with a cool iron to avoid flattening the textured surface of the fabric.

Shirtings, challis, chambray and madras cotton are also suitable, while lightweight wools, Viyella or brushed cotton make warm and comfortable winter blouses.

Take into consideration the colour and pattern of the fabric as well as its nature. If you want to make a feature of the topstitching on the collar, cuffs and button band, don't obscure the effect by choosing a dominating pattern. Topstitching looks most effective on a plain fabric, or one with a small, regular pattern.

Stripes and checks work well on this blouse – remember to allow a little extra fabric if you want to cut the button band on the cross, and for matching the pattern across the seams.

You will need
Fabric according to size

Cutting layouts for classic blouse

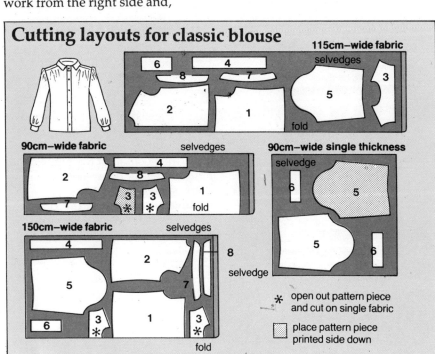

115cm–wide fabric
selvedges
fold

90cm–wide fabric
selvedges
fold

90cm–wide single thickness
selvedge

150cm–wide fabric
selvedges
selvedge
fold

* open out pattern piece and cut on single fabric

place pattern piece printed side down

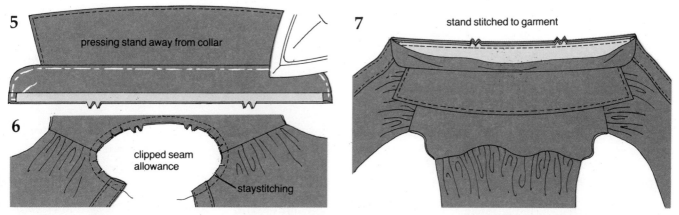

5 pressing stand away from collar

6 clipped seam allowance — staystitching

7 stand stitched to garment

matching notches, pin stand facing over tacked collar and stand. Tack through all thicknesses. Machine stand seam following seamlines carefully. Trim seam, clipping notches at curves to reduce bulk.

5 Turn stand through to right side and press both stand sections away from the collar. Tack close to seamline to keep flat and press.
6 Staystitch neck seamline of blouse. Snip into seam allowance to

staystitching at 2.5cm/1in intervals.
7 With right sides together, matching notches, tack interfaced stand to garment along neck seamline. Machine seam, trim turnings and press towards collar.

Matching thread
0.35m/⅜yd lightweight interfacing
9×1cm/⅜in buttons
Pattern pieces, page 137:
1 Blouse back
2 Blouse front
3 Yoke
4 Button band
5 Long sleeve
6 Cuff
7 Collar stand
8 Shirt collar

Fabric quantity chart

Size	10	12	14	16	18
Bust (cm)	83	87	92	97	102
(in)	32½	34	36	38	40
90cm*	2.30	2.30	2.50	2.60	2.80m
115cm*	2.10	2.10	2.10	2.20	2.20m
150cm*	1.45	1.50	1.50	1.50	1.60m

*without nap.

Allow extra fabric for matching checks or one-way designs.

Preparing to cut out
Position pattern pieces according to the appropriate layout for your fabric width. Cut out carefully and transfer pattern markings to garment sections. Using the same pattern pieces, cut out one collar stand, one collar, two button bands and two cuffs in interfacing.

Right: A back view of the blouse. The gathers in the yoke seam ensure a comfortable fit across the back.

Making the blouse

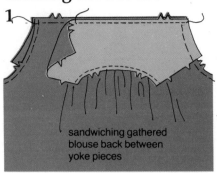

sandwiching gathered blouse back between yoke pieces

Step 1 Staystitch neck and armhole edges within seamline on all pieces. Run two rows of gathering threads between notches on back, draw up to match notches on lower edge of yoke. Tack right side of one yoke section to wrong side of blouse back to form the under yoke. With right sides together, matching notches, tack remaining yoke section to back.

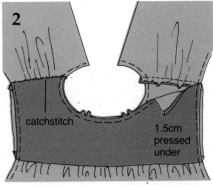

catchstitch

1.5cm pressed under

Machine along seamline, through all thicknesses. Remove gathering threads and press the yoke and under yoke up.

Step 2 Run two rows of gathering threads along upper edges of each blouse front between notches. Draw up the gathers to fit front yoke edges. With right sides together, matching notches,

machine fronts to top yoke. Press seam allowances towards yoke. Press under turnings on front under yoke and bring it down to meet the seam joining fronts to yoke and catchstitch. Topstitch yoke seams.

Step 3 First fitting Tack side seams together and try on. Pin blouse together at centre front. Check width of blouse across back and front measuring about 10cm/4in below shoulders. The armhole seamline should be in line with the end of the shoulder. Check the body width, remembering that the style should be roomy. Take in any excess at side seams. Make similar adjustments to the sleeve seam if you alter the side seam, or the sleeve fit will be affected.

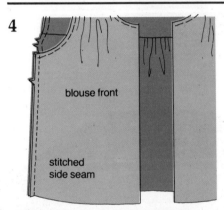

blouse front

stitched side seam

Step 4 Pin, tack and machine the side seams. If you are topstitching the blouse, you may prefer to use a machine flat fell seam instead of an open seam (see Basic seams pages 24–26) to give all the seams a similar appearance.

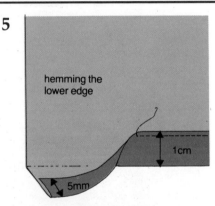

hemming the lower edge

1cm

5mm

Step 5 Hem the lower blouse edge by hand or machine, taking a 1.5cm/⅝in turning. Prepare the button bands and join to each front edge as instructed, making sure the lower finished edge of each band lines up with the hem.

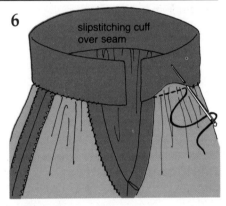

slipstitching cuff over seam

Step 6 Face or bind the lower sleeve opening and attach cuff as instructed on pages 102–105. Prepare collar and collar stand and attach to neckline. Run a row of gathering threads either side of the seamline on the sleeve head and draw up gathers to fit the armhole.

Step 7 Second fitting Tack the sleeve seam, pin and tack into armhole and try on. Pin the blouse together at centre front and check the fit of the sleeve in the armhole. Check that the top sleeve gathers are positioned in a flattering way and that they match each other. Make sure armhole or sleeve are not too tight, remembering that the fit will be looser when the armhole seam is stitched and trimmed.

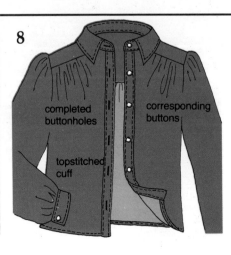

completed buttonholes

corresponding buttons

topstitched cuff

Step 8 Complete sleeve and insert as shown on pages 58–59. Note that this sleeve has a full head and should have a gathered appearance when set in. Topstitch cuff if required. Make hand or machine buttonholes in button band, collar stand and cuffs. Sew on buttons to correspond.

Making a classic tie-necked blouse

The tie-neck blouse is an elegant variation of the shirt in the previous chapter. Make it up in a silky man-made fabric for everyday wear, using the techniques given here, or dress it up for special occasions by making a glamorous version in pure silk crêpe de chine.

Make this tie-neck blouse in exactly the same way as the blouse in the last chapter, but substitute a bias-cut tie for the collar and stand.

The tie-neck blouse needs a soft fabric that gathers well into the yoke or cuffs, and will not form too stiff a bow when tied. For a soft, silky effect, look for polyester, acetate or viscose, or blends of these fibres. Polyester crêpe de chine, surah, foulard, challis and peau-de-soie all fall into this category. For special occasions treat yourself to a fine silk.

You will need
Fabric as given overleaf
Matching thread
0.2m/¼yd lightweight interfacing
9×1cm/⅜in buttons
1 clear plastic press stud
Pattern pieces, page 137 as for the shirt (see page 125) but substitute the Blouse tie (9) for the Shirt collar and stand (7 and 8)

Making up
Make up the blouse in the same way as the blouse in the previous chapter except for the collar details. Follow the instructions for the button band and tie neck overleaf.

Below: A silky polyester crêpe de chine has been used to make this smart tie-necked version of the classic blouse pattern.

Preparing the button band for a neck tie

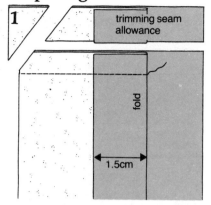

1
trimming seam allowance
fold
1.5cm

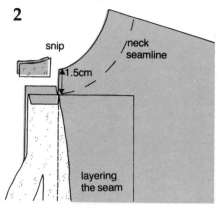

2
snip
neck seamline
1.5cm
layering the seam

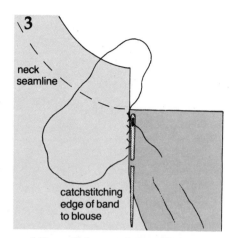

3
neck seamline
catchstitching edge of band to blouse

To ensure that a tie sits well at the neck it is attached to the neckline of the shirt only, not to the button band. So the top edge of the button band must be seamed across the top and bottom before it is attached.
1 Tack interfacing to the wrong side of the button band. Press 1.5cm/⅝in seam allowance to wrong side along one long edge.

Fold button band in half, right sides together, and stitch top and bottom edges taking 1.5cm/⅝in turnings. Trim seam allowances, clip corners and press. Turn band through.
2 With right sides together, position button band 1.5cm/⅝in down from raw edge of blouse neckline at front edge, aligning lower seamed edge with hem. Clip to staystitching at

neckline of blouse, 1.5cm/⅝in in from front. Tack and machine the long front seam, leaving the seam allowance on the upper side of the button band free. Layer turnings, clip corner and press.
3 Press button band forwards. On the inside catchstitch the folded-under edge of the band to the line of the machine stitching.

Making and attaching a neck tie

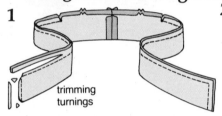

1
trimming turnings

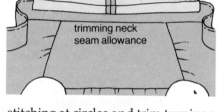

2
trimming neck seam allowance

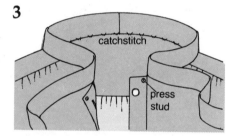

3
catchstitch
press stud

A neck tie is cut on the bias so that it eases to fit the neckline and ties well. It is cut in two sections which are joined at the centre back.
1 With right sides together, stitch the centre back seam and press open. Fold tie in half lengthways, right sides together, and stitch the two tie ends on the seamline as far as the circles, leaving the neckline edge of the tie open. Snip to

stitching at circles and trim turnings only where the seam has been stitched, clipping across corners. Turn right side out and roll seam so that it is positioned to the edge of the tie. Edge tack and press.
2 Working on the right side of the blouse with right sides together and matching notches and circles, pin and tack single layer of neck tie opening to neck edge of shirt on

seamline. Machine seam, ensuring that it aligns with the button band at each side of the front neck. Trim turnings and press up into collar.
3 Fold in seam allowance on free edge of tie opening and catchstitch to neckline seamline. Reinforce junction of tie and button band with a bar tack worked on wrong side. Sew a clear plastic press stud to upper corner of button band.

Fabric quantity chart

Size	10	12	14	16	18
Bust (cm)	83	87	92	97	102
(in)	32½	34	36	38	40
90cm*	2.90	3.00	3.00	3.10	3.30m
115cm*	2.10	2.20	2.20	2.30	2.30m
150cm	1.70	1.70	1.70	1.80	1.80m

*fabric without nap.
Allow extra fabric for matching checks and stripes.

Cutting layouts for tie-necked blouse

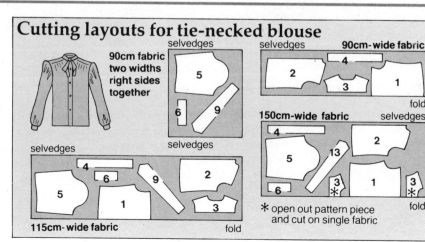

90cm fabric two widths right sides together
selvedges
selvedges
selvedges
selvedges
5
6
9
115cm-wide fabric
4
6
5
9
2
1
3
fold

selvedges
selvedges
90cm-wide fabric
4
2
3
1
fold
150cm-wide fabric
selvedges
4
5
13
2
6
3
*
1
3
*
fold
* open out pattern piece and cut on single fabric

A double-thickness frill

Transform the neckline of the casual blouse with the simple stand collar from the graph patterns on page 137. Use a self or contrasting fabric for the stand or add a narrow double frill to the collar and cuffs for a crisp and elegant variation.

A simple stand collar version of the blouse on page 122 (see pattern page 137) is quick to make. Omit the pattern piece for the collar and turn the stand itself into a collar by neatening the top edge. The blouse can be as casual or smart as you please, depending on your fabric choice.

To make a pretty and feminine blouse from the same pattern, just add some frills. Make double frills and insert them in the top edge of the collar stand and around the cuffs as well. The next chapter shows how to insert single frills either side of the button band.

Adding a frill to an ordinary stand collar changes its proportions slightly – both the frill and stand should be narrow or the frill will be uncomfortably high on the neck. A finished frill of a depth of no more than 2cm/¾in with a collar stand of no more than 2.5cm/1in is ideal. If you wish to make the collar stand even narrower, do not make the alteration at the neck edge or it will not fit the neckline. Instead, trace a line parallel to and below the top edge of the stand pattern, to the new height required.

Below: The frilled blouse looks superb made up in crisp white Swiss cotton. Inset: The plain stand collar looks effective made in a crisp white fabric to contrast with the blouse.

Making a double-thickness frill

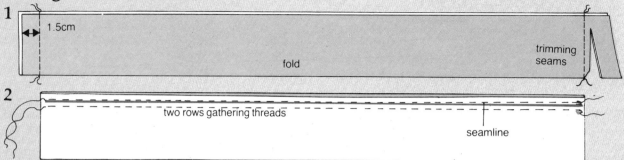

A double frill has a fold along the outer edge with the raw edges inserted into the collar stand or cuff edges.

If you do not have a pattern for a double frill, cut a straight strip of fabric 7cm/2¾in wide (or twice the desired finished width, plus two seam allowances of 1.5cm/⅝in). The length is one-and-a-half to three times the finished length, plus seam allowances, depending on the fullness required. Double frills can be cut on the straight grain or the bias.

1 Fold the strip of fabric in half lengthwise with right sides together and stitch both short ends, taking 1.5cm/⅝in seams. Trim seams, clip corners and turn through.

2 With wrong sides together run two rows of gathering through the double fabric of the frill either side of the seamline.

Making a stand collar without frill

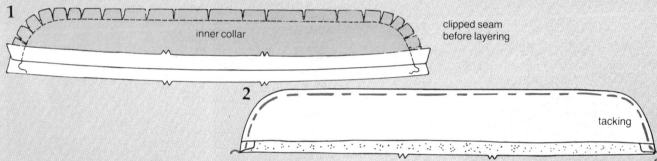

1 Apply interfacing to the wrong side of the outer collar. Press 1.5cm/⅝in seam allowance to wrong side along lower edge of inner collar. With right sides together, lay outer collar over inner collar. Tack around the collar through all layers, leaving the neckline edge open. Machine along seamline and layer the stitched seams. Clip into the seam allowances and cut V-shaped notches at the convex curves.

2 Turn collar to right side, using a blunt knitting needle or a collar-point turner to push out all the seams. Tack close to seamed edges and press.

Apply to blouse neckline as for collar stand (pages 124–125). Topstitch all the way round 2mm/⅛in from the edge for a firm finish.

Making a stand collar with frill

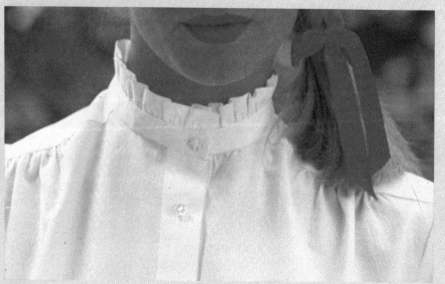

A frill sits best on a collar stand with straight top and front edges.

1 To produce a straight-edge pattern from the rounded one, such as the one on page 137 (pattern piece 7), simply trace the pattern on to tissue paper and continue the line of the top edge of the stand parallel to the lower edge, without curving away.

Left: Close-up of frilled stand collar.

Making frilled cuffs

A frill is inserted at the edge of cuffs in much the same way as in the collar stand. Normally the cuff end which is placed flush to the sleeve opening forms the overlap but in this case take the frill around the short end of the underlap to form a decorative overlap. Adapt the pattern by folding it in half lengthwise. Cut four cuffs to this size, adding 1.5cm/⅝in seam allowance to top edge of each cuff. To make the frill, cut a strip of fabric 7cm/2¾in by length required adding a small amount for extra fullness at the corner. Fold in half lengthways, right sides together, and stitch short edges, taking 1.5cm/⅝in seams. Trim seam allowances, clip corners and turn through.

Run a double row of gathering threads, one each side of the seamline, at the raw edges of the frill, working through both thicknesses of fabric.

1 With right sides together, align the raw edges of the frill with the upper raw edge of the underside of the cuff. Start 1.5cm/⅝in in at the top edge and take the frill down the short side of the cuff nearest the notched lower edge, finishing 1.5cm/⅝in above lower raw edges. Draw up the gathers to fit. Distribute evenly except at the corners where more gathers are required to allow the frill to lie flat when turned through. Pin and tack, then remove pins.

Apply interfacing to wrong side of top cuff. With right sides together,

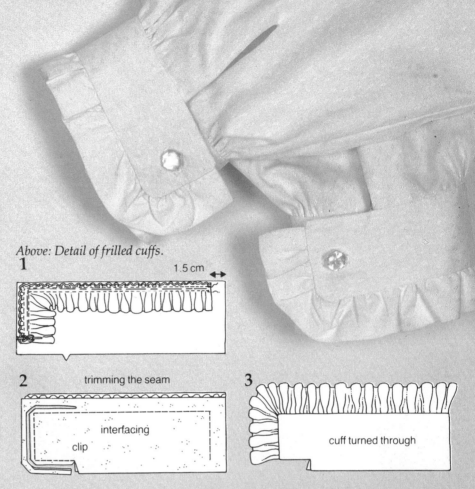

Above: Detail of frilled cuffs.

lay the top cuff over frill and under cuff, sandwiching frill.

Tack the two short edges of the cuff and the long upper edge, sandwiching the frill and going round as far as the notch on the lower edge which now forms the overlap.

2 Machine the seams, taking care not to catch in the free fold edge of frill. Trim the seam, clip the corners

and clip to stitching line at notch on lower edge.

3 Turn the cuff through, pulling the frill gently to ensure the cuff turns through fully.

Press the seams, omitting the frill. Finish the cuffs when attached by sewing the button to the straight edge of the cuff and making the buttonhole in the overlap.

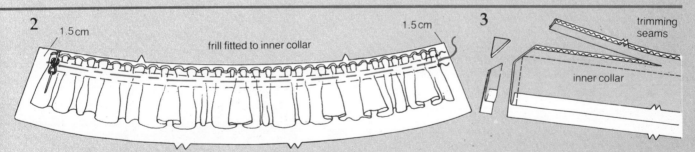

At the front edge of the stand, continue the cutting line up in the same way, until the lines intersect.

2 With raw edges of frill along upper edge of right side of inner collar, pin each end 1.5cm/⅝in from short edges of collar. Draw up gathers to fit, spacing them evenly, pin, tack and remove pins.

3 Apply interfacing to the wrong side of the outer collar. Press 1.5cm/⅝in seam allowance to wrong side along lower edge of inner collar. With right sides together, lay outer collar over inner collar and frill. Tack around the collar through all layers, leaving the neckline seam edge open and being careful not to

catch in the short ends of frill. Machine stitch, cut across corners and trim seams. If the fabric is not too bulky, trim only 5mm/¼in from the upper edge of the seam, as the turnings help keep frill upright. Turn right side out, gently pulling at frill. Tack close to seamed edges and press collar stand only.

Button-through shirt dress with fitted bodice

Choose the fabric carefully, it must be soft enough for the gathered fullness of the skirt to fall attractively but with sufficient body to give shape to the darted bodice. Choose dress weights in natural or synthetic fabrics or blends of both. Soft wool, wool crêpe, jersey, Viyella and brushed cotton are all suitable for cool days. Crisp cottons and cotton blends and silky synthetics are better for warmer weather.

If you are using a boldly patterned fabric use the information given in this and the last chapter to match motifs and as you make up the dress check constantly that right and left sides are level and the motifs correctly aligned.

The buttons are an obvious feature on this dress so choose them carefully, or use covered buttons. Toning plain buttons look effective on patterned fabrics, contrasting ones on plain fabric.

You will need
Dressweight fabric – see fabric
  quantity chart
Matching thread
1m/1yd of 80cm/32in wide
  interfacing
1 press stud
13×1cm/³⁄₈–¹⁄₂in buttons
Optional purchased belt
Pattern pieces, page 138:
   5 Long sleeve
   6 Cuff
   7 Collar stand
   8 Shirt style collar
  15 Dress bodice back
  16 Dress bodice front
  17 Dress skirt back
  18 Dress skirt front
  19 Dress pocket bag

Fabric quantity chart

Size	10	12	14	16	18
Bust (cm)	83	87	92	97	102
(in)	32	34	36	38	40

Long sleeved dress with shirt-style collar

	10	12	14	16	18
90cm**	4.70	4.80	4.90	4.90	5.30m
115cm**	3.20	3.30	3.30	3.40	3.40m
150cm*/**	2.60	2.70	2.80	2.90	2.90m

** without nap.
*/** with or without nap

Cutting out
Make any pattern alterations to bodice (see previous chapter). Position pattern pieces as shown on cutting layouts for your fabric width. Cut out carefully and transfer pattern markings to fabric. Use pattern pieces 7 and 8 to cut a single layer of interfacing for the cuffs. To cut interfacing for the front bodice and front skirt, use the 'attached facing' section of pieces 16 and 18.

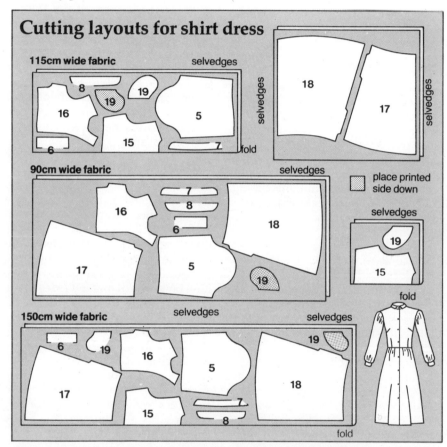

Making up the dress
As it is easier to stitch and press small sections of a garment, complete as much work as possible on the bodice, then on the skirt, before joining them.

Step 1 Machine neaten the outer edge of the front bodice and front skirt facing. Apply interfacing to the front bodice and skirt, catchstitching it along the foldline of the attached facing which will then fold back to cover it. Interface the collar stand, collar and cuffs, and staystitch the neckline edges.

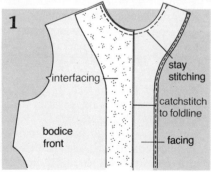

Left: Choose buttons to match one of the fabric colours, or feature the pattern motif on covered buttons.

The shirtwaister – a classic dress

Make yourself this figure-flattering button-through dress using the graph patterns on page 138. The full skirt, gathered into a close-fitting bodice, is ideal for disguising wider hips, while the full and comfortable sleeves guarantee ease of arm movement.

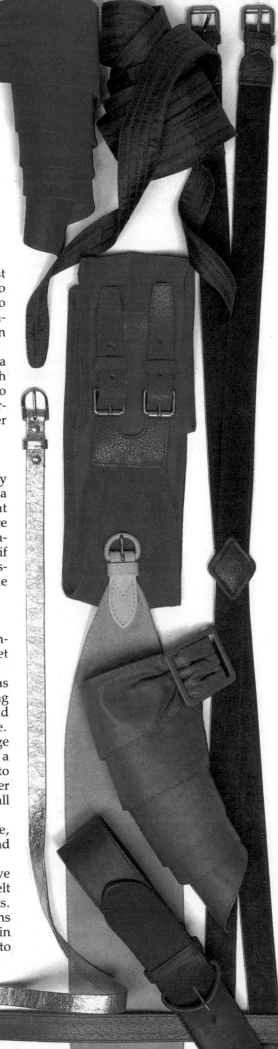

Final fitting and sewing techniques for making up the button-through dress are given in this chapter together with fabric suggestions and making up instructions.

Stitching seams

Great care is needed when using patterned fabric to keep motifs perfectly matched.

Even carefully tacked layers of fabric can move out of alignment during stitching so slip-tack the seams together (see page 80) and leave pins in at right angles while machining. Use an even feed attachment on your machine where possible.

Stitching darts

Bodice waist darts curve slightly inwards following the inner curve from waist to under bust while underarm darts are fairly short and straight – a curve here emphasizes roundness and is not flattering.

You will not be able to match motifs across darts, but it is worth checking where the darts fall before cutting out, to ensure that they will not cut across the design in an ugly way.

Tack darts before stitching and use an even feed attachment on your machine when stitching.

After stitching, press underarm darts down towards the waist, back and front darts towards the centre.

Fitting bodice to waist

The advantage of a waistline seam is that you can adjust the bodice and skirt sections independently but any alterations to the width or length of the bodice will affect the fit of the bodice to the skirt at the waist.

Right: Use different belt widths for the dress (opposite) according to your figure type and the effect you require.

For example, if you take in the waist darts of the bodice you must also draw up the gathers of the skirt to correspond. If the skirt is ungathered, a corresponding alteration should be made to the skirt seams. Check that the waist seam is in a comfortable position. If it is too high it will restrict your movement – too low and the bodice will not fit properly. In both cases the belt will not cover the waist seam.

Pattern matching

Motifs cannot be matched exactly when joining a gathered skirt to a darted bodice except at centre front and back, but it is possible to ensure that the gathers are distributed evenly on the skirt so that the same motif or colour bar occurs at the same position on the right and left sides of the dress.

Choosing belts and buttons

Ready-made belts are easily obtainable but it is not always possible to get just the right colour.

A belt made from the same fabric as the dress or in a toning or contrasting colour adds a distinctive touch and can be made to suit your figure type. A self fabric belt plays down a large waist, a contrast belt emphasizes a slim one. Narrow belts are kinder to short waisted figures whereas wider belts flatter a long back with a small waist.

Whatever type of belt you choose, keep it in place using fabric or thread loops set in the side seams.

If the fabric design has a distinctive motif or colour bar, use it on the belt and repeat it on covered buttons. Make sure that purchased buttons complement the texture on a plain fabric or use shiny buttons and belt to contrast with a matt fabric.

Fitting the bodice

Tack the bodice together and try on.

Align and pin centre fronts from neck to waist and slip shoulder pads in place if required. Check that:

- the fit is easy but not loose at bust and waist.
- waist seamline is at waist level.
- bust darts give fullness at bust level and point towards the bust, stopping 2.5cm/1in from it.
- waist darts are immediately under widest part of bust stopping 2.5cm/1in from bust point on front and below base of shoulder blades on back.
- side seams run vertically from underarm to waist.

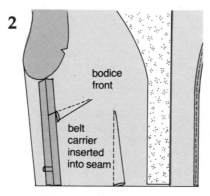

Step 2 Machine back bodice darts and press towards centre back. Machine front waist darts, press towards centre front; and machine underarm darts, pressing towards waist.

Join shoulder and side seams inserting the top of fabric belt carriers (see page 93) 1cm/½in above waistline in each side

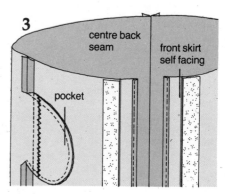

seam if required.
Make up collar and attach to neckline as on pages 124–125.

Skirt
Step 3 Join skirt centre back seam, press open and neaten. Make up pocket bags and attach to side seams (see page 108). Complete side seams.

Joining skirt and bodice
Step 4 Run a double row of gathering threads one either side of the seamline from circle to side seams on front skirt and across full width of back skirt.
With right sides together, matching bodice and skirt side

seams, centres and foldlines, pin skirt to bodice along seamline, drawing up gathers evenly to fit. Include the base of belt carriers if required, at each side seam. Machine. Press seam towards bodice. Trim waist seam allowances to 7mm/⅜in.

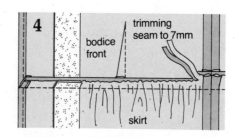

Step 5 Neaten the raw edges by zigzag machining or binding (but not within the area covered by the facing).

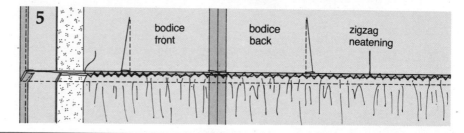

Step 6 Tack fold edge of facing from neck to skirt edge. Press. Catchstitch facing to waist seam. Complete lower edge of facing when the hem is turned up. Make cuffs, attach to sleeves and insert as for blouse (page 126). Complete hem.

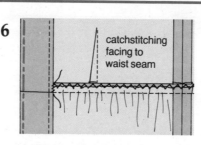

Buttonholes
Step 7 Make ten horizontal buttonholes on right front dress 1.3cm/½in from finished edge. Place the first buttonhole centrally on right collar stand and another 2.5cm/1in above waist seam (to allow for belt). Use

these as markers and space the remainder 9cm/3½in apart – four on the bodice and six on the skirt. Attach buttons on left front to correspond with buttonholes. Secure waist seamline with press stud or hook and eye to prevent it gaping open behind the belt.

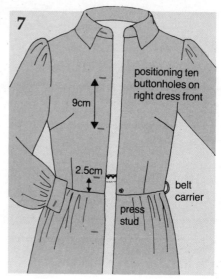

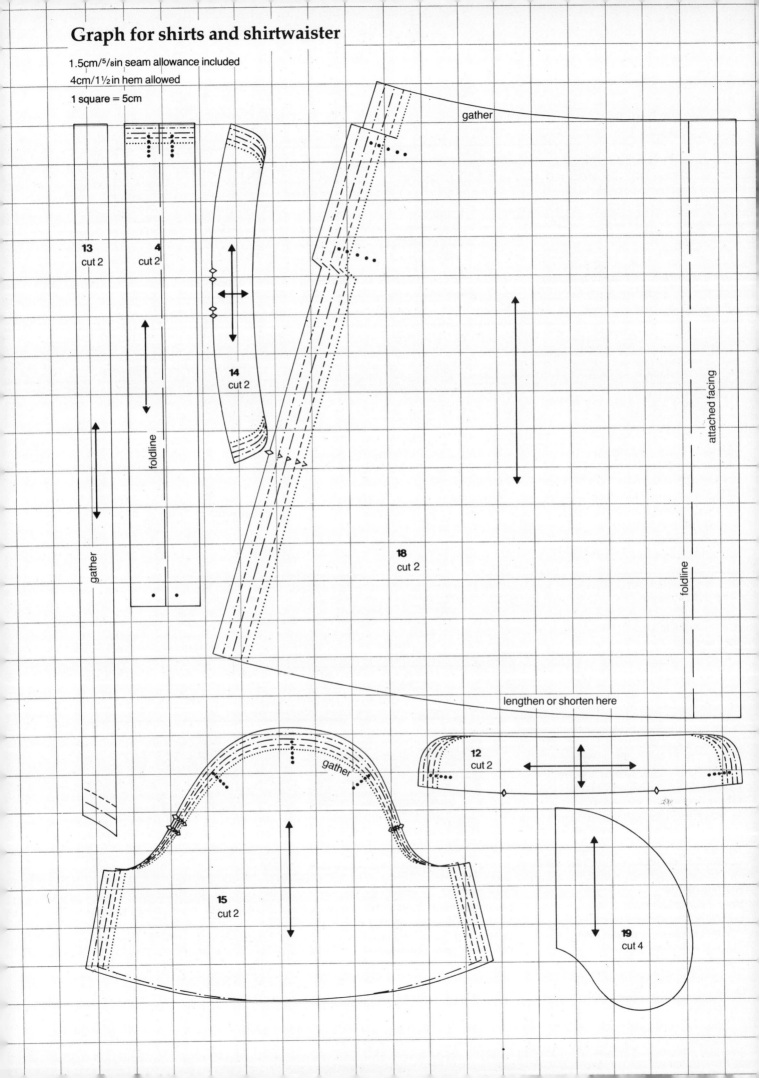

Graph for shirts and shirtwaister

1.5cm/⅝in seam allowance included

4cm/1½in hem allowed

1 square = 5cm

13 cut 2

4 cut 2

foldline

gather

14 cut 2

gather

18 cut 2

attached facing

foldline

lengthen or shorten here

12 cut 2

gather

15 cut 2

19 cut 4

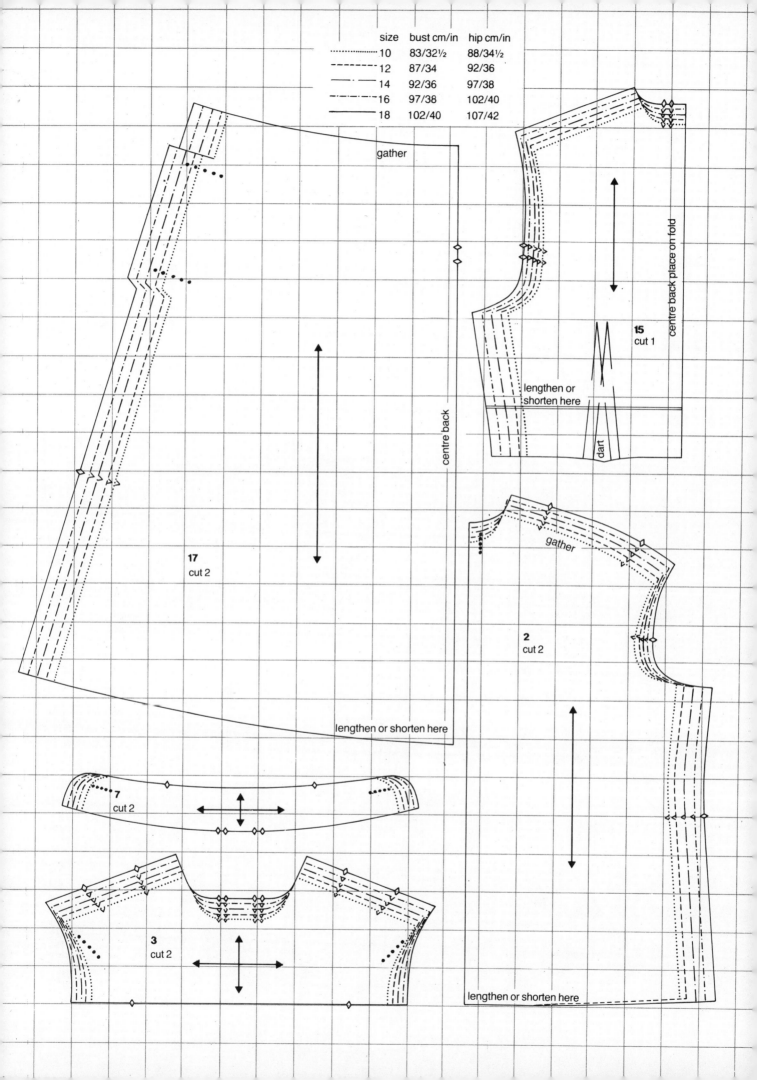

gather

centre back

15 cut 1

centre back place on fold

lengthen or shorten here

dart

17 cut 2

lengthen or shorten here

gather

2 cut 2

7 cut 2

3 cut 2

lengthen or shorten here

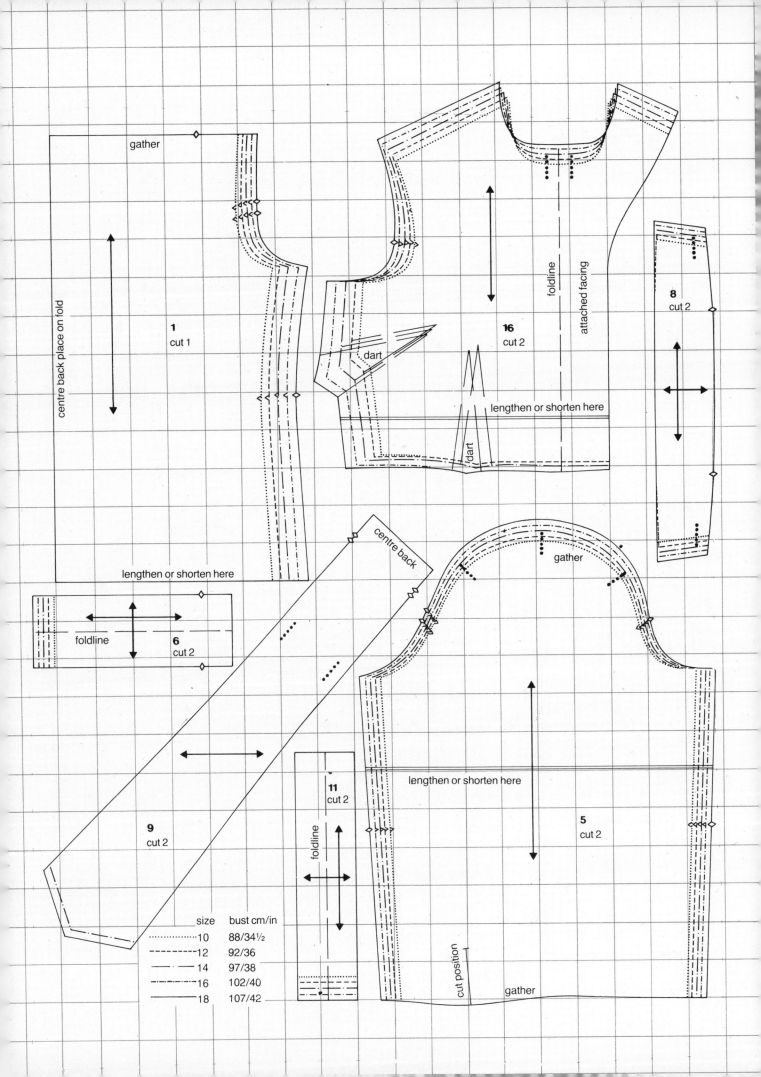

Shorts and trousers

Fashions in length may vary but the basic instructions for making simple summer shorts remain the same. Several new techniques are introduced in this chapter – many of which can be used on other garments. The quick and easy method given for inserting a self-faced fly front zip in the shorts can also be used instead of the more traditional technique described when making up the trousers. Mock turn-ups, faced hip pockets, pocket flaps and a decorative half belt provide stylish touches which can be adapted for use on trousers, skirts and jackets where suitable.

Pattern alterations are important for trousers, especially if you need to disguise figure faults or adapt the leg length. Start with careful measuring up, making basic pattern adjustments as necessary, and then check the fitting stages carefully, using the illustrated guide to common fitting problems when making up.

A half-lining made from the same pattern helps close fitting trousers to retain their shape as well as adding warmth and comfort in wear, particularly if the fabric has a rough texture.

Stylish summer shorts in two lengths

Learn some simple new techniques and make yourself these super summer shorts. The basic design has front tucks, hip pockets and turn-ups and there is a choice of two leg lengths, plus extra design features such as a half-belt or mock back pockets.

You can use the graph pattern on page 143 to make these attractive shorts in two lengths and two sizes; 10–12 (hip 88cm–92cm/34in–36in) or 14–16 (hip 97cm–102cm/38in–40in). The amount of fabric needed is not large so this simple pattern can be used by a beginner as an introduction to trouser making. Many of the techniques are similar to those used in the next three chapters.

Below: Both versions of the shorts.

Fly front zip

This quick and easy method is ideal for casual wear made up in firm fabrics. It gives a smooth, neat finish without the necessity of applying a separate facing or zip shield as given for the true fly front zip described on page 146.

Front hip pockets

The deep, roomy pocket is made using just one pocket pattern piece which is folded into shape.

Mock turn-ups

These are used on the shorter-legged version of the shorts to avoid the bulk of ordinary turn-ups which would interfere with the smooth fit at the top of the leg.

Mock pockets

The 'pockets' consist of decorative flaps which are buttoned-down in position on the back of the shorts. This is another way of avoiding bulk and maintaining a smooth fit.

A decorative half-belt

A half-belt is both decorative and functional, allowing the waistband to be tightened up in wear without altering the garment permanently. The belt consists of two sections which are attached to the back of the shorts and fastened with D-rings. They are positioned so that you can adjust the waistband to fit more snugly by drawing up the half-belt through the D-rings which will prevent it from slipping.

Attaching a front hip pocket

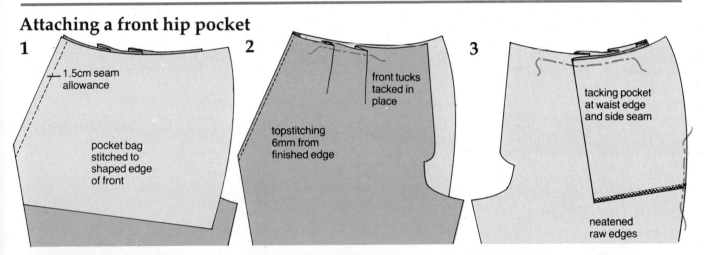

1 With right sides together, matching markings, stitch pocket bags to garment front at side edges.
2 Trim turnings, turn pocket bag to wrong side of garment and press. On right side, topstitch seam 6mm/

¼in from finished edge.
3 On the inside of garment, fold pocket bag, with right sides together along fold line. Stitch across lower edges of pocket bag then zigzag stitch raw edges

together to neaten.
Tack pocket bag at waist edge and down side seams to hold it in position, in preparation for attaching back of garment and waistband.

Fly front zip with self-facing

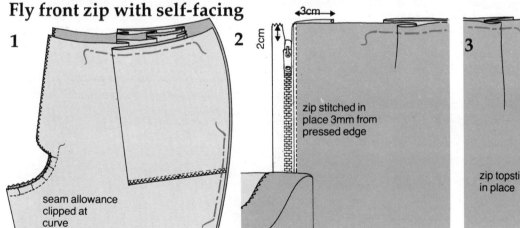
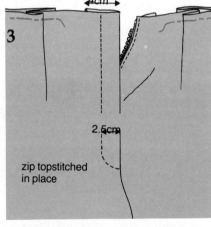

1 With right sides together, stitch centre front seam up to zip marking. Clip into seam allowance at curve and press seam open. Neaten raw edges of seam allowance, continuing the neatening around the curved edge of the fly front facing.

2 On the left front edge, press 3cm/1¼in to wrong side along fly front facing. Place top of zip teeth 2cm/¾in below waist edge and tack through all thicknesses with zip teeth 3mm/⅛in from pressed edge. Using a zipper foot, stitch zip in place.

3 Press 4cm/1½in to wrong side on right fly front facing. Place folded edge so that it just overlaps previous row of stitching and tack through all thicknesses to hold zip in position. From the right side, topstitch 2.5cm/1in from edge, in a smooth curve to base of zip.

Mock pockets

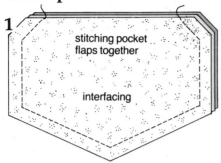

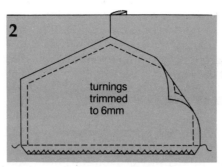

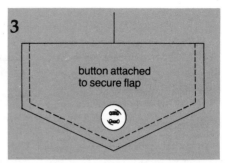

1 Apply interfacing to the wrong side of two pocket flaps. With right sides together, tack an interfaced flap to each of the remaining flaps. Machine stitch around the two short and long shaped edges, following the shaping at the top of the flap. (This gives a neat finish when the flap is stitched in place.)

2 Trim turnings, clip corners and turn right side out and press. Topstitch seamed edges 6mm/¼in from edge. Place right side of flap in position, on right side of garment, with pointed edge towards top of garment. Tack and then stitch raw edge in place, taking a 1.5cm/⅝in turning. Trim turnings to 6mm/¼in and zigzag stitch to neaten edges and secure turnings to shorts.

3 Press flap downwards and attach a button through flap and shorts to hold the flap in position permanently. Reinforce the button position on the wrong side of the shorts with a square of fusible interfacing before stitching.

Mock turn-ups

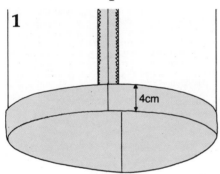

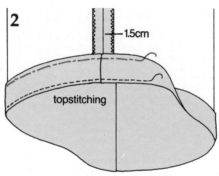

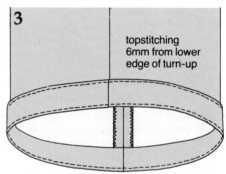

1 Press a 4cm/1½in turning to the wrong side at lower edge.

2 Make another 4cm/1½in turning to the wrong side and tack to hold. Topstitch 6mm/¼in away from outer, folded edge forming a tuck to encase the raw edge.

3 Remove tacking and bring hem down so that tuck turns through to right side. Press tuck upwards and topstitch 6mm/¼in away from lower edge of turn-up.

Making a decorative half-belt

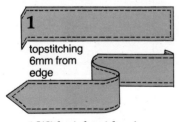

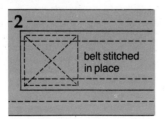

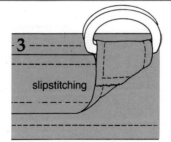

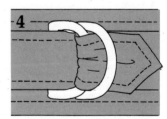

1 With right sides together, fold belt in half lengthwise and stitch around outer edges. Measure 15cm/6in from straight end and cut belt in two. Trim turnings and corners and turn both sections right sides

out. Press. Topstitch 6mm/¼in from seamed edge on both sections. Press under 1cm/½in to wrong side on both raw edges of belt.
2 Place belt sections in position on back

waistband, with pointed section on right back. Stitch them in place by first stitching a square and then stitching diagonally, corner to corner as shown.
3 Thread square end of shorter belt section

through two D-rings and slipstitch securely on wrong side.
4 To fasten, thread other belt section through both D-rings and back through one. Pull up to adjust waistband to size required.

A pair of shorts with a choice of leg lengths

Make up the long version with back pocket flaps and conventional turn-ups, and the short version without back pocket flaps and with mock turn-ups. You can, of course, leave out the back pocket flaps and decorative half-belt in both versions.

Fabric suggestions
Firm cotton, sailcloth, linen, denim and brushed denim, heavy poplin and gaberdine are all ideal for the shorts. Avoid anything too fine and see-through, or too limp, and do not choose thick fabrics, which would make the hip pockets bulky.

You will need
Long version 1.60m/1¾yd of 90cm/36in wide fabric *or.*
1.50m/1⅝yd of 115cm/45in wide fabric
Short version 1.40m/1⅝yd of 90cm/36in wide fabric *or*
1.30m/1½yd of 115cm/45in wide fabric
18cm/7in zip
0.20m/¼yd of 90cm/36in wide interfacing
2×2.5cm/1in D-rings
1×1.5cm/⅝in button (short version)
3×1.5cm/⅝in buttons (long version)
Matching thread

Cutting out
Scale up the pattern from the graph on to dressmaker's graph paper, following the appropriate line for your size. Transfer all notches, pattern markings and cutting instructions. Hem turnings and 1.5cm/⅝in seam allowances are included throughout.
Fold fabric in half lengthwise and position pattern pieces as shown on the appropriate cutting layout. Cut out and transfer pattern markings to fabric.
Cut one waistband and two pocket flaps (if required) in interfacing.

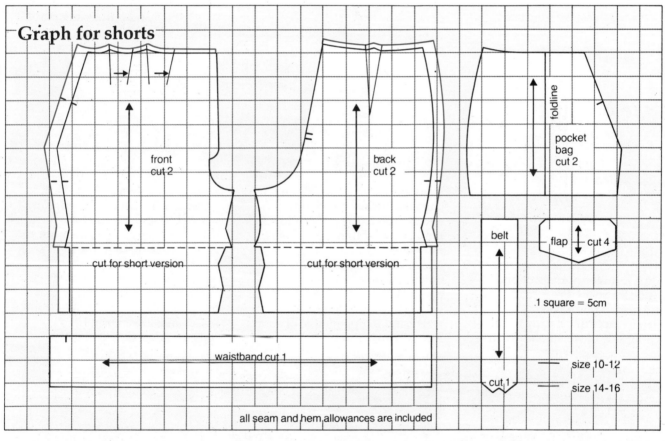

Graph for shorts

front cut 2

back cut 2

foldline

pocket bag cut 2

cut for short version

cut for short version

belt

flap cut 4

1 square = 5cm

waistband cut 1

cut 1

—— size 10-12
—— size 14-16

all seam and hem allowances are included

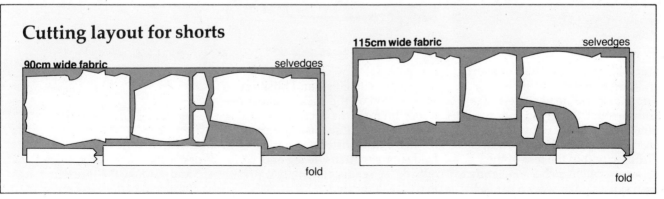

Cutting layout for shorts

90cm wide fabric   selvedges

fold

115cm wide fabric   selvedges

fold

Making the long version of the shorts

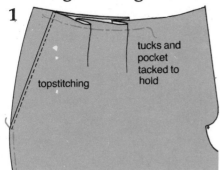

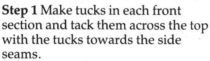

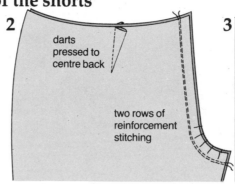

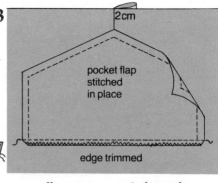

Step 1 Make tucks in each front section and tack them across the top with the tucks towards the side seams.
Make up and attach the front hip pockets, securing them with tacking at waist and side seams.
Step 2 Stitch centre front seam,

leaving 20cm/7¾in open and insert zip following fly front method. Stitch darts in the back of shorts and press towards centre back. With right sides together, matching notches, stitch centre back seam. Work a second row of stitching close to the first, just inside the

seam allowance, to reinforce the seam. Clip into the curves, press seam open and neaten raw edges.
Step 3 Make up and apply mock pocket flaps. Position each flap centrally over back darts, with point of flap 2cm/¾in below upper raw edge; stitch and button into place.

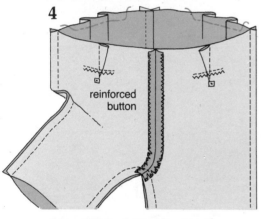

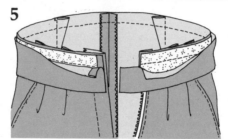

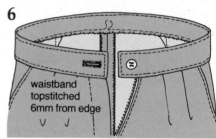

Step 4 With right sides together, stitch front to back at side and inside leg seam. Press seams open and neaten raw edges.
Step 5 Apply interfacing to half of wrong side of waistband. With right

sides together fold waistband in half lengthways. Stitch one short end around to the notch and stitch the other to within 1.5cm/⅝in of raw edges. Trim turnings and corners and snip to stitching at notch. Turn right sides out and press. With right sides together and with extension at left front, stitch waistband to upper edge of shorts.
Step 6 Trim turnings and press

seam towards waistband. Turn under 1.5cm/⅝in on free edge of waistband and slipstitch to previous row of stitching on inside of shorts. Press. Working from the right side, topstitch 6mm/¼in from all edges of waistband starting at centre back. Make a machine or hand-worked buttonhole in centre of right front waistband, 1.5cm/⅝in from finished edge. Sew on button.

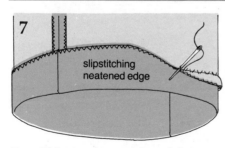

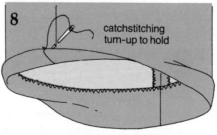

Step 7 Neaten lower edge of shorts and turn 6cm/2½in to the wrong side. Roll back the neatened edge and slipstitch loosely to shorts.
Step 8 Turn shorts right side out and press up 4cm/1½in turn-ups. Working within the fold of the turn-ups, catchstitch them lightly to each side seam or work a bar tack

(see page 61).
Make up the half belt and position each section on the back waistband 2.5cm/1in from the back darts, towards the side seams. Complete the half belt as instructed earlier. Fold shorts with inside leg and outside leg seams matching to press in crease, if desired.

Making the short version
Work as for long shorts, steps 1, 2, 4, 5 and 6. Make the mock turn-ups as instructed earlier.

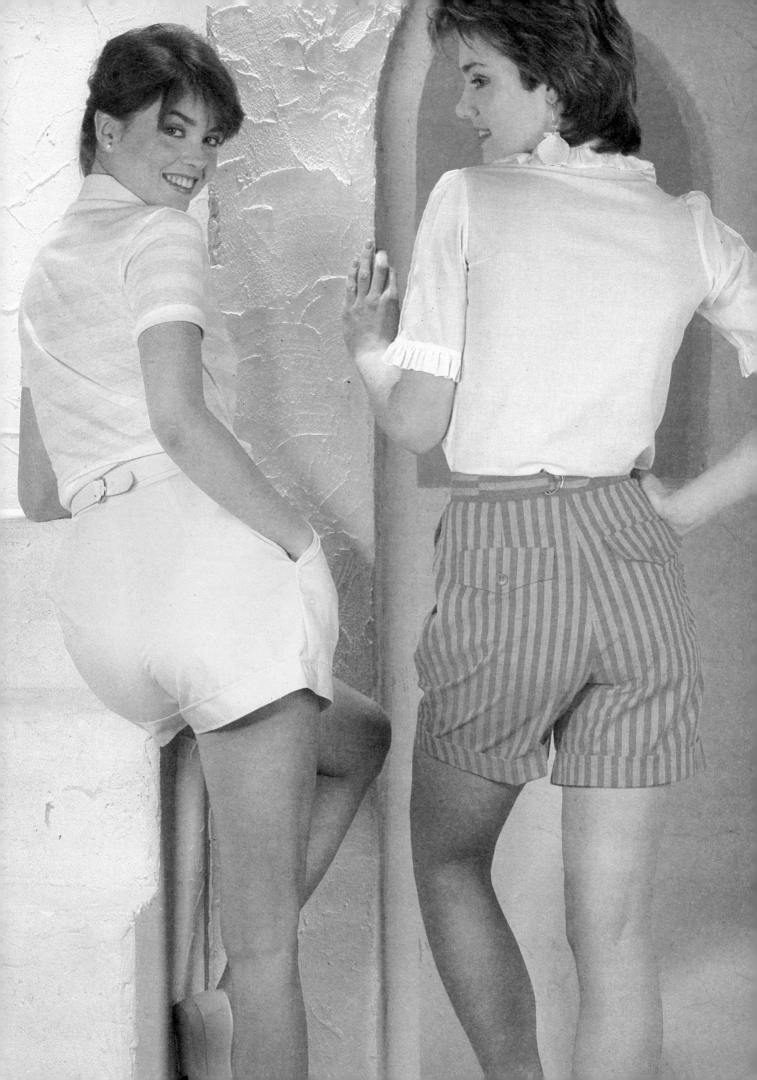

Basic know-how for making well-fitting trousers

Do you avoid making trousers because you are worried about obtaining a good fit? Follow the advice given here and you will find that the secret lies in taking accurate measurements and making pattern alterations before you even start to cut out the trousers.

These trousers from the graph pattern given on page 158 are designed to flatter most figure types. They have front tucks, side slit pockets with topstitching detail, front zip fastening and slightly tapered legs.

If you have already mastered the basic dressmaking processes covered so far, you should have no problems at all when you make up this pattern.

However, many dressmakers find the most difficult thing about making trousers is the fitting. Yet making all major alterations before cutting out will guarantee a good fit.

Pattern alterations

Always choose your trouser pattern size by your hip measurement – the waist line is easier to alter than the hips if it does not match up to your measurements. Before you begin, it is essential to take a full and accurate set of measurements to compare with the paper pattern so that you can make the necessary adjustments. Ask a friend to help you and wear the undergarments you would normally wear under trousers.

Fly front zips

When making up a pattern with a fly front zip, make sure that you buy the right sort of zip. If it is too weak, you will find yourself having to repair or replace it constantly. Choose one that is labelled specially for trousers. It should be straight, with metal teeth and a strong tab which locks when closed. These zips are usually available in basic colours in lengths from 15cm/6in to 23cm/9in.

When inserting the zip, back it the professional way with a zip guard to prevent the zip teeth catching your skin or underclothes. This will also give extra strength to an area of hard wear.

Fabric choice

Choose your trouser fabric carefully – it needs to be soft enough to form the waist tucks and to be comfortable in wear, yet it must be strong and durable enough to withstand quite a bit of strain in sitting and moving.

Inserting a fly front zip with guard

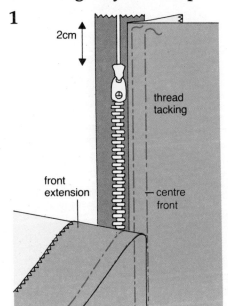

1 Carefully mark seamlines on all sections and thread tack centre fronts. Neaten the edges of the front extensions with zigzag stitching. Turn under the right front extension along seamline and tack to hold, 1cm/½in from folded edge. Fold under left front extension 1cm/½in within seamline to make a narrower turning, and tack.

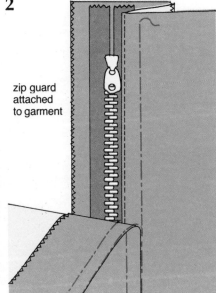

With right side of garment and zip uppermost, place left hand folded edge of opening along teeth of zip with the metal stop 2cm/¾in below top edge of fabric. Pin and tack in place.

2 From matching fabric, and using the selvedge as one long edge if possible, cut a zip guard 6cm/2½in wide, by the length of the

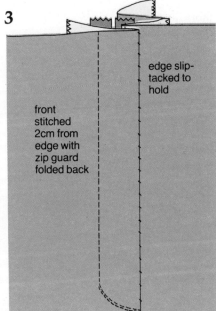

extension. Shape the rectangle to match the curves of the extensions if preferred, and neaten the raw edges.

Place right side of zip guard to back of zip, aligning it to edge of folded back extension of left front. Pin and tack through left front, zip tape and guard close to folded edge.

Working from the right side of the

Avoid a loose, stretchy weave which may split at the seams and pull out of shape. Instead look for a fabric which does not fray readily, with a firm weave that will not show pin or tacking markings. For the best appearance, it should be virtually uncrushable, yet still take a pressed crease.

A particular problem area with trousers is with friction where the trouser legs rub together; this can cause surface roughness – even bald patches in some pure wool fabrics. Ideally, look for a fabric with a percentage of manmade fibre – this helps give some elasticity and helps to prolong its life. Remember, too, that pure wool fabrics, or those with a high percentage of wool may need to be dry-cleaned, so if you think your trousers will get a good deal of wear look for a fabric which is washable.

Cotton, linen mixtures, gaberdine, lightweight wool blends, wool and cotton mixtures, denim, corduroy and synthetics are all suitable.

Fabric requirements, cutting layouts, full making up and fitting instructions appear in the next two chapters.

fabric and using a zipper foot, machine zip in place close to fold. Leaving centre front marking in place, remove other tacking from left front.

3 Lap right front over the zip, matching centre fronts. Slip-tack (see page 80) folded edge to centre front. On the wrong side, fold zip guard back, away from right front so that it is not caught in the stitching. Working from the right side, tack and machine through right front and zip tape 1.5cm-2cm/⅝in-¾in from folded edge, curving towards base of opening. Fold guard back into position and topstitch through all layers of curved section at base only, to reinforce the stitching and hold guard in position. Remove tacking and slip-tacking and press lightly and carefully from the wrong side.

Right: A pair of classically styled trousers with side hip pockets and figure flattering tucks which form a trim, fitted waistline. The slightly tapered legs give a slimming and elongating effect.

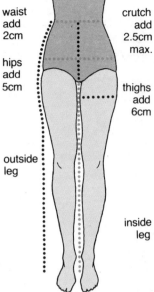

Measuring up

waist add 2cm

hips add 5cm

outside leg

crutch add 2.5cm max.

thighs add 6cm

inside leg

Take all width measurements closely, adding the following allowances for ease, and then check them against the paper pattern but remember that the pattern represents only a *half* garment, and to exclude seams and darts when measuring it.

Amounts for ease
Waist – 2cm/¾in; hips – 5cm/2in; crutch – up to 2.5cm/1in; thigh – 6cm/ 2½in. Inside and outside leg measurements do not require additional allowances, (except for the hem).
If you are unsure of the exact position of your hipline, take a measurement 20.5cm/8in below the waistline. For more advice on taking measurements, see page 20.
To take an accurate crutch depth measurement, sit on a chair, place a piece of string or tape around the waist as a marker and measure from waist to chair, following the line of the hip.

Left: The basic adjustments apply to most patterns.

Making pattern adjustments

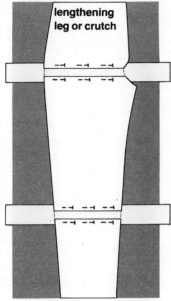

lengthening leg or crutch

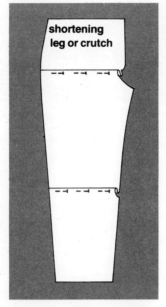

shortening leg or crutch

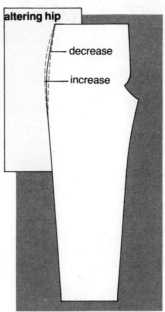

altering hip

decrease

increase

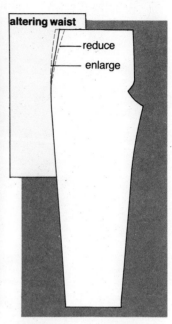

altering waist

reduce

enlarge

Make alterations to length of leg and depth of crutch first, followed by width measurements. Minor adjustments may be made at the first fitting.

Lengthening leg or crutch Cut along the appropriate double alteration lines and spread pattern apart by an amount equal to the extra length required, placing a strip of paper underneath. Ensure that the grain lines are straight and the cut edges parallel and pin or

tape the pattern in place.

Shortening leg or crutch Draw a line above the printed double alteration lines the same depth as the required reduction. Fold the pattern on the alteration line to meet the drawn line and pin or tape in place.

Increasing hip Pin a strip of paper underneath the hip edge of the pattern from waist to crutch level and divide the extra hip width required by four. Draw a new cutting line from the waistline, curving out to the extra

requirement at the hip line and tapering off below the level of the crutch line. Trim away excess paper.

Decreasing hip Use the same principle as for widening the hip but without adding paper, drawing the new cutting line the required distance *within* the original line.

Enlarging the waistline Take slightly smaller tucks or darts. If this alteration is insufficient, make adjustments at the side seams by adding a quarter of the extra

needed on the waist measurement to the waistline, tapering the cutting line down to meet the original line at the hip. Remember to alter the waistband to correspond.

Reducing the waistline Take slightly deeper tucks or darts. If this is insufficient, reduce the waist at the side seams by a quarter of the total reduction required, tapering the new cutting line down to the hipline. Reduce the length of the waistband accordingly.

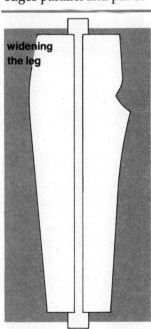

widening the leg

Widening the leg Make minor alterations to the side seams only. If a large alteration is required, affecting the waist and hip as well, leave the side seams as they are and cut the pattern vertically up the centre of the leg from bottom to top. Spread it apart by the required amount, inserting a strip of paper in the gap, and alter the waistband and adjust the tucks accordingly. Do not try and alter the leg part alone as it will distort the finished garment.

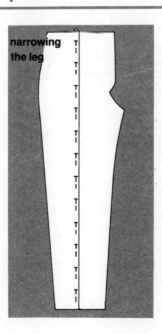

narrowing the leg

Narrowing the leg Take slightly deeper side seams from hip level downwards. If a larger decrease is required, affecting the waist and hips as well, do not try and alter the leg alone as it will distort the finished garment. Make a vertical pleat in the pattern from top to bottom and do not adjust the side seams. Pin or tape it into place. Alter the tucks and waistband to correspond.

149

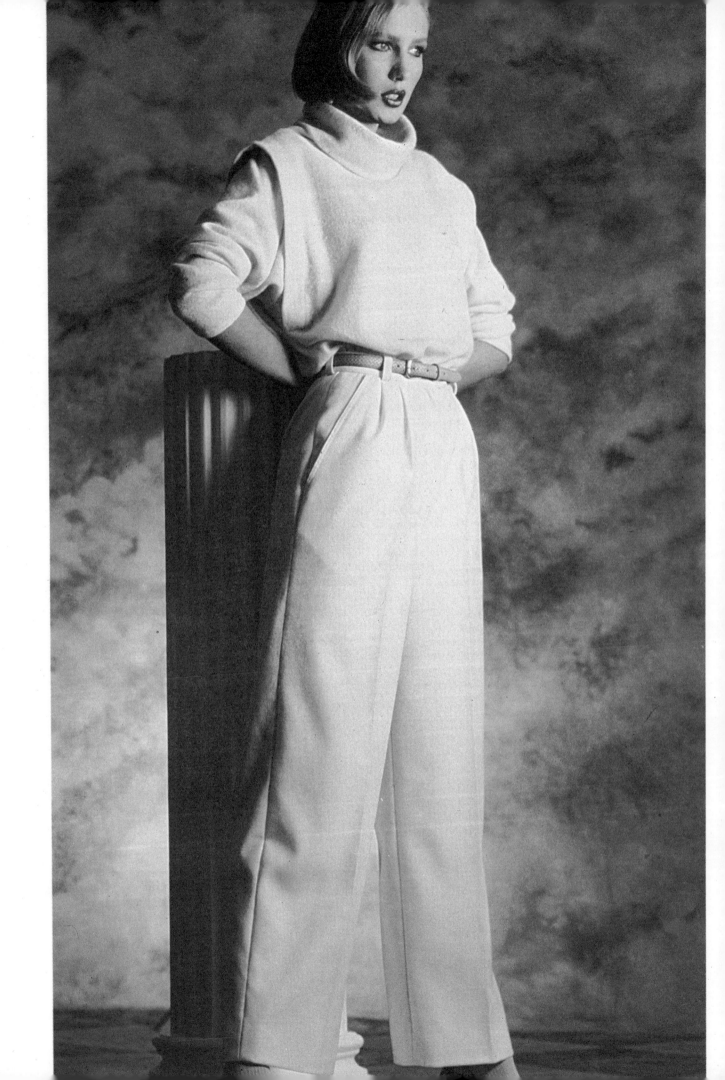

Correcting fitting faults on trousers

*See how easy it is to correct fitting faults and achieve a
smooth look by using the at-a-glance guide
to trouser alterations given in this chapter. Use this when
making up the trousers from the graph on
page 158 or when using any commercial paper pattern.*

Fitting a pair of trousers is slightly
more difficult than fitting a skirt because trousers are generally close-
fitting around the waist, hips and
crutch; it is more noticeable therefore
if they do not fit well. Even though
you learned the basic adjustments for
trouser patterns in the last chapter, the chart overleaf is useful for
pinpointing any other fitting faults
that might appear when the garment
is tacked and tried on. It also shows
remedies to apply when making up.
Use the chart when making up any
fitted trousers pattern and you will
soon learn to recognise the particular
aspects of your figure type that need
attention.

The secret is to make all major alterations to the pattern before cutting
out, saving only minor adjustments
for the making up.

If you have an old pair of well-fitting
trousers, you could use these instead
of adjusting a paper pattern to cut a
new pair. Simply unpick the trousers
carefully, press out the pieces and
either make a copy pattern, or pin the
actual pieces on to your fabric,
adding seam allowances as required.

Preparing to make the trousers

Before cutting out trousers from
the pattern made from the graph (or
from any commercial pattern) make
any necessary length and width
adjustments to all the relevant
pattern pieces following
instructions given on page 149.

Cutting out
Position the pattern pieces for the
trousers as shown on the appropriate
cutting layout below, and cut out.
From leftover fabric cut a
rectangle 6cm×22cm/2½in×8½in to
use as a zip guard. Cut the pocket
and pocket bag pattern pieces (4
and 6) from the lining.
Transfer all pattern markings to the
fabric and mark centre front line
with thread tacking on both front
sections. If you are working on
plain fabric where right and wrong
sides could be confused, then use
tailor's chalk to mark each piece on
the wrong side.
As an aid to fitting before tacking
up the trousers, fold each main leg
piece in half vertically with *wrong*
sides together and press firmly to
give a sharp crease. The back crease
is pressed from crutch level to hem
and the front from the first tuck to
hem. The creases must be on the
straight grain of the fabric. They
should then hang straight at all

*Opposite: To ensure that trousers have a
flattering, smooth fit choose your fabric
carefully and pay attention to pattern
and fitting adjustments.*

times, making it easier for you to
see where fitting adjustments need
to be made. Staystitch all the curves
and the slanted edges of the pockets
on the front sections before starting
to make up the trousers. Full
making up instructions appear on
page 156.

You will need
Fabric according to size
Matching thread
18cm/7in trouser zip
1×15mm/⅝in button
0.15m/⅛yd of 80cm/32in wide
 interfacing
0.50m/⅝yd of 90cm/36in wide lining
0.80m/⅞yd of 90cm/36in wide lining
 for optional half lining.
Pattern pieces, page 158:

1 Trouser front
2 Trouser back
3 Waistband
4 Pocket
5 Pocket facing
6 Pocket bag

Fabric quantity chart
Size	10	12	14	16	18
Waist (cm)	64	67	71	76	81
(in)	25	26½	28	30	32
Hip (cm)	88	92	97	102	107
(in)	34½	36	38	40	42
90cm*		2.50	2.55	2.55	2.55	2.60m
115cm*		2.05	2.20	2.30	2.35	2.35m
150cm		1.30	1.30	1.30	1.50	1.70m

*With or without nap. All other widths
without nap.
Finished inside leg, all sizes, is 77cm/
30½in. Allow extra fabric for longer
lengths and matching checks.

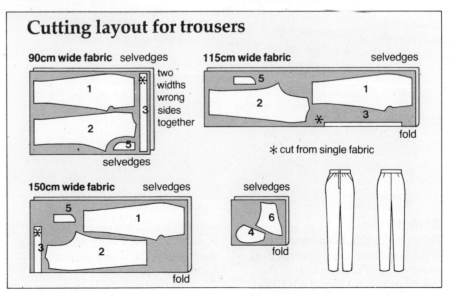

Cutting layout for trousers

90cm wide fabric selvedges
two widths wrong sides together
selvedges

115cm wide fabric selvedges
fold

✳ cut from single fabric

150cm wide fabric selvedges
fold

selvedges
fold

Fitting chart for trousers

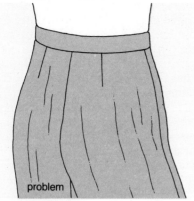

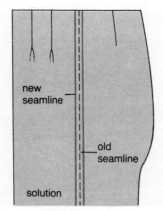

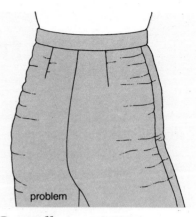

Generally too wide
Fabric hangs in vertical folds throughout.
Solution Take in side seams to give a smooth but comfortable fit and reduce waistband accordingly. Do not alter inside leg seams.

Generally too narrow
Fabric pulls into horizontal folds at waist, hips and thighs.
Solution Let out both inside and

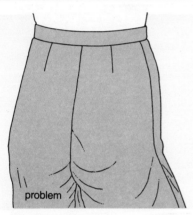

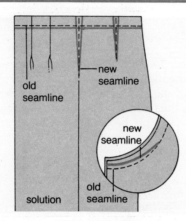

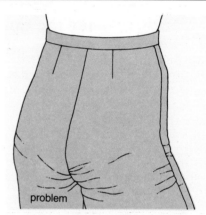

Too long from waist to crutch
Fabric falls in loose wrinkles from crutch down onto upper leg at back and front.
Solution Remove waistband and lift trousers to correct position, then reduce size of waist by taking in at side seams, darts and tucks if necessary. If this is not sufficient, lift crutch seam by a maximum of 1cm/½in as well. Check fit finally with seam allowances snipped around curve and pressed flat.

Too short from waist to crutch
Fabric pulls into tight folds from crutch towards hips on both back and front.
Solution Remove waistband and lower trousers to correct position, increasing size of waist by letting

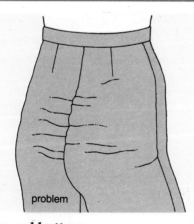

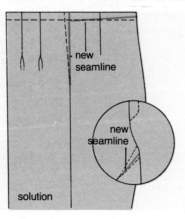

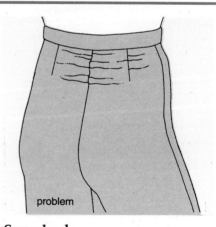

Round bottom
Fabric pulls into horizontal folds across back only. Side seams drag towards back of garment.
Solution Let out upper 10–15cm/ 4–6in of inside leg seams. Raise waistline on back only and shorten darts. Let out the *back* side seam allowance only.

Sway back
Horizontal wrinkles form just below waistband.
Solution Lower waist seamline on back only and increase width of

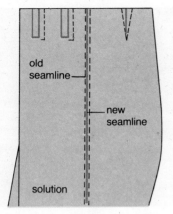

outside leg seams along entire length to give a smooth fit. Release waist darts and tucks a little if necessary and adjust waistband.

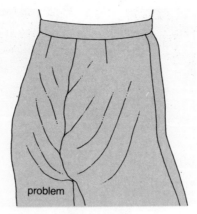

Too wide across back
The fabric hangs in loose, diagonal folds across the seat.
Solution Lower waistline, lengthen

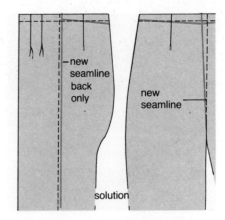

darts and take in *back* side seams only. If necessary, take in at centre back seam by a maximum of 1cm/½in.

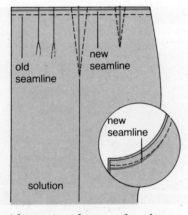

out side seams, darts and tucks. Re-cut the crutch seam in a lower position if necessary, but this will reduce leg length so check whether there is surplus length before making the alteration.

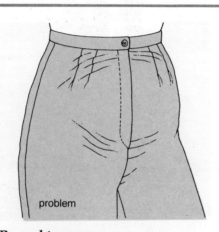

Round tummy
The fabric pulls into horizontal folds just below the waistline. Small wrinkles from crutch towards side seams show on front only.
Solution Let out darts, tucks and *front* side seam allowances and raise

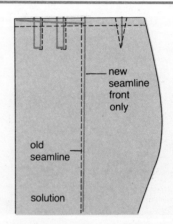

waist seamline to increase width and depth. Shorten darts if necessary.

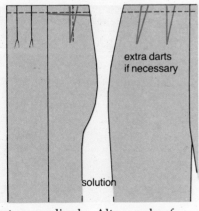

darts accordingly. Alter angle of darts. If this does not correct problem, take four darts instead of two, distributing excess fabric equally.

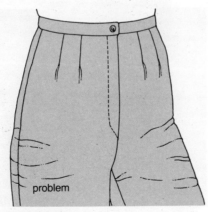

Large thighs
Horizontal and diagonal wrinkles form below hip level and across side seams.
Solution Let out back and front side

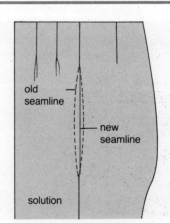

seam allowances from hip to upper thigh.

Making up and half-lining a pair of trousers

This chapter shows you how to complete the trousers made from the graph on page 158. Use the step-by-step making-up instructions together with the pattern alterations and fitting tips on pages 148–149, and add a half-lining for a comfortable, professional finish.

Make up these trousers with or without a half-lining. Amounts of fabric required, cutting layouts together with advice on fitting are given on pages 151–153.

Learn how to make a fabric-covered belt using matching or contrasting fabric for a really professional finish to trousers or skirts.

If you have never before made a pair of trousers, it may help you to pin the paper pattern pieces together first, following the order of making up, so that you understand fully how each stage works. The markings printed on the pattern will help you follow any technique you do not immediately understand. This is particularly useful when making the side slit pockets for the first time, so that you see how the three sections of the pocket fit together.

Half-lining a pair of trousers

If you have chosen a fabric which needs support or a rough wool such as tweed which may irritate the skin, you can half-line your trousers in a similar way to a skirt. This helps to retain the shape of the garment.

Cutting out a half-lining

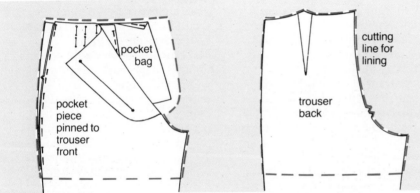

Making the pattern
To obtain the front lining pattern pin together the front, pocket and pocket bag pattern pieces, following the step-by-step instructions for making the trousers but with the tucks released. Turn under the projecting top of the pocket bag. This gives you the basic shape for half the front lining.

Pin these amalgamated front pattern pieces down on to a smooth sheet of tissue or dressmaker's graph paper. Draw round them taking the length to just below seat level, or just above the knee. Trace off a shortened pattern for the back in the same way, giving the basic shape for half the back lining. Transfer dart and tuck markings and any pattern alterations to the pattern pieces before cutting out.

Cutting out the lining
Cut two of each new pattern piece in lining fabric, placing the lower edges of the pattern to the selvedge to avoid making a bulky hem which will show on the right side. Transfer all pattern markings to the lining and make up, inserting it into the trousers before applying the waistband, when all other seams are completed and the zip is in place.

Making up and inserting the half-lining

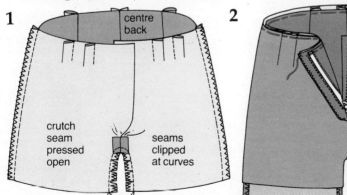

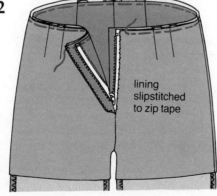

Step 1 Pin, tack and machine darts in back sections and tucks in front pieces. Press.
Join the side seams and centre back seams. Neaten the raw edges with pinking shears or zigzag stitch. Join the crutch seam up to the zip marking and press seam open. Join the inside leg seam, neaten and press. Clip curves.
Step 2 With wrong side of trousers and right side of lining uppermost, slip legs of trousers through legs of lining. Align the waist edges and tack together all around on seamline.
Trim away the excess fabric in the fly facing, fold in the lining seam allowances and slipstitch to zip stitching.

Making up and fitting the trousers

Step 1 Press creases in place on trouser legs (see page 151). With right sides together, matching circles, pin and tack tucks in place on each front.

Step 2 With right sides together, pin and tack darts in trouser back.

Step 3 With right sides together, and matching notches, stitch pocket to trouser front. Trim seam to 6mm/¼in and press it open. Turn pocket through to wrong side of front and lightly press seamed edge from wrong side.

Step 4 Neaten long curved edge of the pocket facing with close zigzag

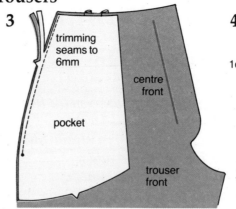

stitching. Place wrong side of pocket facing to right side of pocket

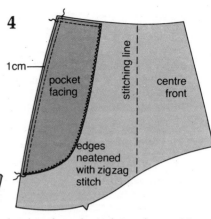

bag, tack and stitch in place taking 1cm/½in turning.

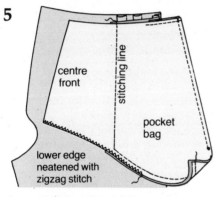

Step 5 With right sides together, matching notches, stitch pocket bag to pocket along lower edge and stitching line parallel to centre front. Trim and neaten lower edge.

Step 6 First fitting Matching centre fronts, tack pocket bag to trousers along centre front, side seam and upper edge.

With right sides together and matching notches, tack left front to left back trouser at side and inside leg seams.

Turn up leg hem and tack.

Repeat for other leg. Turn one leg through to right side and drop it inside the other.

Matching raw edges and relevant markings, tack centre back seam and centre front below zip opening. Fasten ends of tacking

securely, especially on centre front to ensure tacking does not give while trying on. Turn garment to right side and try on. Place a piece of petersham around waist and pin waist seam line of trousers on to it.

Make any necessary adjustments to tucks, darts, side seams and width of leg, ensuring that the leg creases hang vertically. Pin carefully, getting someone to help if possible, then take the trousers off and re-tack any alterations. Try on again to check, then remove petersham at waist.

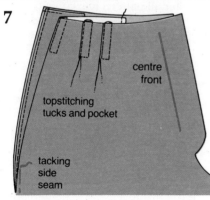

Step 7 Remove tacking at centre back and centre front, and the tacking holding pocket bag in place, in order to expose tucks. With right sides together machine tucks, press them towards centre front and topstitch all round from right side as shown. Re-tack pocket bag and topstitch top of pocket in line with tucks. (If you are careful, and have a free arm on your sewing machine,

all this may be done without removing tacking.)

Step 8 Machine back darts and press towards centre back. Stitch side and inside leg seams and press open. Neaten the raw edges.

Step 9 Second fitting Re-tack centre front and centre back seam as in step 6.

Turn trousers through to right side, re-tack petersham at marked waistline and try on. Lap fly facings and pin into place. At this stage, make any adjustments to crutch seam and waistline, still keeping creases hanging vertically. Alterations to hips can still be made at this stage, but bear in mind that slight creasing around the crutch area will disappear when seam is clipped.

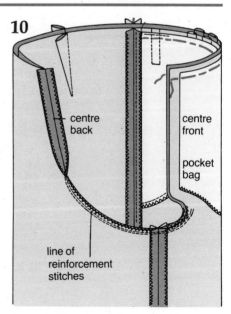

Step 10 Remove waist petersham, re-marking waistline if necessary. Arrange trousers with one leg inside the other as before and

Finishing touches for trousers

Use your knowledge of dressmaking techniques to add some simple finishing touches to the trousers to create an individual look. Mock pocket flaps or a half-belt add interest at the back, while contrast piping used along the pocket edges, or contrast topstitching on the tucks emphasize the lines of the design at the front. You can even add piping to the full length of the side seams, or topstitch them in contrasting thread for effect. Finally, belt carriers in the waistband are a useful addition.

Clockwise: piped seams, turn-ups, half belt, pocket with flap, belt carriers and mock pocket flaps

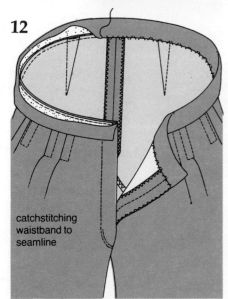

12

catchstitching waistband to seamline

machine crutch seam. Stitch a second row close to the first within the seam allowance, for reinforcement.

Trim curved part of seam close to inner stitching line and zigzag raw edges together to neaten. Press upper part of back seam open and neaten raw edges. Alternatively, clip into the curve up to stitching, neaten, and press seam open. Catchstitch turnings flat at crutch.
Step 11 Insert zip with guard by fly front method (see page 146).
Step 12 Apply interfacing to fold line on wrong side of waistband. Press 1.5cm/⅝in turning to wrong side on long un-interfaced edge. Trim turning to 6mm/¼in, fold band in half lengthwise and stitch 1.5cm/⅝in seams across the two short ends to within 1.5cm/⅝in of raw edges. Trim seams, clip across corners, turn to right side and press. With right sides together stitch interfaced edge of waistband to trousers, aligning one end to the edge of the zip guard and the other to the front folded edge.
Layer seam. Bring pressed edge over to inside and catchstitch all round to previous row of machine stitches.
Step 13 Make a 2cm/¾in horizontal buttonhole centrally on the right front of the waistband, 1.3cm/½in in from the finished edge and attach a button to correspond.

Step 14 Final fitting Try on trousers and adjust leg length.

Step 15 Neaten lower edge and loosely catchstitch hems in place. Press whole garment, including leg creases. If these do not hold well, stitch the crease in place by first tacking and then stitching as close to the edge of the crease as possible. Remove tacking.

Graph for trousers

1.5cm/⅝in seam allowance included
4cm/1½in hem allowed
1 square = 5cm

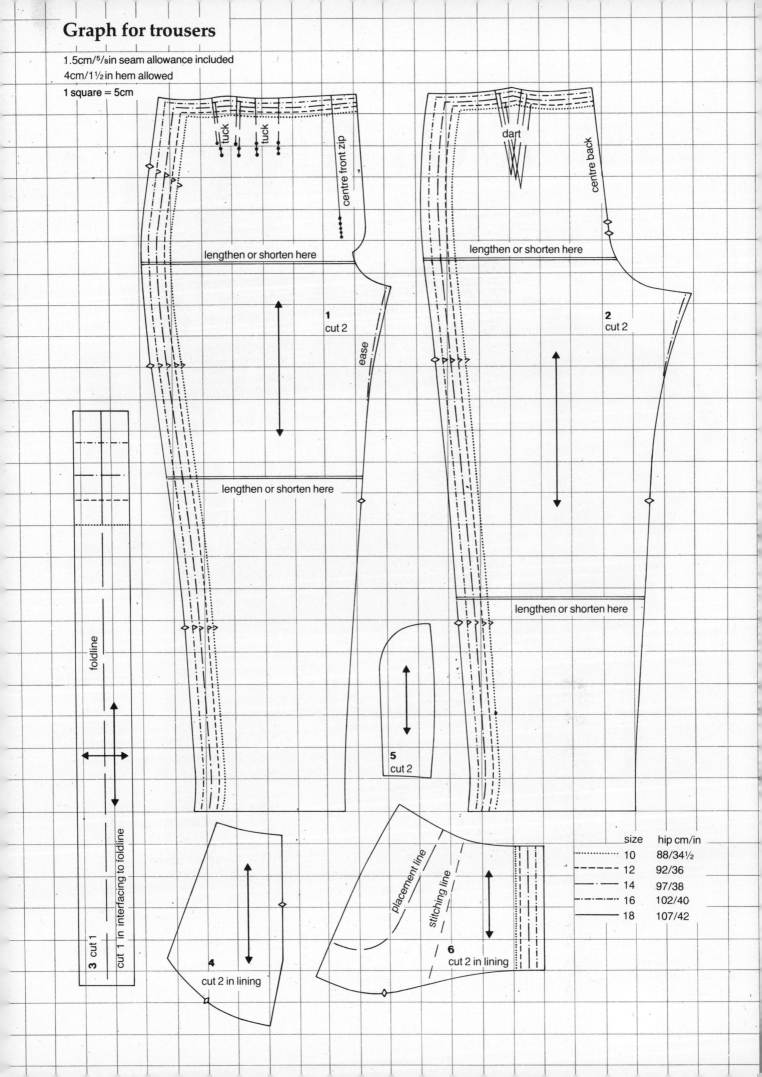

tuck

tuck

centre front zip

lengthen or shorten here

1
cut 2

ease

lengthen or shorten here

dart

centre back

lengthen or shorten here

2
cut 2

lengthen or shorten here

foldline

3 cut 1

cut 1 in interfacing to foldline

4
cut 2 in lining

5
cut 2

placement line

stitching line

6
cut 2 in lining

size	hip cm/in
10	88/34½
12	92/36
14	97/38
16	102/40
18	107/42

PART 2
KNITTING

The knitter's workbox

Knitting is one of the most exciting and rewarding of all the crafts. Every year new and beautiful yarns appear on the market, tools are updated, techniques are modified or rediscovered. This chapter helps you choose the best materials for the job from the wide range available.

alpaca

angora

Basic knitting techniques have remained virtually unchanged for centuries – some of the earliest known knitted items to survive include Arabian sandal socks dating from the third century BC. In Britain the Elizabethan Age was called 'The Golden Age of Knitting', and the knitters were men.

After the frame knitting machine had been invented, the handcraft was continued in Devon and Cornwall by fishermen, and in the Shetlands by sailors.

Today knitting is more popular than ever before – the only problem is choosing from the wide range of yarns and tools available.

Knitting needles are manufactured in a wide range of sizes in order to achieve various tensions. The greater the figure in millimetres, the larger the diameter of the needles. The most durable needles are made from a pale grey, lightweight, plastic-coated metal for smaller sizes. A lightweight, rigid plastic material is used for the larger sizes. These finishes make for smooth knitting and the needles will not break or chip. Almost any colour of yarn shows up against the uniform grey which makes it easier to count stitches.

Pairs of needles For working to and fro in rows to produce a flat section of knitting, needles are manufactured in pairs. Each needle has a smooth working point at one end and a knob at the other. They can be bought in standard lengths of 25/9, 30/11¾ and 35cm/13¾in.

Longer lengths are manufactured but are not so readily available. Large numbers of stitches will need longer needles but personal preference must also be taken into account. Many knitters use long needles so that the left-hand needle can be tucked under the arm to anchor it.

Pairs of colourful plastic needles are also available and children enjoy learning to knit with these. There is a limited range of sizes but they have the advantage of being available in lengths of 15/6, 20/7¾, 25/9¾, 30/11¾ and 35cm/13¾in.

Sets of needles For working in rounds to produce a tubular fabric, needles are manufactured in sets of four or five. Each needle is pointed at both ends. They come in the same size range as pairs of needles and in lengths of 20/7¾ and 30cm/11¾in.

Circular needles These can be used for knitting in rounds or in rows. They comprise two pointed needle ends joined together by a thin strip of flexible nylon. They are not made in as many sizes as pairs of needles and are available in lengths of 40/15¾, 60/23½, 80/31½ and 100cm/39½in. It is important to knit with the correct length of circular needle so that the stitches reach from one needle point to the other.

Other tools Other items in the knitter's workbox include row counters, which fit on to the end of the needle; cable needles – short needles with points at both ends for cabling; stitch holders to keep stitches to be knitted into later while you work the main body of the garment; a needle gauge; a long ruler for measuring sections of knitting; a tape measure for body measurements, a pair of sharp scissors and sewing equipment for joining seams.

Yarn used to mean any natural spun fibre such as wool, cotton or silk, but it now applies to any combination of fibres. The choice is so wide that it is possible to find something to suit all pockets and tastes.

Synthetic yarns are produced by forcing chemical solutions through metal blocks pierced with holes. The size of the holes determines the thickness (denier) of the thread. The extrusion solidifies into long, continuous filaments. Fine filaments are used for tights and stockings. For hand-knitting yarns, thicker filaments are cut into shorter lengths, which are then spun like natural fibres.

All yarns come in standard thicknesses of 2, 3 or 4 ply, double knitting, double double and chunky. The heaviest baby yarn is called quickerknit. Yarns are not spun directly into these thicknesses, but first into plys.

Ply is the term that describes individual spun threads of fibres. These can be fine or coarse and it is a mistake to think that the ply necessarily indicates the finished thickness of any yarn. A Shetland 2 ply can be just as thick as a normal 4 ply.

A yarn containing 4 plys can be made up of three threads of wool and one of nylon, or any combination of natural and man-made fibres.

Twisting the yarn in a variety of ways forms a workable thread that will not break as it is knitted. Untwisted yarn is very bulky and gives a lot of warmth, but it is difficult for the average knitter to use because it pulls apart easily.

Chemical dyeing is a complex process that produces evenly distributed colour of sufficient depth. Natural dyes rarely achieve this overall consistency of colour.

Dyeing is carried out in batches, or

2 ply   3 ply   4 ply

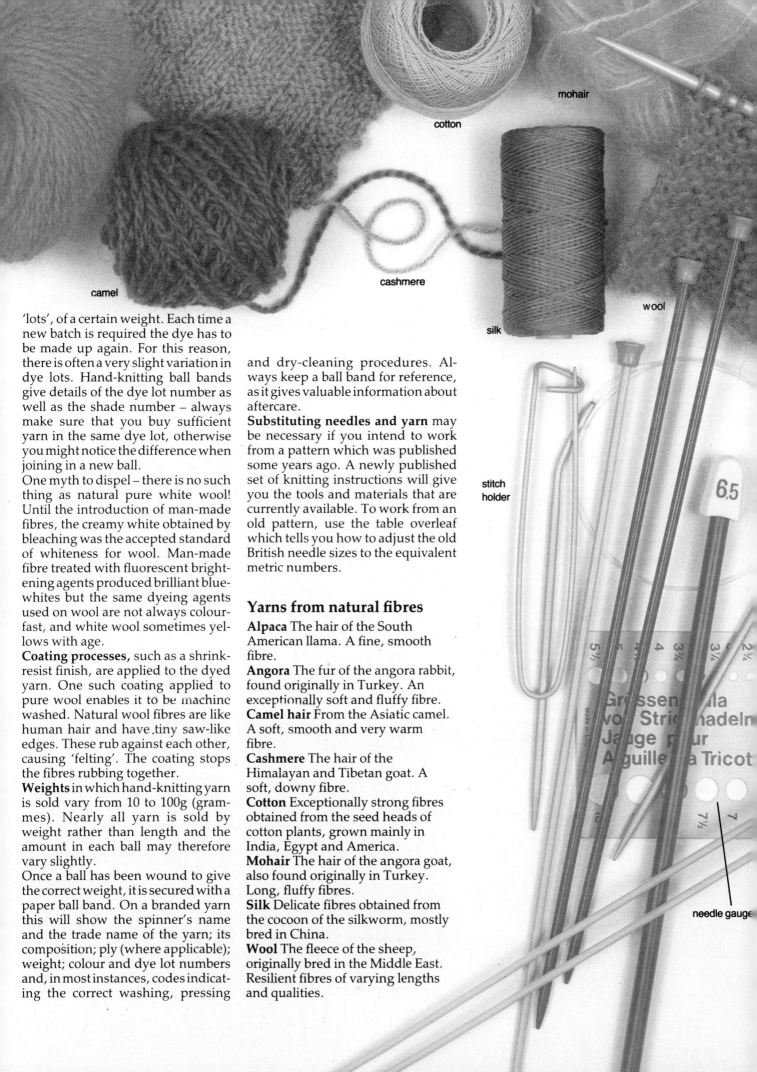

camel

cotton

mohair

cashmere

silk

wool

stitch
holder

6.5

5½   4   3¾ 3¼ 2¾

Grössen   la
wol Stri adeln
Jauge p ur
Aguille a Tricot

7½   7

needle gauge

'lots', of a certain weight. Each time a new batch is required the dye has to be made up again. For this reason, there is often a very slight variation in dye lots. Hand-knitting ball bands give details of the dye lot number as well as the shade number – always make sure that you buy sufficient yarn in the same dye lot, otherwise you might notice the difference when joining in a new ball.

One myth to dispel – there is no such thing as natural pure white wool! Until the introduction of man-made fibres, the creamy white obtained by bleaching was the accepted standard of whiteness for wool. Man-made fibre treated with fluorescent brightening agents produced brilliant blue-whites but the same dyeing agents used on wool are not always colourfast, and white wool sometimes yellows with age.

Coating processes, such as a shrink-resist finish, are applied to the dyed yarn. One such coating applied to pure wool enables it to be machine washed. Natural wool fibres are like human hair and have tiny saw-like edges. These rub against each other, causing 'felting'. The coating stops the fibres rubbing together.

Weights in which hand-knitting yarn is sold vary from 10 to 100g (grammes). Nearly all yarn is sold by weight rather than length and the amount in each ball may therefore vary slightly.

Once a ball has been wound to give the correct weight, it is secured with a paper ball band. On a branded yarn this will show the spinner's name and the trade name of the yarn; its composition; ply (where applicable); weight; colour and dye lot numbers and, in most instances, codes indicating the correct washing, pressing and dry-cleaning procedures. Always keep a ball band for reference, as it gives valuable information about aftercare.

Substituting needles and yarn may be necessary if you intend to work from a pattern which was published some years ago. A newly published set of knitting instructions will give you the tools and materials that are currently available. To work from an old pattern, use the table overleaf which tells you how to adjust the old British needle sizes to the equivalent metric numbers.

Yarns from natural fibres

Alpaca The hair of the South American llama. A fine, smooth fibre.

Angora The fur of the angora rabbit, found originally in Turkey. An exceptionally soft and fluffy fibre.

Camel hair From the Asiatic camel. A soft, smooth and very warm fibre.

Cashmere The hair of the Himalayan and Tibetan goat. A soft, downy fibre.

Cotton Exceptionally strong fibres obtained from the seed heads of cotton plants, grown mainly in India, Egypt and America.

Mohair The hair of the angora goat, also found originally in Turkey. Long, fluffy fibres.

Silk Delicate fibres obtained from the cocoon of the silkworm, mostly bred in China.

Wool The fleece of the sheep, originally bred in the Middle East. Resilient fibres of varying lengths and qualities.

Converting needle sizes

The chart below shows the old British and equivalent metric sizes. A needle gauge giving both sizes will also help you to check old needles, which may not have a size stamped on them.

Imperial	Metric	Imperial	Metric
14	2mm	6	5mm
13	2¼mm	5	5½mm
—	2½mm	4	6mm
12	2¾mm	3	6½mm
11	3mm	2	7mm
10	3¼mm	1	7½mm
—	3½mm	0	8mm
9	3¾mm	00	9mm
8	4mm	000	10mm
7	4½mm		

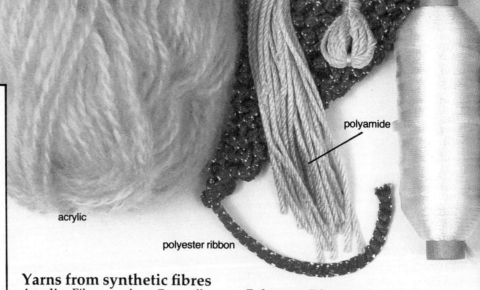

polyamide

acrylic

polyester ribbon

Yarns from synthetic fibres

Acrylics Fibres such as Courtelle and Orlon, derived from natural gas.
Yarns of high bulk and exceptional lightness. They contain pockets of air, which makes them warm to wear.
Polyamides Fibres such as nylon, produced from chemical sources. These fibres are strong yet elastic. They do not absorb moisture, so are not weakened when wet. Nylon fibres feel a little hard but are excellent strengthening agents when combined with wool or acrylics.

Polyesters Fibres such as Terylene and Crimplene, derived from petrol.
These fibres are strong yet light and do not absorb moisture. On their own, they are subject to static electricity, which attracts dirt, but they combine well with other fibres.
Viscose Regenerated fibres such as rayon obtained from the cellulose in waste cotton and wood pulp. These fibres absorb moisture and are good conductors of heat. They are cool to touch and slippery to handle but combine well with other fibres.

Standard aftercare symbols

 A tub indicates that the yarn can be hand or machine washed.

 A hand in the tub means hand wash only.

 A figure in the water shows the correct water temperature.

 Numbers 1 to 9 above the water line denote washing machine programmes.

 Where the tub is crossed through, dry-clean only.

 An iron means the yarn can be pressed – one dot means cool; two dots medium and three dots hot.

 Where the iron is crossed through do not attempt to press the yarn or you may ruin the fabric.

 An empty circle means the yarn can be dry-cleaned.

 An A inside the circle means dry-cleaning in all solvents.

 The letter P means dry-cleaning only in certain solvents.

 The letter F means dry-cleaning only in certain solvents.

 Where the circle is crossed through do *not* dry-clean.

 A triangle means that the yarn can be bleached.

 Where the triangle is crossed through do not bleach.

 Square signs denote drying instructions.

 Three vertical lines in a square mean drip dry.

 One horizontal line in a square means dry flat.

 A circle in a square means tumble dry.

 A loop at the top of a square means dry on a line.

chenille

glitter yarns

viscose ribbon

crepe

knop

slub

bouclé

Fancy Yarns

Bouclé is a loopy textured yarn. Each ply may be of a different thickness, texture and colour.

Chenille is a velvety, tufted yarn which produces a dense fabric.

Crepe is a very highly-twisted yarn, usually 4 ply or double knitting weights.

Glitter yarn is man-made metal threads, used on its own or combined with other fibres.

Slub is an unevenly spun yarn which produces an irregularly textured fabric.

Knop is similar to slub but has small knops in place of thickened streaks.

Converting ounces to grammes

oz balls	25g balls	oz balls	25g balls
1	1	11	13
2	3	12	14
3	4	13	15
4	5	14	16
5	6	15	17
6	7	16	18
7	8	17	19
8	9	18	21
9	10	19	22
10	12	20	23

Abbreviations

A complete list of the abbreviations used in the patterns given in this section can be found on page 246.

Right: This figure-hugging evening top with crossover straps is made from a man-made yarn with a hint of glitter for a touch of glamour.

Casting on and basic stitches

Today's knitting yarns come in a luscious choice of colours and textures. Whether you're an experienced knitter, a bit rusty, or a complete beginner, now is the time to discover how to turn a wealth of traditional stitches into fashionable designs.

Knitting is a straightforward skill that can be picked up in an evening. All you need is a pair of needles, a pattern and some yarn. From there on, learning to knit is like learning to touch-type. It takes a little patience and practice to get the action smooth, with fingers, needles and yarn working in unison. (If you knit jerkily, the knitting will be uneven and bumpy.) There are two basic stitches, knit and purl. They are bread-and-butter stitches, but they combine to produce a vast range of attractive patterns. The following chapters are carefully planned so that skills can be easily acquired. Often techniques are married to projects so that you can make appealing garments as you practise.

How to hold the yarn and needles

1 The needle in your right hand is used to make the stitches, while the needle in your left hand holds the completed stitches.
2 Wind the yarn round the fingers of your right hand so that it flows smoothly and freely over your fingers. This helps you to knit evenly. The main thing is to feel comfortable and relaxed.

PROFESSIONAL TOUCH

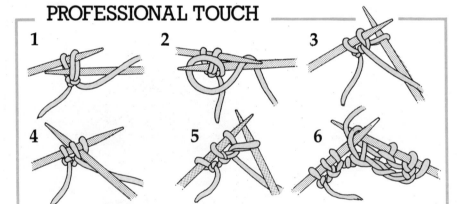

Invisible casting on with two needles

Make a slip loop, then cast on a second stitch.
1 *Insert the right-hand needle from the back to the front between these last two stitches.
2 Take the yarn round the needle as if to purl and **3**, draw the yarn through on to the right-hand needle. Put this new stitch on the left-hand needle taking care not to twist it.
4 Insert the right-hand needle from the front to the back between the last two stitches on the left-hand needle.
5 Take the yarn round the needle as if to knit and draw the yarn

through on to the right-hand needle. Put this new stitch on the left-hand needle taking care not to twist it.
Continue in this way from the point marked with an asterisk (*) until the required number of stitches are made.
With an odd number of stitches begin the next row with a purled stitch – with an even number begin with a knitted stitch.
6 Continue in single rib but on the first row work into the back loop of each knitted stitch, instead of the front.

Casting on with two needles

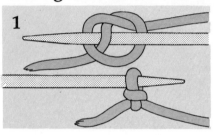

Knitting begins with a slip loop which counts as the first stitch. To make a loop take the main length of yarn across the short end.
1 Using the point of a needle, pull the main length through from the back to the front and leave this loop on the needle.
Draw up the main length to tighten the loop.

Casting on with one needle

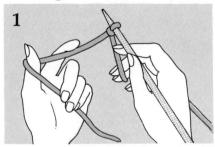

This method uses only one needle because the thumb of the left hand replaces the other needle – so it is sometimes called the thumb method. Begin by making a slip loop about 50cm/20in from end of a ball of yarn. This should be enough yarn to make about 25 stitches in double knitting yarn with 4mm/No 8 needles – leave a

The chapters are also designed to be a useful reference work for experienced knitters – to refresh their memories or unlearn any bad techniques they may have picked up.

Casting on Three methods are given here. Casting on with two needles gives a neat edging and is used with ribbing or stocking stitch. This method is also used when you need to cast on extra stitches further on in the knitting for buttonholes or to extend the shape. Casting on with one needle gives a ridged edge and so is most suitable for use with garter stitch. Experienced knitters will be interested in the invisible casting-on method (below left). This little-known technique gives a professional finish similar to that of an expensive machine-made garment. It is only used with ribbing.

A few helpful hints Hot sticky hands make knitting difficult so always wash your hands. Avoid getting your work dusty by pinning a bag over your work to keep it clean while you knit. Don't stop knitting in the middle of a row, but always continue to the end. Remember not to stick the needles into the ball of yarn as this can split the yarn. When you start to knit a piece which has been left for some weeks, it is a good idea to unpick the last row worked before continuing to knit. This overcomes any distortion of stitches by the needles and eliminates uneven fabric.

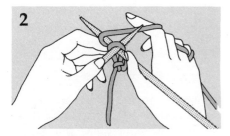

2 Hold the needle with the slip loop in your left hand and the free needle in your right hand, carrying the main length of yarn across your right hand.

3 Insert the point of the right-hand needle into the slip loop from the front to the back, take the yarn under and round the point.

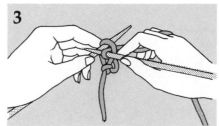

Draw the yarn through the slip loop to make a stitch. Put the new stitch on to the left-hand needle without twisting it.

4 *To make the next stitch insert the needle from the front to the back but this time *between* the two stitches. Take the yarn (as before) under and round the point and draw the yarn

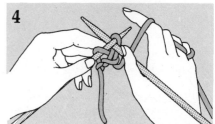

through on to the right-hand needle to make another stitch. Put the new stitch on the left-hand needle without twisting it.

Continue in this way from the point marked with an asterisk (*) until you have cast on the required number of stitches.

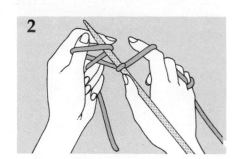

longer end if you are going to need more stitches.

1 Hold the needle with the slip loop in your right hand and wind the main length of yarn round the fingers of your right hand. With the fingers of your left hand hold the end of yarn as shown.

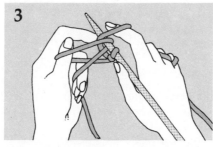

2 *Insert the needle through the loop round your thumb.

3 Take the main length of yarn under and over the point with your right hand and draw the yarn through on to the needle to make a stitch.

4 Leave this stitch on the needle and

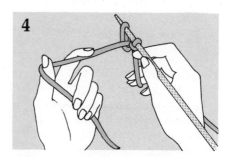

tighten the end of yarn. Wind the end of yarn round your thumb again, ready to make the next stitch.

Continue in this way from the point marked with an asterisk (*) until you have cast on the required number of stitches.

To knit stitches

1

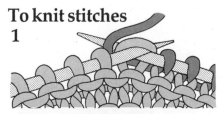

2

3

Hold the needle with the cast-on stitches in your left hand and the free needle and yarn in your right hand.

1 Insert the right-hand needle from the front to the back into the front loop of the first stitch of the row. *Holding the yarn at the back of the work throughout the row, take it under and round the point.

2 Draw the yarn through on to the right-hand needle.

3 Leave this new stitch on the right-hand needle and allow the old stitch to drop off the left-hand needle. One stitch has been knitted and is abbreviated as K1. Insert the right-hand needle from the front to the back into the front loop of the

next stitch. Continue from the point marked with an asterisk (*) until all the cast-on stitches have been knitted on to the right-hand needle. At the end of this row transfer the needle holding the stitches to your left hand, with the yarn again at the right-hand end of the row, ready to start the next row of knitting.

To purl stitches

1

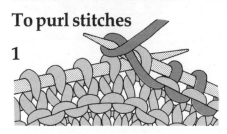

2

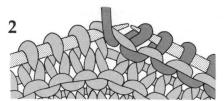

3

Hold the needle with the cast-on stitches in your left hand and the free needle and yarn in your right hand.

1 Insert the right-hand needle from right to left into the front loop of the first stitch of the row. *Holding the yarn at the front of the work throughout the row, take it over the top and round the point.

2 Draw the yarn through on to the right-hand needle.

3 Leave this new stitch on the right-hand needle and allow the old stitch to drop off the left-hand needle. One stitch has been purled and is abbreviated as P1. Insert the right-hand needle from right to left into the front loop of the next stitch.

Continue from the point marked with an asterisk (*) until all the cast-on stitches have been purled on to the right-hand needle. Transfer the needle holding the stitches to your left hand, with the yarn again at the right-hand end of the row, ready to start the next row.

To knit and purl in the same row

1

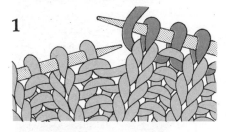

2

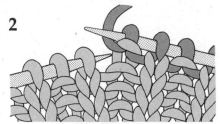

You can build up interesting reversible patterns by knitting and purling in the same row. When changing from a knit to a purl stitch remember to hold the yarn in the correct position. Bring it forward

between the needles to purl and take it back between the needles to knit. If you don't, the yarn will be carried across the right-hand needle and you will find you have created an extra stitch.

Stocking stitch

When the first and every following odd-numbered row is knitted and the second and every following even row is purled, it produces stocking stitch.

The right (knitted) side of this pattern is the smoothest of all knitted fabrics. The wrong (purled) side is called reversed stocking stitch. It does not look the same on both sides.

Garter stitch

(The three stitches shown here are all reversible, which means they look the same on both sides.)

When each stitch in every row is knitted, this is called garter stitch. The effect is a horizontal, ridged pattern.

It can be made quickly and without too much concentration so it is ideal for a beginner. Unlike stocking stitch, a slight unevenness of stitch is acceptable.

Single ribbing

Working single knit and purl stitches alternately across a row – K1, P1, K1, P1 – produces single ribbing, which is reversible. Remember to bring the yarn into the correct position when changing between knitting and purling.

All the stitches which were *knitted* in the previous row must be *purled* and all the purled stitches must be knitted.

It holds its shape very well and is used for cuffs and neckbands.

Basket stitch

This reversible pattern needs a number of stitches cast on which will divide by six, eg 30.

1st row *Knit 3 stitches, called K3, purl 3 stitches, called P3, continue from the * to the end.
Repeat this row 3 times more.
5th row *P3 stitches, K3 stitches, continue from the * to the end.
Repeat the 5th row 3 times more.
These 8 rows form the pattern, which resembles woven basketwork.

Start with a mohair scarf

A mohair scarf is a welcome luxury in cold weather – better still, its fluffiness conceals the uneven fabric that some beginners may produce. The design uses two reversible stitches shown in this chapter. If you wish, the scarf can be worked entirely in garter stitch, single rib or basket stitch. It measures about 18cm × 142cm/7in × 56in.

You will need
5 × 25g balls of Jaeger Mohair Spun, plain or with glitter
One pair 5½mm/No 5 needles

Scarf
Cast on 30 stitches by the one-needle method.
Work 10 rows garter stitch.
Work 16 rows basket stitch. 26 rows in all.
Repeat these 26 rows 11 times more.
Work 10 rows garter stitch.
Page 16 shows you how to cast off and complete your scarf.

Right: Soft and fluffy, this reversible mohair scarf is easy to knit and luxurious to wear.

Casting off and simple seams

Casting off is an art in itself. Discover the different techniques used for casting off on a knitted, purled, or ribbed row and a really original way to deal with that ugly last loop which even experienced knitters sometimes get at the end of the cast off row. Knowing how to join in new yarn and seam sections together properly gives your knitting a professional finish.

Casting off is the method used for finishing off a completed section of knitting or for certain types of shaping such as armholes or shoulders.

When you are ready to cast off, continue to knit or purl the stitches in the cast-off row as the pattern dictates. If the stitches are not cast off in the correct pattern sequence, you will spoil the appearance of the work and make seaming more difficult.

Aim to keep the cast off stitches regular and even, otherwise this edge may pull the whole garment out of shape.

Some instructions emphasize that stitches must be cast off loosely, for example at a neck edge where the fabric needs to be flexible. If you find you cast off too tightly, use one size larger needle in your right hand to work the stitches, before casting off.

Three ways of casting off

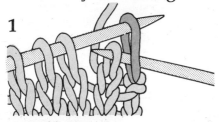

1

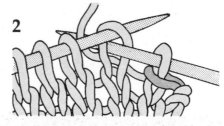

2

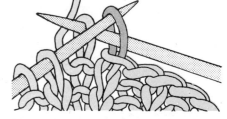

Casting off on a knitted row
Knit the first two stitches in the usual way and leave them on the right-hand needle.
1 *Insert the left-hand needle into the first of the stitches worked on to the right-hand needle. Lift this over the top of the second stitch and off the needle. One stitch has been cast off and one stitch remains on the right-hand needle.
2 Knit the next stitch and leave this on the right-hand needle. Continue from the point marked with an asterisk (*), until all the stitches have been cast off and one stitch remains on the right-hand needle.

Fasten off this last stitch by breaking yarn, leaving an end 10cm/4in long. Draw this end through the last stitch and pull it up tightly.

Casting off on a purled row
Work this in exactly the same way as for casting off on a knitted row, but purl each stitch instead of knitting it, before casting it off.

Casting off on a ribbed row
Rib the first two stitches and leave them on the right-hand needle.
*Insert the left-hand needle into the first stitch worked on the right-hand needle. Lift this over the top of the second stitch and off the needle. Rib the next stitch and leave this on the right-hand needle. Continue from the point marked with an asterisk (*), until all the stitches have been cast off and one stitch remains on the right-hand needle. Fasten off this last stitch.

Seaming

For successful results in knitting you need to pay as much attention when sewing sections together as when knitting them.

Following chapters give full and detailed instructions for different methods of seaming and joining. Each method has a specific purpose and will help to give your garments a professional finish.

The four sections of the mohair T-top overleaf are sewn together using a flat seam, one of the two simple and effective methods given below.

Always tack the pieces together first as this will help you to ensure that you match stitches and row ends. This is important when knitting stripes.

Simple flat seaming

Flat seaming is suitable when you have been knitting with thick yarn. (Use a finer yarn of the same shade if you are sewing up mohair because it is almost impossible to sew with.) Use a blunt-ended sewing needle with a large eye.

Put the right sides of both sections of knitting together and sew from right to left.

Secure the yarn at the beginning of the seam with a few running stitches. Place the first finger of your left hand between the sections.

*Sewing one stitch in from the edge, push the needle through from the back section across to the corresponding stitch on the front section. Pull the yarn through. Move along the width of one row. Push the needle through the front section to the corresponding stitch on the back section. Pull the yarn through.

Continue in this way from the asterisk (*), along the seam. Finish off with running stitches to secure the yarn.

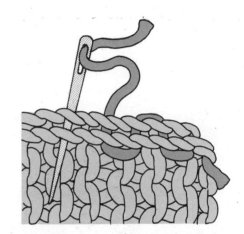

Simple oversewn seam

This method can be used to join stitches to row ends or along any edge where the minimum of bulk is required. It should also be used to join ribbing and fine fabrics.

It draws the edges together very neatly, but take care not to pull the sewing yarn up too tightly as it will form a tight ridge.

As with flat seaming, use a blunt-ended needle with a large eye. Place the two edges together with the right sides facing each other. Secure the yarn at the beginning of the seam with a few running stitches.

*Take the needle over the top of the edges and through one loop at the edge on both pieces. Pull the yarn through.

Continue in this way from the point marked with an asterisk (*), along the seam to give a lacing effect. Keep the stitches even and do not draw them up too tightly. Finish off with a few running stitches to secure the yarn.

PROFESSIONAL TOUCH

Neatening the last loop

Fastening off the last stitch in a piece of knitting can sometimes leave an ugly, loose loop, which makes seaming difficult. There is a simple way to solve this, whether the last stitch has been knitted or purled.

Cast off in the normal way until one stitch remains on the left-hand needle and one on the right-hand needle. Slip the stitch on the left-hand needle on to the right-hand needle without working it or twisting it.

Use the left-hand needle to pick up the back loop only of the last stitch on the row below from the back to the front. Leave this loop on the left-hand needle.

Put the last stitch on the right-hand needle back on to the left-hand needle and work this and the picked-up loop together as one stitch. Use the left-hand needle to lift the first stitch over the top of the second stitch and off the needle. Fasten off this last stitch.

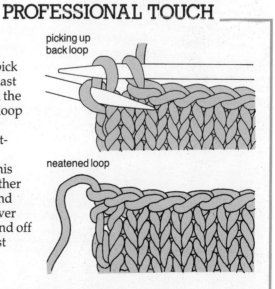

picking up
back loop

neatened loop

Joining in a new ball of yarn

Whether you are knitting with just one colour of yarn or using stripes of different colours, you must always join in a new ball at the beginning of a row, never in the middle. This means you have to judge how much yarn you need to work the last row of the ball. Usually, a piece of yarn about four times the width of the knitting is enough to knit a row.

Joining with a reef knot

Where the same colour is being knitted throughout, join the new ball to the finished one with a reef knot. Take the end of the old ball of yarn from left to right over and under the end of the new ball. Take the same end from right to left over and under the other end, to form a loose reef knot.

When this piece of knitting has been completed, tighten up the reef knot. Darn in the ends along the edge of the fabric, before beginning to seam.

Joining with a slip loop

Where coloured stripes are being

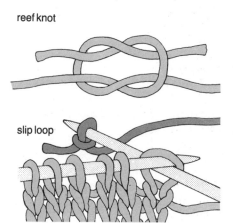

reef knot

slip loop

Left: This sparkling mohair sweater is simple to knit and easy to wear.

T-shaped mohair jersey

Often the most effective designs are the simplest. If you are working with a dramatically beautiful and textured yarn such as mohair, you want to choose stitches and shapes that let the yarn speak for itself, rather than compete. It is a beginner's bonus that the fluffy texture of mohair will disguise uneven knitting.

This T-shaped jersey is knitted in four pieces – two identical pieces for the front and the back, and two identical pieces which combine yoke and sleeves. In this simple pattern none of the pieces needs shaping.

It can be knitted in three colours, as photographed left, or all in the same colour. (If you knit it all in one colour you will need 15 balls of yarn.) As you change colour you change stitch, but you can knit the whole jersey in garter stitch or basket stitch if you prefer.

Sizes

The jersey will fit a medium bust size, 86–91cm/34–36in, loosely Length to shoulder, 57cm/22½in

You will need

7×25g balls of plain Jaeger
 Mohair Spun (67% mohair,
 28% wool, 5% nylon) in
 colour A
5×25g balls of Jaeger Mohair
 Spun with glitter in colour B
3×25g balls of plain Jaeger
 Mohair Spun in colour C
One pair 5½mm/No 5 needles

knitted, such as with the mohair jersey left, join in each new colour with a slip loop. The first stitch will then be in the new colour. Break off the old colour, leaving an end to be darned in along the back of the last row in this colour. Form the end of the new ball into a slip loop. Insert the right-hand needle into the front of the first stitch of the row. Put the slip loop on to the right-hand needle and pull this loop through to complete the stitch in the usual way. Continue knitting with the new colour.

Dropped stitch

This is not easy for a beginner to put right as it must be picked up and worked in according to the pattern. Therefore take care to check the number of stitches at the end of every row. This may seem time-consuming, but it is easier than discovering you have dropped a stitch several rows back. As an emergency measure if you have been unlucky enough to drop a stitch in the row you have

just worked, secure it with a small safety pin. This will stop it unravelling.

On the next row, when you reach the dropped stitch put it back on to the left-hand needle and continue. This may leave an unworked thread, but is not as unsightly as a ladder.

Back and front

With plain yarn in colour A cast on 78 stitches by the one-needle method. This is the bottom of the jersey and should measure 48cm/19in across after you have knitted about 5cm/2in. If it is more than this you are knitting too loosely. Unravel this piece of knitting and start again with 5mm/No 6 needles. If it is less, you are knitting too tightly and should change to 6mm/No 4 needles.
Work 10 rows garter stitch. Break off yarn. Join in glitter yarn in colour B with a slip loop.
Work 16 rows basket stitch. Break off yarn. Join in plain yarn in colour A with a slip loop.
Work 10 rows garter stitch. Break off yarn. Join in plain yarn in colour C with a slip loop.
Work 14 rows stocking stitch. Break

off plain yarn in colour C. Join in yarn in colour A with a slip loop. 50 rows have been worked.
Repeat the first 36 rows once more. Cast off.
Make another piece in same way.

Yoke and sleeve section

With plain yarn in colour A cast on 36 stitches as given for body.
Repeat 50 pattern rows as given for body 4 times in all, then first 36 rows once more. Cast off.
Make another piece in same way.

To make up

Do not press, as this will flatten garter and basket stitch. Darn in all ends – see joining with a slip loop. Check the rows of stocking stitch to see which is the right side of each piece.

With right sides of yoke together and edges without any yarn changes (see diagram), join top arm and shoulder with flat seams, leaving 27cm/10¾in open in centre for neck. Turn in a few stitches at neck edge and lightly stitch down to neaten.
Mark centre of yoke and centre of body pieces with a contrasting coloured thread. Join cast off edge of body pieces to centre of yoke and sleeve sections (see diagram). Join side and sleeve seams.

Above: Two examples of alternative colourways from the Jaeger Mohair Spun range in which to knit your jersey.

Making up guide

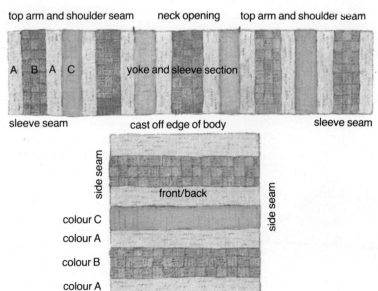

top arm and shoulder seam   neck opening   top arm and shoulder seam

A B A C   yoke and sleeve section

sleeve seam   cast off edge of body   sleeve seam

side seam   front/back   side seam

colour C
colour A
colour B
colour A

How to read knitting patterns

The key to successful knitting lies in following the pattern exactly – and this means knowing how to read and carry out the instructions. Once you understand how patterns work you will always be able to knit a garment as attractive as the one in the picture.

Before you begin to knit – even before you buy the yarn – always make sure to read your pattern thoroughly from beginning to end.

The designer works out tension, yarn thickness and needle size to suit the style of the garment and the pattern of the fabric, and these must be followed exactly for good results. Pay particular attention to the making-up section – even a simple shape may require intricate seaming or trimming.

Pattern writers use abbreviations and symbols in knitting instructions to save space. If in doubt, refer to the list of abbreviations given on page 246 at the end of this section.

Patterns give instructions in full for a specific stitch or technique the first time it is used, followed by its abbreviated form. From then on, only the abbreviation is given.

Symbols also denote working methods. A single asterisk, *, means

Pattern problems

1

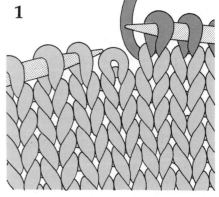

Fortunately there are ways of rectifying your mistakes if you should happen to misread a knitting pattern. If you have misread a pattern row, throwing the following rows out of sequence, follow the instructions opposite to unpick the stitches – only pull your knitting off the needles as a last resort! If you drop a stitch and it has unravelled for a number of rows it will spoil the look of your knitting. You can use a crochet hook to pick it up.

Left: The golden rule when knitting a garment from a pattern is to read the pattern thoroughly from beginning to end even before you go out to buy the yarn.

that the instructions that follow it must be repeated to the end of the row, or until a given number of stitches remains at the end of the row. Further instructions for working these remaining stitches will be given to complete the row.

An asterisk can also indicate that instructions will be repeated at a later stage in the knitting. When knitting a jersey, the pattern for back and front may well be the same to a certain point. A double asterisk, **, signals the end of the repeat.

Any instructions in round brackets, (), apply to all sizes. Instructions shown in square brackets [], denote larger sizes.

The instructions in knitting patterns are divided under a series of headings.

Sizes

This heading gives the finished measurements of the garment, the smallest size first, the larger sizes following in order in square brackets []. Some designs are given only in small sizes because they would not flatter a more generous figure. Some patterned designs are given only in one size because the pattern repeats are so large that one more or less would not give a standard size.

If you underline the figures that apply to your size you will be able to pick them out more quickly as you knit.

You will need

This heading lists the type and brand name of the yarn needed; the needle sizes and any additional tools such as cable needles; and trimmings, such as buttons. Make sure you have everything to hand before beginning to knit.

Tension

This heading gives the key to perfect knitting. Check your tension very carefully, especially if you are using a substitute yarn.

Note

This heading draws your attention to any unusual aspect of the pattern, such as the use of separate balls of yarn to work a coloured pattern.

Making up

This section tells you how to assemble the pieces you have knitted and add any finishing touches. Pay as much attention to these instructions as you did to the rest of the pattern for a really professional finish. Check with the ball band whether you should press the yarn, particularly if you have used a substitute. Sew the pieces together in the order given in the instructions – you may have to add edgings and trimmings before seaming. Never skimp on trimmings – it is better to buy a little too much ribbon than to find yourself short.

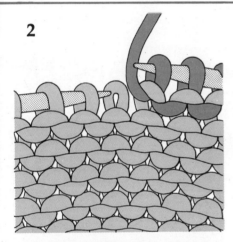

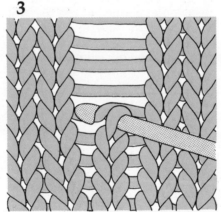

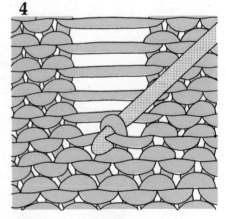

1 To unpick stitches on a knit row
Insert the left-hand needle from the front to the back into the stitch *below* the first stitch on the right-hand needle. Remove the right-hand needle and pull the yarn to unravel the stitch. Keep the yarn at the *back* of the work and repeat this process until the required number of stitches have been unpicked.

2 To unpick stitches on a purl row
Insert the left-hand needle from the front to the back into the stitch *below* the first stitch on the right-hand needle. Remove the right-hand needle and pull the yarn to unravel the stitch. Keep the yarn at the *front* of the work and repeat this process until the required number of stitches have been unpicked.

3 To pick up a dropped stitch on knitted side of stocking stitch
Insert a crochet hook from front to back through the dropped stitch. Put the hook under the thread lying between the stitches on each side of the dropped stitch. Pull this thread through the dropped stitch and leave it on the hook. Repeat this process until the dropped stitch is level with the last row worked. Put the loop on to the left-hand needle and knit it.

If the last row being worked is a purl row, turn the work to the purl side and purl the loop.

4 To pick up a dropped purl stitch in a patterned row
Insert the crochet hook from back to front through the dropped stitch. *Put the hook over the thread lying between the stitches on each side of the dropped stitch and pull this thread through the dropped stitch. Slip the loop on to a cable needle and remove the hook. Insert the hook into the loop again and continue from * until the dropped stitch is level with the last row worked. Put the loop on to the left-hand needle and purl it.

To pick up a dropped stitch in garter stitch
Alternate the knit and purl methods to keep the ridged sequence correct.

Alternative methods of casting on and off

This chapter explores the various ways of keeping your knitting neat to give your garments a professional finish. You can practise keeping in shape by knitting a clinging vest and baggy leg warmers – the ideal gear for exercising to keep yourself in shape too!

If you want to achieve a neat finish, you need to be able to keep the top and bottom edges of your knitting really straight. Depending on the garment you are knitting, you can choose methods of casting on or off to give a firm, elastic or lacy finish.

Casting on neatly

Looped casting on is a variation of the one-needle method. It forms a very loose cast-on edge, ideal for lacy patterns where a hard line would spoil the softness of the fabric. It is not suitable for ribbing or closely textured patterns.

Picot casting on forms a strip of picot loops and is a two-needle method. Instead of casting all the stitches on to one needle, you make a picot loop for each stitch. When you have the right number of stitches, you pick up the loops along one side of the strip with the free needle. The other side of the picot loops forms a dainty edge, ideal for baby garments.

Double casting on forms a very strong but flexible edge just right for husky outer garments. You use two needles, both held in your right hand, to work a variation of the thumb method of casting on.

Invisible casting on gives single ribbing a really professional finish. The ribs appear to run right round the cast-on edge, as with a ready-to-wear garment. You use the thumb method and a length of contrast coloured yarn, which is later removed. After casting on, the stitches are increased on the first row and the next four rows form a very elastic double fabric. You then continue working in single ribbing for the required length.

Casting off neatly

Single decrease casting off forms a very elastic edge and does not leave a hard ridge. It is the perfect method to use when you are working in stocking stitch.

Suspended casting off stops you casting off too tightly. You can use it to cast off in any pattern.

Eyelet hole casting off forms a row of eyelet holes as the casting off row is being worked. It makes an ideal waistband for baby garments, as you can thread ribbon or elastic through the eyelet holes. You need an odd number of stitches to work this method to cast off in any pattern.

PROFESSIONAL TOUCH

Invisible casting on

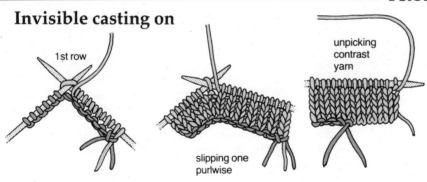

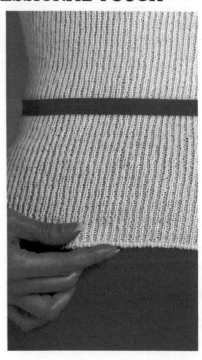

Simple invisible casting on, see page 164, is an easy way of achieving a neat edge over any number of cast-on stitches. This method is worked over an odd number of stitches. Use the thumb method and a length of contrast coloured yarn to cast on half the total number of stitches required plus one extra – 15 cast on stitches will give a final total of 29 ribbed stitches.
Change to the correct yarn and two needles. Begin the double fabric which forms this edge.

1st row K1, *yfwd to inc 1, K1, rep from * to end.
2nd row K1, *yfwd, sl 1 purlwise, ybk, K1, rep from * to end.
3rd row Sl 1 purlwise, *ybk, K1, yfwd, sl 1 purlwise, rep from * to end.
Rep the 2nd and 3rd rows once more.
6th row K1, *P1, K1, rep from * to end.
7th row P1, *K1, P1, rep from * to end.
Continue in rib for the required length. Unpick the contrast yarn used for casting on.

Above: A very neat method of casting on avoiding the common problem of a tight unsightly edge. It gives the appearance of having been cast on by machine.

Looped casting on

Use one needle. Make a slip loop in the end of a ball of yarn and put it on the needle.
1 *Hold the needle in your right hand and loop the yarn round the thumb of your left hand in a clockwise direction.

2 Insert the needle up under the loop just made and remove your thumb from the loop. Pull the yarn up tightly with your left hand. Continue in this way from * until the required number of stitches have been made.

Picot casting on

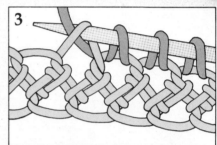

Use two needles, one in each hand. Make a slip loop and put this on the left-hand needle. Cast on one stitch by the two-needle method.
1 *Yfwd and hold at the front ready to take it across the right-hand needle to make an eyelet increase, sl the first st off the left-hand needle

on to the right-hand needle in a purlwise direction, K the second st on the left-hand needle.
2 Lift the sl st over the K st and off the right-hand needle. Turn. Continue in this way from * until the required number of loops have been made. On the last row omit

the yfwd and fasten off.
3 To begin knitting work across these loops just as though they were cast-on stitches. Rejoin the yarn with a slip loop and pick up and knit one stitch into each picot loop along one edge, then continue knitting the rows in the usual way.

Double casting on

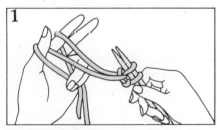

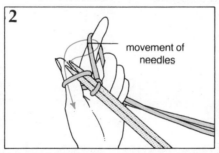

movement of needles

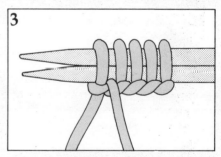

Use two needles, both held in your right hand. Make a slip loop in a ball of yarn as given for the thumb method. Put this loop on both needles. Take the short end of the ball of yarn from the slip loop and the main length from the ball and hold them together in the palm of your left hand.
1 *Put the slip loop end round your thumb in a clockwise direction and the main length round your forefinger in a clockwise direction.

2 Put both needles up and under the loop round your thumb, then down and under the loop round your forefinger and down and under the thumb loop again. Release the loop on your thumb and tighten the stitch on the needles with an upward movement of your right hand, without releasing the ends of yarn held in the palm of your left hand.

3 Continue in this way from * until the required number of stitches have been made. Withdraw one of the needles from the cast-on stitches then continue knitting in the usual way.

Single decrease casting off

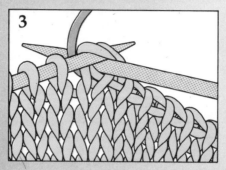

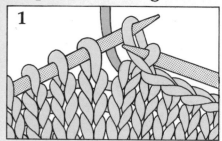

To cast off on a knit row.
1 Use the right-hand needle to knit the first two stitches on the left-hand needle together.
2 *Put this stitch back on to the left-hand needle.
3 Knit this stitch and the next stitch on the left-hand needle together. Continue in this way from * until all the stitches have been cast off. Fasten off.
To cast off on a purl row, purl the stitches together.

Suspended casting off

To cast off on a knit row, work the first two sts in the usual way.
1 *Lift the first stitch worked on to the right-hand needle over the second but instead of allowing it to drop off the right-hand needle, retain it on the point of the left-hand needle.

Camisole, vest and leg warmers

This clinging ribbed camisole (or vest) and matching baggy leg warmers make the ideal gear for exercise classes.

Sizes

To fit 81 [86:91:97:102]cm/ 32 [34:36:38:40]in bust
Camisole length to shoulder, 58cm/ 24in adjustable
Vest length to shoulder, 76cm/30in adjustable
Leg warmers length 70cm/27½in adjustable

The figures in [] refer to the 86/34, 91/36, 97/38, 102cm/40in

You will need

Camisole 4 [4:5:5:5]× 25g balls of Jaeger 3 ply wool (100% botany wool) in main colour A, 1 ball of same in contrast colour B
Vest 6 [6:7:7:7] balls in main colour A, 1 ball in contrast B
One pair 2¾mm/No 12 needles
Set of four 2¾mm/No 12 needles *or* circular needle, 60cm/24in long
1.50m/1½yd ribbon, 5mm/¼in wide

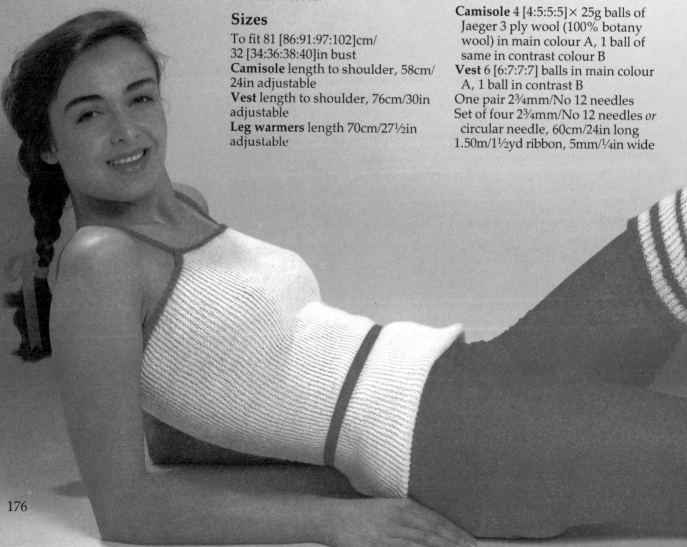

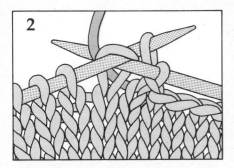

2 Pass the right-hand needle in front of the held stitch and work the next stitch, then slip this stitch and the held stitch off the left-hand needle together. Two stitches remain on the right-hand needle. Continue in this way from * until all the stitches have been cast off. Fasten off.
To cast off on a purl row, purl the stitches before casting them off.

Eyelet hole casting off

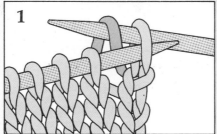

To cast off on a knit row, knit the first stitch on the left-hand needle.
1 *Yfwd and hold across the right-hand needle to make a stitch, lift the first stitch on the right-hand needle over the made stitch and off the needle.

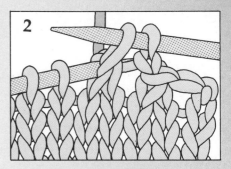

2 Knit the next two stitches on the left-hand needle together, lift the first stitch on the right-hand needle over the knit 2 together and off the needle.
Continue in this way from * until all the stitches have been cast off. Fasten off.
To cast off on a purl row, purl the stitches instead of knitting them and yrn to make a stitch.

Leg warmers 3 × 50g balls of Jaeger Luxury Spun Double Knitting (90% wool, 10% alpaca), in each of two colours, A and B
Sets of four needles in each of sizes 3mm/No 11, 3¼mm/No 10, 3¾mm/No 9, 4mm/No 8 and 4½mm/No 7

Tension

Camisole/vest 45 sts and 42 rows to 10cm/4in over *unstretched* rib worked on 2¾mm/No 12 needles; **leg warmers** 30 sts and 32 rows to 10cm/4in over *unstretched* rib worked on 3¾mm/No 9 needles

Camisole or vest

With 2¾mm/No 12 needles and separate length of contrast yarn cast on 122 [130:138:146:154] sts with the invisible method shown in this chapter. Work the first 6 rows as given.
7th row Using set of four 2¾mm/No 12 needles or circular needle, P1, *K1, P1, rep from * to last 2 sts, K1, then join work into a round by P the last st tog with the first st. 242 [258:274:290:306] sts.
Cont in rounds (see page 60) of K1, P1 rib until work measures 38cm/15in for camisole or 56cm/22in for vest, or required length to underarm. Join in B and work 4 more rows. Using B cast off by the eyelet hole method shown in this chapter.

Straps

With 2¾mm/No 12 needles and B cast on 7 sts.
1st row Sl 1, K1, (P1, K1) twice, K1.
2nd row Sl 1 knitwise, P1, (K1, P1) twice, K1.
Rep these 2 rows until strap measures 40cm/15¾in or length required. Cast off.

Leg warmers

With set of four 3mm/No 11 needles and A cast on 88 sts and arrange in a round. Cont in rounds of K1, P1 rib, working in striped patt as follows:
8 rounds A, 2 rounds B, 6 rounds A, 4 rounds B, 4 rounds A, 6 rounds B, 2 rounds A, 8 rounds B, 4 rounds A, 6 rounds B, 8 rounds A and 4 rounds B.
These 62 rounds form the patt and are rep throughout, *at the same time* when work measures 14cm/5½in from beg change to 3¼mm/No 10 needles, when work measures 28cm/11in change to 3¾mm/No 9 needles, when work measures 42cm/16½in change to 4mm/No 8 needles and when work measures 56cm/22in change to 4½mm/No 7 needles. Cont until work measures 70cm/27½in or required length. Cast off loosely.

To make up

Do not press.
Camisole or vest Take out contrast yarn from lower edge and join ends of first few rows. Sew on straps. Thread ribbon through eyelet holes at top edge to tie at centre front.

This trim camisole top and bright leg warmers keep you warm while exercising.

How to increase

Adding five ways of increasing to your basic techniques widens your knitting horizons considerably. Each of the methods described here has a different purpose. One method, decorative increasing, is used in the pattern for making a shawl for a baby or for yourself.

Whether a jersey fits well or not depends on the basic concept behind its design, and one of the most critical aspects of design is the shaping. Knitting patterns usually indicate when shaping is about to begin but do not always give details of the exact method to use. Knowing which is the best method for the job is the mark of a professional.

To increase means to add or make stitches and there are various ways of increasing the width and varying the shape of knitting. Single stitches added at regular intervals to the ends of the rows gradually change the shape of the knitting, such as when shaping a sleeve. Stitches added at intervals across the row change the shape of the knitting from within, creating panels such as those often found on matinée jackets. Large numbers of stitches added on at the ends of rows alter the outline of the knitting immediately, as with sleeves worked all in one with the body.

This chapter gives you four methods for increasing gradually and one for adding multiples of extra stitches and it gives you the necessary information to select the best method for you. **Working twice into a stitch** is the simplest way of increasing and it is used to make an extra stitch at each end of the same row, as in sleeve shaping. It is abbreviated as inc 1

Working twice into the same stitch

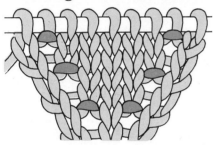 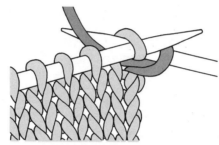 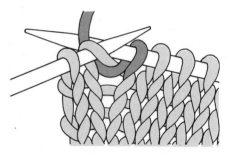

Note: When increasing at the end of a row, work the increase one stitch earlier to ensure that the position of the pip is the same on the right edge as on the left. (Because the extra stitch is formed one in from the edge seaming is easier.)

To increase a knitted stitch at the beginning of a row
Work the first stitch but do not drop it off the left-hand needle. Insert the right-hand needle into the *back* loop of the same stitch and knit it again, then drop the stitch off the left-hand needle.

To increase a knitted stitch at the end of a row
Work until two stitches remain on the left-hand needle. Knit twice into the next stitch as at the beginning of a row, then knit the last stitch.

Increasing between stitches

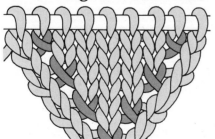 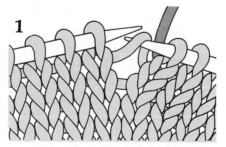 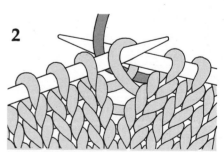

Note: If you work three stitches (for example) and increase one and on the next increasing row you work three stitches and increase one, the increase slants to the right. If you work an extra stitch each time before increasing, it slants to the left.

To make one in a knitted row
1 Work until the position for the increase is reached. Use the right-hand needle to pick up the thread lying between the stitch just worked and the next stitch on the left-hand needle. Put this loop or. the left-hand needle.

2 Knit into the *back* of the loop, this twists the stitch and avoids a hole in the fabric. (Knitting into the front leaves an open space beneath the increased stitch.)

(increase one).

The extra stitch always appears after the stitch it is worked into, making a little 'pip' in the fabric. It is ideal for use in garter stitch where the pip will not show. Do not use it in stocking stitch, particularly in the middle of a row, as it affects the smooth texture of the knitting. Never use this method to increase more than one stitch at a time.

Increasing between stitches is the method used for increasing in the middle of a row. It does not spoil the appearance of the fabric and so is the best method for increasing patterned stitches where the pip increase would spoil the sequence of the pattern. It is also suitable for stocking stitch and can be used to increase at the ends of each row. It is abbreviated as M1 (make one).

This method is particularly useful for picking up stitches on either side of a central stitch, as on v-neck shaping.

Decorative increasing (also known as eyelet hole increasing) is another method for increasing at any point in a row.

It forms an eyelet hole in the fabric and is abbreviated in various ways (see Decorative increasing overleaf), depending on whether you are knitting or purling and forms the basis of most lace patterns. This method involves putting the yarn over or round the needle which makes an extra stitch without knitting one.

Invisible increasing is a useful method of increasing, so called because it is hard to detect. It is used on stocking stitch because it is the only method which does not spoil the appearance of this stitch. It can be used at each end of a row, inside the edge stitches or in the middle of a row and so is very versatile.

This method is particularly useful for increasing three or four consecutive stitches in a row because if you keep the extra stitches fairly loose it does not affect the tension.

Multiples of extra stitches sometimes need to be added to a section of knitting, in which case extra stitches must be cast on. This can be done at the beginning and end of a row, or to replace stitches which have been cast off in a previous row, as for a buttonhole.

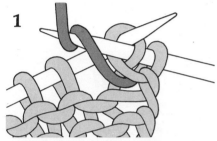

To increase a purled stitch at the beginning of a row
1 Work the first stitch but do not drop it off the left-hand needle. Insert the right-hand needle from left to right through the *back* loop of the same stitch and purl it again, then drop the stitch off the left-hand needle.

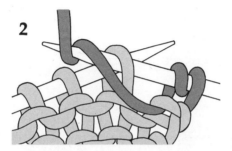

2 Purling twice into the front is not so satisfactory because it forms two loops round the right-hand needle. On the next row you must work into the front of the first loop and into the back of the second loop.

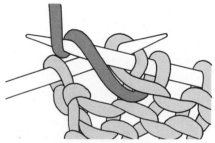

To increase a purled stitch at the end of a row
Work until two stitches remain on the left-hand needle. Purl twice into the next stitch as at the beginning of a row, then purl the last stitch.

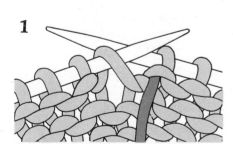

To make one in a purled row
1 Work until the position for the increase is reached. Use the right-hand needle to pick up the thread lying between the stitch just worked and the next stitch on the left-hand needle. Put this loop on the left-hand needle.

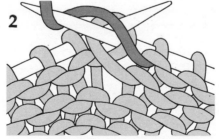

2 Purl into the back of it by inserting the right-hand needle from left to right into the back loop to twist the stitch. (Purling into the front leaves an open space beneath the increased stitch.)

Ribbon threaded through an eyelet increase at the edge of a shawl.

Decorative increasing (eyelet hole)

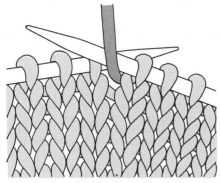

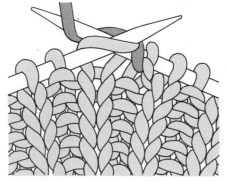

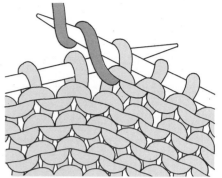

To make a stitch between two knitted stitches
Bring the yarn forward between the two needles. Take the yarn over the top of the right-hand needle ready to knit the next stitch. This is abbreviated as 'yfwd'.

To make a stitch between a purled and a knitted stitch
Carry the yarn, which is already at the front of the work, over the top of the right-hand needle ready to knit the next stitch. This is abbreviated as 'yon'.

To make a stitch between two purled stitches
Take the yarn over the top of the right-hand needle. Bring it forward between the two needles to the front again ready to purl the next stitch. This is abbreviated as 'yrn'.

PROFESSIONAL TOUCH

Invisible increasing

Note: If you work three stitches and increase one and on the next increasing row you work three stitches and increase one, the increase slants to the right. If you work an extra stitch each time before increasing, it slants to the left.

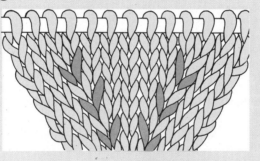

To increase one on a knitted row
Work until the position for the increase is reached. Insert the right-hand needle into the centre of the stitch on the row *below* the next stitch on the left-hand needle.
Knit an extra stitch through this stitch then knit the next stitch on the left-hand needle. The increased stitch slants to the right on the knitted side of stocking stitch.

To increase one on a purled row
Work until the position for the increase is reached. Insert the right-hand needle from the back to the front into the centre of the stitch on the row *below* the next stitch on the left-hand needle. Purl an extra stitch through this stitch then purl the next stitch on the left-hand needle. The increased stitch slants to the left when seen from the knitted side of stocking stitch.

Soft looped shawl

Simple garter stitch is used for this soft, light shawl. Use white for a baby or try a bright colour for yourself. Winding the yarn round the needle at the beginning of the row forms an eyelet increase. Use this as a decorative edging on its own or thread a coloured ribbon through for a splash of colour.

Size
Width across top edge 155cm/62in
Depth from top edge to centre point 82cm/32¼in.

You will need
9×20g balls of Patons Fairy Tale Double Knitting
One pair of 6½mm/No 3 needles
4m/4¼yd of 1cm/½in-wide ribbon

Tension
16 sts and 26 rows to 10cm/4in over garter st worked on 6½mm/No 3 needles.

Shawl
Beg at lower edge, with 6½mm/No 3 needles cast on 2 sts. K one row.
Next row Loop yarn round right-hand needle to inc 1, K to end. 3 sts.

Adding multiples of extra stitches

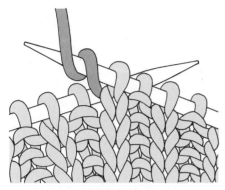

To make a stitch between a knitted and a purled stitch
Bring the yarn forward between the two needles. Carry it over the top of the right-hand needle, then between the two needles to the front again ready to purl the next stitch. This is also abbreviated as 'yrn'.

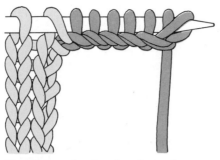

To add at the beginning of a row
Cast on the number of stitches required at the beginning of a row by the two-needle method (pages 164–165). Work across these stitches then continue aling the row. (The easiest way to add stitches at each end is to cast on at the beginning of two consecutive rows.)

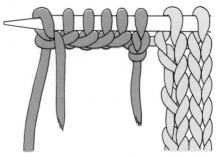

To add at the end of a row
After working across a row, cast on the number of stitches required by the one-needle method (pages 164–5). With a separate length of the same yarn make a slip loop on the left-hand needle. Work into this loop with the right-hand needle and the main length of yarn. Wind the short end round the thumb and use the main length to cast on the number of stitches required.

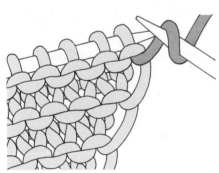

Next row Inc 1, K to end including loop on needle. 4 sts.
Rep the last row until there are 200 sts.
Cast off loosely.

To make up
Do not press. Cut ribbon into two 2m/2⅛yd lengths. Thread through side loops along edges and tie in a bow at centre point at beginning of work. Loop ribbon into bows at top corners and stitch to hold.

Right: This white shawl laced with ribbon makes a perfect christening gift.

How to decrease

Knowing how to reduce the overall width of knitted fabric is an essential part of basic techniques.
Five ways are described here and each has a different purpose.
Practise all these methods so that you can use the correct shaping in your knitting patterns.

Decreasing the number of stitches in the width of a piece of knitting alters its size and shape. Knitting patterns usually indicate when shaping is about to begin but do not always give details of the exact method to use. Each one has a different appearance and purpose and this chapter shows you how to choose the best method for your particular pattern. The samples are worked in stocking stitch so that you can see the angle of decrease clearly, but the methods are the same for other stitch combinations. Depending on which method you use, the decreased stitches slant either to the right or to the left. As a general rule, the slant should follow the line of the knitting. So when decreasing at the beginning of a row, the stitches should slant inwards to the left and at the end of a row they should slant inwards to the right. To work decreases in pairs, one at each end of a row, the decrease at the beginning of the row slants to the left and at the end, it slants to the right. This rule need not apply when the shaping serves a decorative purpose – for example when it highlights the fully-fashioned seams on a raglan-sleeved jersey. Here the decreased stitches are meant to show up and look most effective when worked against the line of the knitting – those at the beginning of the row slanting

Working stitches together

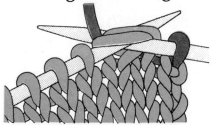

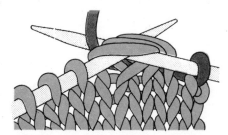

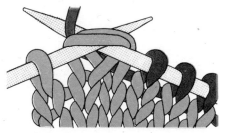

To decrease one knitted stitch at the beginning of a row
Knit the first stitch. Insert the right hand needle through the next two stitches as if to knit them. Knit them both together and drop them off the left-hand needle. The abbreviation for this is 'K2 tog'.

To decrease two knitted stitches at the beginning of a row
Knit three stitches together instead of two. The abbreviation for this is 'K3 tog'.
To decrease one or two stitches in the middle of a row, work until the position for the decrease is reached. Knit the next stitches together as for the beginning of a row.

To decrease one or two knitted stitches at the end of a row
Work until three or four stitches remain on the left-hand needle. Knit the next two or three stitches together as for the beginning of a row and knit the last stitch.

Working stitches together through the back of the loops

To decrease one knitted stitch at the beginning of a row
Knit the first stitch. Insert the right-hand needle through the *back* loops only of the next two stitches. Knit them both together and drop them off the left-hand needle. The abbreviation for this is 'K2 tog tbl'.

To decrease one knitted stitch at the end of a row
Work until three stitches remain on the left-hand needle. Knit the next two stitches together through the *back* loops and knit the last stitch.

To decrease one purled stitch at the beginning of a row
Purl the first stitch. Insert the right-hand needle from left to right through the *back* loops only of the next two stitches. Purl them both together and drop them off the left-hand needle. The abbreviation for this is 'P2 tog tbl'.

outwards to the right and those at the end of the row outwards to the left.

Working stitches together is the simplest way to decrease one or two knitted or purled stitches at any given point in a row. Use it when decreasing at the beginning of a purled row and at the end of a knitted row, but don't work the first or the last stitch together with its neighbour or you will create an uneven edge, difficult for seaming. When stitches are worked together in this way, the decreased stitches all slant to the *right* on the knitted side of stocking stitch.

Working stitches together through the back of the loops is a method which results in the decreased stitches slanting to the *left* on the knitted side of stocking stitch. So use this method when decreasing at the beginning of a knitted row and at the end of a purled row. However, the slip and knit or purl stitch method (detailed below) is simpler and more commonly used.

Slip and stitch decreasing is the simplest method to use at the beginning of a knitted row, using the knit two together method at the end of the same row so that the decreases form pairs, one slanting to the left and one to the right. The slip and knit stitch method results in the decreased stitch slanting to the *left* on the knitted side of stocking stitch.

Slip and purl stitch decreasing creates decreased stitches slanting to the *right* on the knitted side of stocking stitch but is less commonly used than purling stitches together.

Decreasing in a vertical line, as for a gored skirt, is achieved by using both angles of decreasing. Working across the first decreasing row all the decreased stitches should slant to the *right*. Working across the next decreasing row they should all slant to the *left*. By continuing to alternate the angle a vertical line is formed.

Casting off multiples of stitches. Use this method if you need to subtract more than one or two stitches from a section of knitting. This can be done at the beginning or the end of a row, as for the underarms of a jersey. When shaping a neck, a group of stitches is cast off in the centre of a row. Stitches also need to be cast off for details such as buttonholes.

Decreasing in a vertical line

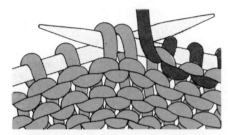

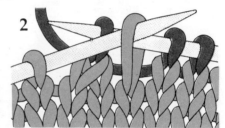

To decrease one or two purled stitches
The methods are the same as for knitting stitches together but the stitches are purled together. Decreasing one stitch is abbreviated as 'P2 tog' and decreasing two stitches as 'P3 tog'.

To decrease two stitches in a vertical line
1 Slip one stitch, knit or purl the next two stitches together, (purling through the back of the loops).

2 Lift the slipped stitch over and off the right-hand needle. The slipped stitch and the two stitches worked together slant in towards each other. The knitted version of this method is abbreviated as 'sl 1, K2 tog, psso' and the purled version as 'sl 1, P2 tog tbl, psso'.

To decrease one purled stitch at the end of a row work until three stitches remain on the left-hand needle. Purl the next two stitches together through the *back* loops and purl the last stitch.

Keeping slants in line
A slip loop in a length of contrast coloured yarn helps you see at a glance where the next decrease should occur in the middle of a row. Slip the loop from one needle to the other without working into it.

To keep a line slanting to the *left* on the knitted side of stocking stitch, the slip loop goes in front of stitches decreased by the 'K2 tog tbl' and 'sl 1, K1, psso' methods.

To keep a line slanting to the *right*, it goes after stitches decreased by the 'K2 tog' method.

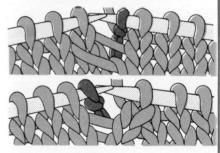

To keep a line slanting to the *right* on the purled side, it goes in front of stitches decreased by the 'P2 tog' and 'sl 1, P1, psso' methods. To keep a line slanting to the *left* it goes after stitches decreased by the 'P2 tog tbl' method.

Slip and stitch decreasing

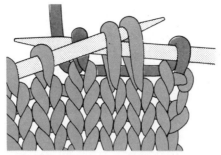

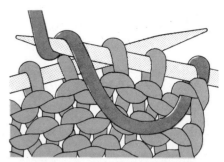

To decrease one knitted stitch at the beginning of a row
Knit the first stitch. Insert the right-hand needle into the next stitch as if to knit it. Keep the yarn at the back of the work and slip the stitch on to the right-hand needle without knitting it. Knit the next stitch on the left-hand needle. Use the left-hand needle to lift the slipped stitch over the top of the knitted stitch and off the right-hand needle. The abbreviation for this is 'sl 1, K1, psso'.

To decrease two knitted stitches at the beginning of a row
Knit the first stitch. Slip the next stitch and the following stitch on to the right-hand needle. Knit the next stitch on the left-hand needle. Lift the two slipped stitches over the top of the knitted stitch and off the right-hand needle. The abbreviation of this is 'sl 2, K1, p2sso'.

To decrease one or two purled stitches at the beginning of a row
The yarn must be kept at the front of the work throughout. Slip one or two stitches on to the right-hand needle as if to purl them. Purl the next stitch on the left-hand needle. Use the left-hand needle to lift the slipped stitches over the top of the purled stitch and off the right-hand needle. These methods are abbreviated as 'sl 1, P1, psso' and 'sl 2, P1, p2sso'.

Note: To decrease one or two knitted or purled stitches in the middle of a row, work until the position for the decrease is reached. Slip and knit or purl the next two or three stitches as for the beginning of a row.

To decrease one or two knitted or purled stitches at the end of a row, work until three or four stitches remain on the left-hand needle. Work the next two or three stitches as for the beginning of a row and knit or purl the last stitch.

Casting off multiples of stitches

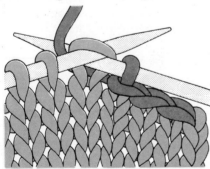

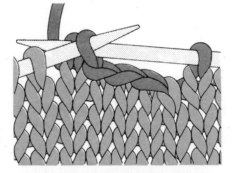

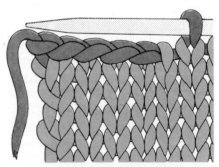

To subtract a number of stitches at the beginning of a knitted row
Cast off the number stated. One stitch remains on the right-hand needle after the casting-off has been completed. This counts as one of the remaining stitches. Continue knitting to the end of the row. The easiest way to subtract a number of stitches at each end of a piece of knitting is to cast off at the beginning of two consecutive rows.

To subtract a number of stitches in the middle of a knitted row
Work until the position for the subtraction is reached. Use the method given for the beginning of a row.

To subtract a number of stitches at the end of a knitted row
Work until the number of stitches to be cast off remains on the left-hand needle. Cast off and fasten off the last stitch. The yarn must be rejoined again at the beginning of the next row to continue knitting. These methods can be used to subtract a number of stitches at the beginning, end or in the middle of a purled row. Purl the stitches instead of knitting them before casting them off.

Tension and textures

The importance of tension cannot be underestimated. It makes the difference between knitting a garment successfully from a pattern and producing a jersey which reaches the knees. Also included in this chapter are four more reversible stitches for you to practise and perfect.

Once you can knit stitches you need to know how to obtain accurate measurements of both the length and width of your knitting, in order to follow a pattern. This is called 'tension'. Many knitters mistakenly believe that tension merely means achieving an even fabric. This is not so and you can never be a proficient knitter until you appreciate how important it is to have the correct tension.

The word tension means the number of stitches and rows to a given measurement which has been achieved by the designer, using a specific yarn and needle size. (Each spinner gives a recommended tension for its yarn on the ball band but this is only a guide and is often different from that called for by the pattern.)

A dressmaking pattern tells you how many metres of fabric are needed and this amount stays the same whether the fabric is chiffon or corduroy. However, in knitting the needle size and thickness of yarn have an effect on the number of stitches and rows needed to arrive at a given measurement. Unless you can obtain the tension called for by the pattern you will end up with a garment either too large or too small. Incorrect tension also alters the texture of the fabric.

The basic steps in knitting soon become as natural as breathing but everyone differs in the way they control the needles and yarn. There is no such thing as 'average' tension. Different people naturally knit more tightly or loosely than others. As you become more experienced your tension may alter with your progress.

Checking tension Always work a sample with the correct yarn and needle size in the stitch given before beginning any knitting. If a pattern gives 22 stitches and 30 rows to 10cm/4in worked over stocking stitch on 4mm/No 8 needles, cast on at least 26 stitches. Allow at least 4 extra stitches and 4 extra rows to enable you to measure the sample accurately. Pin the completed sample on a flat surface. Measure with a ruler and count the number of stitches and rows obtained to 10cm/4in. In this example there should be 22 stitches and 30 rows to 10cm/4in.

Don't be tempted to cheat by stretching the sample. Count the stitches and rows very carefully – even half a stitch makes an overall difference.

Adjusting tension If your sample measures *more* than the tension size given you are working too loosely. Change to a size smaller needles and work another sample.

If your sample measures *less* than the tension size given you are working too tightly. Change to larger needles and work another sample.

Continue experimenting with needle sizes until you obtain the tension

Below: An incorrect tension sample which is too loose, giving 19 stitches and 27 rows to 10cm.

Above: A tension sample giving the correct tension of 22 stitches and 30 rows to 10cm.

Above: An incorrect tension sample which is too tight, giving 26 stitches and 34 rows to 10cm.

given. Most instructions give this as a number of stitches in width and a number of rows in depth. If you have to choose between obtaining one but not the other, the width tension is the most vital. If you cannot satisfactorily adapt the tension to obtain the correct width then cast on the number of stitches given for a smaller or larger size. Length can usually be adjusted by working more or less rows.

Always use new yarn for each sample. If you keep on unravelling the same length of yarn it will become stretched and will not give an accurate tension.

Each design is calculated on the tension achieved with the yarn specified in the instructions. The total amount of yarn is also based on the tension. If you choose to use a substitute it is vital to realise that the amount may vary

and you may not produce the texture of the original fabric.

Reversible patterns

The four patterns below use combinations of knit and purl stitches and form fabrics which look the same on both sides. They can be worked in separate bands or as all-over fabrics. Any of these patterns can be used to knit the bags featured in this chapter.

Moss stitch

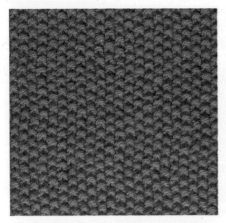

Worked over any number of stitches.
1st row *K1, P1, repeat from * to end, noting that an even number of cast-on stitches will end with P1 and an odd number with K1.
2nd row All the stitches of the previous row which were knitted must be knitted and all the purled stitches purled.
These 2 rows form the pattern.

Double moss stitch

This pattern needs a number of stitches which will divide by 4.
1st row *K2, P2, repeat from * to end.
2nd row As 1st.
3rd row *P2, K2, repeat from * to end.
4th row As 3rd.
These 4 rows form the pattern.

Hurdle stitch

This pattern needs an even number of stitches.
1st and 2nd rows K to end.
3rd and 4th rows *K1, P1, repeat from * to end.
These 4 rows form the pattern.

One pattern – two useful bags

To show how tension controls the finished size and texture, this design has been made in two different yarns and needle sizes. The number of stitches and rows remain exactly the same.

Sizes
Holdall 37cm×34cm/14½in×13½in
Shoulder purse 18cm×15cm/7in×6in

You will need
Holdall 10×50g balls of Patons uncut Turkey Rug Wool
One pair 7½mm/No 1 needles
One pair cane handles

Shoulder purse 3×20g balls of Patons Beehive Double Knitting

One pair 4mm/No 8 needles
1m/1yd of cord for handle
1m/1yd decorative tape or ribbon, optional

Tension
Holdall 10 sts and 16 rows to 10cm/4in over moss st worked on 7½mm/No 1 needles
Shoulder purse 19 sts and 34 rows to 10cm/4in over moss st worked on 4mm/No 8 needles

Holdall
With 7½mm/No 1 needles cast on 36 sts by the 2 needle method.
1st row *K1, P1, rep from * to end.
2nd row *P1, K1, rep from * to end.
Work a total of 110 rows moss st. Cast off loosely.

Gussets
With 7½mm/No 1 needles cast on 8 sts. Work 44 rows moss st. Cast off loosely. Make another piece in same way.

Shoulder purse
With 4mm/No 8 needles cast on and work as given for holdall.

Gussets and handle
These are all knitted in one piece. With 4mm/No 8 needles cast on 8 sts. Work 117cm/46in moss st. Cast off loosely.

To make up
Holdall Do not press. Fold bag in half and mark centre of each side with safety pins. Mark centre of

Using up tension samples

You need not waste any of your experimental samples as the unravelled yarn can be used up in many ways. One useful tip is to wind up some of the yarn and attach it to one of the seams of the completed garment. As this will be washed with the garment it will be in the same condition and can be used for darning and repairs. If the yarn is not too thick it can be used for seaming and completing a garment. Another way of using up yarn is to make a trimming such as a plaited tie-belt for a jersey or a pompom for a pull-on hat.

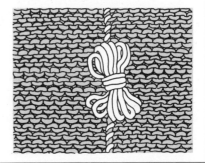

Seeded rib stitch

This pattern needs a number of stitches which will divide by 3.
1st row *K2, P1, repeat from * to end.
This row forms the pattern.

cast-on edge of gussets in same way. Join gussets to bag with a flat seam matching centre markers. Turn right side out. Fold top edges of bag over cane handles and stitch down.
Shoulder purse Do not press. Mark bag and gussets and sew in gussets as given for Holdall. The remainder becomes the handle. Place cord inside the knitted handle length and firmly stitch the open edges together. Thread some decorative tape or ribbon through top edge to tie at front.

Right: Proving the point about tension – the same number of stitches and rows has been used for a sturdy knitting holdall and child's shoulder bag.

Hems, welts, borders and edges

Hems and welts are easily knitted in one with the main pattern. Borders and neck edges are usually worked after the pieces have been sewn together – which entails picking up stitches along a cast-off row or on row ends. The secret of a perfect finish is to pick them up evenly.

Hems and borders play an important part in the successful completion of knitted garments. Any unnecessary bulk must be avoided.

Once the pieces of a garment have been sewn together, it is also necessary to neaten edges, and sometimes these are worked in a different direction to the main line of the knitting. While ribbing is most commonly used where an edge which firmly hugs the contours of the figure is required – as for welts, cuffs and skirt waistbands – hems are used on the lower edge of a skirt or a shaped jacket and it is a simple matter to make provision for these.

Hems on skirts and jackets need firm edges to prevent them dropping or sagging out of shape in wearing. This chapter gives several ways of working neat hems in one with the main fabric to give a turned-under edge.

Turned-under hems are ideal for a garment knitted in stocking stitch or any textured pattern but they are not suitable for light, lacy fabrics. The turned-under section will show through an open fabric and may pull it out of shape. To give minimum bulk, the turned-under section of the hem should be worked in stocking stitch, irrespective of main pattern.

A row of eyelet holes can be added at the folding line of a hem to make a dainty picot finish on baby garments.

Front borders are needed on garments which have a centre front opening. A turned-under border in stocking stitch can be worked in one with the main fabric of a jacket but only when the pattern for the body of the jacket is of a similar texture. Garter stitch, for example, should not be worked in the same row with stocking stitch, because garter stitch stretches widthways and stocking

stitch lengthways.

A cardigan is usually best finished with separately knitted button and buttonhole borders, which are sewn on when the garment is completed.

Edges along which stitches have to be picked up are commonly used to complete garments. This method is used to pick up stitches round the curve of a neckline to work a neckband or collar.

A zip-fastened jacket also has stitches picked up along the front edges to neaten them, before the zip is sewn in place; these must be picked up evenly to avoid stretching or puckering the edge.

Right: Once you turn up the picot hem and begin to seam it, you can see how the row of eyelet holes forms a dainty edge. Inset: Detail of a neatly picked-up ribbed edge on a mohair cardigan.

Turned-under hem

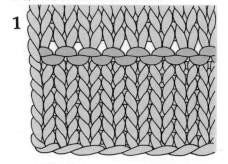 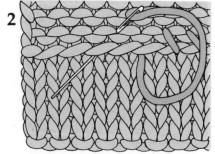

Cast on the required number of stitches with one size smaller needles than given for the main fabric. Begin with a knit row and work an odd number of rows in stocking stitch to the required depth of the turned-under hem.

1 Change to the correct needle size and, instead of purling the next row, knit all the stitches through the back of the loops to form a ridge on the right side of the work which marks the hemline.**

Continue in the main pattern.

2 When the garment is completed and the side seams have been joined, turn the hem up to the wrong side of the work at the hemline ridge. Neatly slip stitch the hem in place.

Picot hem

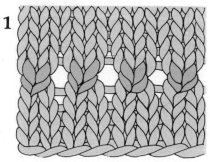

Cast on an odd number of stitches with one size smaller needles than given for the main fabric. Begin with a knit row and work an even number of rows in stocking stitch to the required depth of the turned-under hem. Change to the correct needle size.

1 Next row (eyelet hole row) *K2 tog, yfwd, rep from * to last st, K1.

Double stocking stitch hem

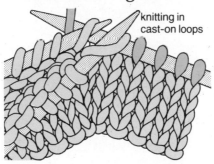

knitting in cast-on loops

2

Purl one row to complete the hem. Continue in the main pattern.
2 When the garment is completed and side seams have been joined, turn the hem up to the wrong side of the work at the eyelet hole row. Neatly slip stitch the hem in place.

Work as given for turned-under hem to **. Begin with a knit row again and work one row less in stocking stitch than the depth of the turned-under section, ending with a purl row.

With an extra needle pick up the loops from the cast-on edge from left to right, with the needle point facing the same way as the main needle. Hold the extra needle behind the left-hand needle. Knit to the end of the row, knitting one stitch from the left-hand needle together with one stitch from the extra needle. Purl one row to complete the hem.

Continue in the main pattern. When the garment is completed join the side seams, including the top section of the hem, then join the turned-under section on the wrong side.

Turned-under front borders

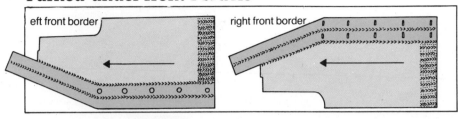

left front border — right front border

Make provision for the border before casting on. Decide on the width of the turned-under part – 3-4cm/1¼-1½in will be sufficient but it will depend on the thickness of the yarn being used. If buttonholes are to be worked, allow sufficient width for a double buttonhole, one in the top part of the border and a corresponding one in the under part.

Cast on required number of stitches. The example shown here is worked over 66 stitches. Double knitting yarn on 4mm/No 8 needles is used to give a tension of 22 stitches and 30 rows to 10cm/4in. This allows for 8 stitches to be turned under, one foldline stitch and 8 stitches for the upper part of the border, with the remaining 49 stitches being used for the body.

To work a left front border
With the right side of the work facing, work in pattern to the last 17 stitches. Work 8 stitches for the top border, slip the next stitch in a purlwise direction to mark the foldline, knit the last 8 stitches for the turned-under part of the border. On the next row, purl the first 9 stitches, then pattern to the end of the row. Repeat these rows for the required length.

Any shaping on the front edge is worked *before* the top border stitches on a right side row.

To work a right front border
With the right side of the work facing, knit the first 8 stitches for the turned-under border section, slip the next stitch purlwise to mark the foldline, work 8 stitches for the top border then pattern to the end of the row. On the next row, pattern to the last 9 stitches then purl to the end. Repeat these rows for the required length.

Any shaping on the front edge is worked *after* the top border stitches on a right side row.

Picking up stitches evenly

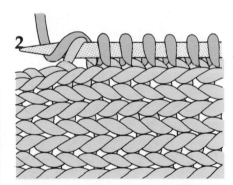

picking up three out of every four row ends

Unless picked-up stitches are evenly spaced, the edge will stretch or pucker. It is a simple matter to pick up stitches along a cast-off row but not so easy to gauge where to pick up stitches on row ends. The picked up edge needs to be very slightly shorter than the main fabric edge.
1 As a general guide, pick up a

Separate front borders

Decide on the width of the border as for turned-under borders. If buttonholes are to be worked, allow one extra stitch on the inner edge of the border so that the buttonhole is central when the border is sewn in position.

To work a border in the same pattern as the welt of the body, such as ribbing, cast on the required number of stitches for the body plus the stitches for the border. Work until the welt is completed.

Picking up edge stitches with a knitting needle

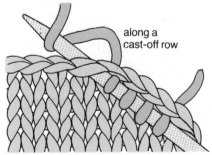

along a cast-off row

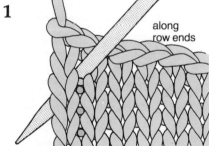

1

along row ends

2

To pick up stitches along a cast-off row, have the right side of the fabric facing you, and a ball of yarn. *Insert the needle from the front to the back under both loops at the top of the cast-off stitch, put the yarn round the needle and pull this loop through, as when working a knit stitch. Leave the stitch on the needle. Continue from the * until the required number of stitches have been picked up using the main

length of yarn to make the stitches.
To pick up stitches along row ends, have the right side of the fabric facing you, and a ball of yarn.
1 *Insert the needle from the front to the back between the first and second stitches in from the edge of the knitting.
2 Put the yarn round the needle and pull this loop through as when working a knit stitch. Leave the stitch on the needle. Insert the

needle between the first and second stitches in from the edge one row along to the left and continue from the * until the required number of stitches have been picked up using the main length of yarn to make the stitches.
To pick up stitches round a shaped edge, such as a neckline, combine the methods of picking up stitches along a cast-off row and along row ends.

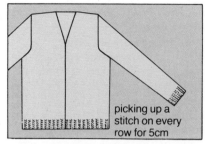

picking up a stitch on every row for 5cm

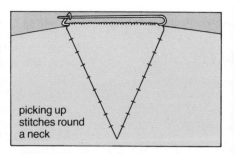

picking up stitches round a neck

Above: Close-up detail of a neckband, showing how the careful spacing of picked up stitches ensures a really snug fit.

stitch on three out of every four successive row ends.

2 If ribbing is to be worked along the edge, it tends to pull up a little from the bottom edges. To overcome this, pick up a stitch on every row end for the first 5cm/2in of the bottom edge.

Round a neck divide edge into equal sections with pins (the back neck stitches have usually been cast off or left on a holder). As an example, if a total of 180 stitches are to be picked up round the front of a V-neck, divide each front edge into nine equal sections. Pick up 10 stitches in each section. This avoids the stitches being too bunched together or too far apart.

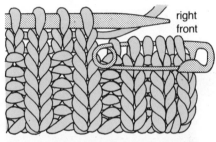

right front

On the right front With the right side of the work facing, work across the border stitches and slip them on to a holder. Continue in pattern on the remaining stitches.

On the left front With the right side of the work facing, work until the border stitches remain and slip them on to a holder. Turn and continue in pattern on the remaining stitches.

When the main piece is completed put the border stitches back on to the same size needle as used for the welt, rejoin the yarn at the inner edge and continue in pattern. *Work about 10cm/4in and tack the border in place along the front edge, easing this in very slightly as you do so – take care not to stretch the main fabric or the border will pucker. Continue from the * until the border is the required length, then cast off. Stitch the border in place along the edge and remove the tacking stitches.

To work a border in a different pattern to the welt, cast on the border stitches separately. Work in pattern until the border is the required length. Continue from the * as given for working a border in the same pattern.

Picking up edge stitches with a crochet hook

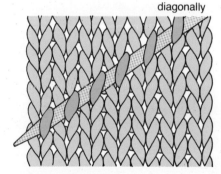

diagonally

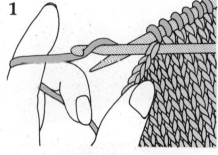

1

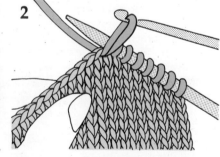

2

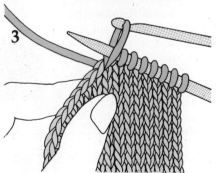

3

To pick up stitches horizontally, vertically or diagonally across a piece of knitting, have the right side of the fabric facing you. Use a double-pointed needle. You will not need any yarn at this stage as the needle is not inserted through the fabric to pull a separate loop. Instead, pick up one loop only from each of the required number of stitches. Join in the yarn and knit across the stitches picked up.

To pick up stitches along a cast-off row, or along row ends, work as given for picking up stitches with a knitting needle. Use a crochet hook to pull the loop through instead of a needle.

1 Insert the crochet hook under the top of the stitch or into the row end, and put the yarn round the hook.

2 Pull the loop through.

3 Transfer the loop from the crochet hook to a knitting needle.

Basic making up: blocking, pressing and seaming

Care taken in the final stages of finishing the pieces of a garment and in the actual making up will give your knitting that professional look. Some modern yarns need careful handling and often a garment can be ruined by incorrect pressing or cobbled seams.

The final preparation and making up of a garment needs as much care and skill as the knitting. The knowledge and time taken to produce a superb piece of knitting to the correct shape and proportions can be wasted if the pieces are badly seamed together or if you don't take the trouble to block and press the pieces where appropriate.

Blocking is the term given to the process of pinning out each individual piece of knitting to the correct size and shape, prior to pressing. Some patterns have a tendency to shrink in width and stretch in length. Others may have a slight bias which needs correction, or scalloped edges which must be pinned into shape. Delicate lace patterns often only need

blocking out and leaving under a damp cloth for a few hours, without actually pressing them.

Diagrams of the pattern pieces give you the finished measurements of each piece and the making up instructions tell you whether or not to press the yarn. The choice of blocking out the pieces, however, will often be left to you. If you are in any doubt, *do not block* – knitting is a wonderfully pliant fabric and will eventually take its own shape.

Pressing is not always essential or even advisable. In the past, knitters did not press any pure wool garments but 'dressed' them over the steam of a kettle, then patted them into size and shape.

The ballband usually tells you if the yarn can be pressed and gives you the iron temperature setting but does not always give you exact details.

If you use a different yarn from the one specified in the pattern, don't

Blocking pattern pieces

To block out each piece you will need a firm table or ironing board. On top of this place a sheet of white carton cardboard. Over this place an ironing pad or blanket.

Place each individual piece right side down on to the prepared ironing board or table. Anchor the piece at each corner with rustless pins. Use a tape measure to check that the width and length are the same as those given in the instructions, when measured in the centre. Gently pat the piece into shape where any increasing or decreasing has been worked and check the measurements, making sure that the side edges are the same length.

Now pin the piece to the board all round the edges. Use plenty of pins evenly spaced and placed at right angles to the stitches and rows. Take great care to ensure that all the stitches and rows lie in straight lines and that the fabric does not have any bias.

If the pieces need blocking but do not require any pressing, cover them with a clean wet cloth, well wrung out. Leave for two or three hours then remove the cloth.

Right: Leave each piece in place until it is dry before removing the pins.

192

forget that the making up instructions may not be appropriate. The instructions may be for a yarn, such as wool, that *can* be pressed but you may have used acrylic and the ballband will tell you this *cannot* be pressed.

Many yarns are blends of man-made fibres so it is not always easy to judge whether they should be pressed. The Pressing guide (right) gives general advice; if in doubt, *do not press*.

Seaming is particularly important for a professional finish. The method you use will depend on the fabric and type of garment. Ribbing and garter stitch should be joined with oversewn and flat seams, page 169.

Backstitch seams are suitable for closely-textured fabrics, such as stocking stitch, and for all shaped edges.

The invisible seam resembles the rungs of a ladder, lacing the pieces together. It is perfect for joining straight edges in any pattern and cannot be detected on a stocking stitch seam – hence its name.

Whichever method of seaming you use, assemble all the pieces in the order given in the instructions. Make sure that stripes or patterns match exactly when pinning the edges together. Use a blunt-ended sewing needle and the original yarn. If it is very thick or textured, use a finer matching yarn.

Hemming is another important detail. Slip stitch is used on turned-under hems or facings as it produces a neat finish. Make sure you do not cast on or off too tightly when knitting an edge which has to be turned under. In hemming you will be matching one cast on or off stitch to one stitch of the main fabric. If the edge is too tight the fabric will pucker. You do not need to pick up every stitch along the edge but keep them regular and fairly loose.

Pressing guide

Pure wool Press under a damp cloth with a warm iron.
Blends of wool and nylon Provided the wool content is higher than the nylon, press as for wool.
Blends of wool and acrylic Do not press.
Nylon Press under a dry cloth with a cool iron.
Blends of nylon and acrylic If nylon content is higher than acrylic, press as for nylon.
Courtelle Do not press.
Acrylic Do not press.
Cotton Press under a damp cloth with a warm or hot iron.
Mohair Steam press very lightly with a warm iron.
Angora Steam press as for mohair.
Glitter yarn Do not press unless stated on the ballband.

Pressing

If the individual pieces have not already been blocked, lay them right side down on to an ironing board.

1 Have the iron at the correct temperature and a clean dry, or damp, pressing cloth as directed. Place the cloth over the piece. Gently but firmly press the whole area of the iron down on top of the cloth, then lift it up again. Do not move the iron over the surface of the cloth as you would when ironing normally. Press each area evenly in this way before going on to the next area.

Once a piece has been pressed, allow any steam to evaporate. Remove the pins if the piece has

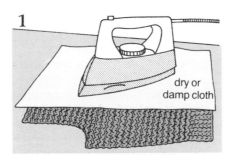

dry or damp cloth

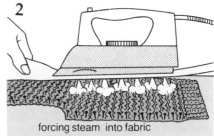

forcing steam into fabric

been blocked and lay it aside ready for seaming.

2 To steam press a piece, use an iron at the correct temperature setting. Place a damp cloth over the piece. Begin at the lower edge and hold the left-hand side of the damp cloth just above the surface of the knitting with the left hand. Allow the iron to come into direct contact

with the cloth but do not press down on to the knitting. This forces the steam down into the fabric. Press each area in this way.

Once a piece has been pressed allow any steam to evaporate. Remove the pins if the piece has been blocked and lay it aside ready for seaming.

SHORT CUT

An easy guide to blocking

Prepare the table or ironing board for blocking the pieces. Choose a piece of evenly-checked gingham – 2.5cm/1in or 5cm/2in squares are ideal. This material must be colour-fast.

Place the gingham over the ironing board, making sure that the checks are in straight rows, horizontally and vertically. Measure the size of the checks and use this to gauge how many stitches in width and rows in depth should cover each one. For example, using a 5cm/2in check gingham, a piece with a side seam length of 40cm/16in and a width of 40cm/16in will require an area of eight checks deep and wide for blocking out. Each check should contain the same number of stitches and rows.

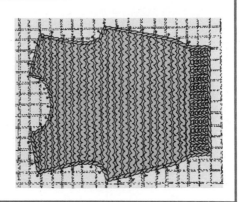

Two new methods of seaming

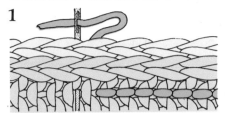

1

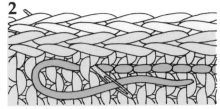

2

Back stitch seam

Place the right sides of the pieces together. Work along the wrong side of the fabric from right to left, one stitch in from the edge. Secure the yarn at the beginning of the seam with two or three small stitches, one on top of the other.
1 *With the sewing needle at the back of the fabric, move along to the left the width of one knitted stitch from the last stitch and push the

needle through both pieces to the front at right-angles to the edge. Pull the yarn through.
2 Take the needle across the front of the fabric from left to right and push it through both pieces at the end of the last sewing stitch to the back. Pull the yarn through.
Continue from the * until the seam is completed. Fasten off with two or three small stitches.

1

2

Invisible seam

With the *right side* of both pieces facing you, lay them one above the other. The seam can be joined from right to left or left to right. Secure the yarn with two or three small stitches one on top of the other on the lower piece. Pass the needle across to the first stitch on the upper piece, pick up the bar between the first and second stitch in from the edge and pull the yarn through.
1 *Pass the needle across to the

stitch on the same row on the lower piece, pick up the bar between the first and second stitch in from the edge and pull the yarn through.
2 Pass the needle across to the next stitch on the next row on the upper piece, pick up the bar between the first and second stitch in from the edge and pull the yarn through.
Continue from the * until the seam is completed, pulling each stitch up to the same tension as the fabric. Fasten off with two or three small stitches.

A neat method of hemming

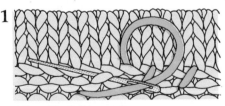

1

2

Slip stitch hemming

Turn in the hem or facing and have the wrong side of the main fabric facing you. Secure the yarn to the hem or facing with two or three small stitches on top of each other.
1 *Insert the needle from right to left and lightly pick up *one thread only* of a stitch to the left on the main

fabric. Pull the yarn through fairly loosely.
2 Move along the fabric to the left, insert the needle into the hem or facing and lightly pick up *one thread only* of a stitch. Pull yarn through. Continue from the * until the hem is completed. Fasten off with two or three small stitches.

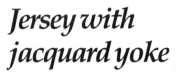

Jersey with jacquard yoke

This stylish jersey features a striking, multi-coloured jacquard yoke. The yarn used is a blend of 80% wool and 20% nylon for added strength. Block out and press each piece as described in this chapter. Make sure the patterns on the raglans match exactly when seaming.

Sizes

To fit 86 [91:97]cm/34 [36:38]in bust
Length to shoulder, 60 [61:62]cm/ 23½ [24:24½]in
Sleeve seam, 47cm/18½in
The figures in [] refer to the 91cm/ 36in and 97cm/38in sizes respectively

You will need

9 [10:10]×50g balls of Sunbeam Trophy Double Knitting (80% wool, 20% nylon) in main colour A
1 ball of same in each of 5 contrast colours B, C, D, E and F
One pair 3mm/No 11 needles
One pair 3¾mm/No 9 needles
Set of four 3mm/No 11 needles
Set of four 3¾mm/No 9 needles

Tension

24 sts and 32 rows to 10cm/4in over plain st st worked on 3¾mm/No 9 needles

Back

With 3mm/No 11 needles and A cast on 106 [114:118] sts.
1st row (Rs) K2, *P2, K2, rep from * to end.
2nd row P2, *K2, P2, rep from * to end.
Rep these 2 rows for 6cm/2¼in, ending with a 2nd row and inc 3 [1:3] sts evenly in last row. 109 [115:121] sts.
Change to 3¾mm/No 9 needles. Beg with a K row cont in st st until work measures 35cm/13¾in from beg, ending with a P row.
Join in colours as required and cont in st st, working first 12 rows from jacquard chart.

Note

For detailed instructions on knitting with two or more different coloured yarns at once see pages 244–5.

Jacquard chart

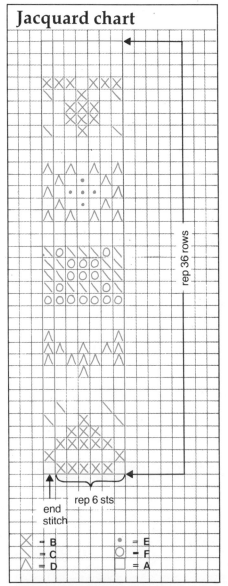

rep 36 rows

rep 6 sts

end
stitch

× = B
○ = C
∧ = D

• = E
○ = F
□ = A

Shape armholes

Cont in patt from chart, cast off 4 sts at beg of next 2 rows.
Next row K1, K2 tog, patt to last 3 sts, sl 1, K1, psso, K1.
Next row Patt to end.
Working throughout in patt from chart, rep these 2 rows until 37 [39:41] sts rem, ending with a Ws row, noting that after completing the 36 rows once, the first 5 rows of next rep should be worked using F instead of B, then on foll rep go back to B.
Leave sts on holder.

Front

Work as given for back, shaping armholes until 57 [59:61] sts rem, ending with a Ws row.

Shape neck

Next row K1, K2 tog, patt 19 sts, turn and leave rem sts on holder. Complete left shoulder first.
Next row Cast off 3 sts, patt to end.
Next row K1, K2 tog, patt to end.
Next row Cast off 2 sts, patt to end.
Next row K1, K2 tog, patt to last 2 sts, K2 tog.
Next row Patt to end.
Rep last 2 rows 4 times more, then cont to dec at armhole edge only on every alt row until 2 sts rem, ending with a Ws row. Cast off.
Return to rem sts on holder, leave first 13 [15:17] sts for centre front neck, rejoin yarn to rem sts, patt to last 3 sts, sl 1, K1, psso, K1.
Next row Patt to end.

Next row Cast off 3 sts, patt to last 3 sts, sl 1, K1, psso, K1.
Complete to match first side, reversing all shapings.

Sleeves

With 3mm/No 11 needles and A cast on 50 [54:58] sts. Work 8cm/3¼in rib as given for back, ending with a 1st row.
Next row (inc row) Rib 7 [9:5] sts, *pick up loop lying between sts and K tbl – called M1, rib 3 [3:4] sts, rep from * 11 times more, M1, rib 7 [9:5] sts. 63 [67:71] sts.
Change to 3¾mm/No 9 needles. Beg with a K row cont in st st, inc one st at each end of 9th [5th:1st] row and every foll 8th row until there are 85 [91:97] sts. Cont without shaping until sleeve measures 43cm/17in from beg, ending with a P row.
Join in colours as required and cont in st st, working first 12 rows from jacquard chart.

Shape top

Cont in patt from chart, cast off 4 sts at beg of next 2 rows.
Cont dec as given for back at each end of next and every alt row until 13 [15:17] sts rem, changing to F instead of B on first 5 rows of second patt rep and ending with a Ws row. Leave sts on holder.

Neckband

Join raglan seams with Rs facing and invisible seam, taking care to

The pattern pieces

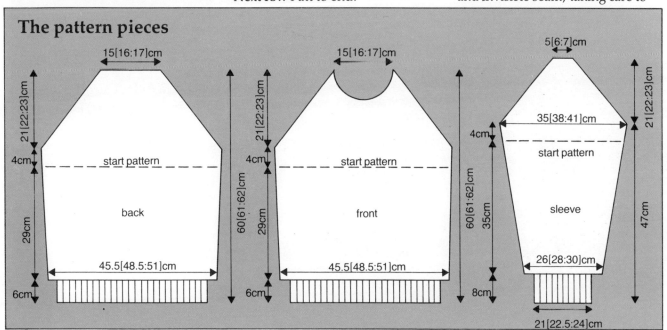

15[16:17]cm
21[22:23]cm
4cm
start pattern
back
29cm
60[61:62]cm
6cm
45.5[48.5:51]cm

15[16:17]cm
21[22:23]cm
4cm
start pattern
front
29cm
60[61:62]cm
6cm
45.5[48.5:51]cm

5[6:7]cm
35[38:41]cm
4cm
start pattern
sleeve
35cm
47cm
21[22:23]cm
8cm
26[28:30]cm
21[22.5:24]cm

match patt exactly.
With Rs of work facing, set of four 3mm/No 11 needles and A, K across sts of right sleeve, back, neck and left sleeve K2 tog at each seam, pick up and K17 sts down left front neck, K across front neck sts on holder, pick up and K17 sts up right front neck. 108 [116:124] sts.
Work 8cm/3¼in in rounds of K2, P2 rib. Change to set of four 3¾mm/No 9 needles. Cont in rib until neckband measures 20cm/7¾in from beg. Cast off very loosely.

To make up

Block out each piece and press under a damp cloth with a warm iron.
Join side and sleeve seams, using oversewing for rib, invisible method for side seams and back st for sleeve seams. Press seams.

Below: Blocking and pressing the pieces of this jersey will improve the final appearance of the finished garment. Inset: Samples knitted in the same yarn as the jersey to give you an idea of some alternative colourways.

Grafting stitches to join seams or repair knitting

Two pieces of knitting can be grafted together to give the appearance of continuous stitches and to avoid an unsightly or uncomfortable seam. Grafting can be worked over stocking stitch, garter stitch or rib and gives a professional finish to a garment.

Where a hard, seamed edge will spoil the line of a garment the alternative is to graft the stitches together to form a continuous piece of knitting without a seam. Grafting works best with stocking stitch, garter stitch or single ribbing; don't use it with highly textured yarn or when you are working a complicated stitch pattern.

Below: The top seam of the hood of these coats has been grafted to give the effect of continuous knitting.

There are two ways of grafting stitches together, the first method is carried out with the stitches to be grafted still on the knitting needles, the other with the stitches off the needle.

Stitches on the needles

Use this method for joining the tops of socks and mittens, where a hard seam would be uncomfortable; for shoulders, where the shaping has been worked in steps by turning the rows rather than by casting off in stages, or for the top of a hood, where a seam would detract from the appearance when the hood is down. The hood of the child's coat featured in this chapter uses this method.

Stocking stitch or garter stitch The two pieces to be joined must have the same number of stitches on each needle and, when the right side of the knitting is facing you, one piece should have the point of the needle facing to the right and the other should have the point facing to the left. Work one row more or less on one of the two pieces to achieve this and break off the yarn, leaving an end about four times as long as the width of the stitches to be grafted together. Be generous, because although the yarn can be rejoined if you run out, the ends will have to be darned in and may show. Thread this long end into a blunt-ended sewing needle.

Break off the yarn on the other piece of knitting, leaving a short end to be darned in later.

Hold the two pieces together with the wrong side of the fabric to the inside and the piece with the long end of yarn at the back. The points of both needles are now facing to the right

and you are now ready to begin grafting at the right-hand edge.

Single ribbing requires two pairs of needles, preferably pointed at both ends. You can use four ordinary needles but you must then ensure that all the points are facing in the correct direction (see below). First the knit stitches on one side are grafted and then the fabric is turned to enable you to graft the knit stitches on the other side.

Strictly speaking, this is not true grafting but nevertheless it is easy to work and makes a satisfactory join.

Stitches off the needles

Use this method to join two pieces which have just been knitted or to repair existing garments. To achieve the best results with this method the knitted stitches should not be too small or have been worked in a yarn which will unravel easily.

The two pieces to be joined must have the same number of stitches on each needle. You need one needle point facing to the right and one to the left so work one row more or less on the last of the pieces to be joined and break off the yarn as for grafting with stitches on the needles.

Remove the needles from the stitches (or, if you prefer, remove them gradually as you work), and place the pieces flat on a table with the exposed loops pointing towards each other and the right sides uppermost.

Place the piece where the long end of yarn is still attached *above* the other piece so that you are ready to begin grafting at the right-hand edge. Work vertically across from one piece to the other.

Grafting stocking stitch edges

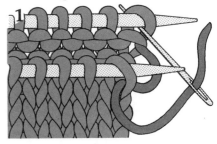

Prepare the pieces to be joined as described under Stitches on the needles and place *purl* sides together with both needles pointing to the right. Thread the long end in to a blunt-ended sewing needle.

1 Insert the sewing needle into the first stitch on the front needle as if to purl it, draw the yarn through and leave this stitch on the needle. Insert the sewing needle into the

Grafting garter stitch edges

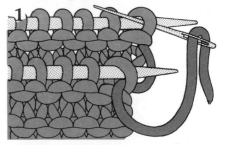

Prepare the pieces to be joined as described under Stitches off the needles and place *wrong* sides together with both needles pointing to the right. Thread the long end in to a blunt ended sewing needle.

1 Insert the sewing needle into the first stitch on the front needle as if to purl it, draw the yarn through

Grafting single ribbed edges

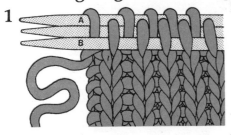

To join two pieces in single ribbing it is much easier if you use needles with points at both ends. However, if you don't have any start with the holding needle pointing to the right on both pieces. Leave a long end of yarn on one of the pieces.

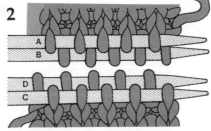

Slip the point of a second needle (needle A) into all the knit stitches on the holding needle (so each knit stitch has two needles through it).

1 Turn the ribbing over so that the points face to the left and slip a third needle (needle B) into all the

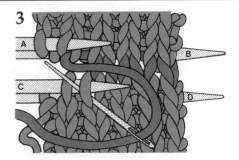

remaining stitches. Remove the holding needle carefully.

Repeat for the other piece of knitting, calling the needles C and D respectively.

2 Lay the two pieces flat on a table as shown with the long end of yarn

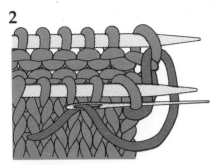

2

first stitch on the back needle as if to knit it, draw the yarn through and leave this stitch on the needle.
2 *Insert the sewing needle into the first stitch on the front needle again as if to knit it, draw the yarn through and slip this stitch off the needle. Insert the sewing needle into the next stitch on the front needle as if to purl it, draw the yarn through and leave stitch on needle.

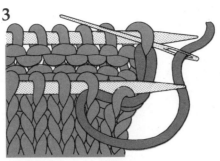

3

3 Insert the sewing needle into the first stitch on the back needle again as if to purl it, draw the yarn through and slip this stitch off the needle. Insert the sewing needle into the next stitch on the back needle as if to knit it, draw the yarn through and leave this stitch on the needle.

4

4 Continue from the * until all the stitches have been worked off both needles. Darn in all the ends.

Reversed stocking stitch edges

With the *knitted* sides facing each other, work as given for stocking stitch, reading knit for purl and purl for knit.
Alternatively, use stocking stitch method, then turn fabric inside out.

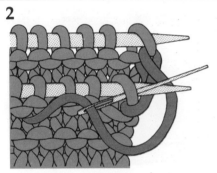

2

and leave this stitch on the needle. Insert the sewing needle into the first stitch on the back needle as if to purl it, draw the yarn through and leave this stitch on the needle.
2 *Insert the sewing needle into the first stitch on the front needle, again as if to knit it, draw the yarn through and slip this stitch off the

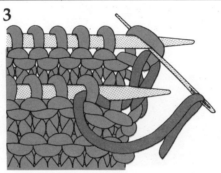

3

needle. Insert the sewing needle into the next stitch on the front needle as if to purl it, draw yarn through and leave this stitch on the needle.
3 Insert the sewing needle into the first stitch on the back needle, again as if to knit it, draw the yarn through and slip this stitch off the

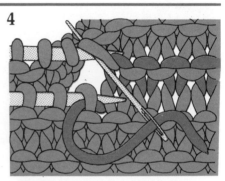

4

needle. Insert the sewing needle into the next stitch on the back needle as if to purl it, draw the yarn through and leave this stitch on the needle.
4 Continue from the * until all the stitches have been worked off both needles. Darn in all ends.

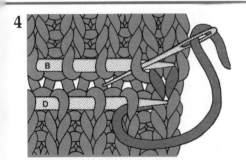

4

at the right-hand edge of top piece.
3 Graft the stitches on needles A and C together as for stocking stitch.
4 Turn the pieces over. Graft the stitches on needles B and D together as for stocking stitch. Darn in all the ends.

Grafting off the needles

Single rib cannot be grafted off the needles because while joining the sets of knit stitches you would unravel the purl stitches that lie in between each of the knit stitches.
Stocking stitch is grafted as you would if it were on the needles

(stocking stitch left and garter stitch right)

except that you work vertically across from the upper piece to the lower piece of knitting instead of from the back to the front needle.
Garter stitch is also grafted as you would if it were on the needles but it is worked vertically as above.

Toddler's coat for a boy or girl

This snug double-breasted coat is worked entirely in garter stitch and is trimmed with twisted rib in a contrasting colour.

The edges of the hood have been grafted together to make a neat and comfortable join.

Sizes

To fit 51 [56:61]cm/20 [22:24]in chest
Length to shoulder, 46 [50:55]cm/ 18 [19¾:21¾]in
Sleeve seam, 22 [25.5:30]cm/ 8½ [10:11½]in
The figures in [] refer to the 56/22 and 61cm/24in sizes respectively

You will need

6 [6:7] × 50g balls of Wendy Shetland Double Knitting (100% wool) in main colour A
1 [2:2] balls of same in contrast colour B
One pair 3¼mm/No 10 needles
One pair 4mm/No 8 needles
Eight buttons

Tension

24 sts and 48 rows to 10cm/4in over g st worked on 4mm/No 8 needles

Back

With 4mm/No 8 needles and A cast on 98 [104:110] sts. K 7 rows g st and mark first row with coloured thread to denote Ws of work.

Shape sides

Cont in g st dec one st at each end of next and every foll 8th [10th:10th] row 14 times in all. 70 [76:82] sts. Cont without shaping until work measures 34 [37:40]cm/ 13½ [14½:16]in from beg, or required length to underarm, ending with a Ws row.

Shape armholes

Cast off 3 sts at beg of next 2 rows. K one row. Dec one st at each end of next and foll 2 alt rows. 58 [64:70] sts.

Cont without shaping until armholes measure 12 [13:15]cm/ 4½ [5:6]in from beg, ending with a Ws row.

Shape shoulders

Cast off 8 [9:10] sts at beg of next 4 rows. Cast off rem sts.

Pocket lining (make 2)

With 4mm/No 8 needles and A cast on 20 sts. Work 24 [28:30] rows g st. Leave sts on holders.

Left front

With 4mm/No 8 needles and A cast on 61 [66:70] sts. Mark first st with coloured thread to denote front edge and work 7 rows g st.
8th row K1, dec one, K to end.
Cont dec one st at beg of every foll 8th [10th:10th] row in this way 6 [5:6] times more. 54 [60:63] sts.

Work 6 rows g st, ending at front edge.

Divide for pocket

Next row K36 [38:41] sts, turn and leave rem sts on holder.
Work 7 [7.5:7.5]cm/2¾ [3:3]in g st ending at pocket opening edge. Leave sts on spare needle.
Rejoin yarn to pocket lining sts, K across these sts then K across rem sts of left front on holder. 38 [42:42] sts.
Cont dec at side edge on every 8th [10th:10th] row as before, work until this side of pocket measures same as front edge, ending at pocket lining edge.
Next row Cast off 20 pocket lining sts, K to end.
Work 14 rows g st across all sts.
Next row (buttonhole row) K3 sts, cast off 3 sts, K to end.
Next row K to end, casting on 3 sts above those cast off in previous row.
These 2 rows are rep on every foll 17th/18th [19th/20th:19th/20th] rows 3 times more, *at the same time* cont to shape side until 47 [52:56] sts rem, then work without shaping until front measures same as back to underarm, ending at side edge.

Shape armhole

Cast off 3 sts at beg of next row. Work one row. Dec one st at armhole edge on next and foll 2 alt rows. 41 [46:50] sts.
Working buttonholes as before cont without shaping until front measures 7cm/2¾in less than back to shoulder ending at front edge.

Shape neck

Next row Cast off 12 [15:15] sts, K to end.
K one row. Cast off 2 sts at beg of next and every alt row 5 times. Dec one st at same edge of every alt row until 16 [18:20] sts rem. Work without shaping until front measures same as back to shoulder, ending at armhole edge.

Shape shoulder

Cast off at beg of next and foll alt row 8 [9:10] sts twice.

Right front

With 4mm/No 8 needles and A cast on 61 [66:70] sts. Mark last st of first row with contrasting yarn to denote

front edge and work as given for left front, reversing all shaping and omitting buttonholes.

Sleeves

With 3¼mm/No 10 needles and B cast on 32 [34:38] sts.
1st row (Rs) *K1 tbl, P1, rep from * to end.
Rep this row 13 times more. Break off B. Change to 4mm/No 8 needles. Join in A.
Next row (inc row) K1 [2:1] sts, *M1, K5 [5:6] sts, rep from * to last 1 [2:1] sts, M1, K1 [2:1]. 39 [41:45] sts.
Work 6 rows g st. Inc one st at each end of next and every foll 8th row 9 [11:12] times in all. 57 [63:69] sts.
Cont without shaping until work measures 22 [25.5:30]cm/ 8½ [10:11½]in from beg, ending with a Ws row.

Shape top

Cast off 3 sts at beg of next 2 rows.
Dec one st at each end of next and every alt row until 37 sts rem. Cast off 2 sts at beg of next 6 rows, and 3 sts at beg of next 2 rows. Cast off rem 19 sts.

Hood

With 4mm/No 8 needles and A cast on 76 [80:84] sts. Work 18cm/7in g st.

Shape top

1st row K29 [31:33] sts, sl 1, K2 tog, psso, K12, sl 1, K2 tog, psso, K29 [31:33] sts.
2nd and every alt row K to end.
3rd row K29 [31:33] sts, sl 1, K2 tog, psso, K8, sl 1, K2 tog, psso, K29 [31:33] sts.
5th row K29 [31:33] sts, sl 1, K2 tog, psso, K4, sl 1, K2 tog, psso, K29 [31:33] sts.
7th row K29 [31:33] sts, (sl 1, K2 tog, psso) twice, K29 [31:33] sts.
9th row K30 [32:34] sts, turn. Leave

both sets of sts on needles and graft edges tog.

Pocket bands (make 2)

With 3¼mm/No 10 needles and A cast on 24 sts. Work 5 rows twisted rib as given for sleeves. Cast off with a K row.

Front bands (make 2)

With 3¼mm/No 10 needles and B cast on 100 [116:130] sts. Work as given for pocket bands.

Armhole bands (make 2)

With 3¼mm/No 10 needles and B cast on 92 [96:100] sts. Work as given for pocket bands.

Hood band

With 3¼mm/No 10 needles and B cast on 120 sts. Work as given for pocket bands.

Neck band

With 3¼mm/No 10 needles and B cast on 134 [136:138] sts. Work as given for pocket bands.

To make up

Do not press. With ridge of cast-off edge uppermost top st pocket bands to edge of pockets. Top st front bands to front edges in same way. Join shoulder seams, noting that buttonholes are on right front for a girl or left front for a boy. Sew neckband right round neck edge. Sew in sleeves. Sew on arm bands to cover seams. Join sleeve and side seams. Sew pocket linings in place. Sew hood band round front edge of hood. Sew hood to back neck just below the neckband on the outside of the coat, easing in place slightly from about 1cm/½in over shoulder seam. Make tassel with B and st to top of hood. Sew on two sets of four buttons for double breasted effect.

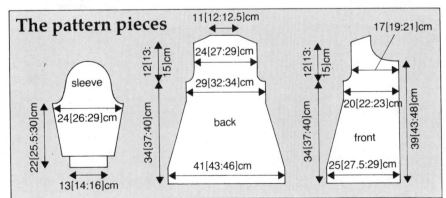

The pattern pieces

sleeve
22[25.5:30]cm
24[26:29]cm
13[14:16]cm

11[12:12.5]cm
12[13:15]cm
24[27:29]cm
29[32:34]cm
back
34[37:40]cm
41[43:46]cm

17[19:21]cm
12[13:15]cm
20[22:23]cm
front
34[37:40]cm
39[43:48]cm
25[27.5:29]cm

Knitting in rounds

Knitting on sets of needles pointed at each end, or on a circular needle, produces seamless, tubular fabrics. You do not turn at the end of each row as in knitting with pairs of needles, so the right side is always facing you, which affects the methods of working even basic patterns.

Knitting in rounds is the ideal way of making socks, gloves, hats, skirts, or anything that would be spoiled by a bulky seam. Jerseys can also be knitted in the round up to the underarms, then divided and continued in rows as normal – in fact this is how trad-itional Aran and Guernsey designs are knitted.

You can knit in rounds with either a set of needles – four, five or six – or a circular needle. (Circular needles can also be used to work to and fro in rows.)

When you are knitting in rounds remember that the right side of the fabric is always facing you as you do not turn to begin another row. If you are working a pattern, the method will be different from when knitting in rows, though the result will be the same.

To cast on with a circular needle

Use the ends of the needle as a pair to cast on the number of stitches required with the method you prefer. Make sure the stitches do not become twisted round the nylon strip which joins the needle ends together. To knit in rounds use the right-hand needle point to work across all the cast-on stitches until you come to the beginning of the round again.

Alternatively, after casting on, turn and use the circular needle as a pair of needles, working the first row without joining it into a round. This is an easier method because it prevents the stitches becoming twisted round the nylon strip, but it does leave a gap in the work. Continue knitting in rounds and join the gap at the beginning with a

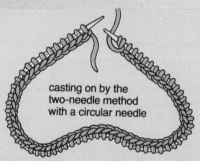

casting on by the two-needle method with a circular needle

few oversewn stitches.
Circular needles are sold in different lengths, to accommodate varying numbers of cast on stitches. The chart on the right lists the minimum number of stitches to cast on for each length of needle, to ensure that you can reach from one needle point to the other without stretching the fabric.

Minimum no of stitches required for circular needles

Tension (sts to 2.5cm/1in)	Needle length			
	40cm 16in	60cm 24in	80cm 30in	100cm 40in
5	80	117	157	196
5½	88	129	173	216
6	96	141	189	236
6½	104	153	205	255
7	112	164	220	275
7½	120	176	236	294
8	128	188	252	314
8½	136	200	268	334
9	144	212	284	353

To cast off in rounds

If you are using a set of four needles, use the free needle to cast off the stitches on the first needle of the round until one stitch remains on the right-hand needle. Put aside the left-hand needle. Use the right-hand needle to cast the stitches off the second needle, and so on. When you get to the very last stitch, fasten off.

If you are using a circular needle, use the right-hand needle point to work the stitches and the left-hand needle point to lift them over and off the needle. When one stitch remains, fasten off.

three needles in use for casting off

one needle free

To cast on with four needles

When you are knitting, the stitches will be divided more or less equally between three needles.

1 Using the method you prefer, you can cast the right number of stitches on to each of the three needles to start with, but be careful that they don't get twisted round the needle before you begin to knit.

An easier method for a small number of stitches is to cast them all on to one needle. Work one or two rows in your pattern, then divide and transfer them to the second and third needles. This way you avoid the stitches getting twisted round the needles, but you will have a gap at the beginning of the work. Use a

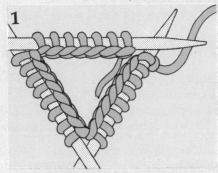

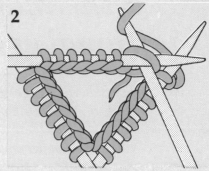

blunt-ended sewing needle and the cast-on end of yarn to join this with a few oversewn stitches.

2 Arrange the three needles in a triangle and use the fourth to begin knitting in rounds.

Work across the stitches of the first needle, then use this to work across the stitches of the second needle, and so on. Always pull the yarn tightly across to the first stitch on each needle to avoid a loose stitch.

Simple patterns knitted in the round

It is easy to convert simple patterns for knitting in the round. Here are the basic ones most often used.

Stocking stitch Work by knitting every round. This simplifies knitting multi-coloured patterns such as Fair Isle.

Garter stitch Work by knitting the first and every odd-numbered round. The second and every even-numbered round must be purled. Alternate rounds of knitting and purling form the ridged effect.

Single ribbing Work by alternately knitting and purling one stitch on the first round. If you begin a round with one knitted stitch you must end with one purled stitch to complete the round exactly. On every following round all the knitted stitches are knitted and the

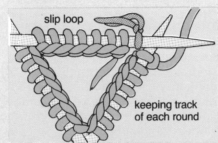

slip loop

keeping track of each round

purled stitches purled.

Single moss stitch Work by alternately knitting and purling one stitch on the first and every odd-numbered round. If you begin a round with one knitted stitch you must end with one purled stitch to complete the round exactly. In the second and every even-numbered round, the knitted stitches must be purled and purled stitches knitted.

Note:

It is easy to lose track of the beginning of each round, whether you are using sets of needles or a circular needle. Mark this point by making a slip loop in a length of different coloured yarn and put it on the needle at the beginning of the first round. Slip the loop from one needle point to the other on every round without working into it.

Fisherman knitting: traditional guernsey patterns

The type of fisherman's garment known as a guernsey – or gansey – originated in the Channel island of that name. As designs were adopted by one port after another, each region developed its own patterns incorporating symbols from their nautical surroundings.

Although traditional navy blue guernsey designs originated on the island of Guernsey, the patterns are also associated with many coastal areas of Britain. Ports, villages and even individual families, developed their own traditional patterns and it was said that fisherfolk could tell at a glance the port from which a sailor hailed by the designs on his jersey.

Most of the patterns have names associated with objects used by the fishermen in their daily work. Ropes of every kind, fishing nets, herring bones, anchors and ladders are all represented.

There are many similarities to Aran knitting – both use combinations of patterns such as cables and moss stitch but while Aran knitting includes relief textures and patterns featuring travelling stitches, the patterns used in fisherman's knitting do not generally stand out in relief against the background, but give the appearance of an even-textured fabric.

These everyday working garments were often knitted by the fishermen themselves – the body and sleeves in stocking stitch with a little pattern decoration on the yoke. More elaborate versions, referred to as bridal shirts, were knitted by young women for their betrothed.

The traditional square shape with a dropped shoulder-line was knitted in the round on sets of five or more needles. The sleeves were knitted from the shoulders to the cuffs which made them easy to unravel and re-knit when the elbows or cuffs wore through. The yarn, techniques and patterns used in knitting the authentic versions made them virtually wind and weatherproof.

The next chapter has a pattern for an authentic guernsey knitted in the round in the traditional navy blue worsted wool, while this chapter has a pattern for a child's jersey knitted in double knitting on two needles. The design uses four of the seven patterns given here and overleaf and experienced knitters will be able to interchange the patterns provided they make allowance for the varying multiples of stitches. The patterns included are as follows:

Ridge and furrow pattern which is made up of two rows of stocking stitch followed by two rows of reversed stocking stitch, repeated as many times as required. Used across the width of the fabric it is an effective way of separating one pattern from the next.

Anchor pattern which is one of the many nautical patterns, can be worked as a border across a row, or repeated one anchor above the other as a vertical panel.

Ridge and furrow pattern

This can be worked over any number of stitches.
1st row K to end.
2nd row P to end.
3rd row P to end.
4th row K to end.
These 4 rows form the pattern.

Ladder pattern

Cast on multiples of 6 sts plus 2 sts, eg 26.
1st row (Rs) P2, *K4, P2, rep from * to end.
2nd row K2, *P4, K2, rep from * to end.
3rd row P to end.
4th row As 2nd.
These 4 rows form the pattern.

Ladder pattern which is said to represent the ladder of life. The purl ridges form the rungs of the ladder. It is best worked as a vertical panel between purl ribs.

Flag pattern which is another nautical symbol representng the jaunty pennant on a fishing boat. It needs to be worked as a vertical panel, preferably against moss stitch.

Betty Martin's pattern which is an example of the kind of simple pattern which would have been passed from one generation to another by word of mouth, becoming known by the name of the knitter who first used it.

Diamond pattern which has a moss stitch diamond shape against a stocking stitch background and can be worked as a border or a vertical panel. There are many variations of this basic shape, some depicting windows, others fishing nets, depending on the area of origin.

Marriage lines which is made up of zigzag lines of purl stitches on a knit background. This represents difficult paths of flashes of lightning – a wry comment on daily life, showing the ups and downs of married life.

Right: The welts of these children's jerseys are knitted in rib instead of the traditional garter stitch.

Casting on for guernseys

This special way of casting on forms a very hardwearing knotted edge. Use the correct yarn and the looped method (see page 175).

Cast on 2 stitches. Use a spare needle to lift the second stitch on the main needle over the top of the first stitch and off the needle.

*Cast on 2 more stitches, then lift the second stitch over the top of the first and off the needle, leaving 2 stitches on the main needle.

Continue from the * until the correct number of stitches have been cast on.

Flag pattern

Cast on multiples of 11 sts plus 3 sts, eg 25.
1st row (Rs) *K1, P1, K1 – **called moss st 3**, K1, P7, rep from * to last 3 sts, moss st 3.
2nd row *Moss st 3, K6, P2, rep from * to last 3 sts, moss st 3.
3rd row *Moss st 3, K3, P5, rep from * to last 3 sts, moss st 3.
4th row *Moss st 3, K4, P4, rep from * to last 3 sts, moss st 3.
5th row *Moss st 3, K5, P3, rep from * to last 3 sts, moss st 3.
6th row *Moss st 3, K2, P6, rep from * to last 3 sts, moss st 3.
7th row *Moss st 3, K7, P1, rep from * to last 3 sts, moss st 3.
8th row *Moss st 3, P8, rep from * to last 3 sts, moss st 3.
These 8 rows form the pattern.

Marriage lines pattern

Cast on multiples of 13 sts plus 2 sts, eg 28.
1st row (Rs) *P2, K5, P1, K2, P1, K2, rep from * to last 2 sts, P2.
2nd row *K2, P1, K1, P2, K1, P6, rep from * to last 2 sts, K2.
3rd row As 1st.
4th row *K2, P3, K1, P2, K1, P4, rep from * to last 2 sts, K2.
5th row *P2, K3, P1, K2, P1, K4, rep from * to last 2 sts, P2.
6th row *K2, P5, K1, P2, K1, P2, rep from * to last 2 sts, K2.
7th row *P2, K1, P1, K2, P1, K6, rep from * to last 2 sts, P2.
8th row *K2, P5, K1, P2, K1, P2, rep from * to last 2 sts, K2.
9th row *P2, K3, P1, K2, P1, K4, rep from * to last 2 sts, P2.
10th row *K2, P3, K1, P2, K1, P4, rep from * to last 2 sts, K2.
These 10 rows form the pattern.

Anchor pattern

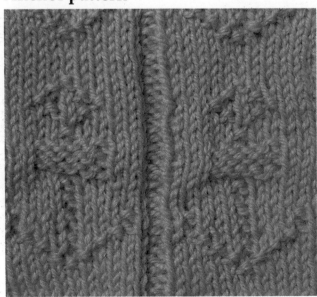

Cast on multiples of 13 sts plus 2 sts, eg 28.
1st row (Rs) *P2, K11, rep from * to last 2 sts, P2.
2nd row *K2, P11, rep from * to last 2 sts, K2.
3rd row As 1st.
4th row As 2nd.
5th row *P2, K5, P1, K5, rep from * to last 2 sts, P2.
6th row *K2, P4, K1, P1, K1, P4, rep from * to last 2 sts, K2.
7th row *P2, K3, (P1, K1) twice, P1, K3, rep from * to last 2 sts, P2.
8th row *K2, P2, K1, P5, K1, P2, rep from * to last 2 sts, K2.
9th row *P2, K1, P1, K3, P1, K3, P1, K1, rep from * to last 2 sts, P2.
10th row *K2, P1, K1, P7, K1, P1, rep from * to last 2 sts, K2.
11th row As 5th.
12th row As 2nd.
13th row As 5th.
14th row As 2nd.

Diamond pattern

Cast on multiples of 13 sts plus 2 sts, eg 28.
1st row (Rs) *P2, K11, rep from * to last 2 sts, P2.
2nd row *K2, P11, rep from * to last 2 sts, K2.
3rd row As 1st.
4th row *K2, P5, K1, P5, rep from * to last 2 sts, K2.
5th row *P2, K4, P1, K1, P1, K4, rep from * to last 2 sts, P2.
6th row *K2, P3, (K1, P1) twice, K1, P3, rep from * to last 2 sts, K2.
7th row *P2, K2, (P1, K1) 3 times, P1, K2, rep from * to last 2 sts, P2.
8th row *K2, (P1, K1) 5 times, P1, rep from * to last 2 sts, K2.
9th row As 7th.
10th row As 6th.
11th row As 5th.
12th row As 4th.
These 12 rows form the pattern.

15th row *P2, K3, P5, K3, rep from * to last 2 sts, P2.
16th row *K2, P3, K5, P3, rep from * to last 2 sts, K2.
17th row As 15th.
18th row As 2nd.
19th row As 5th.
20th row As 2nd.
21st row *P2, K4, P1, K1, P1, K4, rep from * to last 2 sts, P2.
22nd row *K2, P3, K1, P3, K1, P3, rep from * to last 2 sts, K2.
23rd row As 21st.
24th row *K2, P5, K1, P5, rep from * to last 2 sts, K2.
These 24 rows form the pattern.

Right: The yoke of this child's jersey has a combination of traditional patterns. The sleeves are knitted from the sleeve head down to the cuff, so that they can be unpicked and re-knitted to lengthen or repair them.

Betty Martin's pattern

Cast on multiples of 4 sts plus 2 sts, eg 22.
1st row (Rs) *K2, P2, rep from * to last 2 sts, K2.
2nd row *P2, K2, rep from * to last 2 sts, P2.
3rd row K.
4th row P.
These 4 rows form the pattern.

Colourful jerseys with guernsey pattern yokes

This child's version of a guernsey has been modified to suit modern knitting techniques and preferences but uses the special method of casting on.

Sizes

To fit 61[66:71:76]cm/24[26:28:30]in chest
Length to shoulder, 38[42:46:50]cm/15[16½:18:19¾]in
Sleeve seam, 30[33:36:39]cm/11¾[13:14¼:15¼]in
The figures in [] refer to the 66/26, 71/28 and 76cm/30in sizes respectively

You will need

5[6:7:8]×50g balls of Hayfield Brig Double Knitting (100% wool)
One pair 3¼mm/No 10 needles
One pair 4mm/No 8 needles
Set of four 3¼mm/No 10 needles pointed at both ends

Tension

22 sts and 30 rows to 10cm/4in over st st worked on 4mm/No 8 needles

Back

With 3¼mm/No 10 needles cast on 71[77:83:89] sts by the guernsey method.
1st row (Rs) K1, *P1, K1, rep from * to end.
2nd row P1, *K1, P1, rep from * to end.
Rep these 2 rows for 4[4:5:5]cm/1½[1½:2:2]in, ending with a 2nd row.
Change to 4mm/No 8 needles. Beg with a K row cont in st st until work measures 21[24:26:29]cm/8¼[9½:10¼:11½]in from beg, ending with a P row.
Work 14[14:18:18] rows ridge and furrow patt, ending with a 2nd row.

Yoke

1st row P1[4:3:2] sts, (**marriage lines patt** K5, P1, K2, P1, K2), P2 sts, (**Betty Martin's patt** (K2, P2) 3[3:4:5] times, K2), (**diamond patt** P2, K11, P2), (**Betty Martin's patt** (K2, P2) 3[3:4:5] times, K2,), P2 sts, (**marriage lines patt** K5, P1, K2, P1, K2), P1[4:3:2] sts.
2nd row K1[4:3:2] sts, work 11 sts as 2nd row of marriage lines patt, K2 sts, work 14[14:18:22] sts as 2nd row of Betty Martin's patt, work 15 sts as 2nd row of diamond patt, work 14[14:18:22] sts as 2nd row of Betty Martin's patt, K2 sts, work 11 sts as 2nd row of marriage lines patt, K1[4:3:2] sts.
Beg with a 3rd row of each patt, cont in patt as now set until work measures 38[42:46:50]cm/15[16½:18:19¾]in from beg, ending with a Ws row.

Shape shoulders

Cast off at beg of next and every row 7[8:8:9] sts 4 times and 7[7:9:9] sts twice. Leave rem 29[31:33:35] sts on holder for centre back neck.

Front

Work as given for back until work measures 33[37:40:44]cm/13[14½:15¾:17¼]in from beg, ending with a Ws row.

Shape neck

Next row Patt 30[32:35:37] sts, turn and leave rem sts on holder.
Complete left shoulder first. Cast off at beg of next and foll alt row for neck edge 2 sts twice, then dec one st at beg of foll 5[5:6:6] alt rows. 21[23:25:27] sts.
Cont without shaping if necessary until work measures same as back to shoulder, ending with a Ws row.

Shape shoulder

Cast off at beg of next and every alt row 7[8:8:9] sts twice and 7[7:9:9] sts once.
With Rs of work facing, leave first 11[13:13:15] sts on holder for centre front neck, rejoin yarn to rem sts and patt to end. Work one row then complete to match first side.

Sleeves

With 4mm/No 8 needles cast on 61[67:73:79] sts by the thumb method and beg at top. Work 14[14:18:18] rows ridge and furrow patt, then beg with a K row work 2 rows st st.
Cont in st st, dec one st at each end of next and every foll 6th row until 39[43:47:51] sts rem. Cont without shaping until sleeve measures 26[29:31:34]cm/10¼[11½:12¼:13½]in from beg, ending with a K row.
Next row (dec row) P1[3:0:2] sts, (P2 tog, P3) 7[7:9:9] times, P2 tog, P1[3:0:2] sts. 31[35:37:41] sts.
Change to 3¼mm/No 10 needles. Beg with a 1st row cont in rib as given for back for 4[4:5:5]cm/1½[1½:2:2]in. Cast off loosely in rib.

Neckband

Join shoulder seams. With Rs of work facing and set of 3¼mm/No 10 needles K across back neck sts on holder, pick up and K18[18:20:20] sts down left front neck, K across front neck sts on holder, pick up and K18[18:20:20] sts up right front neck. 76[80:86:90] sts.
Work 4[4:5:5]cm/1½[1½:2:2]in in rounds of K1, P1 rib. Cast off loosely in rib.

To make up

Press lightly under a damp cloth with a warm iron. Set in sleeves. Join side and sleeve seams. Fold neckband in half to Ws and sl st down. Press seams.

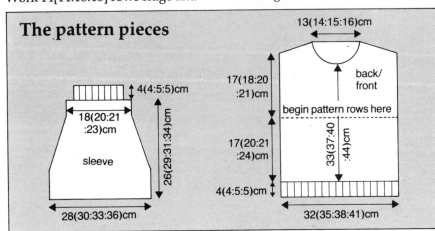

The pattern pieces

4(4:5:5)cm
18(20:21:23)cm
26(29:31:34)cm
sleeve
28(30:33:36)cm

13(14:15:16)cm
17(18:20:21)cm
back/front
begin pattern rows here
17(20:21:24)cm
33(37:40:44)cm
4(4:5:5)cm
32(35:38:41)cm

Guernseys in the round

A true guernsey is so cleverly constructed and cunningly worked that it pays considerable tribute to the inventive knitters of the past. It involves the minimum of technical problems yet creates a garment offering maximum protection and freedom of movement

Authentic fishermens' garments were originally knitted with a special 5 ply worsted wool similar to a double knitting weight and particularly firm and hard wearing. The traditional colour was navy blue but today guernsey wool is available in red and cream as well.

Sets of five long, double-pointed needles, about size 2mm/No 14, were used to knit the garment – four to hold the stitches and the fifth to knit with. These can be replaced by circular needles.

Scottish versions were often knitted with a 6 ply yarn. This was softer than worsted wool and tended to mat together, making the felted fabric completely weatherproof. The needles were also thicker, about 2¾mm/No 12, and shorter, sold in sets of up to eight to take all the stitches.

Knitting the body

To begin the back and front, the welts were cast on separately with two needles, using the wool double and the knotted cast-on method for greater strength (page 205). Once the welts were completed, the front and back were joined into a round for the body, leaving welt flaps open at the sides for ease of movement.

The positions for mock side seams were marked with one or two purl stitches up each side of the body and used as a guide to positioning the increased stitches for underarm gussets. The underarm gusset was incorporated about half-way up the body under the arms to give freedom of movement.

Below: The neck gusset provides extra stitches so that the loose fitting neckband stands away from the neck.

Knitting the armholes

Instead of dividing the work on to two needles at the armhole, authentic designs continued in rounds. The position of the armholes was marked on every round by winding the yarn several times round the needle, before continuing the knitting. These loops were dropped off the needle on the following round and the process repeated until the armholes were the required length. This separated back from front.

When the body was completed, a series of loose strands of yarn would mark the position of each armhole. These loops were then cut in half and the ends darned back into the main fabric. This made a rather bulky edge and nowadays most knitters prefer to divide the work at the underarm and complete back and front separately.

Knitting the sleeves

The stitches for the sleeves were picked up round the armholes, including the underarm stitches of the gusset. The sleeves were knitted from the shoulder down to the cuff – this part received the most wear and could easily be unpicked and re-knitted. Further re-inforcement was added by casting off cuffs with double yarn. The sleeves often appear to be rather short. This is because they were practical, working garments for men whose hands were often in water – and soaking wet cuffs were the last thing a fisherman would want.

Sheringham herringbone and diamond

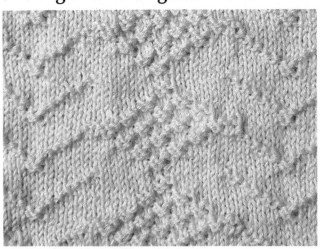

Cast on multiples of 28 sts plus 14 sts.
1st row (Rs) *K6, P2, K12, P2, K6, rep from * to last 14 sts, K6, P2, K6.
2nd row *P6, K2, P12, K2, P6, rep from * to last 14 sts, P6, K2, P6.
3rd row *K5, P1, K2, P1, K9, P2, K2, P2, K4, rep from * to last 14 sts, K5, P1, K2, P1, K5.
4th row *P4, K1, P4, K1, P8, K2, P2, K2, P4, rep from * to last 14 sts, P4, K1, P4, K1, P4.
5th row *K3, P1, K6, P1, K5, (P2, K2) 3 times, rep from * to last 14 sts, K3, P1, K6, P1, K3.
6th row *P2, K1, P8, K1, P4, (K2, P2) 3 times, rep from * to last 14 sts, P2, K1, P8, K1, P2.
7th row *K1, P1, K10, P1, K1, (P2, K2) 3 times, P2, rep from * to last 14 sts, K1, P1, K10, P1, K1.
8th row *K1, P12, K1, (K2, P2) 3 times, K2, rep from * to last 14 sts, K1, P12, K1.
9th row *K6, P2, K8, (P2, K2) 3 times, rep from * to last 14 sts, K6, P2, K6.
10th row *P6, K2, P8, (K2, P2) 3 times, rep from * to last 14 sts, P6, K2, P6.
11th row As 3rd.
12th row As 4th.
13th row *K3, P1, K6, P1, K9, P2, K6, rep from * to last 14 sts, K3, P1, K6, P1, K3.
14th row *P2, K1, P8, K1, P8, K2, P6, rep from * to last 14 sts, P2, K1, P8, K1, P2.
15th row *K1, P1, K10, P1, K15, rep from * to last 14 sts, K1, P1, K10, P1, K1.
16th row *K1, P12, K1, P14, rep from * to last 14 sts, K1, P12, K1. These 16 rows form the pattern.

Fife heart

Cast on multiples of 16 sts plus 3 sts.
1st row (Rs) *P1, K1, P1, K6, P1, K6, rep from * to last 3 sts, P1, K1, P1.
2nd row *K1, P1, K1, P5, K3, P5, rep from * to last 3 sts, K1, P1, K1.
3rd row *P1, K1, P1, K4, P2, K1, P2, K4, rep from * to last 3 sts, P1, K1, P1.
4th row *K1, P1, K1, P3, K2, P3, K2, P3, rep from * to last 3 sts, K1, P1, K1.
5th row *P1, K1, P1, K2, P2, K5, P2, K2, rep from * to last 3 sts, P1, K1, P1.
6th row *(K1, P1) twice, K2, P3, K1, P3, K2, P1, rep from * to last 3 sts, K1, P1, K1.
7th row *(P1, K1) twice, P2, K2, P3, K2, P2, K1, rep from * to last 3 sts, P1, K1, P1.
8th row *K1, P1, K1, P2, K4, P1, K4, P2, rep from * to last 3 sts, K1, P1, K1.
9th row *P1, K1, P1, (K3, P2) twice, K3, rep from * to last 3 sts, P1, K1, P1.
10th row *K1, P1, K1, P13, rep from * to last 3 sts, K1, P1, K1.
11th row *P1, K1, P1, K13, rep from * to last 3 sts, P1, K1, P1.
12th row As 10th.
Rep 11th and 12th rows twice more.
These 16 rows form the pattern.

Knitting the neck

Shaped neck gussets were often included in the neckband so that it made a loose-fitting stand-up collar about 5cm/2in high.

Scottish versions had a button and buttonhole band on one shoulder and a close-fitting neckband. This makes a much neater finish and the neck does not stretch out of shape every time it is pulled over the head. Sheringham herringbone and diamond pattern and Fife heart pattern are used in the guernsey patterns given at the end of this chapter. Two other patterns are also included and can be substituted by experienced knitters.

Sheringham herringbone and diamond pattern makes an all-over pattern for a yoke. The herringbones do not have a centre spine and the diamonds are worked in double moss stitch.

Fife heart pattern is a romantic little motif and would have been worked into a bridal shirt. It makes a useful filler between larger patterns.

Filey cable and herringbone pattern is associated with this fishing port. The cable is a simple twist over six stitches and the herringbone has a centre spine.

Whitby cable and diamond pattern is one of the many patterns associated with this area. The cable is a simple twist over six stitches and the diamond is purled against a knitted background.

Filey cable and herringbone

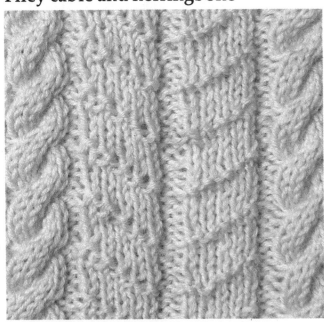

Cast on multiples of 22 sts plus 10 sts.
1st row (Rs) *P2, K6, P2, K5, P2, K5, rep from * to last 10 sts, P2, K6, P2.
2nd row *K2, P6, K2, P4, K4, P4, rep from * to last 10 sts, K2, P6, K2.
3rd row *P2, K6, P2, K3, P1, K1, P2, K1, P1, K3, rep from * to last 10 sts, P2, K6, P2.
4th row *K2, P6, K2, P2, K1, P2, K2, P2, K1, P2, rep from * to last 10 sts, K2, P6, K2.
5th row *P2, K6, P2, K1, P1, K3, P2, K3, P1, K1, rep from * to last 10 sts, P2, K6, P2.
6th row *K2, P6, K3, P4, K2, P4, K1, rep from * to last 10 sts, K2, P6, K2.
7th row *P2, C6B (see page 206), P2, K5, P2, K5, rep from * to last 10 sts, P2, C6B, P2.
The 2nd and 7th rows inclusive form the pattern.

Whitby cable and diamond

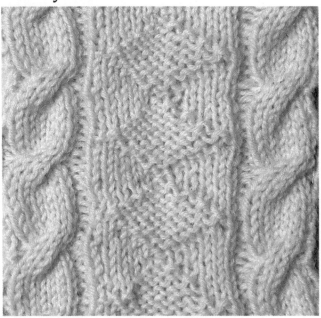

Cast on multiples of 21 sts plus 10 sts.
1st row (Rs) *P2, K6, P2, K11, rep from * to last 10 sts, P2, K6, P2.
2nd row *K2, P6, K2, P5, K1, P5, rep from * to last 10 sts, K2, P6, K2.
3rd row *P2, C6B (see page 206), P2, K4, P3, K4, rep from * to last 10 sts, P2, C6B, P2.
4th row *K2, P6, K2, P3, K5, P3, rep from * to last 10 sts, K2, P6, K2.
5th row *P2, K6, P2, K2, P7, K2, rep from * to last 10 sts, P2, K6, P2.
6th row *K2, P6, K2, P1, K9, P1, rep from * to last 10 sts, K2, P6, K2.
7th row As 5th.
8th row As 4th.
9th row *P2, K6, P2, K4, P3, K4, rep from * to last 10 sts, P2, K6, P2.
10th row As 2nd.
These 10 rows form the pattern.

Authentic guernseys for a man or woman

These jerseys include many of the traditional guernsey features, such as mock side seams and underarm and neck gussets, and the sleeves are knitted from the shoulder to the cuff. To make the garments easier to knit they have been worked on circular needles, instead of sets of needles, and divided at the armholes.

Sizes

To fit 86[91:97:102]cm/34 [36:38:40]in bust/chest loosely
Length to shoulder, 63 [65:67:69]cm/ 24¾ [25½:26½:27¼]in
Sleeve seam, 46 [47:48:49]cm/ 18 [18½:19:19¼]in, adjustable
The figures in [] refer to the 91/36, 97/38 and 102cm/40in sizes respectively.

You will need

16 [17:18:19]×50g balls of Emu guernsey (100% wool)
One pair 2¾mm/No 12 needles
One pair 3mm/No 11 needles
One 2¾mm/No 12 circular needle 100cm/40in long
One 3mm/No 11 circular needle 100cm/40in long
Set of four 2¾mm/No 12 needles pointed at both ends
Set of four 3mm/No 11 needles pointed at both ends
One cable needle

Tension

28 sts and 36 rows to 10cm/4in over st st worked on 3mm/No 11 needles

Body

With 2¾mm/No 12 needles cast on 127 [135:143:151] sts by the guernsey method
Work 7cm/2¾in g st ending with a Ws row. Break off yarn and leave these sts for time being.
Work a second piece in same way but do not break off yarn.

Join body

Change to 2¾mm/No 12 circular needle and cont working in rounds to underarm.
Next round Inc in first st, K to end across second piece, cont across first piece and inc in first st, K to end. Join into a circle taking care not to twist sts. 256 [272:288:304] sts.
Work 6 rounds K2, P2 rib.
Change to 3mm/No 11 circular needle. Commence mock side seams.
1st round *P1, K127 [135:143:151] sts, rep from * once more.
2nd round K to end.
Rep these 2 rounds until work measures 38cm/15in from beg, ending with a 1st round.

Shape underarm gusset

1st round *Pick up loop lying between sts and K tbl – called M1, K1, M1, K127 [135:143:151] sts, rep from * once more.
2nd round K to end.
3rd round *M1, K3, M1, K127 [135:143:151] sts, rep from * once more.
Cont inc in this way on every alt round until there are 292 [308:324:340] sts, ending with an inc round.

Divide for armholes

Next row K19 sts and sl these sts on to a thread for gusset, K127[135:143:151] sts, turn and leave rem sts on spare needle. Complete front first. K 4 rows g st, inc one st in centre of last row on 1st and 2nd sizes only, and dec one st in centre of last row on 3rd and 4th sizes only. 128 [136:142:150] sts.
Next row (Ws) K1, (K1, P1) 1 [3:1:3] times, (K2, P5) 1 [1:2:2] times, *K2, P6, K2, P13, K2, P6, K2*, P42, rep from * to *, (P5, K2) 1 [1:2:2] times, (P1, K1) 1 [3:1:3] times, K1.
Sts are now set for yoke patt. Cont in patt.

Yoke

1st row P1, (P1, K1) 1 [3:1:3] times, (P2, K5) 1 [1:2:2] times, *P2, K6, P2, (K6, P1, K6 noting that these 13 sts are 1st row of heart patt), P2, K6, P2*, (K6, P2, K12, P2, K12, P2, K6 noting that these 42 sts are 1st row of Sheringham herringbone and diamond patt), rep from * to *, (K5, P2) 1[1:2:2] times, (K1, P1) 1 [3:1:3] times, P1.
2nd row K1, (K1, P1) 1 [3:1:3] times, (on 3rd and 4th sizes only K2, P4, K1), on all sizes K3, P4, *K2, P6, K2, work 2nd row of heart patt, K2, P6, K2*, work 2nd row of Sheringham patt, rep from * to *, P4, K3, (on 3rd and 4th sizes only K1, P4, K2), on all sizes (P1, K1) 1 [3:1:3] times, K1.
3rd row P1, (P1, K1) 1 [3:1:3] times, (on 3rd and 4th sizes only P2, K3, P1, K1), on all sizes P2, K1, P1, K3, *P2, sl next 3 sts on to cable needle and hold at back of work, K3 then K3 from cable needle – called C6B, P2, work 3rd row of heart patt, P2, sl next 3 sts on to cable needle and hold at front of work, K3 then K3 from cable needle – called C6F, P2*, work 3rd row of Sheringham patt, rep from * to *, K3, P1, K1, P2, (on 3rd and 4th sizes only K1, P1, K3, P2), on all sizes (K1, P1) 1 [3:1:3] times, P1.
4th row K1, (K1, P1) 1 [3:1:3] times, (K2, P2, K1, P2) 1 [1:2:2] times, *K2, P6, K2, work 4th row of heart patt, K2, P6, K2*, work 4th row of Sheringham patt, rep from * to *, (P2, K1, P2, K2) 1 [1:2:2] times, (P1, K1) 1 [3:1:3] times, K1.
5th row P1, (P1, K1) 1 [3:1:3] times,

The pattern pieces

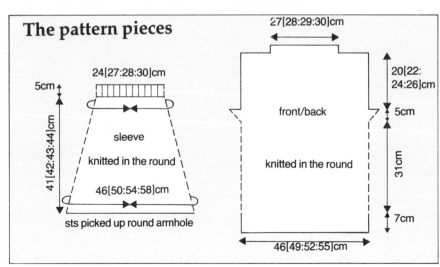

24[27:28:30]cm

5cm

41[42:43:44]cm

sleeve
knitted in the round

46[50:54:58]cm

sts picked up round armhole

27[28:29:30]cm

20[22:24:26]cm

5cm

front/back

knitted in the round

31cm

7cm

46[49:52:55]cm

(on 3rd and 4th sizes only P2, K1, P1, K3), on all sizes P2, K3, P1, K1, *P2, K6, P2, work 5th row of heart patt, P2, K6, P2*, work 5th row of Sheringham patt, rep from * to *, K1, P1, K3, P2, (on 3rd and 4th sizes only K3, P1, K1, P2), on all sizes (K1, P1) 1 [3:1:3] times, P1.
6th row K1, (K1, P1) 1 [3:1:3] times, (on 3rd and 4th sizes only K3, P4), on all sizes K2, P4, K3, *P6, K2, work 6th row of heart patt, K2, P6*, K2, work 6th row of Sheringham patt, K2, rep from * to *, K3, P4, K2, (on 3rd and 4th sizes only P4, K3), on all sizes (P1, K1) 1 [3:1:3] times, K1.
Working 16 row rep of heart patt and Sheringham patt, rep the last 6 rows until armholes measure 20 [22:24:26]cm/7¾ [8¾:9½:10¼]in from beg, ending with a Ws row.

Shape shoulders

Cast off 26 [29:31:34] sts at beg of next 2 rows. Leave rem 76 [78:80:82] sts on holder.
Return to sts on spare needle, with Rs facing rejoin yarn, K first 19 sts of gusset and leave on a thread, K to end.
Complete back to match front.

Neckband

Join shoulder seams. Sl back and front neck sts on to 2 needles from a set of 2¾mm/No 12 needles.
With Rs of work facing and 2¾mm/ No 12 needles, pick up and K1 st from neck edge of left shoulder seam, turn and P1.
Next row K1, then K1 from needle holding front neck sts, turn.
Next row P2, then P1 from needle holding back neck sts, turn.
Next row K3, then K1 from needle holding front neck sts, turn.
Cont in this way until there are 11 sts on needle. Break off yarn and leave sts for time being.
Rep at other side of neck, reading front for back and vice versa. Do not break off yarn.
With Rs of work facing and set of four 2¾mm/No 12 needles K across all sts round neck, inc one st at centre back and centre front. 156 [160:164:168] sts.
Cont in rounds of K2, P2 rib for 5cm/2in. Cast off loosely in rib.

Sleeves

With Rs of work facing and set of

four 3mm/No 11 needles, K across 19 sts of one underarm gusset, pick up and K110 [120:132:142] sts round armhole.
1st round K19 sts, P to end.
2nd round Sl 1, K1, psso, K15, K2 tog, K to end.
3rd round K17, P to end.
4th round Sl 1, K1, psso, K13, K2 tog, K to end.
5th round K to end.
Working in st st, cont to dec in the same way at each side of gusset sts on next and every alt round until 113 [123:135:145] sts rem, ending with a plain round.
18th round Sl 1, K2 tog, psso, K to end. 111 [121:133:143] sts.
19th round K to end.
20th round P1, K to end.
Rep 19th and 20th rounds twice more.
Next round K1, sl 1, K1, psso, K to

last 2 sts, K2 tog.
Next round As 20th.
Keeping mock seam st correct throughout, cont to dec in this way on every 6th [6th:5th:5th] round until 67 [75:77:85] sts rem.
Cont without shaping until sleeve measures 41 [42:43:44]cm/16¼ [16½:17:17¼]in from end of gusset dec 3 [7:5:9] sts evenly in last round, or required length less 5cm/2in.
Change to set of four 2¾mm/No 12 needles. Cont in rounds of K2, P2 rib for 5cm/2in. Cast off loosely in rib.

To make up

Press very lightly under a damp cloth with a warm iron.

Above: This guernsey yoke includes the Fife heart and Sheringham herringbone and diamond patterns.

Simple eyelets and horizontal buttonholes

It is the attention to such simple details as buttons and buttonholes that can give your knitting a professional finish. This chapter deals with various ways of working single and double horizontal buttonholes on separate bands or turned-under facings.

Knitting patterns usually give instructions as to where to place buttonholes and how many stitches to cast off to achieve the correct width in proportion to the garment, but they rarely give the method for how to work them.

Most buttonholes are worked on a buttonhole band which can be knitted separately or as part of a garment. Separate buttonhole bands are often knitted in ribbing on finer needles than the main fabric to form a firm neat edge. Knitted-in bands are often in stocking stitch when the rest of the garment is in lace or some other pattern not suitable for buttonholes. Sometimes, when a stitch pattern extends right to the edge of a garment, extra stitches are worked along the buttonhole edge to make a facing strip which is turned back when making up.

Facing strips are usually worked in stocking stitch to give minimum bulk but remember, if you are working the main fabric in a lace pattern, the facing strip will show through.

This chapter gives methods for working eyelet and horizontal buttonholes and a way of neatening them.

Simple eyelet buttonholes This dainty method is ideal for use on baby garments with small buttons. Eyelets are suitable for buttonholes worked on a buttonhole band whether knitted separately or as part of the main fabric.

Horizontal buttonholes There are several different methods of making horizontal buttonholes all based on the same principle – that a given number of stitches are cast off on one row and replaced by stitches cast on again in the same place on the following row.

Left: Use the method given overleaf to neaten buttonholes on a ribbed band.

One thing to remember when working the first cast-off row for a horizontal buttonhole is that the stitch still on the right-hand needle after the casting off has been completed always counts as one of the remaining stitches of the row.

Which method you choose depends on whether your buttonhole band is knitted separately, as part of the main fabric or with a facing strip and on the size of buttonhole you need and the sort of finish you prefer.

If you are knitting a separate buttonhole band horizontally there is a choice of two methods, one for buttonholes across three or fewer stitches and one for larger buttonholes, which need to be neatened at the corners.

If you are knitting a facing strip to turn back behind the opening edge of the garment, choose the method appropriate for the size of buttonhole you are making, remembering that you have to make a double buttonhole, one in the opening edge of the garment, and a corresponding one in the facing strip.

A third method, which is suitable for edges with a turned-under facing strip and for buttonhole bands knitted at the same time as the main fabric, is slightly harder to work but gives a very neat opening without any hard edges. You can use these tailored buttonholes for big and small buttons so long as you neaten the buttonhole with buttonhole stitch and ideally back it with a firm ribbon. The fourth method, which is suitable for all types of band and size of button, is worked over one row only. You can use this hard-wearing reinforced buttonhole on stocking stitch, garter stitch, moss stitch or ribbing on a right or wrong side row.

Simple eyelet buttonholes

Knit the buttonhole band until the position for the buttonhole is reached. If working a separate band, always end with a wrong side row. If working the band as part of the main fabric, end at the edge where the buttonhole is required. On the next row work the given number of stitches, usually three or four, to the point where the buttonhole is needed. Take the yarn over or round the needle to make an eyelet hole, work the next two stitches together, then work to the end of the row. Work the following row across all stitches.

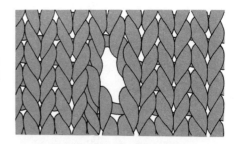

Small buttonholes for separate bands

This method is suitable for buttonholes across three or fewer stitches.
Knit the buttonhole band until the position for the buttonhole is reached, ending with a wrong side row.
On the next row work the given number of stitches in pattern to the point where the buttonhole is needed, cast off the required number of stitches, then pattern to the end of the row.
On the following row replace the cast-off stitches in the previous row with the same number of cast-on stitches, turning the needle to cast on.

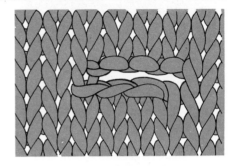

Large buttonholes for separate bands

This method is suitable for buttonholes across four or more stitches.
Knit the buttonhole band until the position for the buttonhole is reached, ending with a wrong side row.
On the next row work the given number of stitches in pattern to the point where the buttonhole is needed.
Cast off one *fewer* than the number of stitches given for the buttonhole, for example, if you are told to cast off four stitches, cast off three of these. Slip the stitch on the right-hand needle back on to the left-hand needle and knit this together with the next stitch to complete the total number of stitches required.
On the following row cast on one *more* than the number of stitches given for the buttonhole, for example, if you are told to cast on four stitches, cast on five instead.
On the next row, work to within

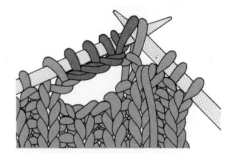

one stitch of this extra cast-on stitch. Work the next stitch together with the extra cast-on stitch to complete the buttonhole.

Buttonholes for edges with a facing strip

Knit the garment until the position for the buttonhole is reached, ending at the edge where the buttonhole is required.
On the next row work the given number of stitches in pattern to the point where the first buttonhole is needed in the facing strip, cast off the required number of stitches. Pattern to the point where the corresponding buttonhole is needed in the main fabric, cast off the required number of stitches, then pattern to the end of the row.
On the following row replace each set of cast-off stitches in the previous row with the same number of cast-on stitches, turning the needle to cast on.

Right: Detail of a double buttonhole — the main fabric is in moss stitch and the facing strip in stocking stitch.

Reinforced buttonholes for all types of buttonhole band

1

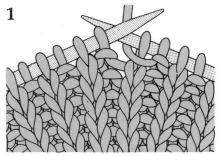

This example has been worked as a separate ribbed band over twelve stitches, with four stitches for the buttonhole.
Knit the buttonhole band in single rib until position for buttonhole is reached, ending with wrong side row.
1 (K1, P1) twice, leave the yarn at the front of the work and sl the next

2

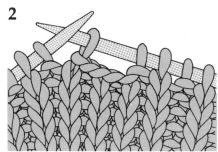

st in a purlwise direction, then take the yarn back between the needles.
2 *Sl the next st on the left-hand needle in a purlwise direction, lift the 2nd st on the right-hand needle over the first st with the point of the left-hand needle and off the needle, rep from * 3 times more.

3

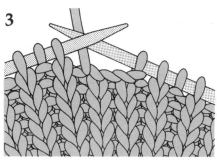

3 Sl the last st on the right-hand needle back on to the left-hand needle, turn the work, pick up the yarn and take it to the back of the work.

4

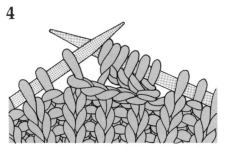

4 **Insert the right-hand needle between the last 2 sts on the left-hand needle and cast on one st, rep from ** 4 times more, turn the work, take the yarn to back of work.

5

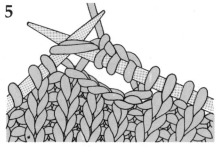

5 Sl the last cast-on st on to the left-hand needle, K this st tog with the next st on the left-hand needle to complete the buttonhole, rib to end of row.

Note: When working the buttonhole row in any other stitch than rib, remember that the yarn must be taken round the first slipped st then left in its correct working position for the stitch prior to the slipped stitch, that is at the back for a knit st and at the front for a purl st.

PROFESSIONAL TOUCH

Buttonhole stitch for neatening

Neaten eyelet and horizontal buttonholes with evenly spaced buttonhole stitches round the opening.
Do not work too many stitches round the opening or the edges will be stretched. Too few stitches and the size of the hole will be reduced and puckered out of shape.
To begin, thread a blunt-ended sewing needle with a length of matching yarn or silk. Make a knot in the other end.
For small eyelet buttonholes the straight loop of each buttonhole stitch must face towards the centre of the hole.
Insert the needle from the back to

the front the depth of one stitch in from the edge of the opening. Pull yarn through, leaving the knot at the back.
*Insert the needle again in the same way, allowing the yarn to curve round and under the needle and pull yarn through. Repeat from * all round the opening and fasten off securely.
For horizontal buttonholes the chain formed by each buttonhole stitch must lie along the opening edges.
Insert the needle from the back to the front at the top right-hand corner of the buttonhole opening. Pull the yarn through, leaving the knot at the back.

*Insert the needle again in the same way, allowing the yarn to curve round and under the needle and pull the yarn through. Repeat from * working clockwise round the opening and fasten off securely.

Tailored buttonholes for knitted-in bands and facings

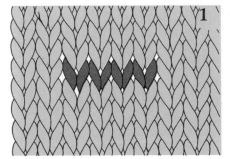

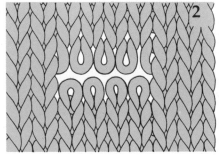

Knit the garment until the position for the buttonhole is reached, ending at the edge where the buttonhole is required.
1 On the next row work the given number of stitches in pattern to the point where the buttonhole is needed. Use a short length of contrasting coloured yarn and work in pattern across the number of

stitches given for the buttonhole. Slip these stitches back on to the left-hand needle and work them again with the correct yarn, then pattern to the end of the row.
2 When the garment section is completed, remove the contrast yarn from each buttonhole very gently, taking care not to let the stitches unravel.

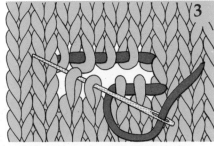

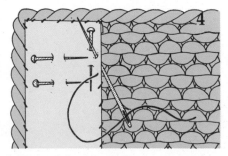

3 Complete each single or double buttonhole by threading a length of the correct yarn into a blunt-ended sewing needle, run this through all of the stitches, matching stitch for stitch on a double buttonhole. Buttonhole stitch single edge to neaten, or ideally, add a ribbon facing and then neaten.
Adding ribbon facing Carefully measure the length and width of the button and buttonhole bands, taking care not to stretch the fabric, to calculate the amount of ribbon you will require. The facing should be wide enough to cover the buttonholes and extend the full

length of the band plus extra to turn under at both ends.
It should be firm and straight grained, such as grosgrain ribbon, and without any tendency to fray.
4 Pin the ribbon in place on the wrong side of the knitting, easing it in evenly without stretching or puckering the fabric and making sure that the buttonholes are correctly spaced. Fold in the turnings at each end and pin in place. Fix a pin to each side of every buttonhole to hold it in place. Slip stitch round all the edges of the ribbon.

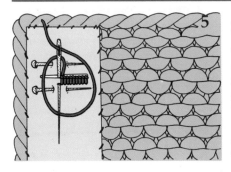

5 Cut through the ribbon for each buttonhole making sure they are the same size and taking care not to cut the knitting. Work round the ribbon and knitting in buttonhole stitch to neaten and hold the edges together.

Right: Use the tailored method for the buttonholes on a man's cardigan.

Button-through cardigan in tweed yarn

This classic button-to-the-neck cardigan is lifted into the couture class by the use of beautiful tweed yarn in a range of mouth-watering colours. All the ribbed edges are worked in a plain toning double knitting. The cardigan can be made in six sizes.

Sizes

To fit 86 [91:97:102:107:112]cm/ 34 [36:38:40:42:44]in bust
Length to shoulder, 51 [52:53.5:54.5:56:56]cm/ 20 [20½:21:21½:22:22]in, adjustable
Sleeve seam, 43 [44.5:45.5:45.5:47:47]cm/ 17 [17½:18:18:18½:18½]in adjustable
The figures in [] refer to the 91/36, 97/38, 102/40, 107/42 and 112cm/44in sizes respectively

You will need

6 [6:7:8:8:9]×50g balls of Sirdar Country Style Double Knitting Tweed (61% acrylic, 28% bri-nylon, 11% wool) in main colour A
2×50g balls of Sirdar Country Style plain Double Knitting (45% acrylic, 40% bri-nylon, 15% wool) in contrast colour B
One pair 3¼mm/No 10 needles
One pair 4mm/No 8 needles
Eight buttons

Tension

22 sts and 28 rows to 10cm/4in over st st worked on 4mm/No 8 needles

Back

With 3¼mm/No 10 needles and B cast on 101 [107:111:117:123:127] sts.
1st row (Rs) K1, *P1, K1, rep from * to end.
2nd row P1, *K1, P1, rep from * to end.
Rep these 2 rows for 6.5cm/2½in, ending with a 2nd row. Break off B. Join in A. Change to 4mm/No 8 needles. Beg with a K row cont in st st until work measures 30.5cm/12in from beg, or required length to underarm, ending with a P row.

Shape armholes

Cast off 6 sts at beg of next 2 rows. Dec one st at each end of next 5 [5:5:5:7:7] rows, then at each end of foll 3 [4:4:5:5:6] alt rows. 73 [77:81:85:87:89] sts.
Cont without shaping until armholes measure 20.5 [21.5:23:24:25.5:25.5]cm/ 8 [8½:9:9½:10:10]in from beg, ending with a P row.

Left: This cardigan fastens neatly to the neck with eight buttons. Use the method given for separate bands.

Shape shoulders

Cast off at beg of next and every row 6 sts 6 times and 4 [5:6:7:7:7] sts twice. Leave rem 29 [31:33:35:37:39] sts on holder for centre back neck.

Left front

With 3¼mm/No 10 needles and B cast on 55 [59:61:63:67:69] sts. Work 6.5cm/2½in rib as given for back. Break off B. Join in A. Change to 4mm/No 8 needles.
Next row K to last 8 sts, leave last 8 sts on safety pin for front band.
Next row P to end.
47 [51:53:55:59:61] sts.
Beg with a K row cont in st st until work measures same as back to underarm, ending at side edge.

Shape armhole

Cast off 6 sts at beg of next row. Work one row. Dec one st at side edge on next 5 [5:5:5:7:7] rows, then at same edge on foll 3 [4:4:5:5:6] alt rows. 33 [36:38:39:41:42] sts. Cont without shaping until armhole measures 14 rows less than back to shoulder.

Shape neck

Next row Work to last 5 [7:8:8:10:11] sts, leave last 5 [7:8:8:10:11] sts on safety pin for front neck.
Next row P to end.
28 [29:30:31:31:31] sts.
Dec one st at neck edge on next and foll 5 alt rows, ending at armhole edge. 22 [23:24:25:25:25] sts.

Shape shoulder

Cast off at beg of next and every alt row 6 sts 3 times and 4 [5:6:7:7:7] sts once.

Right front

With 3¼mm/No 10 needles and B cast on 55 [59:61:63:67:69] sts. Work 4 rows rib as given for back.
Next row (buttonhole row) Rib 3 sts, cast off 3 sts, rib to end of row.
Next row Rib to end, casting on 3 sts above those cast off in previous row. Cont in rib until work measures same as left front to end of ribbing, ending at front edge.
Next row Rib 8 sts and leave these on safety pin for front band, change

to 4mm/No 8 needles and A, K to end.
Break off B.
Beg with a P row cont in st st and complete as given for left front, reversing all shapings.

Button band

With 3¼mm/No 10 needles and B cast on one st, then with Rs of work facing rib across 8 sts on safety pin. Cont in rib until band, when slightly stretched, fits along left front edge to neck edge, ending with a Ws row. Break off yarn and leave sts on safety pin.
Mark positions for 7 more buttons, last to come in neckband with 6 more evenly spaced between.

Buttonhole band

With 3¼mm/No 10 needles and B cast on one st, then with Ws of work facing rib across 8 sts on safety pin.
Work as given for button band, making buttonholes as before as markers are reached, ending at front edge. Do not break off yarn.

Sleeves

With 3¼mm/No 10 needles and B cast on 43 [45:49:53:55:57] sts. Work 6.5cm/2½in rib as given for back. Break off B. Join in A. Change to 4mm/No 8 needles.
Beg with a K row cont in st st inc one st at each end of 7th and every foll 6th row until there are

71 [73:75:79:81:85] sts.
Cont without shaping until work measures 43 [44.5:45.5:45.5:47:47]cm/ 17 [17½:18:18:18½:18½]in from beg, or required length to underarm, ending with a P row.

Shape top

Cast off 6 sts at beg of next 2 rows. Dec one st at each end of next 5 [5:5:5:5:7] rows, then at each end of every foll alt row until 25 [25:25:27:27:29] sts rem. Work one row.
Cast off at beg of next and every row 3 sts 6 times and 7 [7:7:9:9:11] sts once.

Neckband

Join shoulder seams. With 3¼mm/ No 10 needles and Rs of work facing, pick up B and rib across sts of right front band, 5 [7:9:8:10:11] sts on safety pin, pick up and K16 sts up right front neck, K29 [31:33:35:37:39] sts on back neck holder, pick up and K16 sts down left front neck, rib across 5 [7:9:8:10:11] sts on safety pin and sts of left front band.
89 [95:99:101:107:111] sts.
Beg with a 2nd row work 2.5cm/1in rib as given for back. Cast off in rib.

To make up

Press each piece under a dry cloth with a warm iron. Sew front bands in place. Set in sleeves. Join side and sleeve seams. Sew on buttons.

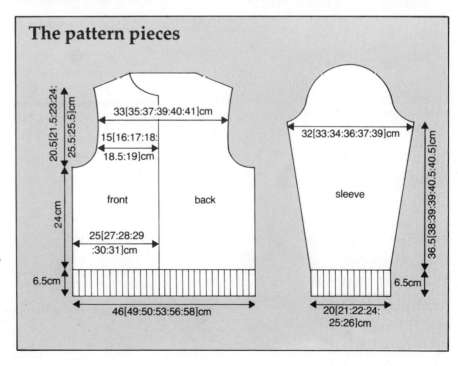

The pattern pieces

20.5[21.5:23:24: 25.5:25.5]cm
33[35:37:39:40:41]cm
15[16:17:18: 18.5:19]cm
24cm
front
back
25[27:28:29 :30:31]cm
6.5cm
46[49:50:53:56:58]cm

32[33:34:36:37:39]cm
36.5[38:39:39:40.5:40.5]cm
sleeve
6.5cm
20[21:22:24: 25:26]cm

The button and buttonhole bands on this cardigan are picked up along the edges. The buttonholes are worked horizontally.

Vertical buttonholes and hand-made buttons

This concluding buttonhole chapter shows how single and double vertical buttonholes are worked on separate bands or as turned-under facings. Learn how to position them so that the buttons do up neatly and how to cover button moulds to match a garment perfectly.

The last chapter dealt with ways of making eyelet and horizontal buttonholes. Although these are probably the best-known methods, vertical buttonholes have the advantage that they can be worked on a narrower button band and there are no loose stitches to mar the appearance.

The fabric is divided at the point where a buttonhole is needed and the two sides are worked separately. The buttonholes are worked on the buttonhole band which can be knitted separately or as part of the garment. Single buttonholes look best worked in a reversible pattern such as moss stitch or rib. If you work them in stocking stitch the edges tend to curl inwards and need to be held in place with ribbon facing.

If the stitch pattern of a garment extends to the edge, work double buttonholes. Knit the facing strip in stocking stitch which is turned back and the edges neatened with buttonhole stitch.

Choosing buttons

Choose buttons which complement the knitted fabric as well as being practical. Fun shapes look decorative but may have sharp edges that will rub and snag the buttonholes. A man's husky jacket looks best when finished with bold leather or wooden buttons; a crisp cotton cardigan is enhanced by the lustre of real pearl buttons and a lacy evening jacket needs the added sparkle of jewelled buttons.

If you are unable to find ready-made buttons suitable for your garment, the answer is to knit covers to fit over a metal or nylon button mould. Do not feel you have to stick to the same yarn as the garment.

Knit the covers using fine needles so that the mould does not show through. To knit smaller or larger covers than those given as examples simply cast on fewer or more stitches increasing and decreasing accordingly.

Consider the thickness of the knitted fabric when choosing buttons. Those with central holes will lie flat on the fabric unless you add a yarn shank but buttons with built-in shanks stand above the fabric to allow for the thickness of the buttonhole band when the buttons are fastened.

Make sure that the buttons you select are the right size to go through the buttonholes without stretching them and that they are the right weight for the fabric – if they are too heavy they will pull the band out of shape.

Positioning buttonholes

Knit the button band first and mark the position of the buttons with pins. Knit the buttonhole band, working the buttonholes to correspond with these markers. They need to be evenly spaced so that the garment does not gape or pucker so knit the same number of rows between each buttonhole.

Positioning buttons

After making up the garment, pin the buttonhole edge over the button band, matching top and bottom edges and securing these points with pins.

Horizontal buttonholes Mark the centre of the buttonholes with pins before removing the buttonhole band, leaving the pins in position.

Vertical buttonholes Mark the position of the button 3mm/⅛in below the top of the buttonhole.

Right: Sample knitted in moss stitch showing vertical buttonholes worked on a separate buttonhole band.

Buttonholes for separate bands and edges with a facing strip

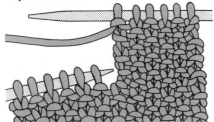

separate bands

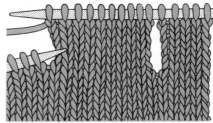

edges with a facing strip

Separate bands

Knit the buttonhole band until the position for the buttonhole is reached, ending on the wrong side. On the next row work the given number of stitches in pattern to the point where the buttonhole is needed, turn the work.
Continue in pattern across these stitches only for the number of rows needed to take the size of the button, ending at the buttonhole opening edge. Break off the yarn. Leave these stitches.
Rejoin the yarn at the buttonhole edge of the remaining stitches and pattern to the end of the row. Work the same number of rows over these stitches as worked for the first part of the buttonhole, ending at the edge away from the buttonhole.
On the next row, work across all of the stitches to close the buttonhole.

Edges with a facing strip

Knit the garment until the position for the buttonhole is reached, ending at the edge where the buttonhole is required.
On the next row work the given number of stitches in pattern to the point where the first buttonhole is needed in the facing strip. Turn the work.
Continue in pattern across these stitches only for the number of rows needed to take the size of the button, ending at the buttonhole opening edge. Break off the yarn. Leave these stitches.
Rejoin the yarn at the buttonhole edge of the remaining stitches and pattern to the point where the second buttonhole is needed in the main fabric.
Repeat from ** to ** working the same number of rows.
Rejoin the yarn at the buttonhole edge of the remaining stitches and pattern to the end of the row. Work the same number of rows over the stitches, ending at the edge away from the buttonhole.
On the next row, work across all of the stitches to close the buttonhole.

Four knitted button covers

Stocking stitch button cover
This example fits a 2cm/¾in nylon button mould, using 2mm/No 14 needles and 4 ply yarn.
Cast on 4 sts. Beg with a K row work in st st, inc one st at each end of every row until there are 12 sts.
Work 6 rows without shaping.
Dec one st at each end of every row until 4 sts rem. Cast off.
Place over button mould, work a row of running stitches round outside edge, draw up and fasten off leaving end to sew on button.

Embroidered button cover
This example fits a 3cm/1¼in met button mould, using 2mm/No 14 needles and 4 ply yarn. Lengths of 3 colours of embroidery silk.
Cast on 6 sts. Beg with a K row work in st st, inc one st at each en of every row until there are 18 sts.
Work 10 rows without shaping.
Dec one st at each end of every ro until 6 sts rem. Cast off.
Embroider design in the centre of the cover and fit as for stocking stitch cover.

Bobble button cover
This example fits a 2cm/¾in nylon button mould, using 2mm/No 14 needles and 4 ply yarn.
Cast on 3 sts. Beg with a P row work in reversed st st, inc one st at each end of every row until there are 11 sts.
Work 4 rows without shaping.
Next row P5 sts, (K1, P1, K1, P1, K1) all into next st, turn and P5, turn and K5, turn and P5, turn and K5, turn and lift 2nd, 3rd, 4th and 5th sts over first and off needle, P5.
Work 4 rows.
Dec one st at each end of every row until 3 sts rem. Cast off.
Fit as for stocking stitch cover.

Moss stitch button cover
This example fits a 3cm/1¼in met button mould, using 2¼mm/No needles and double knitting yarn
Cast on 4 sts.
1st row (Rs) *K1, P1, rep from * to e
2nd row Inc in first st, K1, P1, inc last st.
3rd row Inc in first st, (K1, P1) twice, inc in last st.
Keeping moss st correct as now se cont inc one st at each end of eve row until there are 14 sts.
Work 6 rows without shaping.
Cont in moss st, dec one st at eac end of every row until 4 sts rem. Cast off.
Fit as for stocking stitch cover.

Pleated knitting for skirts

Pleated skirts are casual and easy to wear and provide a useful addition to any wardrobe. The choice of yarn is important if they are to hold their shape and the pleats keep their swing. When knitted from the top down, the length can be adjusted according to fashion.

A knitted pleated skirt is an adaptable and comfortable garment which can form the basis of mix-and-match outfits. Team the skirt given in this chapter with the button-to-neck cardigan on page 218 – they are both knitted in the same tweedy yarn.

A knitted skirt is virtually a tube of fabric which is wider at the hem edge than it is at the waist.

Mock or ribbed pleats can start at the bottom or the top – gradually increase or decrease according to the direction of the work.

The fullness of the skirt depends on the number of stitches at the hem or the amount of increase from the waist. There is no problem of bulk at the waist using either of these methods.

Work inverted pleats from the hem to the waist where they are folded and joined to the waistband. Do not make the pleats too full as this increases the bulk at the waist.

All three methods are joined to a ribbed waistband with elastic sewn in.

Choosing suitable yarns

It is vital to use a yarn which will retain its shape. Bulky yet light-weight fashion yarns, such as mohair, are not suitable. Not only may the skirt seat and drop but the thickness of the yarn will make the skirt clumsy and unflattering. Look for a wool yarn with a nylon content for added strength – 4 ply or double knitting weights are ideal. If the yarn has a crêpe twist or tweed texture so much the better, as these give a firm fabric.

Knit in rounds or rows using finer needles than normally advised for the yarn. This gives a close, firm fabric which hangs well. Use a circular needle to knit in rows or rounds if increasing to a large number of stitches.

Do not line a knitted skirt. The pleats need to swing freely and stitching in a lining only restricts the knitting. Wear a separate waist petticoat to avoid any seating effect.

To plan a pleated skirt in one of the methods given in this chapter, first calculate the width required at the hem and waist and the finished length including the waistband. Use these measurements and the tension obtained with the yarn and needle size of your choice to arrive at the number of stitches which must be cast on at the lower edge if working from the hem up, or at the waist if working down. Remember to allow for the multiples of stitches needed to make the pattern work out correctly.

Left: Team the skirt with the matching cardigan jacket given earlier to make up this attractive outfit.

Mock pleats are the simplest of all to work. They can be knitted on two needles in two sections and joined at the side seams, or in the round.

The fabric is reversible with a knit stitch defining each pleat and separating panels of garter stitch. This method can be worked from the hem up, decreasing as required, or from the waist down, increasing as required and is ideal for a toddler's skirt.

Use waist and hem measurements to calculate the number of stitches to cast on and increase/decrease according to the tension obtained with the yarn and needle size of your choice. Cast on stitches in multiples of eight stitches plus one at hem or multiples of four stitches plus one at the waist and adjust the total accordingly. For example, a total hem width of 112cm/ 44in based on a tension of 28 stitches to 10cm/4in will require 154 stitches for the back and the same for the front. Adjust this to 153 stitches to give correct multiples.

Ribbed pleats can be knitted on two needles in two sections and joined at the side seams, or in the round. A slipped stitch defines the edge of the pleats. This method can be worked from the hem up, decreasing as required, or from the waist down, increasing as required and gives a very slimming line.

Calculate the number of stitches for waist or hem as for mock pleats.

Cast on multiples of 15 stitches at the hem or multiples of eight stitches at the waist. For example, a total hem width of 112cm/44in based on a tension of 28 stitches to 10cm/4in will require 154 stitches for the back and the same for the front. Adjust to 150 stitches to give correct multiples.

Inverted pleats can be worked on two needles or in the round. A slipped stitch defines the edge of the pleats but this method can only be worked from the hem to waist edge. Two extra needles of the same size as used to knit the skirt are needed to close the pleats at the top edge, before adding a waistband. These full pleats give an attractive swirl to a skirt and hang well. You do not need to press them into place.

Calculate the width for hem as for mock pleats and multiply by three to allow for the pleats.

Cast on multiples of 13 stitches plus two to give a pleat fold of four stitches. For example, a total hem width of 188cm/74in based on a tension of 28 stitches to 10cm/4in will require 259 stitches for the back and the same for the front. Adjust to 262 stitches to give the correct multiples.

Ribbed pleats on two needles

Cast on the stitches in multiples of 15 at the hem, or in multiples of eight stitches at the waist.

Working up from the hem
1st row (Rs) *K7, keep yarn at back of work and sl 1 in a purlwise direction – **called sl 1**, K3, P4, rep from * to end.
2nd row *K4, P11, rep from * to end.
Repeat these 2 rows for about one quarter of the length required, ending with a Rs row.
Next row (dec row) *K4, P9, P2 tog, rep from * to end. Multiples of 14 sts.
Next row (Rs) *K6, sl 1, K3, P4, rep from * to end.
Next row *K4, P10, rep from * to end.
Repeat last 2 rows for about half of the length required, ending with a Rs row.
Next row (dec row) *K4, P8, P2 tog, rep from * to end. Multiples of 13 sts.
Next row (Rs) *K5, sl 1, K3, P4, rep from * to end.
Next row *K4, P9, rep from * to end.
Repeat last 2 rows for about three-quarters of the required length, ending with a Rs row.
Next row (dec row) *K4, P7, P2 tog, rep from * to end. Multiples of 12 sts.
Next row (Rs) *K4, sl 1, K3, P4, rep from * to end.
Next row *K4, P8, rep from * to end.
Repeat last 2 rows for length required, ending with a Rs row.
Next row (dec row) *(K2 tog) twice, P2 tog, P4, P2 tog, rep from * to end. Multiples of 8 sts.
With size smaller needles work about 2.5cm/1in K2, P2 rib. Cast off. Join sides. Sew elastic inside waist edge.

Working down from the waist
Work waist ribbing, ending with a Rs row.
Next row (inc row) *Rib 1, inc in next st, rep from * to end. Multiples of 12 sts.
Change to size larger needles.
1st row (Rs) *K4, sl 1, K3, P4, rep from * to end.
2nd row *K4, P8, rep from * to end.
Repeat these 2 rows for about one quarter of the length required, ending with a Rs row.
Next row (inc row) *K4, P7, inc in next st, rep from * to end. Multiples of 13 sts.
Next row (Rs) *K5, sl 1, K3, P4, rep from * to end.
Next row *K4, P9, rep from * to end.
Repeat last 2 rows for about half of the length required, ending with a Rs row.
Next row (inc row) *K4, P8, inc in next st, rep from * to end. Multiples of 14 sts.
Next row (Rs) *K6, sl 1, K3, P4, rep from * to end.
Next row *K4, P10, rep from * to end.
Repeat last 2 rows for about three-quarters of the length required, ending with a Rs row.
Next row (inc row) *K4, P9, inc in next st, rep from * to end. Multiples of 15 sts.
Next row (Rs) *K7, sl 1, K3, P4, rep from * to end.
Next row *K4, P11, rep from * to end.
Repeat last 2 rows for length required. Cast off loosely.

Mock pleats on two needles

Cast on the stitches in multiples of eight stitches plus one at the hem, or multiples of four stitches plus one at the waist.

Working up from the hem

1st row (Rs) P1, *K7, P1, rep from * to end.
2nd row K4, *P1, K7, rep from * to last 5 sts, P1, K4.
Repeat these 2 rows for about a third of the length required, ending with a Ws row.
Next row (dec row) P1, *sl 1, K1, psso, K3, K2 tog, P1, rep from * to end. Multiples of 6 sts plus one.
Next row K3, *P1, K5, rep from * to last 4 sts, P1, K3.
Next row P1, *K5, P1, rep from * to end.
Repeat last 2 rows until work measures about two-thirds of the length required, ending with a Ws row.
Next row (dec row) P1, *sl 1, K1, psso, K1, K2 tog, P1, rep from * to end. Multiples of 4 sts plus one.
Next row K2, *P1, K3, rep from * to last 3 sts, P1, K2.
Next row P1, *K3, P1, rep from * to end.
Repeat last 2 rows for length required. With size smaller needles work about 2.5cm/1in K1, P1 rib. Cast off. Join side seams. Sew elastic inside waist edge.

Working down from the waist

Work waist ribbing. Change to size larger needles.
1st row (Rs) P1, *K3, P1, rep from * to end.
2nd row K2, *P1, K3, rep from * to last 3 sts, P1, K2.
Repeat these 2 rows for about a third of the length required, ending with a Ws row.
Next row (inc row) P1, *inc in next st, K1, inc in next st, P1, rep from * to end. Multiples of 6 sts plus one.
Next row K3, *P1, K5, rep from * to last 4 sts, P1, K3.
Next row P1, *K5, P1, rep from * to end.
Repeat last 2 rows until work measures about two-thirds of the length required, ending with a Ws row.
Next row (inc row) P1, *inc in next st, K3, inc in next st, P1, rep from * to end. Multiples of 8 sts plus one.
Next row K4, *P1, K7, rep from * to last 5 sts, P1, K4.
Next row P1, *K7, P1, rep from * to end.
Repeat last 2 rows for length required. Cast off loosely.

Inverted pleats on two needles

Cast on multiples of 13 stitches plus 2, to give a pleat fold of 4 stitches.

Working up from the hem

1st row (Rs) K5, *P1, K3, keep yarn at back and sl 1 in a purlwise direction – **called sl 1**, K8, rep from * to last 10 sts, P1, K3, sl 1, K5.
2nd row P9, *K1, P12, rep from * to last 6 sts, K1, P5.
These 2 rows form the pattern and are repeated for the length required, less about 2.5cm/1in for the waistband, ending with a Ws row.

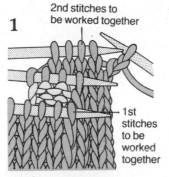

2nd stitches to be worked together

1st stitches to be worked together

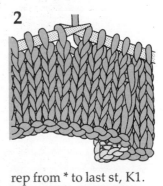

To close pleats

1 Next row K1, *sl next 4 sts on to a spare needle (A), sl next 4 sts on to 2nd spare needle (B) and *turn it round*, place needle A behind needle B and both spare needles behind the left-hand needle.
2 K the next st (the sl st) with one from needle A, K next 3 sts knitting one from all 3 needles, then K next st on left-hand needle tog with last st from needle B (the P st), rep from * to last st, K1.
Change to size smaller needles. Work 2.5cm/1in K1, P1 rib for single waistband, or 5cm/2in for double waistband. Cast off.
Join side seams.
Sew elastic inside single waistband, or fold double waistband in half to wrong side and slip stitch in place, then thread elastic through.

225

Pleated skirt

To avoid bulky pleats at waist level this skirt has a well-shaped hip yoke. Extra stitches are then cast on to give the correct number to form the pleats. To complete the skirt the pleats must be closed at the top and stitched down on the wrong side. The length is adjustable.

Sizes

To fit 91 [97:101]cm/36 [38:40]in hips
Length from waist to hem,
65 [66:67]cm/25½ [26:26½]in,
adjustable
The figures in [] refer to the 97/38 and 101cm/40in sizes respectively

You will need

15 [16:17]×50g balls of Sirdar
 Country Style Double Knitting

Above: This swirling pleated skirt is a flattering style for all ages. It is particularly slimming when worked in tweedy yarn with a nubbly texture.

Tweed (61% acrylic, 28% Bri-
 nylon, 11% wool)
One pair 3¼mm/No 10 needles
One pair 4mm/No 8 needles
One 4mm/No 8 circular needle
 100cm/40in long

Waist length of 2cm/¾in wide elastic

Tension

24 sts and 32 rows to 10cm/4in over st st worked on 4mm/No 8 needles

Back

With 3¼mm/No 10 needles cast on 90 [96:102] sts. Work 2.5cm/1in K1, P1 rib.
Change to 4mm/No 8 needles.

Shape hip yoke

Beg with a K row work 6 rows st st.
Next row (inc row) K1, inc in next st, K22 [24:26] sts, inc in next st, K1, inc in next st, K36 [38:40] sts, inc in next st, K1, inc in next st, K22 [24:26] sts, inc in next st, K1.
96 [102:108] sts.
Beg with a P row work 9 rows st st.
Next row (inc row) K1, inc 1, K24 [26:28] sts, inc 1, K1, inc 1, K38 [40:42] sts, inc 1, K1, inc 1, K24 [26:28] sts, inc 1, K1.
102 [108:114] sts.
Beg with a P row work 9 rows st st.
Next row (inc row) K1, inc 1, K26 [28:30] sts, inc 1, K1, inc 1, K40 [42:44] sts, inc 1, K1, inc 1, K26 [28:30] sts, inc 1, K1.
108 [114:120] sts.
Beg with a P row work 9 rows st st.
Change to 4mm/No 8 circular needle and cont working in rows.

Shape pleats

Next row (inc row) *K6, turn and cast on 7 sts, rep from * to end.
234 [247:260] sts.
Next row (Ws) *K4, P9, rep from * to end.
Next row *K5, keeping yarn at back of work sl 1 in a purlwise direction – **called sl 1**, K3, P4, rep from * to end.
Rep last 2 rows until work measures 20cm/8in from beg, ending with a Rs row.
Next row (inc row) *K4, P8, inc in next st, rep from * to end.
252 [266:280] sts.
Next row *K6, sl 1, K3, P4, rep from * to end.
Next row *K4, P10, rep from * to end.
Rep last 2 rows until work measures 26cm/10¼in from beg, ending with a Rs row.
Next row (inc row) *K4, P9, inc in next st, rep from * to end.
270 [285:300] sts.
Next row *K7, sl 1, K3, P4, rep from * to end.
Next row *K4, P11, rep from * to end.
Rep last 2 rows until work measures 32cm/12½in from beg, ending with a Rs row.
Next row (inc row) *K4, P10, inc in next st, rep from * to end.
288 [304:320] sts.
Next row *K8, sl 1, K3, P4, rep from * to end.

Next row *K4, P12, rep from * to end.
Rep last 2 rows until work measures 38cm/15in from beg, ending with a Rs row.
Next row (inc row) *K4, P11, inc in next st, rep from * to end.
306 [323:340] sts.
Next row *K9, sl 1, K3, P4, rep from * to end.
Next row *K4, P13, rep from * to end.
Rep last 2 rows until work measures 46cm/17¾in from beg, ending with a Rs row.
Next row (inc row) *K4, P12, inc in next st, rep from * to end.
324 [342:360] sts.
Next row *K10, sl 1, K3, P4, rep from * to end.
Next row *K4, P14, rep from * to end.
Rep last 2 rows until work measures 65 [66:67]cm/25½ [26:26½]in from beg, or required length from waist to hem, ending with a Ws row.
Cast off very loosely.

Front

Work as given for back.

To make up

Do not press. Join side seams. Stitch down cast on sts at top of pleats on Ws of work.
Join elastic into a circle. Sew inside waistband with casing st.

Adding elastic to a waistband

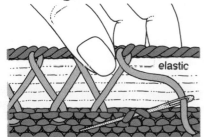
elastic

Below: Stitching elastic into waist.

Measure your waist and cut the elastic into the required length.
For a single thickness waistband, sew elastic into a circle and mark the knitting and the elastic into four sections. Pin the elastic in place on the wrong side of the waistband. Thread a sewing needle with yarn and secure join of elastic to one seam of the knitting. Attach with casing stitch.
*Hold the waistband and elastic over the fingers of your left hand, take the yarn over the elastic and insert the needle lightly through the knitting from right to left and pull the yarn through.
Take the yarn back over the elastic to the top edge of the waistband, insert the needle about 3 stitches along from the previous stitch from right to left and pull the yarn through.
Continue from the * in this way.
Fasten off securely at the end.

For a double thickness waistband, fold the waistband in half to the wrong side and slip stitch in place, leaving a small gap as an opening at the end.
Secure a safety pin into one end of the elastic, small enough to go through the waistband, and thread the elastic through the waistband. Make sure the elastic is not twisted, then sew the ends securely together. When the elastic is in place, sew up the gap.

Neckbands and collars for straight and round necks

Allow sufficient room at the neckline in order to get a garment comfortably over the head. A straight across neckline is easy but where shaping rows are worked as part of the main fabric, the neck edge must be neatened with a neckband or collar.

Details for working the neck of a garment are usually given in full in the instructions but it is also a simple matter to adapt the style of a neckline or collar to suit your preference.

Basic neck shapes are straight across, round, square and V-shaped – either at back, front or both. On all of these shapes you can add front or back vertical openings.

The neatest way to complete the edge is by knitting a neckband or collar in one to avoid uncomfortable seams round the neckline. For all neck shapes except for the straight across neck stitches must be picked up round the edges (page 190), to add the neckband or collar.

To complete a straight neck without a vertical opening, work across the stitches that remain once the shoulder shaping on the back and front is completed. The shoulders and neckband seams are then joined in one, leaving an opening wide enough to pull on easily over the head.

Where a vertical opening is desired at back or front, the piece will have to be divided and each side completed separately, making provision for button and buttonhole bands if required.

To complete a round neck when working on two needles in rows, provision for turning the needles must be allowed.

On a single thickness round neck, a double thickness crew neck or polo collar, seam one shoulder before picking up the neckband stitches, leaving other shoulder unseamed until neckband is completed.

If working single rib in rows, pick up an odd number of stitches and begin and end each row with the same stitch to allow for seaming. If working variations of rib, or in a pattern, make sure you have the correct multiples, plus any edge stitches needed to make the pattern begin and end with the same stitches.

When working single rib on four needles, in rounds, pick up an even number of stitches to ensure the rounds work out exactly. If working in variations of rib or pattern, make sure you have the exact multiples of stitches.

To complete a round-necked collar a centre front or back opening must be left as part of the main fabric, to be closed with a zip or buttons. The collar is worked in rows on two needles and both shoulders can be seamed before picking up the stitches round the neck.

With a centre front overlapped placket opening, a collar is worked in one piece but with a centre back opening, a collar is usually worked in two halves unless the pattern suggests otherwise.

All the examples have been worked in double knitting yarn on 4mm/No 8 needles, using a contrast colour to show the neckline.

Straight necks

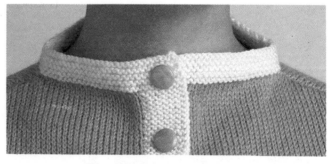

Straight neck without opening
Do not work any neck shaping on the back or front. Work the shoulder shaping as given on the back and front but do not cast off the remaining neck stitches. Work a few rows in garter stitch or ribbing across the neck stitches to give the depth of neckband required. Cast off.

Front overlapped placket opening
Complete back as for straight neck without an opening. Work the front and end with a wrong side row at the required position for the front opening.

On the next row, pattern across half of the stitches for the left side, plus about an extra four stitches for the left front band, then work the last eight stitches to match back neckband and making buttonholes as required for a man. Work as for the back. Complete the shoulder shaping and neckband.

With the right side of the work facing, rejoin the yarn and cast on eight extra stitches for the right front band and work as for left front band, making buttonholes as required for a woman and pattern to end. Complete to match the left shoulder.

Round necks

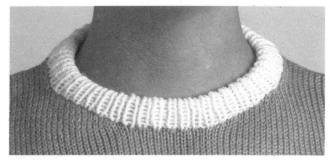

Single round neck in rib
With the right side of the work facing, pick up and knit the required number of stitches round the neck.
Work in rib for 2cm/¾in, or depth required. **
Cast off loosely.

Double crew neck in rib
Work as given for single round neck to **.
Continue in rib for a further 2cm/¾in, or same depth as first part. Cast off loosely.
Fold neckband in half to wrong side and slipstitch in place.

Polo neck in rib
Work as given for single round neck to **.
Continue in rib for a further 12cm/4¾in, or total length required. Cast off loosely.
Fold neckband in half to right side.

PROFESSIONAL TOUCH

Finishing a double crew neck

If a double width round neckband without any openings is folded in half to the inside and stitched in place too tightly, it is often difficult to pull the garment over the head – this is particularly uncomfortable for a baby.

The way to overcome this and give a really elastic neckband is to leave the stitches on a separate length of yarn once the length of neckband has been completed, instead of casting them off. The *loops* are then sewn in place and will stretch to allow the garment to be put on, reverting to the snug fit of the neckband in wear.

Thread a blunt-ended sewing needle with a length of yarn. Secure this with one or two stitches on top of each other at the base of the first of the picked-up neckband stitches.

Fold the neckband in half to the inside, insert the sewing needle into the loop at the top of the same stitch on the separate length of thread and pull the yarn through loosely.

*Insert the sewing needle through one strand at the base of the next stitch and pull the yarn through, then insert the needle into the loop at the top of the same stitch on the separate length of thread and pull the yarn through loosely.

Repeat from * until all the loops have been secured. Fasten off with one or two small stitches on top of each other. Remove the separate length of thread.

Round necks with collars

Single rib collar with front overlapped placket
Begin at the centre front opening with the right side of the work facing and miss half of the cast off stitches at

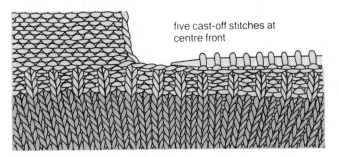

five cast-off stitches at centre front

Peter Pan collar with centre back zip opening
Begin at the centre back opening with the right side of the work facing and pick up and knit the required number of stitches round the neck, having an odd number of stitches.
Work 3 rows in single rib.
Beginning with a purl row continue in stocking stitch to allow for collar to be folded over to right side.
Next row (divide collar) Cast off 3 sts, P to centre 5 sts, cast off centre 5 sts, P to last 3 sts, cast off last 3 sts. Complete this side first. Rejoin yarn.
** Beg with a K row work 5cm/2in st st, or length required, ending with a P row.

the top of the right front band, pick up and knit the required number of stitches round the neck then miss half of the cast off stitches at the top of the left front band, having an odd number of stitches.
If the opening is closed with a zip, pick up and knit the number of stitches round the neck, beginning and ending at the edge of the opening and having an odd number of stitches.
Work 3 rows in single rib.
Next row (Rs) K3, pick up loop lying between needles and K tbl – **called M1**, rib to last 3 sts, M1, K3.
Next row K2, P1, rib to last 3 sts as now set, P1, K2.
Repeat last 2 rows until collar is the required depth.
Cast off *very* loosely.

Next row (dec row) K1, sl 1, K1, psso, K to last 3 sts, K2 tog, K1.
Next row P to end.
Repeat last 2 rows twice more. Break off yarn.
With right side of collar facing, pick up and knit stitches evenly along side edge of half collar, knit across stitches on the needle and pick up and knit stitches along other side edge of collar. Work 2 rows single rib. Cast off loosely in rib. **
With right side of work facing, rejoin yarn to remaining stitches and work other half of collar to match first side from ** to **.
Sew down ends of rib edging at centre front and back.

Polo-necked jersey

This raglan-sleeved jersey in wide stripes of five colours can be made with a polo collar or crew neckband. To make this design in one colour only, add the quantities together.

Sizes

To fit 86 [91:97]cm/34 [36:38]in bust
Length to centre back neck,
64 [65:66]cm/25¼ [25½:26]in
Sleeve seam, 46cm/18in
The figures in [] refer to the 91/36 and 97cm/38in sizes respectively

You will need

Polo neck version 5 [5:6]×50g balls of Chat Botté Kid Mohair (80% mohair, 20% chlorofibre) in main colour A

Crew neck version 3 [4:4] balls of same in A
Both versions 2 [3:3] balls in contrast colour B
2 [2:2] balls each in contrast colours C, D and E
One pair 5mm/No 6 needles
One pair 6mm/No 4 needles
Set of four 5mm/No 6 needles pointed at both ends

Tension

15 sts and 20 rows to 10cm/4in over st st worked on 6mm/No 4 needles using 2 ends of yarn

Note

Two strands of yarn are knitted together throughout

Back

With 5mm/No 6 needles and 2 strands of A, cast on 70 [74:78] sts.
1st row (Rs) K2, *P2, K2, rep from * to end.
2nd row P2, *K2, P2, rep from * to end.
Rep these 2 rows for 9cm/3½in, ending with a 2nd row. Break off A. Change to 6mm/No 4 needles and 2 strands of B. Beg with a K row cont in st st, working 18 rows each in B, C and D, then 14 rows with E, ending with a P row.

Right: As the yarn is used double this jersey is very quick to knit. Shown here with a generous polo collar it can also be made with a crew neckband.

alternative colourways

Shape armholes

Next row With E, K1, K2 tog, K to last 3 sts, sl 1, K1, psso, K1.
Next row With E, P to end.
Rep last 2 rows once more. Break off E.
Cont rep last 2 rows until 28 [30:32] sts rem, working 18 rows with A then cont with B to end.
Leave rem sts on holder.

Front

Work as given for back until 36 [38:40] sts rem in armhole shaping, ending with a P row.

Shape neck

Next row Keeping stripes correct throughout, K1, K2 tog, K10 sts, turn and leave rem sts on holder.
Complete left side first.
Next row Cast off 2 sts at neck edge, P to end.
Next row K1, K2 tog, K to end.
Rep last 2 rows twice more.
Next row P2 tog, P1.
Cast off rem 2 sts.
With Rs of work facing leave first 10 [12:14] sts on holder for centre front neck, rejoin yarn to rem sts, K to last 3 sts, sl 1, K1, psso, K1.
Complete to match first side, reversing shapings.

Sleeves

With 5mm/No 6 needles and 2 strands of A, cast on 34 sts. Work 9cm/3½in rib as given for back, ending with a 1st row.
Next row (inc row) Rib 4 [5:7] sts, *pick up loop lying between needles and K tbl – **called M1**, rib 26 [8:4] sts, rep from * 0 [2:4] times more, M1, rib 4 [5:7] sts. 36 [38:40] sts.
Change to 6mm/No 4 needles. Beg with a K row work 6 rows st st. Break off A. Join in 2 strands of B.
Cont in st st, working stripes as given for back, inc one st at each end of 5th and every foll 10th row until there are 48 [50:52] sts.
Cont without shaping until 14 rows in E have been completed, thus ending with same row as back at underarms.

Shape top

Work as given for armhole shaping

on back until 6 sts rem, ending with a P row.
Leave sts on holder.

Polo neck version

Join raglan seams. With Rs of work facing, set of four 5mm/No 6 needles and 2 strands of A, K across sts of back neck and left sleeve K2 tog at seam, pick up and K12 sts down left front neck, K across front neck sts on holder, pick up and K12 sts up right front neck, then K across sts of right sleeve K last st tog with first st of back. 72 [76:80] sts.
Cont in rounds of K2, P2 rib for 24cm/9½in. Cast off very loosely in rib.

Crew neckband

Join raglan seams. With Rs of work facing, set of four 5mm/No 6 needles and 2 strands of A, K across sts of back neck and left sleeve K2 tog at seam, pick up and K8 sts down left front neck, K across front neck sts on holder, pick up and K8 sts up right front neck, then K across sts of right sleeve K last st tog with first st of back. 64 [68:72] sts.
Cont in rounds of K2, P2 rib for 5cm/2in. Leave sts on a separate length of thread.

To make up

Do not press. Join side and sleeve seams. Fold polo neck over to outside.
Fold crew neckband in half to Ws and sl st in place, sewing the loops on the thread to picked up sts of neck and removing the thread as you go.

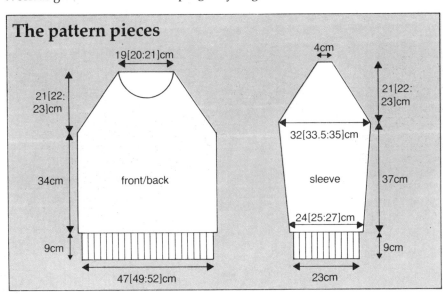

The pattern pieces

19[20:21]cm

21[22:23]cm

34cm

front/back

9cm

47[49:52]cm

4cm

21[22:23]cm

32[33.5:35]cm

sleeve

37cm

24[25:27]cm

9cm

23cm

Polo-neck inset

For extra warmth and comfort knit this simple polo-neck inset to wear under a V-neck jersey, your favourite casual dress or track suit.

Two straight pieces are joined at the shoulders and completed with a polo collar – simply pull it on over your head.

Sizes

To fit 81–91cm/32--36in bust
Length to shoulder, 30cm/11¾in

You will need

3×50g balls of Sirdar Country Style Double Knitting (45% acrylic, 40% Bri-nylon, 15% wool)
One pair 3¾mm/No 9 needles
Set of four 3mm/No 11 needles pointed at both ends

Tension

24 sts and 32 rows to 10cm/4in over st st worked on 3¾mm/No 9 needles

Back

With 3¾mm/No 9 needles cast on 72 sts. K 4 rows g st.
Next row (Rs) K to end.
Next row K2, P to last 2 sts, K2.**
Rep these 2 rows until work measures 30cm/11¾in from beg, ending with a Ws row.

Shape shoulders

Cast off at beg of next and every row 5 sts 4 times and 7 sts twice. Leave rem 48 sts on holder for centre back neck.

Front

Work as given for back to **.
Rep last 2 rows until work measures 24cm/9½in from beg, ending with a Ws row.

Shape neck

Next row K29 sts, turn and leave rem sts on spare needle.
Complete left shoulder first.
Keeping 2 sts at outer edge in g st, cast off 2 sts at beg of next and foll 3 alt rows.
Next row K to last 3 sts, sl 1, K1, psso, K1.
Next row P to last 2 sts, K2.
Rep last 2 rows 3 times more.
17 sts.
Cont without shaping until work measures same as back to shoulder, ending at armhole edge.

Shape shoulder

Cast off at beg of next and every alt row 5 sts twice and 7 sts once. With Rs of work facing, sl first 14 sts on to holder for centre front neck, rejoin yarn to rem sts and K to end.
Next row K2, P to end.
Complete to match first side reversing all shapings.

Polo Neck

Join shoulder seams. With Rs of work facing and set of four 3mm/No 11 needles, K across 38 back neck sts, pick up and K30 sts down left front neck, K across 14 front neck sts, pick up and K30 sts up right front neck. 112 sts.
Cont in rounds of K1, P1 rib for 18cm/7in. Cast off loosely in rib.

233

Inserted pocket techniques

Pockets are a practical and useful addition to a garment and it is easy to add them to a pattern or to change the style to suit your requirements. These inserted pockets can be horizontal, vertical or diagonal and knitted to match the garment fabric.

Choose the style of pocket to fit in with the structure of the main fabric and the shape of the garment. Make sure the fabric is suitable so that it will hold the shape of a pocket without sagging. For example, pockets on very lacy fabrics tend to pull out of shape.

The size of the pocket must also be taken into account at the planning stage. A small pocket on a chunky jacket will look out of proportion while a large pocket on a dainty cardigan would look clumsy and sag out of shape.

If you want to use a pattern that does not include inserted pockets, it is a simple matter to add them. A little pre-planning is necessary and you will also need an extra ball of the yarn.

Horizontal stocking stitch pocket

Check the number of stitches and rows needed to give the correct size. This example is worked over 30 stitches in double knitting yarn on 4mm/No 8 needles on the right front of the cardigan. For any other pattern, make sure the multiples of stitches for the upper side of the pocket will work out exactly. Adjust the number left for the pocket opening and cast on for the lining, as required.

Cast on 30 sts for the inner pocket lining. Beg with a K row cont in st st for the depth of pocket required, ending with a P row. Break off yarn and leave these sts on a holder.

Work the welt or hem as given in the instructions. Cont in the patt for the main fabric to the same depth as the lining, ending with a Ws row.

Next row Work to the position for the opening, sl 30 sts for the pocket opening on to a holder, with Rs of pocket lining sts to the Ws of the main fabric, work across lining sts on holder, then work to end of row.

Complete the right front as given in the instructions. With the Rs of the work facing and a size smaller needles, rejoin yarn to the pocket opening sts on holder. Work 2.5cm/1in ribbing. Cast off loosely. Stitch pocket lining in place.

Vertical basket stitch pocket

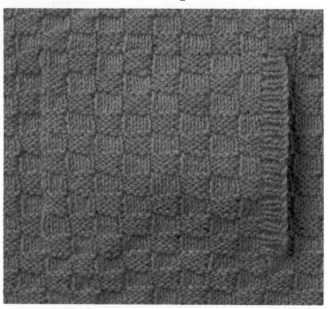

This example is worked over 32 stitches and 40 rows in double knitting yarn on 4mm/No 8 needles on the left front of a jacket. For any other pattern, check that the position for the pocket opening comes at the end of a repeat of the multiples of stitches.

Work in basket stitch pattern of K4, P4 until lower edge of opening is reached, ending at the side edge.

Next row Patt multiples of 4 sts to the position for the opening, turn and leave rem sts on holder.

Next row Cast on 32 sts for pocket lining, P32 then patt to end.

Keeping pocket lining in st st, work the number of rows over these sts to give the depth of pocket, ending at lining edge.

Next row Cast off 32 sts, patt to end. Do not break off yarn. Return to where the work was divided, join in a separate ball of yarn to rem sts and patt to end. Work the same number of rows as for the first side, ending at pocket opening edge. Break off yarn.

Return to the first section, work across all sts in patt to close the opening. Complete the left front as given in the instructions. Stitch lining in place. With Rs facing and a smaller needle size, pick up and knit sts along edge of pocket. Work 2cm/¾in rib. Cast off in rib.

Inserted pockets can be horizontal or vertical. If they are not included in the instructions you must work out the position for each pocket before beginning to knit.

Calculate the width and depth of pocket needed – on a woman's cardigan in double knitting, 12.5cm/5in square is a good size. The opening must be clear of any shaping and front edges.

If a horizontal pocket is to be placed above a ribbed welt you must work sufficient depth in the main fabric to allow the lower edge of the pocket lining to come at the top of the ribbing. The pocket opening edge looks best neatened with the type of ribbing used on the other edges.

If vertical pockets are to be positioned on the fronts of a jacket, you must allow sufficient width in the main fabric from the pocket opening to ensure that the edges of the lining do not overlap the front edges.

A vertical pouch pocket can be placed on the front of a jersey. The pocket opening edges look best neatened with ribbing, as used on the other edges.

Diagonal inserted pockets Before beginning to knit, decide where the pocket opening is to begin and the direction in which it must slant for the right or left front. The opening must be clear of any shaping and allow for a lining to be sewn above the welt, also without overlapping front edges. The slanting edge of the pocket can be neatened with ribbing, as used on the other garment edges.

On all of the inserted pocket techniques, the pocket lining is slipstitched into place on completion of the garment.

Vertical stocking stitch pocket

Check the number of stitches and rows needed to give the correct size. This example is worked over 59 stitches and 46 rows in double knitting yarn on 4mm/No 8 needles across the centre front of a jersey.

Cast on 59 sts for the inner pocket lining. Beg with a K row work 10 rows st st, or the depth required to reach from the top of the welt to the lower edge of the pocket opening, ending with a P row. Leave sts on a holder. Work the welt as given in the instructions, then beg with a K row and work the same number of rows as worked for the pocket lining.

Next row K to the position for the left-hand pocket opening, sl the next 59 sts on to a thread and leave for the time being, K across the pocket lining sts then K to the end of the row.

Beg with a P row cont in st st for 45 rows, or the required depth of pocket, ending with a P row. Leave sts for time being. Do not break off yarn.

Complete the pocket front by joining in a separate ball of yarn to the sts left on the thread and work the same

number of rows as for the first piece. Break off the yarn.

Return to where the yarn was left and join the pocket front and lining.

Next row K to the pocket opening, place the sts of the pocket front in front of the main fabric and K together one st from each needle until all the sts have been worked, then K to end.

Complete the front as given in the instructions.

With the Rs of the work facing and a smaller needle size, pick up and knit the required number of stitches along the left-hand edge of the pocket front. Work 2cm/¾in ribbing. Cast off.

Work along the right-hand edge of the pocket front in the same way.

Stitch base of pocket lining in place.

Below: A close-up view of the vertical pouch pocket on the front of the raglan jersey featured in this chapter. The pocket lining is carefully slipstitched in place at the back.

Diagonal stocking stitch pocket

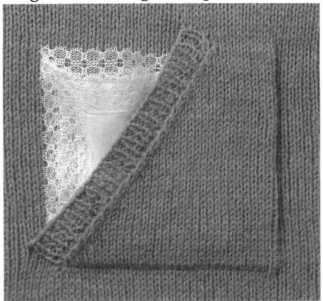

Check where the lower edge of the pocket opening is to begin and the way in which it must slant. This example is worked over 30 stitches in double knitting yarn on 4mm/No 8 needles on the right front of a jacket and slants from left to right.

Work the welt or hem as given in the instructions. Beg with a K row cont in st st until the lower edge of the opening has been reached, ending with a P row.
Next row Work to the position for the opening, turn. Leave remaining stitches on holder.

Dec one st at beg of next row and at same edge on every alt row 30 times in all, ending at front edge. Do not break off yarn.

With separate ball of yarn cast on 30 sts for pocket lining and use this yarn to complete other side of pocket opening.

Beg with a K row cont in st st to give depth of pocket from top edge of welt to lower edge of opening, ending with a K row.

Continue to knit across stitches on holder to end of row. Cont in st st until same number of rows have been worked as for first side, omitting dec, ending with a P row. Break off yarn.

Return to the first section, work across stitches, knitting together one stitch from each needle to join pocket top to main fabric. Complete the right front as given in the instructions.

Complete as given for basket st vertical pocket. Stitch pocket lining in place.

Patch pockets

This quick and simple method can add pockets to an existing garment as well as to the jersey you are knitting. Buy a ball of yarn in a toning or contrasting colour, or use up oddments of yarn of the same thickness to work jazzy stripes or a Fair Isle motif.

Calculate the width and depth of the pocket using an oddment of fabric pinned to the garment. Make sure the pocket does not interfere with any shaping or overlap edges. Large patch pockets are usually positioned with the lower edge just above the ribbing or hem. Smaller pockets look effective as breast

selection of design ideas for patch pockets

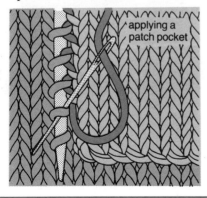

applying a patch pocket

pockets or as a decorative feature on a sleeve.

Knit them in a textured pattern or add cables against a reversed stocking stitch background. Finish the top edge with a few rows of ribbing to match the garment edges or reverse the pattern at the top of the pocket to make a turned down flap.

Apply patch pockets directly on to the garment. Use a fine knitting needle, pointed at both ends, to keep the pocket side edges in line with the main fabric. Pick up every alternate stitch along the line of the main fabric with the needle. Catch one stitch from pocket edge and one from needle alternately.

Work across the row of the main fabric corresponding with the lower edge of pocket in the same way.

Practise knitting with several different coloured yarns by making this collection of eye-catching cushion covers.

Colouring-book stripes and checks

Incredible it may seem, but every one of the exciting striped and checked patterns in this chapter was created simply by using two or more colours and basic knit or purl stitches. So cue yourself in to colour and transform a basic jersey into a unique design.

Working striped (or checked) patterns is a most enjoyable way of experimenting with colour and, at the same time, using up oddments of the same thickness of yarn.

Horizontal and chevron stripes are particularly easy, as only one colour at a time is used in a row. These patterns produce fabrics of a *single* thickness.

Narrow vertical or diagonal stripes use two colours at a time in a row, and produce fabrics of *double* thickness.

The colours used in all patterns of this type are coded for ease of identification, the first colour as A, the second B, the third C and so on.

Horizontal stripes

In stocking stitch, the knitted side will show an unbroken line of colour and the purl side a broken line.

In garter stitch, if an even number of rows is worked in each colour the right side shows an unbroken line of colour and the wrong side a broken one.

All ribbed stitches can be worked in stripes, but if you wish to keep an unbroken line of colour on the right side, the first row of each new colour must be knitted instead of ribbed. If you work in ribbing throughout, a broken line of colour will show on the right side.

When horizontal stripes are worked over an even number of rows, it is a simple matter to change colours. Whatever the pattern, each new colour is brought into use at the beginning of a row and at the same edge. When working narrow stripes with no more than three colours, the two colours not in use can be carried loosely up the side of the work and twisted round the last colour used before you continue to knit with the next colour.

However, to work more than eight rows in any colour – or in more than three colours – do not carry yarns up the side, as this will pull the side edge out of shape. Instead, break off the yarn at the end of each stripe and rejoin it when it is needed again.

To work horizontal stripes over a random number of rows, use a pair of needles pointed at both ends. Each new colour will not necessarily be joined in at the same edge and working an odd number of rows will leave the yarn at the opposite end of the row.

Chevron stripes

Whether regular or random, these are worked in the same way as horizontal stripes. The scalloped effect is achieved by increasing and decreasing at regular points in each row.

Narrow vertical stripes

Two-colour stripes of this type look best worked in stocking stitch as this defines the edge of each stripe. Stitches are worked with the first and second colours alternately, changing at regular points across each row.

The yarn not in use is carried loosely across the back of the work each time it is needed. On a knit row carry the yarn across the back and on a purl row across the front of the work. Take the yarn not in use across in the same position each time – the second colour over the top of the first and the first colour under the second. Do not pull the yarn across tightly or you will pucker the fabric.

Narrow diagonal stripes

These are also best in stocking stitch. The method is the same as for vertical stripes but the position of each stripe is changed by one stitch on every row.

Random horizontal stripes

Stocking stitch stripes

Using A cast on any number of sts. Work in st st, 2 rows A, 1 row B, 3 rows C, 1 row D, 4 rows E, 1 row B, 2 rows A, 1 row E and 3 rows D. These 18 rows form the pattern.

Regular chevron stripes

Using A cast on multiples of 20 sts plus 3, eg 43. Work in g st.

1st row (Rs) Using A, K1, K2 tog, *K8, yfwd, K1, yfwd, K8, sl 1 knitwise, K2 tog, psso, rep from * to last 20 sts, K8, yfwd, K1, yfwd, K8, sl 1, K1, psso, K1.

2nd row Using A, K1, P1, *K8, K1 tb1, K1, K1 tb1, K8, P1, rep from * to last st, K1.

These 2 rows form the chevron patt. Work 2 rows each in B, C, D, E, F & A. These 12 rows form the striped patt.

Regular horizontal stripes   Random chevron stripes

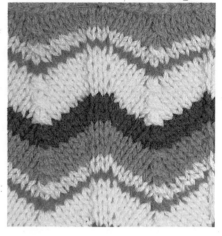

Garter stitch stripes
Using A cast on any number of sts.
Work in g st, 3 rows A, 3 rows B,
3 rows C and 3 rows D.
These 12 rows form the pattern.

Using A cast on multiples of 4 sts
plus 2, eg, 18.
1st row (Rs) Using A, K2, *P2, K2,
rep from * to end.
2nd row Using A, P2, *K2, P2, rep
from * to end.
These 2 rows form the rib pattern.
Rep them once more. Join in B. K
one row then rib 3 rows. Join in C.
K one row then rib 3 rows. Join in
D. K one row then rib 3 rows.
These 16 rows form the striped
pattern.

Using A cast on multiples of 13 sts
plus 2, eg 41. Beg with a K row work
2 rows st st. Commence patt.
1st row (Rs) Using A, *K2, pick up
loop lying between sts and K tbl –
called M1, K4, sl 1 knitwise, K2 tog,
psso, K4, M1, rep from * to last
2 sts, K2.
2nd row Using A, P to end.
These 2 rows form the chevron patt.
Work 2 more rows A, 3 rows B,
6 rows C, 1 row D and 2 rows E.
These 16 rows form the striped patt.

Narrow vertical stripes   Narrow diagonal stripes   Small checked pattern

Using A cast on multiples of 6 sts
plus 3, eg 27. Work in st st.
1st row (Rs) Keeping yarn at back,
K3 A, *K3 B, K3 A, rep from * to
end.
2nd row Keep yarn at front, P3 A,
*P3 B, P3 A, rep from * to end.
These 2 rows form the pattern.

Using A cast on multiples of 4 sts
plus 2, eg 26. Work in st st.
1st row (Rs) Keep yarn at back, K2
A, *K2 B, K2 A, rep from * to end.
2nd row Keep yarn at front, P1 B,
*P2 A, P2 B, rep from * to last st,
P1 A.
3rd row K2 B, *K2 A, K2 B, rep from
* to end.
4th row P1 A, *P2 B, P2 A, rep from
* to last st, P1 B.
These 4 rows form the pattern.

Using A cast on multiples of 4 sts.
Work in st st.
1st row (Rs) Keep yarn at back, *K2
A, K2 B, rep from * to end.
2nd row Keep yarn at front, *P2 B,
P2 A, rep from * to end.
3rd row *K2 B, K2 A, rep from * to
end.
4th row *P2 A, P2 B, rep from * to
end.
These 4 rows form the pattern.

Mosaic patterns in two or more colours

These sophisticated coloured patterns in combinations of horizontal stripes and slipped stitches could not be easier, but they have tremendous impact. Some look best in only two colours, others in as many colours as you wish. Try them out on the cushions overleaf.

Mosaic patterns can be used to create a wonderful variety of coloured fabrics, so don't be put off by their apparent intricacy – they are easy to work. Only one colour is used in any row, some of the stitches being knitted and others simply slipped from one needle to the other. Two rows are worked with the first colour. Then the next two rows are worked with a second colour – again, some of the stitches being knitted and others slipped, but in a different sequence.

Working mosaic patterns

The right side rows are always knitted. Every slipped stitch is slipped with the yarn at the *back* on right-side rows and the same stitch is slipped again with the yarn at the *front* on following wrong side rows. The colours are alternated after every two rows and each slipped stitch – spanning two rows – is caught in again with its own, or an additional colour, on the third row. To begin, cast on with colour A and work the number of rows given.

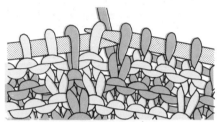

Knitting a right side row
Join in B. Keep the yarn at the *back* of the work, *K the number of stitches given, slip the number of stitches given in a purlwise direction, repeat from * to end.

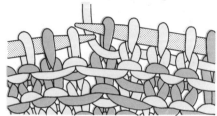

Knitting a wrong side row
Using same colour as previous row, keep the yarn at the back and knit all knitted stitches and bring the yarn forward to the front to slip all slipped stitches of the previous row.

Turret pattern

Using A cast on multiples of 4 sts plus 3, eg 23.
1st row (Rs) Using A, K to end.
2nd row Using A, P to end.
3rd row Using B, K3, *sl 1, K3, rep from * to end.
4th row Using B, K3, *yfwd, sl 1, ybk, K3, rep from * to end.
5th row Using A, K2, *sl 1, K1, rep from * to last st, K1.
6th row Using A, P2, *sl 1, P1, rep from * to last st, P1.
7th row Using B, K1, *sl 1, K3, rep from * to last 2 sts, sl 1, K1.
8th row Using B, K1, *yfwd, sl 1, ybk, K3, rep from * to last 2 sts, yfwd, sl 1, ybk, K1.
9th and 10th rows Using A, as 1st and 2nd.
11th and 12th rows Using B, as 7th and 8th.
13th and 14th rows Using A, as 5th and 6th.
15th and 16th rows Using B, as 3rd and 4th.
These 16 rows form the pattern. To work in more than two colours use different colours for next repeat.

Tricolour pattern

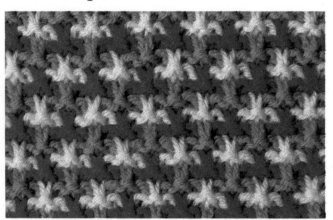

Using A cast on multiples of 4 sts plus 3, eg 23.
1st row (Rs) Using A, *K3, sl 1, rep from * to last 3 sts, K3.
2nd row Using A, K3, *yfwd, sl 1, ybk, K3, rep from * to end.
3rd row Using B, K1, *sl 1, K3, rep from * to last 2 sts, sl 1, K1.
4th row Using B, K1, *yfwd, sl 1, ybk, K3, rep from * to last 2 sts, yfwd, sl 1, ybk, K1.
5th and 6th rows Using C, as 1st and 2nd.
7th and 8th rows Using A, as 3rd and 4th.
9th and 10th rows Using B, as 1st and 2nd.
11th and 12th rows Using C, as 3rd and 4th.
These 12 rows form the pattern. To work in two colours only repeat first 4 rows.

Altering the sequence of knitted and slipped stitches causes parts of each pair of rows to be concealed by slipped stitches in a different colour carried up from the previous row. This way the slipped stitches form a superimposed pattern.

You can use only two colours throughout or introduce more colours in the following rows. In printed patterns the colours are coded as A, B, C and so on, for ease of reference and to allow you to substitute colours of your own choice, if you wish. If you are creating your own mosaic design, it is well worth coding your colours in this way so that you have a handy record of the sequence worked.

Purl or plain All mosaic patterns can be worked in either stocking stitch or garter stitch. If the instructions are for garter stitch and you want to work stocking stitch, simply purl all the wrong-side rows instead of knitting them. To work garter stitch instead of stocking stitch, knit the wrong side rows instead of purling them. If you are using a printed pattern, you may find it helpful to write in these adjustments, to save confusion.

The type of yarn you choose should relate to the effect you wish to achieve. The smooth surface of stocking stitch is complemented by bouclé or fluffy yarns, while the knobbly texture of garter stitch looks best worked in a plain yarn. Both fabrics look stunning when a glitter yarn is introduced as one of the colours. Because stitches are slipped on every row the fabric is very dense.

Stitch requirements The fascinating thing about mosaics is that they can be worked over any number of stitches, so you are not tied to exact multiples of stitches.

Each example given here has an exact multiple of stitches shown but don't let this put you off if you want to experiment. Simply begin each right-side pattern row at the right-hand edge, as given, and work across the row until you run out of stitches, irrespective of what point you have reached in the pattern. Work the return row by knitting (or purling) all the knitted stitches of the previous row and slipping all the slipped stitches. The ends of the rows may not match exactly but these patterns are easy to incorporate into a basic design whether for a garment or household items such as bedcovers or cushion covers.

The easiest mosaic pattern to practise if you are a beginner is the tricolour pattern as this has a pattern repeat of only four rows with the effect being formed by changes in the colour of the yarn.

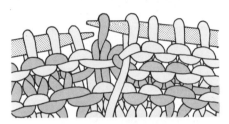

Purling a wrong side row
Using same colour as for previous row, keep the yarn at the front and purl all the knitted stitches and slip all the slipped stitches of the previous row.

Overcheck pattern

Using A cast on multiples of 6 sts, eg 24. P one row.
1st row (Rs) Using B, K5, *sl 2, K4, rep from * to last st, K1.
2nd row Using B, K5, *yfwd, sl 2, ybk, K4, rep from * to last st, K1.
3rd row Using A, K1, *sl 1, K2, rep from * to last 2 sts, sl 1, K1.
4th row Using A, P1, *sl 1, P2, rep from * to last 2 sts, sl 1, P1.
5th row Using B, K2, *sl 2, K4, rep from * to last 4 sts, sl 2, K2.
6th row Using B, K2, *yfwd, sl 2, ybk, K4, rep from * to last 4 sts, yfwd, sl 2, ybk, K2.
7th and 8th rows Using A, as 3rd and 4th.
These 8 rows form the pattern. This pattern is best worked in two colours only.

Zigzag pattern

Using A cast on multiples of 5 sts plus 1, eg 21. K one row.
1st row (Rs) Using B, *K4, sl 1, rep from * to last st, K1.
2nd row Using B, P1, *sl 1, P4, rep from * to end.
3rd row Using A, K5, *sl 1, K4, rep from * to last st, K1.
4th row Using A, K5, *yfwd, sl 1, ybk, K4, rep from * to last st, K1.
5th row Using B, K1, *sl 1, K4, rep from * to end.
6th row Using B, *P4, sl 1, rep from * to last st, P1.
7th and 8th rows Using A, as 3rd and 4th.
These 8 rows form the pattern. This pattern is best worked in two colours only.

241

Greek key pattern

Using A cast on multiples of 6 sts plus 2, eg 26.
1st row (Rs) Using A, K to end.
2nd row Using A, K to end.
3rd row Using B, K1, *sl 1, K5, rep from * to last st, K1.
4th and every alt row Using same colour as previous row keep yarn at front of work to sl all sl sts of previous row and take it back to K all K sts.
5th row Using A, K2, *sl 1, K3, sl 1, K1, rep from * to end.
7th row Using B, K1, *sl 1, K3, sl 1, K1, rep from * to last st, K1.
9th row Using A, K6, *sl 1, K5, rep from * to last 2 sts, sl 1, K1.
11th and 12th rows Using B, as 1st and 2nd.
13th row Using A, K4, *sl 1, K5, rep from * to last 4 sts, sl 1, K3.
15th row Using B, *K3, sl 1, K1, sl 1, rep from * to last 2 sts, K2.
17th row Using A, K2, *sl 1, K1, sl 1, K3, rep from * to end.
19th row Using B, K3, *sl 1, K5, rep from * to last 5 sts, sl 1, K4.
20th row As 4th.
These 20 rows form the pattern. To work in more than two colours use different colours for next repeat.

Pyramid pattern

Using A cast on multiples of 14 sts plus 3, eg 31. K one row.
1st row (Rs) Using B, K8, *sl 1, K13, rep from * to last 9 sts, sl 1, K8.
2nd and every alt row Using same colour as previous row keep yarn at front of work to sl all sl sts of previous row and take it back to K all K sts.
3rd row Using A, K2, *(sl 1, K1) twice, sl 1, K3, (sl 1, K1) 3 times, rep from * to last st, K1.
5th row Using B, K7, *sl 1, K1, sl 1, K11, rep from * to last 10 sts, sl 1, K1, sl 1, K7.
7th row Using A, K2, *sl 1, K1, sl 1, K7, (sl 1, K1) twice, rep from * to last st, K1.
9th row Using B, K5, *(sl 1, K1) 3 times, sl 1, K7, rep from * to last 12 sts, (sl 1, K1) 3 times, sl 1, K5.
11th row Using A, K2, *sl 1, K11, sl 1, K1, rep from * to last st, K1.
13th row Using B, K3, *(sl 1, K1) 5 times, sl 1, K3, rep from * to end.
15th row Using A, K1, *sl 1, K13, rep from * to last 2 sts, sl 1, K1.
16th row As 2nd.
These 16 rows form the pattern. To work in more than two colours use different colours for next repeat.

Razzle-dazzle cushion covers

The attractive cushion covers shown earlier on page 237, can be made in the colours and patterns of your choice. For all three versions shown, the backs and the front 'frames' with their mitred corners are worked as one piece, in garter stitch.

One front cover is worked in Greek key mosaic pattern, one in random stripes and one in square patches – each with a different pattern.

Instructions are given for 40cm/15¾in covers but, if you wish to use one of these designs for a cushion of a different size, it is a simple matter to scale them up or down.

Size

To fit a 40cm/15¾in cushion

You will need

Cushion back all versions, 6×20g balls of Wendy Courtellon Double Knitting (60% Courtelle, 40% Bri-Nylon) in main colour A
Greek key cushion front 1 ball each of same in contrast colours B and C
Striped cushion front Oddments of same in 6 contrast colours
Patchwork cushion front Oddments of same in 6 contrast colours
One pair 4mm/No 8 needles
30cm/12in zip fastener
40cm/15¾in cushion pad

Tension

20 sts and 28 rows to 10cm/4in over st st (20 sts and 40 rows for g st) worked on 4mm/No 8 needles

Cushion back

With 4mm/No 8 needles and A cast on 62 sts. K 2 rows.
3rd row K into front and back of first st – called inc 1, K to last 2 sts, inc 1, K1. **4th row** K to end.
Rep 3rd and 4th rows 7 times more, then 3rd row again. 80 sts.
20th row (opening for zip) K10, cast off 60 sts, K to end.
21st row Inc 1, K9, cast on 60 sts, K to last 2 sts, inc 1, K1.**22nd row** As 4th.
Rep 3rd and 4th rows 9 times more. 100 sts.
Cont without shaping until work measures 40cm/15¾in from beg, ending with a Ws row.
Next row K2 tog tbl, K to last 2 sts, K2 tog.

The pattern pieces

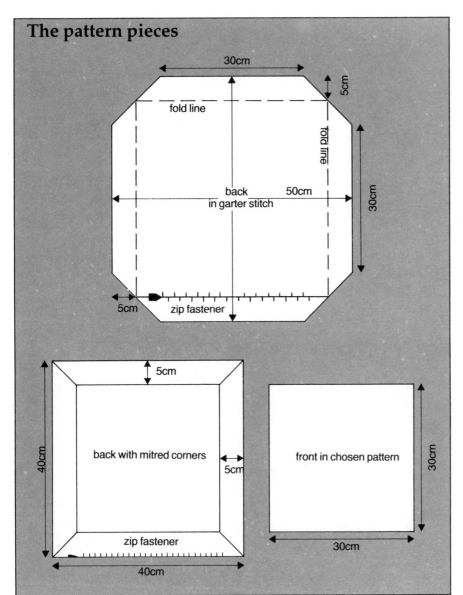

Next row K to end.
Rep last 2 rows 18 times more, then K one row. Cast off loosely.

Greek key cushion front

With 4mm/No 8 needles and B cast on 62 sts. Work 30cm/11¾in in Greek key pattern ending with a 20th patt row. K one row. Cast off.

Striped cushion front

With 4mm/No 8 needles and any colour cast on 62 sts. Work in st st and random stripes, see page 110, for 30cm/11¾in. Cast off.

Patchwork cushion front

This is made up of 9 squares, each in a different pattern, shown here in random stripes, basket st, vertical stripes, small check, diagonal stripes, moss st, double moss st, and overcheck and turret mosaic patt.
For each square cast on 22 sts or the nearest multiple of sts for the patt of your choice.
Work 10cm/4in patt. Cast off.

To make up

Join 9 patches to make a square. Press all cushion fronts lightly under dry cloth with a warm iron. Do not press backs.
Join mitred corners of cushion back. Turn to Ws. Join edges of front to back. Turn Rs out. Sew in zip. Insert cushion pad.

PROFESSIONAL TOUCH

Sizing the cushions up or down

If you have an existing cushion in a different size and would like to make one of these covers, this is how to scale the designs up or down. Use the tension given to calculate how many stitches and rows you must work to give the size required.
Cover back For a width of 30cm/11¾in the instructions were to cast on 62 stitches. To take a size down to 25cm/9¾in, cast on 52 stitches. To take it up to 35cm/13¾in, cast on 72 stitches. Increase at each end of every row as given in the instructions to give a width of 45cm/17¾in (smaller size) or 55cm/21¾in (larger size).

(Both measurements allow for mitred corners.) Adjust the number of rows for the length, then decrease as given in the instructions down to the original number of stitches. When the corners are turned in and mitred the finished size of the back will be 35cm/13¾in (smaller size) or 45cm/17¾in (larger size).
Cover front This is adjusted up or down in the same way by subtracting or adding 10 stitches for every 5cm/2in.
Patchwork cushion front Each patch for this design needs to be 8cm/3¼in square (smaller size), 12cm/4¾in square (larger size).

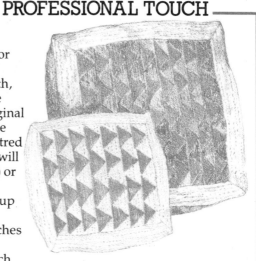

Above: An example of the cushion covers sized up and down from the original measurements given in the pattern.

243

Multi-Coloured Patterns

*In jacquard knitting a single, multi-coloured motif or repeats
of the motif forming a pattern are used to highlight
basic garments. Random pictorial and regular geometric
collage patterns produce all-over fabrics.
These techniques use many colours in any one row.*

Jacquard, random pictorial and regular geometric collage patterns (also called intarsia knitting), use any number of colours in the same row and are worked in stocking stitch.

It is possible to work a small jacquard design using only three colours in any row, by stranding the yarns across the back of the fabric. To strand more than three colours makes the fabric clumsy and untidy. In a random pictorial pattern small areas may have the yarn stranded or woven in across the back, while larger areas need to be worked with

Weaving in yarns across the fabric

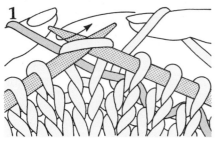

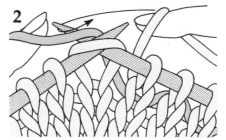

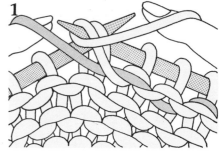

Working a knit row
Keep the yarns at the back of the work throughout and repeat the following action each time a new colour is brought into use.
1 Knit the first stitch with the first colour in the right hand.

2 On the second and every following *alternate* stitch in the first colour, insert the right-hand needle from front to back into the stitch. Use the left hand to place the contrast yarn not being used over the top of the right-hand needle, then knit the stitch with the first colour. The stitches in between are knitted in the usual way.

Working a purl row
Keep the yarns at the front of the work throughout, and repeat the following action each time a new colour is brought into use.
1 To alternate the position of the weaving, purl the first two stitches with the first colour in the right hand.

Working jacquard patterns from charts

Jacquard motifs or repeating patterns use more than two colours in a row. Working from charts, the first and odd-numbered rows read from right to left and the second and even-numbered rows from left to right.

Below: A sample showing a rose motif in double knitting yarn. Embroider the stem afterwards in stem stitch.

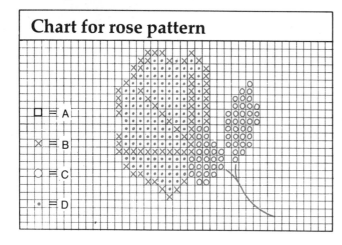

Chart for rose pattern

□ = A
× = B
○ = C
• = D

separate balls of colour. In consequence some areas of the fabric will be of double thickness and others of single thickness so it is particularly important to keep the tension regular and even – otherwise you will emphasize the irregularities already inherent in the design.

The correct method for working all large jacquard motifs, all-over-pictorial or geometric collage patterns and wide vertical stripes is to use small, separate balls of yarn for each colour. As each new colour is brought into use loop it round the previous one to avoid leaving a gap in the fabric. Work with short lengths of each contrast colour or the yarns will become very tangled and difficult to unravel. An alternative is to use bobbins – see Professional Touch overleaf. These patterns form fabrics of single thickness as the yarns are not stranded across the back of the work.

Joining in new colours

On jacquard and pictorial patterns when more than four stitches have to be worked in one colour, weave in the yarn on every alternate stitch. This avoids long, loose strands of yarn on the back of the fabric which catch and snag in wear.

On wide vertical stripes and regular geometric collage patterns, loop each new colour round the last stitch in the previous colour on every row. If you do not, you will produce unjoined stripes or shapes of each colour.

On large motifs and random pictorial patterns, loop the new colour yarn round the last stitch in the previous yarn in any row where the same number of stitches have been worked in one colour, to avoid a gap in the fabric. With such patterns and motifs, however, some stitches will inevitably overlap other areas of colour – in which event the yarn will automatically be looped and the fabric closed.

Changing colours in wide vertical stripes

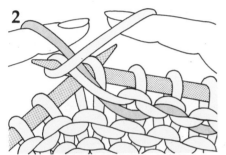

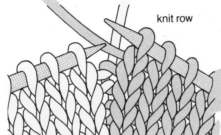

knit row

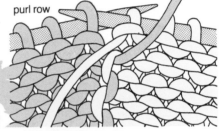

purl row

2 On the third and every following *alternate* stitch in the first colour, insert the right-hand needle from right to left into the stitch. Use the left hand to place the contrast yarn not in use across the top of the right-hand needle, then purl the stitch with the first colour. The stitches in between are purled in the usual way.

Working a knit row
Keep the yarns at the back of the work throughout and repeat the following for each new colour. Knit across the stitches in the first colour. Take this end of yarn over the top of the next colour to be used and drop it. Pick up the next colour under this strand of yarn and take it over the strand ready to knit the next stitch.

Working a purl row
Keep the yarns at the front of the work throughout and repeat the following for each new colour. Purl across the stitches in the first colour. Take this end of yarn over the top of the next colour to be used and drop it. Pick up the next colour under this strand of yarn and take it over the strand ready to purl the next stitch.

Chart for border pattern

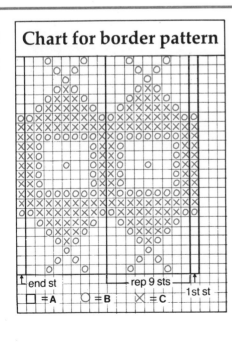

end st   — rep 9 sts —   1st st

□ = A   ○ = B   ✕ = C

Knitting pattern abbreviations

alt	alternate(ly)
approx	approximate(ly)
beg	begin(ning)
ch	chain(s)
cm	centimetre(s)
cont	continu(e)(ing)
cr2L	cross 1 knit st to left
cr2R	cross 1 knit st to right
dec	decreas(e)(ing)
foll	follow(ing)
g st	garter stitch
g	gramme(s)
inc	increas(e)(ing) by working twice into a stitch
K	knit
K up	pick up and knit, as round neck edge
K-wise	knitwise direction
m	metre(s)
MB	make bobble, as specified
mm	millimetre(s)
M1	make one by picking up loop lying between needles and knit through back of loop to increase one
patt	pattern
psso	pass slipped stitch over
p2sso	pass 2 slipped stitches over
P	purl
P up	pick up and purl
P-wise	purlwise direction
rem	remain(ing)
rep	repeat(ing)
Rs	right side of fabric
sl	slip
sl st	slip stitch(es)
st(s)	stitch(es)
st st	stocking stitch
tog	together
tw2B	twist 2 knit stitches to left
tw2F	twist 2 knit stitches to right
tw2PB	twist 2 purl stitches to left
tw2PF	twist 2 purl stitches to right
Ws	wrong side of fabric
ybk	yarn back between needles
yfwd	yarn forward between needles
yon	yarn over needle
yrn	yarn around needle

Pattern symbols

An asterisk, *, in a pattern row denotes that the stitches after this sign must be repeated from that point to the end of the row, or to the last number of stitches given.

Instructions shown in round brackets (), denote that this section of the pattern is to be worked for all sizes. Instructions shown in square brackets, [], denote larger sizes.

PART 3
CROCHET

Starting to crochet

The great advantage of crochet is its versatility. It can be as delicate or as serviceable as you care to make it. Using the techniques given in this section you can learn to make items ranging from a bedspread and light summer tops to a selection of attractive baby wear.

Making crochet chains

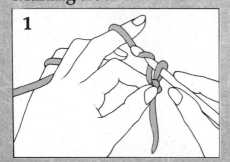

With the slip loop on the hook, begin to make the series of chain stitches which form the foundation row of crochet. The abbreviation for chain stitch is ch.
1 *Hold the end of yarn between the thumb and forefinger of your left hand and the main length of yarn taut across the first and second fingers of your left hand.

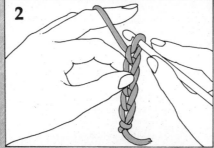

2 With the hook in your right hand catch the yarn in the curve of the hook. This is called yarn round the hook and is abbreviated as yrh. Draw the yarn through the loop on the hook. You have made your first chain and the working loop remains on the hook.
Continue in this way from the point marked with an asterisk (*) until you have made the required number of chains. Take care to move the thumb and forefinger of your left hand up the chain as it is formed to hold each stitch firmly.

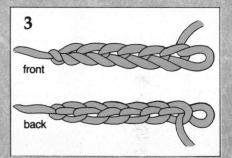

3 Compare your work with the diagram. Each chain is made up of three strands of yarn. Two of the strands form the loop which has been pulled through the previous loop. The third is the strand which has been carried behind this loop, ready to put round the hook again for the next chain.

248

There are many beautiful crochet patterns available. These range from fashionable garments to useful and attractive items for the home. You don't even need to crochet a whole garment but can decorate your linen, blinds or petticoats effectively with a crochet trimming.

Crochet requires even less equipment than knitting – just one hook and the yarn you have chosen. This means it is easily portable. As each stitch finishes with just one loop on the hook, there is little chance of stitches unravelling.

Busy people find crochet ideal because you do not spoil the fabric if you have to stop in the middle of a row.

It can take more yarn to crochet a garment than to knit one but, because most crocheted rows are deeper than knitted ones, you'll find that crochet grows faster than knitting.

Too often crochet instructions look baffling. This chapter details them simply and in full with clear illustrations to start you off on your first project. Each following chapter introduces you gradually to more intricate techniques.

How to hold the hook and yarn

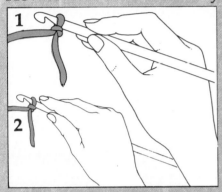

1 Hold the hook comfortably in your right hand between the thumb and the forefinger, just as you hold a pencil. Allow the hook to rest against the second finger.
2 An alternative way of holding the hook is to grasp it from above, just as you would hold a knife.

3 Wind the yarn round the fingers of your left hand in such a way that you can firmly control the flow of the yarn: this helps you to crochet evenly. The most common method is shown above.

Making a slip loop

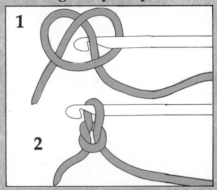

All crochet begins with a slip loop which is placed on the hook.
To make a slip loop take the main length of yarn across the short end.
1 Using the curve of the hook, pull the main length through from the back to the front.
2 Tighten the loop on the hook.

Turning chains

Crochet stitches range in size from slip stitches, which are very shallow, to triple trebles which can be as much as 2.5cm/1in deep. To bring the hook up to the correct height for the stitch being made, you must work extra chains at the start of every row. These are called turning chains and the number varies with the stitch being worked.

Unless otherwise stated in a pattern, the table (below) should be followed:

Stitches	Turning chains
Double crochet	1 or 2
Half treble	2
Treble	3
Double treble	4
Triple treble	5

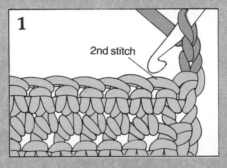

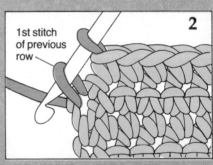

Turning chains always form the first stitch and to compensate for this, the first stitch must be left unworked.
1 Work the first actual stitch of the pattern (such as double crochet overleaf) into the second stitch of the row.
Unless the first stitch is missed after working the turning chain, an extra stitch will be added to the beginning of the row.

2 At the end of a row, work the last stitch of the pattern into the top of the turning chain (which formed the first stitch of the previous row).
Turning chains form a neat edge, which makes seaming easier at the final stage.

Making slipped stitches

These are very shallow stitches and are seldom used on their own. They are used in shaping, or as a linking stitch. (The abbreviation for slipped stitch(es) is ss.)

1 To work back along a foundation row of chains, *insert the hook from the front to the back into the second chain from the hook, yarn round the hook. Draw a loop through and then through the loop on the hook. One slip stitch has been made. Continue in this way from the point marked with an asterisk (*) until you have the required number of stitches.

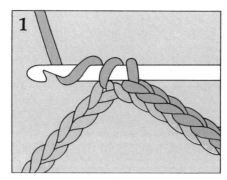

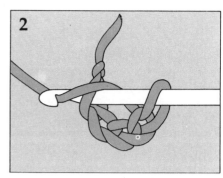

2 To use a slip stitch to join chains into a circle, first make sure that the chains are not twisted. Push the hook from the front to the back

through two of the strands of the first chain made. Yarn round the hook and draw through all the loops on the hook.

Making double crochet stitches

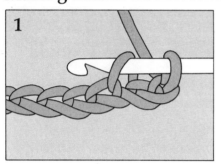

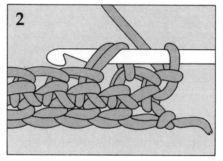

Double crochet worked in firm cotton.

Make the number of chains required plus one extra turning chain. Eleven chains form ten double crochet stitches. (The abbreviation for double crochet is dc.)

1st row Leave the first 2 chains.
1 Push the hook through the top loop only of the 3rd chain from the hook, *yarn round hook and draw a loop through the chain, (2 loops on hook), yarn round hook and draw through both loops on the hook. One double crochet stitch has been made with

the two missed chains forming the turning chain.
Push the hook through the top loop of the next chain and repeat from the point marked with an asterisk (*) into each chain. At the end of the row turn the work so that the last stitch of this row becomes the first stitch of the next row.
2nd row Make 2 chains as the turning chain, miss the first double crochet.
2 *Push the hook under both loops at the top of the next stitch, yarn round

hook and draw a loop through, (2 loops on hook), yarn round hook and draw through both loops on hook. Continue in this way from the point marked with an asterisk (*) into each stitch to the last stitch. This is the turning chain of the previous row. The last double crochet should be worked into the top of this chain. Turn the work.
The 2nd row forms the pattern.

Fastening off

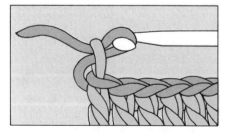

When you have finished you do not need to cast off as in knitting. Instead, the remaining loop on the hook is fastened off securely.
To do this, break off the yarn leaving an end about 10cm/4in. Draw this through the loop on the hook and pull it up tightly.

PROFESSIONAL TOUCH

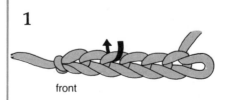

front

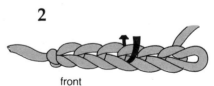

front

A firm foundation

1 To achieve a firm edge when working the first row into a foundation chain, put the hook under *the top strand only* of each chain. This gives the best results for closely textured fabrics such as

those formed by double crochet.
2 A looser edge is obtained when the hook is put under *the top strand and the strand across the back* of the chain. This method is ideal for open, lacy patterns.

Cotton purse and belt

A simple drawstring purse and matching belt using chain stitches and double crochet stitches. The bead trimmings are added at the end.

Sizes

Purse 14cm×16cm/5½in×6¼in
Belt To fit waist sizes 61, 66 and 71cm/24, 26 and 28in. It is designed to leave a gap of 10cm/4in at front of waist when tied. The actual sizes of the crochet are 51, 56 and 61cm/20, 22 and 24in long by 5cm/2in wide.

You will need

Purse 2×25g balls of Twilley's Lyscordet
Oddment in contrast colour
3.00mm/No 10 crochet hook
8 small wooden beads, optional
Belt 2×25g balls of Twilley's Lyscordet
Oddment in contrast colour
3.00mm/No 10 crochet hook
30 small wooden beads, optional

Purse

With 3.00mm/No 10 crochet hook make 37ch.
1st row 1dc into 3rd ch from hook, work 1dc into each ch to end. 36 sts.
2nd row 1ch to count as first dc, work 1dc into each dc, working last dc into top of previous turning ch. This is the purse bottom and should measure 14cm/5½in across after you have crocheted about 5cm/2in. If it is more you are working too loosely. Unravel the crochet and start again with a 2.50mm/No 12 hook. If it is less, you are working too tightly and should change to 3.50mm/No 9 hook. Repeat the 2nd row until the work measures 14cm/5½in from beginning. The next two rows make holes for the drawstring.
Next row 1ch to count as first dc, 1dc into each of the next 2dc, *2ch, miss 2dc, work 1dc into each of next 2dc, repeat from * to last st, 1dc into last st.
Next row 1ch to count as first dc, work in dc to end, working 2dc into each 2ch space.
Repeat 2nd row at beginning of purse 6 times more. Fasten off.
Make another piece in same way.

Above: Polished beads of cream and brown are used to highlight the crocheted belt.
Right: A neat, little drawstring purse.

To make up

Press under a damp cloth with a warm iron. Join sides and lower edge with oversewn seam.
Using 3 strands of contrast yarn together, make a chain about 70cm/30in long. Thread through holes at top. Thread 4 beads on each end of chain, knotting at intervals of 2.5cm/1in. Join ends of chain.

Belt

With 3.00mm/No 10 hook make 135ch for a 61cm/24in waist (66cm/26in waist – 148ch; 71cm/28in waist – 161ch). Work 1st and 2nd rows as for purse. This gives 134 sts for 61cm/24in, 147 sts for 66cm/26in and 160 sts for 71cm/28in.

Repeat 2nd row until work measures 5cm/2in from beginning. Fasten off.

To make up

Press under damp cloth with warm iron. Using 2 strands of yarn make 6 chains in same colour as belt and 4 chains in contrast yarn, about 25cm/10in long.
Alternating colours, sew 5 chains along each short end to tie at front. Trim each chain with 3 beads as given for purse.

Adding trebles and granny squares to your techniques

Half trebles are the shallowest of all the variations of trebles and ordinary trebles are the most commonly used of crochet stitches. To practise working trebles in rounds, make some colourful granny squares. They are fun to make and easy to assemble into useful designs.

You can either work trebles to and fro in rows or you can produce motifs, such as granny squares, by beginning at the centre and working round and round in trebles and chains.

To work to and fro in rows you transfer the stitches just made to your left hand, so that the yarn is ready to start the next row of crochet. This is abbreviated as 'turn'.

To work granny squares in rounds you do not turn at the end of each round but join the last stitch to the first stitch with a slip stitch, so the same side of the fabric is always facing you. All treble stitches begin by putting the yarn round the hook as the first working movement, before inserting the hook into a stitch. This is abbreviated as 'yrh'.

If you study how half treble and treble stitches are made you will see why they look different when worked in rows or rounds. On each stitch the first movement of yarn round the hook forms a horizontal thread at the back of the stitch when it is completed.

Making half treble stitches

1

Make the number of chains required plus one extra turning chain. Eleven chains form 10 half trebles. The abbreviation is 'htr'.

1st row Beg each st with yrh.
1 Yrh, push the hook through the top loop of the 3rd ch from hook, *yrh and draw a loop through the ch, (3 loops on hook), yrh and draw through all 3 loops on hook. One htr has been made with the 2 missed ch

2

forming the turning ch. Yrh, push the hook through the top loop of the next ch and rep from * into each ch. At the end of the row, transfer the hook to the left hand to turn so that the last st of the row becomes the first st of the next row.
2nd row Make 2ch as turning ch, miss first htr.
2 *Yrh, push the hook under both loops at the top of the next st, yrh

Half trebles worked in double knitting.

and draw a loop through, (3 loops on hook), yrh and draw through all 3 loops on hook. Continue from the * into each st to the last st. This is the turning ch of the previous row. Work the last htr into the top of this ch. Transfer the hook to the left hand to turn.
The 2nd row forms the pattern.

Making granny squares using one colour

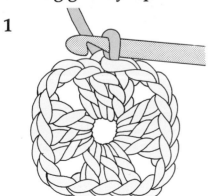

1

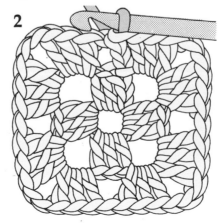

2

Make 6ch. Join with a ss to first of these 6ch to form circle.
1st round 3ch to count as first tr, 2tr into the circle working under the ch, 2ch, work (3tr into the circle, 2ch) 3 times.
1 Join with a ss to 3rd of first 3ch.
2nd round 2ch, working under first 2ch into space make 3tr, 2ch, 3tr – **called 'work corner'**, *1ch, work corner into next 2ch space, rep from * twice more.
2 Join with a ss to first of first 2ch.
3rd round 3ch to count as first tr, work 2tr into first ch space to the

This lies just beneath the two loops at the top of the stitch. When turning at the end of each row this horizontal thread shows on every alternate row. When working in rounds the horizontal thread never shows on the right side of the motif.

Half trebles are deeper than double crochet stitches. When they are used as an all-over pattern, they form firmly textured crochet. They are most commonly used to bridge the gap in height between double crochet and treble stitches.

Trebles are deeper than half trebles. They are the most popular of all crochet stitches and the different ways of forming and combining them produce a great variety of patterns.

Granny squares, or Afghan squares as they are sometimes called, are the simplest and most colourful way of learning to crochet. You can make granny squares in oddments of double knitting yarn, provided they are of about the same thickness.

Half granny squares form a triangular motif which is useful to shape a garment made up of granny squares, such as the neck edge on a waistcoat. These motifs are worked in rows and each row begins with a new strand of yarn joined to the *beginning* of the previous row. As the work is not turned at the end of each row, the crochet looks the same as that of a granny square.

Right: Trebles worked in double knitting.

Making treble stitches

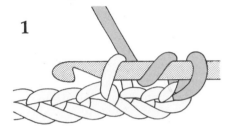

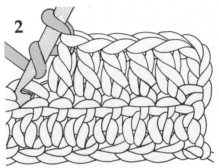

Make the number of chains required plus two extra turning chains. Twelve chains form ten trebles. The abbreviation is 'tr'.

1st row Beg each st with yrh.
1 Yrh, push the hook through the top loop of the 4th ch from hook, *yrh and draw a loop through the ch, (3 loops on hook), yrh and draw through 2 of the loops on the hook, (2 loops on hook), yrh and draw

through 2 loops on hook. One tr has been made with the 3 missed ch forming the turning ch. Yrh, push the hook through the top loop of the next ch and rep from * into each ch. At the end of the row, turn so that the last st of the row becomes the first st of the next row.
2nd row Make 3ch as turning ch, miss first tr.
2 *Yrh, push the hook under both

loops at the top of the next st, yrh and draw a loop through, (3 loops on hook), yrh and draw through 2 of the loops on the hook, (2 loops on hook), yrh and draw through 2 loops on hook.
Continue from the * into each st to the last st. This is the turning ch of the previous row. Work the last tr into the top of this ch. Turn.
The 2nd row forms the pattern.

left of the ss of the previous round, 1ch, *work corner, 1ch, work 3tr into next 1ch space, 1ch, rep from * twice more, work corner, 1ch. Join with a ss to 3rd of first 3ch.
4th round 2ch, work 3tr into next 1ch space, 1ch, *work corner, 1ch, work (3tr into next 1ch space, 1ch) twice, rep from * twice more, work corner, 1ch, 3tr into last 1ch space before ss of previous round. Join with a ss to first of first 2ch.
Break off yarn and fasten off. Darn in two ends on wrong side of square.

Joining granny squares with double crochet

This method of joining granny squares gives an attractive ridged finish, and is a professional alternative to a plain oversewn seam.
Begin at the right-hand corner, with the wrong side of each square together. Insert hook from front to back into the space on both squares. Put a slip loop on the hook, pull this through, yrh, draw through loop on hook. *Insert hook under both loops at the top of next treble on each square, yrh, draw loop through, yrh, draw through both loops on hook. Continue from * into each treble and space to end. Fasten off.

Making granny squares using two or more colours

Make chains and work the first round as for granny square in one colour. Break off yarn and fasten off.

2nd round Join next colour into any 2ch space with a ss, 3ch to count as first tr, work 2tr into same 2ch space, *1ch, work corner as 2nd round of square in one colour, rep from * twice more, 1ch, 3tr into same 2ch space as beg of round, 2ch. Join with a ss to 3rd of first 3ch. Break off yarn and fasten off.

3rd round Join next colour into any 2ch space with a ss, 3ch to count as first tr, work 2tr into same 2ch space, *1ch, work 3tr into next 1ch space, 1ch, work corner, rep from * twice more, 1ch, 3tr into next 1ch space, 1ch, 3tr into same 2ch space as beg of round, 2ch. Join with a ss to 3rd of first 3ch. Break off yarn and fasten off.

4th round Join next colour into any 2ch space with a ss, 3ch to count as first tr, work 2tr into same 2ch space, *(1ch, work 3tr into next 1ch space) twice, 1ch, work corner, rep from * twice more, (1ch, work 3tr into next 1ch space) twice, 1ch, 3tr into same 2ch space as beg of round, 2ch. Join with a ss to 3rd of first 3ch.

Break off yarn and fasten off. Darn in all ends on wrong side of square.

A multi-coloured granny square.

Papoose bag

This simple shape will keep baby warm and cosy in a pram or cot. It can also be used as a carrying bag.

Size
Length when folded, 45cm/18in wide by 81cm/32in long

You will need
4×50g balls of Sirdar Majestic double knitting in main colour A
2 balls of same in contrast colour B
3 balls of same in contrast colour C
2 balls of same in contrast colour D
One 4.00mm/No 8 hook
Note: Each square should measure 9cm×9cm/3½in×3½in. If larger you are working too loosely and should change to a 3.50mm/No 9 hook. If smaller you are working too tightly and should change to a 4.50mm/No 7 hook.
Continue changing hook sizes until you can achieve the correct size.

To work bag
With 4.00mm/No 8 hook make 80 squares in four colours. Work 40 of the squares using D for 1st round and B for 2nd round. Work the remaining 40 squares using B for 1st round and D for 2nd round. Complete each square using C for 3rd round and A for 4th round.

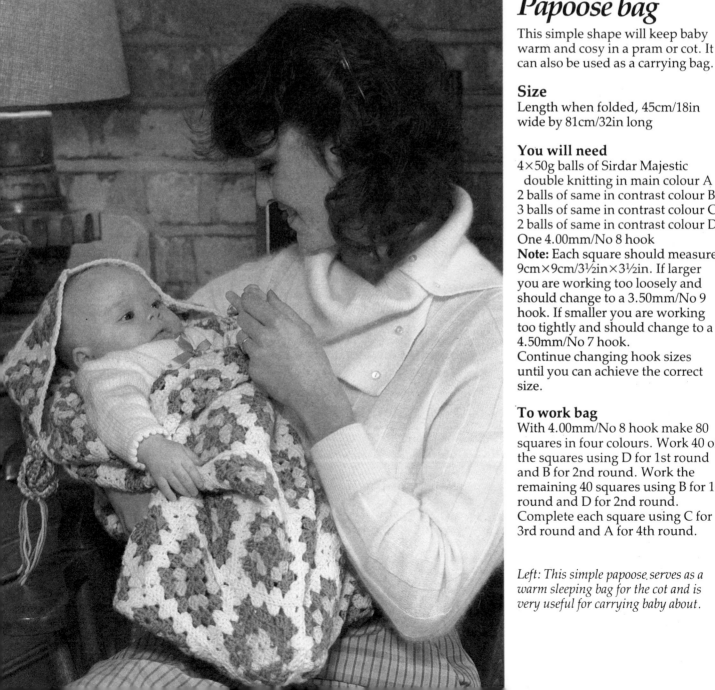

Left: This simple papoose serves as a warm sleeping bag for the cot and is very useful for carrying baby about.

Making half granny squares

Make 5ch. Join with a ss to first of these 5ch to form a circle.

1st row (right side) Using same colour make 4ch to count as first tr and 1ch space, work corner of (3tr, 2ch, 3tr) into circle working under the ch, 1ch, 1tr into circle.
Break off yarn and fasten off.

2nd row Join next or same colour to 3rd of first 4ch at beg of previous row with a ss, 4ch to count as first tr and 1ch space, work 3tr into first 1ch space of previous row, 1ch, work corner into next 2ch space, 1ch, 3tr into last 1ch space, 1ch, 1tr into top of last tr of previous row.
Break off yarn and fasten off.

3rd row Join next or same colour to 3rd of first 4ch at beg of previous row with a ss, 4ch to count as first tr and 1ch space, work 3tr into first 1ch space of previous row, 1ch, 3tr into next 1ch space, 1ch, work corner into next 2ch space, (1ch, 3tr into next 1ch space) twice, 1ch, 1tr into top of last tr of previous row.
Break off yarn and fasten off.

4th row Join next or same colour to 3rd of first 4ch at beg of previous row with a ss, 4ch to count as first tr and 1ch space, work 3tr into first 1ch space of previous row, 1ch, (3tr into next 1ch space, 1ch) twice, work corner into next 2ch space, (1ch, 3tr into next 1ch space) 3 times, 1ch, 1tr into top of last tr of

A half granny square in double knitting.

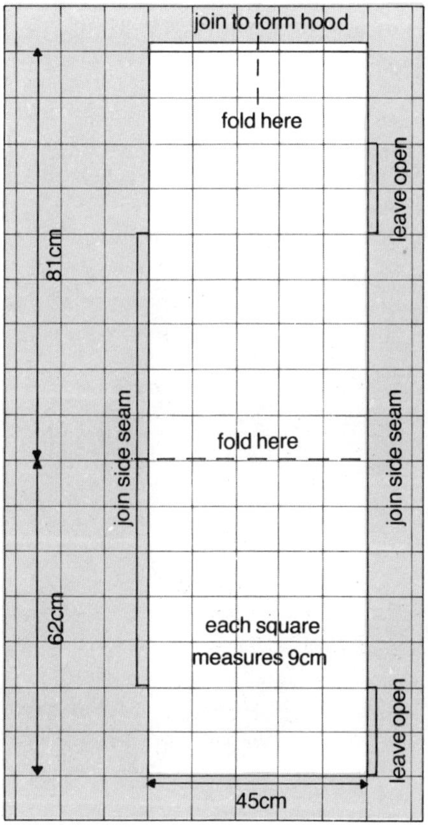

previous row.
Break off yarn and fasten off. Darn in all ends on wrong side of half square.

To make up

Darn in all ends. Press each square under a damp cloth with a warm iron. Using oversewn seam and, matching stitch for stitch, join five squares to form one row. Join 15 more rows in the same way then join rows together. Complete as shown in diagram.
Make two lengths of 100ch, using one strand each of A, B, C and D. Thread through holes at corners of flap and corresponding holes on main section to tie at sides.

(diagram: hooded garment layout)
join to form hood
fold here
leave open
81cm
join side seam — fold here — join side seam
62cm
each square measures 9cm
leave open
45cm

Designing with granny squares

These useful motifs can be made to any size – work more or fewer rounds for a full square, more or fewer rows for a half square. To work more than four rounds or rows, increase by 3tr and 1ch space along each side between corners.

To plan a granny square design, decide on the shape and size of the item. As a simple suggestion, join four squares together and four rows to make one side of a cushion cover, then make the other side the same.

The diagram of the child's waistcoat (below) shows a total of 42 full squares and two half squares. Two rounds (or rows) only are worked to give a 5cm/2in square, using double knitting yarn and a 4.00mm/No 8 hook. This combination of squares should fit a child with a 50cm/20in chest. As a variation sew the squares together as diamonds and fill in the gaps along the edges with half squares.

Use up oddments of any yarn of the same thickness – the more colours, the more original the results. To arrive at the quantity of new yarn you will need, see how many squares you can make from one ball, then divide this number into the total number of squares.

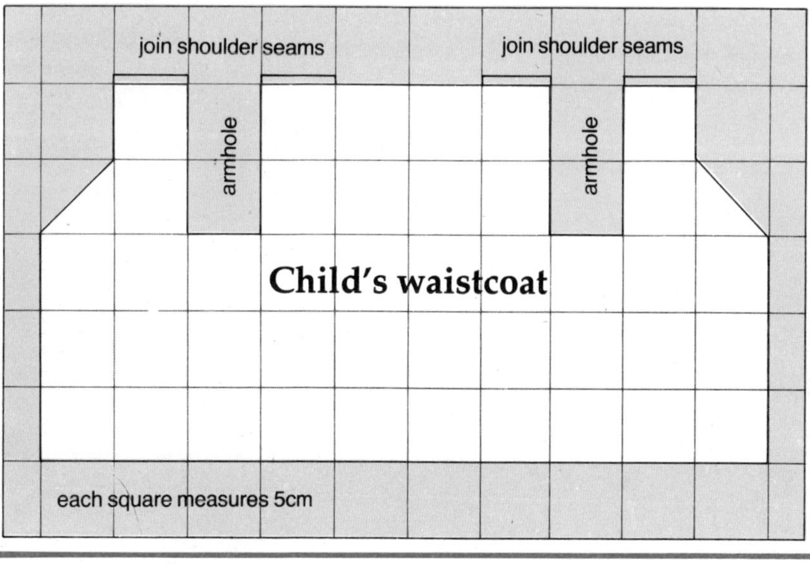

(diagram: child's waistcoat layout)
join shoulder seams   join shoulder seams
armhole   armhole
Child's waistcoat
each square measures 5cm

255

Tools, materials and the importance of tension

Crochet is one of the most versatile of all crafts – you can do it with any yarn from sewing cotton to garden twine. The type of yarn you choose and the size of hook you use will determine the stitch and row tension, and these control the structure and texture of the crochet.

The simple process of working a loop of yarn over a single hook – the basic principle of crochet – can produce an amazingly wide variety of patterns. The craft has tremendous scope and produces unique, almost three-dimensional fabrics, suitable for anything you care to make from summer tops to winter rugs.

Crochet designers choose a yarn and a hook size that will produce the right tension and texture of fabric to complement the style of garment. The measurements of the garment are based on the designer's original tension, so it is vital that you get this right for successful results. Get it wrong and your garment will end up too big or too small.

Basic crochet stitches in standard double knitting yarn are quite loose and deep, so make sure you check your tension carefully. For how to do this, see far right.

Equipping your workbox

Before you start to crochet, in addition to the appropriate hooks, you should have to hand a long, rigid rule for measuring sections of crochet; an unstretchable tape measure for body measurements; small, sharp scissors, and blunt-ended sewing needles with large eyes for seaming. As you acquire new skills you will also need special tools, such as Tunisian hooks.

Crochet hooks are manufactured in a range of metric sizes according to the diameter of the hook shank. If you have a hook made in the UK before conversion to metric, you will find the chart below useful for comparing sizes.

Hooks were originally made of bone, ivory or tortoiseshell. Today sizes 0.60–1.00/7–5½ are made of steel; sizes 1.50–5.00/16–6 are anodized aluminium alloy and larger sizes lightweight plastic. All hooks are pale grey so that most colours of yarn show up well against them. The finish allows the yarn to flow smoothly and evenly.

As each crochet stitch is worked separately until only one loop remains on the hook, the hooks are

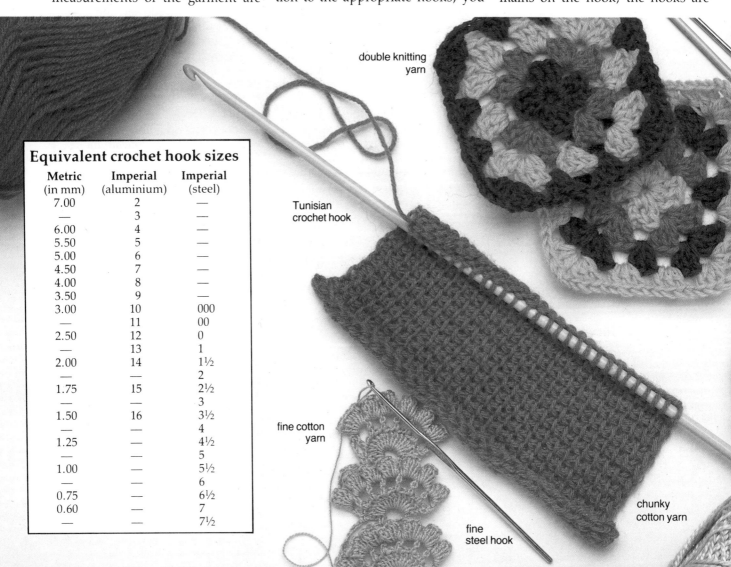

double knitting yarn

Tunisian crochet hook

fine cotton yarn

fine steel hook

chunky cotton yarn

Equivalent crochet hook sizes

Metric (in mm)	Imperial (aluminium)	Imperial (steel)
7.00	2	—
—	3	—
6.00	4	—
5.50	5	—
5.00	6	—
4.50	7	—
4.00	8	—
3.50	9	—
3.00	10	000
—	11	00
2.50	12	0
—	13	1
2.00	14	1½
—	—	2
1.75	15	2½
—	—	3
1.50	16	3½
—	—	4
1.25	—	4½
—	—	5
1.00	—	5½
—	—	6
0.75	—	6½
0.60	—	7
—	—	7½

made to a standard length.

Tunisian hooks are the exception to the standard length because they are designed to hold stitches for working original Tunisian crochet patterns. They have a knob at one end like a knitting needle and are available in 30–35cm/11¾–13¾in lengths.

Materials There is a very wide range of suitable materials. You can use all the standard yarns – natural and man-made fibres in double knitting, 2, 3 and 4 ply and chunky yarns. Exceptionally fine cotton yarns produce delicate lace fabrics and rug yarns, raffia, string and macramé cords give a heavily textured finish. As you gain in confidence, try experimenting with some of these unusual yarns to see what effect they have.

If you have difficulty in obtaining a yarn specified in a pattern or wish to use a different yarn, choose a yarn which crochets to the same tension.

Below: A selection of equipment you will need for your crochet work-box.

aluminium crochet hook

Tension in crochet

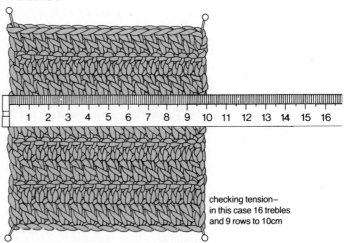

checking tension–
in this case 16 trebles
and 9 rows to 10cm

Always work a sample with the correct yarn and hook size in the stitch given before beginning a crochet project. If the pattern gives 16 trebles and 9 rows of trebles to 10cm/4in worked on a 4.50mm/No 7 hook, make at least 20 stitches and work 11 rows. The extra stitches and rows will make it easier to measure the sample accurately. Lay the completed sample on a flat surface and pin it down. Measure it with a firm rule and, in this example, check that 16 stitches and 9 rows do give 10cm/4in. If not,

you need to adjust your tension.

How to adjust tension

If your sample measures *more* than the tension size given you are working too loosely. Change to a size smaller hook, in this example 4.00mm/No 8, and work another sample. If your sample measures *less*, you are working too tightly. Change to a size larger hook, 5.00mm/No 6, and work another sample. Continue experimenting with hook sizes until you can obtain the tension given.

PROFESSIONAL TOUCH

Double crochet foundation chain

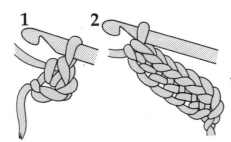

Firm foundation chains can be used to reinforce the lower edge of a design. The double crochet method shown here is most practical for childrens' garments which may get handled roughly. It is also most effective when using a chunky yarn.

Make a slip loop and two chains in the usual way. These count as the first stitch.
1 Insert the hook from the front to the back into the second chain from the hook, *yrh and draw a

loop through, yrh and draw a loop through both loops on hook. The second stitch has been made.
2 Insert the hook from the front to the back into the top loop of the stitch just worked and continue from the * for the required number of chains, plus any turning chains. Twelve double crochet chains will form 10 trebles.
3 On the first pattern row, work under the single loop at the top of each double crochet chain.

Increasing and decreasing: essentials for shaping

Knowing how to increase or reduce the overall size of a piece of crochet is an essential part of basic techniques. Because of the depth of most crochet stitches, shaping must be neatly executed or seaming will be difficult and the finished effect clumsy.

As in knitting, it is possible to increase and decrease in crochet at the beginning and end of a row as well as at any point in the middle of a row. However, it is inadvisable to increase or decrease on the very first or very last stitch of a row as this will give you untidy side edges and make seaming difficult. You will get a much neater edge if you work the increase or decrease after the turning chain at the beginning of a row and before the last stitch (the turning chain of the previous row) at the end of a row.

Increasing and decreasing just after and just before the ends of rows is used for straight-forward shaping such as sleeves and armholes, while increasing and decreasing in the middle of a row is used for multiple shaping such as in the panels of a flared skirt.

The method of increasing is the same whatever stitch is being worked but the method of decreasing varies depending on the stitch. This chapter gives all the basic ways of increasing and several ways of decreasing, including the method needed for the stylish bikini on page 260. The next chapter gives ways of decreasing in trebles which forms the basis for shell and cluster patterns.

To increase one or two stitches

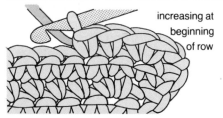
increasing at beginning of row

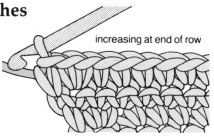
increasing at end of row

increasing in middle of row

At the beginning of a row work the turning chain to count as the first stitch and miss the first stitch of the row to compensate for this. Work two or three stitches in pattern into the second stitch, then continue to the end of the row.

One or two stitches increased in this way at regular intervals above each other give an angle of increase slanting out to the right.

At the end of a row work until two stitches remain. Work two or three stitches in pattern into the next stitch, then work one stitch into the last stitch.

One or two stitches increased in this way at regular intervals above each other give an angle of increase slanting out to the left.

In the middle of a row work until the position for the increase is reached. Work two or three stitches in pattern into the next stitch, then continue to the end of the row.

To keep a straight, vertical line when increasing one or two stitches above each other, alternate the position of the increased stitches.

To decrease one or two stitches in double crochet

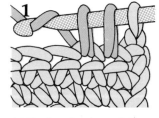

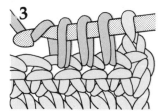

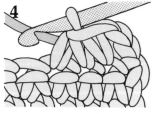

At the beginning of the row to decrease one double crochet, make the turning chains and miss the first stitch.

1 Insert the hook into the next stitch and draw a loop through, insert the hook into the next stitch and draw a loop through, (3 loops on hook). **

2 Yrh and draw through all 3 loops on hook.

To decrease two double crochet work as given for decreasing one double crochet to **.

3 Insert the hook into the next stitch and draw a loop through, (4 loops on hook).

4 Yrh and draw through all 4 loops on hook.

Working two or three stitches together in this way at regular intervals above each other gives an angle of decrease slanting in to the left.

Even shaping for panels

To increase one stitch in a vertical line in the middle or at any point on every alternate or even numbered row, work the first increase in the position given. On the next increasing row, work the increased stitches in the *first* of the previously increased stitches. On the next increasing row work the increased stitches in the *second* of the previously increased stitches. Continue alternating the position of the increases in this way.

To decrease one stitch in a vertical line in the middle or at any point on every alternate or even numbered row, work the

increasing

decreasing

first decrease in the position given.

On the next decreasing row, work the stitch *before* the decreased stitch together with the decreased stitch. On the next

decreasing row, work the decreased stitch and the stitch *after* the decreased stitch together. Continue alternating the position of the decreases in this way.

To increase more than two stitches

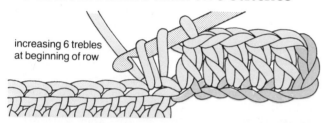

increasing 6 trebles at beginning of row

At the beginning of a row make a number of extra chains before working the turning chain. This should be one less than the total number of extra stitches needed plus the correct number of turning chains. As an example, if 6 extra stitches are required when working in trebles, make 5 extra chains plus 3 turning chains, making 8 in all.

Work the first extra treble into the 4th chain from the hook and one treble into each of the next 4 chains. Six stitches have been increased and the turning chain is now at the beginning of the increased stitches.

1 **2**

joining length of chain

increasing 6 trebles at end of row

At the end of a row use a length of the correct yarn. Make a separate length of chains for the number of extra stitches required.

1 Join this length of chains with a slip stitch to the top of the first stitch of the *previous* row and fasten off.

2 Use the main length of yarn to work one stitch into each of the extra chains to complete the row.

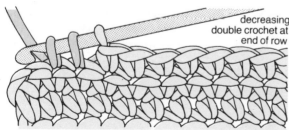

decreasing double crochet at end of row

At the end of a row to decrease one double crochet, work until two stitches plus the turning chain of the previous row remain. Work the next two stitches together as given for the beginning of the row, then work the last stitch.

To decrease two double crochet, work until three stitches plus the

turning chain of the previous row remain. Work the next three stitches together as given for the beginning of the row, then work the last stitch. Working two or three stitches together in this way at regular intervals above each other gives an angle of decrease slanting in to the right.

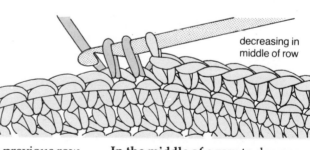

decreasing in middle of row

In the middle of a row to decrease one or two double crochet, work to the position for the decrease. Work the next two or three stitches together as for the beginning of a row, then continue in pattern. To keep a straight line when decreasing stitches above each other, alternate the position of decreased stitches.

To decrease one or two stitches in half trebles

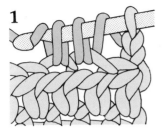 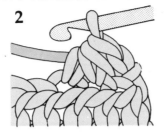 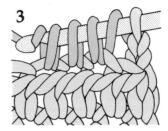 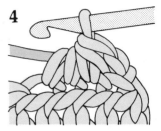

1   **2**   **3**   **4**

At the beginning of a row to decrease one half treble, make the turning chains and miss the first stitch.
1 Yrh, insert the hook into the next stitch and draw a loop through, insert the hook into the next stitch

and draw a loop through. (4 loops on hook). **
2 Yrh and draw through all 4 loops on hook.
To decrease two half trebles work as given for decreasing one half treble to **

3 Insert the hook into the next stitch and draw a loop through, (5 loops on hook).
4 Yrh and draw through all 5 loops on hook.

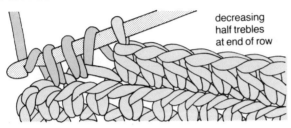

decreasing half trebles at end of row

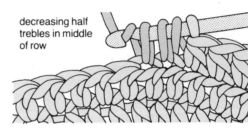

decreasing half trebles in middle of row

At the end of a row to decrease one half treble, work until two stitches plus the turning chain of the previous row remain. Work the next two stitches together as given for the beginning of the row, then work the last stitch.

To decrease two half trebles work until three stitches plus the turning chain of the previous row remain. Work the next three stitches together as given for the beginning of the row, then work the last stitch.

In the middle of a row to decrease one or two half trebles, work until the position for the decrease is reached. Work the next two or three stitches together as given for the beginning of a row, then continue in pattern to the end of the row.

Stylish crocheted bikini

The briefs of this well-shaped bikini are cut high to give a leggy look. Use the slip stitch method to begin the leg shaping, then decrease in double crochet as given for the beginning and ends of the rows.
The bra top is gathered on to a cord and then ties as a halter round your neck.

Sizes

Bra top to fit 76 [81/86:91/97]cm/ 30 [32/34:36/38]in bust
Briefs to fit 81 [86/91:97/102]cm/ 32 [34/36:38/40]in hips
The figures in [] refer to the 81/86cm 32/34in and 91/97cm, 36/38in bust and 86/91cm, 34/36in and 97/102cm, 38/40in hip sizes respectively.

You will need

4 [4:4]×50g balls of Pingouin Coton Perle No. 5 (100% cotton)
One 2.50mm/No 12 crochet hook
One clasp for bra top
Length of elastic for briefs

Tension

24 sts and 32 rows to 10cm/4in over dc worked on 2.50mm/No 12 hook

Briefs back

With 2.50mm/No 12 hook make 92 [96:100] ch and beg at top.
1st row (Rs) Into 3rd ch from hook work 1dc, work 1dc into each ch to end. Turn. 91 [95:99] dc.
2nd row 2ch to count as first dc, miss first dc, work 1dc into each dc

to end. Turn. Rep 2nd row until work measures 2.5 [3:3.5]cm/ 1 [1¼:1⅜]in from beg.

Shape legs

Next row Ss across first 3dc and into next dc, 2ch to count as first dc, miss first dc, work 1dc into each dc to last 3 sts, turn. 85 [89:93] dc. **
Work one row without shaping.
Dec one st at each end of next and every alt row 16 [17:18] times in all,

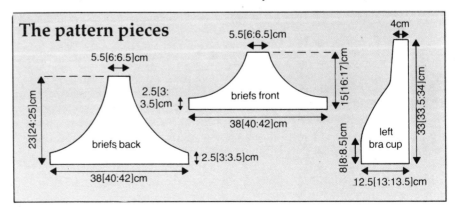

The pattern pieces

briefs back   23[24:25]cm   5.5[6:6.5]cm   38[40:42]cm   2.5[3:3.5]cm

briefs front   5.5[6:6.5]cm   2.5[3:3.5]cm   38[40:42]cm   15[16:17]cm

left bra cup   4cm   33[33.5:34]cm   8[8:8.5]cm   12.5[13:13.5]cm

then dec 2 sts at each end of every alt row 10 times in all. 13 [15:17] dc. Work a futher 3cm/1¼in without shaping. Fasten off.

Briefs front

Work as given for back to **.
Cont shaping legs, dec one st at each end of every row 16 [17:18] times in all, then 2 sts at each end of every row 10 times in all. 13 [15:17] dc.
Work a further 3cm/1¼in without shaping. Fasten off.

Bra top

With 2.50mm/No 12 hook make 31 [33:35] ch for left cup.
Work first 2 rows as given for briefs back. 30 [32:34] dc.
Rep 2nd row until work measures 8 [8:8.5]cm/3¼ [3¼:3⅜]in from beg, ending with a Rs row.
Dec one st at beg of next and every alt row for left-hand edge until 8dc rem.
Cont without shaping until work measures 33 [33.5:34]cm/ 13 [13¼:13½]in from beg. Fasten off.
Work right cup as given for left cup, reversing the shaping by dec at the end of the rows for the right-hand edge.

To make up

Press each piece under a damp cloth with a warm iron.
Briefs Join side seams. With 2.50mm/ No 12 hook and Rs facing work a row of firm dc round each leg. Join crutch. Sew elastic inside top edge using herringbone st.
Bra top Fold 1cm/½in at beg of left and right cups to Ws to form hem and sl st in place. With 2.50mm/ No 12 hook and Rs facing work a row of firm dc round rem 3 edges of each cup. Using 7 strands of yarn make a twisted cord, or crochet cord in ch, about 150cm/60in long. Beg at top of one cup and thread this cord through the hem, then beg at the lower edge and thread through the hem on the other cup. Pull the ends up to gather the front edges and tie cord in a double knot. Use the rem cord to tie at back neck. Sew on clasp to back of bra top.

Left: For modesty's sake you could line the crochet briefs with a pair of white cotton ones – slipstitched in place.

Increasing and decreasing: shells and clusters

This chapter describes how to decrease when shaping in trebles. The working movements for decreasing also form the basis of cluster patterns; those for increasing form the basis of shell patterns. Instructions are given for both – and there's a delightful angel top to make.

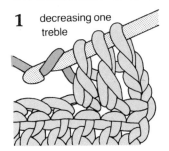

Above: A dainty angel top to crochet in trebles and a simple cluster pattern.

Decreasing in trebles involves one more movement than when decreasing in half trebles. When decreasing in long trebles, each variation requires another extra step to complete the stitch because the yarn is put round the hook more than once to begin each stitch. The yarn is wound round the hook twice to begin a double treble; three times to begin a triple treble and so on.

To decrease groups of any crochet stitches at the beginning or in the middle of a row, such as when mak-

To decrease one or two stitches in trebles

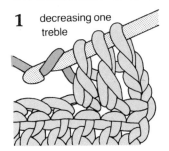

1 decreasing one treble

2 decreasing complete

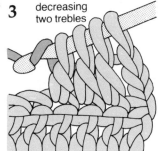

3 decreasing two trebles

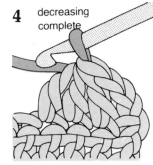

4 decreasing complete

At the beginning of a row to decrease one treble, make the turning chains and miss the first stitch.
1 (Yrh, insert the hook into the next stitch and draw a loop through, yrh

and draw through 2 loops on hook) twice, (3 loops on hook). **
2 Yrh and draw through all 3 loops on hook.
To decrease two trebles work as given for decreasing one treble to **

3 Yrh, insert hook into next stitch and draw a loop through, yrh and draw through 2 loops on hook, (4 loops on hook).
4 Yrh and draw through all 4 loops on hook.

Shell pattern

Make a number of chains divisible by 6 plus 1, eg 7, 13, 19 and so on.
1st row (Rs) Into 4th ch from hook work 5tr, *miss 2ch, 1dc into next ch, miss 2ch, 5tr into next ch – **called 1 shell**, rep from * to last 3ch, miss 2ch, 1dc into last ch.
2nd row 3ch to count as first tr, 2tr into first dc, (edge st), *1dc into 3rd of next 5tr, 1 shell into next dc, rep from * to last shell, 1dc into 3rd of last 5tr, 3tr into 3rd of first 3ch.
3rd row 1ch to count as first dc, *1 shell into next dc, 1dc into 3rd of next 5tr, rep from * to end working last dc into 3rd of first 3ch.
4th row As 2nd but working last 3tr into first 1ch.
The 3rd and 4th rows form the patt.

samples of shell pattern
made in 4 ply yarn

ing the shaping for a neck, slipped stitches are used.

At the end of a row groups of stitches are decreased by leaving them un-worked.

Shell and cluster patterns

These form very pretty, lacy fabrics and they are surprisingly simple to work. Shell patterns are formed by working more than once into a stitch and cluster patterns by working stitches together.

A simple variation of the cluster pattern is used for the skirt and sleeves of the angel top given overleaf, which buttons at the back.

If you prefer to dress the baby in a pretty matinée jacket, however, then simply put it on so that the buttons can be fastened at the front rather than the back.

To decrease three or more stitches

decreasing several trebles at beginning of row

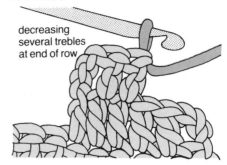

decreasing several trebles at end of row

At the beginning of a row before making the turning chain, slip stitch across the number of stitches to be reduced and into the next stitch of the row. Make the number of turning chains for the stitch being worked and continue in pattern to the end of the row.

At the end of a row work until only the number of stitches to be

reduced remain, noting that the turning chain of the previous row counts as one of these. Leave the stitches unworked and turn, ready to begin the next row.

In the middle of a row work until the position for the decrease is reached, then continue as given for the beginning of the row.

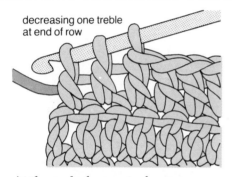

decreasing one treble at end of row

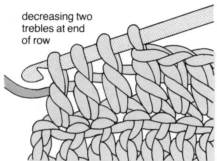

decreasing two trebles at end of row

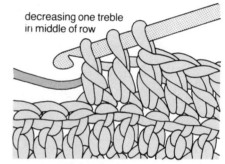

decreasing one treble in middle of row

At the end of a row to decrease one treble, work until two stitches plus turning chain of the previous row remain. Work the next two stitches together as given for the beginning of the row, then work the last stitch.

To decrease two trebles work until three stitches plus the turning chain of the previous row remain. Work the next three stitches together as given for the beginning of the row, then work the last stitch.

In the middle of a row to decrease one or two trebles, work until place for decrease is reached. Work next two or three stitches together as given for beginning of row, then continue in pattern to end of row.

Cluster pattern

Make a number of chains divisible by 4 plus 2 and 1 additional turning chain, eg, 7, 15, 19 and so on.

1st row (Rs) Into 3rd ch from hook work 1dc, 1dc into each ch to end.

2nd row 3ch to count as first tr, 2ch, *keeping last loop of each st on hook work 1tr into each of next 4dc, yrh and draw through all loops on hook – **called 1 cluster**, 4ch, rep from * to last 5dc, work 1 cluster over next 4dc, 2ch, 1tr into 2nd of first 2ch.

3rd row 1ch to count as first dc, 1dc into each of next 2ch, *miss 1 cluster, 1dc into each of next 4ch, rep from * ending last rep with miss 1 cluster, 1dc into each of next 2ch, 1dc into 3rd of first 3ch.

4th row As 2nd but working last tr

into first 1ch.
The 3rd and 4th rows form the patt.

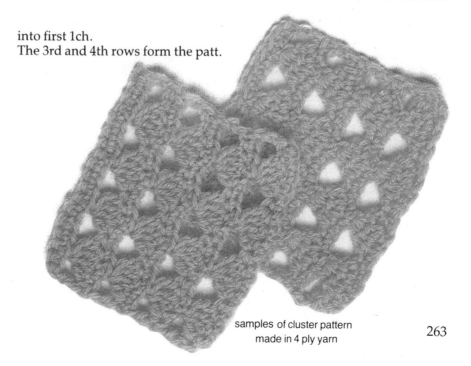

samples of cluster pattern made in 4 ply yarn

263

Fit for an angel

The yoke of this enchanting angel top has increasing in the middle of a row to build up stitches for the sleeves – giving the impression of raglan shaping. The skirt and sleeves are worked in a pretty, lacy pattern.

Sizes

To fit 46 [51]cm/18[20]in chest
Length to shoulder, 28 [29]cm/11 [11½]in
Sleeve seam, 15 [18]cm/6 [7]in
Figures in [] refer to 51cm/20in size only.

You will need

4 [5]×20g balls of Patons Fairytale 2 ply Courtelle/Bri-nylon
One 2.00mm/No 14 crochet hook
One 2.50mm/No 12 crochet hook
Four buttons
One sew-on motif, optional

Tension

29tr and 18 rows of tr to 10cm/4in worked on 2.00mm/No 14 hook

Yoke

With 2.00mm/No 14 hook make 75ch and work in one piece beg at neck edge.
1st row Work 1tr into 4th ch from hook, 1 tr into each of next 11ch, 1ch, 1tr into each of next 11ch, 1ch, 1tr into each of next 25ch, 1ch, 1tr into each of next 11ch, 1ch, 1tr into

Below: Wear the angel top so that it buttons at the front and it becomes a practical matinée jacket.

each of next 13ch.
2nd row 3ch, miss first tr, *1tr into each tr to next 1ch space, (1tr, 1ch, 1tr) into 1ch space, rep from * 3 times more, 1tr into each tr to end.
3rd row 3ch, miss first tr, *1tr into each tr to next 1ch space, (2tr, 1ch, 2tr) into 1ch space, rep from * 3 times more, 1tr into each tr to end.
Rep 2nd and 3rd rows 6 [7] times more, then 2nd row once. 249 [273] tr.

Divide for skirt and sleeves

Next row 3ch, miss first tr, 1tr into each of next 2 [3] tr, *2tr into next tr, 1tr into next tr, rep from * to 1ch space, miss 55 [61] tr for sleeve, 1tr into next tr, **2tr in next tr, 1tr in next tr, rep from ** to next 1ch space, miss 55[61] tr for sleeve, ***2tr in next tr, 1tr in next tr, rep from *** to last 3 [2] tr, 1tr into each tr to end. 205 [223] tr.

Skirt

Change to 2.50mm/No 12 hook. Commence skirt patt.
1st row 4ch, miss first tr, 1dc in next tr, *3ch, miss 2tr, 1dc in next tr, rep from * to last 2tr, 1ch, miss 1tr, 1tr in last tr.
2nd row 1ch, 1dc in first tr, *7tr in 3ch space, 1dc in next 3ch space, rep from * ending 1dc in 3rd of first 4ch.
3rd row 6ch, *1dc in 4th of 7tr, 3ch, (yrh, insert hook into next dc) 4 times, yrh and draw through first 8 loops on hook, yrh and draw through 2 loops on hook – **called**

1Cl, 3ch, rep from * ending last rep 3ch, 1tr into first dc.
4th row *3ch, 1dc into 3ch space, rep from * ending last rep 1dc into 4th of first 6ch, 1ch, 1tr into 2nd of 6ch.
5th row 4ch, 3tr into 1ch space, *1dc into next 3ch space, 7tr in next 3ch space, rep from * ending last rep 4tr in first 3ch.
6th row 1ch, 1dc in first tr, *3ch, 1Cl in dc, 3ch, 1dc in 4th of 7tr, rep from * ending last rep 3ch, 1dc in 3rd of first 4ch.
7th row *3ch, 1dc in 3ch space, rep from * ending last rep 1dc in last 3ch space, 1ch, 1tr in dc.
Rep 2nd to 7th rows until work measures about 25 [28]cm/9¾ [11]in from shoulder, ending with a 2nd or 5th patt row. Fasten off.

Sleeves

With Rs of work facing and 2.00mm/No 14 hook rejoin yarn with a ss to first tr at underarm.
Next row 3ch, 1tr into each tr to end. 55 [61]tr.
Change to 2.50mm/No 12 hook. Work first 7 rows skirt patt. Rep 2nd and 7th rows until sleeve seam measure 15 [18]cm/6 [7]in, ending with a 2nd or 5th patt row. Fasten off.

Back bands

With 2.00mm/No 14 hook and Rs of work facing, join yarn with a ss to lower edge of left back. Work evenly in dc up left back edge, all round neck and down right back edge working 2dc into each row end and 1dc into each tr.
Mark positions on left back edge for 4 buttons, first to come at neck edge and last at bottom of yoke with 2 more evenly spaced between.
Buttonhole row Work 1dc into each dc making buttonholes as markers are reached by missing 2dc and making 3ch.

To make up

Do not press. Join sleeve seams. Sew on buttons. Sew motif on front yoke, if required.

Right: Pretty as a picture – wearing the crochet angel top buttoned at the back. To add a splash of colour, trim with a ready-made motif on the front yoke.

Bloused waistcoat with a scooped neck

Make this useful waistcoat either in a ribbon yarn specially made for knitting or in thick cotton. The welts and borders are knitted in rib and the main fabric is crocheted in a very simple stitch, making it ideal for a beginner.

Sizes

To fit 86 [91:97]cm/34 [36:38]in bust
Length to shoulder, 52 [55:57]cm/20½ [21¾:22½]in
The figures in [] refer to the 91/36 and 97cm/38in sizes respectively

You will need

10[10:11]×50g balls of Pingouin
  Coton Natural 8 fils *or* Tricotine
  (both 100% cotton)
One pair 3¾mm/No 9 needles
One 7.00mm/No 2 crochet hook
Six buttons

Tension

16 sts and 15 rows to 10cm/4in over pattern using 7.00mm/No 2 hook

Back

With 3¾mm/No 9 needles cast on 79 [83:87] sts.
1st row (Rs) P1, *K1, P1, rep from * to end.
2nd row K1, *P1, K1, rep from * to end.
Rep these 2 rows from 7cm/2¾in, ending with a Ws row. Cast off loosely in rib.
Change to 7.00mm/No 2 hook.
Commence crochet patt working into cast-off rib sts. **
1st row (Rs) With Rs of ribbing facing insert hook into first st and make 1ch, work 1dc into first st, *1ch, miss one st, 1dc into next st, rep from * to end. 79 [83:87] sts.
2nd row 2ch and miss first dc, *1dc into 1ch sp, 1ch, miss 1dc, rep from * ending with 1ch over last dc, ss into 1ch worked at beg of previous row.
3rd row 1ch, 1dc into first ch sp, *1ch, miss 1dc, 1dc into next ch, rep from * to end, working last dc into 2nd of the 2ch at beg of previous row.
The 2nd and 3rd rows form the patt,

noting that the 2ch at the beg of 2nd row counts as one st and the 1ch at beg of 3rd row does not count as a st. Cont in patt until work measures 29 [30:32]cm/11½ [11¾:12½]in from beg of ribbing.

Shape armholes

Keeping patt correct, dec 3 sts at each end of next row, 2 sts at each end of next 4 alt rows, then dec one st at each end of next 3 [3:4] rows. 51 [55:57] sts.
Cont in patt without shaping until armholes measure 23 [25:25]cm/9 [9¾:9¾]in from beg, ending with a Ws row.

Shape neck

Next row Patt 9[11:11] sts, turn.
Complete right shoulder first.
Dec 2 sts at neck edge on next row.
Work 1 row on rem 7 [9:9] sts.
Fasten off.
With Rs of work facing, miss first 33 [33:35] sts and leave for centre back neck, rejoin yarn to rem sts and patt to end. Complete to match first side, reversing shaping.

Left front

With 3¾mm/No 9 needles cast on 39 [41:43] sts and work as given for back to **.
Cont in crochet patt as given for back on 39 [41:43] sts until work measures same as back to underarm, ending with a Ws row.

Above: Detail showing crochet stitches worked into the knitted welt.

Shape armhole

Dec 3 sts at beg of next row, 2 sts at same edge on next 4 alt rows, then dec one st at same edge on next 3 [3:4] rows. 25 [27:28] sts.
Cont without shaping until armhole measures 7 [8:8]cm/2¾ [3¼:3¼]in from beg, ending at front edge.

Shape neck

Dec 7 sts at beg of next row, 3 sts at same edge on foll 2 alt rows, one st on next alt row, 2 sts on next alt row, then dec one st at same edge on next 2 [2:3] rows. 7 [9:9] sts.
Cont without shaping until armhole measures same as back to shoulder, ending at armhole edge. Fasten off.

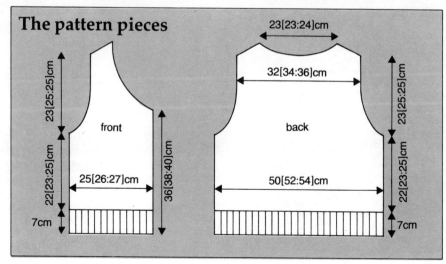

The pattern pieces

front
23[25:25]cm
23[23:25]cm
22[23:25]cm
7cm
25[26:27]cm
36[38:40]cm

back
23[23:24]cm
32[34:36]cm
23[25:25]cm
22[23:25]cm
7cm
50[52:54]cm

Right front

Work as given for left front, reversing all shapings.

Buttonhole band

With 3¾mm/No 9 needles and Rs of work facing, pick up and K61 [65:71] sts along right front edge from lower edge of ribbing to beg of neck shaping.

Work 2nd row of rib as given for back.

Next row (buttonhole row) Rib 4 [4:5] sts, cast off one st, rib 9 [9:10] sts, cast off one st, (rib 11 [12:13] sts, cast off one st) 3 times, rib to end.

Next row Rib to end, casting on one st above those cast off in previous row.

Work one more row rib. Cast off in rib.

Button band

Work along left front edge as given for right front edge, omitting buttonholes.

Neckband

Join shoulder seams. With 3¾mm/No 9 needles and Rs of work facing, pick up and K4 sts across top of buttonhole band, 36 [38:38] sts up right front neck, 43 [43:45] sts round back neck, 36 [38:38] sts down left front neck and 4 sts across top of button band. 123 [127:129] sts.

Work 2nd row of rib as given for back.

Next row (buttonhole row) Rib 2 sts, cast off one st, rib to end.

Next row Rib to end, casting on one st above st cast off in previous row.

Work one more row rib. Cast off in rib.

Armbands

With 3¾mm/No 9 needles and Rs of work facing, pick up and K86 [90:90] sts round armhole.

Work 4 rows K1, P1 rib. Cast off in rib.

Top make up

Do not press. Join side and armband seams. Sew on buttons.

Right: This waistcoat is worked in the ribbon yarn, but the thick cotton alternative (suggested in the You will need) crochets to the same tension and produces the same texture.

Variations on the theme of trebles

Long, ridged and raised trebles each give a new look to a familiar stitch and can be combined in many different ways to produce highly textured fabrics. The warm and elegant bedspread on page 271 is in diagonally arranged squares of raised trebles.

Long trebles are combined with other stitches in lacy, open patterns. With the exception of double trebles, they seldom form a fabric in their own right.

Long trebles are worked by putting the yarn round the hook more than once to begin each stitch. The number of times it goes round the hook – twice for a double treble, three times for a triple treble, four times for a quadruple treble and so on – gives each treble its name.

The extra yarn round the hook for each variation adds another working movement and, correspondingly, one more turning chain is required to bring the hook up to the correct height to begin a new row.

You can put the yarn round the hook as many times as you like, working extra movements to complete each treble variation but beyond a quadruple treble the stitches become very straggly.

Ridged and raised trebles can be worked in any length of treble stitch to produce crunchy, three-dimensional textures.

How to work long trebles

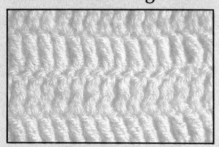

Double trebles worked in double knitting.

Double treble stitches
Make the number of chains required plus 3 extra turning chains. 13 chains form 10 double trebles. The abbreviation is 'dtr'.
1st row Yrh twice to begin each st.
1 Push the hook through the top

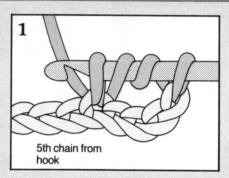

5th chain from hook

loop of the 5th ch from hook, *yrh and draw a loop through the ch, (4 loops on hook), (yrh and draw through 2 loops on hook) 3 times. One dtr has been made with the 4 missed ch forming the turning ch. Begin each st with yrh twice, push the hook through the top loop of next ch and rep from * to end. Turn.

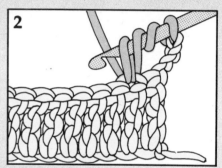

2nd row Make 4ch as the turning ch and miss the first dtr.
2 *Yrh twice, push the hook under both loops at the top of the next st, yrh and draw a loop through, (4 loops on hook), (yrh and draw through 2 loops on hook) 3 times, rep from * to end. Turn.
The 2nd row forms the pattern.

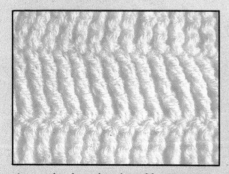

A sample of quadruple trebles.

Quadruple treble stitches
Make the number of chains required plus 5 extra turning chains. 15 chains form 10 quadruple trebles. The abbreviation is 'qd tr'.
1st row Yrh 4 times to begin each st.
1 Push the hook through the top

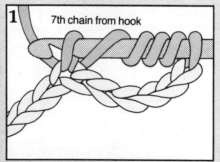

7th chain from hook

loop of the 7th ch from hook, *yrh and draw a loop through the ch, (6 loops on hook), (yrh and draw through 2 loops on hook) 5 times. One qd tr has been made with the 6 missed ch forming the turning ch. Begin each st with yrh 4 times, push the hook through the top loop of next ch and rep from * to end. Turn.

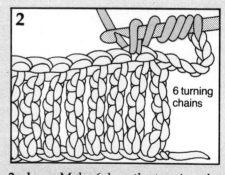

6 turning chains

2nd row Make 6ch as the turning ch and miss the first qd tr.
2 *Yrh 4 times, push the hook under both loops at the top of the next st, yrh and draw a loop through, (6 loops on hook), (yrh and draw through 2 loops on hook) 5 times, rep from * to end. Turn.
The 2nd row forms the pattern.

Ridged trebles are made by working into the front or back loop only of each treble in the row below, instead of under both loops at the top of the stitch.

Working into the back loop produces a ridge on the side of the crochet facing you. Working into the front loop produces a ridge on the side of the crochet facing away from you.

If you alternate these methods row by row a smooth fabric forms on one side and a ridged fabric on the other.

Raised trebles are formed by putting the hook round the stem of the treble in the row below, instead of under both loops at the top of the stitch.

Inserting the hook from the front, behind the treble and out to the front again produces a raised treble on the side of the crochet facing you and a ridge on the side facing away from you.

Inserting the hook from the back, in front of the treble and out to the back again produces a raised treble on the side of the crochet facing away from you and a ridge on the side facing you.

Alternating these methods across a row, or working some raised trebles and some ordinary trebles can produce very interesting basketweave and raised treble patterns. Two examples are shown overleaf.

Right: Raised trebles used in motifs.

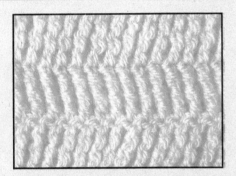

Triple trebles worked in double knitting.

Triple treble stitches

Make the number of chains required plus 4 extra turning chains. 14 chains form 10 triple trebles. The abbreviation is 'tr tr'.

1st row Yrh 3 times to begin each st.
1 Push the hook through the top

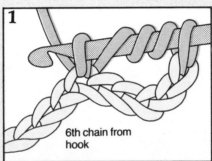

loop of the 6th ch from hook, *yrh and draw a loop through the ch, (5 loops on hook), (yrh and draw through 2 loops on hook) 4 times. One tr tr has been made with the 5 missed ch forming the turning ch. Begin each st with yrh 3 times, push the hook through the top loop of next ch and rep from * to end. Turn.

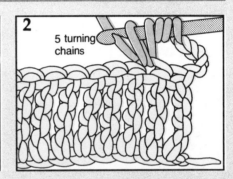

2nd row Make 5ch as the turning ch and miss the first tr tr.
2 *Yrh 3 times, push the hook under both loops at the top of the next st, yrh and draw a loop through, (5 loops on hook), (yrh and draw through 2 loops on hook) 4 times, rep from * to end. Turn. The 2nd row forms the pattern.

How to work ridged trebles

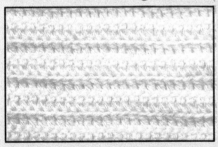

Ridged trebles worked on the right side.

Make the number of chains required plus 2 extra turning chains. 12 chains form 10tr.
1st row Into 4th ch from hook work 1tr, 1tr into each ch to end. Turn.

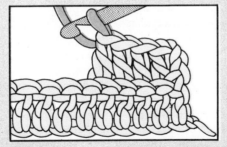

Ridged treble on the wrong side
2nd row Make 3ch as turning ch and miss first tr.
*Yrh, push hook under *back* loop only at the top of next st, yrh and draw a loop through, (yrh and draw through 2 loops on hook) twice, rep from * to end. Turn.

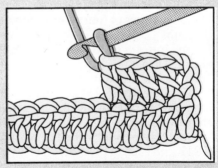

Ridged treble on the right side
2nd row Make 3ch as turning ch and miss first tr.
*Yrh, push hook under *front* loop only at the top of next st, yrh and draw a loop through, (yrh and draw through 2 loops on hook) twice, rep from * to end. Turn.

How to work raised trebles

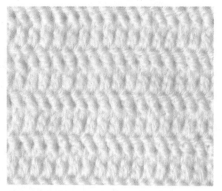

Raised trebles worked on the right side.

Make the number of chains required plus 2 extra turning chains. 12 chains form 10tr.
1st row Into 4th ch from hook work 1tr, 1tr into each ch to end. Turn. Rep the 1st row once more.

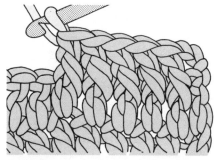

Raised treble on the right side
3rd row Make 3ch as turning ch and miss first tr.
*Yrh, insert hook from front round behind the stem of the next tr and out to the front again, yrh and draw a loop through, (yrh and draw through 2 loops on hook) twice, **called 1RTF**, rep from * to end. Turn.

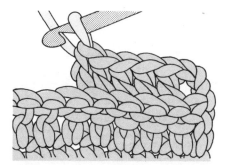

Raised treble on the wrong side
3rd row Make 3 ch as turning ch and miss first tr.
*Yrh, insert hook from back round in front of the stem of the next tr and out to the back again, yrh and draw a loop through, (yrh and draw through 2 loops on hook) twice, **called 1RTB**, rep from * to end. Turn.

Basketweave pattern

Make multiples of four chains plus 2 turning chains, eg 18 chains.
1st row Into 4th ch from hook work 1tr, 1tr into each ch to end. Turn.
2nd row 3ch to count as first tr, work 1RTF into next tr, *1RTB into each of next 2tr, 1RTF into each of next 2tr, rep from * to last 2tr, 1RTB into each of last 2tr.
3rd row As 2nd.
4th row 3ch to count as first tr, work 1RTB into next tr, *1RTF into each of next 2tr, 1RTB into each of next 2tr, rep from * to last 2tr, 1RTF into each of last 2tr.
5th row As 4th.
The 2nd to 5th rows form the pattern.

Raised treble pattern

This looks very similar to basketweave pattern and can be used as an alternative.
Make multiples of four chains plus 2 turning chains, eg 18 chains.
1st row Into 4th ch from hook work 1tr, 1tr into each ch to end. Turn.
2nd row 3ch to count as first tr, 1tr into next tr, *1RTB into each of next 2tr, 1tr into each of next 2tr, rep from * to last 2tr, 1RTB into each of last 2tr.
3rd row 3ch to count as first tr, 1RTF into next tr, *1tr into each of next 2tr, 1RTF into each of next 2tr, rep from * to last 2tr, 1tr into each of last 2tr.
4th row 3ch to count as first tr, 1RTB into next tr, *1tr into each of next 2tr, 1RTB into each of next 2tr, rep from * to last 2tr, 1tr into each of last 2tr.
5th row 3ch to count as first tr, 1tr into next tr, *1RTF into each of next 2tr, 1tr into each of next 2tr, rep from * to last 2tr, 1RTF into each of last 2tr.
The 2nd to 5th rows form the pattern.

A dream of a bedspread

This attractive bedspread is easy to make, very warm and could well become a family heirloom.

The pattern allows for five different colours so you can make it in subtle pale shades which are near to each other on the colour spectrum or – in a plain bedroom – you can go for a more striking effect with vivid pinks, magenta and electric blues. If, on the other hand, your bedroom scheme already contains a number of colours in the curtains, soft furnishings, carpet and wallpaper, you could go for a fully co-ordinated effect, making the bedspread in paler or darker shades of the existing colours.

The squares of raised trebles can be made whenever you have a spare moment – even on bus or train journeys. Then all you have to do is to join them up diagonally, in rows, to produce a ridged effect and give an interesting zigzag edge to the bedspread which makes additional edging unnecessary.

Below: You will be proud to own this easily made bedspread.

Sizes

170cm×233cm/67in×95in

You will need

8×50g balls of Pingouin
 Pingofrance (75% acrylic,
 25% wool) in colour A
8 balls of same in colour B
11 balls of same in colour C
13 balls of same in colour D
16 balls of same in colour E
One 5.50mm/No 5 crochet hook

Tension

Each motif measures 15.5cm/6¼in
diagonally across; 11cm/4¼in
square

Square motif

With 5.50mm/No 5 hook and A
make 4ch. Beg at lower point.
1st row (Rs) Miss 3ch as turning ch,
into 4ch from hook work 4tr.
2nd row 2ch to count as first htr,
yrh, insert hook from front, round
behind the upright stem of next tr
and out to front again, yrh and
draw a loop through, (yrh and draw
through 2 loops on hook) twice –
called 1RTF, work 3RTF round next
tr, 1RTF round next tr, 1htr into
turning ch.
3rd row 2ch, 1RTF round next st,
2RTF round next st, 3RTF round
next st, 2RTF round next st, 1RTF
round next st, 1htr into turning ch.
4th row 2ch, 1RTF round each of
next 4 sts, 3RTF round next st, 1RTF
round each of next 4 sts, 1htr into
turning ch, joining in B.
Break off A.
5th row 2ch, 1RTF round each st to
one st before centre st, 2RTF round
next st, 3RTF round next st, 2RTF
round next st, 1RTF round each st

Baby's cot cover

Choose a soft pastel colour
scheme for this cot cover. As it
needs only 41 squares it is a
much quicker project than the
full bed cover.

Size

77cm/30¼in square

You will need

2×50g balls of Pingouin
 Pingofrance (75% acrylic, 25%
 wool) in colours A, B, C and D
3×50g balls of same in colour E
One 5.50mm/No 5 crochet
 hook

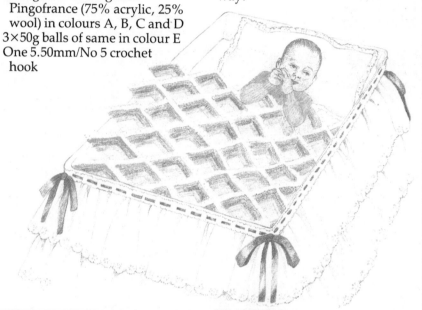

to last st, 1htr into turning ch.
6th row 2ch, 1RTF round each st to
centre st, 3RTF round next st, 1RTF
round each st to last st, 1htr into
turning ch, joining in C. Break off B.
Rep 5th and 6th rows 3 times more,
working 2 rows each in C, D and E.
Fasten off.
Make 305 square motifs in all.

Motifs

Make 41 motifs as given for
bedspread.

To make up

Join 5 squares together as given for
bedspread to form the first row.
Join 4 squares to form the second
row then join this row to the first
row. Join a total of 9 rows in this
way.

To make up

Do not press as this will flatten
pattern. Keeping E at top, join tog
in rows of 11 motifs and 10 motifs
alternately, overlap edges to
resemble fish scales and top stitch
through, see diagram. Make a total
of 15 rows of 11 motifs with 14 rows
of 10 motifs between.

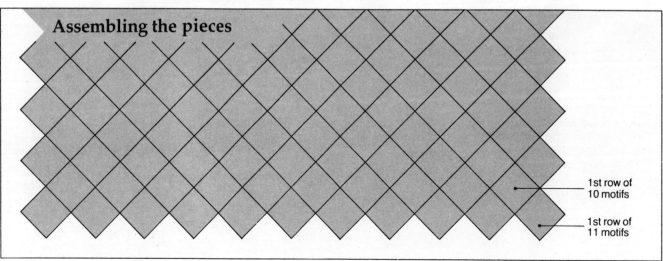

Assembling the pieces

1st row of
10 motifs

1st row of
11 motifs

Basic making up: blocking, pressing and seaming

*Care taken in finishing and assembling the pieces will give
all crochet garments a professional look.
Pure cotton and wool yarns benefit from blocking and pressing
but pure acrylic yarns should never be
pressed. Seams can be crocheted or sewn together.*

More garments are ruined by careless making up than by any other cause – with the possible exception of incorrect tension. Paying attention to the final details of blocking, pressing and joining the pieces together makes the difference between a successful *hand*-made design and a cobbled *home*-made attempt.

Crochet stitches are very quick to work so you may easily finish all the pieces in a few days, but don't be in too much of a hurry to complete the garment. If you want perfect results you should spend as much time in finishing and assembling as in working the pieces.

The principles of blocking and pressing crochet are exactly the same as those which apply to knitting. This chapter gives a step-by-step guide.

Blocking is the process of pinning out individual pieces of crochet to the correct size and shape, prior to pressing. This stage is essential with very open, lacy patterns, or patterns and motifs with shaped edges which need pinning into shape.

Cotton yarns used for household items benefit from a spray of starch after they have been blocked into shape. They can then be left to dry without pressing.

Some patterns do not need starching or pressing but should simply be blocked into shape and left under a damp cloth for a few hours, until dry. Diagrams of the pattern pieces give you the finished measurements of each section and the making up instructions tell you whether or not to press the yarn, but the choice of blocking out will often be left to you. If in any doubt, *do not block* – many of the yarns available today do not take kindly to excessive handling.

Pressing is only advisable if the making up instructions recommend it and the instructions on the ball band permit it. When working a highly textured pattern the instructions will tell you *not* to press as this will flatten the pattern even though the ball band may say otherwise.

Similarly, the instructions may tell you to press the pieces but, if you are using a different yarn from that which the pattern recommends, the ball band may tell you *not* to press the yarn. It pays to check and double check *before* pressing. If in doubt, *do not press*.

Seaming is particularly important for a professional finish. The method you choose will largely depend on the stitch pattern and the type of garment you are crocheting. You can either sew the seams in the usual way, or crochet the edges together to make a focal point of the joins.

Back stitch seams are suitable for closely textured fabrics, such as all-over trebles, and for shaped edges.

Flat seaming is suitable when you have been working with thick yarn, or for a highly textured pattern.

An oversewn seam joins the edges together with the minimum of bulk and is ideal for lacy patterns. Do not pull the sewing yarn up too tightly, however, as this forms a hard ridge. When crocheting seams together use double crochet to join the pieces on the right side for a decorative effect.

For back stitch, flat and oversewn seams use a blunt-ended sewing needle threaded with matching yarn. If you have used mohair or a very thick yarn to crochet, use a finer yarn of the same shade for seaming.

For crochet seams use a hook of the same size as for the crochet pieces, and a matching or contrasting yarn.

Blocking out crochet pattern pieces

To block out each piece you will need a firm table or ironing board on which to work. On top of this place a sheet of white carton cardboard at least as large as the largest pattern piece. Over this place an ironing pad or thick blanket.

Place each individual piece right side down on to the prepared ironing board or table. Anchor the piece at each corner with rustless pins. Use a tape measure to check

that the width and length are the same as those given in the instructions. Always measure across the centre of a piece. Gently pat the piece into shape where any increasing or decreasing has been worked and check the measurements again, making sure that the side edges are the same length.

When you are satisfied that the measurements are correct, use rustless pins to pin the piece to the board all round the edges. Use plenty of

pins, evenly spaced and placed at right angles to the stitches and rows. Take great care to ensure that all the stitches and rows lie in straight lines and that the fabric does not have any bias.

If the pieces need blocking but do not require any pressing, cover them with a clean, wet cloth, well wrung out. Leave for two or three hours then remove the cloth. Do not unpin the pattern piece until it is completely dry.

An easy guide to blocking

Prepare the table or ironing board for blocking the pieces. Choose a piece of evenly-checked gingham – 2.5cm/1in or 5cm/2in squares are ideal. This material must be colour-fast.

Place the gingham over the ironing board, making sure that the checks are in straight rows, horizontally and vertically. Measure the size of the checks and use this to gauge how many stitches in width and rows in depth should cover each one. For example, using a 5cm/2in check gingham, a piece with a side seam length of 40cm/16in and a width of 40cm/16in will require an area of eight checks deep and wide for blocking out. Each check should contain the same number of stitches and rows.

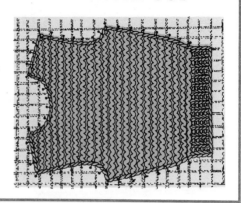

Pressing crochet pattern pieces

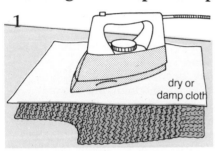

1

dry or damp cloth

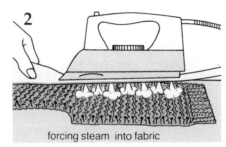

2

forcing steam into fabric

If the individual pieces have not been blocked, lay them right side down on to an ironing board.
1 Have the iron at the correct temperature and a clean dry, or damp, pressing cloth as directed. Place the cloth over the piece. Gently but firmly press the whole area of the iron down on top of the cloth, then lift it up again. Do not move the iron over the surface of the cloth as you would when ironing normally. Press each area evenly in this way before going on to the next area.
Once a piece has been pressed, allow any steam to evaporate. Remove the pins if the piece has been blocked and lay it aside ready for seaming.
2 To steam press a piece, use an iron at the correct temperature setting. Place a damp cloth over the piece. Begin at the lower edge and hold the left-hand side of the damp cloth just above the surface of the crochet with the left hand. Allow the iron to come into direct contact with the cloth but do not press down on to the crochet. This forces the steam down into the fabric. Press each area in this way.
Once a piece has been pressed allow any steam to evaporate. Remove pins if the piece has been blocked and lay it aside for seaming.

Pressing guide

Always check the ball band for the manufacturer's recommended pressing instructions.

Pure wool Press under a damp cloth with a warm iron.
Blends of wool and nylon Provided the wool content is higher than the nylon, press as for wool.
Blends of wool and acrylic Do not press.
Nylon Press under a dry cloth with a cool iron.
Blends of nylon and acrylic If nylon content is higher than acrylic, press as for nylon.
Courtelle Do not press.
Acrylic Do not press.
Cotton Press under a damp cloth with a warm or hot iron.
Mohair Steam press very lightly with a warm iron.
Angora Steam press as for mohair.
Glitter yarn Do not press unless stated on the ball band.

Back stitch seam

Place the right sides of the pieces together. Work along the wrong side of the fabric from right to left, one stitch in from the edge to join row ends, or just under the double loop at the top of each stitch to join stitches to stitches. Secure the yarn at the beginning of the seam with two or three small stitches, one on top of the other.
*With the sewing needle at the back of the fabric, move along to the left about 4mm/¼in from the last sewing stitch when joining row ends, or the width of one crochet stitch when joining stitches to stitches. Push the needle through both pieces to the front at right-angles to the edge and pull the yarn through.
Take the needle across the front of the fabric from left to right and push it through both pieces at the end of the last sewing stitch from front to back. Pull the yarn through. Continue from the * until the seam is completed. Fasten off with two or three small stitches as at the start.

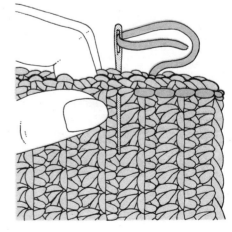

Flat seam

Place the right sides of the pieces together. Work along the wrong side of the fabric from right to left, one stitch in from the edge to join row ends, or just under the double loop at the top of each stitch to join stitches to stitches. Secure the yarn at the beginning of the seam with two or three small stitches, one on top of the other.

*Push the needle through from the back section across to the corresponding row end or stitch on the front section. Pull the yarn

through. Move along to the left about 4mm/¼in from the last sewing stitch when joining row ends, or the width of one crochet stitch when joining stitches to stitches. Push the needle through the front section to the corresponding row end or stitch on the back section. Pull the yarn through.

Continue from the * until the seam is completed. Fasten off with two or three small stitches as at the beginning.

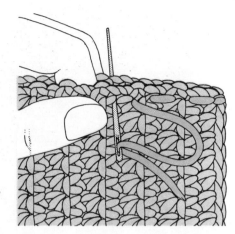

Oversewn seam

Place the right sides of the pieces together. Work along the wrong side of the fabric from right to left, one stitch in from the edge to join row ends, or just under the double loop at the top of each stitch to join stitches to stitches. Secure the yarn at the beginning of the seam with two or three small stitches, one on top of the other.

*Take the needle over the top of both edges and push the needle through from the back section to the

corresponding row end or stitch on the front section. Pull the yarn through. Move along to the left about 4mm/¼in from the last sewing stitch when joining row ends, or the width of one crochet stitch when joining stitches to stitches.

Continue from the * until the seam is completed. Fasten off with two or three small stitches as at the beginning.

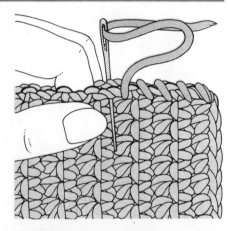

Crochet seam

To join a seam which is not meant to show place the right sides of the pieces together. To make a focal point of the seam, place the wrong sides of the pieces together. Work along the fabric from right to left, one stitch in from the edge to join row ends, or just under the double loop at the top of each stitch to join stitches to stitches.

Insert the hook from front to back through both pieces at the beginning of the seam, place a slip

loop on the hook and pull this through, yarn round hook and draw through loop on hook.

*Insert the hook from front to back through both pieces about 4mm/¼in from the last stitch when joining row ends, or the width of one crochet stitch when joining stitches to stitches, yrh and draw a loop through, yrh and draw through both loops on hook. One double crochet has been made. Continue from the * until the seam is completed. Fasten off.

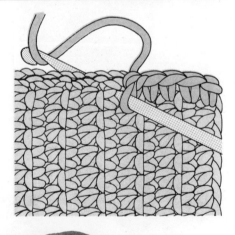

Below: A close-up showing the method used for crocheting a seam to make it a feature of the garment.

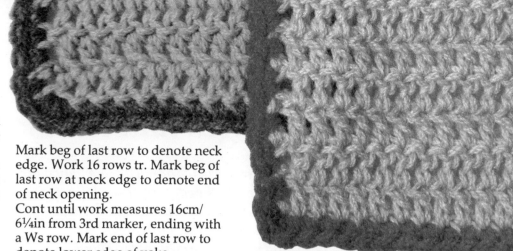

T-shaped jersey

This smart, boxy T-top is worked in simple trebles and joined with double crochet in a contrasting colour. The sleeves and yoke are worked from cuff edge to cuff edge so the length can be adjusted. The two body pieces can also be extended as necessary.

Sizes

To fit 81-86cm/32-34in bust loosely
Length to shoulder, 48cm/19in, adjustable
Sleeve seam, 15cm/6in, adjustable

You will need

6×50g balls of Emu Crêpe Royale Double Knitting (75% Courtelle, 25% wool) in main colour A
1×50g ball of same in contrast colour B
One 4.00mm/No 8 crochet hook

Tension

14 sts and 8 rows to 10cm/4in over trebles worked on 4.00mm/No 8 hook

Body

With 4.00mm/No 8 hook and A make 71ch.
1st row (Rs) Into 4th ch from hook work 1tr, 1tr into each ch to end. 69tr.
2nd row 3ch to count as first tr, miss first tr, 1tr into each tr to end.
The 2nd row forms the patt and is rep throughout.
Cont until work measures 25cm/9¾in from beg, or required length to underarm, ending with a Ws row. Fasten off.
Make another piece in same way.

Back yoke and sleeves

With 4.00mm/No 8 hook and A make 34ch, beg at right cuff and work in one piece. Work 1st and 2nd rows as given for body. 32tr.
Cont until work measures 15cm/6in from beg, or required sleeve length ending with a Ws row. Mark end of last row with coloured thread to denote *lower* edge of yoke.
Cont until work measures 31cm/12¼in from beg, or required sleeve length plus 16cm/6¼in, ending with a Ws row.**

Left: This striking top has minimum shaping on the neck edge only, so is an ideal pattern for a beginner.

Mark beg of last row to denote neck edge. Work 16 rows tr. Mark beg of last row at neck edge to denote end of neck opening.
Cont until work measures 16cm/6¼in from 3rd marker, ending with a Ws row. Mark end of last row to denote lower edge of yoke.
Cont until work measures 15cm/6in from last yoke marker, or required sleeve length to match first sleeve. Fasten off.

Front yoke and sleeves

Beg at left cuff and work as given for back yoke and sleeves to **, ending at opposite edge of work to last marker.

Shape neck

Next row Ss across first 6tr, dec one st, patt to end.
Dec one st at neck edge on every foll row 4 times more. 21tr.
Work 6 rows without shaping.
Inc one st at neck edge on next and every foll row 5 times in all, ending at neck edge, turn, make 8ch, work 1tr into 4th ch from hook, 1tr into each of next 4ch, patt to end. 32tr.
Complete as given for back yoke and sleeves.

Above: Different colourway samples.

To make up

Do not press. With Ws facing pin top edge of back body to lower edge of back yoke between markers.
With 4.00mm/No 8 hook and B, join yoke to body with a row of dc evenly spaced. Fasten off. Join front body and yoke in same way. Join shoulders and upper sleeve seams in same way.
With Rs of right sleeve facing and B, work one row dc round cuff edge, place under sleeve seam tog and join with dc, then cont down side edge of body to lower edge.
Work other side in same way, beg at lower edge of body and ending with a row of dc round cuff, so that join lies the same way on both seams.
With Rs of work facing and B, work one round of dc round neck edge and lower edge of body.

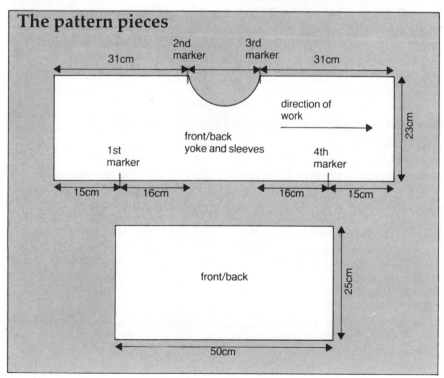

The pattern pieces

297

Basic making up: decorative edges and trims

Once you have assembled your crocheted garment, you may want to neaten or decorate the edges with an applied trim. This chapter includes six trimmings; take your pick, but be careful to work them evenly or you could pull the garment out of shape.

Although there may be no need to add further decoration to a crochet garment once it has been assembled, it is often necessary to work round the edges for a firm, neat finish. Knowing how to apply all types of edges allows you to give a personal touch to any basic garment

Neatening edges

If the edges just need neatening, a single row (or round) of slipped stitches or double crochet, worked close to the edge, will suffice. For more specific purposes, such as neckbands and front edges, work two or more rows (or rounds) of double crochet or treble stitches.

Although the instructions may include details of the type of edging required under the making up section, they are not always specific. For instance, you may simply be told to work in double crochet round all the edges, but not be told how many stitches to work. It is left up to you to experiment to arrive at a number of stitches that will not pucker the main garment or give a fluted edge.

Decorating edges

When a decorative edging is an integral part of a design, full working instructions are usually given but it is often extremely difficult to give precise numbers of stitches so, to some extent, it is still a matter of trial and error.

Experiment by working one double crochet to each double crochet row end or stitch, two double crochet to each treble row end and one double crochet to each treble stitch. If you end up with too many stitches overall and a fluted edge, you could try using a hook one size smaller than the one you used to crochet the garment, but this tends to give a very firm edge, which may not be in keeping with the rest of the garment.

Most crocheters use the same-sized hooks to work the edging, and adjust the number of stitches by missing a stitch every so often. When working along row ends, for example, you may well end up with an equation of, say, 10 double crochet stitches to 12 double crochet row ends. Keep to this equation for an even edge.

Corners always present a problem – there's no need to work into every stitch or row end on an *inner* corner edge but you will need to work more than once into a stitch on an outer corner edge.

This chapter outlines the best way of working a neat even edging and includes patterns for six different trimmings.

Crab stitch edging is worked over two rows and gives a firm, corded effect. It is ideal for finishing front openings which are left unfastened and may therefore have a tendency to curl back or under.

Mock blanket stitch edging takes just one row to work and it is much easier to keep the stitches neat and even than with embroidered blanket stitch. Work in a contrasting colour to give the best effect.

Simple picot edging is worked over three rows and forms a narrow, double edge suitable for neckbands and armbands. When completed, it is folded in half to the wrong side and slip stitched in place.

Curlicue edging makes a corkscrew-type fringe and is worked over one row. The fringing can be as long as you like and closely or widely spaced. Use it to trim the short sleeves of a jersey or in place of a traditional fringe on a shawl.

Shell edging needs exact multiples of stitches and takes two rows to complete. It forms a dainty scalloped edge ideal for baby garments.

Cluster edging also needs exact multiples of stitches and takes two rows to work. It forms a chunky pattern which looks most effective along the front and neck edges of a jacket.

Calculating the number of stitches to pick up

If you want to crochet an edging you must first work out how many stitches you need to pick up as you work along the edge of your garment. This ensures an even edging if you are working in simple double crochet, for example, and is essential if you are working a more decorative edging, requiring exact multiples of stitches.

Pinning out Begin by placing pins all along the edge to be trimmed at 5cm/2in intervals. Experiment by working a little of the edging to see how many stitches you can comfortably pick up between each

pin. Multiply this figure by the number of 5cm/2in intervals to calculate the total number of stitches to go along the edge. For example, if you have pinned out the edge into 10 sections and can pick up five stitches between each pin, the total number for a straight edge will be 50 stitches. If the edging you have chosen is a decorative one requiring, say, multiples of four stitches plus one, adjust the total number of stitches to 49 instead of 50.

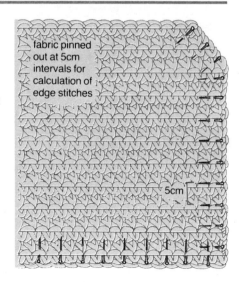

fabric pinned out at 5cm intervals for calculation of edge stitches

5cm

Working a straight edge in double crochet

working along row ends

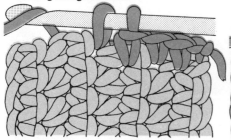

working along last row

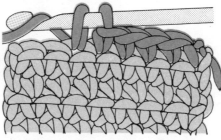

working along foundation row

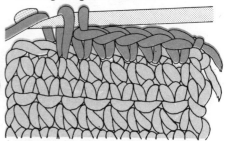

Have the right side of the fabric facing, the hook in your right hand and the yarn in your left hand. Insert the hook from front to back, make a slip loop in the yarn and place it on the hook, pull the loop through and make one chain to form the first stitch.
*Insert the hook from front to back along to the left of the previous stitch, yrh and draw a loop

through, yrh and draw through both loops on hook. One double crochet has been made.
Continue from the * along the edge. If required, turn and work another row of double crochet, working one stitch into each stitch. Fasten off.
If working along row ends pick up the stitches one stitch in from edge.
If working along the last row of the main fabric, insert the hook under

both loops of each stitch.
If working along the foundation row insert the hook where the stitches of the first row were made. If two threads of the commencing chain were picked up for the first row, only one thread will be left for the edging, and vice versa. Do not work under all the threads of the commencing chain as this will distort the fabric.

Working an outer curve in double crochet

For right-angled corners work three stitches of the edging into the corner stitch of the garment and remember to take these extra stitches into account if you are working an edging which needs exact multiples of stitches.
For a gentle curve you need to know how many extra stitches are needed to avoid pulling the edge up too tightly so that it does not lie flat. Mark the beginning and end of the

curve with pins. Measure between these markers with a flexible tape following the exact edge of the curve. Check this length against a previously worked straight edge. Count the number of stitches which were worked to achieve this length on the straight edge. This number is worked round the curve. Work more than once into stitches and row ends at regular intervals to achieve this.

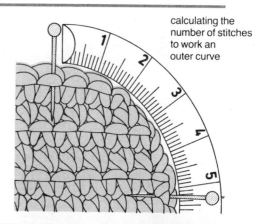

calculating the number of stitches to work an outer curve

Working an inner curve in double crochet

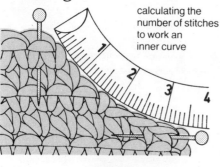

calculating the number of stitches to work an inner curve

You need to know how many fewer stitches are needed to avoid the edge fluting out.
Mark and measure the edge as given for working round an outer curve.
This is the number to work round the inner curve. Work stitches together at regular intervals to achieve this.

working a double crochet edging around an inner curve

Simple picot edging

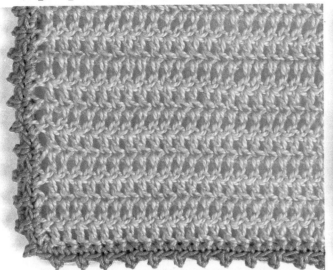

With the right side of the work facing, work one row of double crochet along the edge to be trimmed in the usual way, making sure that you have multiples of 2 stitches plus one. Turn.

Next row Work 4ch to count as next tr and 1ch sp, miss first 2dc, 1tr into next dc, *1ch, miss 1dc, 1tr into next dc, rep from * to end.

Next row 2ch to count as first dc, miss first tr, *1dc into 1ch sp, 1dc into tr, rep from * to end.

Fasten off. Fold the edging in half at the row of trebles and slip stitch in place.

Mock blanket stitch edging

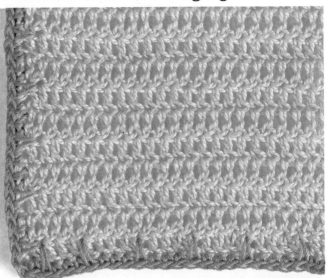

With the right side of the work facing, join in the yarn at the end of the edge to be worked with a slip stitch. Make one or two chains to count as first double crochet, depending on the thickness of yarn. Work two more double crochet in the usual way.

*Insert the hook through the fabric from front to back the depth of one additional row or stitch, yrh and draw a loop through *very loosely*, yrh and draw through both loops on hook, (making one long double crochet), now work 3dc in usual way.

Continue from the * along the edge. Fasten off.

shell edging

decorative edgings worked in toning yarns

Cluster edging

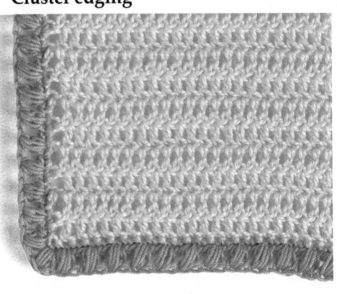

With the right side of the work facing, work one row of double crochet along the edge to be trimmed in the usual way, making sure that you have multiples of 2 stitches plus one. Turn.

Next row 2ch to count as first dc and 1ch space, *miss next dc, (yrh, insert hook into next dc and draw through a loose loop) 4 times into same dc, (9 loops on hook), yrh and draw through all loops on hook, 1ch, rep from * to last 2dc, miss 1dc, 1dc into last dc. Fasten off.

mock blanket stitch edging

Crab stitch edging

With the right side of the work facing, work one row of double crochet along the edge to be trimmed, working from right to left in the usual way.

Do not turn at the end of this row.

1 Begin again at the end of the last row. Make 2 turning chain and miss first st. Insert the hook from front to back under both loops at the top of the next st and draw loop through.

2 Yrh, draw loop through both loops on hook.

Continue along edge. Fasten off.

1

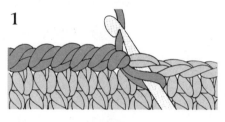

2

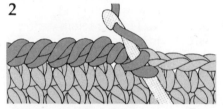

Curlicue edging

With the right side of the work facing, join in the yarn at the end of the edge to be trimmed with a slip stitch. Make one or two chains to count as the first double crochet, depending on the thickness of the yarn.

*To make a curlicue make 20ch, work 1dc into 3rd ch from hook, work 2dc into each ch to end, work 1dc into edging.

Continue from the * along the edge, making curlicues as required at intervals. Fasten off.

Shell edging

With the right side of the work facing, work one row of double crochet along the edge to be trimmed in the usual way, making sure that you have multiples of 4 stitches plus one. Turn.

Next row 1ch to count as first ss, *miss 1dc, 4tr into next dc, miss 1dc, 1ss into next dc, rep from * to end. Fasten off.

Flower-patterned V-necked top

This V-necked crochet top has neat cap sleeves and a double crochet welt. The neck and sleeve edges are finished with a crochet border which folds over to form a pretty picot edge.

Sizes

To fit 86 [91:97:102]cm/ 34 [36:38:40]in bust loosely
Length to shoulder, 62 [63:65:66]cm/ 24½ [24¾:25½:26]in
The figures in [] refer to the 91/36, 97/38 and 102cm/40in sizes respectively

You will need

6 [6:7:7]×50g balls of Neveda Primula Fine (100% wool)
One 2.00mm/No 14 crochet hook

Tension

32 sts and 14 rows to 10cm/4in over patt worked on 2.00mm/No 14 hook

Front

With 2.00mm/No 14 hook make 142 [150:158:166]ch.
1st row (Rs) Into 4th ch from hook work 1tr, 1tr into each ch to end. 140 [148:156:164]tr.
2nd row 3ch to count as first tr, miss first tr, 1tr into each tr to end.
Rep 2nd row twice more.
5th row 3ch to count as first tr, miss first tr, 1tr into each of next 4tr, *2ch, miss 2tr, 1tr into each of next 6tr, rep from * to last 7 sts, 2ch, miss 2tr, 1tr into each of last 5tr.
6th row 3ch to count as first tr, miss first tr, 1tr into each of next 2tr, *6ch, miss (2tr, 2ch and 2tr), 1tr into each of next 2tr, rep from * to last st, 1tr into 3rd of first 3ch.

7th row 3ch to count as first tr, miss first tr, 1tr into each of next 2tr, *3ch, work 1dc under all ch loops of previous rows, 3ch, 1tr into each of next 2tr, rep from * to last st, 1tr into 3rd of first 3ch.
8th row 3ch to count as first tr, miss first tr, 1tr into each of next 2tr, *2tr under next 3ch loop, 2ch, 2tr under next 3ch loop, 1tr into each of next 2tr, rep from * to last st, 1tr into 3rd of first 3ch.
9th row 3ch to count as first tr, miss first tr, *1tr into each of next 4tr, 2tr under 2ch loop, 1tr into each of next 2tr, rep from * to last 3 sts, 1tr into each of last 3 sts.
The 2nd to 9th rows inclusive form the patt and are rep throughout.
Cont in patt until work measures 35 [35:36:36]cm/13¾ [13¾:14¼:14¼]in from beg, ending with a 9th row.**

Shape sleeves and divide for neck

Next row 3ch to count as first tr, miss first tr, 2tr into next tr, work 65 [69:73:77]tr, work 2tr tog, 1tr into next tr, turn. Complete this side first.
Next row 3ch to count as first tr, miss first tr, work 2tr tog, 1tr into each tr to last 2 sts, 2tr into next tr, 1tr into last tr.
Cont in patt, inc one tr at sleeve edge on every row 8 times in all, *at the same time* dec one tr at neck edge on every row as now set 16 [17:18:19] times in all, working extra sts into a complete patt when possible.
Cont without shaping until sleeves measure 22 [23:24:25]cm/ 8¾ [9:9½: 9¾]in from beg of shaping. Fasten off.

Rejoin yarn with a ss to next tr at centre neck, 3ch to count as first tr, miss first tr, work 2tr tog, work 65 [69:73:77]tr, 2tr into next tr, 1tr into 3rd of first 3ch.
Complete this side to match first side, reversing all shapings. Fasten off.

Back

Work as given for front to **.

Shape sleeves

Next row 3ch to count as first tr, miss first tr, 2tr into next tr, patt to last 2tr, 2tr into next tr, 1tr into 3rd of first 3ch.
Cont inc one st in this way at each end of every row 8 times in all.
Cont without shaping until back measures same as front to shoulders. Fasten off.

Welts

With Rs of front facing and 2.00mm/No 14 hook rejoin yarn with a ss to lower edge and work one row dc, working 3dc for every 4 commencing ch.
Cont in dc until welt measures 5cm/2in. Fasten off.
Work along back edge in same way.

Neck edging

Join shoulder seams. With Rs facing and 2.00mm/No 14 hook, rejoin yarn with a ss to one shoulder seam and work an odd number of dc evenly round neck.
Next row 4ch to count as first tr and 1ch space, miss first 2dc, 1tr into next dc, *1ch, miss 1dc, 1tr into next dc, rep from * to end.
Next row Work 1dc into each tr and 1ch space to end, working 2dc at centre of neck and corners of neck. Fasten off.

Sleeve edging

With Rs of work facing and 2.00mm/No 14 hook, rejoin yarn with a ss to beg of sleeve shaping and work as given for neck edging.

To make up

Press very lightly under a damp cloth with a cool iron. Join side seams. Fold neck and sleeve edgings in half at row of tr to Ws and sl st in place. Press seams.

Right: The simple 8 row pattern forms groups of holes that look like flowers.

The pattern pieces

front

22[23:24:25]cm

49[51:54:56]cm

back

35[35:36:36]cm

44[46:49:51]cm

44[46:49:51]cm

Crochet your own buttons and trimmings

Make your own buttons and cords to match the style and, more importantly, the yarn of a garment and add decorative trimmings such as rosettes and spirals for an individual touch. To make them bigger or smaller, just vary the yarn thickness and hook size.

It can be expensive and time-consuming trying to find buttons which match the yarn used for a garment and are the correct size. Buttons which are too small will not remain fastened, and if they are too large they will stretch the buttonhole out of shape. The answer is to make your own buttons from oddments of yarn.

Shaped button covers can be fitted over button moulds – the kind sold for covering with fabric – or old buttons which are the wrong colour.

Tiny round buttons which are too small to take a button mould, need to be filled with a small amount of the same yarn used to make them. These are ideal for baby garments as they are soft and will not press into delicate skin. A firmer button can be made by inserting a bead instead of yarn.

Flat crochet buttons are worked over a plastic ring – a metal one may rust in washing and spoil the buttons. They can also be used as decorative motifs.

The search for trimmings to complement a design or liven up an old garment can be just as fruitless. Cords sold by the metre or yard are costly and very often look too clumsy and rigid. If you go through your stocks of yarn you are bound to find something in a toning or contrasting colour which can be used to make all of the trimmings given in this chapter.

Rosettes, bows and spirals are great fun to make. Scatter little rosettes all over the yoke of a jersey, or just add one or two to the toe of a baby's slipper. Make two or three spirals and attach them to the top of a beret or add two or three flower shapes or a bow above the top of a pocket.

Cords can be thick or thin, depending on the size of hook or yarn thickness. A fine cotton cord threaded with beads makes a colourful necklace; a thicker cord makes an ideal replacement handle for a shopping bag.

Instead of a hook use your fingers to make the simple finger cord worked in two colours.

Each of the fastenings and trimmings shown on the following pages can be enlarged or reduced in size by using a thicker or thinner yarn and adjusting the crochet hook size accordingly.

Left: Trim a knitted waistcoat with crochet buttons and a fine cord.

A selection of crochet trimmings

Making a four-petal rosette
Make 5ch, leaving an end about 20cm/8in long to sew on the rosette. Join with a ss to first ch to form a circle.
1st round 1ch, work 3tr into circle, *1ss and 3tr into circle, rep from * twice more. Join with a ss to first ch.
Fasten off and darn in last end.

Making a five-petal rosette
Make 5ch, leaving an end about 20cm/8in long to sew on rosette. Join with a ss to first ch to form a circle.
1st round 1ch to count as first dc, work 15dc into circle. Join with a ss to first ch.
2nd round *2ch, leaving last loop of each st on hook work 1tr into each of next 3dc, yrh and draw through all 3 loops on hook – called **1 cluster**, work 2dc down side of last tr of cluster then ss into same dc as last tr of cluster, rep from * 4 times more.
Fasten off and darn in last end.

Making a two-colour flower
With A make 5ch, leaving an end about 20cm/8in long to sew on flower. Join with a ss to first ch to form a circle.
1st round *Make 8ch, yrh, insert hook into 2ch ch from hook and draw yarn through, insert hook into each of next 6ch and draw yarn through, yrh and draw through all 9 loops on hook, ss into circle, (1 petal has been made), rep from * 4 times more. Do not join.
2nd round *3ch, ss into commencing ch beyond next petal, rep from * 3 times more, 3ch. Join with a ss to same place as beg of round.
Break off A. Join in B with a ss to any 3ch space.
3rd round *Make 9ch, yrh, insert hook into 2ch ch from hook and draw yarn through, insert hook into each of next 7ch and draw yarn through, yrh and draw through all 10 loops on hook, ss under 3ch of 2nd round, rep from * once more into same ch space**, rep from * to ** 4 times more. Fasten off and darn in ends.

Making a looped-petal flower
Make 4ch, leaving an end about 20cm/8in long to sew on flower. Join with a ss to first ch to form a circle.

1st round *Make 12ch, ss into circle, rep from * 11 times more.
Fasten off and darn in last end.

Making a spiral trimming
Make 20ch, leaving an end about 20cm/8in long to sew on spiral trimming.
1st row Into 4th ch from hook work 2tr, *3tr into next ch, rep from * to end.
Fasten off and darn in last end. The spiral curls into shape.

Making a spiral rosette
Make 14ch. Do not join into a circle.
1st row Into 3rd ch from hook work 3tr and 1htr, *work 1htr, 3tr and 1htr into next ch, rep from * to end. Fasten off. Curl the rosette round into shape. Secure the ends with a few small sts through the centre, leaving an end at the back to sew on the rosette.

Making a bow
This example is worked in two colours, coded as A and B.
Bow With A make 7ch.
1st row Into 3rd ch from hook work 1dc, 1dc into each ch to end. Turn. 6dc.
2nd row 1ch to count as first dc, 1dc into each dc to end. Turn.
Rep 2nd row 16 times more. Fasten off.
Band With B make 5ch.
Work 1st and 2nd rows as given for bow. 4dc.
Rep 2nd row 6 times more. Fasten off.
Gather up centre of bow and sew band in place round middle, securing at back.

Making a round, filled button
Make 4ch. Join with a ss to first ch to form a circle.
1st round 3ch to count as first tr, work 11tr into circle. Join with a ss to 3rd of first 3ch.
2nd round 2ch to count as first dc, miss first tr, 1dc into each tr to end. Join with a ss to 2nd of first 2ch.
3rd round (dec round) Ss into next dc, (work 2dc tog) 5 times, work last dc tog with 1dc into same place as ss at beg of round. 6dc.
Fasten off leaving an end about 20cm/8in long. Fill the button with a separate length of the same yarn wound into a ball, or a small bead.

Above: Pick a pixie hood to trim with several spirals instead of a tassel.

Thread the end into a blunt-ended sewing needle, thread through sts of last round, draw up and fasten off securely. Use this end to sew on the button.

Making a shaped button cover
Make 2ch. Do not join into a circle. Into the first of these 2ch work 8dc. Do not join.
Continue working round and round spirally, without joining, working (2dc into next dc, 1dc into next dc) 12 times in all when there will be 20dc in the round. Do not join.
Next round Work 1dc into each dc to end. Do not join.
Next round (dec round) (Miss 1dc, 1dc into next dc) 10 times. Do not join.
Place crochet cover over button mould, or fill with a separate length of the same yarn wound into a ball.
Next round (dec round) (Miss 1dc, 1dc into next dc) 5 times.
Fasten off leaving an end about 20cm/8in long. Thread the end into a blunt-ended sewing needle, thread through sts of last round, draw up and fasten off securely. Use this end to sew on the button.

Making a flat button
The size of the ring determines the size of the button.
Make 3ch, leaving an end about 20cm/8in long to sew on the button. Join with ss to first ch to form circle.
1st round 1ch to count as first dc, work 11dc into circle. Join with a ss to first ch.
2nd round 1ch to count as first dc, hold the ring *behind* the crochet and working *over* the ring make 1dc into same place as ss, work 2dc into each dc to end in same way. Join with a ss to first ch.
Fasten off and darn in last end.

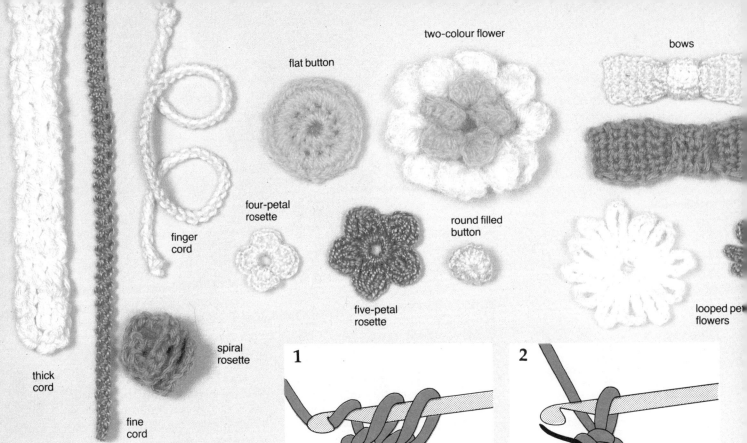

two-colour flower

flat button

bows

finger cord

four-petal rosette

round filled button

five-petal rosette

looped pe[...] flowers

thick cord

spiral rosette

fine cord

1

2

Making a thick cord

Make 6ch. Join with a ss to first ch to form a circle.
1st round 3ch to count as first tr, work 1tr into each ch to end. Do not join. 6tr.
Continue working round and round in tr, without joining, until cord is required length. Fasten off and darn in ends.

Making a fine cord

Make 2ch. Hold the 2ch between the thumb and finger of the left hand.
1 Work 1dc into first of these 2ch, turn work to *left*.

2 Inserting hook into the back loop, work 1dc into foundation loop of 2nd ch made at beginning, turn to *left*.

Dainty slippers for tiny feet

These crochet baby slippers are made from soft, fine cotton. They are trimmed with little rosettes and fastened with small round buttons. Make the trimmings and fastenings yourself using the instructions given in this chapter. This ensures the trimmings match the slippers perfectly.

Size

Length about 11cm/4¼in, to fit a baby of about 3 months.

You will need

One-colour version 1 × 50g ball of Phildar Perle No 5 (100% cotton) in main colour A
Oddment of same in contrast colour B, optional
Two-colour version 1 × 50g ball each of same in colours A and B
One 2.50mm/No 12 crochet hook
Two buttons

Tension

27 sts and 36 rows to 10cm/4in over dc worked on 2.50mm/No 12 hook

Slippers

With 2.50mm/No 12 hook and main colour make 18ch and beg at centre of sole.

1st round Into 3rd ch from hook work 1dc, 1dc into each of next 14ch, 3dc into next ch noting that this is the toe, cont along other side of ch and work 1dc into each of next 15ch, 1dc into first of 2ch at beg, ss into 2nd of these 2ch, *turn*. 36 sts.
2nd round 1ch, 2dc into next dc, 1dc into each dc to toe, 3dc into centre dc at toe, 1dc into each dc to last dc, 2dc into last dc, ss into first ch, *turn*. 40 sts.
Rep 2nd round 3 times more. 52 sts.
6th round 1ch, 2dc into next dc, 22dc, 2dc into next dc, 3dc, 2dc into next dc, 22dc, 2dc into next dc, ss into first ch, *turn*.
7th round 1ch, 2dc into next dc, 23dc, 2dc into next dc, 5dc, 2dc into next dc, 23dc, 2dc into next dc, ss into first ch, *turn*.
8th round 1ch, 2dc into next dc, 24dc, 2dc into next dc, 7dc, 2dc into next dc, 24dc, 2dc into next dc, ss into first ch, *turn*. 64 sts.
Work 4 rounds without shaping, turning at the end of each round. Join in contrast colour at end of 12th round if required.
13th round 1ch, 23dc, work 2dc tog, 13dc, work 2dc tog, 23dc, ss into first ch, *turn*.
14th round 1ch, 23dc, work 2dc tog, 11dc, work 2dc tog, 23dc, ss into first ch, *turn*.
15th round 1ch, 23dc, work 2dc tog, 9dc, work 2dc tog, 23dc, ss into first ch, *turn*.
16th round 1ch, 21dc, work 2dc tog, 2dc, work 2dc tog, 3dc, work 2dc

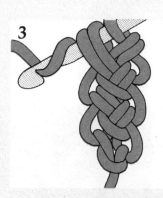

spiral trimming

Making a finger cord

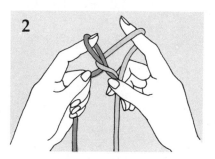

This example of a cord is made without a crochet hook, using the fingers of both hands instead. Use two separate balls of yarn, either in matching or contrasting colours.
1 Make a slip loop in the end of both balls of yarn. Place one loop, coded as A, over the other

and tighten up this loop. Place the other loop, coded as B, on the forefinger of the right hand.
2 Pull a loop of A through the loop of B from the back to the front with the forefinger of the left hand. Gently tighten up the loop of B.

3 Pull a loop of B through the loop of A from the back to the front with the forefinger of the right hand. Gently tighten up the loop of A.

4 Continue alternating the loops in this way until the cord is the required length. Break off yarns. Fasten off securely.

3 *Insert hook into 2 loops at side, yrh and draw through these 2 loops, yrh and draw through 2 loops on hook, turn to the *left*. Repeat from * until cord is required length. Fasten off and darn in ends.

tog, 2dc, work 2dc tog, 21dc, ss into first ch, *turn*. 54 sts.
17th round 1ch, 23dc, work 2dc tog, 3dc, work 2dc tog, 23dc, ss into first ch, *turn*.
18th round 1ch, 23dc, work 2dc tog, 1dc, work 2dc tog, 23dc, ss into first ch, *turn*.
19th round 1ch, 20dc, work 2dc tog, 5dc, work 2dc tog, 20dc, ss into first ch.
Fasten off. 48 sts.
Place a marker on 13th st at each side of heel.

Strap
With 2.50mm/No 12 hook and main colour for one-colour version or contrast colour for two-colour version make 9ch, work 1dc into each of 27 sts between markers at heel, *turn*. 36 sts.
Next row 1ch, 1dc into each dc to end, then 1dc into each of 9ch.
Work 2 more rows dc, making a 4ch

button loop at end of strap on last row. Fasten off.
To reverse strap for 2nd slipper, work 1dc into each of 27 sts between markers, make 10ch, *turn*.
Next row Into 3rd ch from hook work 1dc, 1dc into each of next 7ch, 1dc into each dc to end.

Below: Pretty baby slippers worked in two colours and trimmed with four-petal rosettes on the toes.

To make up
Do not press. With 2.50mm/No 12 hook and main or contrast colour work one row of crab st (page 281), working in dc from left to right instead of right to left, all round top of slipper and strap. Sew on buttons. Trim with small rosette.

Standard abbreviations used in crochet

Pattern symbols An asterisk, *, in a pattern row denotes that the stitches after this sign must be repeated from that point to the end of the row, or to the last number of stitches given.

Instructions shown in round brackets,(), denote that this section of the pattern is to be worked for all sizes. Instructions shown in square brackets, [], denote larger sizes.

alt	alternate(ly)	**htr**	half treble(s)	**st(s)**	stitch(es)
approx	approximate(ly)	**in**	inch(es)	**tog**	together
beg	begin(ning)	**m**	metre(s)	**tr**	treble(s)
ch	chain(s)	**MB**	make bobble, as specified	**tr tr**	treble treble(s)
cl	cluster, as specified	**mm**	millimetre(s)	**2tr tog**	keeping last loop of each
cm	centimetre(s)	**patt**	pattern		stitch on hook work 2tr,
cont	continu(e)(ing)	**qd tr**	quadruple treble(s)		yrh and draw through all
dc	double crochet(s)	**rem**	remain(ing)		3 loops on hook
dec	decreas(e)(ing)	**rep**	repeat(ing)	**3tr tog**	keeping last loop of each
dtr	double treble(s)	**Rs**	right side of fabric		st on hook work 3tr, yrh
2dtr tog	keeping last loop of each	**RTB**	raised treble at back		and draw through all 4
	st on hook work 2dtr, yrh	**RTF**	raised treble at front		loops on hook
	and draw through all 3	**sh**	shell, as specified	**Ws**	wrong side of fabric
	loops on hook	**sl**	slip	**Yrh**	yarn round hook
foll	follow(ing)	**sp**	space(s)		
g	gramme(s)	**ss**	slip stitch(es)		

PART 4

SOFT FURNISHINGS

Bedlinen: flat and fitted sheets

*With such a good choice of sheeting fabric now available it
is a simple and rewarding task to make
bedlinen sets to complement your bedroom decoration scheme.
Here are instructions for making flat
and fitted sheets, and ideas for pretty trims.*

You can save quite a lot of money by
making your own bedsheets – you
only need to stitch hems on flat
sheets or casings on fitted sheets.
There are four standard sizes of bed:

Single beds are   90cm wide×190cm
                     36in wide×75in
         and   100cm wide×200cm
                     40in wide×80in
Double beds are   135cm wide×190cm
                     54in wide×75in
         and   150cm wide×200cm
                     60in wide×80in

There is also an extra large double-size
(king size), not so widely used,
              183cm wide×200cm
              72in wide×80in

Mattresses are about 18cm/7in deep
(though some are slightly deeper).
To fit these bed sizes, purchased
flat sheets are about 180cm/71in
wide×260cm/160in for single, 230cm/
90in wide×260cm/106in for double,
and 270cm/110in wide×280cm/114in

for king size beds.
These sizes allow for approximately
12cm/4¾in tuck-in top and bottom
and 20cm/7¾in at the sides.
Fitted sheets are made to fit tightly
over the mattress with a turned-
under section of about 15cm/6in all
round held in place by elasticated
corners. Sheeting fabric, which is
purchased by the metre, is sold in
228-230cm/89½in-90½in widths.
Fabric joins should be avoided as
seams in sheeting are uncomfortable. If the width of the sheeting fabric is just over or just under the size
you require, you can leave the selvedges at the sides instead of making
side hems. Always check when
buying fabric to see whether you will
need to allow for shrinkage.

*Right: Flat sheets are very simple to sew
and the top turn-back can be trimmed
with a decorative edging for emphasis.*

Flat sheet

Flat sheets are used as top and
bottom sheets with blankets, or as a
bottom sheet with a duvet. By making your own to measure, you can
ensure a good fit.

You will need
Sheeting fabric
Matching sewing thread

Cutting out
Measure the length, width and
depth of the mattress.
To the length measurement add
twice the mattress depth plus twice
the 12cm/4¾in tuck-in allowance
plus 10cm/4in for hems. You can
increase the tuck-in allowance by up
to 30cm/11¾in each end if you wish.
To the width measurement add
twice the mattress depth and twice

the tuck-in allowance (this can be
from 12cm/4¾in to 25cm/9¾in,
depending on the width of fabric) and
add a further 3cm/1¼in for hems.
Cut one piece of fabric to these
measurements.

Making up
Make a double hem down each side
by folding 5mm/¼in and then 1cm/
½in to wrong side of the fabric.
Tack and stitch hems in place. (If
you are leaving the selvedges,
simply omit this stage.)
For the bottom hem, fold 1cm/½in
and then 3cm/1¼in to wrong side to
make a double hem. Tack and stitch.
For the top hem, fold 1cm/½in and
then 5cm/2in to wrong side to make
a double hem. Tack and stitch.
Remove all tacking.

*These sheeting samples
show the wide choice of
styles available.*

measuring a bed

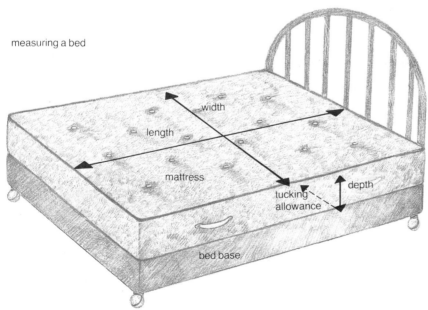

width

length

mattress

tucking
allowance

depth

bed base

Measuring example

Double bed 135cm wide × 200cm

Mattress length	200cm
Mattress depth × 2	36cm
Tuck-in × 2	24cm
Hem allowance	10cm
Total length	270cm
Mattress width	135cm
Mattress depth × 2	36cm
Tuck-in × 2	50cm (or less)
Hem allowance	3cm
Total width	224cm

Note: hem allowance need not be added to the width measurement if selvedges are left on fabric.

Fitted sheet

A fitted sheet is a bottom sheet which has elasticated corners to hold it securely in position on the mattress. It can be used either with a flat top sheet and blankets or with a duvet cover to keep the bed looking neat and tidy even when the duvet or blankets are drawn back.

You will need
Sheeting fabric
1m/1yd of 1cm/½in wide elastic
Matching sewing thread

Cutting out
Measure the length and width of the mattress and add 72cm/28¼in to each dimension.
Cut one piece of fabric to these measurements.

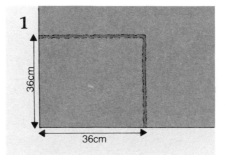

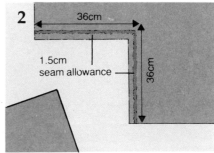

Making up
At each corner, measure 36cm/14¼in from the corner point and mark with tailor's chalk. Measure in from each mark and at right angles draw chalk lines until they meet, forming a 36cm/14¼in square.

2 Leaving a 1.5cm/⅝in seam allowance outside the marked lines, cut out the resulting square.
3 Making up each corner in the same way, place the two cut edges with the wrong sides together. Tack and stitch 5mm/¼in from edge. Remove tacking. Turn so right sides face and stitch 1cm/½in from edge.

Converting a flat sheet to a fitted sheet

If you have made the change from blankets to a duvet, you may find a fitted bottom sheet more convenient to use than a flat sheet. It will give the bed a neat and tidy look even when the duvet is thrown back. If your existing flat sheet is still in good condition, this can easily be converted into a fitted sheet to save the expense of buying new.

You will need
Flat sheet to fit your bed
1m/1yd of 1cm/½in wide elastic
Matching sewing threads

Cutting out
Measure your mattress and calculate the length/width of fabric needed as for a fitted sheet. Either cut off or unpick and press out the hems on your flat sheet depending on the dimension of fabric you need.

Making up
Follow the instructions for making up a fitted sheet.

Right: A fitted bottom sheet hugs the mattress neatly by elasticated corners.

PROFESSIONAL TOUCH

To apply corded trim to sheet edge

To imitate the smart finish found on expensive purchased sheets, one or two rows of cording can be added to the top of an upper flat sheet, so that the cording shows when the sheet is folded over the blankets.
Use pearl cotton (a thick embroidery thread) as the cord and the cording foot on your sewing machine or achieve a similar effect by using a twin needle – if your sewing machine will take one.

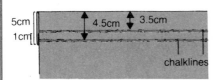

Draw one (or two) tailor's chalk line(s) on right side of top sheet 4.5cm/1¾in (and 3.5cm/1½in) from the folded edge.

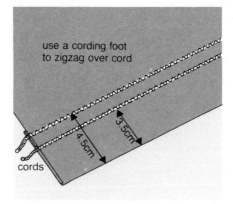

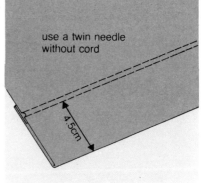

Using the cording foot attachment on your sewing machine, apply the pearl cotton over the chalk line(s). Choose pearl cotton to match the colour of your sheeting, and stitch with a matching sewing thread. Use either a wide zigzag so that the pearl cotton shows through, or conceal it with a close-up zigzag.

Using a twin needle on your sewing machine, tighten the tension so that when you sew two rows of stitching you get a raised area between them. (This method needs no cord.)

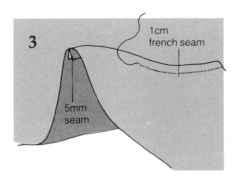

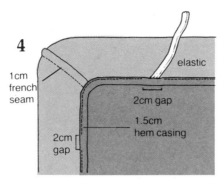

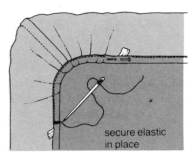

to form a French seam. Remove tacking.

Turn under a double hem, 1.5cm/⅝in and 1.5cm/⅝in, all round outer edge. Tack, leaving 2cm/¾in gaps 34cm/13½in each side of all four corners. Stitch, close to folded edge – except over 2cm/¾in gaps – to form a hem casing.

4 To gather up each corner in turn, cut a 25cm/10in length of elastic and secure one end on a safety pin. Thread safety pin end of elastic through one of the gaps in the casing and along through the casing until the loose end of the elastic lines up with the gap. Securely pin loose end of elastic in place.

5 Continue pushing elastic along casing until you can draw it out through the second gap (in the process gathering up the fabric on the corner). Remove the safety pin, ease the elastic back into casing and pin, then tack in place. Stitch securely with three rows of stitching. Stitch up casing openings.

Pillowcases to match – plain or fancy

You can give your bedroom scheme a new look simply by changing the pillowcases. Though they are usually made or bought in sets with sheets, you can easily make extra pairs in complementary colours, patterns and styles by following the instructions given here.

Pillowcases can have feminine frills in matching or contrasting fabric, or be left plain for a smart tailored look. Either way they provide an inexpensive way to change the look of your bedding to suit your mood – so why not make several pairs in different styles?

Standard pillows are usually about 74cm × 48cm/29¼in × 19in and pillowcases 75cm × 50cm/29½in × 19¾in. There are variations so measure your pillow in both directions before cutting the fabric. When measuring, remember that the case should fit the pillow loosely and add 3cm/1¼in to each dimension.

There are three basic pillowcase styles: the plain one-piece housewife style, the Oxford (which has a flat border), and the frilled pillowcase. All three have an inner flap to hold the pillow in place and eliminate the need for side fastenings on the case. Sheeting or cotton/man-made fibre mixes are best for pillowcases, but it is not essential to use a wide-width fabric; you can cut out a pillowcase along the fabric length providing that the design/pattern is not one-way only.

Right: A vivid combination of bright, bold colours is eye-catching and practical in a child's bedroom.

Housewife pillowcase

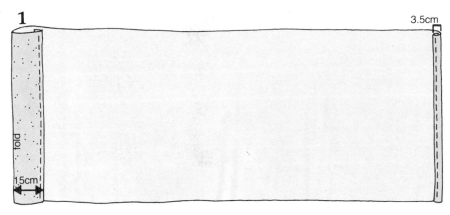

The plain housewife pillowcase is very easy to make because it can be cut from a single piece of fabric with one end folded in to form the inner flap.

You will need

For each pillowcase:
0.55m/⅝yd of fabric 230cm/90in wide *or* 1.75m/1⅞yd of fabric 90cm/36in *or* 120cm/48in wide (one-way designs in the two narrower widths are not suitable)

Cutting out and making up

From the fabric cut one piece 173cm×54cm/68in×21¼in.
1 Turn under a double hem (1.5cm/⅝in and 1.5cm/⅝in) on one short side. Tack and stitch in place.
At the opposite short side, turn under 5mm/¼in, then 3.5cm/1⅜in to make a double hem. Tack and stitch in place.
With wrong sides facing, fold in the short side with narrow hem for 15cm/6in to form the inner flap.

2 Fold the fabric so that the opposite hem meets the fold, enclosing flap.
Tack and stitch both long edges taking 1cm/½in seams. Trim seams to 5mm/¼in. Remove the tacking.
3 Turn through so that right sides face then tack and stitch the long edges again taking 1cm/½in seams (you have now completed French seams). Remove tacking.
Turn pillowcase through to right side. Press.

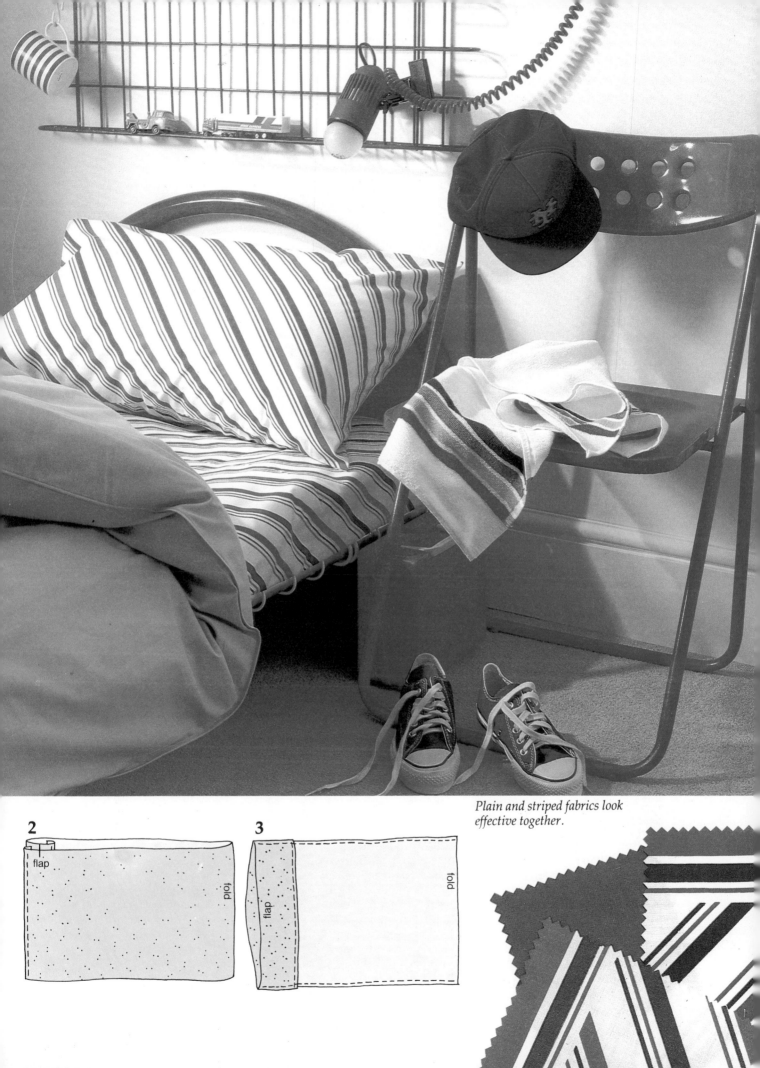

Plain and striped fabrics look effective together.

2

flap

fold

3

flap

fold

Oxford pillowcase

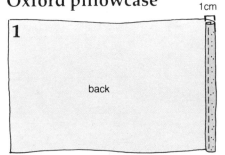

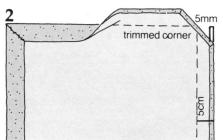

This style has a smart wide border – to give it a decorative, but tailored rather than feminine, finish – and an inner flap to hold the pillow in place.

You will need

For each pillowcase:
0.75m/³/⁴yd fabric 230cm/90in wide *or* 1.25m/1½yd fabric 120cm/48in wide *or* 2.40m/2½yd fabric 90cm/36in wide

Cutting out and making up

From fabric cut the following:
97cm×71cm/38¼in×28in for front
79.5cm×53cm/31¼in×20¾in for back
17cm×53cm/6¾in×20¾in for flap

1 On the back piece, turn under a double hem (1cm/½in and 1cm/½in) along one short edge. Tack and stitch in place.

2 On the front piece, fold 5mm/¼in and then 5cm/2in to the wrong side all round, mitring each corner. Press and slipstitch in place the mitred corners. This mitred hem forms the pillowcase border.
3 On the flap piece, turn under a double hem (1cm/½in and 1cm/½in) along one long edge. Tack and stitch in place.

Frilled pillowcase

This style has a gathered frill all round to give it a soft, feminine look.

You will need

For each pillowcase:
0.90m/1yd fabric 230cm/90in wide *or* 1.70m/1¾yd fabric 120cm/48in wide *or* 2.40m/2½yd fabric 90cm/36in wide

Cutting out and making up

From fabric cut the following:
79cm×53cm/31in×20¾in for front
80cm×53cm/31½in×20¾in for back
17cm×53cm/6¾in×20¾in for flap
For frill cut and join (with narrow flat seams), sufficient pieces of fabric 11cm/4¼in wide to make up a 5.30m/5¾yd length

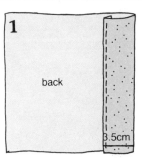

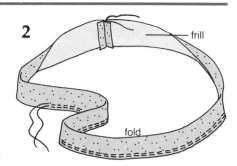

1 Along one long side of flap turn under a double hem (1cm/½in and 1cm/½in). Tack and stitch in place. On one short side of back piece turn under a double hem (5mm/¼in and then 3.5cm/1⅜in). Tack and stitch in place.

2 Stitch together short ends of frill to make a circle, then fold frill in half lengthwise with wrong sides facing. Run two rows of gathering stitches round the frill, 1cm/½in and 1.5cm/⅝in from the raw edges.

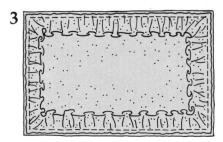

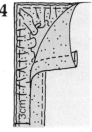

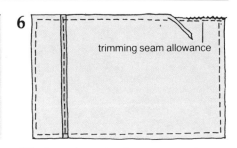

3 Position frill to right side of front, folded edge facing inwards. Pull up the gathering stitches evenly so that the frill fits the front. Tack frill in place.

4 Place back piece to front piece, right sides facing, sandwiching the frill and matching all edges except the short hemmed edge of the back which must fall 3cm/1¼in short of the length of the front.
5 Place flap with right sides down on to back piece, positioned so that the long raw edge lines up with the protruding front edge.

6 Tack and stitch all round the outer edge of the pillowcase taking 1.5cm/⅝in seams, and being careful not to close up the back hemmed edge in the stitching line.
Trim seam allowance to 1cm/½in and machine zigzag stitch the raw edges together to neaten. Remove tacking. Turn pillowcase to right side, folding flap to inside of front piece. Press.

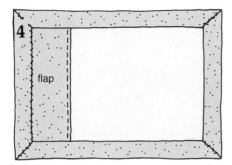
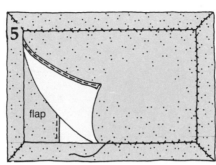
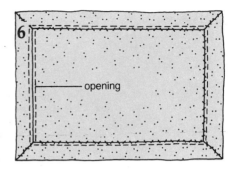

4 With wrong sides facing, place flap to one short side of the front piece, tucking all three raw edges under the mitred hem border by 1cm/½in. Slipstitch mitred hem border to flap along tucked-under long edge.

5 Place back piece to front piece wrong sides facing, with the back piece hem positioned over the flap/ mitred hem border join. Tuck the raw edges on the back piece under the mitred hem border by 1cm/½in. Slipstitch mitred hem border in the back piece round three sides, leaving the flap side unstitched.

6 Working from the back side of the pillowcase, machine stitch all round just 3mm/⅛in inside the mitred hem border edge. Be careful not to catch the back piece opening as you stitch.
Remove all tacking. Press.

Above: Frilled pillowcases give a soft and pretty look, while the Oxford-style ones (right) have a chic tailored finish.

Sheets trimmed to perfection

It is the decorative trim applied to flat sheets along the top turn-back, that lifts them out of the ordinary and gives them a designer look. Such sheets are usually expensive, but fortunately it is an easy matter to add a variety of trims yourself.

All of the design ideas suggested here are simple to add to a sheet as you are making it, or they can be applied to a ready-made sheet.

Zigzagged scalloped edge

This pretty scallop shape gives emphasis to the sheet edge, and the machine zigzag stitching around the scallops can be in a contrast colour for extra appeal.

Cut out a paper template for the scallops (see page 178). You will find it easiest to work with a template about 30cm/12in long and use it repeatedly along the edge. Complete the making up of the sheet, but do not sew a hem at the top. On the right side of the sheet, place the template 5mm/¼in from raw top edge.

If you are working on a ready-made sheet, place the template so that it butts up to the finished hem edge. Draw round the scallop outlines with tailor's chalk.

Machine zigzag along the scallop shapes and then, with small sharp scissors, carefully cut away the fabric close to the zigzagging to give the scalloped shape.

Simple border trim

To contrast with or complement a plain coloured sheet, a border of plain or patterned fabric can be sewn along the top edge.

If you are making the sheet, complete the make up with the exception of a top hem.

If you are adding a border to a ready-made sheet, unpick the hem or cut off the corded edge if the length allows this.

Left: A selection of special decorative trims for flat sheets. From top: zigzag scallop edge; a simple border trim and crisp broderie anglaise with a ruffle.

Cut a piece of fabric for the border 23cm/9in by the width of the sheet, plus 3cm/1¼in. Turn 1.5cm/⅝in to the wrong side on each short edge of border piece and tack. Wrong sides facing, fold the border in half along the length and press. Open flat again.

With right sides facing, place one long edge of border to top of sheet and sew with 1.5cm/⅝in seams. Turn border to wrong side of sheet along the foldline and neatly slipstitch along both short ends and the long edge. Press.

Broderie anglais with a ruffle

A ruffle and broderie anglaise trim with two neatened edges, adds a romantic and delicate look.

Whether you are making the sheet or adding a ruffle to a ready-made one, use a minimum-iron fabric for the ruffle. Otherwise, this type of trim can be time-consuming to iron after each laundering.

Complete the make up of the sheet but turn only a single 1cm/½in hem to the right side along the top edge. Cut a piece of fabric for the ruffle 23cm/9in×1½ times the width of the sheet adding 3cm/1¼in for seams. Turn 1.5cm/⅝in to the wrong side on each short end of ruffle fabric. Wrong sides facing, fold in half along the length and press. Machine stitch across both short ends.

Run two lines of gathering stitches along the length of the ruffle, then gently and evenly pull up the gathering threads until the ruffle fits the width of the sheet.

If you have made the sheet, place the raw edges of the ruffle to the right side of the sheet, 1.5cm/⅝in from the top edge to cover the hem. If you are adding the ruffle to a ready-made sheet, place the ruffle to the right side of the sheet overlapping the top edge by at least 1.5cm/⅝in. Tack ruffle in place, then lay a length of broderie anglaise trim over the ruffle raw edges and sew in place.

Six pillowcase trimmings

Add a personal touch to pillowcases with simple but effective decorative features. Here are six ideas designed to start you off on the creative track. You will find it easier to stitch embroidery, attach braid or work appliqué before you make up the pillowcases.

You can, however, use all but the piping idea on bought pillowcases, if you take care to stitch through only the front piece of the pillowcase.

Satin stitch embroidery

Initials, bows – or both – are simple shapes to embroider.

First mark the outline with tailor's chalk, then satin stitch by hand or by machine along the outline. Embroidery looks effective on all styles of pillowcase.

Ric rac for emphasis

The bright colours of ric rac braid make a bold colour emphasis as a pillowcase trim, and this is especially jolly for a child's bedroom.

Tack the braid in place, then stitch along the centre. Remove tacking. This type of trim can be added to all styles of pillowcase.

Piping adds style

Piping is a sure way to give a pillowcase style, but it is not suitable for the Oxford pillowcase. You can add piping most successfully to a frilled pillowcase, between the case and frill, or to the seams on a housewife style (except at the opening). For either style, insert piping between the seams (see page 87) during the making up of the pillowcase.

Points for visual interest

For an unusual pillowcase trim on a frilled or Oxford style, cut the edge into points using a template as your guide (see page 88). Machine zigzag the raw edges with a close stitch and, for a strong visual impact, do this in a contrast colour.

Appliqué accents

Simple motifs cut from fabric can be appliquéd in place down one side, or all round a pillowcase – and this decorative feature can be used on all styles of pillowcase.

Cut out the motifs and tack securely in position. Sew all round with a close machine zigzag stitch.

Lacy looks

Lace is guaranteed to enhance even the most simple of patterns, or to soften the effect of a plain colour. If you are making the pillowcase in the frilled style, you could make the frill from lace as a pretty alternative to fabric.

On a purchased housewife style pillowcase, you can neatly slipstitch a length of lace all round the outer edge. A lace frill is not suitable for an Oxford style pillowcase.

Right and below: Pillowcases acquire a touch of class with a special trimming.

Duvet covers: frilled or reversible

Duvet covers are quick and easy to make using the extra wide sheeting now available. There is a wide range of this easy-care fabric. Choose bold bright colours to make a focal point, a different pattern on each side for versatility or add a frill for a pretty finish.

It is easy to see why more people are changing to duvets – they are light and warm and bed making becomes just a matter of straightening the bottom sheet and shaking the duvet. Duvet covers are best made up in an easy-care cotton and polyester sheeting which, apart from being washable, needs minimal ironing. It can be bought in wide widths so the front and back can each be cut out in one piece, without having to join fabric. Nowadays poly/cotton sheeting is available in a wide variety of plain colours, geometric patterns and floral designs, so there is something to suit any bedroom. It is just as simple to make up the basic cover in two complementary fabrics so that turning the duvet over gives a completely new look.

Duvets should be about 40cm/18in wider than the bed to allow for covering the occupant as well. Duvet covers tend to fall into two sizes: 140cm × 200cm/4ft 6in × 6ft 6in for single beds and 200cm/6ft 6in square for small or standard double beds. King-size duvet covers are 230cm × 205cm/7ft 6in × 6ft 11in and, at the other end of the scale, cot covers are usually 100cm × 120cm/40in × 48in.

Measuring up

If your duvet is not a standard single or double size, measure it and add about 5cm/2in to each dimension for the cover as this should be loose fitting like a pillow case. Alter the fabric requirements accordingly.

Add seam allowances to the finished measurements of the cover: 4cm/1½in to the width and 9.5cm/4in to the length.

This allows for an opening along the bottom edge. If you want a side opening, reverse the seam allowances for width and length and, when making up, apply the instructions given for the bottom edge to one side.

Right: Colour match different patterns, such as the spots and stripes shown here, or use contrasting colourways of the same pattern to make an unusual and reversible duvet cover.

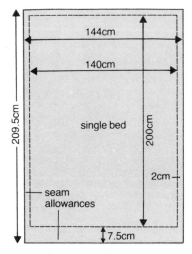

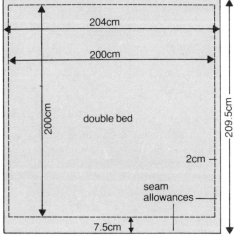

Making the plain duvet cover

A plain duvet cover is simply made by stitching two pieces of fabric together to form a large bag with an opening at one end. The quantities are given below and as sheeting is usually 228cm/90in wide it can be more economical to cut the length of the duvet across the width of the fabric, pattern permitting. Simply double the width of the cover, including seam allowances, to calculate the fabric needed.

You will need
Single: 2.9m/3⅛yd wide sheeting
1m/1⅛yd press fastener tape
Matching thread
Double: 4.1m/4½yd wide sheeting
1.6m/1¾yd press fastener tape
Matching thread

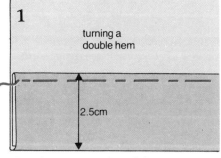

Cutting out and making up
Cut front and back pieces to the required size, including seam allowances, keeping to the straight grain of fabric.
1 On the bottom (opening) edge of each piece, turn a double hem (2.5cm/1in and 2.5cm/1in) to the wrong side. Pin, tack and machine stitch.

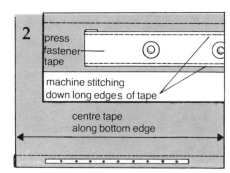

2 Separate the press fasteners and pin one half of the tape to the **right side** of each piece, placing it centrally to the width and next to the stitching. Ensure that the press fasteners correspond on both tapes. Turn raw ends under and use a zipper foot, if you have one, to machine stitch down the long edges of each tape.

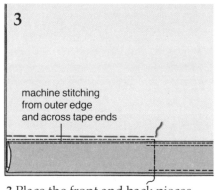

3 Place the front and back pieces right sides together, fasten poppers and tack in from each side to just past the tape ends next to the hem edge. Machine stitch from each outer edge along the tacking, then down across the hem and the tape ends.
The other three sides are stitched with French seams.

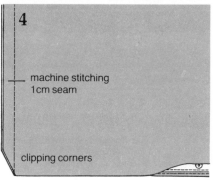

4 With wrong sides together, stitch a 1cm/½in seam down both sides. Trim seam allowance and press. Clip off corners to reduce seam bulk.

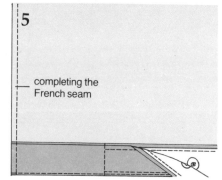

5 Fold cover so that right sides are together and stitch side seams again with 1cm/½in allowance to complete the French seams.
Turn cover right side out and repeat steps 4 and 5 to join top edge with a French seam.
When the cover is complete, turn right side out and press well.

Making a frilled duvet cover

The quantities given below allow for a 12cm/5in deep frill. To calculate the amount of fabric for the frill alone simply subtract the quantities given for the plain duvet from the quantities given for the frilled version.

This duvet will not, of course, be reversible, so add any trimmings to the front cover only.

You will need

For a single duvet:
3.5m/3⅞yd wide sheeting
1m/1⅛yd press fastener tape
Matching thread
Trimmings if required
For a double duvet:
4.9m/5⅜yd wide sheeting
1.6m/1¾yd press fastener tape
Matching thread
Trimmings if required

Cutting out and making up

Cut the back and front pieces as for the basic cover.
Cut 15cm/6½in deep strips across the width of the remaining fabric until you have enough to form a strip 1½–2 times the length to be frilled (about 8m/9yd and 10m/11yd for single and double covers, respectively).

1 — machine stitching a double hem — 1cm — 14cm — machine stitching a double hem — 1cm

2 — stitching a double row of gathering threads along each section — mark dividing 6 equal sections

1 Join the frill lengths into one long strip with 5mm/¼in and 1cm/½in French seams. Neaten the short ends by turning a narrow double hem, 5mm/¼in and 1cm/½in, to the wrong side and stitching. Neaten the lower long edge with a double hem (5mm/¼in and 1cm/½in) turned to the wrong side and stitched.
2 Divide the frill strip into six equal lengths and mark. Run two rows of gathering stitches along each section, placing the stitches on either side of the stitching line, which will be 1.5cm/⅝in from the raw edge.

Stitch the hems on the bottom edges of the cover (step 1 of plain duvet cover). Measure down one side, along bottom edge and up the other side on front cover piece and mark this length into six equal divisions.

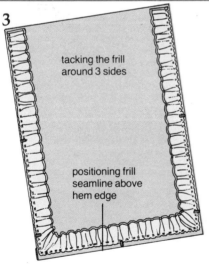

3 tacking the frill around 3 sides

positioning frill seamline above hem edge

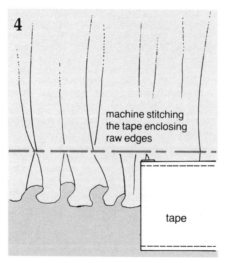

4 machine stitching the tape enclosing raw edges

tape

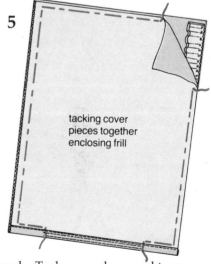

5 tacking cover pieces together enclosing frill

3 With right sides and raw edges together, pin the frill around the three edges of the front cover, pulling up the gathers evenly so that each section of the frill fits one section of the cover. Allow slightly more fullness at each corner. Start and finish at the top edge seamline and position the frill seamline close to the folded hem edge but not over it. Tack all round.

4 Pin, tack and stitch the press fastener tape into position as for the basic cover but enclosing the raw edge of the frill.
5 Place the cover pieces right sides together and tack a 1.5cm/⅝in seam round the three unfinished sides. Take care not to catch the frill in the top edge seam. Tack in from each side of the bottom edge, next to the hem edge, until just past the tape

ends. Tack across hem and tape. Machine stitch all round the cover following the tacking. Trim down seam allowance on raw edges, then zigzag together to neaten.
Turn cover right side out through opening, spread out frill, and press.

Right: Fold the frill in half widthways to make a reversible cover. Bands of Offray ribbon make an attractive trim.

Trimming with lace for luxurious effects

Transform your bedlinen by adding beautiful, delicate lace trimmings. Cobweb-fine lace and fine white cotton give a romantic look while heavier lace has an old-fashioned splendour. Lace trims and inserts can also be added to curtains and tablewear where appropriate.

For centuries, fine lace trimmings have been used to make functional soft furnishings appear as luxurious and decorative additions to the home. Now that machine-made lace is available in an abundance of patterns, designs and textures, an old-fashioned richness of style and character can be added to bedlinen you have made yourself or bought, at relatively little cost.

Use lace as edgings or insertions to soften a patterned fabric, add interest to a plain colour or to highlight an unusual shape. Gather it into frills, or appliqué individual motifs cut from a length of lace, for different effects. Choose a fine, delicate lace for a romantically feminine touch, or a richer, heavier lace to echo a country or Victorian look.

Choosing lace

When picking a lace trimming from the confusing array so often available, it's important to be quite clear as to how it will be applied – whether you will use it as an edging or an insertion, whether it is to be flat or frilled, and whether one, both or neither edges will show. A wide lace trimming with a decorative finish along both edges, for example, would be ideal as a topstitched border or an insertion but unnecessarily bulky – and expensive – when

gathered into a frill or inserted in a seam.

The same design of lace is often available in a variety of widths – choose one to suit the proportions of the item it is to decorate.

For a frilled edging, buy either pre-gathered lace or enough to gather up effectively (at least 1½ times finished length).

Try to match the fibre content of the lace to that of the fabric, choosing a cotton lace for a cotton fabric, nylon for synthetics and so on. This not only gives a better finished look, but also simplifies laundering. A nylon

Below: Mass together lots of lovely lacy items to transform a basic bed – or any dull corner – into a strikingly pretty focal point. Mix old lace and new for a really decorative effect.

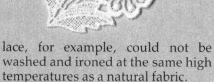

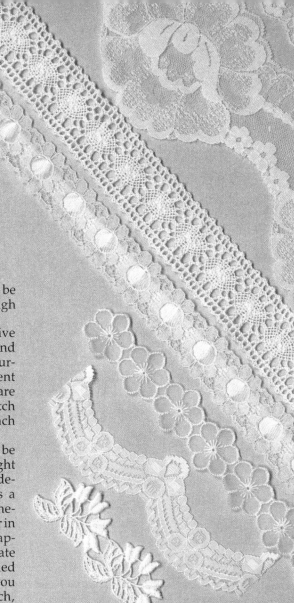

lace, for example, could not be washed and ironed at the same high temperatures as a natural fabric.

Avoid putting antique or expensive hand-made lace that should be hand washed or dry cleaned on to furnishings that will require frequent machine washing, unless you are willing to remove them and stitch them on again by hand after each laundering.

Most modern laces are designed to be machine-stitched in place. A straight edge automatically provides a guideline for stitching; if the lace has a scalloped or shaped edge, machine-stitch either around the shaping or in a straight line just within the shaping. Lace with particularly intricate edges, however, should be attached by hand and so is best avoided if you have a large area of lace to attach, such as down the edges of long curtains.

selection of lace samples

Sewing guidelines

Whether attaching lace by hand or machine, always use a fine sharp needle to avoid snagging and a fine thread in a fibre to match that of the lace.

When machine-stitching lace, it is advisable to practise stitch length and tension on a spare piece of lace and fabric if possible: the tension may have to be loosened slightly to prevent puckering. Tack tissue paper over any lace that will lie on the underside of the fabric while machining, to prevent threads catching in the feeding mechanism. The tissue can be torn away after stitching.

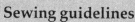

PROFESSIONAL TOUCH

Joining lace trimmings

To join two pieces of lace trimming unobtrusively, or when joining one piece into a circle, overlap the ends – if possible at a point where the pattern matches – and oversew or zigzag stitch the overlapping edge. With small, sharp scissors, trim away the surplus fabric from the underside, close to the stitching.

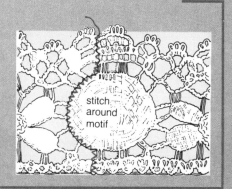

stitch around motif

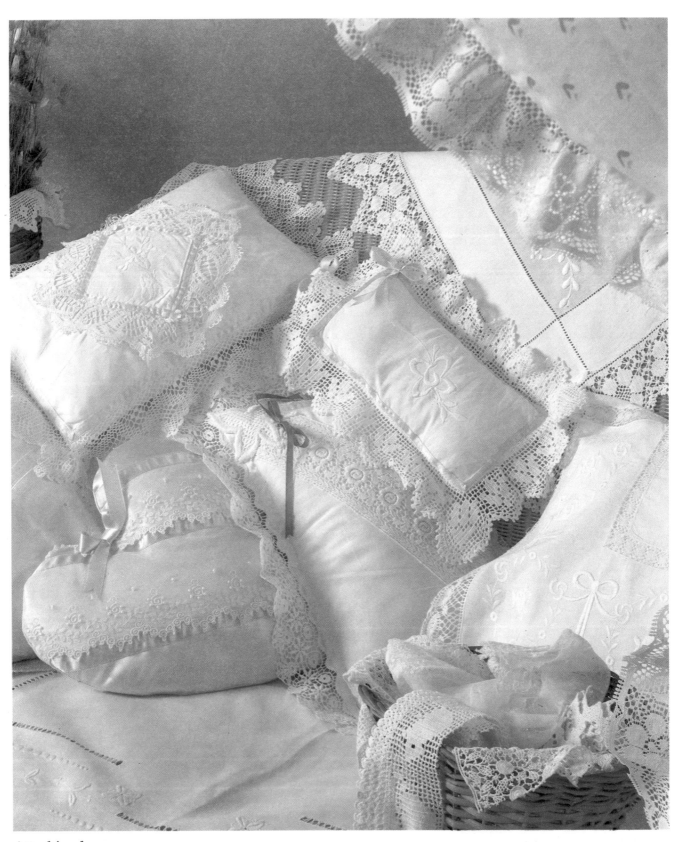

Attaching lace

Where possible, attach lace as part of the making up process as this saves work, enables you to secure raw ends in seams and gives a more professional finish. The exception is when adding precious and very expensive hand-made or antique lace which will need to be sewn on by hand and removed for laundering.

When stitching a lace trimming in place take the smallest possible seam allowance (5mm/¼in or even less on a pre-finished edge) from the lace so as not to lose too much of the pattern, but take the normal seam allowance in the fabric to which it is being attached.

As a seam trimming

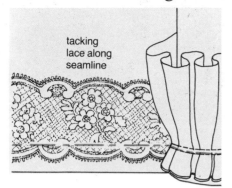

Insert lace edging into the seams on items such as pillow cases and cushion covers.

With right sides facing, tack the lace along the seamline on one piece of the main fabric so that it will lie sandwiched between the two pieces of fabric while stitching the seam. A fabric frill can be inserted in the seam at the same time.

Left: Lace inserts and frills can also be used on other kinds of soft furnishings such as tablelinen, lampshades, curtains and cushions. White lace complements most colour schemes and always creates a fresh and pretty effect. For a bolder, more dramatic look, dye lace trims in rich or strikingly bright colours, using the appropriate commercial dye.

As an edging

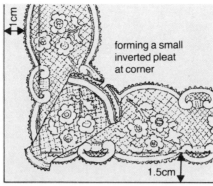

Attach a lace edging before making the hem on such items as sheets, tablecloths and napkins where there is only a single thickness of fabric.

Mark the fold of the hem on the right side of the fabric and tack the lace right side down with the plainer edge overlapping the hemline by about 5mm/¼in and facing outwards. Form the lace into a small inverted pleat at all corners so that it will have enough fullness to fan out. Machine stitch along the hemline, then fold under and complete hem as usual, leaving the main part of the lace falling below the fabric edge.

As a border or appliqué

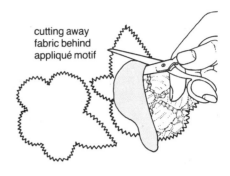

Simply tack and topstitch lengths of lace in position on the right side of the fabric to form a border. Where possible, let the short raw ends overlap the seamline so they will be caught and hidden in the seams; otherwise turn under the ends to neaten.

Motifs can be cut from lengths of lace and appliquéd on to a fabric background.

To create appliqué with an openwork effect, pin and tack a lace motif to the right side of the fabric and stitch all round the edge with particularly close zigzag stitches, or oversew by hand. Using small sharp scissors and being extremely careful not to cut into the lace, carefully cut away the main fabric from behind the motif.

As an insertion

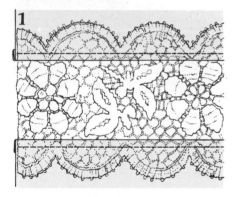

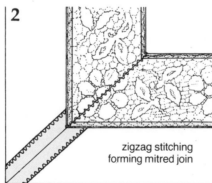

Lace inserted flat, between two areas of fabric, because it is unbacked, will show up well against the dark wood of furniture underneath, a pretty lining or undercloth, or the light of a window.

1 If the lace has prettily finished edges, tack a very narrow hem along each of the fabric edges. Tack the lace edges on the right side of the fabric over the hems and topstitch in place, catching down hem turnings at the same time.

If the lace edges are to be hidden, seam one edge of the lace to one piece of fabric, right sides facing and taking only a narrow seam allowance on the lace. Seam the other edge of lace to the second piece of fabric in the same way. Zigzag stitch or oversew turnings together and press away from the lace so as not to show through.

2 If the lace insertions are to meet at a corner, overlap the two ends at right angles and zigzag stitch across at 45° to form a mitred join. Trim away the surplus fabric on both sides, cutting as close to the stitching as possible.

Bed valances in three different styles

A bed looks neater with a valance round the edge concealing the base and legs. The style can be frilled, pleated or plain with pleated corners – they are all quick and easy to make. Co-ordinate the colours and add trimmings to match the bedlinen.

A bed valance fits between the mattress and the base of a bed, hanging down to cover the base, the bed legs and the space under the bed. A valance is particularly necessary for a bed with a duvet and no bedspread to cover the divan base, but it can also be a decorative extra used in conjunction with a bedspread which isn't quite floor length.

The base fabric covers the bed base, fitting under the mattress, and the valance skirt is attached around three sides leaving the head end free. The skirt can be frilled, box pleated or plain with a single inverted pleat at each corner – choose a style to suit the bedroom.

Make it up in an easy-care polyester/cotton sheeting which matches the bedding or complements a throw-over bedspread. Extra wide sheeting requires fewer joins for the skirt and none at all for the base, but to economise use sheeting for the skirt and a cheaper washable fabric, such as an extra wide calico, for the large area hidden under the mattress.

Measuring up

For the valance base, measure the bed base both lengthways and widthways. Add 4.5cm/1¾in to the length and 3cm/1¼in to the width measurements for seam allowances. The base can be cut in one piece from wide sheeting but if you use a narrower fabric, you need to join sections with flat felled seams. For the depth of the valance skirt, measure from the top of the bed base to the floor. The average height is between 30–35cm/12–14in. To this measurement add 6.5cm/2½in for hem and seam allowance.

The finished length of the valance skirt is measured from one head corner, round the base to the other corner (but not across the head end). The actual skirt piece will be cut according to the style of valance.

Right: The deep-coloured valance contrasts with the prettiness of the bedding. If your bedlinen is rather plain, brighten it up with a frilled valance or one in a patterned fabric.

Making a gathered valance

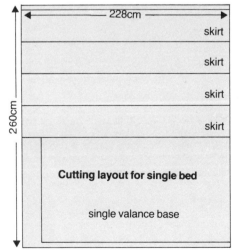

Cutting layout for single bed

single valance base

228cm

skirt

skirt

skirt

skirt

260cm

The frilled valance is particularly quick and simple to make.

You will need

For a single bed 90cm/3ft wide:
2.6m/2⅞yd sheeting 228cm/90in wide
For a double bed 135cm/4ft 6in wide:
3.1m/3½yd sheeting 228cm/90in wide
Thread
Trimmings if required

Cutting out and making up

Cut out the valance base with the length across the width of the fabric. Join widths if necessary on narrow fabrics.

The skirt should be 1½–2 times the finished length to allow for gathering. Cut strips across the width of the fabric to make up the length, allowing 3cm/1¼in seam allowances for each join and the two ends.

Fold a double hem (1.5cm/⅝in and 1.5cm/⅝in) along the top edge (head end) of the valance base and machine stitch. Pin, tack and stitch the skirt pieces together into one long strip with French seams.

Fold a double hem (1.5cm/⅝in and 1.5cm/⅝in) at each short edge of skirt strip and machine stitch.

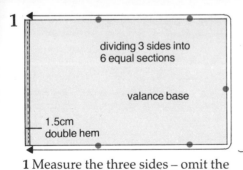

1 Measure the three sides – omit the hemmed end – of the base piece and mark into six to eight equal sections. Divide the skirt strip into the same number of sections and mark.
2 Turn a double hem (2.5cm/1in and 2.5cm/1in) along base edge of skirt and machine stitch or hem by hand.

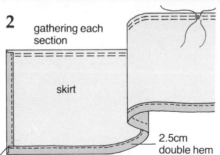

Add any trimmings at this stage. Run two rows of gathering stitches along each skirt section, placing the stitches on either side of the stitching line which will be 1.5cm/⅝in from the raw edge.
3 With right sides together pin the skirt to the base, matching one skirt

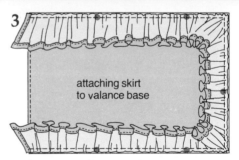

section to one base section in turn and drawing up gathering stitches evenly to fit. Allow slightly more gathering round each corner. Tack and stitch skirt in place with 1.5cm/⅝in seams. Trim seam allowance and zigzag stitch together to neaten. Press well to complete.

Making a pleated valance

Box pleats require more fabric than a frill but make a smart valance with a neat finish.

You will need
For a single bed:
3.8m/4¼yd sheeting 228cm/90in wide
For a double bed:
4.2m/4⅝yd sheeting 228cm/90in wide
Thread
Trimmings if required

Cutting out and making up
Measure up for the valance base and skirt depth as before. Cut out the base piece with the length across the width of the fabric. The skirt should be three times its finished length to allow for pleating. Cut strips across the fabric width until you have sufficient length, allowing 3cm/1¼in seam allowances for each join and the two ends.

Decide on the size of pleat you require, finding a figure that will divide evenly into the width of the bed, eg six pleats 15cm/6in wide or nine pleats, 10cm/4in wide, for a 90cm/3ft bed.

Hem the top edge of base piece, join the skirt strips together with French seams and hem the short and lower edges, as for the gathered valance.

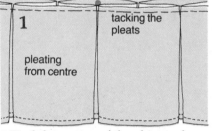

1 **pleating from centre** / **tacking the pleats**

2 **attaching skirt to valance base**

1 Find the centre of the skirt and begin pleating out from this point, folding and pinning the fabric into even box pleats. Try to position the pleats so there will be an inverted pleat formed at each corner.

2 Place the pleated skirt around the three sides of the base with right sides and raw edges together. Adjust the last pleats as necessary to acquire the exact finished length – if they have to be slightly smaller or larger it will not be very noticeable at the head end. Pin, tack and stitch together with a 1.5cm/⅝in seam. Trim seam allowance slightly and zigzag raw edges together to neaten.

Turn right side out and press well to complete.

Making a plain valance with pleated corners

Make the plain valance in a heavier fabric for a more tailored look.

You will need
For a single bed:
2.2m/2½yd sheeting 228cm/90in wide
For a double bed:
2.6m/2⅞yd sheeting 228cm/90in wide
Thread
Trimmings if required

Cutting out and making up
Measure up for the valance base and skirt depth as before. Cut out the base piece with the length across the width of the fabric. The skirt is made from five pieces – two sides, one end and two pleat

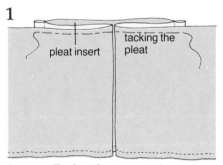

1 **pleat insert** / **tacking the pleat**

inserts. Each side piece is the bed length plus 10.5cm/4in, the end piece is the bed width plus 18cm/7in and each pleat insert is 18cm/7in. Cut out across the width of the fabric. If a narrower fabric is used, add seam allowances and join widths as necessary. Hem top edge of base as for the gathered valance.

2 **attaching the skirt matching centre of pleats to corners**

Join the skirt pieces together with French seams (1cm/½in and 1cm/½in seam allowances) to form a continuous strip working in the following order: one side piece, one pleat insert, end piece, second pleat insert and remaining side piece. Hem lower edge and short ends of skirt as for the gathered valance.

Above: Box pleats – simple but smart.

Right: Corner pleat of a plain valance.

1 Mark the finished length of each side piece and of the end piece (working from a central point) on the skirt. Use the excess between to form an inverted pleat; the pleat insert becomes the back of the pleat. Pin and tack the two pleats firmly.

2 Place skirt to base with right sides and raw edges together, matching centre of pleats to corner points of base and clipping into seam allowance on each pleat insert at the corner point. Pin, tack and stitch in place with a 1.5cm/⅝in seam. Trim down seam allowance and zigzag stitch raw edges together to neaten. Press well to complete.

Beautiful bedspreads made to measure

Frilly and feminine or bold and smart, whatever your bedroom décor, there's a style of fitted bedspread to complement it. Choose a pretty gathered style, one with a stylish box pleated skirt, or a classic design with crisp corner pleats.

It is not always easy to buy a fitted bedspread in a suitable fabric, in the style that suits your room scheme and in a size that will perfectly fit a particular bed. However, making your own bedspreads enables you to achieve a perfect fit in the style and colours of your choice.

All fitted bedcovers consist basically of a top panel that lies over the top surface of the bed and a skirt to fit around the sides. The top panel can be a feature in itself, perhaps made from quilted fabric or a co-ordinating print, but it is the skirt that has the most scope for design variations. A gathered skirt is ideal for a pretty floral print or broderie anglaise and can be trimmed with ribbons or frills. For a stylish look choose box pleats or a plain skirt with corner pleats.

Measuring up

Make up the bed with the normal amount of bedding and, if desired, the pillows. For a tailored fit over high pillows, you will need to include triangular side gussets at the top end when making up the bedspread, although this isn't necessary with a low pillow. However, rather than having a hump of pillows under the bedspread, you may prefer to measure up without them and put the pillows inside pretty daytime covers so that they lie on top of the bedspread during the day as a decorative feature.

The top panel Measure the length and width of the top of your bed and add 3cm/1¼in seam allowances to each dimension to calculate the size of top panel to cut from fabric. If the fabric is not wide enough to cut this in one piece, allow an extra 3cm/1¼in for each seam needed to join widths. Plan the seam positions carefully for the best possible visual effect, having a whole width of fabric down the centre of the panel with an equal amount added on either side rather than one join in the middle of the panel.

The skirt Measure from the top of the bed to within 1cm/½in of the floor for the finished height of the skirt and add 4.5cm/1¾in seam allowance and hem.

Measure down both long sides of the bed and across the foot end as a basis for calculating the width (the longer dimension) of the skirt.

For a gathered skirt, multiply this measurement by 1½ to allow for fullness.

For a skirt with corner pleats, measure each side separately so that seams can be positioned at the corners behind a pleat where possible. Add 40cm/16in to the measurement across the width of the bed and 20cm/8in to the length of each side to allow for pleats and side hems.

For a box pleated skirt, multiply this measurement by 2¼ for spaced pleats or by 3 for continuous pleating.

Optional side gussets Cut a right angled triangle for a paper pattern. Measure the width of the pillows and add 10cm/4in to this measurement for the long base edge of the triangle. Measure the height of the pillows when they are lying fairly flat, rather than puffed up, for the short side of the triangular gusset which lies at right angles to the base. Join these two lines with a curved line that follows the shape of the pillows, then add 1.5cm/⅝in seam allowance all round.

Estimating fabric requirements

Draw out a small scale plan (eg 1cm/½in representing 10cm/4in) of the top panel, side gussets (if any) and skirt.

If your fabric is plain or has a design such as a stripe that can be used sideways to good effect, cut the skirt in one piece along its length to avoid seams. If this would prove uneconomical or if a patterned fabric must be used the right way up, join widths to make up the skirt. You may also have to join widths for the top panel. Subtracting 3cm/1¼in from each fabric width to allow for seams, mark out seam positions to estimate how many widths of fabric are needed for each piece.

Multiply the number of widths by the length to calculate the amount of fabric needed for each piece. Make sufficient allowance for matching patterns when either the top panel or the skirt must be made from more than one width of fabric. After buying your fabric and lining (if you choose to use it), thread is the only other requirement.

Cutting out

Each bedspread consists of a top panel and skirt. Cut out the necessary number of widths to make up each piece to the size calculated by measuring up, allowing for pattern matching.

Right: The simple styling of the straight-skirted bedspread with corner pleats emphasizes the bold stripes of a crisp cotton fabric.

Left: Insert fabric-covered piping cord in the seam around the top panel to add a professional finish to a pretty gathered bedspread.

machine stitches as gathering stitches 1cm/³⁄₈in and 1.5cm/⁵⁄₈in down from the top edge. Do not stitch the gathering threads in one continuous length as they would then be impossible to pull up: stitch for lengths of about 60cm/24in and gather up the skirt in sections.

Joining top panel and skirt
With right sides facing, pin the two side edges of the skirt to the top (head) end of the top panel and pin the centre of the skirt to the centre of the bottom edge of the top panel, matching tailor's tacks. Pull up the gathering threads until the skirt fits around the three sides of the top panel, with even gathering all along. Pin, tie off threads securely, tack, and then stitch the skirt in place. Clip into the seam allowance on the curved corners to ease the fabric, if necessary. Remove tacking and press seam.

Bedspread with gathered skirt

The top panel of the bedspread can be lined for extra weight and warmth. Alternatively use a ready-quilted fabric for the top panel and the matching unquilted version for the skirt.

Making up
Take 1.5cm/⁵⁄₈in seam allowances for flat seams, 5mm/¼in then 1cm/³⁄₈in for French seams.

Preparing the top panel Join fabric widths, if necessary, to make up the top panel. Use French seams if the top panel will be unlined, flat seams if it will be lined. Trim the two lower corners of the top panel to a gentle curve, using an object such as a saucer as a guide to ensure that both corners are the same. Mark the centre of the lower edge with a tailor's tack.

If lining is required, cut out, make up and trim to the same size. If the bedspread is to be unlined, zigzag stitch round the three sides of the panel, omitting the top end, to neaten.

Adding side gussets If including these, zigzag along the two longer sides to neaten, and, with right sides together, stitch a curved edge to each side edge at the top of panel, as in the diagram. Treat the base of the side gusset as the new edge of the top panel. If lining the top panel, join side gussets to lining in the same way.

Preparing the skirt Using French seams, join the skirt pieces together to make one continuous length. Zigzag stitch along the top edge to neaten and mark the centre of the top edge with a tailor's tack. Insert two rows of the largest

Completing the bedspread
Turn 5mm/¼in and then 1cm/½in to the wrong side to make a hem along the skirt sides and panel top edge and stitch. Turn 1.5cm/⁵⁄₈in and then 1.5cm/⁵⁄₈in to the wrong side to make a double hem along the bottom edge of the skirt and stitch.

To line the top panel press 1.5cm/⁵⁄₈in seam allowance to the wrong side all round the lining, clipping into the seam allowance on the curved corners. Press the top panel/skirt seam towards the top panel and pin the lining and top panel together, wrong sides facing, enclosing all seam allowances. Slipstitch by hand all round the edge of the lining to attach it to the top panel.

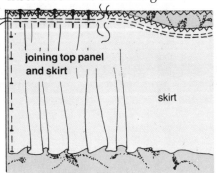

adding side gussets
snip edge of base and spread to fit curve
gusset

joining top panel and skirt
skirt

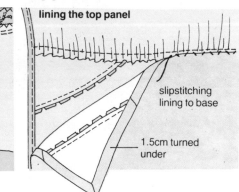

lining the top panel
slipstitching lining to base
1.5cm turned under

Fitted bedspread with corner pleats

Make this unlined, fully lined or line just the top panel. Use French seams (5mm/¼in and 1cm/⅜in) for joining widths of fabric on any parts that will be unlined to eliminate raw edges. Otherwise, use 1.5cm/⅝in flat seams.

Making up

Prepare the top panel as for the bedspread with a gathered skirt but, before curving the corners, draw a short chalkline at 45° to each of the lower corners. Curve away just the very tip of the corners.

To mark the pleat position measure 1.5cm/⅝in from the curved edge along the diagonal chalkline and mark with a tailor's tack.

Join the side gussets, if needed, to the top panel as before.

Prepare any lining required for the top panel in the same way.

Prepare skirt by joining widths where necessary to make side and end panels (see Measuring up, page 312). Join a side panel to both short ends of the end panel to make a continuous strip with a side, end, side sequence of panels.

If you are lining the skirt, cut out and join pieces of lining fabric to the same size as the fabric skirt. Place fabric and lining wrong sides facing and tack together along the top edge. From now on, treat the skirt fabric and lining as one.

Mark the exact centre of the top edge of the end panel with a tailor's tack. Also mark the centre of the

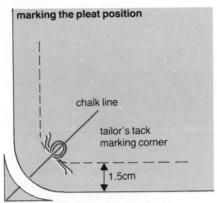

marking the pleat position

chalk line

tailor's tack marking corner

1.5cm

lower edge of the top panel with a tailor's tack.

Joining skirt and top panel

With right sides facing and matching the two central tailor's tacks, pin the end panel of the skirt to the lower edge of the top panel as far as the corner tacks.

With the top edge of the top panel and the short side edge of the skirt together, pin the long side edges of panel and skirt together as far as the corner tack, so that the surplus skirt fabric lies on top of the skirt at the lower corners.

To form the corner pleats, fold the surplus fabric at each corner into an inverted pleat, with the centre lying on the corner tack. Clip into the seam allowance on the back part of the pleat so that it will spread around the curved corner. Tack and stitch the skirt in place, catching down the pleats. Neaten the raw edges of this seam unless the top panel is to be lined.

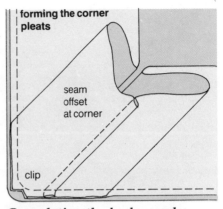

forming the corner pleats

seam offset at corner

clip

Completing the bedspread

Complete an unlined bedspread, or one that has the top panel only lined, in the same way as one with a gathered skirt, adding a lining to the top panel if required.

Complete a fully lined bedspread by pressing a 1.5cm/⅝in turning to the wrong side along the head (top) end of the bedspread (ie skirt sides and top panel). Trim the side edges of the skirt lining so that they lie almost on the fold, tucked under the fabric turning. Turn in the raw edge of the fabric again to make a 1cm/⅜in hem right across head end of bedspread and stitch.

Turn up a double hem (1.5cm/⅝in and 1.5cm/⅝in) around the lower edge of the skirt, trimming and tucking in the lining edge as before, and mitring the corners for neatness. Attach lining to top panel as for the bedspread with gathered skirt.

Bedspread with box pleated skirt

10cm/4in is a good average size for box pleats whether spaced 10cm/4in apart or butted together.

Making up

Cut out and prepare the top panel as for the bedspread with gathered skirt, with side gussets if needed.

Join the skirt pieces into one continuous strip with French seams. Zigzag stitch the top edge to neaten and mark the centre of this edge.

Turn up a double hem (1.5cm/⅝in and 1.5cm/⅝in) along the bottom edge and tack. Rule a vertical chalkline 5cm/2in either side of the central tailor's tack and then every 10cm/4in along the entire length of

the valance. Using these lines as a guide, press in and tack each pleat, spaced or butted.

Joining skirt to top panel. With right sides together and matching centre tailor's tacks, tack the skirt to the top panel, clipping into the seam allowance around curves. If necessary, adjust the pleats or the spaces between at each end of the skirt so that you do not end with part of a pleat, then trim the short ends of the skirt to level them up with the edge of the top panel. Stitch round 1.5cm/⅝in in to join skirt and top panel.

Completing the bedspread

Turn in a double hem (5mm/¼in

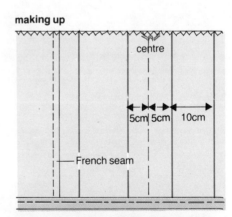

making up

centre

5cm 5cm 10cm

French seam

and 1cm/½in) along the head edge of the bedspread, mitring the corners with the lower hem, and tack. Machine stitch the hem all round the bedspread to complete. Line the top panel, if required.

Practical and decorative fabric bedheads

If you can sew a cushion cover, you can make yourself a striking new bedhead. Simply make up a gusseted cushion incorporating hanging tabs and suspend it from a decorative rail above your bed. Or make a loose quilted cover to put over an existing headboard.

As well as being functional, bedheads can also look very decorative covered in a fabric which co-ordinates with the room or adds a splash of colour.

If the bed already has a fixed headboard, you can make a slip-over cover to give it a new look. If not, you can create a bedhead by simply hanging a cushion from a wooden or brass curtain rail fixed to the wall.

Slip-over bedhead covers

These can be made for most types of fixed headboards, such as the wooden ones normally supplied on a divan bed or padded ones which have become worn or soiled. The bedhead can be any shape, you will have to make a paper pattern of the bedhead before cutting out the fabric for the cover if it is not simply rectangular.

Slip-over covers look best made in quilted fabric as this disguises any indentations in the original bedhead and is more comfortable to lean against. If you buy ready-quilted fabric, making the cover is a very simple matter. However, if you wish to match the cover to curtains or bedding, you can quilt your own fabric.

Hanging bedheads

These are suitable for divans without headboards. To make a hanging bedhead, fix a brass or wooden curtain pole to the wall and hang a cushion – or a pair of cushions – from it.

The pole, measured between end stops, should be at least as wide as the bed. To position it on the wall, sit up in bed and mark the point on the wall where the cushions should be. (You should be able to rest your head in the centre of the cushion.) The pole should be about 6cm/2½in above top edge of cushion to allow for tabs.

You need only one cushion for a single bed. For a double bed, choose either a pair of cushions or one long one. Each cushion will require at least three hanging tabs, an extra-long cushion for a double bed five or more, depending on the width of the bed.

Types of cushion This chapter gives instructions for making two styles of cushion. A solid foam block with a gusseted cover gives a firm long-lasting bedhead with a smartly tailored look; a cushion without a gusset, filled with wadding, feathers or foam chips, is simpler to make and just as decorative, but offers less support. The width of the cushion should correspond to the pole width and is generally the width of the bed. For a pair of cushions, deduct 5cm/2in from the pole width to allow for the central gap, then divide the measurement in half for the finished width of each cushion.

Cushions can look attractive slightly inset each side of the bed, in which case cut down your measurements accordingly.

Left: To quilt your own headboard cover choose a suitable design such as this floral trellis pattern and quilt along the printed lines and round flower shapes. Below: A slip-on cover made to match a quilted bedspread.

A quilted slip-over bedhead cover

Transform an old-fashioned bedhead with a simple-to-make quilted cover. The instructions given below are for a gusseted cover, but if the wood of your bedhead is thinner than 5mm/⅜in, omit the gusset.

You will need

Enough quilted fabric to cut the front, gusset strip and (optional) the back of the bedhead cover
or fabric and wadding to quilt yourself
Plain fabric for the back of the cover if not using quilted
Matching thread
50cm/½yd strong cotton tape for the ties
Paper to make pattern
Bias binding if required

Making a pattern

Stick together enough large sheets of paper from which to cut the headboard pattern. If the headboard is easily removed from the bed (most simply bolt or screw into place), lay it on the paper and draw round the shape. If you cannot remove the headboard, use very accurate measuring to draw up the pattern. Cut out the paper pattern adding an extra 1.5cm/⅝in seam allowance all round. If your headboard has supporting struts jutting out at the back, make a separate back pattern, drawing round these. Leaving a seam allowance, cut out the strut shapes. Measure the thickness of the bedhead to give the gusset width. Measure up both sides and around or across the top, following any shaping, to give the gusset length. Add seam allowances all round.

making up

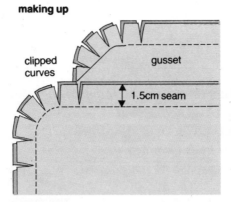

clipped curves · gusset · 1.5cm seam

attaching cover to headboard

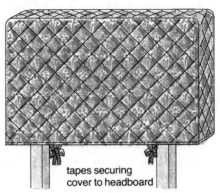

tapes securing cover to headboard

Cutting out

Cut the front and the gusset strip from quilted fabric. Cut the back from either plain or quilted fabric.
Note If you are not using ready-quilted fabric, cut a piece of fabric 10cm/4in larger all round than the front pattern piece (quilting tends to 'shrink' the fabric a little). Tack a layer of medium-weight polyester wadding to the wrong side, then machine stitch diagonal parallel lines in both directions to quilt the two layers together. When the quilting is complete, cut out a more accurate pattern piece. There is no need to quilt the back of the bedhead or the gusset strip, although you should back the gusset strip with a strip of wadding to make it look even.

Making up

If you have cut strut shapes from the back piece, neaten the edge with bias binding (see pages 320–3).
With right sides together, tack the gusset strip around the sides and top of the front cover piece. Snip into seam allowance to go round curves and corners. Stitch taking 1.5cm/⅝in seam allowance.
Tack and stitch the other side of the gusset strip to the back piece in the same way. (If you are not adding a gusset, simply place back and front pieces right sides together and stitch around sides and top.)
Carefully snip away the wadding from seam allowances to reduce bulk and clip across any corners. Trim away 1.5cm/⅝in of wadding around the open base edge, then turn the unbacked fabric over to the wrong side and turn in the raw edge to make a double hem. Stitch the hem and turn the whole cover to the right side.

Attaching cover to headboard

Cut the cotton tape into four and attach two lengths to the base edge of front piece of cover and two lengths to correspond on the back piece. Position them just inside the supporting struts of the bedhead. Slip the cover over the bedhead an tie back and front tapes together in a double bow. The cover will remain securely in place but is easily removed for laundering.

Solid foam bedhead cushion

Read pages 90-93 first for detailed instructions on cutting out and making a gusseted cushion cover to cover a block of foam.
Foam suppliers will cut foam blocks to the exact size you require; 4cm/1½in is a suitable depth for the foam, but this can be varied according to choice and the distance of the pole from the wall. To prolong the life of the foam, make an inner cover from calico in the same way as a gusseted cushion cover, slipstitching it on to the foam block.

You will need

Foam block 4cm/1½in thick cut to the required size
Enough fabric to cover back, front and side strips of foam and to make tabs
The same amount of calico minus tabs
Thread
Hanging pole and fixings

Cutting out

Using the foam block as a guide, make paper patterns. You will need a front and a back, four gusset strips to fit top, bottom and side edges, and at least two tab strips for the cushion. Each tab consists of two strips 10cm×20cm/4in×8in plus seam allowances. Add 1.5cm/⅝in seam allowance round all pieces before cutting out.

Making up

Place two tab pieces right sides facing and stitch down the two long edges. Turn right side out and press. Repeat to make all the tabs.

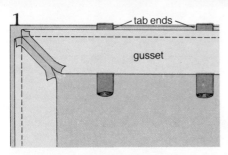

1

tab ends

gusset

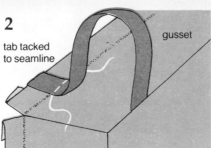

2

tab tacked
to seamline

gusset

Above: Piped seams add a professional finish to an attractive pair of hanging bedhead cushions. Choose a fabric to match or co-ordinate with your curtains and bedding.

1 Tack one end of each of the tabs into position on the right side of the front piece, raw edges together. Join the short edges of the gusset strips to form a continuous strip,

leaving 1.5cm/⅝in unstitched at each end of each seam. With right sides together, stitch gusset to front piece, enclosing tab ends.
2 Tack the free end of each tab to the

seamline on the opposite edge of the top gusset.
Tack the back piece to the gusset and stitch round except along lower edge, making sure that only the tab ends are caught in the stitching. Clip corners, trim seams and turn right side out. Press well, insert the foam block and slipstitch opening.

Tablecloth, mats and matching napkins

To complement both china and furnishings, a tablecloth, placemat and napkin set is quick and easy to sew. To add colour contrast, the edges of the cloth and mats can be trimmed with bias binding, and the napkins made in a plain colour.

Whether you create family meals most of the time or entertain regularly, you'll still be keen to put on a good show with a table setting.

A square or rectangular tablecloth always looks handsome and helps to unify the look of a table and will also cover up a worn table top. If possible, choose a washable fabric that requires a minimum of ironing.

Placemats can be used on their own or can be teamed with a tablecloth and laundered separately if the cloth itself is not soiled.

Napkins should be a generous size to give plenty of cover. Bear in mind that reversible fabrics look better than fabrics only printed on one side.

Colour planning

The fabric chosen for the tablecloth and mats (photographed right) is a good example of the versatility of table-linen in colour co-ordination. It is checked in primary colours on a white background and the edges of the cloth and placemats are finished with bright blue bias binding, picking up one of the primary colours from the checks. The napkins are made in a plain blue to match the blue on the main fabric and to co-ordinate with the bias binding trim.

All corners on the checked tablecloth and placemats are mitred to give a neat accurate 90° square without bulkiness. Alternatively, corners can be rounded and edged with bias binding, or can be finished with a turned-under hem.

As another variation, the placemats can be made up in a ready-quilted fabric to give a softer look. (Polyester wadding used in ready quilted fabrics gives only minimal heat insulation, so use cork mats underneath with hot plates.) Napkins can be made up in plain fabric and trimmed round the edges with bias binding cut from strips of the same fabric used for the cloth, mats or other furnishings.

Remember when using a fabric tablecloth and fabric placemats that the fabric will not protect your table from hot dishes and plates. With tablecloths you need a layer of heat-resistant protective material such as an old blanket or Bulgomme (heat resistant rubberised cotton) between the cloth and table top.

Measuring up

The tablecloth Measure your table top and add an overhang all round. As a rule the cloth should overhang the table to the height of the chair seats.

In many cases, especially if you have a family-sized dining table, standard-width furnishing fabrics are not wide enough to make a cloth without a fabric join. For a centre seam, join two fabric widths together with a flat seam, and cut an equal amount from each width to make up the cloth size so that the seam lies exactly across the centre of the table. Alternatively, to avoid bumps on the table top, join the fabric with a whole width in the centre and a part width either side.

With the bias binding method of finishing raw edges, you need not add any seam allowance to the cloth measurements. For hemmed edges, add 2cm/¾in all round.

Placemats should either be large enough to take a complete place setting or just a dinner plate. (Plates are usually 25cm/10in diameter, but measure your own.) For raw edges finished with bias binding, you need

not add any seam allowances, but for hemmed mats, add 2cm/¾in all round to placemat measurements.

Napkins can be any size but 30cm/12in is a good standard size. Add 2cm/¾in all round the napkin for a hem.

The bias binding Measure all round adding 2.5cm/1in for joining.

Right: The tablecloth and placemats have been made up in the same fabric and are trimmed with co-ordinating bias binding. The napkins match the binding.

Below: This placemat, trimmed with bias binding and co-ordinated with a plain-coloured napkin, is large enough to accommodate a dinner plate and cutlery.

Attaching bias binding to straight edges

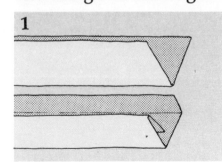

These instructions are for 25mm/
1in-width bias binding which is the
most suitable for trimming
tablecloths and mats.
1 Fold the bias binding in half along
the length, wrong sides facing. On
each long raw edge turn 5mm/¼in to
wrong side. Press. (Most commercial

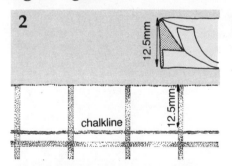

bias bindings are pre-pressed in this
way, and you only need to complete
this step when you make your own
bias binding strips.)
2 Measure between the centre fold
line and one of the outer fold lines.
Using this figure, measure in from
the raw edge of the mat or cloth and

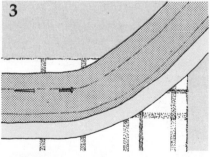

chalk a line along the right side of the
fabric at this depth.
3 Lay the fabric and bias binding
right sides facing, pinning one outer
edge fold line of the binding to the
chalk-marked line on the fabric.
Pin along one side of the
square/rectangle to the corner.

Mitring square corners with bias binding

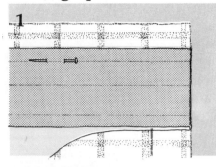

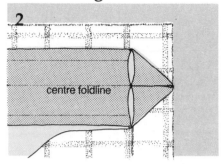

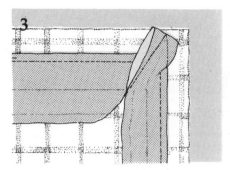

With tailor's chalk, mark a vertical line on the bias binding to correspond with the raw edge of the fabric corner. Unpin a few centimetres of binding.
1 Right sides facing, fold the binding along the line you've marked.

2 Fold in each side at a 45° angle, on to the centre fold line. Press and then open out again.
3 Hand sew along the pressed lines. Pin binding to fabric as far as chalk-marked corner on fabric. Turn corner, making sure none of the

corner binding is trapped. Continue pinning, mitring each corner, then tack. If binding needs joining, tack to within 5cm/2in of join.
4 To join the two ends of the binding, cut one end of binding to a 45° angle. Butt the other end of binding to the

Finishing curved corners with bias binding

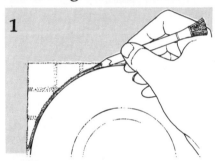

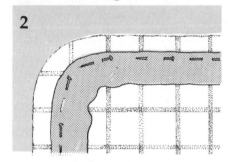

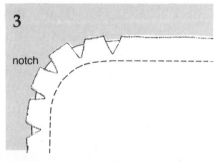

1 To make a rounded corner on a mat experiment by drawing round drinking glasses or saucers to get the curve you want. For a tablecloth, a dinner plate will give a larger curve.
2 Pin the bias to the raw edges of the mat or cloth in the same way as for the square-edged mats but, on the

corners, gently ease the binding to follow the shape of the curve. (Because this binding is cut on the bias (cross) of the fabric, it has a natural stretch which allows it to be eased into shape.) Tack in place, then sew. Remove tacking.

3 If the curve of the fabric is very tight, notch the main fabric almost to the stitching line to give more stretch to the fabric.
Continue to attach the binding in the same way as for the square-edged mats.

Cutting your own binding

Commercially produced bias binding comes in a wide range of plain colours but, if you want a specific colour or pattern to tone with your other furnishings, you can cut bias strips from fabric, and join the strips to make a continuous length of bias binding.
1 To find the bias (cross) of the fabric, lay the piece of fabric flat and fold over one corner at a 45° angle to the selvedge (or lengthwise grain of the fabric). The diagonal fold line is the bias.

Left: The placemat is made in ready-quilted fabric for extra body and the napkins edged with matching bias strips.

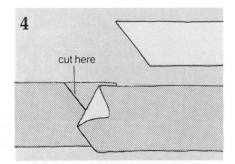

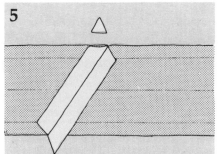

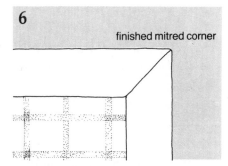

angled piece, overlapping by 1cm/
½in on the shortest edge. Cut a
complementary angle that overlaps
the first by 1cm/½in.
5 Right sides facing, tack the two
pieces together with 5mm/¼in seams
and hand sew. Press flat. Cut off

excess triangular corners from the
seam allowance. Tack this loose
length of binding along the chalk
line. Sew binding in place along the
chalk line and remove tackings.
Turn binding to wrong side of fabric
so that centre binding fold is exactly

on the raw edge of the fabric. Turn
each corner with care.
6 The corners will be square, with a
diagonal stitching line (the mitred
corner). Tack binding in place on the
reverse side of the fabric, then slip
stitch. Remove all tackings.

Mitring corners

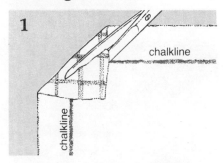

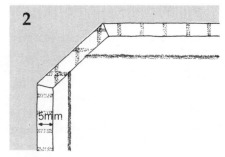

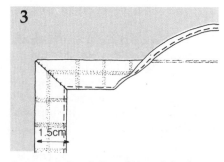

As an alternative to bias binding, and
for the napkins, fabric edges can be
neatened with a hem and mitred
corners.
When measuring up, allow an extra
2cm/¾in all round. With tailor's
chalk, mark a foldline all round
on the wrong side, 2cm/¾in from

the raw fabric edges.
1 Fold each corner at 45° until the
diagonal touches the point where
the foldlines meet. Cut off the
folded corner leaving 5mm/¼in of
the hem allowance.
2 On the straight edges and corners
turn in 5mm/¼in and tack. Now turn

in remaining 1.5cm/⅝in of the hem
allowance on the sides, along the
foldline.
3 The corners fold to make a diagonal
join (mitre). Tack hem and corners.
Slip stitch diagonal mitre joins and
sew hem by machine, or slip stitch by
hand. Remove tackings.

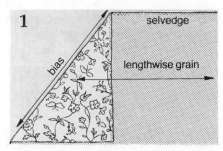

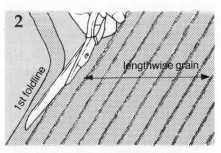

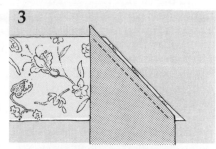

2 Mark this foldline with a ruler and
tailor's chalk, then mark a series of
parallel lines. These should be 3.5cm/
1½in apart if you want 2.5cm/1in
finished-width bias binding. For
other widths of binding, take the
finished binding width and add
1cm/½in (5mm/¼in to each edge for

folding to wrong side) and mark your
parallel lines to this width.
3 Join the strips by placing two
lengths at 90°, right sides facing, so
the two diagonals match, leaving an
equal amount of triangular-shaped
fabric each side of the seamline.
Tack. Check the two lengths are level

with each other and, if necessary,
adjust the seam to level the pieces.
Sew with a 5mm/¼in seam. Press
seam open and clip off extending
triangular shapes. Press 5mm/¼in
to wrong side down each long edge,
then fold the binding in half along
the length and press.

Circular tablecloths

Pretty circular cloths not only protect a table – they enhance it, providing an effective way of complementing a decoration scheme or livening up one that needs a little extra dash and style. Here are instructions for making long and short versions plus a topcloth for either.

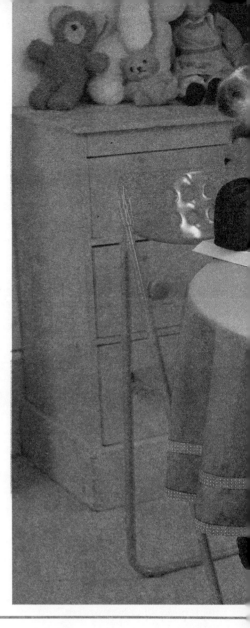

Circular tablecloths are not simply a means to protect a table surface or to conceal a less than perfect one. They also provide a charming way to co-ordinate colours and patterns in decorating schemes.

Don't be deterred by the prospect of cutting a perfect circle of fabric. Simply fold the fabric into four, as shown below, and mark just a quarter of the fabric. Then cut through all layers and you will have a perfect circle.

Measuring up for a short cloth

Measure from the centre point of the table, across the table top and down over the edge to the desired drop. For a short cloth, an average drop is 25-30cm/10-12in from the table top or to just reach a chair seat.

Double this measurement (to give you the diameter) and add 2cm/¾in hem allowance.

Choose the widest possible fabric so that you can cut this cloth in one piece. If joins are unavoidable, make them at the edges of the cloth, not at the centre (see page 326).

Measuring up for a long cloth

Measure from the centre point of the table, across the table top and down to the floor. It is easier if you have help with this stage. If not, weight the tape measure down on the table top and take care not to move it as you measure downwards.

Double this measurement (to give you the diameter) and add 2cm/¾in hem allowance.

Unless you choose a very wide fabric, you will have to join two widths to make up the total diameter. For a really large table, you may need to join three widths.

Right: Strong, plain colours can be both practical and eye-catching.

Cutting out and making up a short cloth

Cut out a square of fabric to the final measurement (diameter plus hem allowance).

1 Fold the fabric in half lengthways, right sides facing, and then in half again widthways, wrong side facing. Lay the folded fabric flat on the floor, or on a table. Pin the edges together, then tack all round to hold the four layers securely together.

Tie a length of string round a short pencil and measure the string to half the diameter plus hem allowance measurement (as above). Tie a single knot in the string to mark the exact length required. Push the drawing pin through the knot and into the folded fabric at the innermost corner (the one with only folded edges). To protect your flooring or table, place a thick piece

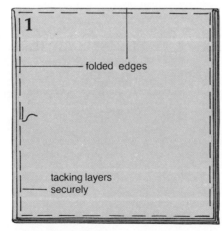

of card or a cork mat under the fabric corner.

If the fabric is particularly fine, use a map pin with a fine point, in preference to a drawing pin.

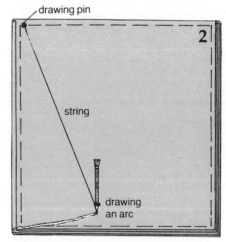

2 Keeping the string taut and the pencil upright, draw a pencil line on the fabric from one corner to another, forming an arc. Remove the drawing pin and string. Tack along the curve just inside the pencil line, through all four thicknesses.

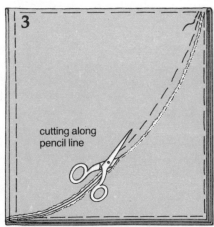

3 Cut out the fabric along the marked pencil line. Remove the tacking, and open out the fabric. To finish the raw hem edge, either make a double hem, or make a single hem with bias binding to give stretch on the curve.

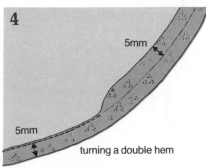

turning a double hem

4 To make a double hem, turn 5mm/ ¼in and then a further 5mm/¼in to the wrong side and tack in place. Slipstitch by hand, or machine stitch. Do not be tempted to make a deeper hem than 5mm/¼in, as the curve will pucker.

5 To make a hem with bias binding, use 13mm/⅝in width bias binding. Right sides facing, and raw edges matching, sew one long edge of the binding to the hem edge with a

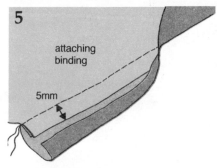

5mm/¼in seam allowance. Press seam towards the binding. Turn binding to the wrong side of fabric and fold remaining long edge of binding to the wrong side by 5mm/¼in (if not pre-folded when purchased). Tack binding in place. The natural stretch in the bias binding will ease the hem in to place without puckering. Stitch binding in place by machine, or by hand using slipstitch.

Cutting out and making up the long cloth

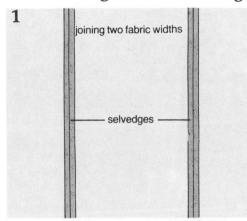

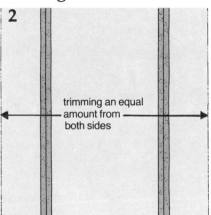

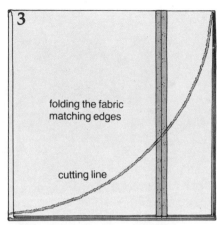

If you have chosen a wide-width fabric, cut a square of fabric to the final measurement (diameter plus hem allowance).

1 If you cannot cut the total square from one piece, cut two (or possibly three for a large table) widths of fabric equivalent to the diameter plus the hem measurement, matching the pattern if necessary. If you have to use two fabric widths, cut one of them in half along its length and tack one to either side of the complete fabric

piece with selvedges together. (This is so that you do not have an unsightly join in the middle of your cloth.) Sew together with 1.5cm/⅝in seams. Press the seams flat, or make fell seams.

If you have to join three pieces of fabric, take 1.5cm/⅝in seams. Press the seams flat, or make fell seams.

2 To adjust the *total* width of the joined fabric to the diameter plus hem allowance measurement required for the cloth, trim an *equal* amount from each side piece of

fabric, remembering to allow 2cm/¾in for a hem. Your fabric will now be a square.

3 Fold the square of joined fabric (or single fabric if you have used a wide width) into four, matching the edges together.

Cut the fabric in a curve to half the diameter plus hem measurement and make up in the same way as for the short circular cloth.

Below: A long cloth looks particularly pretty with a deep, bound ruffle.

A topcloth for emphasis

A square or round topcloth used with a long circular cloth can be made in a contrasting or co-ordinating fabric for extra emphasis.

Cut the topcloth from one piece of fabric to avoid unattractive joins. The raw edges can either be hemmed or given a decorative finish.

Place the long circular cloth on your table and measure the size for the topcloth – this will depend on personal choice – what looks best for the proportions of your table and for the fabric you've used for the cloth. As a general guide, a topcloth should be about 10cm/4in larger than the diameter of the table.

Square or round topcloth Cut a square or circle of fabric to size, allowing 1cm/½in for hems all round. Turn a double hem (5mm and 5mm/¼in and ¼in) all round to wrong side, mitring each corner on a square cloth. Tack, then machine stitch or slipstitch by hand. Remove tacking.

Right: Beautiful tablecloths transform a simple table into a design feature.

Decorative hem finishes

These finishes for hems are very effective applied to the edge of a topcloth, but they can also decorate the hem of a short or long circular cloth.

A border, whether in a plain or patterned fabric, accentuates shape and colour. For a square topcloth, you can use a ready-made fabric border or cut your own strips of fabric.

Cut four lengths of border fabric and join them together with mitred corners. Turn the border edges to the wrong side all round and press. Hem the cloth and apply the border to the topside of the cloth, topstitching in place. For a border round the hem of a short or long circular cloth, the border fabric must be cut on the cross (bias) to give the necessary stretch round the curve of the hem.

Motifs, particularly flower shapes, make a very pretty edging on a cloth. Hem the cloth. Then appliqué the motifs on to the edge of the cloth, or sew to the cloth so that they overhang the edge. Cut out the motif shapes, tack in place on the cloth and satin stitch or machine zigzag all round the raw edges.

A bound ruffle is particularly decorative. Hem the cloth. Then cut strips of fabric the required width of ruffle and join to form a strip at least one and a half times the circumference of cloth. Bind both long edges and join short edges to form a circle. Run a double gathering thread along ruffle, draw up to fit cloth edge and topstitch in place along gathering lines.

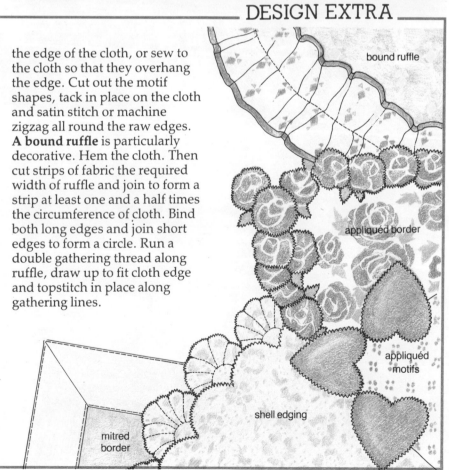

bound ruffle

appliquéd border

appliquéd motifs

shell edging

mitred border

Decorative fitted tablecloths made to measure

Update a dull room by covering a small table in a strikingly pretty, ruffled cloth and using it to display plants, flowers or a collection of favourite items. A fitted, skirted cloth, whether round or square, has endless scope for design variations.

Make a pretty, gathered tablecloth to transform an old table into an attractive piece of furniture, ideal for displaying plants, photographs, lamps or ornaments. If you are unable to find a suitable table lurking in the loft or a junk shop, inexpensive chipboard tables, usually small and circular, are available from many mail order firms.

Making the cloth from two pieces – the shaped top and gathered skirt – enables you to achieve a perfect fit, whatever size and shape your table. It can also be a more economical use of fabric than making a full-length cloth from one complete circle or rectangle, and gives endless scope for design variations.

A deep hem ruffle gives a rich, flounced effect but could be replaced by contrasting bands of fabric, lace insertions or frills, tucks, braid or edge trimmings. To emphasize a

Below: On a ruffled circular cloth, piping and binding in ivory satin trim a subtly patterned, crisp glazed cotton. The overall effect is extremely pretty without being over 'fussy'.

highly patterned fabric, it could, of course, simply be omitted.

The seam between top and skirt also gives scope for adding decorative extras: choose anything from simple piping to a ruched valance or a flamboyant, swagged frill.

Choosing fabrics

The best fabrics to use are those which are washable and easy-care, so a cotton and synthetic mixture, such as polyester/cotton sheeting, is ideal. Seersucker, gingham, lawn, calico, dressweight cottons and lightweight curtain fabrics are equally suitable, but may need more careful ironing! Check whether your material is shrink-resistant, and if not, wash it first, before cutting out. Also ensure that any decorative trimmings are washable, shrink-resistant and colour-fast. Cotton piping cord – as opposed to ready-made piping – should always be pre-shrunk by washing.

Measuring up

Measuring area of table top If the table is circular measure the diameter, add on 4cm/1½in for seams and allow a square of fabric to this size. If the top is square or rectangular, measure length and width and add 4cm/1½in to each dimension.
For the skirt length, measure from the table top to 1cm/½in above the floor and add 2cm/1in for the top seam allowance and a further 2cm/1in lower hem allowance. If adding a frill or ruffle, deduct ¼-⅓ of the skirt length for this before adding seam allowances to both pieces.
Estimate skirt fullness by multiplying by 1½ the circumference of a round tabletop (or the sum of the four sides for a square or rectangular table) and then adding 4cm/2in for seams. The fullness of a frill or ruffle should be 1¼-1½ times this calculated measurement.

To estimate fabric requirements with the least wastage, draw out a rough plan of the cutting layout. With some fabric designs, it may be possible to cut the skirt piece (and frill) down the length of the fabric to avoid seams. If not, and you need to join widths of fabric, allow for extra seams and pattern matching.

Cutting out and making up

Cut out the top piece and required number of skirt and ruffle pieces.
To cut out a circular top piece, fold the square of fabric to a quarter of its size and draw an arc from corner to corner as for a short circular tablecloth (see pages 324–5) before cutting the exact circle. With the fabric still folded in four, cut a small inwards notch in the folded edges of the two outer corners to mark the quarter points of the circle.

Making up

Matching patterns if necessary and with French seams (8mm and 1.2cm/⅜in and ⅝in turnings), join short sides of skirt piece(s) to form a circle. Similarly join ruffle pieces into a circle. Turn up and stitch a double 1cm/½in hem around lower edge of skirt and both long edges of ruffle. (Alternatively, omit seam allowances on ruffle and bind the edges.)
For circular and square cloths, fold the skirt piece into four and mark the quarter points by notching into seam allowance of top edge. Matching these notches to those in the circular top, or to the corners of a square top, will ensure an even amount of fullness on each side. For rectangular cloths, notch the half-way points to correspond with opposite corners, then mark remaining corners according to the ratio between long and short sides. Insert a double row of gathering stitches between each pair of notches 2cm and 1.5cm/¾in and ½in from top edge.
Adding ruffle Insert a double row of gathering stitches, in easy-to-draw-up sections, about 2.5cm/1in from top edge of ruffle and pull up to fit lower edge of skirt. Topstitch ruffle to edge of skirt.

Joining skirt to top

If piping is required, tack it around the seamline (2cm/¾in in) of the top piece, corded edge inwards and raw edges pointing outwards.
Pulling both threads together, draw up each section of gathering to fit the appropriate side (or quarter) of the top and even out gathers. Matching notches of skirt and top and with right sides facing, pin and tack skirt around edge of top. Machine stitch, keeping notches together and pivoting fabric around needle at corners on a square or rectangular cloth.
Remove tacking, trim seam to 1cm/½in and neaten by zigzagging or oversewing raw edges together. Press seam downwards behind skirt so that finished cloth lies smoothly.

DESIGN EXTRA

Decorative details

For a more elaborate effect, add a ruched or swagged valance to a fitted tablecloth. Simply drape an inserted frill into swags and hold with ribbon bows or use vertical lines of curtain tape to form deep ruching on a valance strip.

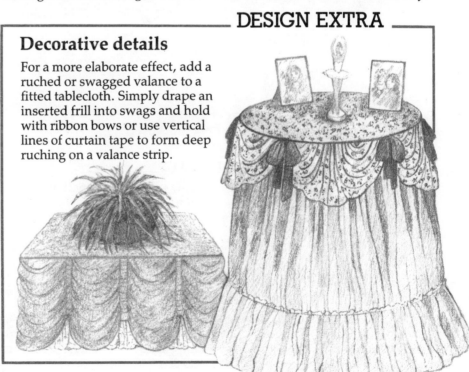

A simple slip-on lampshade

There is no complicated fitting, no special shaping, no taping and sewing to the frame – this is the simplest of lampshades to make. If you attach it to the frame by an elasticated casing at the bottom and a ribboned casing at the top, you can slip it off the frame for cleaning.

Lampshades can be expensive to buy and it is sometimes quite difficult to find exactly what you want to suit your room. The answer is to make your own, combining a frame of your choice with a fabric that co-ordinates with your colour scheme.

Lampshades are surprisingly easy to make and the slip-on style shown here is the simplest of all.

Choosing a frame

To make a simple slip-on lampshade, you will need a frame with a round or oval top and bottom ring. The top ring should be smaller in diameter than the bottom ring and the struts must be straight, or bowed out as in a tiffany. Avoid frames with a shaped or scalloped bottom.

Preparing a frame

Lampshade frames are available in plain metal or coated with white plastic. Plain metal frames must be painted, or they will rust and mark the shade.

Before painting a frame, remove any rust by rubbing down with sandpaper and file off any rough or sharp spots. Paint the struts and rings with white enamel paint, but do not paint the gimbal (the centre ring that attaches to the light bulb holder and pivots for angling the shade).

Is lining necessary?

A lining always makes the shade look neater inside, but whether or not it is necessary depends on the fabric you choose.

With a very thin fabric the light bulb may well be visible through the shade when the light is on, and a lining will solve this problem.

Medium and heavyweight fabrics, particularly in darker colours, should not need lining to conceal the light bulb, but can be lined for a professional finish.

Lining will of course add extra bulk to the shade fabric. If the top ring of the frame is very much smaller than the bottom, as with the large tiffany, this could make it impossible to gather up the fabric tightly enough to fit. In this case, use a lightweight lining such as lawn.

Choosing the lampshade fabric

The thinner and lighter the fabric, the more light will penetrate through the shade. A thick, dark fabric will throw the light from the top and bottom of the shade. If the shade has a narrow top and a wide bottom it will throw a pool of light and be ideal for hanging over a dining table.

You will need

A lampshade frame
Fabric to make the shade
Matching sewing thread
Elastic for the bottom casing
Ribbon for the top casing

Right: A large tiffany shade on a hanging pendant is ideal for lighting a working or eating area. The shade can be made up in a fabric to match furnishings such as curtains or tablelinen.

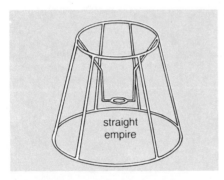

straight empire

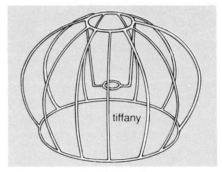

tiffany

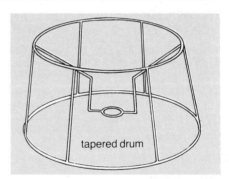

tapered drum

Calculating the amount of fabric

For the amount of fabric needed, measure the height of your frame following the curve or slope of the side (A). To this measurement add 4cm/1½in at the top for the casing (B) which will form a gathered frill that stands 1cm/½in above the ring and hides it.

Add an allowance for the elasticated casing at the bottom (C). The depth of the finished bottom casing should be one fifth the height of the frame, (for a 30cm/11¾in high frame you need a 6cm/2¼in casing). So, to calculate casing allowance, double the size of the finished casing and add 5mm/¼in (D). (For a 6cm/2¼in casing add 12.5cm/4⅞in fabric allowance.) Remember that the casing at the bottom of the shade should not prevent heat escaping from the light bulb.

For the width of fabric needed, measure the circumference of your lampshade at the widest point and add 2cm/¾in for seam allowance.

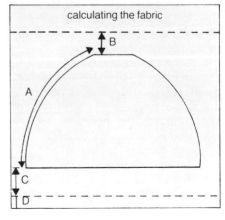

calculating the fabric

Making up the shade

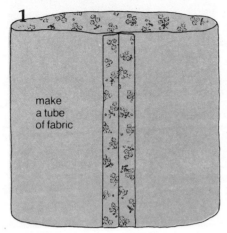

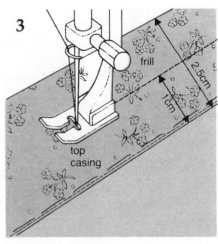

Cut out a piece of fabric to the dimensions required and an identical piece in lining fabric (if applicable).

1 With right sides facing, join the fabric with a 1cm/½in seam to make a tube.

Note: If the circumference is greater than the width of your fabric, join two pieces of fabric. Measure half the circumference on the frame and add 2cm/¾in for seam allowances. Cut two pieces of fabric to these

measurements and, with right sides facing, join with a 1cm/½in seam. Repeat for the lining fabric.

For unlined shades neaten the seam edges with a machine zigzag stitch or oversew by hand. Press flat. If you are lining the lampshade fabric, make up fabric and lining in the same way, but do not neaten the seam edges.

2 Place fabric and lining wrong sides together and tack round all edges. From now on, treat the fabric

and lining as one.

3 Turn 5mm/¼in to wrong side along top edge of fabric and tack. Turn a further 2.5cm/1in to wrong side and tack.

Sew along lower edge of turn and again 1cm/½in higher up to make a casing for the ribbon. Remove tacking.

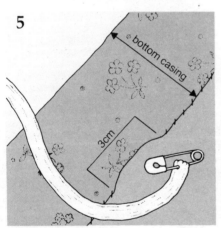

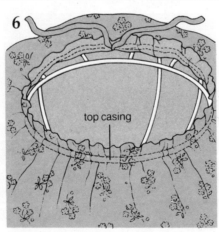

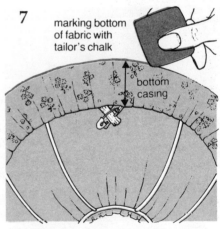

5 Slipstitch along the edge of this casing, leaving a 3cm/1¼in gap. Attach a small safety pin to one end of the elastic and thread it through bottom casing. Pin elastic ends together to secure. Measure top edge, add 20cm/7¾in, and cut a length of 4mm/¼in wide ribbon or tape to this length. Thread ribbon through the top casing as for elastic. Gently pull the fabric over the frame, aligning at least one seam with a metal strut and the top casing with the top ring of the frame.

6 Pull up the ribbon in the top casing until the fabric fits the ring, adjusting so that the gathers are even and a small 1cm/½in high frill stands above it. Knot the two ends of the ribbon around the ring to hold the fabric in place.

7 Unpin the elastic in the bottom casing and pull it up underneath the frame until the fabric is taut. Pin the elastic together.

At this point, if you are adding a frill or trim, mark the bottom point of the lampshade frame all round with a line of tailor's chalk. Untie the top ribbon and remove the fabric from the frame.

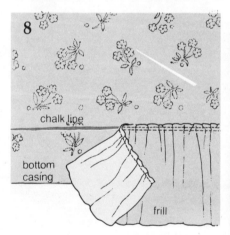

4

slot for ribbon

casing

4 With a small pair of pointed scissors, cut a slit on the inside of the casing through only one layer of fabric (and lining if applicable) just large enough to slot the ribbon through. Overcast the edges of this slit to neaten.
Turn 5mm/¼in to wrong side along bottom edge and tack, and then turn fabric again to the wrong side to the depth of the bottom casing (which you have already calculated) and tack.

Finishes for the bottom edge

The bottom of the shade can be left plain, or a sewn-on trim can look attractive. Beads can give an ethnic feel, a frill can make use of a co-ordinating fabric while lace can make your lampshade softly feminine.

To add a frill of fabric or lace, measure round the bottom of the frame and cut a piece of fabric or lace 1½ times this length. Neaten both long raw edges on frill with a double hem and join to make a circle. Gather up evenly to fit the bottom of the frame. Topstitch to the chalk-marked bottom line on the shade, see step 7 below left.
For a beaded bottom edge, calculate how many beaded fringes you need, slot beads on to thread accordingly, then neatly sew ends of threads to chalk-marked line, see step 7 below left.

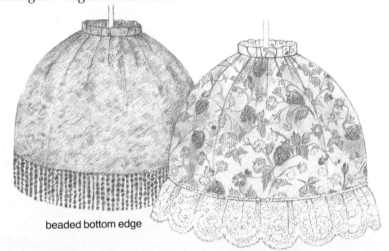

beaded bottom edge

frilled bottom edge

8

chalk line

bottom casing

frill

8 Unpin the elastic and attach the frill or trim along the chalk-marked line, taking care not to sew over the 3cm/1¼in gap left in the casing. Add the finish of your choice. Replace fabric on frame, knotting top ribbon in place and pulling bottom casing elastic up to fit. Sew the elastic together securely and cut off any surplus. Close the gap in the casing with slipstitch.

Right: The method used for the tiffany has here been adapted to make a shade for a straight empire frame.

Quick and easy shades

Make a simple but eye-catching lampshade to add the finishing touch to a newly-decorated room or to brighten a dull colour scheme. Choose the pretty handkerchief shade for an informal room, the elegant drum shade for classic styling.

It can become expensive to buy new lampshades every time you re-decorate, but don't let an old shade spoil a

Left: A handkerchief or drum shade (inset) can be made in about two hours.

new room scheme. With a piece of fabric left over from making curtains or cushions, or a pretty remnant, you can make a new shade in less than an evening.

The handkerchief shade is basically just a square or a circle of fabric draped over a utility ring or a small metal coolie shade. A circle of fabric falls into even folds, whereas a square produces the true 'handkerchief' points. Use a fairly lightweight fabric that drapes easily. and add a lacy trim for extra effect.

The drum-shaped shade is equally simple to make and requires very little fabric. Self-adhesive pelmet stiffening gives the fabric enough body to stand between two single lampshade rings.

Safety note Neither lampshade should be used with a high wattage bulb which might introduce a fire risk.

Stiffened drum lampshade

Use pvc-coated rings, choosing the appropriate fitting for the style of lamp, so that no taping is required.

You will need
Two lampshade rings of same diameter, one with lampholder
Piece of 'Pelmform' the height of shade by the circumference plus 2.5cm/1in
Rectangle of main fabric a little larger than this
Same size rectangle of lining fabric
Clear fabric adhesive
Braid trim

Making up
Ensure that Pelmform is the exact size required and that all corners are right angles. Press lining and fabric to remove creases. Place Pelmform on a flat surface and peel away protective paper from one short edge. Anchor edge of wrong side of fabric to this and smooth fabric on to Pelmform, peeling away backing as you go and taking care to keep fabric centred and wrinkle-free. Turn Pelmform over and fix lining in place in the same way. Trim edges of both fabric and lining.

Gluing overlap Place stiffened fabric around rings and hold in place close to top and bottom edges with clothes pegs, adjusting to get a good tight fit. Lightly pencil in overlap line on the inside of shade. Remove fabric from rings and trim overlap to about 1cm/½in. Apply adhesive lightly to the wrong side

of overlap end and position the other end of the shade on to it, making sure it fits true to the line. Place shade, seam down, on a flat surface and weight the seam with a strip of wood or card with a weight on top, for at least half an hour.

Gluing in the rings Position one ring inside the shade about 1cm/½in from the appropriate edge. Run a thin line of adhesive around the inside of the shade about 3mm/⅛in from the edge, push the ring back to this and hold in place with clothes pegs until the adhesive has set. Glue second ring to opposite edge in the same way.

Completing shade Stick or stitch decorative braid around the top and bottom edges of shade to neaten.

Handkerchief style lampshade

To prevent a fire risk, use a low wattage bulb and make sure that the fabric falls well away from it.

You will need
Dropped pendant lampshade ring, large utility ring or small coolie shade
Enough fabric to cover (see below)
Matching bias binding
Trimming for outer edges (optional)

Measuring up
Measuring correctly is important as the fabric should hang slightly below the bulb on all sides. Attach the ring to the lampholder, insert the bulb and measure from the central flex out to the ring and down to the base of bulb. Add at least 2.5cm/1in to this measurement and double the final figure to give the minimum size of circle or square needed: increase the size for a deeper shade. A 90cm/36in square of fabric is generally suitable for a 20cm/8in ring.

Cutting out and making up
Fold the fabric into quarters, cut a hole 3cm/1¼in in diameter from the centre as shown and mark outer line for circle, if desired.
Neaten the raw edge around centre hole with bias binding. Neaten outer edges with a narrow double hem, catching in any edge trimming as you go.

cutting line for handkerchief style lampshade

fold

cutting line for centre

folds

1.5cm

Remove bulb and ring and slip shade over the light flex. Replace ring and bulb and arrange the fabric into evenly-draped folds.

Sun-ray pleated lampshade

*One of the simplest of all lampshades to make, but also one
of the most stylish, a sun-ray pleated
lampshade is ideal for both table lamps and ceiling lights.
Make one from a remnant of fabric sprayed
with fabric stiffener to brighten a dull room.*

There's no excuse for naked light
bulbs or dull old shades: a bright and
cheerful-looking pleated shade can
be made in very little time, for very
little money.

Simply spray your fabric with an
aerosol stiffener (sold for making roller blinds), press into concertina
pleats and attach to a frame. There's
no time-consuming taping of the
frame, no complicated hand stitching, no neatening or trimming of
edges, but the finished shade can
look strikingly attractive.

Choosing fabric Any closely-woven
lightweight furnishing fabric or
heavyweight dress cotton can be
used, but avoid sheers or loose-
weave fabrics. Use left-over pieces
from curtains, cushions or loose covers to create a perfectly co-ordinated
look.

Always test fabric spray on the
wrong side of a spare piece of fabric
before treating the main piece.

Choosing a frame Making sure it has
the correct gimbal fitting for the type
of light (table lamp, pendant light or
standard lamp), choose a straight-
sided round frame of your required
size. The finished effect depends on
the frame shape. Choose one with a
silhouette to suit the base. It can be
either drum-shaped or one with
tapering sides: the method of covering is the same for either.

Alternatively, use a pair of lampshade rings as, except on a very large
frame, the stiffened fabric does not
need the support of side struts. One
ring should have the appropriate
gimbal fitting, the other being just a
plain circle. The larger the lower ring
in proportion to the top ring, the
more sloping the sides. Two rings of
the same size will produce a drum-
shaped pleated shade.

Both rings and frame should be the
pvc-coated type which needs no
finishing, as they are not taped.

You will need

Pair of lampshade rings of required
  sizes or a suitable frame, pvc-
  coated
Medium weight fabric (see below)
Roller blind fabric-stiffening spray
Length of straight rod or dowel
Clothes pegs
Strong thread (button thread)

*Right: Making your own lampshade
gives you a wide choice of colour and
design. The glowing blues and greens of
this richly printed glazed cotton ensure
a really eye-catching effect.*

Measuring up and preparing the fabric

Measure around larger ring and
double this measurement, then add
on 10cm/4in for shrinkage and
turnings. Decide on required height
of shade (or length of sloping sides)
and add 2.5cm/1in to allow for
shrinkage. Cut a rectangle of fabric
to these measurements and press to
remove creases. If more than one
piece of fabric is needed, allow a
2cm/¾in overlap.

Using clothes pegs, attach dowel to
one short edge of fabric and
suspend dowel from a clothes line
(out of doors, if possible, when
there's no wind). Spray the wrong
side of the fabric evenly all over
with fabric stiffener and allow to dry.
Remove dowel and press fabric on
wrong side. Trim fabric to required
depth of lampshade sides by double
the circumference of lower ring plus
2cm/¾in, making sure that all
corners are true right angles.

Making up the pleated shade

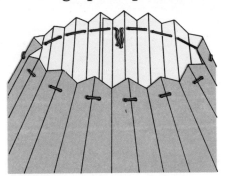

Using a medium-hot iron (and
steam if necessary), carefully press
the whole piece of fabric into 2cm/
¾in wide concertina pleats, parallel
to short edges, taking care to keep
top and bottom edges level. These
pleats form the sun-ray effect when

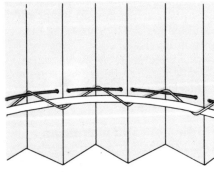

opened out.

1 Thread a large needle with a long
length of strong button thread and
work along each long side of the
shade in turn, picking up a tiny
amount of every inner pleat fold
2.5cm/1in from edge as shown.

Arrange the pleated fabric around
the large ring, overlapping the
join(s) so that the raw edges lie
inside pleats, trimming away the
end pleat sections if necessary.
When pleats fit snugly around ring,
tie ends of gathering thread
securely together.

2 Attach the pleated fabric to the
ring by whipping the gathering
thread to the ring with another
length of thread as shown, stitching
through the shade at the join to
anchor the overlap, and tying ends
securely together.

Join the top ring to shade in the
same way, then carefully distribute
the pleats evenly around the shade
to complete.

Stylish lampshades – pleated to perfection

Clever lighting can transform a room and these pretty pleated lampshades add the finishing touch. Choose a fabric to emphasize your colour scheme or to match your curtains, cushions or bedspread, for either a smart drum-shaped frame or fashionable coolie shade.

The hand-pleated method of covering lampshades can be used on any frames with sloping or straight sides. A straight drum-shaped shade is quick and easy to cover with even pleating, while a coolie shade, where the top ring is much smaller than the bottom ring, looks particularly effective because the pleats fan out from the top. Frames with bowed sides or with fancy shaping on the top or bottom edges are not suitable.

As these lampshades are unlined, choose a medium-weight fabric with a suitably dense weave. If the fabric is too thin or has an open weave the light bulb and frame will show through. Too dense and thick a fabric will be difficult to form into pleats and won't give enough light. If you do want to use a thin fabric, then you can back it with a soft or medium-weight iron-on Vilene.

The lampshade frames are covered with tape, a technique used in traditional lampshade making.

You will need
Lampshade frame
Strong white cotton tape, 13mm/ ½in wide
Fabric to cover frame
Matching sewing thread
Fabric glue
sand down any rough spots and paint the frame, except the gimbal (see page 330).

Preparing the frame
If the frame is not plastic coated, sand down any rough spots and paint the frame, except the gimbal (see page 174).

Right: An oval drum-shaped shade is pleated in the same way as a round one.

Taping the frame

This method of taping is used for any lampshade where the fabric or lining have to be stitched to the frame.
Every strut and the top and bottom rings of the frame must be taped. The tape, which is wound very tightly around the metal, acts as the securing base for the stitches that hold the fabric cover in place.
Measure all round the top and bottom rings, and along each strut (but not the gimbal) and multiply this figure by three to give the total length of tape needed.
The tape used should be a strong cotton – not bias binding – and you must be able to tug very hard on the tape without any danger of it breaking.
If you want the tape to match the colour of the inside of your fabric

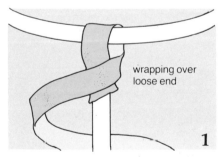

wrapping over loose end

1

(or the lining, for more complicated shades with linings) dye it with cotton fabric dye.
To start the taping, cut a piece of tape to three times the length of one of the struts.
1 Starting at the top front of one strut, wind the end of the tape over the top ring, round behind, and across to wrap over the loose end.
2 Work down the strut, wrapping the tape diagonally, so that each wrap of the tape slightly overlaps

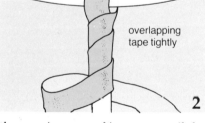

overlapping tape tightly

2

the previous one. You must pull the tape *very tightly* as you wrap – once the taping is complete it must not be able to move on the strut.
3 When you reach the bottom ring, pass the tape round the bottom ring and back through the last loop to make a knot. Leave the loose end of tape dangling for the time being. Tape each strut except one using this method.
Measure the top ring, the bottom ring and the last untaped strut and

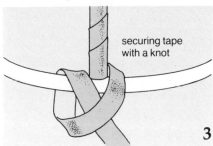

securing tape with a knot

3

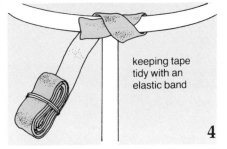

keeping tape tidy with an elastic band

4

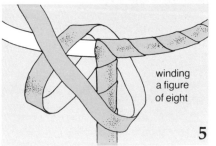

winding a figure of eight

5

cut a piece of tape three times this length.

Wind up the tape and secure it with an elastic band, leaving about 20cm/8in loose from the bundle. This will keep the tape neat as you work and you won't have to spend a lot of time untwisting it. Once the 20cm/8in is used up, free another length.

4 Start taping the top ring at the join with the untaped strut. Hold the end of the tape against the ring at this point, then wind the tape to the

inside of the ring and back over the ring again catching the loose end under it. Work right round the top ring as on the struts.

5 When you reach the join between each strut and the top ring, wind the tape round the strut and ring in a figure of eight.

When you have worked all round the top and arrived back at the untaped strut, wind round this in a figure of eight and then tape down its length. When you reach the

bottom of the strut, wind round it in a figure of eight and continue to tape the bottom ring in the same way as the top.

As you reach each bottom ring/strut join, trim off the surplus tape from the bottom of the strut leaving a 1cm/½in end. Work the figure of eight over this end to secure it.

To finish off, trim off any surplus tape to leave 5mm/⅜in. Turn this 5mm/⅜in in to the wrong side and handstitch to the bottom ring.

Cutting out the fabric

For a drum-shaped shade, measure the circumference of one ring and multiply this figure by three. For a coolie shade, measure the circumference of the larger bottom ring and multiply this figure by 1½. Add 10cm/4in to these measurements to give the total length of fabric needed.

If you have to use more than one width of fabric to make up this length, allow an extra 10cm/4in on each extra piece for joining. (Do not sew the fabric pieces together to join, they simply overlap.)

To calculate the height of fabric needed, measure along one strut and add 5cm/2in.
Cut out a piece of fabric to these measurements.
To stiffen the fabric, cut out both the fabric and iron-on Vilene slightly over size. Iron the Vilene on to the wrong side of the fabric before cutting out accurately.
The side edges of the fabric, unless selvedges, must be machine zigzagged to prevent fraying. The top and bottom edges are left raw as they are neatened with bias binding.

If you are using purchased bias binding, measure the circumference of the top ring and the bottom ring and cut a length of binding to each measurement plus 2.5cm/1in. If you are not using purchased bias binding, cut bias strips (see page 323), 4cm/1½in wide from fabric and join to make up lengths to fit the top and bottom rings plus 5cm/2in to allow for joining.

Right: By making your own lampshades you have a wider choice of colours and shapes. Neaten raw edges with bias strips to match or contrast with main colour.

Attaching fabric to a drum frame

Measure around the top ring between one strut and the next and decide on the size and number of pleats to fit within this to give a pleasing effect and to suit the fabric. *For example* if the measurement between struts is 12cm/4½in, six 2cm/¾in pleats would be suitable.
Mark with chalk an overlap allowance of one pleat from the edge of the fabric. Using tailor's chalk, mark out the pleat positions along both edges of fabric, at least for the first section, after which you may be able to pleat up by eye. For each pleat, mark its width, then twice its width for the underlap.

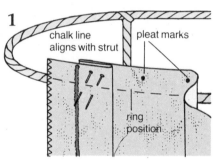

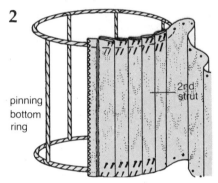

1 Keeping to the straight of grain and leaving the overlap allowance free, fold in the first pleat and pin to the frame so that the chalkline lies on a strut, and the top edge overlaps the frame top by 2.5cm/1in.

2 Pin the pleats into place around the top of frame between the first two struts, then pin round the lower edge of that section keeping pleats taut, straight and even. If lower ring is larger, adjust pleats.

Attaching fabric to a sharply sloping frame

Because of the size difference between the rings, it is necessary to measure the bottom (larger) ring to calculate the amount of fabric available for each pleat.
Measure around the bottom ring, from one strut to the next and multiply this figure by 1½.
Now measure the distance between two struts on the top ring, and decide on a visually pleasing number of pleats to fit within this. *For example* if the measurement between struts on the top ring is 6cm/2¼in, six pleats would be suitable. If the total amount of fabric available for pleating this section, taken from measuring the bottom ring, is say 30cm/12in (20cm×1½ or 8in×1½) then you have 30cm/12in of fabric in which to form six pleats between struts on the top ring. Six pleats within 30cm/12in of fabric gives you 5cm/2in for each pleat.

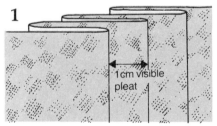

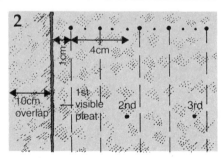

1 The pleats can be overlapped as shown, so (following through the example from above) 1cm/½in forms the visible pleat on the right side of the fabric and the other 4cm/1½in is incorporated into the back of the pleat.
This method may seem to involve a fair amount of mathematics, but it does give a professional look with very even pleating.
2 Using the figures you have calculated mark up the fabric leaving 10cm/4in for the overlap (this is tucked into the last pleat to

give a neat finish). Use tailor's chalk and mark out the pleat lines on just the first section (the total amount of fabric to be used between two struts).
If you feel skilled enough you can pin the fabric on to the frame by eye without marking the pleats first, but accurate markings, at least on the first section, give a more professional finish.
Fold the first pleat on the top edge, so that the required size of pleat is shown on the right side and the surplus is folded behind.

joining new fabric

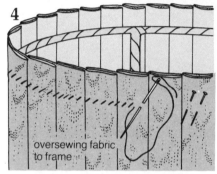

oversewing fabric to frame

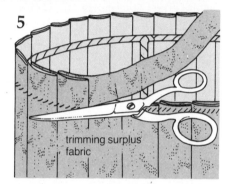

trimming surplus fabric

3 If you have to join the fabric, slip the neatened end (or selvedge) of the new fabric behind or into the last pleat so that no join is visible on the right side of the shade.

4 Oversew all round the top of the frame from the outside, making sure each pleat is firmly stitched on to the taped ring. Repeat round the bottom ring and remove all pins.

5 Trim off the surplus fabric from above the top ring and below the bottom ring, carefully cutting close to the stitching so that the fabric is flush with the frame.

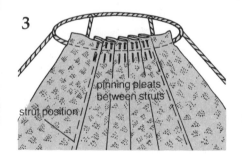

pinning pleats between struts

strut position

spacing out pleats around bottom ring

Trimming the shades

trimmed edge

attaching binding with fabric glue

3 With the overlap fabric left free, pin the pleats to the first section of the top ring as for the drum shade. The last pleat should just reach the next strut.
Check that the spacing of the pleats looks even, then mark the rest of the fabric along the top edge with the same pleating divisions.
4 Now form the same number of pleats in this first section on the bottom ring. Follow the foldline of pleats but pleat up only a tiny amount of fabric so that the pleats are very shallow. Pin them

individually to the bottom ring, making sure that the spacing is even. Pleat each section between struts in this way, pinning the pleats in place to the top and then fanning out on to the bottom ring.
If you have to add another width of fabric, slip the new piece of fabric behind the last pleat (behind several pleats on the top).
To complete the pleating, pin the last pleat over the first overlap. Oversew all round the top and bottom of the frame and trim off the surplus fabric as for the drum shade.

Press 5mm/⅜in to the wrong side on each long edge of the bias binding (this may be pre-pressed on purchased binding) and stick down with fabric glue. Allow glue to dry. Fold the binding in half, wrong sides facing, along its length, press, unfold and glue the wrong side. Stick the binding around the edges of the frame with the centre foldline over the raw edges of the fabric. Join the two ends of the bias by cutting one end at a 45° angle, turning 1cm/½in to the wrong side and lapping it over the other end.

Elegant tailored lampshades with fitted linings

A smartly tailored and lined lampshade adds a distinctive touch and is easy to make. Choose an attractive fabric – a remnant will do – to cover an empire or a drum-shaped frame and line it in a pale colour to help reflect the light or to give a warm glow.

A fitted lampshade cover with a balloon lining gives a professional and elegant effect but is surprisingly simple to make. The lining conceals the struts of the frame and helps to reflect light. It also disguises the outline of the bulb when using fine fabrics.

Almost any classic frame with a straight base edge can be used (see below), but spherical or tiffany shades are not suitable for this method.

Choosing fabrics

Soft, easily draped fabric, such as fine cotton, silk, satin and crêpe, are suitable for both the lining and the shade. Crêpe-backed satin is particularly easy to work with. Avoid stiff fabrics with no stretch or those which fray or split easily such as nylon or 100% polyester. If you have to choose a fabric that frays badly, use French seams at the joins.

The shade fabric can be light or dark and should tone with the room furnishings. Choose a pale-coloured lining fabric to increase light reflection. A cream or white gives maximum light while a pale pink or peach sheds a warmer glow, a good choice for a bedroom, for example.

Cutting out

The fabric is usually cut on the cross which makes it easier to mould round the frame and gives a smooth finish. If you are using a patterned fabric where the pattern dictates that the fabric must be cut on the straight, choose a frame which has fairly straight sides.

Preparing the frame

Remove any rough edges from the frame with fine sandpaper before taping, covering and lining as described earlier on pages 330–1 and 338–41.

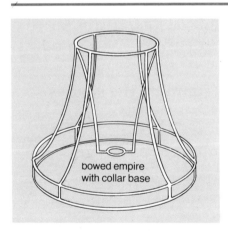

bowed empire with collar base

tall drum

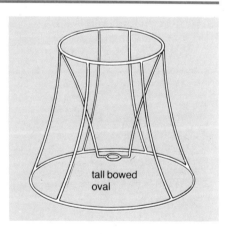

tall bowed oval

suitable lampshade fabrics

Making a lined lampshade

The instructions given here are for a classic shade with the fabric cut on the cross. If you must use your fabric on the straight grain, cut two rectangles and make up in exactly the same way. Keep the vertical grain as straight as possible, especially at the point halfway between the seams.

You will need

A prepared and taped frame
A square of shade fabric which, when folded crosswise, will cover half the frame and allow 4cm/1½in turnings all round.
The same amount of lining fabric
Thread to suit fabric
Enough braid, velvet ribbon or bias strips to trim top and bottom edges
Fine steel glass-headed pins
Tailor's chalk or light pencil

Right: This elegant shade made from furnishing fabric trimmed with ruched velvet would be expensive to buy but is economical to make for yourself.

Preparing the cover and lining

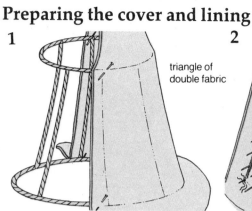

1

2

triangle of double fabric

wrinkle-free fabric pinned and marked

Fold the square of shade fabric in half diagonally to form a triangle, right sides together.

1 With the folded edge running parallel to the base of the frame, lay the triangle of double fabric over half of the frame. Hold with four pins, one at the top and bottom of two opposite struts.

Place pins halfway down the two

outer struts and in the centre of the top and bottom semi-circle of frame. Pulling the fabric taut, pin outwards from these central pins, working round the frame until the fabric is securely pinned all round and completely smooth and taut. Re-pin wrinkled areas as many times as necessary for a perfect finish.

2 When the fabric is absolutely

wrinkle free, mark with tailor's chalk or light pencil down the two pinned struts on the wrong side of the fabric. Tailor's tack at each end of the lines to mark the position of the top and bottom rings of the frame. Carefully remove the fabric from the frame, keeping the two layers pinned together and cut along the fold.

With the two triangles of fabric still together, right sides facing, stitch along the two pencil lines, extending the seams by about 2cm/ 1in at each end. Trim down seam allowances to 5mm/¼in and press to one side.

Cut, pin and fit the lining in exactly the same way. As you are working on the *outside* of frame, stitch 3mm/ ⅛in inside the marked lines to make the lining slightly smaller to fit *inside* the frame.

Fitting the cover to the frame

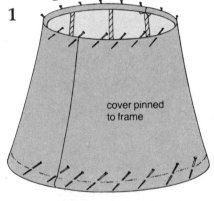

1

2

cover pinned to frame

oversewing using double thread

1 Slip the cover right side out over the frame. Position the seams along two opposite struts so that they will be less noticeable when the light is switched on. Use the tailor's tacks

as a guide to positioning.

Pin at strut ends and then around top and bottom of the frame, pulling the fabric taut and smooth and re-pinning where necessary until the cover is a perfect fit.

2 Using double thread and small even stitches, oversew the fabric to the tape around the top and bottom rings. Remove pins as you go but keep the fabric taut. Trim off surplus fabric close to stitching.

Fitting the lining to the frame

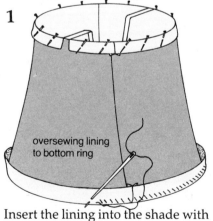

1

oversewing lining to bottom ring

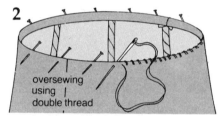

2

strip covering raw edges round gimbal

lining trimmed close to stitching

Insert the lining into the shade with the wrong sides of fabric and lining together and matching side seams to those on the outside cover. Pin at strut ends to hold in place. Wrap the surplus fabric over the edge of

the outer cover and, working from the outside of shade, pin around the top and bottom rings, pulling the lining taut as before. Make a slit in the fabric to fit round the gimbal where it joins the top of the frame.

1 Oversew lining in place around the top and bottom rings on the outside of the frame, making sure that the stitches do not show on the lining inside. Trim excess fabric close to the stitching. The stitches and raw edges of fabric will be covered by the trimming.

Cut two short strips 2.5cm/1in wide from the surplus fabric, fold in half lengthwise and press. Press the long raw edges of the fabric in towards the centre fold.

2 Cover the raw edges of the lining around the gimbal with these strips, placing them under the gimbal, over the top ring and pinning the ends (trimmed to fit) to the outside of the cover, close to the top edge of the lampshade.

Trimming the frame

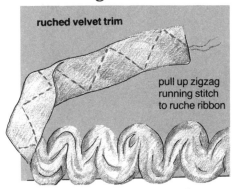

ruched velvet trim

pull up zigzag running stitch to ruche ribbon

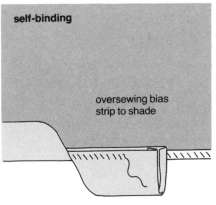

self-binding

oversewing bias strip to shade

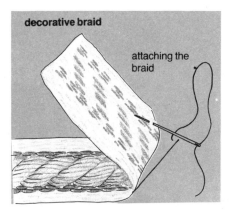

decorative braid

attaching the braid

Neaten the shade with either a decorative trimming or a subtle self-binding.

Velvet ribbon trimming is one of the quickest and easiest to apply. The texture of the velvet covers the stitching and raw edges without looking lumpy, unlike ordinary ribbon which is not usually heavy enough. Simply stick it into place using a fabric glue such as Copydex, folding in the ends so that they butt together neatly. You must be extremely careful not to get excess glue on the shade.

For a ruched velvet ribbon trim, cut the ribbon twice the required length. Stitch a zigzag line down the centre of the ribbon using small running stitches. Draw up the thread until the ribbon fits the frame, adjusting the gathers for an even scalloped effect. Catchstitch the ribbon to the shade instead of gluing, positioning it so that the scallops slightly overlap the edge.

Self-binding gives a more tailored finish. Cut a bias strip of fabric, double the required width of binding plus 1cm/½in and long enough to go round both the top and bottom edges of the frame. Fold the strip in half, widthways, wrong side in and tuck in the short ends.

Pin the bias strip to the edge of the shade so that the raw edges overlap the shade by 5mm/¼in and the folded edge lies outside the shade. Oversew the strip to the shade, stretching it slightly as you go. Fold the binding over on to the shade

cover – if it has been stretched properly while sewing, it should be flat without needing the top edge slipstitched down.

Decorative braid or fringing can be glued into position but as these trimmings have a tendency to fray easily, the less experienced lampshade maker will find it easier to stitch them on.

Working from behind the braid, take tiny stitches alternately through the top and bottom edges, catching them to the shade fabric. The thread zigzags along behind the braid; do not pull it too tightly or the stitches will leave an imprint on the right side of the braid.

Below: This method of making lampshades is suitable for any size of light fitting.

Cushions for comfort

*Cushions are just about the most versatile of home furnishings.
They provide a splash of colour, tone or contrast,
and give added comfort to a sofa or chair. Once you have
learned how to make the basic cushion shapes, you
can add frills, piping or fancy borders for a decorative effect.*

To make a simple cushion cover all you need is a front, a back, and a method for opening and closing. Before you set to work with the scissors cutting out the fabric, decide on the type of opening you want to use, as this determines the cutting measurements.

A zip, Velcro or overlap opening is the most satisfactory type if you're likely to be laundering the cushion cover frequently, because this makes the cushion pad easy to take out and put back.

A hand sewn opening, although easier to make in the first place, needs to be carefully unpicked and resewn each time the pad is removed.

Choose any furnishing fabric to make up a cushion cover. You can create a bold show mixing style, colour and pattern by buying up fabric remnants or, if you're sewing curtains, loose covers and other furnishings for your home, use left overs from cutting out the fabric to make co-ordinating covers at no extra cost.

The cushion cover itself is sewn to fit over a cushion pad. Never put fillings straight into your cushion cover. All filling has to be enclosed in its own inner cover to give a cushion pad that can be removed from the cushion cover for laundering.

Re-use the pads you've got already if they're still in good condition. If you're buying a new pad, manufactured cushion pads are available in a large number of sizes and shapes, square, rectangular and round, so you should be able to find one with the dimensions to suit your needs.

Right: Cushions in a mixture of shapes and sizes add subtle touches of colour to this cool grey living room.

Making square and rectangular cushion covers

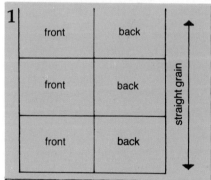

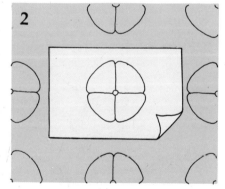

Measuring and cutting

Use a tape measure to size up your cushion pad. It's important to measure right over the pad to take account of its padded out shape. Measure in both directions to find the size of the square or rectangle you will need for the cover and to these measurements add 1.5cm/⅝in seam allowance all round. For a plump-looking cushion, do not add seam allowance so that, after you have sewn the cover together, it fits tightly over the pad.

For each cushion cover, cut a front and a back piece (two sections for the back piece if you've chosen to have a back zip opening, page 349). Lay the fabric on a flat surface and with a ruler and tailor's chalk mark up the sizes of the squares or rectangles.

1 Mark all the squares/rectangles on the straight grain of the fabric with the pattern (if applicable) running in the same direction.

If the fabric has a definite bold pattern, place this centrally on the cushion cover for best effect. To do this, cut a piece of tracing paper to the size of your square/rectangle.

2 Place the tracing paper pattern on the fabric, centring over the main design.

When you're cutting several covers from the same fabric, it helps to estimate the total amount of fabric if you draw up a plan first. On a small piece of paper, mark up the width of your fabric and then draw on, with measurements, the number of fabric pieces needed. Make sure that the combined measurements across the width come close to, but do not exceed, the width of your fabric. To estimate the total length of fabric you will need, simply add up the measurements of the pieces marked down the length.

Hand-sewn side opening This is the simplest of cushion covers to make, its only disadvantage is that you have to resew the opening when the cover is cleaned.
Right sides facing, tack the two pieces of fabric round three sides 1.5cm/⅝in from outer edge with a 90° right angle at each corner. On a rectangular cover, leave a short side untacked. To give rounded corners tack a curve instead of a right angle at each corner. After sewing, trim fabric and notch almost to the seamline.

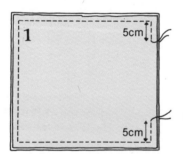

1 On the untacked side, tack 5cm/2in of the seam from both ends, leaving the centre of the seam open. Sew all seams with a 1.5cm/⅝in seam allowance leaving the untacked sections open.

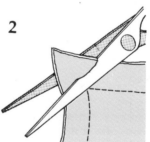

2 On each corner, cut the seam allowance diagonally close to the stitching to reduce bulk. Neaten the raw edges by zigzagging on a sewing machine.

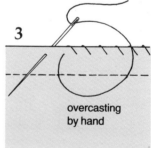

overcasting by hand

3 Alternatively overcast by hand to neaten. Turn to right side and add the cushion pad. Tack the opening closed. Handstitch opening with slip stitches. Remove tacking.

347

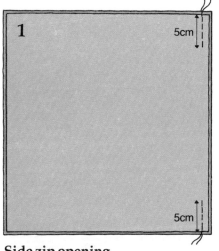

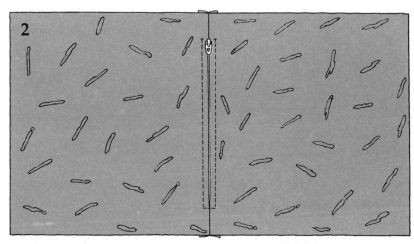

Side zip opening

Lay the two squares/rectangles right sides facing.

1 On one side (short side for a rectangle) tack together for 5cm/ 2in from each corner along seam allowance. Sew. Remove tacking. Press these short seams flat and press seam allowance to wrong side between the sewn seams. Lay the zip, which should be the same size as

the opening, face up on a flat surface and with wrong side of fabric to zip, place open section of seam over the zip teeth. Tack zip in place.

2 On the right side of the fabric, sew down both sides of the zip and across the bottom close to the teeth using the zipper foot on your machine, or as close to the teeth as you can get with the normal sewing foot. Remove tacking. Open the zip and

with right sides of the two pieces of fabric facing, tack and sew round the other three sides. Remove tacking. Neaten raw edges. Turn to right side.

Other opening methods In place of a zip you can use a length of press stud tape or Velcro. Make up cover in the same way as for a hand-sewn side opening. Place tape or Velcro on either side of the opening and slip stitch or machine in place.

Making round cushion covers

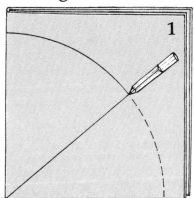

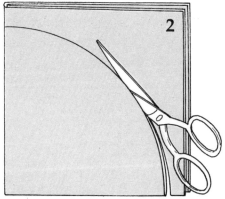

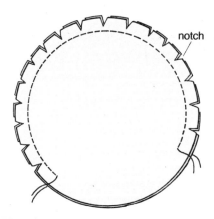

Measuring and cutting

The success of a round cover depends on cutting a perfect circle from the fabric. Measure across the diameter of your cushion pad and add 3cm/1¼in (1.5cm/⅝in seam allowance each side). Cut a square of paper slightly largely than the diameter plus seam allowance.

1 Fold this paper square into four sections. Tie a length of string securely round a pencil and cut this off to half the diameter of the cushion plus 1.5cm/⅝in seam allowance. Again for a plump cushion do not add the seam allowance, and you will get a snug fit. Lay the folded paper on a

board and pin the loose end of the string to the point of the folded corner with a drawing pin.

Hold the pencil upright and, at full extent of the string, mark the paper with the pencil in a curve.

2 Take out drawing pin and cut along the curve through all four layers of the paper. Open out the paper and you will have a perfect circle.

This circular paper pattern can be made up in tracing paper if you want to see through the pattern to centre it over a fabric design.

Cut two circles of fabric for each cover. A different pattern has to be made for the back of the cover, if you are placing a zip in the back (right).

Hand-sewn side opening

This is the easiest of round cushion covers to make up, as there is no fastening. However, the opening will have to be unpicked and re-sewn each time for washing.

Right sides facing, lay the two circles of fabric together and tack round the circumference with a 1.5cm/⅝in seam allowance, leaving an opening sufficient to squeeze in cushion pad. Sew. Remove tacking. Notch into the seam allowance all round (except the opening) close to stitching line. Turn cover through to right side and add cushion pad. Tack opening closed and slip stitch by hand. Remove tacking.

Creative cushion covers

Once you're familiar with the basic cushion-making skills, you can think more creatively in design terms. Always remember to sew on any motifs or decoration *before* assembling the cushion pieces.
As a taster, the ideas (shown right) are simple and effective.
Simple machine patchwork is marvellously quick and uses up odd scraps of fabric.
Ribbons can be sewn on in a plaid design or as a decorative border.
Cotton lace, backed by a piece of taffeta in a contrasting colour, looks pretty for a bedroom.
Appliquéd motifs are fun to make up. As a short cut, you can cut out a motif from left-over curtain material.
A fabric with a regular pattern or printed with squares, diamonds or stripes is easy to quilt and makes a soft padded cushion cover.

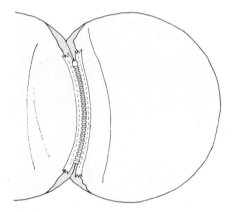

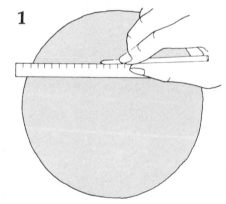

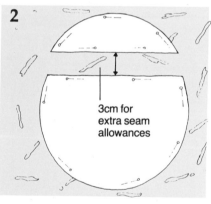

Side zip opening

Choose a zip long enough to take the pad. Pin the two circles together right sides facing, leaving an opening in the seam allowance the length of the zip. Tack along the seam allowance for 2.5cm/1in either side of the opening. Sew. Remove tacking and pins. Press short seams flat. Pin the zip into the opening between the stitched seams. This seam is on the curve, so ease the fabric slightly. Tack and sew.
Open the zip and place the two fabric circles right sides facing. Tack together round remaining circumference. Sew. Remove tacking. Notch the seam allowance. Turn to right side and insert pad.

Back zip opening

A back zip is easier to sew into a round cushion and looks neater because the zip is sewn between two pieces of flat fabric. Using the circular paper pattern, as before, cut just one piece of fabric (for the front of the cover). Choose a zip length about 10cm/4in shorter than the diameter and using the same circular paper pattern.
1 Mark a straight line across the paper pattern where the zip is to be fitted (you can place this centred or off centre) and cut the paper pattern across this line.
2 Position the two paper patterns on the fabric and mark an extra 1.5cm/⅝in seam allowance along

both straight cut edges. Cut out with the extra seam allowance. Right sides facing, match the two straight edges and tack together. Sew 5cm/2in from either end along the seam allowance. Remove tacking. Sew in zip (as for square cushion cover). Open the zip. Right sides of the front and back circles facing, tack together and sew all round taking 1.5cm/⅝in seams. Remove the tacking. Turn the cover through to right side and add cushion pad.

Single frill with bias edge

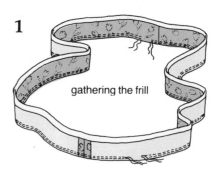

gathering the frill

This cushion cover has a frill made from a single thickness of fabric, the outer raw edge of which is finished with bias binding.

Cutting out and making up
Cut out two squares or rectangles of fabric to the cushion pad size with a 1.5cm/⅝in seam allowance all round. The finished width of the frill is a matter of personal choice, but you will find that a frill any wider than 7cm/2¾in finished width is rather floppy. Add 1.5cm/⅝in to finished width of frill for seam allowance. To calculate the length of frill required, measure all round the cushion cover and double this

Add contrast bias for impact.

figure to give an ample frill. For a thick fabric which is more bulky to gather, one-and-a-half times the length is sufficient.
For very fine fabrics only you may need two to three times the measurement.
To the frill length measurement add 3cm/1¼in seam allowance for joining the two short ends and add 3cm/1¼in for any joins that are necessary to make up the length. Cut out the frill and, with 1.5cm/⅝in seams, join the lengths to make a circle.
Neaten the outer raw edge of the

frill with bias binding.
1 Sew two lines of gathering stitches on the inner edge of the frill, 1.5cm/⅝in and 1cm/½in from raw edge. Work gathering stitches along half the length, then cut the stitching threads. Make gathering stitches along the remaining length in the same way.
With right side of frill facing right side of one of the main cushion cover pieces, and raw edges matching, gently ease up the gathering threads along half the frill length, until this exactly fits two sides of the cover fabric. Make slightly more gathers on the corners to allow sufficient fullness.

Pleated frill

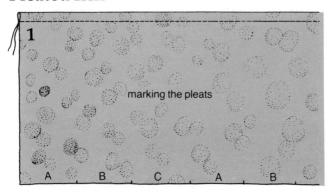

marking the pleats

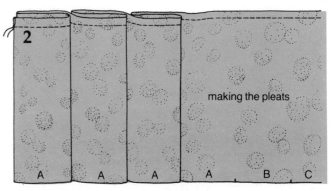

making the pleats

A pleated fabric frill gives a crisp finish to a round or rectangular cushion cover. Piping can also be inserted into the seam for extra decorative effect.

Cutting out and making up
Cut out two squares or rectangles of fabric to the cushion pad size, with a 1.5cm/⅝in seam allowance all round. To calculate the amount of fabric length needed for the frill, measure all round cushion pad and cut fabric to three times this length plus 3cm/1¼in seam allowance for joining the two short ends and add 3cm/1¼in seam allowance for any

joins that are necessary to make up the complete frill length.
To calculate the amount of fabric width needed for the frill, decide on the finished width and add 2.5cm/1in for seams.
Cut out the frill fabric and join the pieces to make one length. On the outer long edge turn a 1cm/½in double hem (5mm/¼in and then 5mm/¼in) to the wrong side and sew.
To pleat up the frill mark the fabric into 3cm/1¼in sections along its length with tailor's chalk. Mark on the right side of the fabric, within the 1.5cm/⅝in seam allowance.
1 Starting at one edge, and using

tailor's chalk, lightly mark each section in a series of consecutive As, Bs and Cs along the length.
2 Make the pleats by folding and pressing the fabric on the right side on the chalk marks so that the mark between A and B is pressed and touches the mark between C and the next A. Continue along the length. From the right side, all the As should be visible and the Bs and Cs folded to the inside. Pin the pleats and tack. Machine 1cm/½in from raw edge. Remove tacking. Tack the pleated frill in place, as for the single frill with bias edge. (To add piping to the seam see under

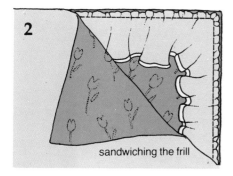

sandwiching the frill

Match and fit the remaining half of frill to the other two sides of the fabric in the same way. Tack the frill in place. Machine 1cm/½in from raw edge. Remove tacking and gathering threads.

At this stage add a side zip, if you want a zip opening.

2 With right sides together, place the second piece of cover fabric on the first, sandwiching the frill inside, and tack all round. Sew all round, allowing a 1.5cm/⅝in seam, and leaving an opening to insert the pad, if a zip has not been added. Remove tacking, turn through to the right side and insert the pad.

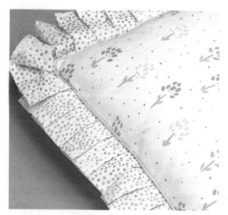

A pleated frill is smart and looks good on round and square cushions.

Professional Touch, right.)

If you want to add a side zip, do so at this stage.

Right sides facing, place the second cushion piece over the first, sandwiching the frill. Sew all round with a 1.5cm/⅝in seam and leave a gap for inserting the cushion pad if a zip has not been added. Remove all tacking. If you have added piping, use a zipper foot to get close up to the piping with the stitching line. Turn through to right side and insert the pad.

Covering piping cord

You can buy piping cord from haberdashery departments. It comes in several thicknesses, and your choice will depend on how prominent you want it to be – the thicker the cord, the more it will stand out from the seam. Piping cord has to be covered with fabric cut on the bias. Either you can make your own bias strips from spare fabric or buy ready-made bias binding. In either case, you will need enough bias fabric to go right round the piping cord and to allow at least 1cm/½in on each edge for seam allowance. So for piping cord that is 12mm/½in in diameter, you will need bias strips at least 3.2cm/1⅜in wide.

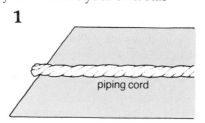

piping cord

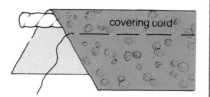

covering cord

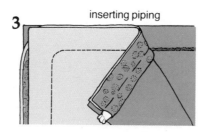

inserting piping

joining ends

1 Press the bias strip flat and place the piping cord along the centre, on the wrong side of the fabric.

2 Wrap the fabric round the piping cord and tack the fabric together as close to the cord as possible. Sew, using a zipper foot to get the stitching line close to the cord. Remove tacking.

Adding piping to a seam

Mark seam allowance (1.5cm/⅝in) on the right side of either the front or back of the cushion cover, using tailor's chalk.

3 Place the piping on the right side of the cover, matching the stitching line of the piping to the marked seam allowance line. The raw edges of the bias piping cord fabric must face outwards to the raw edges of the cushion cover. Tack the piping in place. At each corner, curve the piping round slightly to avoid a sharp angle.

To join the piping first make a

Added to a seam, piping gives a professional and expensive look.

join in the bias strip along the grain. Join the piping cord by allowing an extra 5cm/2in when you cut the cord to length.

4 Overlap the two ends by 2.5cm/1in and at each end unravel the twisted cords and trim each separate cord to a slightly different length. Intertwine the cords at each end to make a smooth join.

Place front and back of cushion cover together. Tack together, except for the opening and taking a 1.5cm/⅝in seam, stitch as close to the piping cord as possible using the zipper foot on your machine. Sew the piping cord in place along the open edge. Remove tacking.

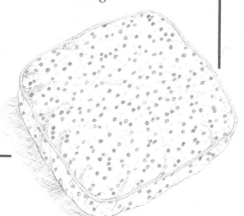

Zigzagged pointed frill

1 strip of fabric

cushion cover

2 fold

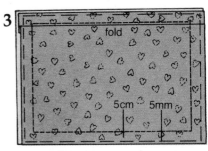

3 fold

5cm   5mm

This fancy edge is cut to shape with the help of a template and the raw edges neatly finished with a machine zigzag stitch. This type of cover is not suitable for a zip.

Cutting out and making up
Cut out two squares or rectangles of fabric to the cushion pad size plus an extra 8cm/3¼in on both the length and width. Also cut one strip of fabric 8cm/3¼in by the length of the rectangle or square.
1 Place 8cm/3¼in wide fabric strip wrong sides facing on one cushion cover rectangle/square, and with raw edges matching to one of the edges (a long edge if making a rectangular cover). Tack in place.

Take the other rectangle/square and turn 5cm/2in to the wrong side along one edge (long edge if a rectangle). Trim the turn to 3cm/1¼in.
2 Lay the two rectangles/squares together, wrong sides facing, matching raw edges and placing the folded edge of one rectangle/square so that it overlaps the attached strip on the other rectangle/square.
3 Tack all round cover, 5mm/¼in, then 5cm/2in from the raw edges.

Machine along the 5cm/2in tacking line, working from the back, so that the opening is not machined closed. Turn to right side.
To make the pointed frill You will need a cardboard template to cut an evenly pointed edge between the 5cm/2in machined line and the edges of the cushion cover. To make the template, cut a piece of card 30cm × 4.5cm/11¾in × 1¾in. Draw a central line through the length. Mark along

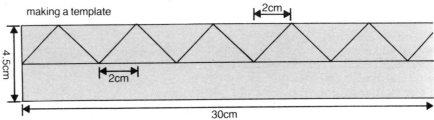

making a template

4.5cm

2cm

2cm

30cm

Double gathered frill

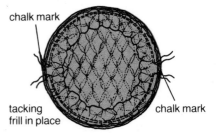

chalk mark

tacking
frill in place

chalk mark

This frill is made from a double thickness of fabric. If you are using a fabric with a one-way design, you can create an interesting visual effect by cutting the frill fabric so that the design runs in the opposite direction to that on the cover.

Cutting out and making up
Cut out two circles of fabric to the cushion pad size with a 1.5cm/⅝in seam allowance all round. If you want to insert a back zip, do so at this stage.
To calculate the length of frill needed measure the circumference of your cushion pad with a tape measure. For full gathers cut the frill to double this measurement, adding 3cm/1¼in seam allowance for joining the two short ends and

This frill can be made in either a matching or a contrast fabric.

another 3cm/1¼in for each join necessary to make up the length. Decide on the finished width of the frill, double this measurement and add 3cm/1¼in seam allowance. Join the fabric strips to make up the total length, with 1.5cm/⅝in seams. Join the two short ends.
Fold the frill fabric in half lengthways, wrong sides facing and press. Work two rows of gathering stitches through the layers, 1.5cm/⅝in and 1cm/½in from the raw edges. Work the gathering along half the length, then cut the threads. Resume the gathering along the remaining length.
Fold one of the cushion cover circles

in half, and mark the raw edge at each end of the fold with a tailor's chalk line. Open flat again.
With raw edges matching, and frill length to right side of marked cover piece, place each break in the gathering threads on one of the chalk marks. Gently pull up the gathering threads, evenly around the circumference.
Tack frill in place. If you want to insert a side zip, do so at this stage. Right sides facing, lay the remaining circle of fabric on the first, sandwiching the frill. Tack together and then machine with a 1.5cm/⅝in seam, and leave a gap to insert the pad if a zip has not been added. Remove tacking.
Turn through to right side and insert the pad.

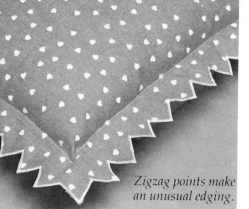

Zigzag points make an unusual edging.

this line every 2cm/¾in and along outer edge of card every 2cm/¾in.
4 Join up the marks with diagonal lines to make a series of points. Cut along the diagonal lines. Lay the template with the straight edge along a section of the stitching and with tailor's chalk mark around the points on to the fabric. Continue in this way all around the cushion cover. At each corner, turn the template at an angle of 45°.
Using a small size, close machine zigzag, stitch along the marked points.
Using small sharp scissors, carefully cut away the fabric close to the zigzag stitching, so that you have a pointed frill. Insert pad.

Gathered corners with piping

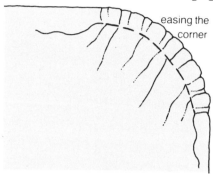

easing the corner

Gathered corners create a plump cushion.

This style of cover, suitable for a rectangular or square cushion, has slightly gathered corners.

Cutting out and making up
Cut out two squares or rectangles of fabric to the cushion pad size, with a 1.5cm/⅝in seam allowance all round. Curve each corner by drawing round a saucer or a glass with tailor's chalk. Cut the fabric along the chalked curves.
On both cushion cover pieces work a gathering thread round each corner and gently ease up gathering threads so that each corner is reduced by 3-4cm/1¼-1½in.

Cover the piping cord and stitch to the right side of one cushion cover piece (see Professional Touch on page 351), following the curves on the corners.
If you want to add a side zip, do so at this stage.
Lay both cushion pieces right sides facing and tack together. Sew all round with a zipper foot as close to the ridge of the piping as possible leaving a gap to insert the cushion pad if you have not added a zip. Turn through to right side and insert pad.

Overlap frill with trimmed edge

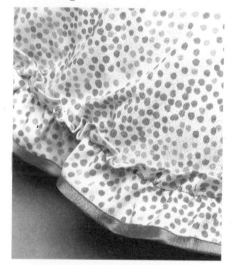

This frill looks best on a round cushion but can be used on a square too.

This is a double fabric frill with the folded edge gathered on to the top edge of the cushion cover. The two raw edges are joined together with satin bias binding.

Cutting out and making up
Cut out two circles of fabric to the pad size with a 1.5cm/⅝in seam

1 gathering frill to fit cushion

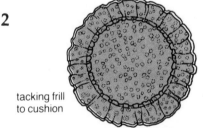

2 tacking frill to cushion

allowance all round.
If you want to insert a back zip, do so at this stage.
Calculate the length and width of frill needed as for the double gathered frill, but do not add a seam allowance to the finished width, as the raw edges are bias bound.
Cut the frill in fabric, join and press in half as for the double gathered frill. Tack the two raw edges together and neaten the raw edges by enclosing them in toning or contrasting bias binding.
Work gathering stitches in two halves along the folded edge as for the double gathered frill.
1 Gather up the frill to fit the circumference of the cushion, placing folded edge of gathered frill 4cm/1½in in from the raw

edge of the right side of fabric circle, so that the frill overlaps the circle by 4cm/1½in all round. Tack in place.
2 Top stitch frill to the circle of fabric, 2cm/¾in from the folded edge. Remove tacking and gathering threads.
Fold the frill to the centre of the fabric circle.
Insert a zip at this stage, if you are adding a side zip.
Place the remaining circle on first circle, right sides facing, and tack together all round through both layers of fabric – make sure the frill does not get caught in the stitching. Sew with a 1.5cm/⅝in seam and leave a gap to insert the cushion pad if a zip has not been added. Turn through to right side and insert pad.

Gusseted cushions for a perfect fit

Make feather filled cushions luxuriously deep and foam filled cushions neatly tailored, by adding a third dimension – a side gusset – to the cover. Even the plainest of kitchen chairs can be transformed with a bright, comfortable cushion.

Adding a gusset to a cushion cover allows for a deeper, more tailored shape. The gusset, or welt, as it is sometimes known, is a strip of fabric forming the sides between the top and bottom pieces of the cover. The three-dimensional shape produced can be emphasized by piped seams or a decorative or contrasting gusset.

A zip inserted in one side makes it easier to remove the cover for cleaning. If you do not want a zipped opening (or for an inner cover), omit the instructions for a zip. Leave one side unstitched, except for 5cm/2in at the corners, then slipstitch together after inserting cushion pad or stuffing. For soft fillings such as

feather, down or foam chips, simply add the zip to one side of the cover and squash the cushion through the opening. For solid fillings such as foam pads, you may have to extend the zip around the adjoining sides – in which case, take this into account when measuring up for the cushion cover fabric.

Before you begin making up these cushions, read the previous chapter for basic instructions.

Right: This antique wooden bench is made more comfortable with a firm, gusseted seat cushion in an attractive print. The round, feather-filled cushions are made in plain, toning fabrics.

Making square and rectangular cushions

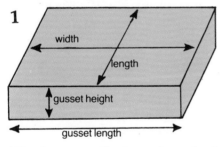

1 For the top and bottom piece of the cushion cover measure the surface of the pad in both directions and add an extra 1.5cm/⅝in seam allowance all round.

For gusset pieces, measure the width and height of each side of the pad and add 1.5cm/⅝in seam allowance all round. The back gusset piece will be cut in half along its length for the zip to be inserted, so add an extra 3cm/1¼in to the height of this piece. For each cushion cover, cut out from fabric one top piece, one bottom piece and the four gusset pieces – one back, one front and two sides.

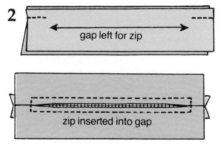

2 Cut the back gusset piece in half along its length and place the two halves right sides together. Rejoin the cut edge by tacking for approximately 5cm/2in from each corner along the seamline, leaving a central opening to fit the zip. Stitch, press the seam flat and insert the zip.

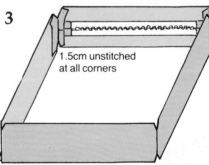

3 With right sides facing, and taking a 1.5cm/⅝in seam allowance, join the four gusset pieces together to form a square or rectangle. Leave 1.5cm/⅝in at each end of seams unstitched but secure ends of stitching firmly. Press seams open.

4 Matching seams to corners and with right sides facing, pin and tack gusset to one main piece. Machine in place with a 1.5cm/⅝in seam. To ensure a neat square finish at the corners, insert the machine needle right into the fabric at the corner, lift the presser foot, then turn the fabric to correct position for the next row of machining, pivoting it around

Making round cushions

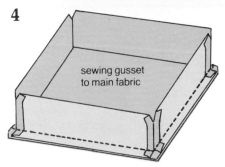

sewing gusset to main fabric

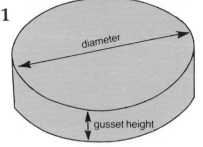

diameter

gusset height

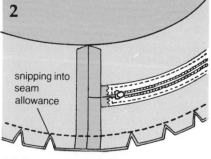

snipping into seam allowance

the needle. Replace presser foot and continue stitching.

Snip diagonally across seam allowance at corners, close to stitching, to eliminate bulk. Open the zip, then attach remaining main piece in the same way. Press all seams towards gusset. Turn cover through to right side and insert cushion pad.

1 Measure the diameter of the cushion pad and add 3cm/1¼in to give the diameter of the circles to cut for the top and bottom of the cushion cover.

Measure the circumference and the height of the pad. Cut one gusset piece as a rectangle measuring half the circumference plus 3cm/1¼in by the height plus 3cm/1¼in.

Cut a second rectangle for the zipped half of the gusset but adding a further 3cm/1¼in to the height. Cut this piece in half along its length, place the two halves right sides together, rejoin at each end and insert zip as for square cushion.

Make up gusset as for square one, but forming a circle.

2 With the zip open and right sides together, attach top and bottom circles to the gusset, snipping into the seam allowance all the way round to ease the fabric and give a neat appearance to the seam on the right side. Press all seams towards gusset. Turn cover through to right side and insert pad.

A bolster cushion is simply a variation of a round gusseted cushion, with the gusset height extended to the required length of bolster. Cut the gusset in one piece and insert the zip in the seam.

355

Making shaped cushions

Many chairs have arms or staves that jut out into the seat, so the cushions must fit an irregular shape. If you already have cushion pads to fit the chair, cut the pattern pieces to fit these – adding 1.5cm/⅝in seam allowance all round. If not, make a paper pattern of the seat shape.

1 Measure the width and depth of the chair seat and cut a piece of paper a little larger. Lay the paper on the seat and fold in the edges to the exact outline of the seat. Cut out this shape and check its accuracy by laying it on the seat once more; adjust if necessary. If a back cushion is needed for a sofa or armchair make a paper pattern in the same way, remembering that it will sit on top of the seat cushion, so measure up from the height of this. You can now use these patterns to have pieces of foam cut for the pads. Depending on the amount of padding required, the usual depth for seat pads is 5-10cm/2-4in. Alternatively, you could use your pattern to make up an inner cover in ticking or down-proof cambric, omitting the zip. Stuff with feathers, feather and down or foam chips and sew up opening. Feather cushions look soft and luxurious

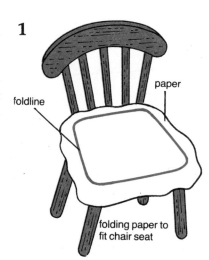

1 foldline / paper / folding paper to fit chair seat

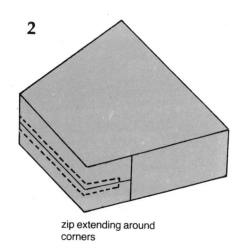

2 zip extending around corners

but a foam pad retains its shape better and looks neater.

2 After measuring up the shaped pad, calculate the length and position of the zip. On a wedge-shaped cushion, the zip can be inserted into the gusset but it should extend at least 5cm/2in around each adjoining side, so the back gusset piece must be lengthened and the sides correspondingly shortened.

3 For cushions with curved sections cut out to accommodate the arms of the chair, insert the zip into the widest part of the bottom piece of the cushion cover, where it will not show. Cut across your paper pattern where the zip is to go and add 1.5cm/⅝in seam allowance to each edge, before cutting from fabric. The gusset will then consist of side pieces simply joined at the corners, or wherever is most inconspicuous, depending on the irregularity of the shape.

Cut out and make up as for square cushions, placing zip in gusset or main bottom piece as necessary.

Attaching the cushion to the chair

Although the cushions simply lie in place on sofas and easy chairs, when used on wooden upright chairs, stools and rocking chairs they need to be firmly attached. Ties are the simplest solution. They can be made from coloured ribbons or cord, purchased bias binding or tape, or bias strips cut from spare fabric. (Fold raw edges of bias strip to centre, fold strip in half lengthways to enclose them, tuck in short raw ends and slipstitch together). For each tie you need about a 30cm/12in length.

Ties for chairs Place the ties as near to the back corner of the cushion pad as possible, matching up their position to the struts of the chair. Securely stitch centre of tie to cover, then simply tie round chair strut.

Ties for stools Add a tie to each lower corner of the cushion and tie behind stool legs or, for a decorative finish, cross ties behind the legs and tie a bow in front.

Velcro fastenings Use Velcro as an

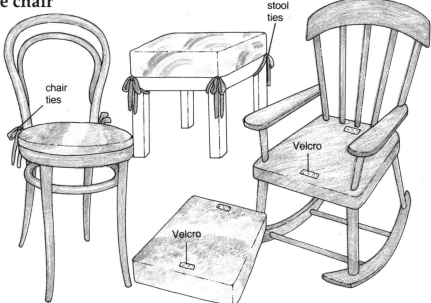

chair ties / stool ties / Velcro / Velcro

alternative to a tie for an invisible fixing – two 5cm/2in lengths are sufficient for one cushion. Stitch one half of each Velcro piece to centre front and centre back of the cushion's underside about 3cm/1¼in

in from the edge. Using a clear household adhesive, stick the backs of remaining Velcro pieces to chair seat to correspond. Allow glue to dry completely before putting cushion in place.

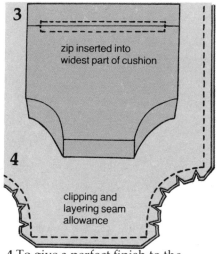

3

zip inserted into widest part of cushion

4

clipping and layering seam allowance

4 To give a perfect finish to the cushion cover, once the stitching is complete, trim away some of the seam allowance to layer the seams and reduce fabric bulk. Snip into the seam allowance on curves, cutting away small V shapes on inner curves, clipping right up to – but not through – stitching line. At the corners, snip off the seam allowance diagonally.

Press all seams towards the gusset. Turn through to right side – all the seams should now lie perfectly flat.

Right: Soften the seat of a rocking chair with a pretty piped cushion.

Finishing touches

To make cushions really special – and individual – add one of the following finishes:

Piped edges These give an elegant tailored finish. Use them to pick out one of the colours on a patterned fabric, or pipe in a toning or contrasting colour to add emphasis to a plain cover. Make up the piping and tack it in position round the edges of both main pieces. Make up covers, sewing the gussets in place using a zipper or piping foot and stitching as close to the piping as possible.

Mix and match fabrics Many fabric ranges now include co-ordinated patterned or plain fabrics, matching borders and positive/negative designs. Use an alternative to the main fabric for the gusset, and perhaps also use the alternative fabric for scatter cushions.

Pleated gussets Join gusset strips to make three times the required length plus seam allowances. Pleat up, tack and then stitch along just inside seamline to hold pleats firmly in position before inserting gusset.

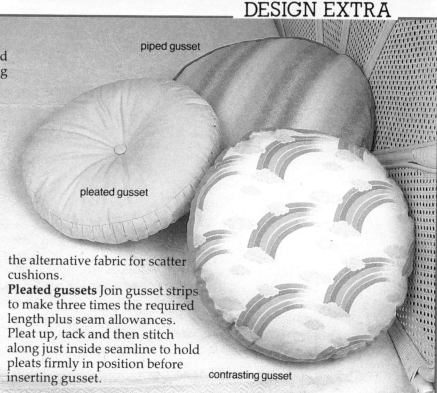

piped gusset

pleated gusset

contrasting gusset

Soft seating: sag bags and floor cushions

*If you're short of space – or of money – for extra seating,
then floor cushions or sag bags provide
the answer. They make comfortable, inexpensive seating units
that can easily be tucked out of the way,
and firm foam cushions will even double as a mattress.*

Use floor cushions or sag bags to replace traditional settees and armchairs for a relaxed informal look that is inexpensive to create and easily varied. They are also ideal as extra seating that can be brought out for visitors then pushed into the background, or into a cupboard, when not required.

Choose a firm furnishing fabric or a tough fabric such as corduroy for the covers. A reasonably dark shade is more practical but all the covers are zipped and easily removed for cleaning.

Sag bags have always been popular with children and teenagers but they are surprisingly comfortable for adults too. Sink into a sag bag and the polystyrene bead filling moulds itself to support your favourite sitting position. This sag bag has a handy

Above: Sag bags are great fun and surprisingly comfortable. For maximum safety, use a fire-retardant polystyrene granule filling.

strap at the top which makes it easy to move around – try one in the garden on a sunny day.

Fabric-covered foam blocks make particularly versatile floor cushions – stack three together against the wall as a simple chair, tie them in line to form a single mattress, use more for a settee, or simply sit on one!

A foam specialist shop will cut the foam to the exact size you require. It is advisable to make a cotton inner cover to protect the foam and help to prevent the corners and edges crumbling with age. This inner cover does not need a zip as it will not need to be removed for cleaning.

Before making up your floor cushion, read pages 354–5 for detailed instructions for cutting out and making up a gusseted cover.

Making a sag bag

Make the sag bag by sewing together six identical pattern pieces, rather like the segments of an orange, and adding a circular zipped base.

Fill the bag with polystyrene granules or beads to about two-thirds of its capacity – the surplus space means you can push the bag into the most comfortable shape for sitting on.

You will need

3.40m/3¾yd of fabric 120cm/48in wide
46cm/18in zip
Matching thread
2.70kg/6lb bag of polystyrene granules

Preparing the pattern pieces

Enlarge the segment pattern piece given below by drawing a grid on which one square equals 5cm/2in and copying the outline on to it square by square. (A 1.5cm/⅝in seam allowance is included.)
Using this as the paper pattern, cut six segment shapes from your fabric. On the wrong side of each segment, draw a chalk line about 5cm/2in down from the pointed end (see graph below).
Cut two strips of fabric each 35cm × 6cm/14in × 2¾in for the handle.
Cut a circle 64cm/25in in diameter for the base. Fold the circle across the diameter and cut in half.

Graph for pattern piece

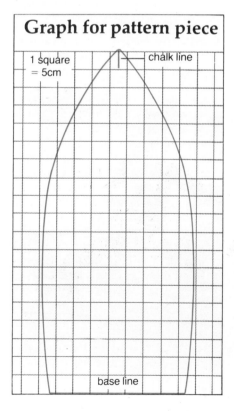

1 square = 5cm

chalk line

base line

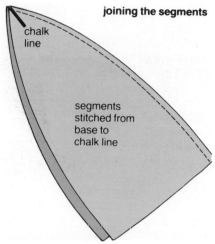

joining the segments

chalk line

segments stitched from base to chalk line

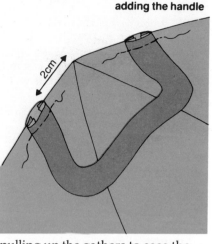

adding the handle

2cm

Making up

Joining the segments Place two segments right sides together. On one side only, tack and then stitch from the base up to the point where the seamline meets the chalk line. In the same way attach a third segment to the free side of one of the first two, stitching as far as the chalk line.
Repeat this procedure to join the remaining three segments together as a separate half.

Adding the handle Make up the handle by placing the two strips right sides together and sewing down both long edges. Turn right side out, press and tack the ends to the outside edges of one set of three segments 2cm/1in below the top point, raw edges together.
Place the two sets of three segments together, right sides facing, sandwiching the handle ends, and tack and stitch the two remaining outer edges from base to chalk line. Turn right side out and the handle will protrude from the seams. Reinforce the point at which the segments meet with a little hand stitching – this gives added strength to the area most under stress. Press the seams open, then run a double row of gathering stitches around the base, just within the seam allowance.

Making the base Place the two halves of the circle right sides together and stitch along the straight edge for 9cm/3½in from each end. Press the seam allowances open and insert the zip in the central gap.
With the zip open, and right sides facing, pin the base of three segments around half of the circle,

pulling up the gathers to ease the fitting. Pin the other three segments to the remaining half of the circle; gather, tack and stitch all round. Turn right side out through the open zip.

Filling the sag bag

Fill about two-thirds of the bag with polystyrene granules.
As a precaution against the bag being opened accidentally or by an inquisitive child, hand stitch the pulling tab of the zip to the base of the bag.
Save any left-over granules as they do tend to crush down a bit with time and wear, and the sag bag may need topping up.

Laundering the cover

To empty the bag for laundering, shake the granules to the bottom of the sag bag, hold over a large open plastic sack and open the zip. Gently shake the granules from the sag bag into the plastic sack – it is easier if you have a helper so that one person can hold the plastic sack while the other tips up.
Turn the sag bag cover inside out, pick out any remaining granules caught in the seams or stuck to the inside of the fabric and wash or dry clean according to the type of fabric.
If your sag bag is likely to be washed frequently, it is worth making an inner cover which can be removed complete with the polystyrene granules while the outer cover is being laundered. Make the inner cover from an inexpensive fabric such as calico, following the sag bag pattern but omitting the handle and zip.

359

Making foam block cushions

Cover a block of foam with a simple gusseted cover and you have a comfortable floor cushion. Make more than one cushion, inserting ties into the seams, and the potential variations of seating are endless.

The instructions are for a versatile 75cm/30in square cushion, 18cm/7in deep, but alter the measurements to suit your needs, remembering to adjust the fabric requirements accordingly.

You will need

75cm/30in square block of dense, seating quality foam approximately 18cm/7in deep
2.5m/2¾yd of fabric at least 80cm/32in wide for the top cover
The same amount of a firm plain fabric such as pre-shrunk calico for the inner cover, if required
70cm/28in zip
Thread
Strong cotton tape about 15mm/⅝in wide to make the ties

Cutting out

For the top cover cut two pieces of fabric 78cm/31¼in square, three gusset strips each 78cm/31¼in wide and 21cm/8¼in deep, and one strip for the back gusset piece the same width but 24cm/9½in deep.
Cut the inner cover pieces to the same dimensions but make all four gusset strips 21cm/8¼in deep. These dimensions include 1.5cm/⅝in seam allowances.

Making up

Make up the inner cover in the same way as a gusseted cushion cover, insert the foam block and hand stitch the opening together. Make the top cover in the same way as a gusseted cushion cover but cutting the back gusset piece in half, widthways, and inserting the zip between.

Adding ties If you wish to link cushions together, insert ties in the seams while making up.

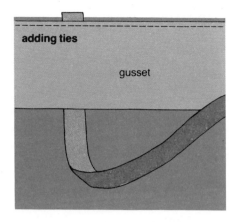

adding ties

gusset

Cut a 30cm/12in length of cotton tape for each tie required. (If you cannot buy the colour of tape to match or contrast with your cushion, dye white tape with a commercial fabric dye.) Eight lengths of tape – two on two opposite sides on both top and bottom – give complete versatility.

Below: Vary the shape and size of cushion to suit your needs – a half-size cushion makes a good back-rest.

Soft floor cushions

These giant floor cushions are quick and easy to make using ready-made cushion pads filled with foam chips or feathers. Simply measure the pad and make up a basic cover as described on pages 346–8, inserting a zip in the side seam for easy removal for cleaning. A combination of large and small floor cushions can make versatile, cheap seating. Use them to replace conventional chairs – an arrangement of low level tables and cushions as shown here gives a feeling of space to a small area and is inexpensive to create. Choose one dominant colour or a combination of toning colours for the best effect. These cushions are made up in a series of black and white checked fabrics, the checks decreasing with the size of the cushions, to give a co-ordinated yet varied look. Alternatively, one or two large

Above: Floor cushions replace the conventional three-piece suite to provide interesting and versatile seating at a fraction of the cost.

cushions are a useful addition to sofa and chairs and a pile of bright covers can add a splash of colour to a dull corner. Bear in mind when choosing fabrics that floor cushions will get a greater amount of wear than a sofa cushion so use a tough furnishing fabric.

Simple unlined curtains – the lightweight look

Unlined curtains involve a minimum of sewing and are the simplest type to make up. Join fabric widths, neaten side hems, add heading tape, sew bottom hems and you're there. Sheer fabrics – the kind that let in lots of light and give you privacy too – are highly suitable for making up by this quick method.

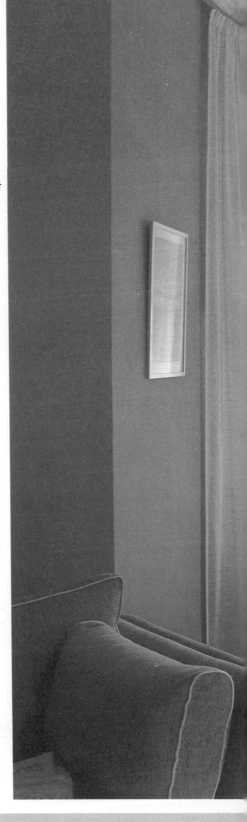

Unlined curtains are ideal for use in kitchens, bathrooms, playrooms or on any window where insulation and light exclusion are less important than a cheap and cheerful effect and easy laundering. Unlined curtains are also the simplest to make.

Double hems neaten edges and standard curtain tape attached to the top has pockets for the hooks which hang the curtain on the track. For curtains that do not need to be drawn back, a cased heading hung on elasticated wire or a length of dowelling is an even cheaper alternative.

Choosing and buying fabrics

All furnishing fabric departments include a wide range of plain and printed cottons ideal for unlined curtains. Many dressmaking fabrics are also suitable, although they may tend to fade more quickly.

There is also a wide choice of semi-transparent fabrics, usually in man-made fibres and often incorporating a woven thread pattern. Curtains made from these sheer fabrics usually remain drawn to provide privacy while letting in light and are also excellent for disguising a far from scenic view.

Instructions for measuring up for curtains are given on page 364 but bear in mind that some washable fabrics have a tendency to shrink: if in doubt buy an extra 10% of fabric length (10cm/4in for every metre/yard). Either wash the fabric before cutting out or make up with all the excess incorporated in the bottom hem. The curtain can then be let down after the first wash.

The sewing thread should match the fibre content of the fabric. A polyester thread is best for man-made fabrics. Sheers, man-made fabrics in particular, tend to slip when machining so tacking is essential. Fine pins and machine needles should be used and the tension set fairly loose. Use a scrap of spare fabric to test stitch size and tension before beginning. Fabrics which are very slippery or have an open weave can be machined by placing tissue paper between the machine base plate and fabric – to be torn away later.

Joining widths Curtain fabrics come in fairly standard widths. Try to buy the widest possible to avoid seams, but if necessary, join widths with a flat or French seam. See page 382 for matching patterns.

Selvedges, if they are woven more tightly than the rest of the fabric, should be trimmed off before seaming to prevent puckering. If selvedges are left, they should be clipped every 10cm/4in along the edge.

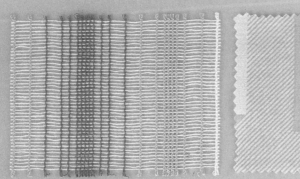

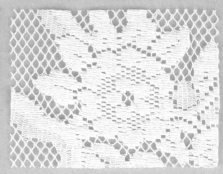

Above: In this bay window corner, full length sheer curtains soften the effect of plain roller blinds.
Left: The variety of fibres and weaving/printing techniques makes for an abundant choice of sheer fabrics, from fine nets to heavier lace designs and open weaves.

Measuring up

The curtain track or pole can be either in the window recess (most net curtains are hung in this position) or outside the recess and just above the window frame.

If the track is *outside* the recess, it should extend, if possible, 15cm/6in on each side of the window frame so that the curtains can be pulled back from the glass area during the day for maximum light. The height of the track above the window will depend on the best visual effect for the curtain length you choose. Lightweight sheer fabrics hung *inside* a window recess can be supported by a thin pole or elasticated wire slotted through a casing at the top of the curtain. A pole can also look good outside the recess.

How much fabric do you need? This method of calculating the total amount of fabric needed should be used for all curtains, lined or unlined. You may find that a pocket calculator is helpful.

1 Measure the total width needed

2 Work out number of fabric widths required

3 Multiply fabric widths by length to arrive at a total amount.

For a six-step guide to calculating your fabric needs see far right.

Width Measure the width of your track or pole using a steel tape or wooden rule. Multiply this figure by 1½ to 3 times depending on the heading tape. Standard heading tape, such as Rufflette 'Standard', needs at least 1½ – 2 times the track width in fabric. Light sheers can use up to three times. To the total width required, add on 2.5cm/1in for each side hem on the curtains (5cm/2in for sheers) and add the overlap for each curtain if the track is in two overlapping halves. Divide this total figure by the fabric width chosen for number of fabric widths needed. Err on the generous side, rounding up to full widths as you will need 3cm/1¼in seam allowance for each width join.

Length Measure the curtain length (see diagrams below). Add 4cm/1½in for top heading hem (Standard heading tape) and 15cm/6in for bottom hem. For sheer fabrics double this bottom hem allowance and add 6cm/2¼in for top hem for cased heading.

Pattern repeats If your fabric has a definite pattern, you must make an allowance for matching. As a guideline, add one extra pattern repeat for every fabric width. Pattern matching is covered in detail on page 382.

Six-step guide to fabric calculation

Taking curtain track width and finished curtain length, follow this step-by-step method to arrive at the total quantity of fabric required.

1 Measure width of track

2 Multiply track width by 1½-2 (for Standard heading tape) or by up to 3 times for other heading tapes and add side hem allowances (double for sheers). Add overlap fabric allowance if applicable.

3 Divide this figure by the width of fabric to give number of fabric widths.

4 This will probably not work out to a whole number of widths, so round this figure up to the next full width.

5 Multiply the number of fabric widths by length of curtain with top hem and bottom hem allowances to give total fabric needed.

6 This total has now to be divided between the number of curtains (generally two).

sill length

just below sill length

floor length

How long should your curtains be?

This is a matter of personal choice, and depends on the size of the window, your style of furnishings and the visual effect you want but basically curtain lengths fall into three categories: sill length, just below sill length (15–20cm/6–8in) and floor length.

Making up the curtains

Preparing to cut

You need a large flat surface that will take the complete length of your curtain and a full width of the fabric. A large table is best, or clear an area of floor space to work on. If you work in cramped conditions, you're likely to make mistakes in measuring and cutting out. You'll need space for an ironing board too.

Cutting out

It's vitally important that you start with a straight cut across the width. If the fabric has a straight thread pattern (the weft) across the width, pull out a thread for a straight line, otherwise cut at a right angle to the selvedges. Line up the pattern repeat (if necessary) before cutting subsequent widths.

Joining widths

Seam widths of fabric together to make up the total width for each curtain. If the curtain contains full widths and a half, place the half width on the outer side of the curtain. Use a flat seam if the edges are selvedges or for raw edges that can be neatly finished off. To hide raw edges use fell or French seams.

Seams for joining widths

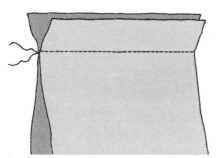

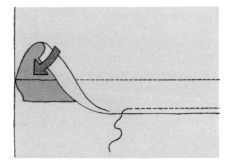

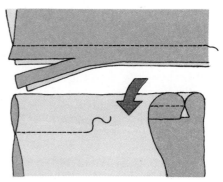

Flat seam
Right sides of fabric facing and edges matching, pin the two layers of fabric together and tack. Stitch 1.5cm/⅝in from edges. Remove tacking, press seam open. If the fabric edges are selvedges, clip seam allowance every 10cm/4in along the selvedge to prevent fabric puckering.

Fell seam
Right sides facing, make a flat seam of 1.5cm/⅝in. Press open. Trim one seam allowance in half. Fold other seam allowance over trimmed one and tack down to enclose raw edge. Top stitch through all layers. Remove tacking and press. One stitching line will show on right side of fabric.

French seam
Wrong sides facing, make a flat seam of 5mm/¼in. Trim to 3mm/⅛in. Press. Turn so right sides face and seam is on the fold. Tack the two layers together. Sew 1cm/½in down from first seam. Remove tacking. All raw edges are enclosed in seam and are to the reverse of the fabric. No stitching line shows on the right side of fabric.

Side hems

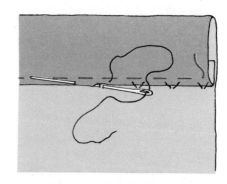

To neaten sides, turn 5mm/¼in of the hem allowance to wrong side and press. Fold remaining 2cm/¾in of hem allowance to wrong side. Tack. Stitch through all layers by machine or slipstitch. Remove all tacking. Slipstitch by passing the sewing needle through 1cm/½in of hem fold, picking up a single thread of the main fabric and then passing through 1cm/½in of fold again. Repeat down hem. Remove tacking. Sheer fabrics should be finished with a double side hem to look neat and prevent raw edges from showing through. Fold the 2.5cm/1in hem allowance to the wrong side and press. Fold over again to same size. Tack through all layers. Machine stitch or slipstitch in place.

PROFESSIONAL TOUCH

Hems for open weave fabrics

As with all sheer fabrics, side and bottom hems must be sewn with double turnings. You'll need to plan the placing of these hems so that the weave or pattern matches when the hem is turned under and also so that there's a maximum of solid pattern area available to sew through. In approximately the right position for the first turn of the hem, mark,

with tailor's chalk or tacking, a vertical line between the pattern repeats (horizontal for bottom hems).
1 Mark again between the next line of pattern repeats.
2 Fold the fabric to the wrong side along the first marked line, and the pattern of the main fabric and turned under hem should match. Tack.

3 Turn the hem again along the second line. Tack and stitch. Remove tacking.
If the pattern is large, mark a suitable hem allowance and match pattern areas as best as possible. Use French seams to join widths taking care to match the pattern repeat as for hems.

Choosing the right heading tape

A heading tape is designed to take up the fullness of the curtain fabric in even gathers or pleats. Various styles of ready-made heading tapes are available, and the choice will depend on the gathered/pleated effect you personally find most pleasing. Standard tape gives an evenly gathered heading while deeper tapes are made to create various pleat effects – eg, Rufflette Regis produces very close deep pleats. Cartridge wider pleats and Tridis, fan-shaped triple pleats (see pages 376 and 377).

The synthetic fibre version of Standard tape is particularly suitable for sheers and lightweight fabrics. When you buy heading tape, check with the retailer how much fullness of fabric is required for the tape chosen. Rufflette Standard Tape for example requires a minimum of 1½ times track width, Regis 2½ times.

Attaching Standard heading tape

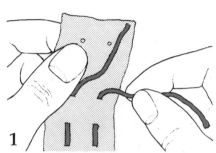

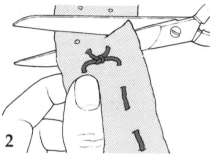

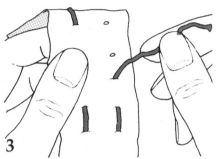

Measure finished width of curtain and add 4cm/1½in at either end for neatening. Cut a piece of heading tape to this length.
1 At the end where the curtains will overlap, pull 4cm/1½in of each cord free at the back of the tape.

On the wrong side of the heading tape, tie the 4cm/1½in of free cords together securely with a knot.
2 Trim off the surplus tape to leave 1.5cm/⅝in beyond the knot and press this seam allowance to the wrong side of the tape.

3 At the other end of the heading tape, gently ease out 4cm/1½in of cords on the right side. These cords will be used to pull the tape and fabric into gathers. Turn surplus tape to wrong side and press.

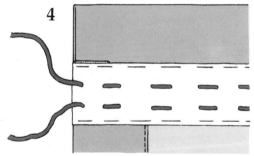

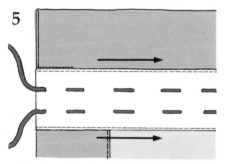

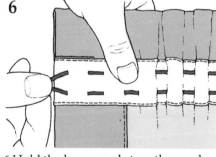

Turn 4cm/1½in at the head of the curtain to wrong side and press. Position the tape on the wrong side of curtain with top edge no more than 2.5cm/1in below the head.
4 Tack, tucking knot at centre side edge to wrong side.

5 Machine stitch the heading tape to curtain. Do not stitch across the short end with the loose cords. Stitch both long edges in the same direction as this will prevent any puckering while sewing. Remove tacking.

6 Hold the loose cords together and gently push tape up to gather the fabric until fully pleated.
Then ease out evenly until curtain is the right width.
Tie loose cords together. Insert tape hooks about every 8cm/3in.

Bottom hems

At bottom edge, turn 1cm/½in to wrong side and press. Turn balance of hem allowance to wrong side and pin. (For sheers see previous page.) Tack hem. Press complete curtain and hang on the track or pole for several days to allow fabric to 'drop'. Check level and height of hem and adjust if necessary. Slipstitch hem by hand and remove tacking. Sheer fabrics need a double hem, to hide raw edges, and look best with machined hems. Fold half the hem allowance to the wrong side and press. Fold the same amount again and tack hem (see diagram right). Hang for a few days. Check height and level and machine or slipstitch the hem. Remove tackings. Press.

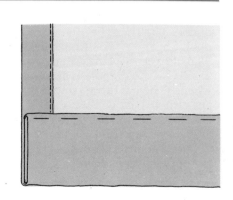

Choosing, making and caring for net curtains

Net curtains come in a wide range of plain, patterned and frilled sheer fabrics. Learn the most economical way of buying curtaining to suit the proportions of your window and keep unsightly joins to a minimum using these cutting and sewing techniques.

Net, lace and sheer curtains let in light while retaining privacy. They also filter harsh sunlight without totally obscuring the view, adding a fresh, decorative touch to the room scheme. Forget the old image of yellowing nets hanging limply from drooping wire – with recent developments in the design and manufacturing of sheer fabrics and hanging methods, there are now endless ways of styling them to create attractive window treatments.

Traditionally, net or lace curtains are hung permanently across the window recess, with heavier curtains on top. This gives scope for adding colourful trimmings, for using frilled or shaped curtaining, and for making use of modern curtain headings. Alternatively, try decorative lacy drapes over a simple roller blind, which is pulled down for warmth and privacy, or make a pretty sheer or net fabric into an Austrian blind, trimmed to echo the colours of top curtains.

Below: Modern net and sheer fabrics give you privacy with style.

Buying net curtain fabric

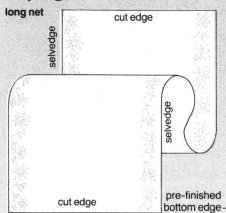

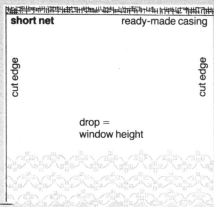

As seams in sheer curtains, particularly nets, tend to be very obvious against the light of a window, curtain net fabrics are sold in a wide variety of widths and drops to eliminate the need for seaming widths together.

Buying nets can be confusing – you can choose the fabric either in a suitable width (long nets) or with a suitable drop (short nets).

Long nets are sold in widths up to about 300cm/118in so that most curtains can be made from one piece of fabric, avoiding joins. The selvedges of the fabric form the side edges of the curtain. Measure the width of the window area to be covered and multiply this by 1½-3, according to the amount of fullness required, to calculate the width of curtain to buy.

Measure the height of the window area and add allowances for a top casing or turning, and a bottom hem, to calculate the length of curtaining to buy.

Short nets are ideal for windows that are wide rather than tall. They are manufactured so that the two edges of the fabric become the top and bottom of the curtain. One edge is pre-finished into a bottom hem, often with a frill, scallop or some other decorative finish, and the other edge has a casing to take either an elastic wire or a hanging rod. You therefore buy the *width* of fabric (called the drop) to fit the *height* of your window.

To determine the length of fabric to buy, multiply the width of the window area to be covered by 1½-3 times, according to how much fullness you require. The cut edges become the sides of the curtain and should be neatened with narrow double hems.

If you cannot buy the exact width that provides the drop of fabric that

Caring for and hanging net curtains

Some lace and sheer fabrics, particularly those in natural fibres such as cotton, can shrink by as much as 10% so buy sufficient fabric to allow for this if necessary. Wash and dry the fabric before cutting out so that any shrinkage has already occurred before making it up.

Check washing instructions when purchasing sheers as some of the more delicate fabrics can be damaged by machine washing. If in any doubt, wash gently by hand. If nylon nets turn yellow after a while try soaking them in a nylon whitener.

Net curtains are generally very light in weight so the method of hanging

does not have to be as bulky and strong as a standard type of curtain track. Nor do they need to be drawn back and forth as they are usually positioned permanently across the window.

Elasticated wire, with a small hook screwed in at each end, is the cheapest and most often used way to hang permanently positioned nets. This plastic-coated wire simply threads through the casing at the top of the curtain and, stretched taut, hooks to screw eyes inserted at either side of the window frame. It is suitable for small lightweight curtains but, unless put under very strong tension, tends to sag with large or

a selection of
sheer curtain fabrics

you need, buy the next size up and carefully unpick the top casing. Trim away any surplus fabric and remake the casing to the required depth so that the fabric is the exact drop required.

Stitching techniques for nets

Because of the transparency of nets, care must be taken in making hems and seams. Avoid seams where possible. If you have exceptionally large windows and cannot make a curtain from just one width of fabric, rather than joining fabric widths, make up two (or as many as necessary) separate curtains. Hang them next to each other and conceal the overlapping edges of the fabric in the folds of the curtain.

Hems should be double so that the raw edge of the fabric lies at the fold of the hem. If you have a deep hem on a patterned fabric and the pattern showing through the hem looks unsightly, insert a ribbon or a strip of fabric (the same width as the hem depth) into the hem so that only the solid colour shows through. The ribbon or fabric strip must have the same fibre content as the curtain, as should sewing thread and any heading tape used. See pages 365 and 371 for details of sewing hems and cased headings on sheer or net curtains.

Right: A length of lacy net transforms a bare window in a matter of minutes. Simply machine hem the ends and drape over a wooden pole and side brackets.

heavier curtains.

Curtain rods, designed for net or lightweight curtains that will not need to be drawn back and forth, also thread through the casing but – being in a rigid material – will not sag. Most of the rods designed for net curtains consist of two sections slotted together so that they are telescopic and easily adjustable to the exact size of the window. The rods simply sit on small hook-type fittings attached to the window frame. At least one manufacturer supplies the fittings backed with self-adhesive pads so they are easy to attach even to metal window frames.

Curtain track is required when net or lace curtains may need to be drawn back, perhaps to open French doors or to reveal large windows on a sunny day. Several tracks are specifically designed to be suitable for nets and lightweight curtains, and can be fixed to the wall or to the underside of a window recess. The curtains must have a taped – rather than a cased – heading so that hooks can be inserted to hang them on the track.

Heading for net curtains A cased heading is simple to make (see page 371) and gives a pretty gathered effect, but you may prefer to use a curtain heading tape for a more stylish finish. Some ordinary curtain tapes tend to be too heavy for nets and even those that are lightweight must be used with proper curtain track. However, a translucent man-made fibre tape specifically designed for nets is now available. It draws the fabric into neat pencil pleats, but differs from other pencil pleating tapes in having bars on the back that simply thread on to an elasticated wire or narrow rod for hanging. Alternatively, the tape also has pockets which enable it to be hung with curtain hooks from a curtain track or decorative pole.

Attach the heading tape to the top of the curtain in the usual way, then pull up the two cords to form the pleating.

Cased headings

Not all curtains have to be hung from tracks. When positioning fixed curtains either inside a window recess or in front of the window, a quick and effective method is to use an elasticated wire, or a brass or wooden rod, slotted through a casing at the top of the curtain. This is particularly suitable for lightweight sheers which are not to be drawn back and forth, and are used to give permanent privacy at a window. When estimating fabric for this method, allow 12cm/5in for the heading (more if rod is thick).

Turn 6cm/2½in to wrong side on top of curtain and press. Fold over again 6cm/2½in. Tack. Sew along lower edge of hem and again 2.5cm/1in higher up. Remove tacking and press. This forms the casing. If the rod is thicker than 1cm/½in diameter, measure the diameter and add 1.5cm/⅝in to give a casing depth into which the rod will slip easily. Add 3.5cm/1¾in and double this total figure. Make up as above, but with a deeper casing. Insert rod or wire through the casing, easing the fabric into gathers.

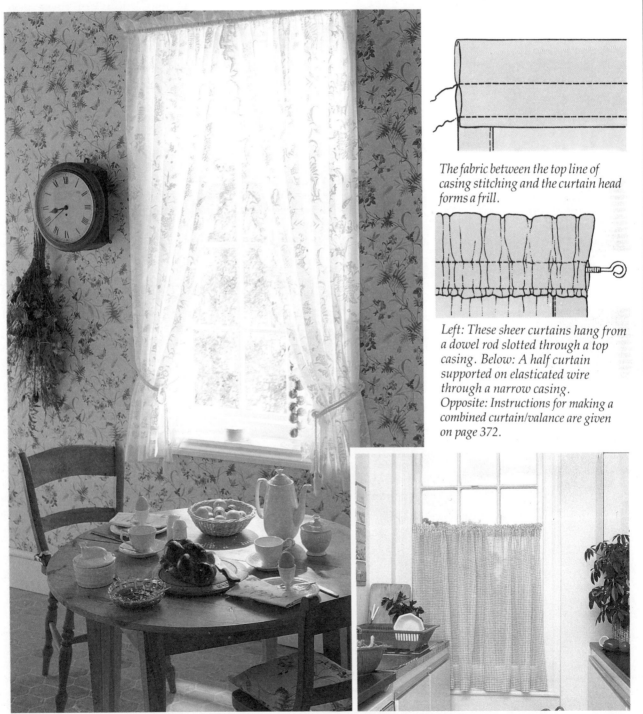

The fabric between the top line of casing stitching and the curtain head forms a frill.

Left: These sheer curtains hang from a dowel rod slotted through a top casing. Below: A half curtain supported on elasticated wire through a narrow casing. Opposite: Instructions for making a combined curtain/valance are given on page 372.

Creative ways to style net curtains

Use one of the many lovely net, lace, sheer or semi-sheer fabrics now in the shops to transform a bare window into a pretty and eye-catching room feature. Style the fabric into cross-over curtains, valanced curtains or a dramatic full-length drape.

Make pretty curtains from net, lace, sheer or semi-sheer fabric to dress a window in a kitchen, bathroom, hall or landing where heavier, drawn curtains are not always necessary. Use them in other rooms, too, during the summer when heavy curtains benefit from being cleaned and 'rested' away from the strong sunshine which fades and ages them.

Many styles of ready-made net curtains are now available in the shops, but making your own is economical and enables you to achieve a perfect fit for windows that are not a standard size. You also have a wider choice of fabric and can add trimmings to match your room scheme. Details of buying and sewing sheer fabrics, making a cased heading and how to care for net curtaining are given on pages 367 to 371. This chapter gives design ideas and making up instructions for three decorative styles of window dressing using these delicate fabrics. Choose from curtains with a combined valance, cross-over draped curtains or a simple but eye-catching draped valance over a decorative curtain pole.

Combined curtain and valance

A valance and lightweight side curtains sewn in one eliminates the need for two rods or wires and ensures a neater, less bulky heading. The curtains are gathered and fixed at the top so they cannot be drawn back and forth. Instead, they look very pretty draped to the sides and held with fabric or brass tie-backs which are easily released.

A separate strip of fabric joins the curtain and valance and forms the cased heading so the curtains can be hung on a decorative pole, simple rod or wire (see page 370).

Measuring up and cutting out
Cut a strip of fabric for the casing the length of the pole or the width of the window (whichever is the longer) plus side hem allowances. The depth of the strip must accommodate the wire or pole plus 1cm/½in seam allowance on each long side. Neaten the short side edges with narrow double hems if necessary.

Measure up and cut out the curtains in the usual way allowing at least 1½ times the window width for fullness, and sew side and lower edge hems. Trim the top of each curtain so that it will just reach the hanging rod. Run a row of gathering stitches 1cm/½in below this edge and pull up each curtain to exactly half the width of the casing strip. Tie the gathering threads securely and spread the gathers evenly over the width.

The depth of the valance is a matter of personal taste and varies according to the proportion of the window. Add 3cm/1¼in seam allowance to the required depth and allow approximately twice the width of the window for the width of the valance. Neaten the side edges with a narrow double hem (1cm/½in and 1cm/½in). Hem the bottom edge in a similar way or add a lace or frilled edging, trimming away any excess hem allowance. Omit hems if using selvedges. Run a gathering thread along the top edge of the valance and pull up to the width of the casing strip.

Making up the curtains and valance

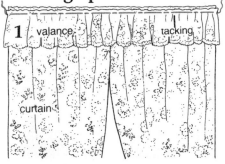

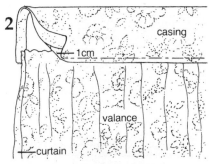

Lay the curtains out flat, right side up and with the two inside edges butted up together. Lay the valance across the two curtains, wrong side down, matching gathered edges.
1 Tack securely together along the top edge.

2 Turn 1cm/½in to the wrong side along all the edges of the casing strip and tack to hold. Fold the strip in half, lengthwise, wrong sides facing, and place over the top gathered edges of the curtain/valance, overlapping it by 1cm/½in so that the raw edges are enclosed in the casing. Tack in place.
Machine stitch the length of casing in place, sewing 5mm/⅜in from the edge through all layers – curtain, valance and both sides of the casing.

Remove all tacking, press well and thread on to a rod or wire to hang. Hold the curtains to the sides of the window with a simple tie-back. Choose from a length of silken cord (adding tassels to the ends), matching or contrasting ribbon or a length of delicately scalloped and embroidered broderie anglaise with the raw edge neatened. See pages 370, 371 and opposite for ideas.

Prettily draped cross-over curtains: the top edges can be overlapped either partially or completely.

Cross-over draped curtains

These are gathered up with the usual amount of fullness but are wide enough to overlap at the top so that while draped back to the sides of the window, forming attractive folds, they do not leave a large area of bare window.

The two curtains are sewn together at the top and hang on a single rod or wire, so they can't, of course, be drawn back and forth.

To maintain a straight lower edge on the curtain, the draped inside edge of each curtain requires a greater length of fabric than the straight outer edge. The hems are therefore angled.

Measuring up and cutting out

Allow at least 1½ times the window width for the width of *each* curtain.

1 Measure the length of the straight shorter outside edge from the hanging wire or rod to the window sill. To calculate the length of the longer inner edge, drape a tape measure from one end of the rod to a suitable tie-back point on the opposite side of the window and down to the window sill. Add the

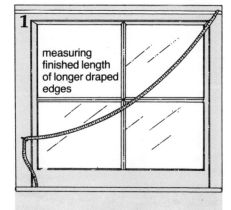

same allowance for the top casing and bottom hem to each of these measurements.

Cut both curtains to the longer length then lay right sides together and mark off the shorter length along one side. Cut diagonally across from this point to the opposite lower corner to angle the hem. This ensures that one curtain slopes in the reverse direction to the other.

Neaten side and lower edges with

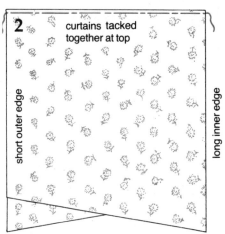

narrow double hems, adding a frill to the longer inside edges if required (see page 402).

2 With right sides upwards, lay one curtain on top of the other and tack the straight top edges together. Complete the heading, treating the two curtains as one, either adding a heading tape or making a casing. Hang the curtains and drape them back to the sides, holding them with fabric tie-backs or decorative curtain holders.

All-in-one valance and side curtains

The dramatic effect of this draped valance falling into side curtains is simply achieved by securing a long length of reversible lacy curtaining over a decorative curtain pole. This creative style of window dressing is pretty rather than practical and ideal as a replacement for heavier curtains during the summer.

Measuring up

To calculate the amount of fabric required, drape a tape measure (or a piece of string) from one end of the pole to the other, allowing it to droop in the curve you want for the valance. Add this measurement to the length needed for the side curtains (twice the height from floor to pole) plus hem allowances on both sides. This gives the length of fabric required.

If you are using a patterned fabric with a one-way design, the curtain will have to be cut in two so that the pattern will be upright on both sides. Add enough extra fabric to join two pieces together with a narrow French seam. The design should be level on both side curtains, so that the same part of the pattern lies at the lower edge on each, and you may also need to allow extra fabric for this.

Making up

As this type of curtain is not drawn across the window, one width of fabric is normally sufficient, and therefore side hems are unnecessary. Cut a fabric with a one way pattern in half across the width and join the top edges of the two halves with a narrow French seam so that the pattern will be upright on both side curtains. Neaten the lower edges with a narrow double hem, a pretty satin binding or with a lace or frilled edging.

Measure the length of the drop from each end and, with tailor's chalk, draw two lines across the width of the fabric to mark the central area allowed for the valance drape. Lay the fabric over the pole with the curtains falling behind and the valance in front of the pole. Adjust the fabric so that the two curtains hang well, then adjust and pin folds at both ends of the valance so that it falls in a pleasing way. Take down the curtains/valance carefully and secure the folds at each end of the valance with a few hand stitches. Remove pins and re-hang to check the final effect, adjusting if necessary.

To prevent the fabric slipping off the pole, cut two 5cm/2in pieces of 'stick and sew' Velcro fastening. Stitch the sew-on halves of the Velcro to the ends of the valance on the wrong side, at a point where the fabric has been folded several times so that they will not show.

Replace the curtains/valance on the curtain pole and stick the self-adhesive halves of the Velcro to the pole to correspond with the sewn on halves. Add extra Velcro if the valance shows a tendency to slip.

Below: Lengths of border-patterned Terylene net create a strikingly pretty window dressing.

Curtain heading tapes and detachable linings

All curtains, with the exception of sheers and curtains with a deliberately delicate look, gain from a lining. Adding a lining will cost you more in money and effort, but the curtains will hang better, look more professional and provide valuable insulation.

Curtains shut out the dark, protect the sleeper from the dawn and give privacy. A lining acts as a barrier between the curtain and window and fulfils several vital functions:
– it cuts down light penetration through the curtain fabric (especially important in bedrooms)
– it provides insulation, helping to cut down on draughts and cold air from the windows
– it weighs down the curtain, giving it more 'body' and a better hang
– it protects the curtain fabric from the damaging effects of sunlight, and to some extent from dirt and dust

– a detachable lining can be removed for separate laundering
– on really draughty windows where one lining is not enough, an interlining of a fine blanket-like material sewn to the curtain fabric before the lining is attached gives a further layer of insulation. Interlinings are dealt with on page 386.
The fabric generally sold as curtain lining' is 100% cotton. The weave is close and dense to cut out light and draughts. Thermal curtain-lining fabric, which has a special coating on one side, is a little more expensive to buy, but provides extra insulation.

Choosing the lining method
There are several ways to line curtains. Which method you choose depends on the size of the curtain and the weight of the fabric and, of course, your personal preference.
Detachable linings are suitable if the curtain and lining fabric have different laundering requirements, or if you want to add a lining to an existing unlined curtain. The curtain and lining are completely separate and just held together at the top by virtue of sharing the same curtain hooks.
Sewn-in linings are suitable for small or lightweight curtains. They are joined to the curtain down the side hems and across the top. They are covered in the next chapter.
Locked-in linings are suitable for large or weighty curtains. In addition to being attached to the curtain across the top and down the sides, the lining is invisibly lock-stitched to the curtain fabric at regular intervals from top to bottom over the whole curtain. Locked-in linings are dealt with on pages 384–5.

Below: The lining in these curtains gives them extra body and a good hang.

Creating a heading for your curtain

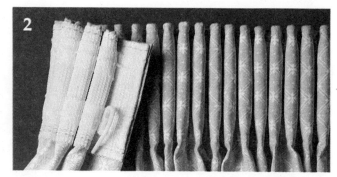

The easiest way to create a decorative heading is to use a ready-made curtain heading tape. This has cords running through it to pull both tape and fabric up into gathers or pleats, and pockets for hanging hooks.
The basic heading styles are:
1 Even gathering
2 Pencil pleating
3 Triple pleating
4 Cylindrical pleating
There are other tapes which create different visual effects, but they are less widely available. If you do use tapes other than the four styles above, follow the manufacturers' instructions for the amount of tape and fabric needed and attaching method. Hand-made headings – hard work but very professional-looking – are dealt with on pages 388–91.

How much fabric?

The type of heading you use determines the amount of fabric needed for both curtains and lining, so choosing a heading should be your first consideration. A gathered heading needs only 1½ times the track width of fabric, although up to 3 times can be used for sheers. Pencil pleats need 2¼ to 2½ times and triple and cylindrical pleats twice the track width.

How much tape?

You need as much tape as the finished flat width of each curtain plus an extra amount for accurate placing of the pleats and neatening. Check with the shop assistant how much you need – for triple pleating allow 30cm/12in extra per curtain.

Which heading?

The type of heading you choose depends on the look you want. Each style of heading tape shown is suitable for any weight of fabric, but there are some general guidelines to follow.
For short curtains the shallower tapes such as 'Rufflette' brand gathered tape, pencil pleating, triple pleating and cylindrical pleating look best. A deep heading tape might look top-heavy on a short curtain.

Pencil pleating

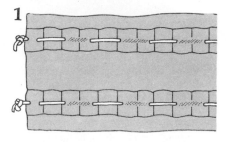

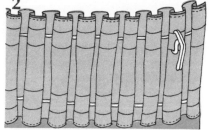

For each curtain, cut a piece of tape to the curtain width plus at least 7cm/2¾in for neatening edges.
1 At the edge of the tape which will be at the centre, pull 4cm/1½in of cords free and knot. Trim surplus tape to within 5mm/¼in of knots and turn edge to wrong side. (The right side of the tape has pockets.) At the other end, pull 5cm/2in of cords free and turn tape to wrong side. Place wrong side of tape to wrong side of curtain 3mm/⅛in down from the top edge with the tape the correct way up. (Rufflette brand tape has a yellow line at the bottom.) If you are not sure which way up the tape should be, insert hooks and check the hang on your track. Tack the tape to the curtain 3mm/⅛in in from each long edge and, from the wrong side of the curtain, machine the tape each side in the same direction. Machine both short edges, taking care not to stitch across loose cords. Hold cords, pull up fabric to maximum pleating, then ease to correct width.
2 Knot the cords to secure, and insert hooks at either end and at about 8cm/3in intervals along the tape. (With Rufflette Regis, use R40 hooks) If you want the curtain to cover the track, add hooks to the bottom row of pockets. If you want it to hang below, use the top row.

Triple pleating

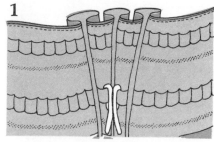

At the edge of the tape which will be at the centre, cut across the first pleat to free the cords. Knot each cord and trim surplus tape to 5mm/¼in. If the curtain tracks overlap turn 4cm/1½in of tape to the wrong side of this centre edge. If the curtains are to butt up, turn 9cm/3½in. The amount of tape turned back on the centre edge governs the pleat position. Neaten this edge and cut tape to fit curtain width allowing at least 6cm/2¼in at the outer edge for neatening. Free 5cm/2in of the cords from outer edge, free from tape with scissors point. Trim off surplus tape to within 5mm/¼in of cords and fold to

For long curtains extra-deep versions of pencil and triple pleating give the best proportioned look, but standard depth tapes can also be used if preferred. With sheer fabrics, even a simple gathered tape gives a neat heading on long curtains.

Fabric choice and laundering

Curtain tapes are suitable for any weight or type of fabric and are washable and dry cleanable, so you should launder curtains according to the washing instructions of your curtain fabric. Use the lowest heat when ironing synthetic fibre tapes.

Which curtain track?

Which curtain track you use depends on whether you want the curtain to conceal it (as in most plastic tracking), or to be suspended below. Poles fall into this second category.
Some tapes such as Rufflette brand gathered (Standard), pencil pleating (Regis), triple pleating (Tridis) and cylindrical pleating (Cartridge) have hook pockets positioned so that they can be used with either type of hanging. Deep triple pleating (Deep Tridis) and deeper pencil pleating (Deep Regis) are manufactured in two versions, one for covering the track, the other for a suspended heading.

How to attach a heading tape

The easiest tape to sew to a curtain head is gathered tape (see page 366).

Above: The photographs show,
1 gathered heading (Rufflette Standard),
2 pencil pleating (Rufflette Regis),
3 triple pleating (Rufflette Tridis) and
4 cylindrical pleating (Rufflette Cartridge).

For pencil, triple or cylindrical pleating tape, turn a minimum hem allowance of 6mm/¼in at the top of curtain to the wrong side and press. When attaching tape, be careful to knot the cords on the correct end of the curtain, depending on whether it is to be hung on the left or on the right. The cord ends are knotted and turned to the wrong side on the centre edges of each curtain. Never cut off surplus cords at outer edges.

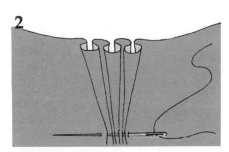

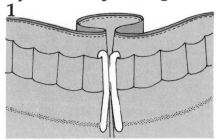

Cylindrical pleating

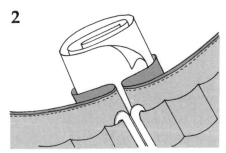

wrong side.
Sew in place as for pencil pleating. Pull the cords and push up the tape and fabric to form the first set of pleats. Move along, forming pleats and tie a slip knot with the cords.
1 This style of tape needs a two-pronged hook (Rufflette R10). One hook is inserted behind each pleat set, each prong into an adjacent pocket. Add a hook at both the centre and outer edge. Use the bottom pockets for covering the track, the top for suspending the curtain.
2 To keep the pleats tight, a small neat tack can be sewn through the base of the front of each pleat.

At the edge of the tape which will be at the centre, cut across the first pleat to free the cords. Knot each cord and cut tape to within 5mm/¼in of knots.
If your two curtain tracks overlap, turn 2.5cm/1in to wrong side of this centre edge. If the curtains are to butt up, turn 5cm/2in to neaten. Cut the tape to fit the curtain width allowing at least 6cm/2¼in at the outer edge for neatening. Free 5cm/2in of the cords from outer edge, picking cords out with a scissor point if they are not visible. Trim tape to within 5mm/¼in of cords. Attach tape as for pencil pleating.

Hold the cords and push the tape up into pleats, keeping each pleat tight. Tie a slip knot to secure cords.
1 The same hooks are used as for the triple pleating, one for each pleat and one at each end, placed in the bottom row of pockets for covering the track or the top row for suspending.
2 For extra pleat definition, each pleat can be stuffed with rolled-up tissue paper.

Making a detachable lining

Detachable linings are the simplest of all to make. These completely separate linings are attached to the main curtains by sharing the same curtain hooks.

The main advantage of a detachable lining is that the curtain and lining can be laundered separately. This could be useful if the fabric and lining have different laundering requirements – in some cases the lining may be dry cleanable only (as with thermal lining material) and the curtain fabric washable, or vice-versa.

Even if both the curtain and lining are washable, the combined weight of both sewn together often makes the curtain a very heavy and bulky item to wash by hand. If the curtain is large it may be too bulky to fit in a domestic washing machine. A detachable lining which can be separated from the curtain reduces this bulk.

A special heading tape is available for detachable linings. It is designed to be used in conjunction with a heading tape on the curtain sharing the same hooks. Some curtain tracks have combined hooks and gliders with an additional ring for hooking on a lining.

Detachable linings use less fabric than sewn-in linings since, whichever type of heading is on the curtain, only 1½ times the track width in lining is necessary.

This type of lining can easily be added to existing unlined curtains.

Measure up and cut out the main fabric and lining, using the same

Above: A strip of contrast fabric sewn to the inner edge and bottom of each curtain accentuates the draped shape. Instructions for making contrast fabric borders are given on pages 402–3. The pleated tie-back is shown opposite.

basic method as for unlined curtains (see page 364), but allowing sufficient fabric width for the heading of your choice.

Make up the main curtain in exactly the same way as for an unlined curtain, attaching the heading tape of your choice.

Make up the lining as for an unlined curtain, but leave the top as a raw edge and attach lining heading tape to this raw edge as described in the instructions (right).

Attaching lining heading tape

1

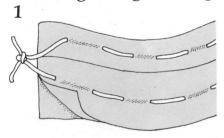

2

1cm

3

This tape (Rufflette brand) is made up of two 'skirts', one skirt fitting each side of the top of the lining fabric.

The right side of the tape is the corded side.

Remember to make a left and right-hand version for a pair of curtains.

Cut a length of lining tape to the width of the curtain plus at least 10cm/4in for neatening the ends.

1 At the end of the tape that will be at the centre, pull the two cords free and secure with a knot. Trim off surplus tape up to the knot.

2 Ease the two skirts apart and slip the top of the lining between the skirts, with the corded side on the right side of the lining.

Place the knotted end at the centre edge of the curtain lining, overhanging the end of the lining

by 1cm/½in.

Turn 5mm/¼in and then remaining 5mm/¼in at knotted end of tape to wrong side of lining. Pin tape in place.

At outer edge of tape, pull 4cm/1½in of each cord free and trim surplus tape so that it overhangs lining by 1cm/½in. Neaten with a double hem 5mm/¼in and 5mm/¼in to wrong side of lining, leaving the

4

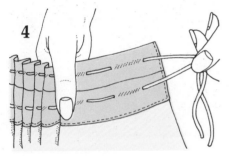

5

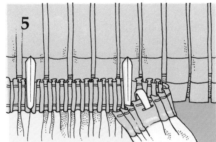

6

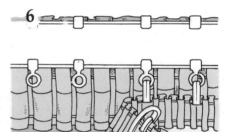

loose cords free for gathering up. Tack tape in place.

3 Stitch tape in place, close to the bottom edge and down both sides, being sure not to catch the loose ends of the cords into the stitching. Remove tacking.

4 Hold the two cord ends and gently pull the cords at the same time as pushing up the fabric and

tape until the fabric is fully gathered. Now ease out the gathers until the lining is the required fullness for the curtain.

5 Insert curtain hooks, spacing evenly at about every 8cm/3in through slits on top of the lining tape. With wrong side of lining and wrong side of curtain facing, fit the hooks through the pockets on the

curtain heading tape, so that both lining and curtain hang from the same hooks.

6 For curtain tracks that have combined hook/gliders with rings for lining hooks, the lining tape should be fitted with hooks which then fit through the rings under the main curtain hooks.

DESIGN EXTRA

Pleated curtain tie-back

This is a quick and simple way to make a professional looking pleated tie-back using curtain heading tape. The most suitable style of tape to use is pencil pleating, either Rufflette Regis (7.5cm/3in deep) or Deep Regis (13.8cm/5½in).

Measure round the full bulk of the pulled back curtain and lining. Cut fabric to 2½ times this length plus 3cm/1¼in and to same depth as the heading tape plus 3cm/1¼in. Cut tape the same

length.

All round the fabric, turn 1cm/½in to wrong side and tack. Centre tape on wrong side of fabric. Neaten the short ends of the tape as for a curtain head. Stitch tape in place and pull up to pleat. To hold the two ends of the tie-back together, sew a ring to each end on the wrong sides. Slot the rings onto a hook screwed into the wall, positioned so that the tie-back holds the curtain in a generous drape.

Sewn-in curtain linings for a permanent finish

If your curtain fabric and lining can be laundered together, the sewn-in method of curtain lining is ideal. Its advantage is that it gives you a neat finish down the side hems and across the top. The hem of the lining is left free from the curtain for the best possible hang.

With this method, curtains and lining are attached by being sewn together down the side hems and across the top. Both long and short curtains can be lined like this.

Before reading this chapter read through pages 364–6 and 375–7 for basic curtain making techniques.

Long, heavy curtains are best lined by the locked-in method which secures curtain and lining with vertical lines of stitching (see pages 384–5).

Measuring up and cutting out

Calculate the amount of fabric needed for each curtain using the same basic method as for unlined curtains, but allowing sufficient fabric width for the heading of your choice. Measure up for the lining fabric in exactly the same way as for the curtain fabric, but cut the lining fabric to 1cm/½in less than the *finished* width of curtain, and do not add the hem allowance at the top. The top hem allowance on the curtain is 4cm/1½in for gathered heading tape and a minimum of 6mm/¼in for other heading tapes (including gathered tape when used as a suspended heading).

Right: A pleated frill on these bedroom curtains gives them a soft, but not too feminine, designer touch.

Making a sewn-in curtain lining

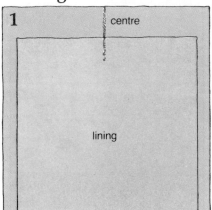

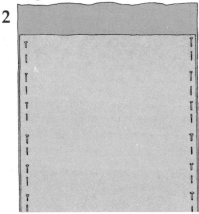

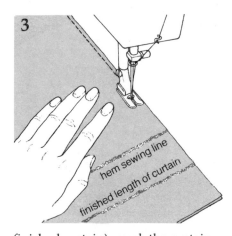

With flat seams, join the curtain fabric widths together to make up each curtain, and join the lining fabric widths to make up each lining. Fell or French seams are not necessary since the edges of the flat seam will be hidden between the lining and the curtain.

1 Mark the centre point on the wrong side of both the curtain fabric and the lining with tailor's chalk.

2 Position lining on curtain fabric, right sides facing with top of lining 4cm/1½in (or hem allowance) below the curtain fabric. Pin the raw edges together down both sides. You will find that the curtain fabric is wider than the lining, so allow the curtain fabric to form a few gentle folds in order to match the raw edges exactly.

Measuring from the top of the lining fabric (ie, the top of the

finished curtain), mark the curtain length required with tailor's chalk on to both the lining and the curtain fabric. Also mark the position of the hem. The hem allowance for the bottom edge is generally 15cm/6in, 1cm/½in being turned under first, followed by 14cm/5½in.

3 Sew both side seams with a 1cm/½in seam, sewing from the top of the lining to within 10cm/4in of the hem sewing line.

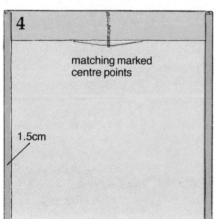

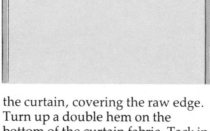

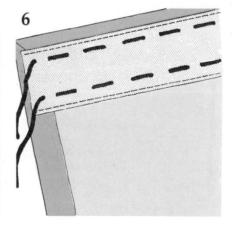

4 Turn curtain fabric and lining through to the right side. Press lining and curtain fabric flat, matching the centre marked points on lining and fabric. The curtain fabric overlaps on the lining side by 1.5cm/⅝in down each side edge.
5 Turn curtain fabric to the lining side at the top of the curtain, folding along the top edge of the lining.
6 Attach heading tape to the top of

the curtain, covering the raw edge. Turn up a double hem on the bottom of the curtain fabric. Tack in place.
For extra neatness and less bulk on the corners you can mitre each corner.
Turn up a double hem to the wrong side on the lining fabric, so that the lining hangs about 2cm/¾in above hem level of curtain fabric. The depth of the lining hem should be

the same as, or less than, the curtain fabric hem, so you will have to trim off the surplus lining fabric to make the hem to the correct depth. Tack hem in place.
Pull up the heading tape to make the curtains the correct width for the window. Hang the curtains in place for several days to give the fabric time to 'drop'. Adjust the hems if necessary and then slipstitch.

Mock mitres on hem corners

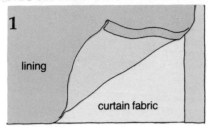

1 lining   curtain fabric

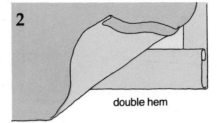

2 double hem

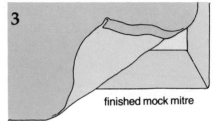

3 finished mock mitre

A mitred corner makes a neat finish on a curtain hem. A true mitre should be a 45° angle, but with curtains, the bottom hem is deeper than the side hems and a mock mitre is by far the simplest method.

To make this mock mitred corner you have to cheat with the angle

of the mitre. Only one side of the corner (the deeper bottom hem side) is mitred, and this is not at a 45° angle.

The lining and the curtain fabric are sewn together to within 10cm/4in of the hem sewing line (see page 380).

1 Turn in and press the

remaining side hem allowance on the curtain fabric.

2 Turn up a double hem at the bottom.

3 Fold the bottom hem allowance under at an angle on the corner until its top edge touches the side hem allowance. Sew in place with slipstitches.

Matching patterned fabrics

When working with patterned fabric, take care to match the pattern correctly along each seam. On the selvedge edge of the fabric, measure the distance between one pattern and the next identical one. This is called the 'pattern repeat' and you will often see it quoted on furnishing fabric details. You need to know the length of the pattern repeat when you are measuring up for curtains as you must buy extra fabric for matching the pattern. Unless you are making curtains for a very narrow window, each curtain will be made up of more than one width of fabric. With a patterned fabric, the pattern must be matched at each seam and also at the centre of a pair of curtains where they join when closed.

1 Before cutting your first piece of curtain fabric, make sure the end is cut exactly straight (at right angles to the sides.) With tailor's chalk mark a line across the width to

indicate the top hem allowance. For the best effect, you need to show the complete pattern, or a representative proportion of it, along the top edge of the curtain. If your tailor's chalk line intersects the pattern at a visually unbalanced point (perhaps cutting through a flower pattern so that the heads would be turned to the wrong side for hem allowance and stalks left at the top of the curtain) then alter the top hem allowance. Re-position the tailor's chalk line and cut off any surplus fabric to leave just the hem allowance.

2 Cut this first piece of fabric to the required length (drop of curtain plus top and bottom hems) and lay right side up on a large table or on the floor. Lay out the rest of the fabric, right side upwards, and match the pattern to the first cut piece.

Cut the second piece of fabric so that you have two identical pieces.

Right: Even if you are making up curtains in a small overall pattern like this design, it's important to match the pattern when cutting out the fabric widths and when seaming them together.

Continue in this way until you have cut all the required fabric pieces.

To seam two pieces together

Mark the centre of each pattern repeat on the fabric selvedges (or the cut side edges) with a pin. Lay the two pieces of fabric, right sides facing, matching the pins in the selvedge edges, and pin along the seamline. Turn the fabric to the right side and check that the pattern is matching exactly – make adjustments if necessary.

Tack along the seamline. Remove all pins and then turn the fabric to the right side and check again that the pattern is matching. Sew the seam and remove tacking.

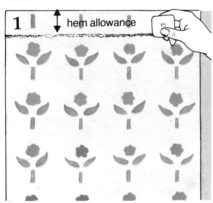

1 hem allowance

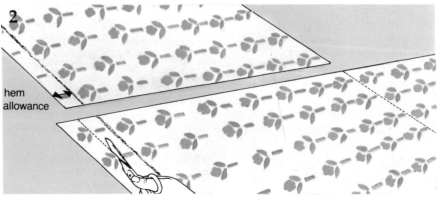

2 hem allowance

Pleated perfection

A pleated curtain frill gives a soft designer look to curtains used in any room.

Cut the curtain lining as for a sewn-in lining, but to the same width as the curtain fabric.

To calculate the fabric needed for the pleated frill, double the finished frill width (say 6cm/ 2¼in) and add 5cm/2in (ie total width of 17cm/6½in). For length allow three times the finished curtain drop and add 3cm/1¼in. Wrong sides facing, fold the fabric in half along its length. Make pleats in either box pleat style (below left) or side pleat style (below right), by marking the pleat spacings with tailor's chalk down the frill fabric and folding and tacking in place.

Neaten the top short edge with a 5mm/¼in and 1cm/½in double hem.
1 Place frill to right side of curtain, matching raw edges and with neatened short edge to finished top of curtain. Cut off any left-over trim at hemline and neaten the edge. Tack in place.
2 Lay lining fabric right sides facing to curtain fabric, matching raw edges and sew both side hems taking 2.5cm/1in seams. Continue making up as for sewn-in linings.

If you have a ruffler attachment for your machine, you can use this to make side pleats quickly from a single fabric thickness. Use half the frill width, and neaten the frill edge with a double hem.

box pleats

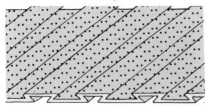

side pleats

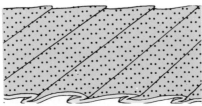

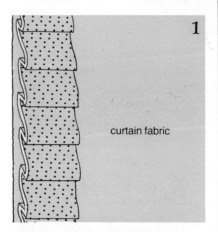

curtain fabric

1

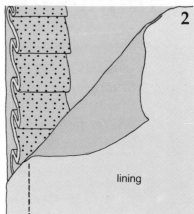

lining

2

Locked-in and decorative linings and interlining

Locked-in linings give a really professional look to large curtains and help them to hang beautifully.
Add interlining for an even more luxurious touch or a thermal lining for extra insulation. Alternatively, turn the lining itself into a decorative feature.

Curtain linings no longer have to be dull beige sateen. They are now available in a wide range of colours and even thermal lining, coated with a layer of insulating material, can be silvery white or rich cream, as well as beige.

Locked-in linings help to give large curtains a really professional finish. For ultra-elegant curtains, add inter-

Above: Wide curtains often suffer from bunched up linings but with the lining locked-in they hang beautifully.

lining as well. This helps curtains to look luxuriously thick and to drape well, and will insulate windows almost as effectively as double glazing.

There is no real reason why a closely-woven dress print or furnishing cotton should not be used as a lining. The extra expense is justified by the decorative effect. Reveal the lining by making it into a decorative border or simply drape the curtain back attractively. Follow one of these two ways of showing off decorative linings for an attractive window treatment.

Curtains with locked-in linings

Locking is a means of joining curtain fabric and lining together at intervals down the length. Held against the lining in this way, the fabric of large, wide or heavy curtains drapes well and falls in graceful folds. Lining also protects the fabric from direct sunlight and dust, and provides more effective insulation.

Cutting out

Measure and cut out curtain fabric as for unlined curtains (see page 364), allowing sufficient width for the heading and adding 4cm/1½in top hem, 10cm/4in bottom hem, 4cm/1½in for each side hem and 3cm/1¼in for each seam joining fabric widths, if necessary. Cut lining to the same width, joining widths if necessary, but to the *finished* curtain length.

Right: Locking in the lining.

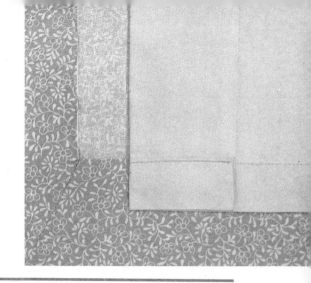

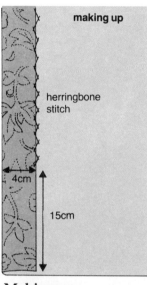

making up

herringbone stitch

4cm

15cm

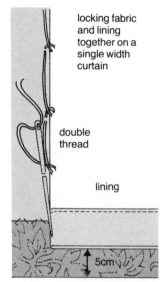

locking fabric and lining together on a single width curtain

double thread

lining

5cm

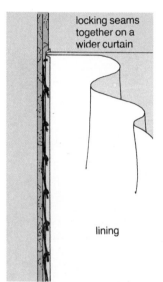

locking seams together on a wider curtain

lining

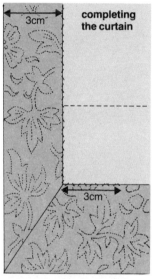

completing the curtain

3cm

3cm

Making up

Press a 4cm/1½in turning to the wrong side down each side of the curtain, making sure it is straight with the grain.
Herringbone stitch down these edges using a large stitch and picking up just a thread on the main fabric so the stitches will not show on the right side. End stitching about 15cm/6in above lower edge to allow for hem.
Turn up and press a 10cm/4in bottom hem, making sure it is absolutely straight. Fold into a mock mitre in the corners (see page 382). Fold in 2cm/¾in along the top edge of hem, then tack and slipstitch down taking care not to make stitches noticeable on the right side of curtain.
Make a hem along the bottom edge of lining, turning 1.5cm/⅝in then 3.5cm/1⅜in to the wrong side, and machine or hand stitch.

Locking together

Lay curtain fabric out flat, right side down, on a large table or the floor.

Place the lining on top, wrong side down, with the lower edge 5cm/2in above lower edge of curtain.
On a single width curtain fold back one third of the lining, aligning top and bottom edges to make sure the fold is straight and smoothing it down with your fingertips.
Using double thread and working from right to left, pick up two threads on the lining and then the same on the curtain fabric. Leave a loop of thread running along for about 10cm/4in, then again pick up a thread or two in the lining and fabric, bringing the needle out into the loop of thread like a large blanket stitch. Continue working along the length of the curtain in this way, leaving the thread fairly loose so that it does not pull on the fabric.
Fold the lining back over the fabric and smooth flat, then fold back a third of the lining on the other long side and stitch in the same way.
On a wider curtain, the seams should be locked together and further lines of locking stitches

made at approximately 40cm/16in intervals (dividing each width into thirds). Begin at the seam nearest to the centre of the curtain, folding back the lining and stitching as above, and work outwards from this. When locking two seams together, stitch through the seam allowances only so no stitches have to be made on the main fabric of curtain or lining.

Completing the curtain

Trim the lining width so the edges are even with the curtain edges then turn in 3cm/1in down each side of lining. Tack the lining down without stretching it, then neatly slipstitch it to the folded-in edge of the curtain. Remove tacking, then slipstitch lining around each lower corner for about 3cm/1¼in leaving the remaining hemmed edges free. Measure the required length from bottom to top at intervals and turn in the top hem. Press and tack down, then attach the heading tape, covering the raw edge in the usual way.

a selection of curtain
linings and interlinings

Curtains with interlining and linings

An interlining adds a luxurious, almost padded effect to curtains, as well as providing effective window insulation. Most curtain fabrics can be interlined except, of course, sheers and nets.

The most popular interlining is a brushed cotton, which resembles a thin fluffy blanket. A domette is a finer, fluffy fabric suitable for interlining more delicate curtaining. There are also synthetic versions which drape very well but do not help to block out the light.

Interlined curtains are an extension of curtains with locked-in linings, so read those instructions first.

Cutting out

Cut out and join widths of curtain fabric and lining. Cut out interlining to the same size as curtain fabric.

Making up

To join widths of interlining, butt the edges together, or very slightly overlap them, and oversew or herringbone stitch to hold. You can join with a zigzag machine stitch, but take care not to stretch the interlining in doing this.

Spread the interlining out flat on a table or the floor and lay the curtain fabric, wrong side down, on top, smoothing it out evenly all over. Fold back the fabric and lock it to the interlining, as for locking in linings. Stitch two rows of locking on each width of fabric and a row on each seam.

When the locking is complete, smooth down the fabric over the interlining and tack the two together all round the edge.

Turn the curtain over so that the interlining is uppermost, fold in a 4cm/1½in turning down each side and herringbone down. Fold up a 10cm/4in single thickness bottom hem, mitring corners, and herringbone this to the interlining.

Adding lining

Do not make a hem on the lining but lay it right side up on the interlined side of curtain with side and bottom edges together. Lock the lining to the interlining and complete curtain as before except along the lower edge of lining, which should be turned in and slipstitched down as for the side edges.

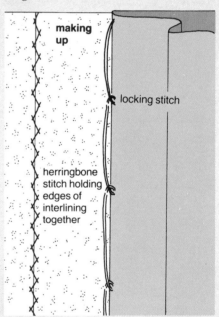

making up

locking stitch

herringbone stitch holding edges of interlining together

Curtains with lining borders

A very attractive way of showing off a decorative lining is to use it to form a border down each side of the curtain. This does not involve any extra work when making up curtains by the sewn-in lining method, as it is simply a reversal of the normal procedure of wrapping the fabric on to the lining side.

Whether it is plain or patterned, toning or contrasting, choose your lining carefully so that it highlights the curtain fabric. Use a pretty print to enliven plain curtains, or frame a geometric or floral pattern with a plain border in a strong colour.

Making up

Follow the instructions on pages 380–1 for curtains with sewn-in linings, but cut the *linings* rather than the curtain fabric to the larger size. For a 5cm/2in border down each side of the curtain, cut the lining 10cm/4in wider than the curtain fabric. Make up the curtains in the normal way but press them so that a strip of lining forms a border down each side edge before completing top edge and finishing the bottom hem.

Diagonal draping

Turn simple curtains into an unusual and decorative room feature by using a pretty or eye-catching fabric rather than a plain lining fabric and draping back the curtain corners to reveal it. Choose the lining to complement your curtains and perhaps to bring a splash of colour or an interesting pattern into the room. Adapt the idea to give a fresh new look to existing but rather dull curtains or economise by using old but attractive curtains as the lining fabric for a new pair.

The method of making up is extremely simple but the two fabrics must be compatible, needing the same type of cleaning and care, and both must be pre-shrunk as you will not have a hem to let down. You will need the same amount of lining as curtain fabric.

Making up

Measure up (see page 364) and cut curtain fabric and lining to exactly the same size, joining widths if necessary.

Place the curtain fabric and lining right sides together and stitch round three sides, leaving the top edge open. Clip off corners of seam allowance, turn right side out and press well. Turn the top edge over to the lining side and lay the curtain heading tape in position, covering raw edges. Machine stitch in place.

Gather up the top to required width and hang the curtains, then sew a small brass ring to the sides or lower corners. Fold back the curtain edges to reveal the lining and mark the appropriate position on the wall behind each curtain for a hook. Screw in a small brass hook at each side and hook the ring over this to hold curtain in place. At night, simply slip the ring off the hook so the windows can be completely covered.

Below: A stunning flower print adds an eye-catching touch to plain curtains. The higher the rings are placed, the more lining is revealed.

Hand-made pleated headings for professional-looking curtains

Give curtains a really special, custom-made look with hand-stitched, pinch-pleat headings. Follow the professional method of making triple or goblet pleats, rather than using tape, to create fuller, more graceful curtains with perfectly-positioned pleats.

When you have splashed out on a luxurious and expensive fabric to make really special curtains, add the ultimate professional finish with a hand-stitched heading.

Although more time-consuming than using commercial heading tape, making pinch pleats by hand enables you to choose the exact depth of pleat that suits the proportions of your curtains or of a printed fabric design.

By being able to put more fullness in the pleats and spacing them more closely, you can make fuller curtains which will hang more gracefully. Hand-made curtains also have a softer appearance as there are no lines of machine stitching running across the top. And adding this exclusive finish may cost less than ready-made tape.

Left: Curtains with goblet pleated headings fall into graceful folds.

Types of pinch pleating

Triple pleats are the most popular form of pinch pleated heading, but goblet pleats provide an unusual variation and are even easier to make. Being one of the few styles of curtain heading that – as yet – it is not possible to create with commercial heading tape, goblet pleating invariably adds a very unusual, custom-made finish to your curtains.

The pinch pleat method can also be adapted to make a valance with clusters of pleats (they can be groups of four or five pleats – not necessarily three) spaced irregularly or more widely than usual, to echo vertical window divisions or just to add an individual touch.

Buying materials

The only items needed to make curtains with hand-stitched headings – apart from the curtain fabric, lining and possibly interlining – are some stiffening and hooks. White, buckram-type stiffenings made specifically for curtain headings in suitable widths are widely available. Select a width about 2cm/¾in greater than the required depth of pleat. Choose either steel pin hooks that simply slip behind the pleat stitching or traditional brass sew-on hooks.

You will need

Curtain fabric
Matching thread
Lining fabric
Interlining if used
Curtain buckram slightly deeper than required heading pleats, twice width of flat curtain
Pronged steel hooks or sew-on hooks and strong thread (1 hook for each pleat plus 4 for edges)

Measuring up and preparing the curtains

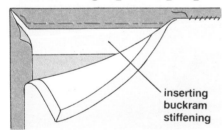

inserting buckram stiffening

Measure up as described on page 10, adding 14cm/5½in to the finished length for top and bottom hems.

For triple pleats, the width of each curtain should be two and a half times the width of half the curtain rail, which allows 10-17cm/4½-6in for each pleat, depending on the spaces between, and creates luxuriously full curtains.

For goblet pleats, twice the width is sufficient. Allow 4cm/1½in for each side hem, and 3cm/1¼in for each seam joining fabric widths, if necessary.

Cut out the curtains, joining widths as necessary. Cut lining to finished size of curtains and lock to prepared curtains (see page 385) but without stitching over heading area.

Inserting buckram stiffening Fold back top edge of lining and slip buckram underneath turnings of curtain fabric, trimming to fit, so that edges of buckram lie level with top and sides of curtain. Tack stiffening securely in place and re-position lining on top, smoothing it down.

Turn in top raw edge of lining to lie about 1cm/½in below top edge of curtain and slipstitch down taking care not to let stitches go through front of curtain.

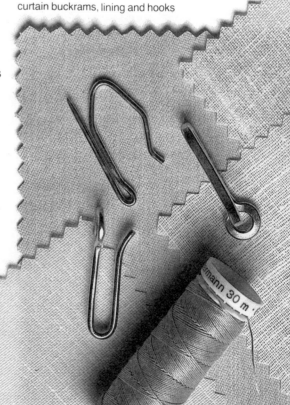

curtain buckrams, lining and hooks

Calculating pleat sizes

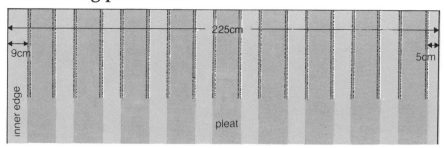

To ensure a perfect finish, spend some time calculating the size and spacing.

Number of pleats
Measure the required finished width of each curtain (half rail length) and, at each end, subtract 5cm/2in or the width of any overlap or return. Assuming a rough average figure of a triple pleat every 10cm/4in of finished curtain, calculate the number of pleats that will fit this width, with a pleat positioned at either end.

Example

Width of finished curtain (half track length)	90cm
Overlap at inner edge	9cm
Flat area at outer edge	5cm
Distance between first and last pleat	76cm
Number of pleats	9

Size of each pleat
From the width of the *flat* curtain, subtract the size of the *finished* curtain (including overlap) to calculate the amount of fabric left over for pleats. Divide this measurement by the required number of pleats to find the amount of fabric allowed for *each* pleat.

Example

Width of flat curtain	225cm
Width of finished curtain	90cm
Difference to be taken up in pleats	135cm
Number of pleats	9
Fabric for each pleat = $135 \div 9 =$	15cm

Size of each space
To calculate the exact size of the spaces between pleats, divide the finished curtain width (less the return, overlap or 5cm/2in at each end) by the number of pleats less one.

Example

Width of finished curtain	90cm
Less 5cm one end and 9cm overlap other end	76cm
Number of pleats less one	8
Size of each space = $76cm \div 8 =$	9.5cm

Making a goblet pleated heading

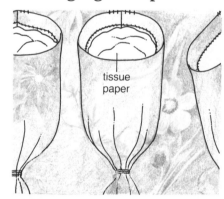

An unusual variation of pinch pleats, goblet pleats have the advantage of requiring slightly less width of fabric than triple pleats.

Calculating pleat sizes
Allowing 9-13cm/3½-5in for each goblet pleat and about the same amount for each space, calculate exact sizes as above.

If your flat curtain is exactly twice the finished size and there is no overlap or return, simply divide the flat width by an even number of pleats and spaces, for example, a 120cm/48in curtain would have twelve 10cm/4in pleats/spaces; that is six pleats, five whole spaces and a half space at either end.

Forming the goblet pleats
Mark out and stitch each pleat as for triple pleated headings (Step 1) as far as stitching from top edge to bottom of stiffening at each pleat. Instead of forming three pleats, pinch together the base of each pleat (folding the fabric into three or

Making a triple pleated heading

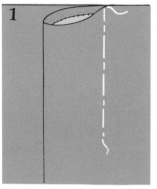 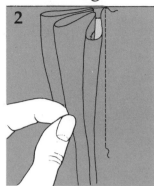 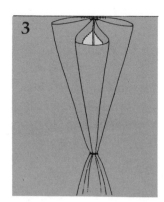 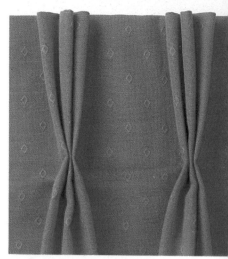

Calculate the exact size of spaces and pleats (see left) and then, using tailor's chalk and a ruler or set square, draw vertical lines to mark their position along the top edge of the curtains.

1 Bring together the two lines marking the first pleat, wrong sides of curtain facing, to form a single large pleat. Tack and stitch (by machine or by hand) from top edge of curtain to lower edge of stiffening, making sure that stitching is at a true right angle to curtain edge.

Repeat for each pleat: each curtain should then be the required finished width (half track length).

2 Hold the centre fold of each pleat between thumb and forefinger just above lower edge of stiffening, and push pleat inwards towards the stitching line, forming three small, evenly sized pleats. Catch the pleats together with a few small handstitches just above lower edge of stiffening.

3 At the top edge of curtain, catch the triple pleats together at the back and also anchor the back edge of the a few unobtrusive hand stitches using matching thread.

---

four small pleats) and catch the folds together with a few hand stitches at the base only.

To form the goblet shape, round out the top of each pleat and catch to the top edge of curtain about 1cm/ ½in out, on either side, from the first stitching line. To ensure that the goblet shape stays nicely rounded, lightly stuff each pleat with a piece of crumpled tissue paper. (Don't forget to remove this when cleaning curtains.)

Attaching hooks

If curtains are to hang just below a decorative wooden pole, attach the curtain hooks as close to the top edge as possible without protruding. If the curtain heading is to cover the rail, position the hooks lower down, according to depth of rail and style of gliders.

If using sew on hooks, attach one at each end of each curtain and one behind each pleat, stitching on very securely with strong button thread. If using pronged hooks, insert behind the stitching at each pleat. Insert the corner hooks by making two vertical rows of stitching at each end of curtains and inserting a hook between the rows.

PROFESSIONAL TOUCH

'Dressing' curtains

All curtains, whether or not their headings are made by hand, will drape more effectively if they are properly 'dressed'. To do this, hang the curtains half drawn open. Starting from the top, run your fingers down the curtain emphasizing each natural fold made by the heading. If necessary, a gentle tug on the lower hem edge, level with a heading pleat, will help the fabric fall into a natural pleat. Start from the outer edge and work along each curtain, drawing back the curtain as you create the draping.

If the curtain heading hangs below a decorative pole, push each space between pleats backwards. If the curtain covers the track, pull the space areas of fabric forwards.

When the curtains are fully drawn back into perfectly-draped folds, tie three lengths of cord or strips of soft fabric around each curtain and leave for as long as possible – at least overnight or preferably two or three days – to 'train' the pleats.

When the cords are removed, the curtains will retain the beautifully draped effect and will 'hang' well for quite some time, but repeat when re-hanging curtains after cleaning.

Traditional fabric pelmets

Custom-made to suit the proportions of your window and the styling of your room, traditional pelmets can be expensive to buy. With modern materials, however, they are simple to make yourself, cost very little, and add the same distinctive finish to your windows.

Pelmets are horizontal panels of stiffened fabric which, positioned at the top of curtains, cover curtain track and balance the proportions of a window. They are particularly attractive on tall windows and are also effective when used to link together adjoining sets of windows.

Below: The border from a printed curtain fabric is ideal for a straight pelmet.

Covered in a furnishing fabric to complement your curtains and shaped to suit the style of your décor, a pelmet never fails to add a distinctive touch to a room.

The material traditionally used to stiffen fabric pelmets is buckram interfacing, a woven fabric which has been treated to become rigid. More modern alternatives include self-adhesive non-woven materials, such as Rufflette Pelmform. This has a peel-off backing paper printed with several different pelmet silhouettes to follow when cutting out and with a grid to simplify drawing out your own design. One type of Pelmform is velour-backed thus eliminating the need for lining. These stiffenings can be bought by the metre from furnishing fabric departments.

Almost any furnishing fabric, except very open weaves and sheers, can be used to cover the pelmet. If using buckram, back your chosen fabric with bump interlining or an iron-on interfacing for a smooth finish.

Attach your pelmet to the pelmet board with touch-and-close fastener – Sew 'n' stick Velcro is ideal. This makes adding decorative braid (traditionally applied to cover tack-heads) purely a matter of choice.

Hanging a pelmet

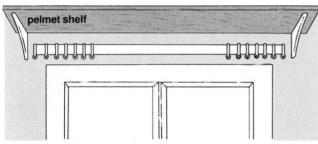

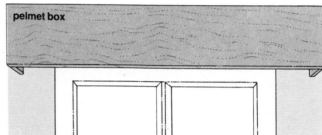

Pelmets must be attached to a firm support, called a pelmet board.

A pelmet shelf – simply a wooden shelf about 10-15cm/4-6in deep permanently attached to the wall just above the curtain track and/or architrave – is adequate for most windows. It should extend about 6cm/2½in beyond each end of the track.

A pelmet box, which also has narrow front and side box-style sections, gives the extra rigidity which may be needed for wide or particularly deep pelmets.

On deeply recessed windows, the pelmet board can be just a simple flat panel fixed across the top of the window area, level with the wall. When putting up a new pelmet shelf or box, bear in mind that, as the top edge of the pelmet will lie level with the top edge of the pelmet board, this will form the top edge of the window area. Consider therefore, the height and depth of the pelmet in relation to the window and to the height of the ceiling, not forgetting that the pelmet must be low enough to cover curtain track, before positioning a pelmet board.

Once screwed to the wall, a pelmet board becomes a permanent fixture which will probably outlast several pelmets. A pelmet, on the other hand, should be easy to remove for cleaning, while decorating, or to be replaced by a new one. Touch-and-close fastener, such as Velcro, is therefore ideal for attaching it. Tack or glue the hooked half of the Velcro all along the top edge of the front and sides (or returns) of the pelmet board (or use the self-adhesive half of Sew 'n' stick Velcro) and stitch the other half to the pelmet lining while making up.

Choosing fabric and a shape for your pelmet

Whatever the room scheme, pelmets can be pretty and decorative, classic and elegant, or stylishly simple to complement it. Choose a firmly-woven fabric to match, contrast or co-ordinate with your curtains and echo the style of the fabric design in the pelmet shape you choose – a prettily scalloped shape, for example, would not suit a sharp geometric print.

You can, if using Pelmform, follow one of the shapes printed on the backing paper. Alternatively, draw up your own design, perhaps copying or adapting one of the styles illustrated here, devising your own shape, opting for a simple rectangle, or following the outlines of motifs printed on the fabric.

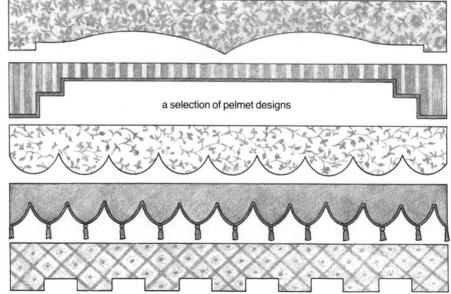

a selection of pelmet designs

Making a fabric pelmet

Put up a pelmet board, selecting the most suitable method of making a pelmet. This varies according to the type of stiffening used.

You will need

Buckram or Pelmform for stiffening
Fabric to match or contrast with
  curtains
Lining fabric (unless using one-sided Pelmform)
Interlining such as bump (if using
  buckram)
Paper to make a template
  (wallpaper is useful because of its
  length)
Velcro fastening
Decorative braid and fabric
  adhesive if desired

Making a template

Measure the length of the pelmet board including returns (short side ends) and cut a straight strip of paper to this length and slightly deeper than the widest section of your chosen pelmet shape. Fold the paper in half crosswise and mark the central point with a crease, and also crease the position of the corners.

Open out the paper and draw the intended shape on it, working from the centre out to the corner folds, and measuring accurately to make sure that any repeated shapes are of equal size and spacing. The returns can be shaped or left plain as desired. Fold the paper in half again and cut the shape from the doubled paper to ensure both sides are the same. Trim the top edge if necessary to make the template the exact size and shape of your finished pelmet, and check its proportions against your windows, adjusting if necessary.

Cutting out

Using the template, cut out the pelmet shape from buckram or Pelmform. Both are available in narrow widths so that the length can be cut from one piece without

Making up with traditional buckram

The traditional method of making a buckram pelmet involves a lot of hand sewing which takes time but gives a very professional finish. If your machine has a zip or piping foot, use the quick method.

Traditional method Place bump interlining centrally on the wrong side of the main fabric, and lock stitch together at intervals (see page 385). Place the buckram centrally on top of the bump interlining. Clipping into the border of fabric around curves or at corners, and trimming away excess where necessary, fold the fabric edges on to the wrong side of the buckram.

If using iron-on buckram, which is glue-impregnated, dampen the edges and stick down the fabric turnings by ironing in place. Otherwise slipstitch the edges of the fabric to the buckram.

Turn in the raw edges of the lining to make it 5mm/¼in smaller all round than the pelmet, clipping and trimming as necessary; press. Stitch the soft half of a strip of Velcro to right side along top edge of lining. Position the lining centrally on the wrong side of the buckram and slipstitch all round to hold.

Quick method Lock interlining to the fabric as above (or use iron-on

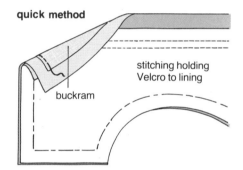

quick method

stitching holding
Velcro to lining

buckram

interfacing). Smoothing out the fabric, tack buckram to interlined side. Stitch the soft half of the Velcro 4cm/1½in down from the top edge of the lining strip. Lay fabric and lining right sides together and tack securely all round edge of

Making up with self-adhesive stiffening

Backings such as Rufflette Pelmform may cost a little more than buckram but are available in different widths for economy and are extremely simple to use. They are particularly helpful if you wish to follow one of the ready printed designs to shape the pelmet edge. Choose between velour backed or double-sided adhesive styles.

Ready-backed type The back of this type of stiffening is coated in a velour-style finish to make lining unnecessary and the front is self-adhesive.

Using your template, cut out the pelmet shape you require. If

ready backed

removing backing
paper and
smoothing fabric

following one of the printed outlines for the lower edge, place the centre of your template either in the exact centre of a scallop or at the point between two shapes.

Ease the backing paper away from the centre of the pelmet shape and cut it across the width. Peel back the paper for a little way on either side of the cut and place the wrong side of your fabric centrally on the exposed area of adhesive. Continue peeling back the paper while smoothing the fabric onto the stiffening adhesive, working from centre outwards so fabric remains absolutely smooth and wrinkle-free.

Press the backing and fabric firmly together and then, using sharp scissors, trim the fabric edges in line with the backing. Stick or tack the coarser hooked side of Velcro to the

Right: Trimming emphasizes the unusual shaping of a plain fabric pelmet.

much wastage; joins are not advisable as they tend to create ridges and will reduce the rigidity of the pelmet.

If using buckram, cut out the same shape in bump, for interlining, butting the edges together and herringbone stitching to join widths. Cut out fabric and lining 2.5cm/1in larger all round than the template. Plain fabrics can sometimes be cut along the length to avoid joins but if your fabric has a one-way design or a definite nap, you may need to join widths with narrow flat seams to make up a strip large enough for the pelmet. To avoid a centre seam, join extra fabric to either side of a central panel. Press seams open.

buckram. Trim lining level with top edge of buckram.

Using a zipper or piping foot, machine stitch as close to the edge of the buckram as possible around sides and lower edge.

Trim the seam to 1.5cm/⅝in, clip into curves and angles and across corners, then turn right side out. Press well, creasing the edges and smoothing the seam towards the lining side rather than the right side.

Press the top edge of fabric over the lining, turn in the raw edge, trimming if necessary, and slipstitch to lining just above the Velcro strip.

pelmet board. The velour backing clings to this without needing the other half of Velcro. Although not generally necessary except as a decorative effect, or on fabrics that have a marked tendency to fray, it may be advisable to stick a decorative braid around the cut edges for a neater finish.

Double-sided adhesive type This does need lining but it gives a more professional finish.

Cut the lining and the stiffening to the finished shape. Stitch the soft half of Velcro along the top edge on the lining, 2.5cm/1in down.

Stick the main fabric onto right side

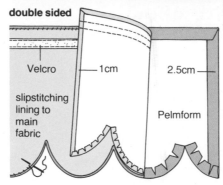

double sided

Velcro — 1cm — 2.5cm

slipstitching lining to main fabric

Pelmform

of stiffening as above but leaving a 2.5cm/1in turning all round. Clip into the turning around curves and into angles.

Press a 1cm/½in turning to the wrong side all round lining piece.

Removing the backing paper as you work, fold the fabric edges onto the wrong side of the pelmet, smoothing down so that they adhere.

Working from the centre outwards, stick wrong side of lining to wrong side of pelmet, overlapping the fabric edges. Slipstitch round lining to secure in place.

Add any braid trimmings required, slipstitching in place.

Attach hooked half of Velcro to pelmet board to correspond with soft half and press pelmet in place to hang. Do not use Pelmform for silk fabrics.

Curtain valances to frame your windows

Elegant and formal or frilly and charming, a curtain valance adds a decorative feature to your window. The wide choice of easy-to-make styles can be fitted on a pole, shelf or curtain track and only the hand-pleated headings require much sewing skill.

Curtain valances are often confused with pelmets, but in fact a pelmet is a rigid fitting, either in wood or fabric-covered wood, whereas a valance is a soft fabric drape. Both are used to disguise the tops of curtains and the curtain track, as well as enhancing the proportions of the window or adding a decorative feature.

The curtain valances shown here can be hung on tracks, poles, rods or a simple shelf-style fitting, above an existing curtain.

Style and proportion

If possible, hang the curtains before finally deciding on the style and depth of the valance.

The style will depend on the fabric the curtains are made from and on the way the room is furnished. A gathered valance made from a fresh, printed cotton will give a pretty, country look, while a valance of regular or grouped pleats will provide a more formal touch for heavier fabrics. A draped valance can be used for either look depending on the lightness of the fabric and on the surrounding furnishings.

The depth of the valance depends on the proportions of the window and personal taste. It can be used to improve the look of a window. For example, a deep valance will lower a tall narrow window, or help to obscure an unsightly view, while a shorter valance allows in the maximum of light through a small or shaded window.

There are no hard and fast rules that set the size of valance in relation to the curtain. If you start with the valance being one sixth of the curtain drop, this gives a point from which to

Left: Bound edges and a fabric-covered batten add style to a gathered valance.

work. Bear in mind that the valance must cover the track on which it is hung, the curtain track and the heading of the curtains.

Valance fittings

There are four main methods for fitting curtain valances: rod or tube, wooden pole, shelf or track.

Rod or tube fitting If the valance is hanging within a recess, or if the side view is not critical, it can be made with a simple cased heading and threaded on to a narrow rod, tube or curtain wire, fixed with brackets or hooks at each end.

Wooden curtain pole fitting The valance can be hung from the rings of a wooden curtain pole with decorative ends and brackets. The pole should be approximately 12cm/5in longer than the curtain track and project far enough from the wall to allow for the curtains. The actual measurement of this projection will be determined by the depth of the brackets used.

Curtain track fittings A simple curtain track is suitable for a valance if it is fitted with extended brackets to clear the curtains; alternatively fittings are available to clip the valance track straight on to the curtain track brackets.

The valance track must extend forward from the wall at least 4cm/1½in in front of the curtain track so that it does not interrupt the free movement of the curtains.

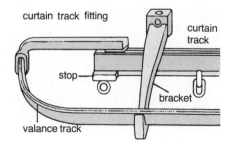

curtain track fitting

curtain track

stop

bracket

valance track

It is not practical to fix valance track above decorative curtain poles that extend away from the wall.

If both curtain and valance are to hang within a window recess, the valance track is the same width as the curtain track. Otherwise it should be longer and of the pliable type so that the ends can be bent back towards the wall to form sides or returns.

The valance is fitted to the track in the same way as a curtain, using curtain tape and hooks.

Shelf fittings If you cannot find a suitable track, pole or rod, fix a simple shelf supported by angle iron brackets above the curtain track. It should be 12cm/4¾in longer than the curtain track (unless in a recess) and protrude from the wall for 4cm/1½in more. Either attach the valance to the front and side edges of the shelf with upholstery tacks, gluing a decorative braid on top to hide the tack heads, or screw eyes round the shelf and attach the valance on to these with curtain hooks. The latter method allows the valance to be taken down for washing.

Measuring up

To find the depth most suitable for your valance, measure one sixth of the curtain drop and cut a strip of paper to this depth and as wide as your curtains. Carefully pin the paper to the top of the curtains in the correct position covering both tracks. Stand well back from the window and check the proportion of the valance in relation to the length of the curtains.

If it looks too deep, unpin the paper and trim off some of the depth. Repin and check again, repeating until you find the correct depth.

If the paper valance looks too shallow, make a new paper pattern with plenty of depth, and trim off until the correct proportion is reached. Remember that ultimately this is a matter of personal taste.

The depth of the fabric needed will be the paper pattern depth plus 2cm/¾in for the lower seam allowance, and a top seam allowance which varies according to the type of heading. The width of the fabric required depends on the type of heading used and fullness required.

If you have to join fabric strips to make up the width, join with 1.5cm/⅝in flat seams, neaten and press.

Making a valance with a taped heading

This style of valance is made as if it were a very short curtain (see pages 364–6 and 375–7). Choose the appropriate curtain tape to give a gathered, pencil pleated or triple pleated heading. Position the tape so that the valance will completely cover the track but still clear the ceiling. A standard gathering tape can be positioned 2cm/1in down from the top edge so that it creates a small upstanding frill along the top.

The valance can be made with just a single thickness of fabric like an unlined curtain or it can be given more body with an iron-on interfacing, in which case it should be lined for a neat finish. A valance with a triple-pleated heading particularly benefits from being interlined and lined.

The depth of fabric required will be as described plus a top seam allowance

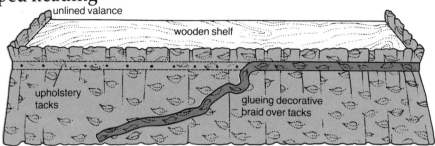

of 4cm/1½in. The width will depend on the manufacturer's recommendation for the type of heading tape used.

An unlined valance

Measure up, cut out and join the fabric. Neaten the side and lower edges as for cased heading valances. Turn in the seam allowance along the top edge and pin the curtain tape into position to

cover the raw edge. Turn in the raw ends of the tape – but not the pulling up cords – and tack and stitch it in place.

Pull up the cords until the valance is the correct width and tie the ends to secure. Even out the pleats or gathers, insert curtain hooks and hang the valance in the same way as a curtain.

If you are using a wooden shelf fitment, line up the curtain tape

Making a valance with a hand-pleated heading

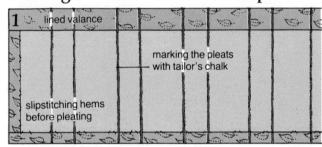

A pleated valance looks best if made with a stiffened fabric – interfaced and lined as the interlined valance with heading tape.

With a strip of paper, work out the size and type of pleat that will suit your valance and fit evenly into its length. Cut a piece of fabric of

sufficient depth and width (join pieces if necessary) to make the valance. Three times the finished width required, plus seam allowances, will be sufficient for continuous knife or box pleats. Allow 4cm/1½in for the top seam allowance.

Make up the valance in the same way as the lined version with curtain tape but, after folding over top seam allowance, do not add tape.

1 Following the pleat size from your experimental paper strip, mark out the valance into even divisions

Making a valance with cased heading

This is the easiest valance to make and hang as the supporting rod, tube or wire is simply threaded through the cased heading.

Measure the depth as described and add 6cm/2½in top seam allowance to enclose a rod up to 2cm in diameter between two rows of stitching.

For the width of fabric required allow one and a half to two times the length of the rod or pole.

Cut out your fabric to the required measurements, joining widths if necessary with 1.5cm/⅝in flat seam or French seam.

1 Turn a double hem (5mm/¼in and then 1cm/½in) to the wrong side down each side edge and stitch. Turn a double hem (1cm/½in and 1cm/½in) along the lower edge and stitch. (Alternatively, trim off lower seam allowance and bind edge with a contrasting binding.)

2 On the top edge, turn the seam allowance to the wrong side, then turn in the raw edge by 1cm/½in and stitch. Make another row of stitching 4cm/1½in above this one to form a channel through which the rod is threaded.

Press well and add any trimmings

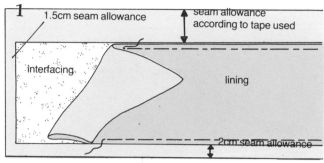

1 1.5cm seam allowance · seam allowance according to tape used

interfacing

lining

2cm seam allowance

2 attaching tape over raw edges

hems slipstitched in place

with the facing edges of the shelf and attach the valance with upholstery tacks. Cover the tack heads with a decorative braid or a fabric-covered batten glued in place.

A lined valance

An interfacing such as iron-on Vilene can be added to give your fabric more body and a crisper look. There are several weights available – select the weight that, together with your fabric, will give the desired thickness.

A lining is necessary to give a neat finish and also protects the valance from sunlight.

Cut out the valance as for an unlined one, and cut the lining and interlining to the exact finished measurements without seam allowances. If necessary, join fabric widths and lining widths.

1 Position the interfacing to the wrong side of the fabric within the seamlines. Following the manufacturer's instructions for heat setting, dry iron the interfacing on to the fabric.

Lay lining on top of interfacing right side upwards and tack in place.

2 Turn in double hems along side and lower edges as for the cased valance, slipstitching down to the lining. Finish the top edge with heading tape.

using tailor's chalk on the wrong side. Fold and press the pleats, one by one, and tack in position.

2 Place a length of plain tape about 2.5cm/1in wide, on the wrong side of the valance to cover the raw edge (as with the heading tape) and sew in place.

You can hand sew the tape if you do not want the stitching lines to show on the right side, but you must be sure to stitch through all but the front layer of fabric in order to secure the pleats in place.

If necessary, neatly catchstitch the top edges of the pleats together on the right side.

Sew rings or hooks to the tape to attach the valance to its support.

before threading on to the rod. This method can be adapted for a simple gathered heading attached around a shelf fitting. Instead of adding the second row of stitching along the top edge, insert two rows of gathering stitches and pull up to the appropriate size. Nail it around the edge of the shelf and cover the nail heads with braid or a neatened bias strip of fabric. Turning in the ends of the braid to neaten, use fabric adhesive to glue in place.

Right: Rufflette Tridis tape gives regular triple pleating; hand-made pleats can be grouped or spaced out.

Draped valance with cascades

Complex swagged valances can be time consuming to make, but this simple draped valance with its cascades on each side gives an equally sumptuous effect for relatively little time and effort.

Choose a lining that is colour matched or use the same fabric for both valance and lining as it will tend to show. If you wish to use a sheer fabric for an unlined valance, omit any seam allowances and bind edges.

The valance is draped over a pair of wooden or metal brackets – such as the type used with curtain poles. Position the brackets just above and slightly outside each end of the curtain track.

Measuring up

To calculate the amount of fabric needed, use a tape measure (or a length of string) and drape it over the two brackets allowing it to drop into a gentle swag between them to hide the curtain track and headings. Allow it to hang down at either side of the window frame to measure the depth of cascade required.

Measure the total length of the tape or string (A–A) to give you the total width of fabric needed, adding 3cm/1¼in for seam allowances. Measure the drop of the swag between the two brackets (B–B) and also the distance in a straight line between the two brackets (C–C).

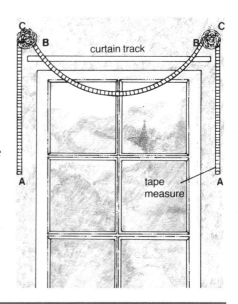

Making up the draped valance

Cut a piece of fabric the width from A to A plus 3cm/1¼in, joining widths if necessary, with a depth of 120cm/47¼in.

1 With tailor's chalk, mark the distance B–B centrally on one long side of the fabric. Draw diagonal lines to join B to A on each side and cut the fabric along these two lines. Now cut a piece of lining fabric to exactly the same size and shape. Tack the lining fabric and valance fabric together right sides facing. Sew the lining and valance fabric together all round, taking a 1.5cm/⅝in seam and leaving a 20cm/7in gap for turning through. Trim the seam to 1cm/½in and clip off each corner close to the stitching line. Turn to the right side and slipstitch the opening closed. Press. On the lining side, mark the distance between the two C points centrally on the longest side.

2 Join points C and B with chalk lines, then sew a length of standard heading tape along each line. Knot the ends of the cord at the B edge, leaving them loose for pulling up on the C edge.

Pull up the cords in the heading tape to gather the fabric and then lay the gathers over the brackets. Adjust the cascades if necessary. If the fabric shows a tendency to slip, tie the ends of the heading tape cords around the brackets so that they don't show.

Right: The valance can be draped over brass curtain holders or wooden brackets.

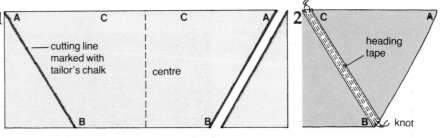

400

Decorative curtain borders for a stylish finish

Add a decorative edging when making up new curtains or to highlight an old pair. Choose a style which suits the room – a frilled edge for a pretty finish, a piped edge for elegance or a bold contrast border or appliqué motif for a striking feature.

Below: Bear in mind the proportions of your curtains when choosing the width and position of a border and use bold colour contrasts for a dramatic effect.

Give curtains a designer style finish by adding a frill or piping to the edges or by applying a fabric border or appliqué motifs. These can easily be incorporated when making up new curtains, but the ideas can be adapted to brighten up an old pair if you unpick hems and sewn-in linings as necessary.

Cut out the curtain fabric and join widths if necessary, following instructions given on pages 364–5 and 380–2. For curtains with sewn-in linings, cut the lining to the *same width* as the curtain fabric.

Take 1.5cm/⅝in seam allowances throughout unless otherwise stated. Bear in mind the proportion of your curtains when deciding which edges are to be decorated. The most usual position is down the inner edge where the curtains meet, but outer and hem edges can be bordered too.

Making a gathered frill

A frill, whether applied to lined or unlined curtains, can be either a single or double thickness of fabric. Double thickness is generally preferable so that the right side of the fabric will show on both sides of the frill, but a single thickness is more suitable if the fabric is bulky.

To calculate the length of fabric for a frill, multiply the length of the edge to be frilled by one and a half to two times. The finished width of the frill should be about 10cm/4in for an average-sized curtain.

For a double-thickness frill cut fabric to the required length (joining strips if necessary), and to double the finished width of the frill plus 3cm/1¼in for seam allowances. Fold the fabric in half along its length, wrong sides facing, and run two rows of gathering threads along the raw edge of the frill, just inside the seam allowance and stitching through both layers of fabric. If you are using a machine, gather in sections no longer than 1m/1yd to make it easier to pull up the threads without breaking.

For a single-thickness frill cut fabric to the required length (joining strips if necessary), and to the width of the finished frill plus 3cm/1¼in for seam and hem allowance. Neaten one long edge with a double hem, 5mm and 1cm/ ¼in and ⅜in. Run two rows of gathering threads along the other long edge, within the seam allowance.

Applying the frill

Gathered frills can be applied to both lined and unlined curtains.

Unlined curtains Pull up the gathering threads until the frill fits between the top and bottom hem lines of the curtain fabric. With right sides and raw edges together, tack frill to curtain fabric. Sew frill in place with a 1.5cm/⅝in seam and zigzag raw edges together to neaten. Press frill out from curtain. This method is also used for curtains with detachable linings.

Lined curtains Pull up the gathering threads until the frill fits between the top and bottom hem lines of the curtain fabric. With right sides and raw edges together, tack the frill to the curtain fabric. Place the lining and curtain fabric right sides together, sandwiching the frill, and sew side seams with 1.5cm/⅝in seams. Trim the seam allowances and turn right side out so that the frill protrudes from the seam.

Complete curtains in the usual way.

Making fabric borders

A ready-made printed border is the easiest kind to apply. They are available in different widths and a wide variety of colours and designs to match or complement a particular range of wallpapers and fabrics.

You can make your own borders from furnishing fabrics to match or contrast with your curtains. Choose fabrics of similar weight as the curtains to ensure they hang well.

Borders can be applied to the edges of both lined and unlined curtains. Decide which edges of the curtain are to be trimmed and the width of the border in proportion to the curtain.

Making the border strips

Cut strips of fabric the length of each border plus 2cm/1in seam allowances all round. Try to cut each section in one continuous strip – if you join strips match the pattern, if there is one, as necessary.

With tailor's chalk, mark the finished side edges and the top and bottom hem foldlines on to the right side of each curtain.

Press the seam allowance to the wrong side on both long edges.

Applying the border

Tack the border to the right side of the curtain fabric, one edge close to the side chalk line. Turn under the short edges to lie along top and bottom hem lines.

If the borders continue around the bottom of the curtain, form a mitre at the corner where they join. Fold the ends at a 45° angle and press. Cut away the excess fabric, leaving a small seam allowance. Slipstitch the mitred edges together or, with right sides together, machine along foldline and open out.

Machine topstitch the borders on to the curtains, then make up the curtains in the usual way.

Making an appliqué border

For a really original touch, appliqué can be used to form a border around a curtain. The motifs can be applied to both lined or unlined curtains before making up. It is best to choose one or two simple motifs to repeat along the edge to form the border.

Making the appliqué motif

To check that the design is in proportion to the curtain, pin a paper pattern on to the curtain fabric to judge the size and position. When you are satisfied with the pattern make an accurate template of the motif. Position it on the right side of the curtain fabric and draw round the template as often as necessary until the appliqué has been accurately marked out.

Use the template to cut out the appliqué shapes from the border fabric. Choose a fabric which matches the weight of the curtain fabric if possible, but if a lightweight fabric is chosen back the motifs with iron-on Vilene.

Applying the motifs

Place each motif within its chalk outline and tack to the curtain. Use a close zigzag stitch to machine over the raw edges of each motif. If you do not have a swing needle

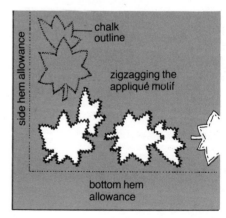

machine, sew round the raw edges with a close buttonhole stitch.

When the appliqué is complete, make up curtains in the usual way.

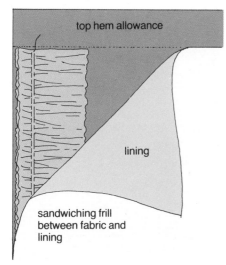

top hem allowance

lining

sandwiching frill
between fabric and
lining

*Right: A gathered curtain frill
emphasizes a pretty fresh cotton print.
Highlight a matching frill with piping
in an accent colour or choose a
contrasting fabric. Echo the frill on
tie-backs, cushions or a bedspread.*

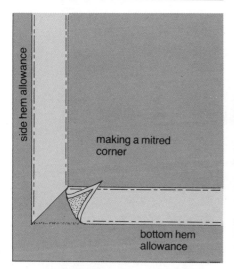

side hem allowance

making a mitred
corner

bottom hem
allowance

Making a piped edge

Piping down the inside and possibly even the outside edges of curtains provides a subtle accent of colour. The piping is inserted between two layers of fabric so this trimming is not suitable for unlined curtains or those with detachable linings.

Making the piping

Cut piping cord to the exact finished length of each edge to be piped. Cut bias strips of fabric wide enough to cover the cord plus 3cm/1¼in seam allowance. Join bias strips to 3cm/1¼in longer than edge to be piped. Wrap the fabric strips, right sides outwards, around the cord and tack the two layers together as close to the cord as possible. Using the zipper foot on your sewing machine, stitch close to the cord. Remove tacking. Alternatively, you can use purchased ready-made piping.

Applying the piping

Tack piping to the right side of the curtain fabric, raw edges together. Place the lining and curtain fabric right sides together, sandwiching the piping between. Tack through all layers close to the piping cord, then machine stitch with a zipper foot.

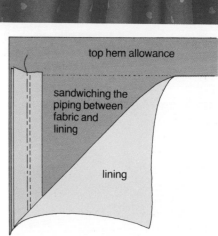

top hem allowance

sandwiching the
piping between
fabric and
lining

lining

Turn the curtain and lining through to the right side, so that the piping protrudes from the seamline. Make up curtains in the usual way.

Curtain tiebacks for a designer look

Tiebacks can be both pretty and practical. Choose a simple curved band or add piping, pleats or flounces for decoration. They make plain curtains more interesting, hold full ones back from a window or door or tie back the hangings round a four-poster bed.

They're only small, and often sadly forgotten, but curtain tiebacks are very useful and can give a new lease of life to a pair of dull or old curtains. A remnant of fabric is all that is needed – choose it to match the curtains, or to tone or contrast.

Make the tiebacks perfectly plain, or pipe them, add a ruffle, pleats or scallops; make them straight or gently curved.

As an alternative to using fabric, a length of chunky dressing gown cord makes a graceful, elegant tieback for full-length velvet curtains. Other ideas can come from furnishing braids, dress trims and ribbons.

You will need
Fabric Most light, closely woven furnishing fabrics are suitable. Don't try to use heavy brocades or velvet as they will not make up successfully – the fabric is too bulky. Both sides of the tieback can be of furnishing fabric, but if you haven't got enough, or the fabric is expensive or bulky, you can use a toning lining fabric for the backing.
Interfacing Use pelmet buckram or firm Vilene interfacing.
4 small curtain rings and two hooks for fixing to wall
Sewing thread
Paper for making patterns

Measuring up
To calculate where to place the tieback and how long and wide it should be, loop a tape measure around the curtain about two-thirds down from the top and arrange the curtain into the curve or folds you want. Note the measurement on the tape measure as this gives the length of the finished tieback. While the tape measure is still in place, make a small pencil mark on the wall to indicate the position for fixing the hook.

For sill-length curtains, the depth of the tieback should be no more than 10cm/4in, but for longer curtains it may be enlarged proportionally. Instructions given here are for 10cm/4in depth tiebacks. Seams throughout are 1.5cm/⅝in unless otherwise stated.

Right: This attractive square bay window is ideal for four separate curtains. The tiebacks hold them back during the day to allow in plenty of light.

Making a straight-edged tieback

This is very simple to make up and any of the variations shown overleaf can be added.

Cut a paper pattern to the length required × 10cm/4in deep. Pin the pattern to a double thickness of fabric and cut out (or cut out once in fabric and once in lining), allowing an extra 1.5cm/⅝in all round for seams.

Pin the pattern to a single thickness of interfacing and cut out without any seam allowance.

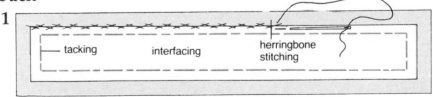

1 tacking — interfacing — herringbone stitching

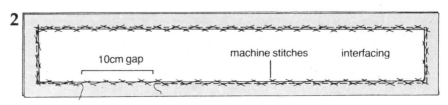

2 10cm gap — machine stitches — interfacing

1 Lay the interfacing centrally on the wrong side of one piece of fabric. Tack together. Herringbone stitch all round the edges of the interfacing to catch to fabric. Work the herringbone stitch from left to right, first taking a small stitch horizontally in the tieback fabric and then diagonally opposite and lower down on the interfacing. The stitches should not show on the right side of the tieback fabric.

2 Place the two tieback pieces right sides facing and tack together all round, leaving a 10cm/4in gap for turning through to the right side. Machine with the interfacing uppermost, being careful to sew close to, but not over, the edge of the interfacing.
Trim the seams and clip diagonally across the corners. Remove tacking. Turn through to right side and slipstitch the open edges together to close. Press.

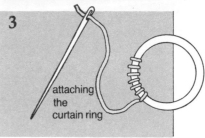

attaching the curtain ring

3 Sew a curtain ring to the middle of each short edge. Working on the wrong side of the fabric, overcast the ring just inside the edge so that most of the ring protrudes.

Making a shaped tieback

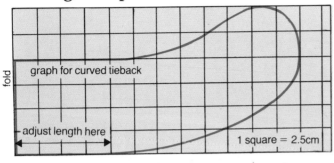

graph for curved tieback

fold

adjust length here

1 square = 2.5cm

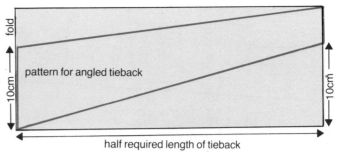

fold

pattern for angled tieback

10cm

10cm

half required length of tieback

A curved tieback gives an elegant shape that echoes the graceful lines of a draped curtain.

Cut a piece of paper to the length of the tieback × 15cm/6in deep and fold in half widthways. Divide into 2.5cm/1in squares and scale up the diagram shown to draw in the curve.

Cut out the paper pattern, open out flat, and cut out twice in fabric, with an additional 1.5cm/⅝in all round for the seam allowance. Cut out once in interfacing.

Continue to make up as for the straight-edged tieback.

An angled tieback gives a stream-lined shape that is easy to emphasise with trimmings.

Cut a piece of paper to the length of the tieback × 15cm/6in.

Fold the paper in half widthways and mark a point 10cm/4in up on each short side. Join points to diagonally opposite corners as shown to make the tieback shape. Make up as for a straight tieback.

Trimming tiebacks

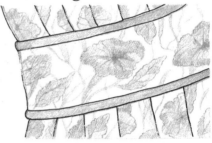

A plain tieback looks very smart but it also lends itself to additional trim-mings that create a softer, crisper or more feminine look.

Piped edges Piping in the seam line emphasises shape and can provide a contrast colour. Either cover the piping cord with bias strips cut from the same fabric as the tieback or use purchased bias binding, 2.5cm/1in wide. Cover the cord and apply to the right side of one piece of the tieback, raw edges together.

Continue making up the tieback as before, but sandwiching the piping between the two layers of fabric. Use a zipper foot to sew the seam, stitching as close to the piping as possible.

Left: Cut tieback patterns in paper and adjust their proportions to suit your curtains. These curved tiebacks were narrowed down to allow for the addition of a deep frill.

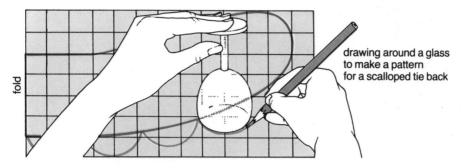

drawing around a glass to make a pattern for a scalloped tie back

A scalloped tieback can be made straight or curved.

Draw up a pattern for the basic shape of tieback you require but on deeper paper. Using a suitable size curve – an egg-cup or the rim of a small wine glass – draw a series of even-sized scallop shapes along the lower edge of the paper pattern. Start with a full scallop at the fold and, when you reach the end, adjust to finish with either a half or a complete scallop.

Cut out the paper pattern and open out flat. Cut out twice in fabric with an additional 1.5cm/⅝in all round for the seam allowance. Cut out once in interfacing without a seam allowance.

Continue to make up the tieback as before, sewing carefully around the scallop shapes and snipping into the curves – taking care not to snip the stitching – before turning through to the right side.

As an alternative, you can zigzag the edges of the scallops with a contrasting coloured sewing thread. Cut out the fabric as for the scalloped edge and attach the interfacing. Right sides facing, sew the two pieces together along the top and two side edges only. Turn to the right side and press.

On the scalloped edge, trim the seam allowance so that the fabric and interfacing edges match. Tack the two scalloped edges together around the edge of each scallop. Using a contrast coloured sewing thread and a close machine zigzag stitch, machine very carefully around the curve of each scallop, so that the zigzag stitch covers the raw edges of the fabric.

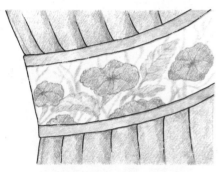

Bound edges Binding all round the edges gives the chance to introduce a contrast colour, or to pick up a plain colour from a patterned fabric. Again, you can use bias strips cut from the fabric or purchased bias binding. Cut out the fabric and interfacing to the shape you require, without any seam allowance.

Wrong sides facing, sandwich the interfacing between the two pieces of fabric, and tack together around the edges. Round off any corners slightly to make it easier to apply the binding. Attach bias strips or bias binding, slipstitching in place on the wrong side.

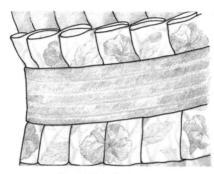

Pleated edges These are most suitable for straight-edged tiebacks. Cut from fabric two pleating strip pieces 11cm/4½in wide × three times the length of the tieback plus 3cm/1¼in.

Right sides facing, fold each pleating strip in half lengthways and sew across each short end. Turn right side out and press. Press in knife pleats, 1.5cm/⅝in wide, all facing in the same direction, along the total length of each pleating strip.

Lay the two pleated strips, one along either long edge, on the right side of one tieback piece, raw edges matching and 1.5cm/⅝in in from the short edge at each end. Adjust pleat depth slightly if the length is not quite accurate. Tack in place. Continue to make up as for the straight-edged tieback.

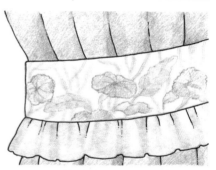

Frilled edges Open the pattern flat, and cut two pieces in fabric with an extra 1.5cm/⅝in seam allowance all round. Measure along the bottom edge of the tieback and cut enough 7.5cm/3in wide pieces of fabric to give a frill piece double this measurement when they are joined. Turn a double hem (5mm/¼in and then 1cm/½in) to the wrong side along one long edge of the frill piece and along the two short edges. Sew two lines of gathering threads along the remaining raw edge, 1cm/½in and 1.5cm/⅝in from the edge. Place the frill on one tieback piece, right sides facing and with raw edges together. Pin each end of the frill 1.5cm/⅝in in from the side edges of the tieback, and pull up the gathering threads until the frill, when evenly gathered, fits along the edge of the tieback. Tack in place. Continue to make up the tieback as for the straight version, being careful not to catch the free ends of the frill in the side seams.

Practical café curtains

These curtains were traditionally used in French cafés to cover the lower half of the window. They are easy and economical to make in a variety of styles – simply gather the top with a taped heading or cut a scalloped edge which can be plain or pleated.

Traditional café curtains cover only the lower half of a window, giving privacy without too much loss of light. They hang from brass or wooden poles, known as café rods, and because of their rather informal look they are most often used in kitchens and bathrooms. They can be unlined to give maximum light but, as with any curtain, a lining does protect the fabric and give added insulation.

Several variations on the traditional single curtain across the lower part of the window are shown below right. You can add a curtain valance at the top of the window. You can combine a single lower curtain with a pair of short upper curtains which can be opened to let in daylight and drawn together at night. Alternatively both lower and upper curtains can be pairs. Café curtains often have a simple gathered top, but perhaps the most distinctive style is the scalloped top, either plain or with triple pleating between the scallops. This chapter concentrates on how to make up this highly decorative variation.

For either style, fix the support brackets and place the pole in position so that the exact drop of the curtain can be measured before cutting out.

The pole for the lower curtain is positioned at least halfway up the window, coinciding with a window bar if there is one at about the required level. The finished curtain should be sill length.

For a valance or top curtains, the pole can be fixed either just above the window frame or within the recess. The top curtains should overlap the lower curtain by about 10cm/4in.

Choosing fabrics

The plain scalloped style of café curtain should be made in a furnishing fabric with a reasonable amount of body or it will not hang well. The other styles, however, do not neces-

Right: Disguise an uninspiring view with a pretty café curtain made with a cased heading and a frilled hem.

sarily need to be made in curtaining at all – choose a printed dress cotton, fresh gingham, cotton lace or a sheer fabric such as voile to complement the style of the room.

Simple gathered café curtain

This can be made in the same way as ordinary curtains with a simple cased heading and threaded on to a narrow rod or a curtain wire. (See pages 364–5 and 371 for making up instructions.) Alternatively, use a curtain heading tape to gather or pleat the top, insert hooks and hang it from the rings of a wooden or brass curtain pole. (See pages 375–7 and 380–2 for lined and unlined versions.)

Scalloped café curtain

An attractive scalloped edge shows to full advantage on a café curtain. It can also be a very economical use of fabric as the curtain is virtually flat – at the most slightly undulating – rather than gathered. If a fuller look is required, pleats can be formed between each scallop.

Curtain rings or hooks are sewn on to the strips between scallops to hang the curtain. Alternatively, crocodile clips are available which hook into the curtain rings and clip to the top of the curtain.

You will need to make a paper pattern for the scalloped edge before cutting out the curtain. The scallop size given overleaf will suit most average windows but it can be adjusted for a particularly large or small curtain. If you want to line the curtain, cut both fabric and lining and join using the sewn-in lining method (see page 380). Tack the top edge of the lining level with the foldline of the curtain top before sewing the scalloped top.

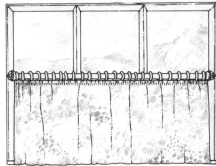

simple gathered café curtain

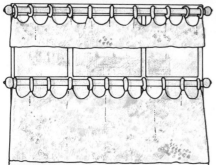

café curtain with valance

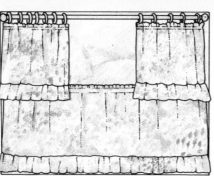

café curtain with pair of upper curtains

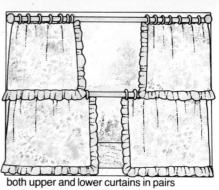

both upper and lower curtains in pairs

Making a plain scalloped curtain

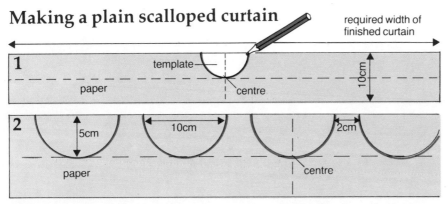

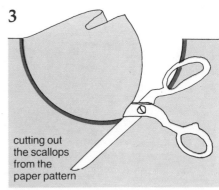

The scalloped top gives style to a flat curtain. Because there is no fullness, choose a furnishing fabric with a fair amount of body rather than a soft or sheer material.

Cutting the pattern An exact semi-circle makes a scallop that is visually pleasing. Use a pair of compasses or a suitable size saucer to draw a circle 10cm/4in in diameter on to thin card. Cut out the circle then cut it across the diameter to make a semi-circular template. Measure the width of the window fairly generously as the curtain will be flat but not absolutely taut. Cut a strip of paper to the required width of

the finished curtain by 10cm/4in deep. Fold in half along the length and width to find the centre.
1 Place the template in the centre of the strip as shown – between the top edge and the centre line – and draw round it to mark the centre scallop.
2 Leaving a 2cm/1in space between each one, and working from the centre to one edge, lightly pencil in further scallops. Ideally, the last scallop will finish about 2cm/1in from the edge but, if you end up with a half scallop, either increase the width of the paper pattern (which will give your curtain a

softer less flat effect) or adjust the spacing between scallops and redraw the pattern. Repeat from the centre to the other end.
To work out the number of scallops and the spacing between them mathematically, take 2cm/1in (the ideal for the space) from the finished curtain width (to allow for a space at both ends) then divide this measurement by 12cm/5in (ie the size of one scallop plus one space). This will give you the number of scallops that will fit the width. If it is not a whole number, adjust the space between scallops until it is.

Making a pleated scalloped curtain

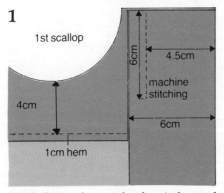

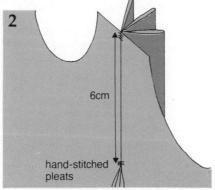

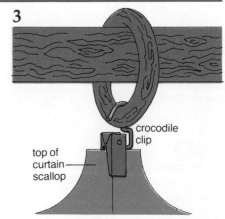

With this style a triple pleat is formed between each scallop to give the curtain more fullness.
Cutting the pattern Work out the number of scallops to fit across the width either by making a rough paper pattern or by calculating mathematically as for the plain scalloped curtain.
Having worked out the number of scallops required, make up a new paper pattern, leaving 12cm/5in between each scallop for the pleats. Although you will increase the fabric width you still have the same number of scallops as for the plain scalloped curtain.

Cutting out and making up Use the paper pattern to cut out the width of the curtain fabric, adding hem and seam allowances and joining widths if necessary, as for the plain version.
1 To form the pleats, fold the fabric between each scallop in half and, starting 4.5cm/2in from the fold, stitch down for about 6cm/2in from the top edge.
2 Make two folds within this pleat to form a triple pleat and tack in place.
Neatly hand stitch the pleats at the front at a point 6cm/2in from the top edge and at the back on the top edge to hold in place. Remove tacks.

Complete the hem along the lower edge as for the plain scalloped curtain.
3 Stitch a curtain ring or hook to the corners of each space between scallops or behind each set of pleats, depending on how much support your fabric needs. Alternatively, hang the curtain with crocodile clips which do not require stitching.

Right: A pleated scalloped curtain is bright and practical for the recess of a kitchen window. With an all-over print, the fabric can be used horizontally and cut in one piece.

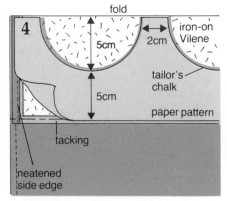

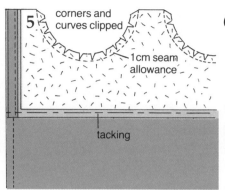

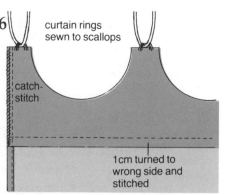

With these measurements, draw scallops along the whole strip.

3 When the paper pattern is completely drawn up, cut away the scallops.

Cutting out and making up Cut the curtain to the pattern width plus 3cm/1¼in seam allowances. If more than one width of fabric is needed allow 1cm/½in seam allowances, join selvedges and press seams open. Cut to the finished length plus a 5cm/2in bottom hem allowance and 10cm/4in for the top turning.

Neaten side edges by turning in 5mm/¼in and 1cm/½in and stitch.

Along the top edge of curtain, turn 10cm/4in of fabric to the right side and tack down. Cut a strip of iron-on Vilene 2cm/1in less than the curtain width and 9cm/3½in deep and iron on to the turned-over flap next to the fold and within the side seams.

4 Place the paper pattern on the flap with the straight edge of the scallops to the fold and draw round the scallop shapes with tailor's chalk. Remove pattern and machine stitch round each scallop following chalk lines.

5 Leaving 1cm/½in seam allowances, cut away each scallop.

Clip across corners and into seam allowances around each curve, remove tacks and turn flap to the wrong side of curtain, carefully turning out each scallop.

6 Turn 1cm/½in to the wrong side along bottom edge of flap and stitch. Catchstitch side edges together.

Sew a curtain pole ring centrally on the wrong side of each space between scallops. Complete the curtain by turning up and stitching the lower hem.

Shower curtains – meet splash with dash

Keep splashes in check with a practical shower curtain. Choose a stylishly simple version or combine it with a fabric or towelling curtain for an elegant and luxurious effect. Eyelets and rings make hanging the curtain quick and simple.

A curtain provides an inexpensive but effective method of keeping the splashes in check while having a shower. The shower curtain must have a waterproof surface and be long enough to tuck inside the bath or shower tray so that splashes of water are diverted by the curtain down the plug hole.

Shower curtains usually hang from a simple rail – you can buy shower rails from chain and hardware stores. There are expanding rails with suction ends which don't need to be screwed into the wall or through tiles and flexible rails which can be angled to fit around two or three sides of the shower.

The shower curtain is attached by means of large plastic rings which you simply thread on to the shower rail and clip together through eyelet holes made along the top edge of the shower curtain.

Inserting eyelets is very simple. You will need a large size of eyelet – 1cm/½in diameter – and a pair of eyelet pliers, or a kit which includes eyelets and a small hammer to insert them. The kit is much cheaper than the eyelet pliers.

You can of course hang the curtain by attaching a synthetic curtain heading tape and hooking this with curtain hooks on to the shower rail rings.

A basic shower curtain is made from a single unlined thickness of water-repellent rot-proof fabric, but to give your bathroom a more luxurious look, add an outer curtain that hangs over the outside of the bath. This can be made from normal curtaining fabric which, as it is protected by the inner curtain, can be trimmed and frilled to suit bathroom furnishings. The fabric side of the curtain must be completely detachable from the plastic or nylon side for laundering, so both plastic and fabric are made up as single thickness curtains and just joined together by sharing the same hooks on the rail. If your shower curtain hooks/rings will not take the bulk of two curtains or if you wish to gather the fabric curtain, use the curtain-tape method described on page 364–6 and insert a split ring to correspond with each eyelet on the ungathered plastic curtain.

Left: Waterproof rip-stop nylon, ideal for shower curtains, is available in strong, stylish colours.

Measuring up

Ready-made shower curtains are designed to fit along an average sized bath or around a shower and are about 180cm/70in square. This is a good standard size but, of course, not everyone's circumstances are standard. It is important that the curtain is of adequate size for the bath or shower, so measure up carefully before buying the fabric.

Shower curtains do not need to be gathered when pulled around the shower as gathering bunches up the curtain, trapping moisture and preventing the fabric drying off effectively. The outer curtain should not get wet so it can be gathered for a more draped effect.

The width Measure the curtain rail for the width of your shower curtain. The waterproof curtain should not be more than 1¼ times the measurement of the rail, but a perfectly flat shower curtain is quite adequate. Add 3cm/1¼in to each side for double side hems. Unless you are making a narrow shower curtain for a built-in shower unit, you will find that the fabrics generally available are not wide enough to make a shower curtain from a single width. Add 3cm/1¼in for each join in the fabric width.

The length Measure from the shower rail down to a point at least 20cm/8in inside the bath or almost to the floor in the shower tray. Add 6cm/2½in for a bottom double hem and 6cm/2½in for the top double hem to take the eyelets.

Choosing the fabric

The fabric for an unlined shower curtain, or for the shower side of a lined curtain, must be waterproof and unlikely to rot. Various synthetic materials such as 100% nylon, 100% pvc and 100% vinyl are available, usually in 130cm/51in widths, in patterned or plain colours. Rip-stop nylon, available from kite and sail shops, is also suitable and comes in a better range of bright colours.

Do not use pins on the fabric if they are likely to leave permanent holes. Hold the layers together with paper clips and use a wedge-pointed needle in the sewing machine.

These synthetic fabrics are not machine washable and should be wiped down with a soft cloth and non-abrasive cleaner.

Once a shower curtain is wet from use, it must be left as flat as possible to dry off. If it is drawn back and bunched up when wet, mildew can easily form and this is almost impossible to remove.

For a lined shower curtain, the fabric facing out into the bathroom does not need to be waterproof and can be chosen to co-ordinate with wallpaper, window curtains or other furnishings.

Towelling (but not the stretch variety) is an excellent choice, as it absorbs moisture but dries out quickly. The same colour towelling can be used for accessories such as bathrobes, towels and bath mat to give a co-ordinated effect which is essential in a small bathroom.

If you are using towelling, add at least 10% to your measurements and pre-wash the towelling before making up, to allow for its natural shrinkage.

A basic shower curtain

In the instructions below the 'right' side of the shower curtain is that which faces into the bathroom; the 'wrong' side faces into the bath or shower.

You will need
Waterproof fabric
Nylon or polyester thread
Eyelet kit or eyelet and pliers
Chinagraph pencil
Rail and rings

Cutting out and making up
Measure up as above and cut out including seam and hem allowances. Join widths if necessary with French seams (see page 365).
If it is necessary to join widths of fabric the joins should be evenly spaced for the best visual effect. For example, if you are joining two pieces, join the two full widths and then cut off any excess from both sides so that the join is in the exact centre of the curtain.
On both side edges of the curtain, turn a double hem (1.5cm/⅝in and 1.5cm/⅝in) to the wrong side. Machine stitch in place close to the fold.

On the top edge, turn 3cm/1¼in then 3cm/1¼in as a double hem to the wrong side and machine stitch close to the lower folded edge.

Positioning the eyelets
To position the eyelets along the top hem, mark the fabric evenly about every 15cm/6in along the width of the curtain and about 1cm/½in down from the top edge. A chinagraph pencil makes a clear mark on plastic fabric and can be removed later with a soapy cloth. Check that you have sufficient shower curtain rings for the number of marks. If you do not have

enough and are unable to buy any more to match, adjust the spacing evenly to tally with the number of rings. Follow the instructions supplied with the eyelet pliers or kit to make the holes and insert the eyelets.

Hanging the curtain
Hang the shower curtain by threading the rings/hooks on to the rail and clipping them through the eyelets.
Turn a double hem, 3cm/1¼in and 3cm/1¼in, along the bottom edge to the wrong side, and machine stitch in place close to the fold.

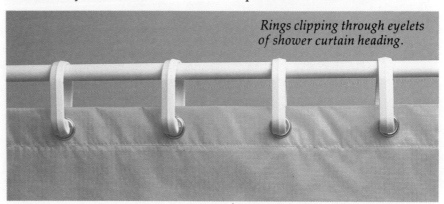

Rings clipping through eyelets of shower curtain heading.

Making a roller blind

*Roller blinds are an attractive alternative to curtains, and
need a fraction of the amount of fabric. They
can be used as sunshades or to block out an ugly view and are
simple to make from a kit. You can buy pre-stiffened
blind fabric or stiffen a furnishing fabric yourself.*

Blinds serve the same function as curtains, but they can also be used to cut out bright sunlight. When not in use they roll up out of the way, but their main advantage over curtains must be that they are so economical to make.

You need buy only the amount of fabric to cover the window area, plus a minimal amount top and bottom – there is no extra needed for pleats and gathers as in curtains and no need for lining fabric (although of course, lining fabric and fullness do make curtains better insulators.) Roller blinds are useful at windows with radiators or furniture underneath them because they cover only the glass and need not hang below the sill. They look crisper and sharper than curtains and complement the clean lines of a modern room.

The blinds are quick and easy to put together. The straight bottom edge is the simplest to make, but the bottom of the blind can also be finished with decorative scallops or zigzag cuts. Alternative finishes are dealt with in the following chapter.

Right: A roller blind is ideal if you have furniture just beneath the window.

Decide whether you are going to hang your blind inside or outside the window recess – blinds are generally hung inside the recess.
1 Measure the width of the recess. If you are hanging the blind outside the recess, add 6cm/2¼in to allow for overlap. Buy a roller blind kit. They come in a range of standard sizes and, unless the width you need is a standard size, buy the next size up and cut the roller to fit. A 275cm/109in width is about the widest roller on sale.
2 Lay out the pieces of the roller kit to check you have everything you need. In most kits there is a wooden roller with a spring fitted at one end, an end cap and pin for the other end, two brackets, a wooden batten for the bottom of the blind,

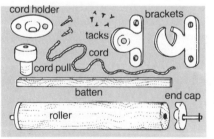

tacks, cord, a cord holder and a pull. Check the roller kit instructions for the positioning of each bracket. Normally two different brackets are supplied in each kit. The slotted bracket, which takes the spring end of the blind, usually goes on the left-hand side, unless you have chosen a non-reversible fabric. In this case, the roller can be fitted so that the fabric rolls over the front of

it with the right side of the fabric showing on the roller, rather than under the roller and down the back in the usual way.

If the fabric is non-reversible, fit the slotted bracket to the right-hand side of the recess for this alternative rolling up method.

If fixing your blind to the inside of the recess, position the brackets as close to the sides of the recess as

possible so that the maximum area is covered by the blind. Screw in the brackets tightly, making sure they are absolutely level.

If fixing it to the outside of the recess, the brackets should be at least 3cm/1¼in from the recess edge and at least 5cm/2in above it to prevent light from the window showing round the top and sides of the blind.

Cutting the roller to size

Measure the distance between the brackets with a steel or wooden rule and saw the roller to this width, making an allowance for the end cap, which you still have to fit.

Fix the end cap and pin to the sawn end of the roller, following instructions supplied with the kit. The roller is now ready to take the fabric.

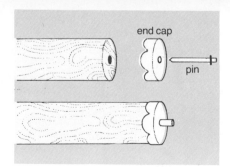

Choosing and preparing the fabric

Use either commercially pre-stiffened fabric or a furnishing fabric, which you can stiffen at home.

Pre-stiffened roller blind fabric has been commercially treated to make it stiff, fray-resistant and, in some cases, spongeable and fade-resistant too. The fabric can be bought by the metre, in widths up to about 2m/2¼yd. Patterns without one-way designs can be used either vertically or horizontally to get the most economical use from the fabric.

Furnishing fabric as blind material There are several do-it-yourself stiffening agents for roller blinds on the market. Choose a medium-weight fabric – too thin and it will not stiffen satisfactorily and will crease when rolled up – too thick and it will not roll up evenly. Many fabrics shrink slightly when stiffened, so treat the fabric before cutting it to size. Follow the instructions for stiffening provided with the product, testing a sample piece of fabric first to see if it is colour fast and can be stiffened.

Measuring up for the fabric Measure the full width of your roller (excluding the protruding pin ends) and deduct 1cm/½in to arrive at the finished fabric width. Measure from the brackets down to the window sill, or to just below the sill for a blind hung outside the recess. Add 18cm/7in to allow for fixing round the roller and for a casing at the bottom for the wooden batten, to arrive at the fabric length. Pre-stiffened fabric will not fray when cut, and home-stiffened fabric should not do so either, so no

Cutting out and making up the blind

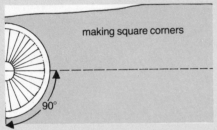

making square corners

90°

joining fabric widths

1.5cm

Work on a flat surface to prevent the fabric from creasing.
Cut the pre-stiffened or home-stiffened fabric to size using a

sharp cutting knife or scalpel and a steel ruler or straight-edge tool as a cutting guide.
Square corners Each one must be an

exact right angle, or the blind will always roll up unevenly and hang badly. Use a protractor or a carpenter's try square to mark exact 90° angles before cutting out.
Joining fabric widths The same method of joining widths can be used for both types of fabric. Overlap the two pieces of fabric by 1.5cm/⅝in and topstitch down both edges to secure.
Neatening fabric edges Pre-stiffened fabric is fray resistant and the

Fitting the batten

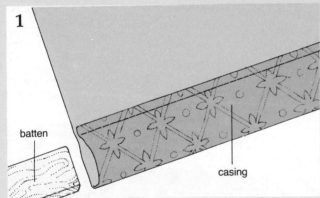

1

batten

casing

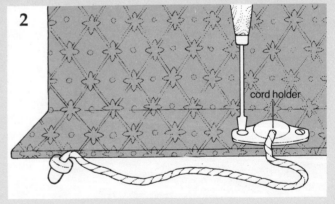

2

cord holder

Saw batten to 1cm/½in less than the width of the blind.
Turn a single hem about 4cm/1½in deep to wrong side along bottom edge. Check that the batten will slide easily into this space, and make the casing deeper if necessary.
1 Machine stitch close to the edge of the casing edge. On pre-stiffened fabric a zigzag stitch is preferable if your machine does this.
Slip the batten into the casing and sew up both ends with tiny overcast

stitches.
If you do not have a sewing machine, cut the batten to size and fold the fabric to make the casing. Spread both sides of the batten with a fabric glue. Position it carefully inside the fold and weight down with heavy objects, such as books or kitchen weights, until the glue has dried.
You need to position the batten differently if the blind is to have a decorative bottom finish. (These are dealt with in the following chapter.)

To attach cord holder and cord
Push one end of cord through the hole in the cord holder, and knot behind it to secure.
2 Position cord holder at the centre of the batten casing, and screw in through the material. Generally the cord holder is fixed to the front of the blind, but you can screw it to the back to hide it from view.
Attach cord pull to end of cord.

allowance needs to be made for side and bottom hems.

If fabric has to be joined to make up the width of the blind, allow 1.5cm/⅝in seam allowance on each piece of fabric. Position the joins at equal intervals for the best appearance. **Patterned blinds** that have joins or are to hang close to one another, such as three blinds at a bay window, should be pattern matched (see page 382). When you measure up for the fabric make an allowance for the pattern repeats so that you can match them.

edges will not need neatening. Furnishing fabric should be fray-resistant once it has been stiffened, but if it does have a tendency to fray, zigzag the edges on a sewing machine. Never turn under a side hem, as this will give you an uneven thickness of fabric on the ends of the roller.

Right: Roller blinds team successfully with curtains; the two can be made up in complementary or matching fabrics.

Fixing the fabric to the roller

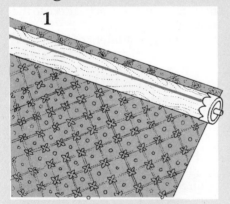

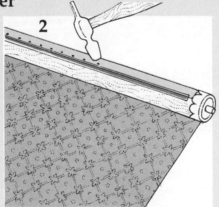

1 Lay the fabric flat, right-side upwards, and place the roller on the fabric at the top.

If you are making a blind in a non-reversible fabric and you have chosen the method of rolling the fabric over the roller rather than under it, you must lay the fabric *wrong* side upwards.

Lift the edge of the fabric over on to the roller, lining up with one of the horizontal marks on it. If your roller has no horizontal lines, clamp it in a carpenter's vice, or ask someone to

hold it very still for you, and mark a straight line at right angles to the ends along the length of the roller. Fix the edge of the fabric temporarily along this line with a length of sticky tape.

2 Hammer the small tacks provided with the kit through the edge of the fabric into the roller, spacing them evenly along it. Peel off the sticky tape.

(If you own or can borrow a staple gun, you'll find stapling the fabric to the roller is easier.)

Hanging the blind

Roll the fabric up tightly around the roller and fit it into the brackets. Pull the blind down to its full extent. You should now find that the tension is correct and when you give the cord a very gentle tug, the blind should roll up. If the tension is not correct, the blind will be sluggish and jerky as it rolls up or it may not roll up at all. Try again. Lift the extended blind out of the brackets and roll the fabric up round the roller. Put the blind back in the brackets and pull down again. Repeat until you get the correct tension, but be careful not to over-tension the blind or the spring may break.

Decorating roller blinds

Cut the lower edge of a blind into scallops, zigzags or a variety of wave shapes so that it remains a decorative feature of the room, even when pulled up. Add a braid trim to match your furnishings and finish the pull cord with a wooden acorn or a tassel.

Roller blinds are economical to make and practical to use but if you feel they leave windows looking rather bare when rolled up, add a decorative edging. Trim the lower edge of the blind into a dramatic wave shape, or cut a repeated shape such as scallops, inverted scallops or zigzags – choosing a style to suit the furnishings of the room.

Braid or lace trimmings can be added either to a straight edged blind or, if the fabric is likely to fray, to a cut, shaped edge.

On scalloped, zigzag and wave edged blinds, position the batten that straightens the lower edge of the blind above and well clear of any shaping or trimming. When the blind is pulled up, the shaping will still be visible, adding an attractive touch to the window.

There are two ways of making the batten casing and either can be used with any style of decorative edging given here.

The tuck method of making a blind casing leaves no surface stitching showing but is only suitable for plain fabrics and patterns without an obvious design as it interrupts the pattern.

The topstitched casing method leaves the main drop of fabric uninterrupted and requires less fabric but does involve a double row of stitching across the width of the blind. Make the batten casing but do not insert the batten until the lower edge is complete.

When planning a shaped edge, do not be tempted to draw the shaping directly on to the blind fabric as a mistake in measuring or drawing out could leave an ugly mark. Work out the proportions of the shaping, make up a paper pattern, then draw round this to transfer the exact pattern to the blind fabric.

If you are not confident of being able to draw a curve, you will find a flexible curve a worthwhile investment. This is a length of flexible plastic which is easy to bend into smooth, neat curves and retains its shape until re-positioned.

Preparing materials

Details of measuring up, materials required and basic making up instructions for roller blinds are given on pages 414–17. Add an extra 5cm/2in to the length of fabric to cut for a blind with a shaped edge.

Attach the brackets of the roller blind kit to the window and trim the wooden roller to fit. Cut the fabric 1cm/½in narrower than the roller and zigzag the edges to prevent fraying, if necessary.

A stiffened material called Pelmform, described on page 393, has a variety of shapes printed on it for use when making pelmets some of which are also suitable for decorative blind edges.

Making a scalloped blind

This method is also suitable for blinds edged with inverted scallops, zig-zags and wave shapes.

Prepare and cut out the fabric then make a batten casing following one of the two methods below. The blind will only roll up as far as the batten so adjust the depth of scallop to suit the proportions of the window.

The tucked casing is suitable for plain or semi-patterned fabrics. Measure 13cm/5in up from the lower edge of blind fabric and mark on the side edges. Measure 9cm/3½in up from these points and mark again.

Fold the fabric across the width, right sides facing, to bring the two sets of marks together. Finger press the fold (an iron may damage stiffened fabric), then stitch across the width of the fabric 4.5cm/1¾in below the fold (between marks on either side), forming a tuck on the

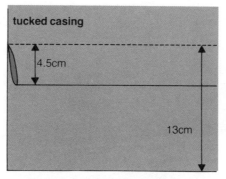

wrong side of the blind. Stitch across one end of the tuck to complete the casing and finger press tuck downwards.

The topstitched casing involves stitching a separate strip of fabric to the wrong side of the blind to form the casing and so does not interrupt the pattern.

Cut a strip 9cm/3½in deep from the bottom edge of the blind and zigzag the edges if they are likely to fray.

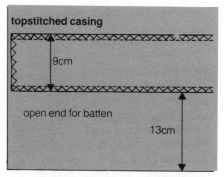

Lay the blind fabric wrong side uppermost and position the casing strip, also wrong side up, across the width 13cm/5in up from the lower edge.

Hold in place with adhesive tape or paper clips, as pins may leave permanent marks in the blind. Topstitch down both long edges and across one short edge, leaving the remaining short edge open to insert the batten later.

Planning the scallop pattern

For a scalloped edge (or one with any other repeated shape) to look its best, the width of the scallops has to be carefully calculated so that an exact number fit across the lower edge of the blind. A measurement of between 12cm/4½in and 14cm/5½in at the widest point of each scallop is a reasonable average size but you will be able to judge whether the proportion is correct after making the pattern and laying it against the blind.

To calculate the number of scallops that you need, divide the blind width by an estimated scallop width.

For example, if your blind is 132cm (or imperial equivalent) wide and you would like scallops about 14cm wide, divide 132 by 14. This gives 9.4 as the number of scallops. Obviously, a part scallop looks unbalanced so take the nearest whole number i.e. 9, and divide the width of the blind by this number to give the *exact* width of each scallop. In the example, 132 divided by 9 gives a scallop size of 14.7cm.

Left: Shallow inverted scallops, neatened and defined by a narrow trimming, add interest to a simple blind and echo the shaped edge of a pretty net curtain.

Cutting out the pattern

Cut a strip of paper 13cm/5in deep by the width of your blind and mark it out into sections *half* the calculated scallop width.

Fold the paper *concertina fashion* along the marked sections. On the unfolded edge at one end of the paper, make a mark 6cm/2¼in up from the bottom. Using a flexible curve for absolute accuracy, draw half a scallop curving from the bottom folded corner to the mark. Cut along the curve through all thicknesses of the paper and open the paper out. You will now have a paper pattern of even scallops to fit the width of your blind.

Note: If you are making a wide blind and the bulk of the folded paper is too much to cut through, cut two strips, each exactly half the blind width. Cut each into scallops, and then join the two pieces with adhesive tape to make a pattern to fit the complete blind width.

Shaping the blind edge

Lay the pattern on the wrong side of the blind, with the shaped edge close to the lower edge of the blind, and hold in place with adhesive tape.

With a sharp tailor's chalk pencil, carefully draw round the shaped

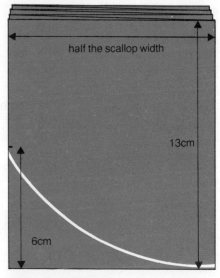

edge of the pattern. Remove the pattern and check that the outline is smooth and even.

Cut the fabric along the shaping line with a scalpel, DIY cutting knife or a special rotary cutting wheel (sold as a dressmaking/craft aid). Zigzag stitch around the shaping if it is liable to fray.

Insert the batten into the casing and hand stitch or machine stitch the remaining open edge to close. Attach the cord holder and cord to the back of the batten, attach the blind to the wooden roller, and hang it at the window.

Shaping variations

Follow the method of making up a scalloped blind, but choose one of the variations below for the shaping.

Inverted scallops

Calculate the width of these and prepare the pattern as for the scallop edged blind.

Having folded the paper concertina fashion to half a scallop width, mark 4cm/1½in (or your required scallop depth) up on the folded edge of the top piece of paper. Draw half an inverted scallop (like a shallow rainbow) from this point to the lower unfolded corner. Cut through all thicknesses and unfold to make the pattern.

Zigzags

Estimate the number and width of zigzags that will fit across the blind, using the same calculation method as for scallops – 10cm/4in wide is an average size. Half the width is a good guide to estimating the height of zigzags, but alter proportions to suit your blind.

Fold a strip of paper concertina fashion to half the width of a zigzag, as for scallops, but mark the top unfolded edge the required

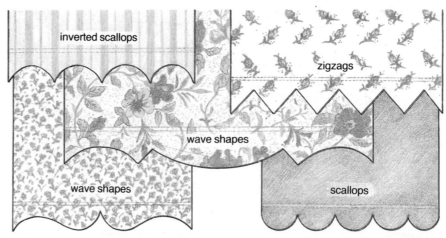

height of zigzag (about 5cm/2in) from the bottom. Rule a straight line from this mark down to the bottom corner on the folded side.

Cut along the line through all layers and unfold to make the pattern.

Wave shapes

These differ from repeated shapes such as scallops and zigzags as one shape covers half the width of the blind and is reversed to cover the other half.

Cut a strip of paper 12cm/4¾in deep by the width of the blind and fold in half, short ends together.

For a deep wave shape, draw a line across the full width of the folded paper 6cm/2¼in up from the bottom edge. For a shallower shape, draw the line about 4cm/1½in up from the bottom edge. Draw two or three evenly spaced vertical lines and use these and the horizontal line as a guide, when you are designing your required shape. A flexible curve makes this easy to do.

Cut out the shape through both layers of paper, unfold and check that the shape is visually pleasing, altering if necessary, before using as the pattern.

Adding a decorative trimming

In addition to, or instead of, cutting the bottom of your blind into a decorative shape, glue a pretty braid trimming – with or without fringing, tassels or bobbles – to the blind edges.

Use any type of braid trim along the bottom of a straight edged roller

blind, but to attach braid around a curved shape, you must use bias cut braid or a flexible woven braid that will bend around the curves without puckering.

If the ends of the braid are liable to fray, either neaten with a zigzag stitch or turn a small amount of braid to the wrong side at each end and glue.

Use a fabric adhesive such as Copydex and follow the manufacturer's instructions to simply glue the braid along the edge of the blind.

A beautiful fabric print, which might be lost in the folds of a curtain, shows to perfection on a roller blind. The elegant wave shaped cut edge increases the stylish effect.

Austrian blinds

A pretty fabric teased into soft swags and gentle gathers makes an Austrian blind a charming alternative, or addition, to curtains. It looks impressively complicated but is easy to make by simply adding tape, rings and cord to an unlined curtain.

An Austrian blind – not to be confused with the ruched festoon blind described in the next chapter – gives a designer look to any room.
When completely lowered it looks like an unlined gathered curtain. The blind is pulled up by cords which are attached to rings and tapes running vertically up the back of the blind. Three types of tape can be used:

Plain woven tape (non-stretch) which has no pockets or bars. Rings have to be sewn on. Buy this about 2cm/¾in wide.
Dainty tape made by Rufflette. A lightweight, narrow curtain heading tape that is ideal for the vertical tapes on Austrian blinds. It has regular pockets for the rings to slot into, which also makes the job of spacing the rings much easier.
Austrian blind tape supplied in Rufflette's Austrian Blind Kit. This tape has regularly spaced bars for holding the cord so rings are not required.
The spacing of the rings and the ac-

Measuring up for an Austrian blind

To calculate how much fabric to buy, first measure your window.
For the width – as a general guide you will need 2-2½ times the window measurement. Check the instructions for the curtain heading tape you are using at the top of the blind, and be sure to allow enough fabric width to form the heading pleats. For all but the narrowest of windows, you will have to use more than one width of fabric.

For the drop – take the window height measurement and allow an extra 20cm/7¾in for hems. Add an allowance for pattern matching the width of fabric, if necessary. Multiply this total drop measurement by the number of fabric widths needed to arrive at the amount of fabric you need.
You will need extra fabric for a frill along the bottom edge, or if you add bows (see Design Extra on page 425).

The amount of tape needed depends on the size of blind you are making – (see above for the types of tape available). The total width of the fabric is divided into sections by vertical lines of tape spaced about 40cm/15¾in apart. You will need sufficient tape to run from top to bottom of the blind along each vertical division and down each side of the blind fabric.

Joining and hemming the fabric

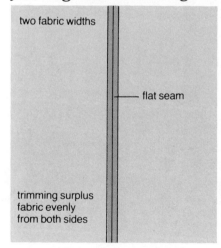

For most windows you will have to join at least two pieces of fabric to make up the width of the blind.
For two fabric widths Join widths together with a flat seam of 1.5cm/⅝in and then trim seam allowance to 5mm/¼in. Cut any surplus fabric evenly from both widths.
For three fabric widths, position a complete width in the centre, and join the widths together with flat

seams of 1.5cm/⅝in. Trim the seam allowance to 5mm/¼in. Cut any surplus fabric evenly from both side widths. Down each side edge of the blind, turn a 2cm/¾in hem to wrong side and tack in place. Do not make this hem if you are adding side frills. For a plain bottom edge, turn a double hem (2cm and 2cm/¾in and ¾in) to wrong side and sew in place. Do not make this hem if you

are adding a bottom frill.
If you are adding a frill, make up and sew it in place (see Design Extra on page 425).

Right: A prettily trimmed frill emphasises the luxurious festooned effect of an Austrian blind. Piping and binding pick up the print colouring and a row of extravagantly styled bows adds a final flourish.

tion of pulling up the cords raises the blind into swags and gathers which form the characteristic appearance of an Austrian blind.

The swags and gathers raise up from the bottom, so the higher you pull up the blind, the more gathers are formed. Once you have raised the blind into the most visually pleasing position, you keep it in place by securing the cords around a cleat on the window frame.

An Austrian blind can be used at a window in addition to normal curtains, to give an extra soft look. Many people prefer to have both so that the blind can be left in a swagged position for decorative effect and the curtains can be drawn for privacy.

Because of its soft, frilly look, an Austrian blind can be used very effectively to make a feature of a plain window. You can use sheer fabric and most light furnishing fabrics, leaving the blind quite plain or adding a frilled bottom edge – trimmed and piped if you wish. You could also add frills down the side edges, or a set of bows to jolly up the top of the blind.

You will need
Fabric (as calculated opposite)
Matching sewing thread

Wooden batten 2.5cm/1in×5cm/2in ×width of your window
Curtain track and fittings of the same width as the batten
You will also need (unless you have purchased Rufflette's Austrian Blind Kit in which the items *below* are included):
Tape (as calculated opposite)
Small metal curtain rings (also known as split rings)
Non-stretch cord (about double the amount of tape required)
Screw eyes (one per length of tape)
Curtain heading tape to fit the total fabric width
1 cleat

Tapes, rings and cords

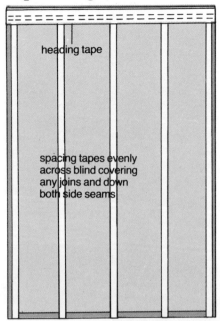

heading tape

spacing tapes evenly across blind covering any joins and down both side seams

Attaching the tapes Wrong sides facing upwards, lay the blind fabric on a large flat surface – the floor is the best place.

With tailor's chalk, mark on the vertical lines for positioning the tape. These must be evenly spaced – about 40cm/16in apart – across the fabric to give good sized swags. If you have joined fabric to make up the complete width, each join must be covered by one of the lengths of tape to disguise the seam. This may mean that you have to adjust the distance between the marked vertical lines slightly – but you must still keep them evenly spaced.

The tape is positioned along these marked lines and also down both outer edges of the blind.

If you are using plain woven tape, cut it into lengths equal to the blind

fabric drop plus 1cm/½in. Turn 1cm/½in to wrong side on one end of each tape. Place each length of tape along a marked vertical line (or seamline) with the folded end to the bottom edge of the blind and raw end to the top edge. Place a length of tape down each side of the blind. Tack the tapes in place, then sew down both long edges of the tape.

If you are using Dainty tape or the Austrian blind kit tape, cut each length at exactly the same point on the tape so that when all of the cut lengths are in position the pockets or bars line up across the width. Apply as for the plain tape, ensuring that the pockets or bars face upwards.

Sew heading tape to the top of the blind, as for a curtain, but do not gather up yet.

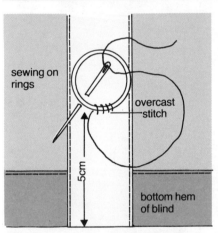

sewing on rings

overcast stitch

5cm

bottom hem of blind

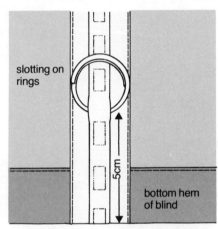

slotting on rings

5cm

bottom hem of blind

Sewn-on rings If you have used plain woven tape on your blind, you will need to sew rings to the tape using overcast stitch. Starting at the bottom left-hand corner, sew the first ring to the tape, placing it 5cm/2in from the bottom edge. Continue up the tape

attaching the rings, spacing them evenly about 20cm/8in apart. Repeat for the other tapes, starting from exactly the same point at the bottom for each one. It's very important to space the rings accurately, because if they do not line up horizontally the blind will not hang evenly.

Slotted-in rings Starting at the bottom left-hand corner, slot a ring through a pocket on the first length of tape, about 5cm/2in from bottom edge. Continue spacing the rings accurately as for the sewn-on rings; you will find them easy to space as you simply count the number of pockets between each ring. *Note:* the tape supplied in the Rufflette Austrian blind kit has retaining bars instead of rings. When all the rings are in place, pull up the cords in the heading tape at the top of the blind, gathering up the fabric evenly until it is the correct width for the window.

Cording the blind Lay the blind flat, wrong side upwards. Starting at the bottom left-hand corner, measure the length of the blind, plus the top width plus one metre extra. Cut a piece of cord to this

Hanging the blind

1 Take the batten of wood and fix the curtain track along one of the 5cm/2in sides, close to the top edge. Pull up curtain tape to fit track and insert hooks. Lay the batten on the floor and fit the blind to the curtain track. Turn over so that tape side of blind faces upwards and, with a pencil, mark on the underside of the batten where each tape meets the batten. Remove blind from track.

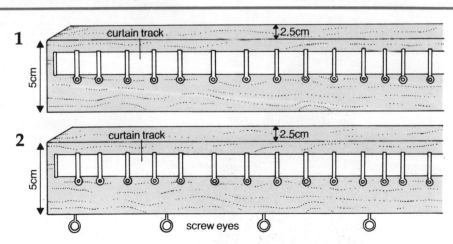

1

curtain track

2.5cm

5cm

2

curtain track

2.5cm

5cm

screw eyes

Adding frills and bows

Frills and bows add extra
softness and charm to an
Austrian blind, and they are easy
to make up and attach.
For the frill Cut and join
sufficient 10cm/4in wide strips of
fabric to make up double the
width of the blind. Turn a double
hem (5mm and 5mm/¼in and
¼in) to the wrong side along one
long edge and both short edges.
On remaining long edge, sew
two lines of gathering stitches
1cm/½in and 1.5cm/⅝in from the
edge. Draw up gathering threads
until the frill exactly fits the
bottom of the blind.
With right sides facing, tack and
then sew raw edges of frill and
blind together, with a 1cm/½in
flat seam. Insert piping between

frill and blind at this stage if
desired. Remove tacking and
neaten seam with zigzag or
overcasting stitch.
A row of bows are a clever way
to conceal the seams in the fabric.
For each bow, cut a strip of fabric
70cm×6cm/27½in×2¼in. Fold in
half lengthways, wrong sides
facing, and cut each end into a
point. Trim all edges with bias
binding, or bias strips cut from
fabric. Tie each fabric strip
into a bow. Stitch bows to blind
along gathered heading.

*Right: Designer touches give a really
professional finish to an Austrian blind.
Piped seams, a flouncy frill, contrasting
binding or a row of bows – choose one
or add them all for maximum effect.*

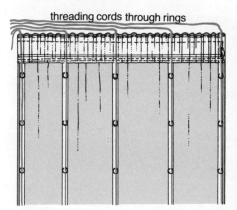

threading cords through rings

measurement.
Tie this first cord in place to the
bottom ring, or bottom bar, of the
tape in the bottom left-hand corner
and thread it up through the other
rings/bars.
Add cords to the other tape lengths
in the same way, working across to
the right-hand side of the blind.

2 Fix a screw eye in place on each
pencil mark along the batten. Screw
each end of the batten to the
window frame.
Hang the blind on the curtain track.
3 Thread the left-hand cord through
the first screw eye and then through
all the screw eyes to the right-hand
side of the batten.
Repeat for the other cords.
Attach the cleat about half-way
down the right-hand side of the
window frame.

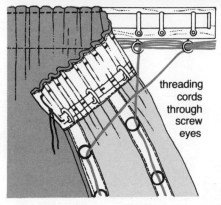

threading cords through screw eyes

*Above: In a sheer fabric, an Austrian
blind lets in softly filtered light.*

To check that the blind pulls up
properly, pull the cords evenly
together, so that the fabric gathers
upwards into soft swags.
Lower the blind, so that it is flat and
tie the cords together in a knot,
trimming ends to make a neat bunch.
Pull the blind up once more, until it
is in the desired position and secure
the cords around the cleat.

Elegantly ruched festoon blinds

Even more sumptuous than an Austrian blind, a festoon blind remains ruched into soft swags not only when pulled up but also when fully covering the window. Emphasize the pretty scalloped effect of the lower edge with a matching or contrasting frill.

Transform a dull window by making a strikingly decorative ruched festoon blind, highlighting the scallops of the lower edge with a deep gathered frill. Choose a richly printed furnishing fabric, or use a sheer voile for a translucent blind to team with heavier side curtains.

A festoon blind is very similar to an Austrian blind but retains the ruched swags whether raised or lowered and so creates an even more dramatic effect. Read the previous chapter on making Austrian blinds and adapt, as described here, to make a festoon blind. Vertical lines of curtain tape – lightweight Dainty Tape is ideal – gather up the extra length.

A rod or batten encased in matching fabric, stitched to the back of the blind, ensures that the bottom edge hangs well and is easy to raise and lower smoothly. Choose a metal rod about 1cm/½in in diameter or, adding curtain weighting tape to increase the weight if necessary, a wooden batten about 2cm/¾in deep.

Below: Piping and a frill add to the decorative effect of a festoon blind.

You will need

Fabric for the blind, frill and batten casing (see Measuring up)
Rufflette Dainty tape for vertical tapes (see Measuring up)
Blind cord about twice length of tape
Rufflette Standard curtain heading tape to fit width of prepared blind fabric plus turnings
Small split curtain rings
Screw eyes
Metal rod or wooden batten to fit finished blind width
Wooden heading batten, curtain track and hooks to hang blind
Cleat to hold cords
Note: The tape in an Austrian blind kit does not create permanent ruching.

Measuring up

To calculate how much fabric to buy, measure the width and drop of your window (or the area to be covered by the finished blind).
Multiply the width by 1¼ times for a medium-weight fabric or by 1½ times for lightweights and sheers, to find the width of fabric needed. You may need more than one width of fabric to make up this size.
Multiply the drop by 1½-3 times (again, the bulkier the fabric, the less you need; only a fine sheer needs 3 times the drop) to find the required length of blind fabric.
Calculate how much fabric you will need to buy by multiplying the required length by the number of widths needed. You will also need sufficient 20cm/8in-deep strips of fabric to make up a piece 1½ times the width of prepared blind fabric for the frill and a strip of fabric 8cm/3in deep by the width of the finished blind to cover the rod or batten.
Add allowances for pattern matching as necessary.
Calculate the Dainty tape needed as for an Austrian blind, page 70.

Cutting out

Allowing for pattern matching where necessary, cut out lengths of fabric to make up the area of the blind. Also cut 20cm/8in deep strips to make up a frill piece 1½ times the blind fabric width, and a strip for batten casing (see Measuring up).

Making up and hanging the blind

Join widths of fabric if necessary, as for an Austrian blind, page 70. Press a 2cm/¾in turning to the wrong side down each side edge of the blind and tack.
Press a 4cm/1½in turning to the wrong side across the top edge; tack.

Adding the frill

Join the strips of fabric to make up the frill with 1cm/½in flat seams and press seams open. Fold the strip in half along its length, right sides facing, and stitch across both short ends, 1cm/½in in. Fold strip right side out, press and insert two rows of gathering stitches, in easy-to-gather sections, through both thicknesses along the open edge. Pull up the gathering threads until the frill fits the width of the blind, tie the thread ends securely and even out gathers.
Tack the frill across the bottom edge on the right side of the blind, raw edges together, and stitch 1.5cm/⅝in in from the edge. Remove tacking, zigzag stitch or oversew raw edges together; press upwards.

Attaching tapes and rings

Lay the fabric out flat on the floor, wrong side uppermost and, using a tailor's chalk pencil, mark the position of the vertical lines of Dainty tape. Position the two outer tapes 1cm/½in in from the side edges; space the remaining tapes evenly between them 25–40cm/10–16in apart. If possible, arrange the

attaching tapes and rings

spacing so that a line of tape will cover any seams joining fabric widths. Cutting 1cm/½in in front of a tape pocket each time, so that they will line up horizontally on the blind, cut the appropriate number of lengths of tape each 5cm/2in longer than blind (excluding frill). Freeing the ends of the gathering cords, turn in 1cm/½in at the lower end of each length of tape, and pin into position from the frill seam to the edge of top turning. Ensure that the edges of the side hems and any seams are covered by tape and that the tape pockets line up. Stitch long edges of each tape.
Freeing the top ends of gathering cords on vertical tapes as shown in diagram, stitch standard heading tape across top of blind covering raw edge and tape ends.
Slot split rings through the tape pockets every 20–25cm/8–10in or so, placing the first ring about 10cm/4in up from the bottom of the tape, with the final ring just below the heading tape.
Gather up each line of tape to the finished length of the blind. Even out the gathering so that the rings line up horizontally across the back of the blind and tie the ends of the cords to secure. Just below each pocket, catch the cords of the gathering tape to the fabric with small invisible handstitches to hold the gathers in place as heavy fabrics may slip when hanging.

Adding a rod or batten

Fold the strip of casing fabric in half lengthwise, right sides facing, and stitch across one short end and down long raw edges with a 1cm/½in seam. Turn right side out.
Slip the rod, or a batten plus weighting tape, into the casing and slipstitch the open end closed.
Lay the blind out flat, wrong side upwards and place the covered rod just below the lowest row of rings as close to the scallops as possible without being visible from the right side. Stitch the top edge of the casing securely in place at the points where it crosses the vertical tapes, making sure the stitches are unnoticeable on the right side.

Cording and hanging

Attach cords and hang the blind in the same way as an Austrian blind.

Roman blinds for a soft pleated effect

Softer than a roller blind and less fussy than an Austrian blind, a Roman blind suits most windows and rooms, and is quick and economical to make. It is also easy to hang and to operate – the pull cords which raise it form attractive layered folds.

A Roman blind is an economical and unusual way of covering a window. When fully lowered it looks similar to a roller blind, but when pulled up, a system of rings and cords on the back concertina the fabric into soft horizontal pleats. There is, therefore, no need to stiffen the fabric, or buy a spring-loaded roller blind kit. A wooden batten running across the blind close to the bottom edge keeps it in shape and hanging straight.

Choosing fabrics

A Roman blind is made from a double thickness of fabric – top blind fabric and lining. The top fabric must not be too sheer or flimsy or it will not fall into crisp pleats. Most smoothly woven furnishing fabrics are suitable – choose one to match your upholstery or the colour scheme of the room. The lining can be ordinary curtain lining, an insulating lining or a complementary fabric that will also look pretty from the outside of the house. Choose closely woven fabrics for both blind and lining and the blind will be light-tight enough even for a bedroom.

The blind is quick and simple to make. After joining fabric and lining, simply stitch vertical lines of tape down its length. Sew rings to the tapes and pass cords through them – when pulled, the cords raise the blind by pleating up the fabric.

Tack the blind to a length of wood for hanging, and fix it to the wall with small angle iron supports, available from most hardwear or DIY suppliers.

Measuring up

The width Measure the width of the window area to be covered by the

Below: An elegant set of Roman blinds.

blind. If the blind is to be hung inside a recess or within a decorative window frame, make sure that the finished width will allow enough clearance for the blind to be raised and lowered without catching on the sides. If the blind is to hang outside a recess, overlap each side by at least 3cm/1¼in. For either style of hanging, add 3cm/1¼in to the finished width measurement for side seams.

It is possible to make a blind for a smallish window from a single piece of fabric. If you do have to join widths of fabric for a larger window, balance the joins evenly – for two widths the join should run down the exact centre of the blind; for three widths, use a complete width for the centre panel with an equal amount of fabric on either side.

For each join required, add 3cm/1¼in to make a 1.5cm/⅝in flat seam.

The length Measure the total drop required and add 3cm/1¼in for top and bottom seams and 1cm/½in for

overlapping the blind fabric on to the wooden heading. If you are hanging the blind outside a recess, add any overlap required at the top or bottom.

The tape Calculate the amount needed in the same way as for an Austrian blind (see page 422).

The finished width of the blind is divided into equal sections by vertical lines of tape spaced at approximately 30cm/12in intervals across the width – with a length of tape on each side edge. To work out the amount of tape required, calculate the number of lengths of tape needed and multiply this by the finished length of the blind plus 2cm/¾in.

You will need
To make the blind
Fabric for the front of the blind (see measuring up)
The same amount of lining fabric
Matching sewing thread
2cm/¾in wide cotton tape (see measuring up)

Non-stretch cord about twice the length of tape
Small plastic or metal curtain rings
Wooden batten about 2cm/¾in wide 1cm/½in shorter than finished width of blind

To hang the blind
A piece of 5cm×2.5cm/2in×1in wood to fit the finished width of blind, for the heading
A metal screw eye for each vertical line of tape
Tacks or staples to attach blind to wooden heading
Angle irons to attach wooden heading to window frame
Cleat to hold cords in place

Cutting out
Cut the fabric to the required length and join widths, if necessary, with 1.5cm/⅝in flat seams. Press seams open. Trim away any excess width taking an even amount from each side. Cut out and make up lining to the same size.

Making up the Roman blind

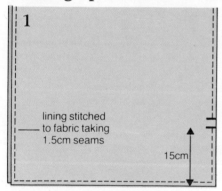

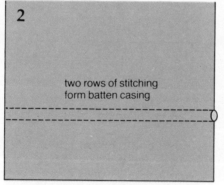

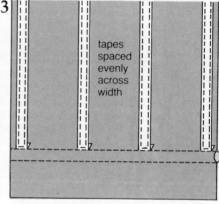

Joining fabric and lining Lay the lining fabric wrong side upwards flat on a table or the floor and measure 15cm/6in up from the bottom on one side edge. Mark this point with tailor's chalk.

Measure the wooden batten, add 5mm/¼in to the width and make a second mark on the lining this distance above the first.

1 Lay fabric and lining right sides facing and tack together all round. Sew down both sides and across the bottom edge taking 1.5cm/⅝in seams leaving a gap between the two marks on *one* side of the fabric to insert batten. Turn right side out. Turn 1.5cm/⅝in to the wrong side on both fabric and lining top edges and press. Tack and topstitch the folded edges together close to edge.

2 Lay the fabric out flat with the lining uppermost. With a ruler and tailor's chalk, mark two parallel lines for the batten casing in line with the gap left in the stitching on one side. Sew along these marked lines to form the batten casing.

Attaching tape and rings Mark the position of the vertical tapes on the lining side of the blind by drawing lines with tailor's chalk from the top of the blind to the batten casing. Begin by marking the position of a line of tape 1.5cm/⅝in in from each side edge. Divide the remaining fabric into equal sections with lines for tapes spaced about 30cm/12in apart, adjusting the spacing to suit your blind depth. It is *vital* that the tapes are evenly spaced.

3 Once you have marked the tape lines and checked that the spacing is even, pin and tack the tapes in place, turning 1cm/½in to the wrong side at the top and bottom ends. The tapes should run from the top edge ending at, but not overlapping, the batten casing. Sew the tapes in place, down both long edges and across the bottom edge. Remove tacking.

With tailor's chalk or pins, mark the ring positions about 15cm/6in apart along each line of tape. The first mark should be just above the batten casing and the last approximately 18.5cm/7in down from the top edge of the blind. It is important that the rings are *exactly* aligned horizontally so that the blind pulls up evenly.

4

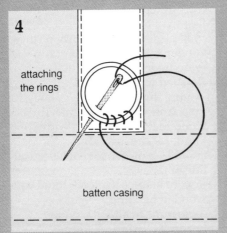

attaching the rings

batten casing

5

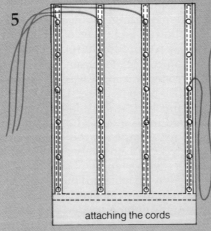

attaching the cords

ease it into the stitched casing and neatly hand sew the casing closed.

5 To attach the cords, lay the blind flat on the floor, lining side upwards and tie a length of cord securely to the bottom ring on the left-hand side. Pass the cord through every ring in this first line of tape and across to the left-hand edge of the lining. Allow 1m/1yd or a length that you will be able to reach when the blind is hanging, and then cut the cord.

Repeat for each line of tape, taking the cord up to the top of the blind, across to the left-hand edge and adding approximately 1m/1yd extra before cutting to form the hanging cords which are pulled to operate the blind.

4 Sew on a ring at each mark, using overcast stitching worked through the tape and lining but not the top blind fabric.

Adding batten and cords Check that the length of wooden batten is 1cm/½in less than the width of the blind; trim it if necessary. Gently

---

Hanging the Roman blind

Preparing the wooden heading Cut the 5cm×2.5cm/2in×1in piece of wood for the heading to the width of the blind and attach the screw eyes to a wider side, positioning them to correspond with the lines of tape on the blind.

Screw as many angle irons as are necessary to support the blind to the same side of the wood as the screw eyes, placing the bend of the angle iron in line with the edge of the wood.

Below: Use Rufflette Austrian blind tape rather than tape and rings, and thread the cords through the loops.

1

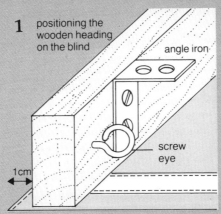

positioning the wooden heading on the blind

angle iron

screw eye

1cm

1 With the blind flat on the floor, lining side upwards, lay the narrow edge of the wooden heading (angle irons uppermost), on to the fabric 1cm/½in down from the top edge. Wrap the 1cm/½in strip of blind fabric on the wider side of the wood without screw eyes and tack or staple it securely in place. Make sure that the strip of fabric turned on to the wood is absolutely straight and even or the blind will hang askew.

2

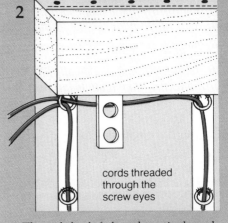

cords threaded through the screw eyes

2 Thread the left-hand vertical cord through the screw eye above it so that it hangs on the left side of the blind. Work across the blind threading each cord through the screw eye directly above and through the other screws along the wood to the left-hand side. When all cords have been inserted loosely knot the dangling ends together. Hold the wood and blind up to the window in the required position and attach the angle irons to the window frame or wall.

Untie the cords and trim to an even length of about 1m/1yd (or as required) then re-tie neatly together.

Pull the bunch of cords downwards and the blind above the batten will pull up in even folds, from the bottom upwards.

Screw a cleat to the window frame in a position within easy reach; wind the cords around this to hold the blind up at the required level.

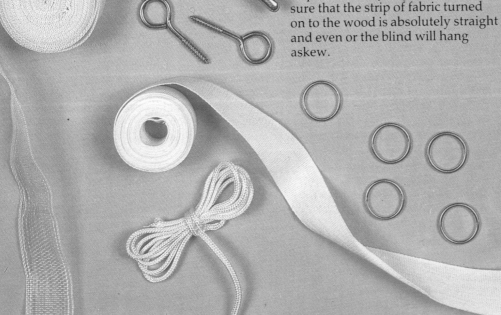

Trimming a Roman blind

Emphasize the neat, clean lines of a Roman blind with a sharply contrasting trim.

Use a flat tape or straight strips of fabric with raw edges pressed under for the trim. A width of 2.5cm/1in wide gives a bold effect.

Make up the blind as far as attaching the tapes to the lining side. Add the trim before attaching the rings.

Lay the blind out flat, right side upwards, and tack the trim in place down both sides and across the bottom edge, mitring the corners. Set the trim about 1.5cm/⅝in in from the edge so that the blind fabric forms a narrow border.

Machine the trim in place, topstitching down both edges, but do not machine over the batten casing. Remove the

Above: On a border-printed fabric, adjust width by making a tuck and only trim lower edge of the blind.

tacking and back stitch by hand along the trim where it crosses the casing, stitching through the top layer of fabric only, so as not to obstruct it.

Press well, sew on the rings and continue to make up the blind in the normal way.

Furnishing fabric guide

Cushions

Almost any fabric can be used, from heavy tapestry weaves to lightweight cottons; the limiting factor is the amount of wear the cushion is likely to get. Avoid very loose weaves and choose fabrics with easy care or washable properties for cushions which will get a lot of use. Remnant counters are a good source of some luxurious fabrics if only a small amount is required. For a co-ordinated look, save offcuts from your curtains and upholstery. Ready-made cushion pads are available but if you intend making your own, suitable fabrics are calico, cambric, cotton sheeting and lining material. If the filling is feather or down, use a down-proof ticking.

Curtains

Traditional curtain fabrics are brocade, velvet, linen and cotton and nowadays there is a wide range of man-made fabrics developed for use in soft furnishing. Some manufacturers produce a range of matching or co-ordinating wallpapers and fabrics, the latter often in two weights suitable for curtains and upholstery. Do not confine yourself to the furnishing-fabric departments – many dressmaking fabrics can also be used successfully for curtains.

Acetate
Man-made fibre made into silky-looking fabrics, often combined with cotton or linen in brocades and open-weave effects. Drapes well but is not very strong. Usually washable; does not shrink.

Acrylic
Synthetic fibre used for lightweight yet strong and crease-resistant fabrics such as velvet and satin. Washable but some varieties may need drycleaning.

Balloon fabrics
A very closely-woven cotton fabric used for cushion interlinings as it is downproof.

Brocade
A heavy fabric with the pattern woven in using a jacquard weave. Cotton, linen or silk is woven with, for example, rayon or acetate to produce a silky pattern on a dull background, or vice versa. Used for curtains.

Buckram
A loosely-woven cotton or linen fabric which is stiffened with glue size. It will not remain stiff if washed. Used for curtain pelmets and tiebacks.

Calico
A hard-wearing, medium-weight plain weave cotton fabric which is often used for cushion interlinings.

Cambric
A lightweight plain weave cotton or linen fabric used as a backing fabric or for lightweight curtains.

Casement cloth
A medium-weight cotton fabric in a closely-woven plain weave dyed in plain colours and used for lightweight curtains and blinds.

Chintz
A printed cotton fabric with a glazed finish. The glaze can be treated chemically to withstand washing. Used for curtains, blinds and cushion covers.

Cotton
Natural fibre which is strong and wears well. Used for many types of fabric, including glazed cotton, which has a shiny finish and resists dirt. Other varieties include velveteen, cotton satin, sateen and towelling. Washable.

Cretonne
A firm plain weave cotton fabric often printed with patterns which have a shadowy outline. It can be reversible and is used for curtains, blinds and cushion covers.

Fibreglass
Man-made fibre which is flame-resistant. Dryclean.

Folkweave
A loosely-woven soft fabric made from a coarse cotton yarn. Often printed with a striped pattern but the colours have a tendency to run if washed. Used for curtains.

Hessian
Made from jute, a natural fibre, it is cheap and comes in a wide range of colours. The loose weave may droop. Dryclean. Used for curtains.

Lace
Synthetic or cotton lace with an all-over pattern is used for lightweight curtains.

Lawn
A sheer, lightweight smooth-woven fabric made from cotton or linen which can be blended with man-made fibres. Use for cushion interlinings or lightweight curtains.

Linen
A plain weave with uneven surface texture made from natural fibre which can be blended with man-made fibres. Used for curtains and blinds.

Milium
Man-made fibre for aluminium-backed curtain lining with good insulation properties. Available in silver, white and cream. Dryclean.

Moiré
Watermark-patterned fabric which gives a waved effect. A fairly stiff, shiny fabric made from silk and from rayon and other man-made fibres. Used for all soft furnishings.

Nylon
Synthetic fibre used for fabrics of all weights and types. Varieties include nylon velvet and nets. Can fade, and may discolour in sunlight. Washable.

Polyester
Synthetic fibre often blended with natural fibres – does not shrink or fade. Drapes well, very strong and used for its sheer and opaque qualities.

The main requirements when choosing fabric are that it drapes well, has stable colours and will not fade excessively in sunlight, wears well and will not shrink or stretch when washed or hung. The fabric label should guide you on these points but, if in doubt, consult the sales assistant. Check whether the fabric is washable or needs to be drycleaned as this will affect your choice of lining and interlining.

Blinds

Closely-woven fabrics which do not have a tendency to fray are most suitable for roller blinds. Light-weight or flimsy fabrics will crease on the roller unless they are dipped, painted or sprayed with fabric stiffener. This has the added advantage of allowing the fabric to be sponged clean. Pvc or pvc-coated fabrics are particularly suitable for bathrooms or kitchens as long as they are not too heavy and bulky fabrics in general should be avoided as they will not roll up successfully.

Some soft-furnishing departments sell made-to-measure roller blind fabric which is spongeable, fade-resistant and does not fray. The patterns are designed specifically for use on a blind.

Austrian and ruched festoon blinds should be made up in a fabric which drapes well and which is not too stiff to gather up in swags across the width. Suitable fabrics include moiré, soft cottons, slubbed satin, dupion and sheer voile.

Roman blinds must be lined and an aluminium-backed lining such as Milium will give added insulation. Choose a firm, closely-woven fabric such as linen-look types or chintz. The fabric must not be too stiff or the blind will not fall in even pleats.

Pvc

A non-porous finish made from polyvinylchloride and applied to woven or knitted base fabrics. Used to make kitchen or bathroom blinds.

Rayon

Also known as viscose. Man-made fibre used in taffeta, linen-look types and velvet. Drapes and wears well but tends to fray so care needed when making up. Hand wash.

Ripstop nylon

A lightweight man-made fabric which comes in a range of bright colours. Used for shower curtains.

Sateen

A strong lightweight cotton fabric which has a sheen on one side. Often used for curtain linings.

Satin

A special weave in which threads 'float' over the base threads to give a surface sheen. Made from silk, rayon or man-made fibres and used for curtains and cushion covers.

Silk

Natural fibre fabric in all weights and types. May fade in bright sunlight. Dryclean or hand wash with care.

Ticking

A closely-woven, strong cotton or linen fabric, often with a characteristic stripe. Used for cushion interlinings.

Velvet

A warp-pile fabric made from silk, cotton or man-made fibres. Used for curtains.

Velveteen

A short, closely-set piled fabric on a cotton base. The heavier weights are suitable for curtains.

Viscose

See Rayon

Standard aftercare symbols

 A tub indicates that the yarn can be hand or machine washed.

 A hand in the tub means hand wash only.

 A figure in the water shows the correct water temperature. Numbers 1 to 9 above the water line denote washing machine programmes.

 Where the tub is crossed through, dry-clean only.

 An iron means the yarn can be pressed – one dot means cool; two dots medium and three dots hot.

 Where the iron is crossed through do not attempt to press the yarn or you may ruin the fabric.

 An empty circle means the yarn can be dry-cleaned.

 An A inside the circle means dry-cleaning in all solvents.

 The letter P means dry-cleaning only in certain solvents.

 The letter F means dry-cleaning only in certain solvents.

 Where the circle is crossed through do *not* dry-clean.

 A triangle means that the yarn can be bleached.

 Where the triangle is crossed through do not bleach.

 Square signs denote drying instructions.

 Three vertical lines in a square means drip dry.

 One horizontal line in a square means dry flat.

 A circle in a square means tumble dry.

 A loop at the top of a square means dry on a line.

Index

Acknowledgments

Artwork by Lindsay Blow, Bill le Fever, Sharon Finmark, Eugene Fleury, Chris Hurst, Susie Lacone, Coral Mula, Colin Salmon, Sue Sharples, Jill Shipley, Sara Silcock, Sheila Tizzard, Catherine Ward and Charmian Watkins.

Photographs by courtesy of Burda, Butterick, Camera Press, J. & P. Coats Ltd., Coloroll, Curtain Net Advisory Bureau, Designers' Guild, Dulux, French Wools (Pingouin) Ltd., Laura Ashley, Maudella, Mayfair, McCalls, Rufflette, Sanderson, Simplicity, Style, Swish and Vogue; and by Jan Baldwin, Brian Boyle, Tom Belshaw, Jon Bouchier, Alan Bramley, Steve Campbell, Bill Carter, Allan Grainger, Chris Harvey, Clive Helm, Hank Kemme, Di Lewis, Monique Leluhandre, Liz McAulay, Spike Powell, John Suett, Tinc Tedaldi, Jerry Tubby and Nick Wright.

Graph patterns copyright Maudella Patterns Co. Ltd., and copyright Eaglemoss Publications Ltd.

Text by Pam Dawson (Knitting and Crochet), Joy Mayhew (Dressmking) and Carolyn Watts (Soft Furnishings).